'Superb ... This is a universal story of fear and loathing in political life. Shipman is wonderful, and unsparing, in revealing the levels of unpleasantness and stupidity of the operation inside 10 Downing Street'
RICHARD ALDOUS, *The American Interest* Top Books of 2017

'Shipman is a first-rate journalist'   MATTHEW D'ANCONA, *Guardian*

'Wherever you sit on the political spectrum, it is so, so good'
ELLIE MAE O'HAGAN

'*Fall Out* [is] the finest book on UK politics I've read in years'
NICK BRYANT, BBC

ALSO BY TIM SHIPMAN

All Out War: The Full Story of Brexit

writing. He ~~~~
seventeen years writing about p~~ ~~
Westminster for the *Daily Mail* and the *Sunday Ex*~ ~~
Washington correspondent for the *Sunday Telegraph* during Bar~
Obama's historic first election campaign. He has covered five general
elections, three presidential elections, two wars and more leadership
contests than he can count. He popularised the word 'omnishambles' in
Westminster long before George Osborne based a budget on the idea.
Tim was chairman of the Parliamentary Press Gallery in 2012. He was
shortlisted for the Political Journalist of the Year award at the British
Press Awards in 2015, 2016, 2017 and 2018. He lives in south-east
London with his wife and more than two thousand books. This is the
second he has written himself.

Praise for *Fall Out*:

'If journalism is the "first rough draft" of history, then Tim Shipman is
the master of the second, tidied up, version of events. There is plenty in
Fall Out to keep the gossips entertained. A mixture of political thriller,
psychological analysis and campaign diary, this is a page-turner for
anyone interested in politics'   RACHEL SYLVESTER, *The Times*

'This extraordinary book … reads like a roaring farce … jam-packed
with fresh, illuminating details … Shipman's writing has admirable clarity and drive … For anyone who wants to relive the past year … this
book is a must'   CRAIG BROWN, *Mail On Sunday*

'*All Out War* was the best political book published last year … its trium-
phant sequel … is even better … A masterpiece of its type'
     ALEX MASSIE, *Spectator*

'It reads like a gripping thriller, except it's more frightening because it's all true and it's happening right now. The way he writes is very dramatic and he also humanises politicians in a way I aspire to do myself'

JAMES GRAHAM, author of *This House*, *Ink* and *Coalition*

'The doyen of ... high-class gossip is ... Shipman, whose *All Out War* was last year's bestselling guide to the referendum campaign. Its sequel takes up where that left off ... Shipman's books are fast becoming classics'

GABY HINSLIFF, *Guardian*

'Readers who enjoyed the lucid prose and unrivalled access that made the first book such a treat will love its sequel'

STEPHEN BUSH, *New Statesman*

'*Fall Out* is really quite brilliant. I thought *All Out War* was exceptional, but amazingly he's managed to write a book which is even better'

ANDREW SPARROW, *guardian.co.uk*

'Shipman ... a major-domo with a notebook in his waistcoat pocket ... bends over backwards to be fair ... It is crammed with detailed description and the transcribed thoughts of those who were there when the key decisions were taken'

ANDREW MARR, *Sunday Times*

'Excellent ... engrossing ... a witty phrase-maker ... Shipman does a fine job of making sense of the period since the Brexit referendum ... illuminating'

ANDREW RAWNSLEY, *Observer*

'It carries on from his first book, *All Out War* and is just as good ... The British equivalent of Robert Caro's series of biographies of Lyndon Johnson – and I can't give his books any higher praise than that'

IAIN DALE, LBC

'A dazzling display of journalistic skill and world-class storytelling'

IMRAN AHMED, author of *The New Serfdom*

'Shipman ... returns to his role as the chief biographer of Brexit with a worthy sequel'

SEBASTIAN PAYNE, *Financial Times*

FALL
OUT

A YEAR OF POLITICAL MAYHEM

TIM SHIPMAN

WILLIAM
COLLINS

William Collins
An imprint of HarperCollins*Publishers*
1 London Bridge Street
London SE1 9GF
WilliamCollinsBooks.com

First published in Great Britain by William Collins in 2017
This William Collins paperback edition published in 2018

1

A catalogue record for this book is
available from the British Library

ISBN 978-0-00-826442-0

Printed and bound in Great Britain by
CPI Group (UK) Ltd, Croydon

MIX
Paper from
responsible sources
FSC   FSC® C007454
www.fsc.org

This book is produced from independently certified FSC paper
to ensure responsible forest management

For more information visit: www.harpercollins.co.uk/green

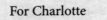

For Charlotte

fall out v.

    1 quarrel

    3 come out of formation

fallout n.

    1 radioactive debris caused by a nuclear explosion or accident

    2 the adverse side effects of a situation

The Concise Oxford Dictionary (1991 edn)

'It is not the critic who counts; not the man who points out how the strong man stumbles, or where the doer of deeds could have done them better. The credit belongs to the man who is actually in the arena, whose face is marred by dust and sweat and blood'

Theodore Roosevelt, 23 April 1910

'Everybody has a plan until they get punched in the mouth'

Mike Tyson

CONTENTS

PART ONE: GENESIS
The Battle for Brexit
September 2016 to March 2017

PART TWO: HUBRIS
The Chiefs
September 2016 to March 2017

PART THREE: NEMESIS
The General Election
February to June 2017

PART FOUR: CATHARSIS
The Fall Out
June to December 2017

ACKNOWLEDGEMENTS

This is the second book I never intended to write. Just as with *All Out War*, my 2016 book on the Brexit referendum campaign, *Fall Out* is the product of extraordinary events. The original intention was to add a few chapters to *All Out War* to bring the Brexit story up to date with the declaration of Article 50 in the spring of 2017. Then Theresa May called a general election and the inexorable logic of writing a sequel overwhelmed me. The fallout from the EU referendum and the general election is still with us. It was perhaps the most extraordinary of my lifetime. It led the Tory Party to fall out with itself and fall out of formation.

This book is based on more than one hundred interviews conducted primarily between July and October 2017. Last time I listed most of the primary sources. This time I have not done so since many more of them are still in prominent posts and most were reluctant to be named. That said, only a very small number of people refused to cooperate. Those who talked to me include fifteen members of Theresa May's Downing Street staff, twenty ministers, including thirteen of cabinet rank, more than twenty-five Tory campaign staff, more than a dozen senior figures in the Labour Party, the shadow cabinet, Jeremy Corbyn's office and the trade unions, as well as civil servants, special advisers, diplomats, former ministers, MPs and pollsters.

During the time covered by this book I interviewed Theresa May three times and accompanied her on her visit to the White House. I also conducted on-the-record interviews with David Davis, Boris Johnson, Damian Green, Michael Gove, John McDonnell, Nigel Farage, Arron Banks and Michael Fallon. I have drawn on the unpublished transcripts of these conversations.

As before, some people agreed to certain observations being 'on the record' but most of the time we spoke on the understanding that I would construct a narrative of events without signalling the origin of every fact and quote. Where I have directly quoted someone or attributed thoughts or feelings to them, I have spoken to them, the person they were addressing, someone else in the room who observed their behaviour, or someone to whom they recounted details of the incident or conversation. You should not assume that the obvious source is the correct one. Many of those who spoke to me off the record have written newspaper articles, given interviews or spoken publicly about their views. Where this is the case I have footnoted published sources in the text.

I will repeat a couple of stylistic warnings I issued in *All Out War*. Westminster is a profane place and I have sought to capture the language of the age. Be warned. Peers are referred to by the name by which they are best known. Knights of the realm are 'Sir' on first usage then stripped of their titles. In no one's world is Stephen Gilbert, Lord Gilbert of Panteg and anyone who has tried to call Lynton Crosby 'Sir' gets a look that discourages repetition.

The Brexit negotiations and the general election are a complex series of interlocking and overlapping events. In seeking to impose narrative order not everything is presented in strictly chronological order. This felt necessary to prevent *Fall Out* descending into a recitation of 'one damn thing after another'. Part One covers the negotiations over Brexit between September 2016 and March 2017, when Theresa May triggered Article 50. Part Two covers the internal battles of the May government – which pitted her chiefs of staff against other senior members of the administration – to try to explain how the culture they had created affected the election campaign and their own demise. Part Three covers the election and Part Four the subsequent leadership plotting and its implications for Brexit, culminating in the phase one exit agreement in December 2017.

With events still live there are many people who will not like what they find in these pages. We do not know yet how Brexit will end or how the 2017 election will impact on the future history of the Conservative Party, still less whether 2017 represented the beginning of the end or the end of the beginning for Theresa May and Jeremy Corbyn. I have sought to honestly convey the events as they seemed to the participants at the time. My personal view is that Britain must make the best of its future. Good people on both sides of the referendum result have a role to play.

Capitalising on the benefits of Brexit requires a cold-eyed understanding of the complications.

While people have behaved with conviction as well as ambition they have not always behaved well. I have known Nick Timothy and Fiona Hill for a decade. If I have highlighted some of the extremes of their characters as they were experienced by others, I can only say my own contacts with them have almost always been positive. Both are dedicated public servants and – away from the stresses of office – charming company. If they did not always seem so to colleagues, it is worth remembering that all the best political operators I have known – Damian McBride, Dominic Cummings and Alastair Campbell among them – have been divisive figures.

At HarperCollins I am deeply indebted to the incomparable Arabella Pike, whose image will adorn the next edition of the Illustrated Oxford Dictionary alongside the word 'sangfroid'. I hope she persuades David Cameron to file quicker than I did. Iain Hunt and Robert Lacey dealt with a mountain of words with similar forbearance. I'm also grateful to Marianne Tatepo, who sorted the pictures and much else besides and the legendary Helen Ellis. My agent, Victoria Hobbs, and all at A. M. Heath kept up my morale at key moments.

Special thanks must go again to my Sancho Panza, Gabriel Pogrund, who contributed acute reporting, several insightful interviews and the fastest transcription services in the West. Hannah McGrath let me see unpublished material from election night. I am also grateful to both old comrades – George Greenwood, Harriet Marsden and Oliver Milne – and new – Sebastien Ash, Megan Baynes, Isabelle Boulert, Tony Diver, Caitlin Doherty, Emily Hawkins, Anna Hollingsworth, Michael Mander, Conor Matchett, Holly Pyne and Josh Stein – for their help in turning more than one hundred hours of interviews into seven hundred thousand words of transcripts. I'm grateful to Natasha Clark for the introductions to such a keen young team.

At the *Sunday Times*, I am indebted to Martin Ivens, Sarah Baxter and Ben Preston for offering space to the political reporting on which this book was built. Ray Wells was generous with his time sourcing the pictures. There is no better wingman in covering Brexit than Bojan Pancevski, the king of the Brussels correspondents and no wiser partner in crime than Caroline Wheeler, who held the fort when this book took over. Richard Kerbaj helped with the fallout from the terrorist attacks.

Elsewhere in Westminster, I'm grateful to Jim Waterson for guiding me through the digital election battle and David Wooding for sharing a transcript.

My greatest debt remains to my family, particularly my amazing wife Charlotte, who have put up with more absences than anyone should have to endure – and to Kate and Michael Todman for indulging a mono-syllabic house guest for the second summer in succession.

Tim Shipman
Westminster, Preggio, Camerata, San Nicolo,
Church Knowle, Studland and Blackheath
July–October 2017

TIMELINE

2016

23 Jun – Britain votes to leave the European Union by a margin of 52 per cent to 48 per cent

29 Jun – Other 27 member states agree a 'no negotiations without notification' stance on Brexit talks and Article 50

13 Jul – Theresa May becomes prime minister and pledges to create 'a country that works for everyone'

7 Sep – May insists she will not give a 'running commentary' on Brexit negotiations

24 Sep – Jeremy Corbyn re-elected as Labour Party leader

30 Sep – Carlos Ghosn, Nissan's CEO, says he could scrap potential new investment in its Sunderland plant

2 Oct – In Brexit speech to party conference, May says she will trigger Article 50 before the end of March and create a Great Repeal Bill to replace the 1972 European Communities Act

5 Oct – In main speech to party conference, May criticises 'citizens of nowhere'

6 Oct – Keir Starmer appointed shadow Brexit secretary

27 Oct – Nissan says it will build its Qashqai and X-Trail models at its Sunderland plant, protecting 7,000 jobs

2 Nov – At *Spectator* awards dinner May compares Boris Johnson to a dog that was put down

3 Nov – High Court rules that only Parliament not the government has the power to trigger Article 50

4 Nov – *Daily Mail* calls the judges 'enemies of the people'

8 Nov – Donald Trump elected the 45th president of the United States

14 Nov – *FT* reveals the EU wants a €60 billion exit bill from Britain

15 Nov – Boris Johnson tells a Czech paper the UK will 'probably' leave the customs union and is reprimanded by May

19 Nov – Johnson accused of turning up to a cabinet Brexit meeting with the wrong papers

20 Nov – Sixty pro-Brexit Tory MPs demand Britain leaves the single market

21 Nov – Trump calls for Nigel Farage to be made British ambassador to Washington

7 Dec – MPs back government amendment to opposition day debate saying the government must set out its Brexit plans but also that Article 50 should be triggered by the end of March

8 Dec – Johnson calls Saudi Arabia a 'puppeteer' in the Middle East, sparking a rebuke from Downing Street and fears he will resign

11 Dec – Fiona Hill's 'Trousergate' texts to Nicky Morgan, banning her from Downing Street, are published

15 Dec – BBC reveals that Sir Ivan Rogers has privately warned ministers a post-Brexit trade deal might take ten years

2017

4 Jan – Ivan Rogers resigns

10 Jan – Corbyn announces a wage cap in his 'Trump relaunch'

17 Jan – In speech at Lancaster House May announces Britain will seek a hard Brexit leaving the single market, the customs union and the jurisdiction of the European Court of Justice. She says 'no deal is better than a bad deal'

24 Jan – Supreme Court votes 8–3 to uphold the High Court ruling

25 Jan – Downing Street says Brexit plans will be set out in a white paper

27 Jan – May meets and holds hands with Trump at the White House

1 Feb – Article 50 bill passes second reading by 498 votes to 114

2 Feb – White paper published echoing the Lancaster House speech

7 Feb – Government defeats amendment 110 which would have given Parliament the right to a vote on Brexit following a deal with Team 2019 Tory rebels

9 Feb – Article 50 bill passes Commons by 494 votes to 122

16 Feb – May's aides hold strategy meeting at Chequers for the 2020 election

17 Feb – Tony Blair makes a speech urging Britons to 'rise up' against Brexit

7 Mar – House of Lords amends Article 50 bill to guarantee a 'meaningful vote' on Brexit deal. Lord Heseltine sacked

8 Mar – In his spring budget, Philip Hammond raises National Insurance contributions for the self-employed

13 Mar – Nicola Sturgeon confirms she will ask for permission to hold a second referendum on Scottish independence, playing into Ruth Davidson's hands

14 Mar – Article 50 bill finally gets royal assent

15 Mar – May forces Hammond into humiliating U-turn on National Insurance

17 Mar – George Osborne named editor of the *Evening Standard*, overshadowing May's Plan for Britain

29 Mar – May signs letter triggering Article 50

18 Apr – May announces that she is calling a general election

26 Apr – May dines with Jean-Claude Juncker at Downing Street. Details of the meal leak and are blamed on his chief of staff Martin Selmayr

4 May – In local elections Tories make big gains

10 May – Labour manifesto leaks

16 May – Labour manifesto published

18 May – Conservative manifesto published, includes plans for a controversial social care policy

21 May – Polls show Tory support 'dropping off a cliff'. Lynton Crosby says care could lose the election

22 May – May U-turns, scrapping the care plan but insisting 'nothing has changed'. Manchester Arena terror attack that night leads to a pause in the campaign

24 May – In Downing Street meeting, May is warned the numbers are bad

3 Jun – London Bridge terror attack puts police cuts at the top of the agenda

8 Jun – General election: the Conservatives win 317 seats, down thirteen and lose their majority. Labour gains thirty seats

9 Jun – May visits the queen and says she has a deal with the DUP then fails to apologise for losing seats

11 Jun – Nick Timothy and Fiona Hill resign as chiefs of staff

12 Jun – May apologises to 1922 Committee and endures criticism from ministers in cabinet

14 Jun – Grenfell Tower disaster plunges the government into a new crisis and May into a 'personal crisis'

19 Jun – First round of Davis–Barnier Brexit negotiations

26 Jun – Andrew Mitchell and Nicky Morgan tell One Nation dinner Theresa May should resign

6 Jul – CBI demands a transition period with no time limits

20 Jul – Second round of Davis–Barnier talks

31 Aug – Third round of Davis–Barnier talks ends in fractious deadlock

7 Sep – Select group of cabinet ministers shown policy paper by Oliver Robbins setting out plans for May's Florence speech

12 Sep – Philip Hammond tells Lords Economic Affairs Committee there must be a 'status quo' transition

15 Sep – Boris Johnson publishes 4,200-word article in the *Daily Telegraph* challenging May's authority on Brexit

18 Sep – Oliver Robbins leaves DExEU to run Cabinet Office Brexit unit

22 Sep – During speech in Florence, May says Britain will seek a status quo transition lasting 'about' two years and hints the UK will pay €20 billion to the EU in that time

30 Sep – Johnson sets out his four 'red lines' for Brexit

4 Oct – Theresa May's conference speech descends into disaster

16 Oct – May dines with Jean-Claude Juncker. A leak suggests she was 'begging' for help

19 Oct – At Brussels summit, May pleads with EU leaders to get the trade talks moving

22 Nov – Hammond's second budget of the year cuts stamp duty for first-time buyers

4 Dec – DUP pulls the plug on May's exit deal, plunging the talks into fresh crisis

8 Dec – May strikes phase one Brexit deal when Commission pronounces that 'sufficient progress' has been made on money, citizens and the Irish border

Introduction

FOUR MINUTES TO TEN

The first clue that something was wrong was the look on Fiona Hill's face. One of Theresa May's two chiefs of staff emerged from the safe space reserved for the senior staff at the rear of the war room in Conservative Campaign Headquarters. She was looking for the other chief, Nick Timothy. Hill was a thin and elegantly dressed brunette in her early forties whose waif-like appearance concealed a backbone of pure galvanised steel. 'Where's Nick?' she asked. Her voice was a sweet Scottish lilt that belied a tongue which could crack like a whip. Hill was a figure of authority but her voice betrayed her nervousness. 'Her face was just white,' a witness recalled.

In the weeks to come those who were there would see the next few moments unfold again and again in their mind's eye like a Martin Scorsese film, indelible images that jump-cut into a portrait of unfolding disaster. A member of the Conservative media team, which Hill had commanded for the previous seven weeks, said, 'I looked at her and thought, "That's not somebody who's been told good news." She grabbed Nick and took him to the Derby room.' It was Thursday 8 June. Election day. The aide looked at his watch, so he would remember the time. 'The moment I knew it was fucked was at 9.56 p.m.,' he said.

Nick Timothy looked both like he meant business and like an egghead – fitting for one of the best Conservative policy brains of his generation. Like many political players he was a figure of contradictions, sometimes easy company, smoothly charming to both men and women. He spoke with an accent that betrayed a little of his Midlands upbringing and a great deal of the relentless inner drive that had taken him from working-class Birmingham to the pinnacle of a Conservative government. Thirty-seven and balding on top, Timothy had become a recognisable public figure thanks to the lustrous beard he wore, which would not have looked out of place on a nineteenth-century Russian novelist. In Tory circles 'Timmy' was most usually compared to the 3rd Marquess of Salisbury, the last Tory prime minister to sit in the House of Lords.

When Hill and Timothy emerged from the side room and made their way to the safe space again, others, anxious now, stood rooted to the spot. 'The two of them were the only people moving,' one recalled. A Conservative special adviser – a 'spad' to all those in Westminster – turned to Liz Sanderson, one of May's Downing Street staff, and asked what sort of percentage lead the Tories would need in the exit poll to have a good night. 'I don't know what good is supposed to look like,' the adviser said. As Big Ben struck ten, the BBC's David Dimbleby announced that Britain was on course for a hung Parliament. The Conservatives were set to lose seats. 'It dropped on the screen and I thought, "Well it ain't fucking that." I burst into laughter because that is my reaction to anything totally catastrophic.'

No one else was laughing. 'The whole place was like someone had been murdered,' another spad recalled. There was a paralysing quiet. 'Panic looked like the most wonderfully British panic, which was total fucking silence,' a Downing Street official said. 'The air just went from the room. It was like a vacuum.'

Hill and Timothy spoke to Theresa May by phone. The prime minister was at home in her Maidenhead constituency. They agreed to await the results. Inside, May prepared for the worst. She had already had a little cry. After a seven-week campaign which was supposed to be a victory lap, May had taken her party backwards. Over the next eight hours, her expected majority of sixty or more dissolved into a net loss of thirteen seats. Conservative staff fell into a deep depression. The campaign had not been enjoyable but the prospect of victory had kept them going. Now that was gone. 'I felt like Andy Dufresne in *The Shawshank Redemption*,' one spad said. 'I had crawled through a mile of shit and there was supposed to be a boat or money or Morgan Freeman coming to hug me at the end. Instead, it was just a pile of poo, and I was stuck in a pond with the rain pouring down on me.'

The political implications were as acute as the personal. A prime minister who had seemed impregnably strong was suddenly dangerously weak and fighting for her career. An election called to strengthen Britain's hand in negotiations on the country's exit from the European Union –

'Brexit' as it was now known to everyone – had left the UK disempow-ered at a critical moment in her history. May's two closest aides, who had been as dominant a duopoly as 10 Downing Street has ever seen, saw their power evaporate. Timothy and Hill had helped to create the public being of Theresa May. They were her greatest cheerleaders and defend-ers. Now they were to be sacrificial lambs for the disaster that was unfolding, their best service to throw themselves to the wolves so that she might escape their jaws.

It had all been very different on results night a year earlier. Nick Timothy was in a remote Sicilian mountain-top village with his then fiancée Nike Trost on the night of the EU referendum. He was a convinced Brexiteer but did not think Leave would win. Halfway through the night his phone began beeping with messages saying 'Are you watching?' Timothy took out his laptop and began live streaming Sky News as the biggest electoral earthquake in modern political history unfolded. His partner, a German citizen, realised what was happening and groaned, 'Oh my God!' By dawn it was clear that, after forty-four years, Britain had voted to leave the European Union by a margin of 52 per cent to 48 per cent.

Over his hotel breakfast, Timothy watched David Cameron resign as prime minister. A German family at the next table lectured him about how bad the result was for Europe. The Italian woman who owned the hotel was more enthusiastic: 'This is British Brexit, it's the Italians next!' As the sun came out Timothy and Trost booked their flights home. He knew this was a defining moment in his life. By then he had already spoken with the two other women in his life: Theresa May and Fiona Hill. For a decade they had discussed how to make the Conservative Party more electable and had quietly positioned May for a tilt at the top. Timothy had a leadership campaign to run, perhaps a country to run. This time he was convinced he would win. This is a play with many actors, but overwhelmingly it is the story of those three people and how they took charge of the most complex political conundrum since the Second World War, one which unfolded in the small hours of 23 June 2016.

The road that brought them to that moment four minutes before ten has many tributaries. The first came in a geography tutorial meeting at Oxford University in the mid-1970s when the young Theresa Brasier turned to a fellow student, Alicia Collinson, and first expressed a desire to become prime minister. Collinson was already the girlfriend of another future cabinet minister, Damian Green, and the two students spent their university years in a social circle around the Conservative Association and the Oxford Union which included others who would find future fame in Westminster: Alan Duncan, Michael Crick and Philip Hammond. Brasier's most significant meeting in those years – famously at the instigation of Benazir Bhutto, the future leader of Pakistan – was with Philip May, a president of the union who was to become her husband in 1980 and her 'rock' thereafter.

The serious, dogged devotion to 'public service' and May's occasionally pious insistence that her only goal was to 'do what I think is right' appeared to come from her father, Anglican vicar the Revd Hubert Brasier. The cabinet colleague who said, 'She is extraordinarily self-contained,' sought an explanation no deeper than her status as an only child, the death of both her parents in her mid-twenties and the Mays' subsequent discovery that they could not have children. Hubert Brasier died in a car crash in October 1981; his wife Zaidee succumbed to multiple sclerosis a few months later. Bill Clinton, Tony Blair and Barack Obama all lost parents when they were young.

When Andrea Leadsom, against whom May faced off for the Tory leadership in July 2016, questioned her suitability for the job because she was not a mother, it was Leadsom who was forced to drop out. Yet the questions she raised about May's emotional intelligence were to become a feature of her difficulties eleven months later. Leadsom had been the third major rival to self-immolate. George Osborne had gone down with David Cameron's ship after lashing himself to the mast of the Remain campaign during the EU referendum. Then, as the battle to replace him began, Boris Johnson showed less commitment to victory than his campaign manager, Michael Gove, would have liked, prompting Gove to declare him unfit for the top job, a shot fired from such an angle that it ricocheted into Gove's own foot. The result was that May inherited the Tory crown without either her colleagues or herself learning what she was like under sustained fire during a campaign. They were soon to know.

Those looking for clues about the sort of prime minister she would be would have found contradictory messages from her past. After twelve years at the Bank of England and a council career in Merton, south-west London, where she crossed paths with another future colleague, Chris

Grayling, May became an MP in the Labour landslide of 1997. These were the darkest days of opposition. She was the first of her intake into the shadow cabinet two years later. Initially, May was seen as a moderniser. As the first female party chairman in 2002, she delivered a few home truths from the conference platform, urging the grassroots to change. 'You know what people call us? The nasty party.' Katie Perrior, May's press mouthpiece at the time, recalled, 'The traditionalists around Iain Duncan Smith, the Tory leader, were ordering Mrs May to remove the words "nasty party" from the speech. On the floor below, a gang of modernisers including Mrs May, staring two huge electoral defeats in the face, were thinking there was not much to lose and were determined to press on.'[1] May did not endorse the 'nasty party' label but to many members she had legitimised criticism of her own team. Yet, her analysis that the public were losing faith in politics was ahead of its time.

May's appointment as home secretary by David Cameron in 2010, when the coalition government was formed, added further layers of complexity to her politics. Cameron joked that he and May were the only two ministers who supported the Tory commitment to reduce net immigration to the 'tens of thousands'. Yet May also led a crackdown on police 'stop and search' powers, which she felt were directed unfairly at young black men, and a crusade to stamp out modern slavery. May was hard to categorise politically. Nick Timothy said, 'Those things aren't mutually exclusive but hearing it from the same person leads people to think, "I don't really understand what that person stands for." She doesn't allow herself to be put into ideological boxes.'[2] Colleagues think being home secretary changed her. A former special adviser said, 'If you spend years and years saying something you do end up believing it. When she was shadow work and pensions I used to work with her on things like parental leave. She was into gender equality and social liberalism. Being home secretary for six years does something to you.' Willie Whitelaw, who lost the 1975 leadership contest to Margaret Thatcher and then became her home secretary, is said to have remarked that no home secretary should ever become prime minister because they spend their time trying to stop things from happening rather than leading from the front.

The pattern May set in the first decade became a blueprint for her premiership – pathological caution punctuated by moments of great boldness and bravery. She fought a tenacious and ultimately successful battle to deport Abu Qatada, the 'hate preacher' branded Osama bin

Laden's ambassador in Europe – in the face of a Human Rights Act that appeared to make it impossible. She woke up one morning in 2012 and used the human rights of Asperger's sufferer Gary McKinnon as reason *not* to deport him to face hacking charges in the United States, a decision that took guts even if it did virtually guarantee the support of the *Daily Mail*, which had been campaigning for McKinnon, in a future leadership contest. Former Home Office official Alasdair Palmer said, 'When she is convinced that her cause is right, May can be determined, even obstinate.'

In the Cameron cabinet, May was an oddity, someone the Cameroons would have liked to ignore but knew they could not. Her abilities and virtues stood in direct counterpoint to those of Cameron and his side-kick George Osborne. Where Cameron excelled at presentation and pulling victory from the jaws of defeat with glib displays of concentration and political charisma, May was a grinder, a determined reader of documents who moved towards her conclusions with all the facility of a static caravan on a low loader. Having reached those conclusions, she was unbending in their defence however inconvenient her colleagues found it.

Where Cameron was open, May was secretive. One civil service official said May and her Home Office permanent secretary Helen Ghosh 'would go for weeks without speaking'. May regularly kept both Number 10's staff and her own in the dark about her intentions. A longstanding aide added, 'She'll tell you the truth. If she doesn't want to tell you, she won't make any bones about it, she just won't tell you. That's not an insult, it's just that she's keeping her own counsel.' Where Osborne was imaginatively political and tactical, May obsessed about doing the right thing after due consideration, sticking to her principles. 'Politics,' she was fond of saying, 'is not a game.' Cameron and Osborne revelled in being the best game players in town.

While the Cameroons shared dinner parties as well as political views, May dined in the Commons with her husband. In her leadership launch speech, she explained, 'I don't gossip about people over lunch. I don't go drinking in Parliament's bars.' A senior party official said, 'She is the least clubbable politician I know.' Alasdair Palmer had a typical lunch experience: 'She lacks the personal charm of most politicians. Conversation was not easy. Somewhat to my alarm, May had no small talk whatsoever. She was perfectly comfortable with silence, which I found extremely disorienting.'[3] This detachment would continue in Downing Street, where one aide observed, 'She's so removed from the world her colleagues live in.' The aide said, 'Gavin [Williamson, the chief whip] would come in and explain that this MP was having an affair. The "ins and outs" stuff the whips call it. She'd just be exasperated and say, "Why can't they just do the job."'

There was a peculiarly English social edge to May's differences with the Cameroons. They were public schoolboys, easy company in the salons of the capital; she was a provincial grammar-school girl with no small talk. Although she and Cameron shared a home counties Conservatism, his social circle touched the lower hem of the aristocracy while May was the product of genteel vicarage austerity. Cameron's Christianity, it was said, 'comes and goes' like 'Magic FM in the Chilterns'; May's was steadfast if seldom talked about. Where Cameron's approach to those less well-off found voice in a Macmillanite soft paternalism, May's simmered with the determined rage of one disgusted by injustice, but a rage that her buttoned-up personality never quite allowed her to express in a way that would have turned voters' heads.

May's ordinariness was on display when she moved into Downing Street. The new prime minister was asked whether she wanted the gents' loo outside her office converted for her use. It had previously been for the sole use of Cameron. May replied, 'Absolutely not, I'm not wasting a penny of taxpayers' money. I'll go down the corridor like everybody else.' The same humble approach ensured she went door-knocking in her constituency every weekend. Hill explained to friends, 'She thinks if she underestimates Corbyn and Labour then it will come back to bite her in the bum. She doesn't take her majority for granted.' Another aide saw it as a chance of escape: 'There is a point where she has had enough of being in Number 10. It's a decompression thing, when she goes back and has that connectivity with people that she is comfortable with. When she doesn't have that she gets ratty and you can see the pressure start to build on her.'

May preferred people with knowledge rather than rank. 'She didn't want senior bullshitters,' a Downing Street aide said, 'she wanted younger people who knew what they were talking about.' A civil servant saw the same down-to-earth approach: 'The custodial staff in Number 10 and the ones who take her tea or sandwiches, they were all happier when she arrived after Cameron because she would address them by name. They felt that she treated them like people who were helping her rather than lackeys.'

May's social awkwardness and secrecy meant even close colleagues knew little about her. Some who worked closely with her were perplexed by the efforts of journalists and MPs to discover the 'real' Theresa May. One Tory who worked for her said, 'I'm not sure there's much there. She's very sensible. There's no interest in ideas. Philip is a very sweet man but it takes a certain type of character to marry someone who is so bland. Their conversation is completely banal.'

May appeared determined, even when she became prime minister, to deny there was any such thing as 'Mayism'. 'She's quite anti-intellectual,' a former minister said. 'She's not a great thinker. To admit of an "ism" would be to suggest there was a great Heseltinian long-term plan to be leader – which of course there was.' The plan, though, was not May's but that of Nick Timothy and Fiona Hill.

The fact that Theresa May seemed the only possible option for prime minister by 13 July 2016 was the work of her two closest aides, who were rewarded with the top staff jobs in Downing Street – for ever more known as 'the chiefs'. Nick Timothy grew up in a working-class family in the Tile Cross district of Birmingham. His father left school at fourteen and worked his way up from the factory floor to become head of international sales at a local steel works. His mother did secretarial work at a school. Margaret Thatcher converted his parents to the Tory Party and Timothy was politicised by the 1992 general election because the Labour Party was threatening to close the grammar school – Edward VI Aston School – which had given him a chance in life. He went on to get a first-class degree in politics from Sheffield University and then landed a job in the Conservative research department, where his path first crossed with May's.

May and Timothy quickly realised they were political soulmates. Over a period of fifteen years they fashioned an analysis of how the Conservative Party should reposition itself to broaden its appeal, with 'a conservatism that is about the welfare and interests of the whole of the country across class divides and geographical divides' and the belief that 'there needs to be more of a role for the state'. Katie Perrior said, 'For her it was always about putting the party back in touch with ordinary working people – the Conservatives should no longer be the party of the rich and the privileged.'[4] A colleague of Timothy said, 'He wanted to complete the process of Tory modernisation, but his brand of modernisation was always about class.' Timothy was adamant that he was not 'Theresa's brain', the title he had been awarded by journalists. 'Suggesting I'm the creator of those ideas is absurd and insulting to her,' he said. 'I do think there's more than a hint of sexism.'[5] A cabinet minister close to May agreed: 'The idea that she is this wax palette which can be inscribed by this curious pair is not correct. She has a very, very strong sense of public service and believes from a place deep within herself that injustice is wrong.' Like May, Timothy was a man of contradictions. 'He's very traditional,' a close friend said. 'Even as a twenty-something he had a flat that looked like a man in his mid-forties. It's all old-fashioned paintings and dark antique furniture.' Yet this arch-Brexiteer's two longest relationships had been with European women, a Belgian and a German.

In 2006, Timothy met Fiona Hill outside The Speaker pub in Westminster and the cerebral staff officer acquired an artillery commander. 'I just immediately knew we were politically in the exact same place,' she told friends. Hill had a blunter approach, once declaring, 'We fucking hate socialism and we want to crush it in a generation.' Hill also came from a poor background, growing up in Greenock outside Glasgow. She forced her way into a job on the *Scotsman* newspaper, writing football reports and features, developing the news sense and sharp elbows that would take her to Sky News, where she worked on the newsdesk and met her husband, Tim Cunningham, whose name she was to take until they divorced. When she joined the Conservative Party press office in 2006 Timothy introduced her to May. 'They know each other inside out,' said one who has worked closely with both. 'Sometimes Fi can say something and Nick will say, "That was literally in my head." They both like working hard. It sounds too pious to say they believe in fairness, but they do – and that is what they share with Theresa.'

Hill and Timothy were equals but Hill's media background meant she was seen by the outside world as primarily a communications professional. As someone who had helped May develop legislation on modern slavery and domestic violence it grated. 'She's very sensitive about the idea that Nick is the policy brain and she's just a comms person,' a colleague said. Hill was also resentful of claims that she was May's personal stylist, even though she did advise her on clothes. On one foreign trip Hill erupted with rage when the events team passed her

May's handbag. It made her late for a meeting with Vladimir Putin. 'They never give Nick the handbag,' she complained to Katie Perrior. 'What am I? The fucking handbag carrier?' When Perrior said she would take the handbag instead, Hill attacked: 'This is why you don't have any gravitas – because you're willing to take the handbag.' In pointing out the different treatment of Timothy and the senior women, Hill had a point.

Colleagues say Hill's most important attribute – in matters of both policy and appearance – was to act as May's cheering section, boosting her morale. 'Fi operates as the emotional support: "You're fine, you look great, you don't need to care about this",' a colleague said. At one meeting in Downing Street May had been put off by something. 'Fi leant across and put her hand on her arm and said, "Don't worry, we said there would be days like this,"' a witness said. 'I thought that was a tragic sight, but it also illustrated how connected she is to both of them. They are literally the people who reach out and put an arm around her and tell her it is going to be all right.' A senior Home Office official agreed: 'Theresa was unable to take big decisions without the clear steer and guidance of Fiona.'

The relationship between Timothy and Hill was compared by colleagues to that between brother and sister or even lovers, which they had never been – often fractious but with a united front presented to the world. 'They never let a cigarette paper come between them in public,' a colleague said. Another observed, 'They're like siblings, they fight a lot. They don't care what they say about each other. But there's a loyalty there. It doesn't matter what they've done, it doesn't matter how bad the other person's behaved, they'll always cover the other's arse.'

Timothy and Hill had a devotion to May which surpassed the usual relationship between politician and staff. A former minister who discussed May with Timothy recalled, 'I was talking about her appeal, I said, "I know this sounds almost religious which it's not," and he said something like, "Yes, it is religious."' Timothy was joking but his zeal left an impression on the MP: 'That was a glimpse of how strongly her supporters had come to see her as the messiah.'

Together, 'the twins' set themselves up as May's gatekeepers. 'You had to go through them for everything,' a senior Border Force official said. Some said May's personal limitations and lack of feel for people meant she needed Hill and Timothy's guidance. 'She didn't have the character to elicit the information she might want,' a Home Office official said, 'or know what's true and what's not true. You and I will hear a story and know if it's right or not. I think she found that very difficult. She became reliant on others to do that screening, shielding, interpreting on her behalf.' Others disliked the way Hill and Timothy substituted their judgement for May's. When Alasdair Palmer, a Home Office speech-writer, did once see the home secretary alone, he wrote the speech to reflect May's views and then submitted it to the twins. Hill asked, 'Have you been talking to the home secretary?' Palmer said he had. 'I thought so,' she said. 'I don't think she should say these things.' Palmer suggested that was up to May. 'It's up to me,' Hill said.[6]

Their determination to go to any lengths to protect May led to disaster in June 2014. Hill's downfall came as a result of a feud between May's team and Michael Gove, then the education secretary, over the issue of extremism in schools. Gove briefed journalists from *The Times* that the Home Office was to blame for the failure to tackle the so-called 'Trojan Horse' plot to take over schools in Birmingham. He singled out for crit-icism Charles Farr, director of the Office for Security and Counter-Terrorism, saying officials only took on Islamist extremists when they turned to violence, an approach Gove compared to 'just beating back the crocodiles that come close to the boat rather than draining the swamp'. At that time Farr was in a relationship with Hill.

Furious, she retaliated by releasing onto the Home Office website a letter May had written to Gove, accusing his department of failing to act when concerns about the Birmingham schools were brought to its atten-tion in 2010. The document was published in the small hours of the morning, after Hill and Timothy had enjoyed a night out at the Loose Box restaurant in Westminster with journalists from the *Daily Mail*. To make matters worse, Hill gave quotes to journalists suggesting Gove had endangered children. 'Lord knows what more they have overlooked on the subject of the protection of kids in state schools,' she said. 'It scares me.' Following an investigation by Sir Jeremy Heywood, the cabinet secretary, David Cameron ordered that Hill be sacked, and that Gove issue a written apology to both May and Farr.

Hill found work at the Centre for Social Justice, a thinktank founded by Iain Duncan Smith, where she wrote a report calling for more effort by the authorities to tackle modern slavery, before taking up a post at lobbying firm Lexington Communications.

Timothy got his comeuppance a few months later in December 2014 when he and Stephen Parkinson – another of May's Home Office special advisers – were kicked off the list of Conservative candidates for refusing to campaign in the Rochester by-election. The decision was taken by Grant Shapps, then the party chairman, who had decreed that all candidates and special advisers had to help out. Shapps felt they 'thought themselves above the process' and made an example of them. May phoned Shapps twice to ask for their reinstatement and also collared him in the margins of a cabinet meeting, but he stood firm. He reflected afterwards that, despite being a cabinet colleague for three years, it was the only time May had bothered to talk to him. It was a ripple in a pool which was to have further implications later.

In July 2015, Timothy became director of the New Schools Network. Yet he continued to exercise influence from afar, contacting his protégé Will Tanner, another special adviser, regularly about the running of May's office. A year later the gang was back together in Number 10. An MP close to May summed up the relationship: 'She wouldn't be in Downing Street without their support. And she wouldn't have got to Downing Street, if she didn't have something about her. What Nick and Fi added to that was the ability to make the political weather. Very few people are capable of that.'

Thrown into the deep end, May's authenticity made her popular. A cabinet colleague said, 'There are a very small collection of politicians who are immediately attractive to the public, because they're normal human beings, they see someone who's true to themselves – Ken Clarke is the classic example. You will never hear Ken say something in private that he would not say in public. The PM is the same.' During the leadership contest, Clarke had given May a helping hand, calling her a 'bloody difficult woman'. May adopted the phrase as her calling card. Those looking for her weaknesses might have reflected that Clarke had explained her better than she had ever managed herself.

There were other clues too about what was to come. During the leadership election one of her aides said, 'A large number of MPs said I'm backing Theresa because she came to my constituency for the dinner fifteen years ago, and I've never forgotten it. She has met and engaged with a huge number of people, and most of those people really like her. The problem is people who've never engaged with her. And that's where her appeal falls short. She can't stand on a stage.' An official who worked with May in the Home Office said, 'She instils loyalty in people when you're close. At a distance, it's much more difficult to get that. She doesn't reach out to people. She knows who she is and expects you to come to her.' Knowing how difficult that was for May, Hill and Timothy devised for her a 'submarine strategy' whereby she kept her head down, surfacing rarely to make carefully planned set-piece interventions. At the Home Office, where most news is bad news, it was a shrewd strategy. May dodged public scrutiny but made three of the boldest speeches of the Cameron years – a 2013 party conference speech which was a leadership pitch in all but name; a 2014 warning to the Police Federation that officers should 'face up to reality'; and a party conference speech in 2015 in which she threw raw red meat to the party faithful on immigration that earned her the appellation 'Enoch Powell in a dress'.

In Number 10, Hill and Timothy took the same approach. On the steps of Downing Street May gave a very well received speech vowing to 'fight against the burning injustices' of poverty, race, class and health and make Britain 'a country that works for everyone'. When it came time to set out May's plans for Brexit, they knew it was the moment to write a big speech.

PART ONE

GENESIS

THE BATTLE FOR BREXIT

September 2016 to March 2017

'BREXIT MEANS BREXIT'

It all began with a phrase and an idea. The phrase, in a perfect encapsulation of so much that was to follow, was part Nick Timothy, part Theresa May. The two of them and Fiona Hill were in May's parliamentary office. It was July 2016 and David Cameron had resigned. The Conservative leadership contest was under way and they were discussing how May, a leading though not prominent Remainer, could reassure the party base that she would respect the results of the EU referendum. As they tossed around phrases, Timothy said, 'Brexit means Brexit,' at which point May chimed in, mimicking the jingle-like cadence Timothy had used and adding the coda, '… and we'll make a success of it'.

It was a phrase, as Timothy was to put it, 'with many lives'. The immediate purpose 'was to be very clear that she, as someone who had voted remain, respected the result and Brexit was going to happen'. In the months to come the phrase evolved. 'It also became a message to people who didn't like the result that they had to respect it. Brexit had to mean actually leaving and limiting the relationship, not having us effectively rejoin.'

'Brexit means Brexit' was a statement of intent, but there was still the question of what that meant in practice. Britain had voted to leave the European Union, but the destination had not been on the ballot paper. The Leave campaign deliberately never specified which model of future relationship should be pursued. Public debate dissolved into whether the UK would mimic Norway, Switzerland, Turkey or Canada.

Norway was a member of the European Economic Area (EEA) along with all twenty-eight EU countries, plus Liechtenstein and Iceland, giving it full membership of the single market, an area of 500 million people within which the free movement of goods, capital, services and labour – the 'four freedoms' – was guaranteed. While outside the European Union, Norway paid money into the EU budget and had to agree to all the standards and regulations of the market, except those on agriculture, fisheries, and justice and home affairs. The downside was that Norway was a 'rule taker, not a rule maker' and had no say over the future rules of the market.

Switzerland was a member of the European Free Trade Association (EFTA) but not of the single market, and its access to the market was governed by a series of more than one hundred bilateral agreements with the EU governing key sectors of the economy, though crucially not its banking or services sector. The Swiss made a smaller financial contribution to the budget than Norway and had to implement EU regulations to enable trade. A referendum in 2014 to end the free movement of people had led to retaliation from the EU.

Turkey, like Andorra and San Marino, was in a customs union with the EU, while outside the EEA and EFTA. That meant it faced no quotas, tariffs, taxes and duties on imports or exports on industrial goods sold into the EU and had to apply the EU's external tariff on goods imported from the rest of the world. The deal did not extend to services or agricultural goods.

Canada had just concluded a comprehensive economic and trade agreement (CETA) with the EU after seven years of negotiations, which eliminated tariffs on most goods, excluding services and sensitive food items like eggs and chicken. The deal gave Canada preferential access to the single market without many of the obligations faced by Norway and Switzerland, for goods that were entirely 'made in Canada', but for Britain it would not have given the financial services sector 'passporting' rights to operate in the EU.

The alternative to all these models was to leave with no deal and revert to the rules of the World Trade Organisation (WTO), which imposed set tariffs on different products. Supporters of free trade said the average 3 per cent tariffs were not burdensome but on cars, a key industry for Britain, they were 10 per cent. Removing all tariffs would also be expected to see the market flooded with cheap food and steel, threatening the UK's farming and manufacturing.

At this point the phrase 'soft Brexit' was taken to mean membership of the single market and the customs union, while 'hard Brexit' meant an alternative arrangement, though these terms were to evolve.

This approach was anathema to May, who rejected all attempts to compare the deal Britain might negotiate to any of the existing models. She told her aides, 'That's entirely the wrong way of looking at it.' From the beginning May knew she wanted a new bespoke deal for Britain. The prime minister, with encouragement from Hill, saw the process as similar to negotiation she had carried out as home secretary in October 2012 when she opted out of 130 EU directives on justice and home affairs and then negotiated re-entry into thirty-five of them, including the European Arrest Warrant, several months later. 'We have already done what was in effect an EU negotiation,' a source close to May said. 'We know how it works, we know what levers to pull and we know how to get what we want out of a negotiation.'

The first thing they wanted – the big idea – was a dedicated department to run Brexit. May, Hill and Timothy believed the 'bandwidth' in Whitehall was seriously lacking. 'We knew we'd have a big challenge to get preparation for Brexit up and running quickly,' a source close to May said. During a meeting in Nick Timothy's front room the weekend before May became leader they decided they would create a standalone department, a move that put noses out of joint at the Foreign Office and the Treasury in particular. 'We know Whitehall, we know how it works,' the source said. 'Unless you have a standalone department heading in the same direction then everyone works in silos.' It was the first of many decisions with far-reaching consequences made on the hoof.

The idea of a new department for Brexit was enthusiastically supported by Sir Jeremy Heywood. The owlish cabinet secretary was a problem solver par excellence who had made himself indispensable to four prime ministers in succession, but his enemies saw a mandarin whose first priority in all situations was to maintain his own power base. As the official who had carried out the review that led to Hill's departure from the Home Office, Heywood was understandably on edge after Team May's arrival in Number 10. Under Cameron, the cabinet secretary had been driven to Downing Street every morning and then walked through Number 10 to the Cabinet Office. It was a symbol of his status. 'When she came in that changed, he went through the Cabinet Office door,' a senior civil servant said. 'That was symbolic, putting him in his place.'

Heywood and May were well acquainted. They had dined together when she was home secretary. 'He used to say that he didn't look forward to these dinners because they had run out of things to talk about by the main course,' a fellow mandarin recalled. However, the dinners served a purpose on both sides. 'She did it because she was paranoid about what the centre was saying about her and it was a way of finding out,' the mandarin said. Heywood, meanwhile, was spying for Cameron, who wanted to know what May wasn't telling him. 'In the Home Office she pulled up the drawbridge,' said the mandarin. 'It was like Gordon Brown times two.'

Keeping his job meant Heywood supporting the creation of new departments, even though that put him at odds with other senior civil servants like Sir Ivan Rogers, Britain's permanent representative in Brussels – effectively the UK's ambassador to the EU. Rogers – an intense character with a high forehead who spoke at one hundred miles an hour – felt that setting up new departments would consume the time and energy of officials that could have been better directed at the details of a potential deal.

The other issue facing Heywood was that almost no preparations had been done for Brexit, since Cameron had banned the civil service from working on contingency plans in the run-up to the referendum. The cabinet secretary had hoped to spend the summer getting the civil service ready but the earlier-than-expected end to the Tory leadership contest put paid to that. 'We were caught flat footed,' a senior civil servant admitted. One of May's team said, 'I remember thinking when I got to Number 10 that the absence of any real thinking about this massive issue the country was facing was really quite remarkable.' Some said Heywood should have ignored Cameron. 'It's rather shocking that they did no preparations for Brexit,' a Tory peer said. 'They had a moral duty to prepare. People should have called for Jeremy's head.'

The Department for Exiting the European Union (DExEU, pronounced Dex-ee-oo) was born out of the European and Global Issues Secretariat, a group of forty officials in the Cabinet Office, and quickly cannibalised the European affairs staff of the Foreign Office as well on its way to engaging more than four hundred staff. From early in her leadership campaign, May knew who she wanted to run DExEU – David Davis. 'DD', as he is known in Westminster, had been a whip during the passage of the Maastricht Treaty and then John Major's Europe minister, jobs he had done with the devil-may-care bravado of an ex-SAS territorial, which remained the most interesting line on his CV and gave him an air of menacing charm that he had put to good use over the years. Davis finished second to Cameron in the 2005 leadership contest before throwing away his frontbench career as shadow home secretary with a maverick decision to resign his seat and fight a by-election to highlight civil liberties issues. That finished him with the Cameroons and paved the way for May to become home secretary. Davis became May's most obstreperous backbench opponent during her time at the Home Office. A vociferous critic of the snooper state, he even joined forces with Labour's Tom Watson to take ministers to court over the government's surveillance powers. However, these confrontations had bred mutual respect not contempt – and crucially had even impressed Hill, whose stance towards May's political enemies more usually resembled that of a lioness protecting her cubs. She told a friend, 'He's an absolute pro and having been on the receiving end of his campaigning for things like counter-terrorism laws I know how good he is. When he came onto the leadership team we really hit it off.'

Having been given a chance to do a serious job in government, Davis resolved to make himself useful to May and not allow policy differences to open between DExEU and Downing Street. 'He decided he wanted to be a political consigliere to her,' a source said. Davis's attempts to ingratiate himself with May went to extreme lengths. 'She and DD had this hideous flirting thing going on,' said one official who attended their meetings. 'She twinkled at DD. It was awful, it was like your grandparents flirting. Everybody wanted the ground to open up and swallow them whole.'

At Hill's instigation, and with Katie Perrior's encouragement, James Chapman – a former political editor of the *Daily Mail* who had been George Osborne's special adviser – joined as Davis's special adviser and chief of staff. The appointment raised eyebrows since it was a leap to go from the man most determined to stop Brexit to work for the minister now charged with delivering it, but Chapman was highly intelligent, calm under pressure and brought a deep knowledge of the Eurosceptic press, who would have to be kept on side through the negotiations. It was to be a mistake for both him and Davis.

To start with, DExEU was 'a total and utter shambles'. Four ministers were crammed into 9 Downing Street, where there had previously been just one. 'The department didn't function properly,' said one official. 'One of the floors was a courtroom which we couldn't change because it was a listed building. The press office people were sitting in the dock in the

Supreme Court of the Colonies.' The brass plaque on the front door still read 'Chief Whip's Office'.

DExEU was able to coax highly regarded officials to join from across Whitehall since Brexit was a career opportunity, but the civil service had to implement an outcome in which many did not believe. In Brussels, Ivan Rogers gave his staff a pep talk: 'You're going to be integral to the biggest negotiation the country's ever done and your expertise is valued. But if you can't work for a government that's delivering a Brexit – and that may be a hard Brexit – don't do it. Walk out.' Very few did. But DExEU officials were hamstrung by not knowing May's planned destination. 'It could be anything from staying in the EEA to hard Brexit,' an official said. 'They didn't really know where to start.'

The architecture created by Heywood and the chiefs created two problems, which would hamper the government's planning for the next year. As the lead department, DExEU was both a key participant and expected to be an honest broker with other departments. A cabinet minister said, 'DD was both a player and the referee.' The resentments led to briefings against Davis and his new department. 'There was a turf war,' said a senior DExEU official. 'The Foreign Office was massively put out and wanted to demonstrate that DExEU didn't know what they were doing. We had to fight against that backdrop. It was Jeremy Heywood's fault. There should never have been a separate department.'

The second problem concerned the official who was to play the most important role in the Brexit negotiations. Oliver Robbins was appointed not only permanent secretary at DExEU, the most senior mandarin in charge of the department, but also the prime minister's personal EU envoy – her 'sherpa', in Brussels parlance. Tall, mild-mannered and bespectacled, Robbins was a labrador of a man but with the brains of a fox. Just forty-one when he got the jobs, he had little EU experience. What he did have was the patronage of Jeremy Heywood – who was grooming him as a successor – the trust of Theresa May, from a spell as second permanent secretary in the Home Office, and the power of incumbency as David Cameron's last Europe adviser. He had also served as the prime minister's principal private secretary during the handover from Tony Blair to Gordon Brown and as the director of intelligence and security in the Cabinet Office. He combined his Rolls-Royce CV with bags of intelligence and sharp elbows clothed in a slightly old-fashioned pompous bonhomie.

Ivan Rogers told Robbins he was taking on too much. 'You've got two impossible jobs,' he said. 'Try sticking to one impossible job. The only job that really matters is sherpa because you have to be her eyes and ears around the circuit. You need to be the person to whom people transmit messages if they want to get them to the prime minister. If you're not that, you're toast.'

Robbins disagreed. 'It would be harder to do one job and not the other,' he said. A year later it was decided this was a mistake.

Robbins had May's trust. On foreign trips, other officials watched jealously as he talked to the prime minister alone, without Hill or Timothy listening in. 'He was allowed to have conversations with her one on one,' a colleague said. A senior mandarin who worked closely with Robbins described him as 'an upwards manager', good at ingratiating himself with his bosses, less so with his peers.

Robbins' split role created tensions with David Davis. 'DD and Olly didn't see each other regularly enough and Olly was travelling an enormous amount,' a colleague said. Robbins' office in 70 Whitehall was a ten-minute walk from Davis's in 9 Downing Street. 'The consequence was they hardly ever saw each other. You want your minister and your permanent secretary – who is also the PM's sherpa – to be talking to each other all the time and they didn't.' That meant May's two key advisers on Brexit 'weren't properly aligning where they were headed'. The official said, 'DD was therefore saying things in public that were contrary to what Olly thought was a sensible position.'

It was clear to Davis that Robbins put more time and effort into the Downing Street half of his job. 'His primary concern was the relationship with Nick [Timothy] because he knew nothing was decided by anyone else,' a DExEU source said. Robbins was not alone in this attitude. Those who had served in the Cabinet Office's EU secretariat could not see the point of DExEU. 'There was resentment among the officials that they had ministers at all,' said a source close to Davis. 'They just thought they should report to Number 10.' Davis war-gamed various scenarios for the Brexit negotiations but could never get Robbins to discuss 'the plan' – the strategy for the negotiation, which cards Britain held and when they should be played. More than one official concluded, 'It was all in Olly's head. It wasn't really a properly functioning relationship.'

DExEU was not the only new department established that summer. May also ordered the creation of a Department for International Trade

(DIT) to drum up deals with countries outside the EU. She handed the keys to Liam Fox, a former defence secretary and Brexiteer whose cabinet career had ended in controversy under Cameron but who was an enthusiast for free trade and travel and had cleverly cultivated May for years. 'Liam would take her out for lunch, which no one else could bear to do,' a special adviser recalled. DIT was slower to get off the ground but cannibalised UK trade policy and UK Export Finance, took the Defence Export Services Organisation from the Ministry of Defence and grabbed UK Trade and Investment, the part of the Foreign Office which was supposed to promote business out of Britain's embassies overseas. It would take until January, six months after the department was set up, to get a permanent secretary: Antonia Romeo, another Heywood protégée. It was not until June 2017 that Britain acquired a lead trade negotiator. Crawford Falconer, an experienced New Zealander, took the job after the first choice, Canadian Jonathan Fried, walked away at the final stage because Heywood refused to raise the £260,000 salary.

When tackling Brexit, May had learned three crucial lessons from David Cameron's renegotiation with Brussels before the referendum. The first was to ask for what Britain wanted, rather than making an opening offer calibrated to what the rest of the EU might accept. The second was to at least look like you were prepared to walk away from the talks to maximise leverage. The third was not to broadcast her negotiating position in advance to the media or MPs. A sound tactic this might have been, but by September 2016 May's reticence in spelling out what Brexit really meant had led to claims she was 'dithering'. The only announcement had been a reassurance to farmers and universities, on 13 August, that until 2020 they would keep the same level of subsidy outside the EU as they enjoyed inside it.

MPs on both sides of the EU divide were twitchy. Ken Clarke, the former cabinet minister and arch-Europhile, accused May of running a 'government with no policies'. As the party conference approached – it was to be held, appropriately, in Timothy's home city of Birmingham – May knew she had to add flesh to 'Brexit means Brexit'.

The prime minister's challenge was to reassure Brexiteers that she would honour the result of the referendum, despite her decision to vote Remain and despite insisting to those who voted to stay that she would get the best deal possible. The first part of the equation was made easier by May's less than enthusiastic support for Cameron. 'She was a reluctant Remainer,' said one adviser, 'but she's never been any fan of the EU. She was absolutely comfortable in her own skin about why we were leaving.' Timothy was a longstanding Brexiteer and Fiona Hill, while also a Remain voter, was quickly reconciled to the result and an enthusiast for the opportunities Brexit offered. May saw her first priority as confirming the triumph of the 52 per cent, both to prevent civil disorder and protect her own position within the Conservative Party. She told her closest aides, 'We need to keep this country stable because this could get quite messy.' The senior Eurosceptics, including veterans like Bill Cash, Bernard Jenkin and John Redwood, plus Steve Baker – the leader of the backbench Eurosceptic forces during the referendum campaign – were agitating. 'It was a hugely tense moment leading up to conference,' one sceptic said. 'Was she going to do Brexit properly or not? All hell could have broken loose.' A Downing Street aide said, 'We had to be absolutely clear with the party that Brexit really did mean Brexit – and with some parts of the country. Any confusion would have led to real disruption and calls for another referendum.' May's view was, 'We live in a democracy, democracy has spoken. Now we have to enact it.'

Tory leaders usually give their big conference speech before lunch on the Wednesday. May was keen to lay out her vision for Britain, but if that was not to be drowned out by Brexit she would need to deliver it separately – and first. Timothy said, 'It's unsustainable to wait until Wednesday to hear from Theresa when it's her first conference as leader.' Hill agreed: 'We need two speeches and a plan for Europe. Then we can have a big conference speech about our domestic agenda.' May was 'already there' and agreed immediately. She would give a short speech on the Sunday on Brexit.

Used to governing by speech, May's aides say she used the writing process to define policy, rather than have the speech reflect a pre-ordained line. Timothy discussed with May what she wanted and then wrote a text. The finer points were clarified in 'an iterative process' involving May, Timothy, Hill, Jojo Penn, the deputy chief of staff, and Chris Wilkins, the head of strategy who had penned May's 'nasty party' speech fourteen years earlier. 'The first draft is a hypothesis that either she agrees with or not,' one of those involved said. 'Nick being Nick would write the most "out there" option and it would get reined in. The process of drafting and editing gets Theresa to the point of, "Yes, that's what I want to say."'

Timothy and May were clear on three things: leaving the European Union meant leaving the jurisdiction of the European Court of Justice in Luxembourg, and leaving with it the single market and customs union over which its judges held sway. Anything else, Timothy believed, would leave May open to the charge that she was trying to undermine the referendum vote, and put the other EU countries in a position to claim that Britain wanted the benefits of EU membership – free access to markets – without the downsides – the cost and the need to accept rules made elsewhere. By opting out of all these areas, May could then try to negotiate some of the benefits without being tied to the institutions. 'Nick's view,' a Downing Street aide said, 'was that you're always going to be accused of cherry picking and they're going to say you can't cherry pick. Therefore, we should try and forge our own way forward with a new relationship. Nick largely wrote the speech and took pleasure in doing so.'

In the speech, May was to say, 'There is no such thing as a choice between "soft Brexit" and "hard Brexit". This line of argument – in which "soft Brexit" amounts to some form of continued EU membership and "hard Brexit" is a conscious decision to reject trade with Europe – is simply a false dichotomy.' May explained her new deal 'is not going to be a "Norway model". It's not going to be a "Switzerland model". It is going to be an agreement between an independent, sovereign United Kingdom and the European Union.' Timothy said later, 'If you seek a partial relationship the danger is that you will be in the worst of all worlds, where you will be a rule-taker with none of the advantages of being in, but you will also sacrifice some of the advantages of being out.'

There was a demonstrable logic to all this but it is extraordinary that these, the foundational decisions of Britain's withdrawal strategy, which would shape the next two years of negotiations, were taken, in essence, by two people. The cabinet certainly had no chance to debate them.

Timothy knew where the decisions would take the country but recognised the plan was too controversial to announce so bluntly while emotions were still raw about the referendum result. It would be three months before May admitted publicly, in another speech at Lancaster House, that she wanted to leave the single market and the customs union. 'You need to conduct the negotiation in a way that takes all of the people with you,' a source close to May said. 'I think if we'd said we no longer want to be in the single market at party conference, it would have looked on the EU side like an aggressive statement.'

To distract attention from these major decisions – and to settle key issues of concern – May used interviews with the *Sunday Times* and the *Sun on Sunday* to launch the first of two major announcements from her speech. The government would convert the *acquis* – the existing body of EU law – into British law so that nothing would change on day one of Brexit. Individual laws could then be changed by Parliament in the usual way. The way this was to be accomplished was by a 'Great Repeal Bill' which would also do away with the European Communities Act 1972, the legislation that gave direct effect to all EU law in Britain. The paper was briefed with some suitably Churchillian rhetoric from the speech: 'Today marks the first stage in the UK becoming a sovereign and independent country.'

The rhetoric of repeal was clever since it disguised the fact that the plan was to take every hated Brussels directive for four decades and write them into British law. In private, Davis referred to it as 'the Great Continuity Bill'. Government lawyers had said it was impossible to do anything else, but in an environment where ministers like Andrea Leadsom were proposing to start tearing up regulations and the *Daily Mail* was running a 'scrap EU red tape' campaign, the move took some guts.

May delivered the second announcement during an interview on the BBC's *Andrew Marr Show* on the Sunday morning, pledging to trigger Article 50 of the Lisbon Treaty – the mechanism for kickstarting two years of Brexit negotiations – by the end of March 2017. May had bought time during the leadership election by saying she would not trigger Article 50 before the end of the year. Senior civil servants in DExEU and Ivan Rogers in Brussels had warned her that announcing a timetable was a bad idea because the moment Britain fired the starting gun, 'you lose pretty much all the leverage you have', putting Britain on a countdown clock where the other twenty-seven countries set the rules of the negotiation.

On 29 June, five days after the referendum result, the other twenty-seven member states had agreed a policy of 'no negotiations without notification' and – to the surprise of some British officials – they had stuck to it ever since. Rogers told May the best way of forcing the EU to compromise would be to say, 'We intend to invoke in March, but I give you no cast-iron commitment. The moment I've seen your draft guidelines document we'll invoke.' So confident was Rogers that the prime minister had listened that he told friends in Brussels just days before the conference that May would not invoke Article 50 until the end of 2017. It was proof that even the most experienced civil servants don't always read the politics of a situation accurately. As one of May's senior aides recalled, 'We couldn't get through conference without putting a line in the sand. We had to say something about timing.' David Davis was involved in the discussions over the timing, suggesting that the vague 'before the end of the first quarter' be changed to 'by the end of March', which he believed to be 'specific sounding' and 'hard to demur from later'.

Figures like George Osborne were arguing that no progress would be made in the negotiations until after the German elections in September 2017, so May should delay triggering until then. In retrospect it is possible to conclude that Britain would have been in a stronger position in the talks if the prime minister had set a firm date of October 2017 to trigger Article 50 and announced that Whitehall would spend the next year preparing for the UK to leave without a deal in order to maximise leverage in the negotiations. A minister said, 'She might just have got away with that.' But May was a new prime minister who did not wish to antagonise the Eurosceptics. Choosing 31 March as T-Day, Timothy said, 'I don't think it is sustainable to take longer.'

Later that day, May opened her speech by dismissing those who 'say that the referendum isn't valid, that we need to have a second vote' or were planning to 'challenge any attempt to leave the European Union through the courts'. She said, 'Come on! The referendum result was clear. It was legitimate. It was the biggest vote for change this country has ever known. Brexit means Brexit – and we're going to make a success of it.' In addition to the two main factual announcements, the most important passage of the speech came when the prime minister made clear that controlling immigration was her top priority, above even economic prosperity. 'We are not leaving the EU only to give up control of immigration again,' she said. A May adviser observed, 'It's logical we'd leave the single market because we don't want free movement. By conference we knew that. The vote for Brexit was about controlling immigration. Everything else flows from there.'

May also announced, 'Our laws will be made not in Brussels but in Westminster. The judges interpreting those laws will sit not in Luxembourg but in courts in this country. The authority of EU law in Britain will end.' This was not, as some have suggested, a line smuggled past a confused prime minister. 'The PM was very clear that the jurisdiction of the ECJ had to come to an end,' a close aide said. 'She thinks that is one of the major things that people voted for.' Yet that decision had huge implications which were far from fully understood in the cabinet and some corners of Downing Street when May delivered her speech. The ECJ's remit ran across dozens of agencies and thousands of regulations, from the regulation of medicines and nuclear materials to aviation safety.

While Davis was aware of much of what May was going to say, he had not seen the speech and nor had Oliver Robbins. 'The ECJ wasn't mentioned before the conference speech as a red line,' a DExEU official said. 'It was conjured up by Nick Timothy to get very Eurosceptic conference delegates and the Tory press cheering. They were terrified of people saying, "She's a remainer." There was no discussion or debate whatsoever. I don't believe Olly Robbins knew what she was going to say. The speech was not shared with any of the ministers. The chancellor didn't see it. He was livid. Even DD was furious. He agreed with most of what she said but he didn't know exactly what she was going to say.' Months later, after leaving government, James Chapman, Davis's chief of staff, said, 'The repeal bill was Nick's idea. We thought that was the big announcement. Instead of which he basically announced hard Brexit. She hamstrung the whole negotiation from the start.' In interviews that evening May denied that she had decided to leave the single market. 'All options are on the table,' she said. But according to a DExEU official, 'The pound crashed because anyone with any sense could work out that this means hard Brexit.'

May risked accusations that her tone was divisive too. She also used the Sunday speech to train her guns on the vocal minority in her party who were demanding that MPs have a vote on Brexit. 'Those people who argue that Article 50 can only be triggered after agreement in both Houses of Parliament are not standing up for democracy, they're trying to subvert it. They're not trying to get Brexit right, they're trying to kill it by delaying it. They are insulting the intelligence of the British people.' Later that week, in her main conference speech, she was no more conciliatory, attacking liberals who found the referendum result 'simply bewildering' and the Brexit voters' 'patriotism distasteful, their concerns about immigration parochial, their views about crime illiberal, their attachment to their job security inconvenient'. May was aligning herself clearly with the 52 per cent who backed Leave. While this was understandable politically, the prime minister missed an opportunity that week to put herself above both warring factions and stake a position as a national leader in a way that might have given her greater freedom of manoeuvre in the months ahead.

The influence of May's team was also evident in a policy announced by Amber Rudd, the new home secretary, in her conference speech – a plan to force firms to reveal the percentage of their workers who were foreign. The proposal unleashed a storm of protest and would see Rudd reported to the police for 'hate speech' the following January.

Having said what she wanted to say, the prime minister made clear that the media and the public would have to get used to another infor- mation drought on Brexit: 'There will always be pressure to give a running commentary on the state of the talks. It will not be in our best interests as a country to do that.'

When it came to speaking about herself, though, May was learning to open up. After a fashion.

The truncated leadership election meant that Theresa May was denied the chance to properly introduce herself to the nation or properly outline her political philosophy. Conference gave her the opportunity. Before her interviews with the *Sunday Times* and the *Sun on Sunday*, commu- nications director Katie Perrior had prepped May to respond more openly than usual to more personal questions. Her voice wavering slightly, she talked about the death of her parents and her love of the *Great British Bake Off* and even contributed her mother's recipe for scones.

The interviews were well received but they might not have been if the public had known the agonies that went into the preparations. May was not comfortable talking about herself, a prerequisite of modern politics. 'Why do they want to know this stuff?' she asked her aides. Perrior and press secretary Lizzie Loudon had also lost parents when they were young. Loudon tried to help out. She told May, 'My dad died and it's really sad for me that he can't see me here because I know he would be really proud. But in some way I feel like he would know that I would be doing something like this.' A colleague said, 'When the PM was asked the question by the interviewer she repeated Lizzie's words. She just pick-pocketed the explanation. It was an appropriation of her emotional response. You think: "You yourself don't feel anything".' Another Downing Street aide said, 'If you are prime minister, you have a duty to communicate what you do. You can't resent the questioning but she does resent the questioning.'

May's morale was boosted that week by Fiona Hill, who sent her home with a CD of the high-octane Rolling Stones song 'Start Me Up', which she judged to be what May needed as walk-on music for her set-piece speech. 'She got totally into it,' a member of the team said. 'I love it,' said May.

The main conference speech was a collaborative effort between Nick Timothy and Chris Wilkins, who had been friends for years after meeting in the Conservative Research Department. Wilkins was short and bald and shared Timothy's view that the Conservatives needed to broaden their appeal to the poor. He understood May's philosophy and the cadences of her speech. Timothy found him to be the only person he was comfortable writing with. Timothy had prepared a mini-manifesto for May which she had never used during the leadership election, and he passed on this and a couple of pages of notes laying out the substantive argument. Wilkins fashioned a first draft which the two could 'knock about' between them, with Fiona Hill and others making suggestions for improvements.

The keynote speech was a symphony on the riff May had played during her first speech in Downing Street, promising to make the Tories the 'party of workers' and go after 'rogue' businesses. She pledged to govern for the whole nation: 'We will take the centre ground.' It contained a bold declaration (for a Conservative) that she was not ideologically averse to state intervention. 'It's time to remember the good that government can do,' she declared, though her definition of government appeared to be a dig at David Cameron: 'It's about doing something, not being someone.' A May aide admitted, 'It clearly was designed to define ourselves against what had come before.'

For Wilkins, the most important theme of the speech was its depiction of May as an agent of 'change'. When he was writing the speech,

Wilkins had studied the language in Tony Blair's 2005 conference address, which used the phrase 'We are the change-makers' to try to depict a party in power for eight years as fresh and dynamic. May's team hoped she could pull the same trick, using the constant refrain that 'a change has got to come'. Wilkins recalled, 'We even played the song "A Change Has Got to Come" over the speakers in the hall before she walked on as a little in-joke.' This approach was to become important again months later when May called the general election.

The change message was drowned out, however, by one small phrase in the 7,500-word text, a line penned by Timothy which had barely been glanced at since the first draft. In words that cemented her reputation for plain speaking, May concluded, 'If you believe you're a citizen of the world, you're a citizen of nowhere.' The jibe was aimed at irresponsible jet-set businessmen. A source said, 'It was basically an attack on Philip Green,' the former boss of BHS who had sold the firm for a pound with a black hole in its pension fund. But, to Wilkins' and Timothy's surprise, some Remain voters and many Cameroons saw it as a totemic symbol of May's hostile approach to internationalism, multiculturalism and immigration. One observer summed up the speech, with its statist slant and red meat for the faithful, as 'part Ed Miliband, part *Daily Mail*'.

There was a second gaffe as well. In explaining that the economy had failed to help many since the economic crash, May had said, 'While monetary policy, with super-low interest rates and quantitative easing, provided the necessary emergency medicine after the financial crash, we have to acknowledge there have been some bad side effects.' Her words appeared to be a breach of the convention, established when the Bank of England was granted independence in 1997, that politicians refrain from commenting on monetary policy, and it caused a temporary fall in the pound. A former cabinet minister said, 'They got a real shock. They had no idea that markets paid attention to these things. It was just amateurishness. I know Mark Carney was staggered by it. He thought it was unbelievably incompetent. She said "we're the fifth largest economy in the world" and I think by the end of it we were the sixth.'

Business leaders disliked much of May's rhetoric about rogue bosses. Chris Brannigan, the debonair head of government relations whose job it was to act as the link man with business leaders, was unable to placate them in advance since he had not been told what was going to be in the speech. Carolyn Fairbairn, the new boss of the CBI, Britain's biggest business group, walked past him 'with a face like thunder' as May finished.

On the EU front, May's speech was welcomed in Westminster as much-needed clarity and by the Brexiteers as proof of May's commitment to their cause. But the citizens of the world and those running the other EU countries joined the City in reacting with horror.

In interviews during conference week, May had made clear that she was keen to start 'preparatory work' with Brussels before she invoked Article 50. Both she and David Davis pledged that Britain would respect the existing rights of the three million EU citizens in Britain, as long as the 1.5 million Britons elsewhere in the EU were protected. Ministers saw that as an easy, early win. It was one the rest of the EU did not want to give them. Jean-Claude Juncker and officials from France, Germany, Poland and Slovakia all reasserted the position that there would be 'no negotiation before notification'. While some welcomed the clarity over timing and the acceptance that May was not trying to hold on to all the benefits of membership, Joseph Muscat – the Maltese prime minister who would hold the EU presidency in 2017 – spoke for many when he said, 'Any deal has to be a fair deal, but an inferior deal.'

While attention at home was focused on the timetable for triggering Article 50 and the Great Repeal Bill, the Europeans were transfixed by May's blanket rejection of ECJ oversight. 'My sense of that was that they hadn't fully realised what they'd said on jurisdiction and how radical it was,' commented a diplomat. In Brussels, Rogers and his colleagues began to hear from their EU counterparts, 'Clearly you're leaving the single market and the customs union. Why then can't we just get on with it?'

Nick Timothy had defined British policy on Brexit. Now Theresa May had to guide her cabinet to the same place without admitting the policy was already set in stone.

'NO RUNNING COMMENTARY'

Two moments in early September summed up Theresa May's approach to Brexit negotiations during the autumn of 2016. In the first Prime Minister's Questions after the summer break, May said she would not give a 'running commentary' on the talks. She then took a call from the French president, François Hollande. Six weeks earlier, May had shocked Westminster by putting on hold an £18 billion deal for French company EDF Energy to build the Hinkley Point C nuclear power station, a joint venture with a Chinese state-owned firm. Now, having studied the evidence herself, May gave the green light. Hollande asked why she had thrown the deal into uncertainty. The prime minister replied, 'It is my method.'

Alasdair Palmer, who worked for May at the Home Office, said, 'She likes to consider the evidence carefully before coming to a conclusion. That takes her time. That is why she likes to set up inquiries and consultations – processes that delay decision taking and help reassure her that the decision that eventually emerges will be the right one.' She would not be bounced into decisions. 'I've seen people trying to grab her in the margins of a meeting and say, "Can we do this?" and she'll ask them to produce a piece of paper, and not take the decision now,' a senior cabinet minister said. 'She has always been like that.'

May embarked upon a laborious series of cabinet discussions about Brexit, in which her desire to keep her destination hidden from the public seemed at times to fly in the face of the clear signals that she had sent in her party conference speeches. It was a process in which the prime minister herself seemed to want reassurance that the roadmap she and Nick Timothy had agreed was the right one.

The prime minister had made a big thing of returning to cabinet government after the Cameron years but Brexit was not discussed by the full cabinet. Instead, May appointed a dozen-strong cabinet subcommittee (the European Union Exit and Trade Committee). In keeping with her penchant for secrecy the membership was not published until it leaked in mid-October. Every cabinet minister who had campaigned to leave the EU – David Davis, Boris Johnson, Liam Fox, Chris Grayling, Priti Patel and Andrea Leadsom – was included, half the committee, when they represented just a quarter of the full cabinet. The other five members, all Remain backers, were Philip Hammond, Amber Rudd, Damian Green, Greg Clark and party chairman Patrick McLoughlin.

May let everyone have their say and ministers initially praised the way conclusions had not been preordained on her sofa before the meeting as they had been in the Cameron days. One cabinet minister said, 'There's proper consideration of the issues.' Soon, though, some realised these discussions seldom led to decisions at all. 'They were deliberations not decision making,' one cabinet minister said. 'The decisions were still made in Downing Street.' Another present for the meetings described them as 'fairly odd'. 'Cameron meetings were always chaotic and vociferous. Hers were calm, more measured, but you don't really get a real debate with her. You lodge some points and some observations and she absorbs. But it's terribly difficult to gauge whether you are getting anywhere.' To those paying attention, it seemed obvious that May had decided to leave the single market and the customs union, but the prime minister denied it publicly and in private let her warring ministers fight it out, occasionally showing her displeasure. A senior cabinet minister said, 'She has a very healthy impatience, a slightly Thatcherian quality. She gives that heavy sigh and there's a rolling of the eyebrows.'

In the early meetings, each of which lasted around two hours, Boris Johnson and Philip Hammond emerged as the key antagonists at the head of the blocs of Remain- and Leave-supporting ministers. 'Boris would make rousing speeches about how it was all going to be brilliant and how we should all be saying positive things about Brexit,' a cabinet colleague recalled. 'Phil used to get pretty annoyed about that and say, "It's not that simple." Phil was pretty punchy about staying in the single market and even more so on the customs union.' A source close to May said, 'Hammond and Boris wound each other up, pulling faces when the other one was saying stuff.' Another witness said, 'Boris would chunter through Phil's interventions.'

The two men could not have been more different. Johnson, the Dulux dog lookalike with papers spilling from the distended pockets of his suit, was a man of feral political instincts whose yearning for positive publicity belied an essential shyness. By contrast, Hammond was buttoned up in both tailoring and manner. His accountant's eye for the bottom line had garnered him one nickname 'Spreadsheet Phil', his allergic reaction to the media and soporific delivery another ironic appellation: 'Box Office'. Hammond had a sense of humour drier than a Jacob's cream cracker in the Sahara but his lugubrious politics and appearance, that of a purse-lipped Jar Jar Binks, almost invited the question, 'Why the long face?'

Since no work had been done by the civil service to prepare for Brexit, these early meetings were information-gathering exercises rather than policy-making forums. Civil servants despaired at the level of knowledge around the table. 'It is not possible to underestimate the level of knowledge in the cabinet at that point,' one official said. 'When those things were said at conference I would be quite careful about assuming that the implications were really clear. A big part of the job for officials was educating politicians about the implications of the political narrative that they had established.' This even included Davis. A civil servant said, 'He thought he knew a lot but most of what he'd written was wrong in some way: legally, diplomatically or just plain not correct. You had to put evidence in front of him and use facts.'

May also faced a steep learning curve. Her experience as home secretary was valuable. But having done the same job for six years she lacked expertise outside her brief, particularly in economic affairs. A senior civil servant said, 'I didn't have a sense that outside the world of justice and home affairs she knew what she thought very much.'

A senior cabinet minister summed up the Brexit committee discussions as 'an educational process'. He said, 'There hadn't been a stroke of work done under Cameron, so this was all from scratch. The initial meetings covered what the questions were, then by late autumn we were beginning to get options. In the new year we started answering those questions.'

To their colleagues some Brexiteer ministers seemed more interested in justifying the way they voted in the referendum than preparing for Brexit. Andrea Leadsom, the environment secretary, stood out to colleagues as one who read her thoughts from the departmental brief in front of her. 'Andrea turns up and says what officials have told her to say,' a source close to May said. Another aide characterised the contributions of Leadsom and Priti Patel, the international development secretary, as 'pretty vacuous', their comments a combination of 'departmental briefs' and 'occasional prejudices'.

DExEU officials told Leadsom she would need to hire five hundred more staff but she initially recruited only thirty. 'They've got to redesign forty years of agriculture policy and the entire system of subsidy,' a DExEU source said. 'Meetings with her were embarrassing.' A cabinet colleague said, 'She was completely out of her depth at the beginning. She is a genuine and decent person, but massively underpowered for what was needed at secretary of state level. She's very stubborn and basically not really bright enough.' Several ministers recalled that Leadsom's most memorable contribution in cabinet that year was nothing to do with Brexit. Leadsom had been subjected to ridicule from MPs when she used leadership hustings in June 2016 to discuss the neonatal charity she had set up, which advocated massaging babies' brains. During a health discussion that autumn, she raised the subject again, to the bemusement of her cabinet colleagues. One said, 'She only ever talks about exports of British produce and babies' brains.'

Philip Hammond's time as foreign secretary during Cameron's renegotiation gave him an advantage over most of his colleagues. Combined with the institutional clout of the Treasury, he quickly began to assert himself. The chancellor was 'very gloomy' about Brexit for three reasons. A former minister with whom he discussed his concerns that autumn said, 'One was the economic cost of it. The second was they could see the impact on financial services. Companies were making decisions about whether to leave. Third, they were feeling a bit overwhelmed by all the problems – like creating a customs system at the border.'

A cabinet committee paper discussed in mid-October warned that the Treasury could lose up to £66 billion a year in tax revenues if there was a hard Brexit. It also predicted a worst-case scenario that GDP could fall by as much as 9.5 per cent after fifteen years if Britain left the single market and traded on World Trade Organisation terms. 'In headline terms trade would be around a fifth lower than it otherwise would have been,' it said. The paper drew on the work Treasury officials had done for George Osborne during the referendum campaign. Jeremy Heywood ordered a rewrite of key sections for 'more balance', but even the revised draft drew complaints from Brexiteers that Hammond was 'trying to make leaving the single market look bad'.[1] Publication of the leak drove the pound to a thirty-one-year low against the dollar.

Hammond's vociferous stance and the institutional activism of the Treasury enraged the senior Brexiteers. 'The Treasury for months after the vote was absolutely determined to frustrate the outcome as much as it possibly could,' a senior cabinet minister said. 'They believed that membership of the single market would be seen by everybody as an unalloyed good. But to leave the EU you have to leave the legislative rule-making system, which is the single market.'

Realising after the first cabinet committee meeting on Brexit that they needed to stick together, Boris Johnson, Liam Fox and David Davis met in a waiting room in 10 Downing Street to confirm to each other that they accepted the logic that Brexit meant leaving both the single market and the customs union. 'If you're going to do it, do it right,' Johnson said. 'It's like Theresa says, you've got to stop thinking about what we hold on to, you have to imagine Britain free and think of what you want.' Fox's ability to secure free trade deals depended on Britain leaving both arrangements: 'To be in the single market would mean unrestricted free-dom of movement which is politically not possible,' he said. 'To remain fully in the customs union we're not allowed to have separate free trade agreements with the rest of the world outside of the EU.' Fox regarded these arguments as 'unanswerable'.

Davis was sceptical of the 'clever people with a uniform set of views' in the Treasury and the 'gravity model' they used on trade, which decreed that the closer you are to a country the more you trade. He believed it was ineffective because services were 'weightless' and traditional constraints on long-distance trade, like transport costs, were a small fraction of what they had been decades earlier. 'David felt they massively overestimated the negative impact of a no-deal WTO scenario and then underestimated the advantages of deals with the rest of the world because they're all a long way away from us,' a source said. When Hammond told him there might be a 25 per cent fall in trade, Davis replied, 'That's bollocks!'

Despite her conference speech, May did not wish to be boxed in or hurried into stating her views publicly. 'The system was moving too rapidly to tell her what the right answer would be without giving any evidence,' one mandarin admitted. Some officials found it difficult to adapt from the free-wheeling briefings of the Cameron days to a female prime minister who wanted things done more formally. Both Mark Lyall-Grant, the national security adviser, and Andrew Parker, the director general of MI5, attracted May's ire for interrupting her, talking over her and 'mansplaining' in condescending tones.[2] Ivan Rogers had a similar effect. Some saw the same trait in Hammond, who did not trouble to disguise his disdain for those with lesser intellects or job titles. A cabinet minister said, 'He was patronising. Boris, in particular, had a rough time at some of these meetings.' Another cabinet colleague explained, 'He thinks Boris is a plonker.' May's team saw Hammond's spats with Johnson as evidence that he, too, was seeking to justify his vote on 23 June: 'It does feel a little bit like an exchange of blows over things that are long gone. Phil made such a song and dance about his Euroscepticism over the years – then he campaigned to stay in. Having then lost he feels he can't re-rat.'

When May made Hammond her chancellor, the conventional wisdom was that they were old university friends and that she wanted someone she could trust next door. While they were Oxford contemporaries, Hammond had a very different approach to economics from May and Nick Timothy and felt himself to be no less able than May. Hammond told a former cabinet minister, 'If Theresa May can be the prime minister, so can I.' The source said, 'They're not friends. He doesn't like her.'

Hammond's personality also irritated May's team. A cabinet colleague said, 'There is something mildly Aspergic about him. Philip is not very user friendly.' The chancellor clung to the security blanket of single market membership long after others had given it up as impossible. A senior mandarin said, 'Phil was beating a dead horse. That's the charm and the irritation of the man. He usually picks the wrong battle.'

For his part, the chancellor became highly frustrated that he was blocked by the chiefs from seeing May alone, without their presence. A Downing Street official said, 'Philip used to get very frustrated that he could not see the PM. He thought he had the right to see her any time he liked.' A senior civil servant said Hammond would hover outside May's office but would be intercepted by Timothy or Hill: 'He would want to see her on her own but they would say, "You're not going in there without us."' Another Downing Street source said, 'He was made to feel unwelcome. They never spoke to DD like that.'

In October it was reported that Hammond had threatened to resign, in part because he had been excluded from the 8.30 a.m. planning meeting in Number 10 at which George Osborne had been an habitué. In fact, Hammond had never threatened to resign but he had told friends that he had thought about doing so. 'He went around – in a gallows humour kind of way – saying, "Well, I won't be in this government very long,"' one ally said. 'He doesn't get on with her at all.' Fiona Hill put 'face time' with Hammond in May's diary but the chancellor demanded meetings about the autumn statement alone with May, which the chiefs viewed as unacceptable. Hammond's marginalisation was also painful for his officials. 'The Treasury was running the country under George Osborne and Gordon Brown,' one said nostalgically. As a result of this episode it was agreed that Hammond would have regular dinners or breakfasts with May. 'Phil insisted on having his weekly time with her,' a fellow minister said. Nick Timothy explained later, 'They go for dinner or breakfast with one another probably every fortnight.'[3] The arrangement was publicised by Hammond's aides. By contrast, David Davis was able to wander in to see Hill and Timothy – both of whom were firm DD fans – whenever he liked.

May's aides believed Hammond – while not a leaker to the media himself – was too ready to sound off to people who shared his thoughts with journalists. A cabinet colleague said, 'Philip talks too freely.' A May aide stated, 'On Brexit he quite willingly talks against her to Mark Carney, who tells everyone in his circle and that feeds back. I think he's a bit naïve, actually.' In discussions with third parties Hammond did little to disguise his scepticism about May's approach. 'The economy almost certainly will slow down,' he said privately. As chancellor, Hammond wanted more headroom in the public finances to cushion against turbulence. His personal assessment that autumn, shared with political and media contacts, was that a Remain vote would have provided 'a growth kick of half a per cent of GDP a year for several years' and that growth in 2017 would have been 2.5 per cent, a figure he now expected to be just 1 per cent. Nick Timothy, in particular, regarded Hammond's views on the economy as excessively pessimistic. A DExEU official said, 'The way they talked to the chancellor of the exchequer was totally outrageous. I've seen DD in meetings roll his eyes as Hammond tries to say something sensible about Brexit. They don't want to hear anything about problems.'

As the autumn went on the daunting complexity of Brexit became clearer to the cabinet. At the end of September, Carlos Ghosn, the CEO of Nissan, warned that he could scrap potential new investment in the car firm's Sunderland plant unless the government promised to compensate the company for any tariffs imposed after Brexit. WTO rules stipulated tariffs of 10 per cent on car imports and exports, wreaking havoc with cross-border supply chains. One senior cabinet minister admitted, 'Brexit was a surprise for the Japanese and they don't like surprises.'

Theresa May and Greg Clark, the business secretary, set to work to put Nissan's mind at rest. They did not offer tariff relief but privately made clear that Britain would be pursuing a bespoke trade deal with the aim of keeping tariffs at zero and borders as frictionless as possible. A minister said, 'Assurances were given about investment in training but there were no financial inducements.' It was enough for Ghosn to announce, on 27 October, that Nissan would build its new Qashqai II and X-Trail models in Sunderland, safeguarding seven thousand jobs. It was a propaganda win for the Brexiteers. The Remainers responded by pointing out that insurance giant Lloyd's of London was planning to open a series of subsidiary offices elsewhere in the EU so they could continue to operate post Brexit.

Ministers were quickly aware that moving EU law into British law could not be done at the stroke of a pen, since many laws referred to rulings by the European Commission or various EU regulatory bodies. Each of these would need to be rewritten to refer to new British regulators. A cabinet minister said, 'People made an initial scan and thought, "Fuck!" The number of statutes affected started off in the tens of thousands. It came down significantly to around one thousand.' The number fell because government lawyers 'found ways of doing things once' which would 'cross over to other statutes'.

Davis set up fifty-eight projects inside DExEU to analyse the implications of Brexit for different sectors of the economy and public life and make recommendations about which had to be protected. Separately, Davis asked a bright civil servant called Tom Shinner to oversee a risk register of key projects and institute a 'critical path analysis' which would send alarm bells to Davis if progress on preparing for Brexit was too tardy. May's conference speech brought home to civil servants across Whitehall what was at stake. 'You could go from no impact on the automative industry if you replicate tariff-free trade to total disaster if we have hard Brexit with all the tariffs,' one said. 'We realised that we had to prepare for the worst-case scenario.'

The implications of May's approach to the European Court of Justice raised alarm bells in several departments. The court played a role in overseeing Euratom, the nuclear materials regulator, the Open Skies Agreement, which gave British airlines parity of access to European airports; the European Medicines Agency, which regulated medicines; and the European Broadcasting Union, which granted licences to television companies, prompting the Discovery Channel to warn ministers they might have to relocate elsewhere in Europe. Ivan Rogers sought to explain to ministers some of the benefits of ECJ oversight. 'On aeroplanes, access to the single market means planes can land at EU airports and return from them. Membership of the single market means you get slot, gate and lounge allocation on the same terms as local airlines – not 3.00 a.m. slots a mile away from the terminal, and the airlines can fly within the EU, not just to and from the EU. Access means that your banks can only lend via a local subsidiary. Membership means there is no need for your banks to be separately supervised, regulated, managed and capitalised subsidiaries in other countries. Access means that Scotch can be sold into France or Germany; membership of the single market means that all taxes and duties for comparable products to Scotch must be the same as for Scotch, and if they are not, we can take them to the ECJ and say, "Why are they not?"'[4]

In each case a new deal or a domestic solution was possible, but they would need to be found. A DExEU official said, 'It was clear we were leaving not just the single market but every European agency. The Department of Health people said, "We can't leave the European Medicines Agency". Well, you just have. When we asked each department what their preferred outcome was they all said, "Everything to remain as it is."' That meant officials needed to concentrate on finding ways to replicate the status quo and resist contingency planning for a scenario in which there was no deal. Davis was forced to 'kick them hard' to prepare.

After initial concerns that the Brexit secretary did not like detail and would not put in a full five-day week, by Christmas most saw him as a serious figure striving to get to grips with the task in hand. 'My aim,' he told his staff, 'is to imagine a huge Venn diagram of the different groups – politicians, the City, industry, the diplomatic corps – and find somewhere in that bloody great Venn diagram where everybody overlaps.' At the centre of the diagram, Davis sought to 'ensure Number 9 and Number 10 [Downing Street] are as close as they sound like they are'. A cabinet minister observed of May, 'It takes her time to make decisions. It also takes her time to trust people. You have to work at it.'

Despite Philip Hammond's agitation, the cabinet quickly came to the view that Britain would leave the single market. Their most heated debates throughout autumn 2016 concerned whether the country would remain a full member of the customs union, within which countries set common external tariffs and do not require customs checks. Also at issue was whether the UK could begin negotiating its own free trade deals with other countries, which was not possible with full membership.

In October a leaked cabinet paper showed ministers had been warned that pulling out of the customs union could lead to a 4.5 per cent fall in GDP by 2030 and the clogging up of trade through ports like Dover and Holyhead. It estimated that the UK would need to grow trade with its ten largest partners outside the EU by 37 per cent by 2030 to make up the difference. But the cabinet Brexiteers did not believe the Treasury's figures, after their referendum campaign warnings about an immediate economic shock had proved incorrect. Davis dismissed them as 'pessimistic', while Johnson branded the modelling 'Project Fear crap' reminiscent of the referendum campaign.

Hammond, backed up by Greg Clark, challenged Fox's Department for International Trade to quantify the benefits that could be accrued from new trade deals with non-EU countries, but the figures were not forthcoming. 'This was why Hammond was saying, "We're not leaving the customs union" – because he didn't believe these other trade deals are going to make up the difference,' a senior civil servant said. Trade deals with even friendly countries like the US, Australia and New Zealand presented difficulties, since they would open the border to hormone-infused beef, chlorinated chickens from the States and cheap lamb from Australasia. 'The Welsh Office said, "Hang on a minute, that will kill the Welsh lamb industry,"' a source recalled.

There were also practical problems at the border. A former minister said, 'Phil told me that for every hour at Dover, 30 kilometres of lorries go through. They just don't have any system at all for stopping and checking them.' Customs were installing a new computer system, the Customs Declaration System, a fact which raised alarm bells following previous government IT failures. Officials advised Davis that they would need one thousand lorry bays to inspect incoming freight at Dover. There were currently ten. The dawning realisation that Britain would also need thousands of new customs officers strengthened the hand of Hammond and other ministers who were pressing for a transitional arrangement, to buy Britain more time to move from EU membership to the new order. Put simply, unlike May and Davis the chancellor believed there was no chance of having the necessary people and systems in place by the end of March 2019. 'That's why the Treasury began to kick back violently,' a source said.

As the row rumbled on, Fox remained confident that Britain would be outside the customs union, a view he was quick to share with EU officials. A DIT trade strategy paper leaked in September warned that staying in the customs union 'would constrain our ability to act independently' and could also be 'portrayed by some that remaining means we have not left the EU'. A senior civil servant observed, 'Liam, of course, was fighting for his job. But unless May was going to sack him and shut his department down, the customs decision was taken on the day they created DIT.'

However, when Ivan Rogers sought clarity from Downing Street he was told nothing had been decided. In Number 10, despite her conference speech, allies say May was engaged in the search for a halfway house. 'On the customs union, I think she genuinely wanted to try and find another way,' one said. With some ministers, May even used an old phrase of Tony Blair's. 'She kept saying, "Maybe there's some third way …"' When quizzed by reporters, May would say, 'It's not a binary decision.' A source close to the prime minister explained, 'Membership itself is a binary choice but access is not.' There was even talk of keeping certain sectors of the economy or parts of the country inside the customs union – an idea soon dropped as impractical. This hedging created friction with the Brexiteers, particularly Boris Johnson, who wanted a clear statement that the UK was leaving.

Johnson compared the customs union to the Zollverein, the nineteenth-century arrangement which broke down tariff barriers between German states while maintaining tariffs with the outside world. He wanted Britain to 'come out of the Zollverein' as it related to the rest of the world, but retain free movement of goods between the UK and the rest of the zone. The foreign secretary was unable to keep his views private. On a trip to Prague on 15 November he told a Czech newspaper,

'Probably, we will need to leave the customs union.' He also dismissed the notion that freedom of movement was a founding principle of the EU, with customary relish, as 'bollocks'. May was not amused. Her official spokeswoman Helen Bower told journalists, 'The foreign secretary reflected the government's position which is that a decision hasn't been taken.'

On his return, Johnson was summoned to Downing Street for a 'meeting without coffee' with May and Timothy. 'Boris, why are you so obsessed with the customs union?' May asked. The foreign secretary replied, 'It doesn't make any sense.' They had a long argument. Johnson pointed out, 'You could have frictionless trade from outside the customs union and continue to have goods and services circulating inside the single market.' He cited the example of integrated automotive supply chains that cross the US-Canadian border. Johnson left and told aides that May was concerned business would be 'spooked' by the idea of leaving the customs union. Privately he was critical that Davis was not backing him up. A source close to Johnson said, 'DD's position was, "God, it's all so difficult" because he had a vested interest in intensifying the magnitude of the task in order to intensify his triumph when it comes. Boris was worried that the whole tone of the government was becoming defeatist.'

Johnson did have an ally in Fox. In a wing of the Foreign Office overlooking Whitehall, which had been annexed by DIT, the international trade secretary got on with the job as if he had no doubts Britain was leaving. He saw four main tasks. The first was securing Britain separate 'schedules' at the World Trade Organisation, in effect deciding how much of the EU's trade concessions would be taken over by Britain. It was not just a case of taking ownership of a fixed percentage. The vast bulk of New Zealand lamb coming into the whole EU ended up in Britain, for example. Fox argued that the schedules should apply based on the percentage of any quota ending up in the UK market.

The second task was arranging deals for Britain with countries who already had a free trade deal with the EU so that the UK could keep trading with them on the same terms after Brexit. That meant trying to transplant forty agreements covering fifty-eight countries. Two were worth a disproportionate amount of the trade: Switzerland and South Korea. Fox told those countries, 'We want to adopt the EU FTA [free trade agreement] into UK law. We'll come to a more bespoke agreement that's more liberal later on.'

The third task was to begin talks to secure new free trade agreements. He regarded the US as the main target, but Australia, New Zealand and the Gulf Cooperation Council all indicated interest, with China and India as the other main prizes. This work could not begin in earnest until Davis made progress on trade talks with the EU, because these countries wanted to know what access to the EU a deal with Britain would bring. A paper prepared for a cabinet Brexit committee meeting in September (leaked in November) showed that the DIT had divided countries he wanted Britain to trade with into 'gold' and 'silver' categories.

The fourth and final strand of his work was to talk to Britain's EU partners about how the EU negotiations, led by Davis, would affect world trade. Fox warned that they had a responsibility not to damage global prosperity: 'If Europe comes to an agreement that limits trade and investment that will impact the global economy.' He explained his approach in a speech in Manchester on 29 September, vowing to make Britain a 'world leader in free trade' and exploit the 'golden opportunity' to forge new links. He urged the EU to avoid tariffs which he said would 'harm the people of Europe'.

Things weren't plain sailing, though. Fox received legal advice that there was a 'high risk' that the European Commission would take Britain to court and seek to fine the UK if he sought to sign or negotiate trade deals with third countries while it remained in the EU. The paper revealed that even discussing a trade deal with a country not actively negotiating with the EU would still 'carry a medium/low risk' of being sued by Brussels. A Downing Street official said, 'There was a lot of bravado from ministers about what they were going to achieve, which very quickly proved to be unrealistic and legally impossible.' Some civil servants believed that Fox's focus on trade tariffs – and his belief that a trade deal with the EU would be the 'easiest in the world' – was missing the point, since the real problems were encountered trying to secure a deal on services, where the refusal to recognise professional qualifications and other non-tariff barriers were more significant. 'It's not all about tariffs,' a senior mandarin said. 'Liam believes you just unilaterally disarm and then take all your tariffs down.'

Ivan Rogers also warned Downing Street that the belief of Brexiteers that they could just walk away from the EU with no deal and keep trading on the same terms if neither side erected tariffs was incorrect. Unless the UK signed a trade deal it would automatically revert to the status of a third country after Brexit. He told May, 'You have to be on the list of countries permitted to export into the EU market. Secondly, individual firms then have to be approved, and thirdly individual consignments have to be cleared before the goods or services are allowed on the EU market. That applies to all non-member states until you have a preferential agreement.'[5]

Hammond and the Treasury were also fighting for the financial services industry, which would need special 'passporting' deals to trade in the EU. 'He was of the view that if the FTA doesn't cover financial services, it's not worth having anyway,' a senior official said. May, schooled by Timothy in a distaste for City fat cats, saw it as less of a priority. 'She was not persuaded by the City arguments,' a cabinet minister said. 'They concluded they would be a sacrificial victim.' Davis, who had chaired the Future of Banking commission back in 2010, believed the banks had captured the Treasury. Privately he had been heard to describe bankers as 'the most overpaid useless bunch of wankers I've ever met in my life'.

There were also problems getting DIT fully up to speed. Ivan Rogers warned Jeremy Heywood that the EU trade directorate was, with its US counterpart, the best in the world. 'We have within a very short space of time to build one of the best three trade negotiating authorities in the world.'[6] DIT was not ready for battle.

In seeking to forge a compromise on the customs union, Davis argued that it was perfectly possible to have a frictionless border if Britain secured a free trade agreement with the EU. His 'grand simplifying principle' of the agreement was that Britain would start with total regulatory alignment with the EU and 'if in doubt, keep it as open as it is now'. In the absence of tariffs, a new customs deal would have to settle 'rules of origin' – designed to stop a country like China using the UK as a 'landing craft' to flood the EU market – and how to equate standards on safety, hygiene, data, consumer rights and the environment between the two jurisdictions. He argued that 92 per cent of goods consignments, whose contents could be electronically pre-notified, would take just five seconds to clear customs. Only 8 per cent would have to be inspected.

Ivan Rogers helped get Hammond to understand how isolated he was becoming. They met before the chancellor travelled to a meeting of EU finance ministers on 6 December. 'I think you're fighting a completely losing battle on the customs union, I understand why you're fighting it but I think you're on a loser,' Rogers said. Hammond argued that the future benefits of free trade deals would never match those of single market and customs union membership. 'I'd like to see a reputable cross-government cost-benefit analysis, because it will only show one thing.' Rogers replied, 'If this were about cost-benefit analysis we wouldn't be here at all.' Instead, Rogers urged Hammond to concentrate his efforts on persuading May to secure a transitional arrangement which would keep Britain inside the customs union while a full-blown agreement could be drawn up. 'That's all you're going to get,' he said.

In her conference speech May had said, 'Every stray word and every hyped-up media report is going to make it harder for us to get the right deal for Britain.' But all the bickering meant the cabinet committee leaked relentlessly as the two sides manoeuvred for position. A paper on trade found its way to the *Sunday Times*, details of an immigration discussion to the *Daily Telegraph* and another on security to the *Sunday Telegraph*. *The Times* got hold of a handful of leaks, most notably a paper circulated in November ranking various industries as high, medium and low priorities in the Brexit negotiations. The high-priority industries included pharmaceuticals, car-making, clothing, aerospace, banking and air transport. The steel industry and the business services sector were unimpressed to find themselves in the lowest category.[7]

After initially distributing the key papers a week in advance, Jeremy Heywood began numbering every document, limiting them to hard copies, so they could not be emailed on, and sending them out only the night before or on the morning of meetings. A cabinet minister said, 'You knew perfectly well that if you discussed anything in cabinet it would be outside three minutes after cabinet finished. You cannot have an argument with someone when they're having a three-way discussion with the newspapers at the same time.' Suspicion fell on Johnson and Hammond, but also on Priti Patel, Chris Grayling and Liam Fox, who was liked by May but regarded as an oddball by the chiefs. Fox's cabinet colleagues delighted in spreading a story – vehemently denied by Fox himself – that he had been locked in his hotel room on the orders of the chiefs for several hours during May's trip to India.

As a former journalist who knew Sam Coates – the principal recipient of the Brexit committee papers – James Chapman was quizzed by MI5 officers, who demanded access to both his and his wife's mobile phones.

'We can see you've been talking to him,' one of his interrogators said. Chapman had won a reputation among journalists for never telling his former colleagues anything useful, so the experience was distressing. 'I've never leaked a cabinet document in my life,' he said. Chapman had already decided to leave government and was in talks with the public affairs company Bell Pottinger. Embarrassingly, his private email was full of messages about the possibility of a new job.

The primary leaker was never identified but senior officials in Downing Street, including Katie Perrior, came to suspect that the chiefs were responsible for some of the leaks in a bid to keep journalists occupied and that they had pointed the finger of blame at Chapman to cover their tracks. In October Laura Kuenssberg, the BBC's political editor, found out, half an hour before the decision was announced, that Heathrow was to be allowed to build a third runway.

Earlier, ITV's Chris Ship had broken the news of May's decision to approve Hinkley Point. Perrior was quizzed by security: 'Do you ever speak to Chris Ship?'

'Yes.'

'How often?'

'Several times a week.'

'Why do you do that?'

'Because I'm the director of communications ...'

The leak inquiries were inconclusive but Hill and Timothy had not been required to submit their own phones. When most of the autumn statement appeared in the public domain in advance, Hammond told May he suspected one of her staff of trying to undermine him. This time Perrior suggested that everyone – including May, Hammond and Jeremy Heywood – hand in their phones to ensure there was no excuse for the chiefs to be excluded. She knew the chiefs had been briefing because Timothy was taking her through the plans when they were interrupted by an official informing him that a Sunday newspaper journalist was waiting for him in the next room. The officials charged with the leak inquiry discovered that the chiefs talked to journalists so often that it was impossible to tell if they were behind the specific leaks.

In early December, Jeremy Heywood issued an edict that the 'spate of corrosive leaks' must come to an end. In a memo to mandarins he ordered senior officials to use only government-issue phones, allowing all their communications to be monitored, and warned that anyone leaking would be fired, whether or not there was a threat to national security. Within a few days, Heywood's memo itself had been leaked to the *Mail on Sunday*.

May's government took security very seriously. Every minister in the Brexit department was given an MI5 briefing when they got the job. 'They told us that we were going to be the most targeted department in Whitehall,' one minister said. David Davis took this to heart, carrying around his computer and iPad in a metal briefcase containing a 'Faraday cage' to block all wireless, cellular, GPS and WiFi signals. At his home he stored them in a biscuit tin. He was also told by the security services to ditch his Apple watch to prevent foreign spies using it to listen to his conversations. He replaced it with a Garmin smart watch, advertised as 'for athletes and adventurers'. Asked if it was 'government issue', Davis said, 'You must be joking – that's a thousand-quid watch.' When embarking on foreign trips ministers were warned that they might be approached by 'honey trap' agents from foreign powers and jokingly told, 'You might even want to get changed under your bedclothes.' The warning led to a story in the *Sun on Sunday* that Theresa May herself had been advised to disrobe under the covers or risk being filmed naked – a leak for which Boris Johnson was blamed.

The paranoia extended to Downing Street, where Fiona Hill was highly security conscious after living with a former spy for several years. 'Fiona banned us from talking on mobiles in case people were listening,' said a DExEU official. 'If you wanted Fiona you had to call her on her landline.' Six years at the Home Office had made the prime minister, too, wary of security issues. One of her staff asked May how she kept her wardrobe refreshed: 'I don't know how you find the time. I go home at midnight, I sit on the John Lewis website and I get it all delivered. Do you online shop?'

May said, 'I'm the former home secretary, of course I don't shop online.'

By November May's desire for secrecy around Brexit meant progress was slow. Number 10's sensitivity was well summarised by a memo written by a Deloitte consultant in the Cabinet Office on 7 November, which leaked to *The Times* eight days later. It warned that Whitehall was struggling to cope with more than five hundred Brexit projects and the fact that 'no common strategy' had emerged among cabinet ministers. The memo said May's predilection for 'drawing in decisions and details to settle matters herself' was holding up decision-making.

The prime minister was described as 'personally affronted' by the wording. The official response was, 'This is not a government report and we don't recognise the claims made in it.' But for all too many people it had hit the nail on the head.

Within a month Deloitte had a meeting with Sir Jeremy Heywood and John Manzoni, the chief executive of the civil service, and – under threat of further punishment – agreed not to bid for any further government contracts for six months. Deloitte's treatment excited comparisons between May's operation and both Stalin and Colonel Gaddafi, while business voices complained that her team 'don't want to hear difficult messages' and were guilty of 'government by rage'.[8] MP Anna Soubry, a Remainer, said Deloitte had been 'bullied'. Ministers told to keep quiet, not accept lunch invitations from journalists and refused permission by Downing Street to make announcements on the government 'grid' felt much the same way.

The very next day, 16 November, the Institute for Government (IfG), a thinktank close to senior mandarins, warned that Brexit represented an 'existential threat' to the operations of some departments: 'Whitehall does not have the capacity to deliver Brexit on top of everything else to which it is already committed.' The IfG said May's 'secretive approach' was hampering preparations, with the result that they looked 'chaotic and dysfunctional'. It said, 'Silence is not a strategy. Failure to reveal the government's plan to reach a negotiating position is eroding confidence among business and investors.'[9]

The same day the IfG report was published, Sir Simon Fraser, the former permanent secretary at the Foreign Office, appeared in front of the new select committee shadowing DExEU and said the government did not yet have a 'central plan' for Brexit.

May and her team thought they had signalled clearly where they were heading, but her cabinet was divided and Whitehall was in open revolt. To make matters worse, the European Commission was now playing hardball too, over the most contentious issue of all.

Money.

THE ENEMY GETS A VOTE

It is lost to history whether Martin Selmayr was an admirer of General James 'Mad Dog' Mattis, the American general who was to become Donald Trump's defence secretary, but he certainly understood one of Mattis's favourite aphorisms about war – 'the enemy gets a vote'. While the debate in cabinet and the British media was almost entirely consumed with what Britain wanted from a new deal with Brussels, senior Eurocrats had their own ideas and were beginning to flex their muscles. They didn't come any more senior, or more aggressive, than Selmayr, the chief of staff to European Commission president Jean-Claude Juncker.

A German lawyer in his mid-forties, Selmayr was regarded – with good reason – as the most powerful man in Brussels. To some he was the most gifted protector of the European dream. To a generation of British diplomats he was a menace who regarded the UK as an obstruction to his schemes and had fully earned his nicknames, 'the Rasputin of Brussels' and 'Monster of the Berlaymont', the Commission's headquarters. Said hardly ever to sleep, Selmayr harboured a peculiar animosity towards the British and their media, who had, in his words, a 'foot on the brake of history' – though Selmayr once claimed, 'I only read the British press once a year, when I go to holiday in Spain, when one's blood pressure is low.' A 'true believer' in the European project, he was on record as saying, 'Brexit cannot be a success,' fearing that anything but a catastrophic Brexit could damage the European project. In early November he set out to make it so.

On 4 November, the *Financial Times* – Selmayr's preferred British outlet – ran a story saying that the European Union was to demand an exit bill of €60 billion from Britain. Ivan Rogers, Britain's ambassador to the EU, warned London that Selmayr was trying to 'explode the whole thing' by making an impossible demand. A British diplomat said, 'Selmayr enjoys lobbing grenades into the UK debate. Unlike other EU figures, he is skilled in dealing with the media.'

The exact genesis of the Commission's calculations was a mystery even to many in Brussels. Other member states told British officials that they had never seen the figure before and suggested it had been 'plucked from the sky' by Selmayr. Nonetheless there would be money to pay. Britain's departure was hugely inconvenient for the other twenty-seven member states because it removed a net contributor to the EU budget that paid around 12 per cent of the bills, in 2016 a sum of around £9.5 billion. In 2013, the UK had signed up for the so-called Multi-annual Financial Framework (MFF) which dictated budget contributions through to 2020, a year after Brexit. Confronted by his opposite numbers about Britain ceasing to pay its dues, Rogers said, 'They are not our dues because we will have left, so we do not have any financial liabilities at that point.' EU officials told him, 'You have exploded a bomb under the Multi-annual Financial Framework.'[1] Countries in Eastern Europe which received EU structural funds would only get €88 for every €100 they had budgeted. The issue united countries that were net contributors and recipients. 'One thing they can all agree on is that we are the rogues who have ceased to pay our dues,' Rogers said.

The second part of the bill was the UK's share of the so-called *reste à liquider*: the gap, in European Union accounting jargon, between commitments made by member states and the actual payments handed over, a figure that had ballooned over the years and would be more than €200 billion by 2018. Britain was also expected to pay its share of the pensions for EU officials accrued during its membership and fees for initiatives like the Erasmus university scheme and the Horizon 2020 scientific research budget if it wished to remain part of those initiatives. On the other side of the ledger, Britain could argue that it owned a share of EU assets like its buildings and had around £9 billion invested in the European Investment Bank.

If the money was a burden, it was also Theresa May's best leverage in negotiating a new trade deal. Rogers told MPs, 'The mere fact of our exiting during the period of the framework causes them immense financial difficulty.'[2] His advice to May was, 'Money will unlock a lot.' But that stance – continuing to pay into the budget even after Brexit – was anathema to most Eurosceptics. It also put UKREP – the UK team in Brussels

– at odds with officials in Whitehall, who took legal advice over whether Britain could be forced to pay anything. A House of Lords committee later concluded Britain could not be made to pay. To Rogers it was a matter of politics, not law.

Selmayr had first clashed with May when she was home secretary and he could see that her tactics for Brexit were an echo of her negotiation when Britain opted out of all EU justice and home affairs directives and then back into some of them. EU officials believed the Brexit process was far more complicated and described May's approach as 'deluded'. Selmayr's other beef with May was that he had personally spent hours thrashing out the details of concessions she had demanded as home secretary during David Cameron's ill-fated renegotiation before the EU referendum. Having sweated to satisfy May, he was furious when she virtually sat out the campaign. A British diplomat said, 'May was pushing to get extra things into the package but she never then made much of it in the referendum campaign, which Martin hasn't forgotten.'

Selmayr's power derived in part from his hold over Juncker, whom British officials dismissed as a drunk. David Cameron had tried to stop Juncker getting the presidency of the European Commission and his aides had spread stories – apparently accurate – about the former Luxembourg prime minister drinking brandy for breakfast. 'I've been to four or five things when he has been shitfaced,' one official said. 'Off his trolley, hugging and kissing people.' Rogers' advice to May was that she would have to find a way to 'go around Selmayr' to do business with Juncker directly. 'Before he became a total pisshead he was a very sinuous, agile, clever, schmoozing politician,' a senior official said. 'Even now there are flashes through the alcoholic haze where you think, "This guy's got a very considerable brain."' The problem was that Juncker's knowledge of Britain was twenty years out of date. Recognising that he was 'a total address book politician', one diplomat asked Juncker, 'Who do you know in British politics?' Juncker replied, 'There's John Major, who I got along well with in the past, Ken Clarke, Peter Bottomley.' As a roster of out-of-touch Europhiles with no skin in the new game it was hard to top. Hearing this, Rogers had sought to impress on London that someone should tell Juncker the home truths about political reality in Britain. 'You need people who can be private channels,' Rogers said. 'That's how the game works and every other European power does it.'

Dinner with Jean-Claude Juncker would have to wait but efforts to get May to bond with EU power brokers were made, to the bewilderment of some of them. Donald Tusk, the president of the European Council – the body of member state governments – was ushered in for a series of private chats and faced the same fate as many an MP and journalist. 'There were Pinteresque pauses in all their bilaterals,' an official said. Tusk complained, 'She doesn't say anything!' and was told, 'That's not her style. Don't take it personally.' Martin Schulz, the president of the European Parliament, was invited to Downing Street in late September 2016. After his meeting with May, he texted a senior British diplomat to complain, 'She didn't say anything at all. Why have we come all the way to Downing St for that?'

These meetings raised questions about whether May would be able to do the human end of the negotiations, the 'walk in the woods' with fellow leaders that helped get a deal over the line. A Downing Street aide said May's silences were partly a function of insecurity. 'When you give her a brief to learn, she's brilliant, but she doesn't want to reveal what she doesn't know so she won't say anything.' A senior European government official described May as 'almost reciting from her notes'.[3] At the European Council meeting in Brussels that December, May appeared isolated as television footage showed other leaders greeting each other warmly while she stood awkwardly to the side. She was quickly branded 'Billy no mates' on social media.

The Commission was regarded in Britain as a rather ridiculous organisation. It took Rogers to point out, 'They are really pretty good at negotiating against people. Lots of people who have been doing it for thirty years. They have vastly more information at their disposal about where the twenty-seven are coming from than we do, because they are talking to all these people all the time.'[4] He urged Jeremy Heywood to appoint a slate of a dozen negotiators under Oliver Robbins to lead on individual issues because he could not get across all the detail himself. The plan was rejected. Robbins would be up against Michel Barnier's deputy Sabine Weyand, a 'very smart' German with three decades of trade negotiations behind her, and Didier Seeuws, a former chef de cabinet to Herman van Rompuy, the former Council president. Robbins would need to know everything from customs procedures to the life cycle of pelagic fish.

David Davis regarded the Commission as a smaller version of the Treasury – a group of people with a belief in the European project who were caught up in a 'cauldron of emotions' by Britain's vote to leave. He believed that they would be 'brought back to reality' by the governments of the individual member states. Throughout the summer and autumn Davis travelled Europe meeting fellow ministers and special interest groups, trying to work out who might have interests that would align with Britain's. The first thing he and David Jones, another of his Brexit ministers, found in their travels was that the rest of Europe was still traumatised by Britain's decision to leave. Many could not comprehend that Brexit would even happen, so used were they to EU governments holding repeat referendums until they got the result they wanted. Another cabinet minister said, 'Their initial reaction was one of extreme disappointment, charged with irritation that they were now going to go through a traumatic process which is of our making.' Another minister estimated, 'It took about three or four months before EU ministers came to terms with the fact that we were actually leaving.' At a general affairs council meeting in Bratislava, David Jones was introduced to the Commission's vice president, Frans Timmermans, whose first words betrayed his angst: 'Well, how long do you intend to remain shackled to this corpse?'

In a bid to curry favour, ministers found themselves procuring tickets for a Liverpool football game for one senior EU politician. Davis also considered roping in Aston Martin 'in the national interest' to give Guy Verhofstadt a spin in one of their cars. The Belgian MEP, who was the European Parliament's point man on Brexit, raced vintage sports cars. Davis needed all the tricks of the trade ahead of his first meeting with Verhofstadt on 22 November. When asked about the Belgian in Parliament two months earlier, the Brexit secretary had quoted the biblical line, 'Get thee behind me Satan'. Davis meant he would not be tempted to comment, but the media wrote that he had called Verhofstadt the Devil. When they met, Verhofstadt entered into the spirit of things, greeting Davis with the words, 'Welcome to hell.' The talks were not quite that bad, but at their conclusion Verhofstadt's MEP colleague Manfred Weber said, 'I have not heard much as to how the British government wants to tackle Brexit and what Brexit really means.' Verhofstadt was regarded in Downing Street as a voluble nuisance, but his role was important since the European Parliament would have to rubber-stamp a future trade deal. Davis had identified him as one of thirty key interlocutors – one in each of the twenty-seven countries, plus the Commission, the Council and the Parliament. He believed he needed to meet each of them three times in order to develop a relationship of trust.

In order to facilitate all this travel, Davis demanded the use of the prime minister's official aircraft, dubbed TheresaJet by Westminster journalists, and the Queen's Flight of the Royal Air Force, which is also used by ministers. 'DD felt he was the "real" foreign secretary and so therefore thought he should be allowed to use the prime minister's plane and to catch a royal flight,' a DExEU official recalled. The request led to 'an enormous battle'. Michael Fallon, the defence secretary, gave the green light but Simon Case – May's principal private secretary at Number 10 – and Oliver Robbins, who regularly flew EasyJet, both resisted. 'Olly totally disapproved and kept blocking the plane,' the official said. 'He didn't really see why DD should be whisked by private jet across Europe.' Davis won the day when he told Fiona Hill he would not do the trips unless he got his way.

The most important relationship for Davis to develop was that with Michel Barnier, the French former commissioner for financial services who had been appointed as the lead negotiator for the Commission. Barnier was, in Davis's words, 'very French', a smooth and debonair character – in contrast with Davis, who sported the twisted nose of a boxer with more bravery than ability. The two had known each other since the days when they were both Europe ministers in the 1990s. Now they were friendly adversaries. Officials hoped Barnier would take a more pragmatic approach than Martin Selmayr. 'Barnier is a vain, hopeless and tedious individual but he's not as vicious as he's made out to be,' one undiplomatic diplomat said. 'He actually wants to do a deal.' Davis was similarly encouraged by a belief that Barnier wished to become European Union president when Juncker stood down in 2019 – perfect timing for Barnier if he could land a deal with Britain that spring.

Barnier's hands were tied by the negotiating mandate he had been given by the member states. In their first substantive conversation, Barnier repeated the mantra, 'no negotiation without notification', and told Davis Britain's demand that the divorce arrangements be negotiated alongside the new trade deal was a non-starter. The EU wanted the exit bill settled first, along with a solution to the Irish border and the thorny issue of citizens' rights. Yet when the conversation turned to Northern Ireland, Barnier said, 'You must not attempt to do the Northern Irish and Irish resolution bilaterally.' Barnier had been involved on the EU side in the Good Friday Agreement talks which had secured peace in Ulster. He said, 'I was very involved in this and I'm very keen that the Commission is involved in the resolution of the Northern Irish border problems.' Davis readily agreed and reported back to May, 'He spent the whole meeting saying "no negotiation without notification" and then began negotiating.'

Other ministers had similar experiences, meeting their opposite numbers in member states, who said they could not negotiate separately and then spelled out how they wanted Brexit to work. One minister said, 'Mostly this is to do with the rights of citizens. The Poles have got one million citizens in this country, the Romanians have got about 400,000, there's a very big Portuguese population here too.' The ministers sent the message: 'We want to look after the interests of your nationals but similarly we think it's entirely reasonable that you should undertake to protect the rights of British nationals.'

Despite the mutual interest in a deal on citizens' rights, the issue and that of immigration remained the ones that most soured relations between the government and their European allies throughout the autumn and winter of 2016. The issue was a legacy of the period immediately after the referendum when David Cameron considered a unilateral offer to EU citizens that they could remain in Britain. According to an editorial in George Osborne's *Evening Standard* in June 2017, 'In the days immediately after the referendum, David Cameron wanted to reassure EU citizens they would be allowed to stay. All his cabinet agreed with that unilateral offer, except his home secretary, Mrs May, who insisted on blocking it.'[5] May said that was 'not my recollection', but she had been the only leadership candidate not to support a unilateral offer to EU citizens. A former special adviser corroborated Osborne's claim, saying Michael Gove had tried to have Number 10 issue a statement saying that EU nationals were secure, only to be told by one of Cameron's senior aides, 'You can't because Theresa won't sign it off.'

As time went by, senior Conservatives expressed concern that May had not done more to resolve the issue, which they saw as toxic to the party's brand. One Tory adviser said, 'It was an early example of Theresa's tin-earedness. We could have vetoed every single piece of policy, until they gave us a guarantee over nationals. The tone was as much of a problem as the substance. It spiralled into a complete crisis for us. Three million people – the majority of whom are in London – think we're awful.' As he began to tour Europe, Davis realised the issue was poisoning the well for the negotiations. 'Every meeting we went to with an ambassador, a minister or prime minister, they would say "The problem with this is what's going on with our citizens."' May believed it would betray British citizens in Spain and other EU countries if they were not considered as part of a deal. 'She was adamant that she'd said it in the leadership campaign and it had to be done,' a DExEU official said, 'and they said, "We've got to think about our people in Europe."'

May's attempt to resolve the issue was a disaster that raised fresh questions about her operation. When she visited Angela Merkel in Berlin on 18 November, the prime minister offered a deal to guarantee reciprocal rights for EU citizens. Merkel refused and was privately irritated, since she had told her Europe adviser, Uwe Corsepius, to make clear to Oliver Robbins in advance that she would not countenance any attempt to peel her away from the united line of the EU27. After the meeting Corsepius contacted a British official with a 'poisonous' complaint about Robbins: 'I warned you in advance! Did Olly not transmit back what I said to him?' If Robbins had warned May her advances would be rebuffed, he was ignored. Even after Merkel had rejected May's proposal in their meetings, the prime minister had still ploughed on, robotically repeating her prepared talking points. As a source revealed, 'Merkel's view was: "What part of 'no' do you not understand?"' The incident strengthened a growing view in Whitehall that May's manner was ill-suited to the kind of personal interactions that grease the wheels of European negotiations and that Robbins was reluctant to give her bad news. A senior figure who saw May afterwards said she was 'intensely stunned' by Merkel's reaction. 'It went very badly.'

The German chancellor was in no mood to help, in part because her efforts to deliver a renegotiation deal for David Cameron had been in vain. 'Merkel feels like she really did go the extra mile to get the best possible package for us in February and she was assured that we would win the referendum,' a senior cabinet minister said. 'She feels like we've let her down.'

On 28 November, eighty MPs – most of them Tories – signed a letter to Donald Tusk, the Council president, urging him to intervene to resolve the citizens issue. Coordinated by Steve Baker and Michael Tomlinson, it said people are 'not cards to be traded "tit for tat" in a political playground' and criticised Barnier's refusal to allow formal talks on the matter. It was the first offensive operation by the European Research Group (ERG), a collection of Tory MPs which had been revived that month under Baker's chairmanship. The signatories included former cabinet ministers Michael Gove, Iain Duncan Smith and John Whittingdale. The issue was sufficiently toxic that Tusk and others assumed the letter had been organised by Downing Street. The following day a message was passed to Baker by Denzil Davidson, one of May's Number 10 EU advisers, asking him to 'please stop doing this'. An ERG source said, 'We were just pissing off people at the very top of the EU and that was not what they wanted.' Baker put out a message on the ERG WhatsApp group asking Eurosceptics to stand down. In his diary he wrote, 'At No 10's request suspended operations.'

While the issue of EU citizens already in Britain soured relations with Brussels, what to do about those wanting to come after Brexit was dividing the cabinet. In mid-October Amber Rudd, the home secretary, presented a paper to the Brexit committee proposing a post-Brexit visa regime that would see all European Union workers being forced to prove they had secured a skilled job before being allowed into Britain – along with a seasonal worker scheme for the agricultural and construction industries. Hammond resisted the plans, arguing that permanent low-skilled migrants might also be required.[6] Rudd and Davis had a difficult balancing act to strike, respecting those voters who backed Brexit to take back control of immigration with the need to keep the NHS, the care sector and the hospitality industry, all heavily reliant on migrants, fully staffed.

On 1 December, Davis made a speech to the Welsh CBI cautioning Brexiteers not to expect sudden changes to Britain's immigration system. 'As we take back control of immigration by ending free movement as it has operated before, let me also say this, we won't do so in a way that it is contrary to the national and economic interest. No one wants to see labour shortages in key sectors. That wouldn't be in anybody's interest.' In this Davis had the support of Boris Johnson and Liam Fox, both of whom were liberal on immigration. The disagreement was with May, who had made her name at the Home Office talking tough and who felt she could not betray the wishes of Brexit voters. 'The whole of her government was designed to please the *Daily Mail*,' a disgruntled official claimed. 'The Tory Party is going to meet its commitment to get immigration down to the tens of thousands without doing anything because no European will want to come. We'll have to have immigration from India and places. I'm not sure that's what people were voting for.'

It cannot have been easy for May, having to learn the job of prime minister in a period where every decision she made had the potential to alter the path of history. Throughout the autumn, May's staff say, she gradually became more confident. An MP who spent a lot of time in Downing Street said, 'At the beginning, there was an anxiety in the room which infected everyone else. She wasn't always 100 per cent clear about what she was looking for and people weren't sure what they should be giving her. There were awkward moments, silences, and an uneasiness. Over time, that dissipated as she clearly grew more confident, relaxed and assertive. She knew what to ask for but she also relaxed.' A Downing Street aide agreed: 'I think she definitely grew in the job.'

But even as she became more assured, aides say, May was also showing signs of exhaustion. 'She was already fatigued by the time she got to Christmas – even more into the new year,' another aide recalled. 'Things dried up and became that little bit slower. I realised we had just sucked the soul out of her. The chiefs didn't look after her. They used her to get what they wanted – it was relentless.'

May got a 'really bad cough and cold that just lingered for ages and did wear her down'. One meeting in December 2016 was abandoned when she was gripped by a coughing fit. 'For all that Fiona or Jojo went on about caring about her, it was Simon [Case] who sorted out getting a glass of water and said, "We don't need to do this meeting now,"' one of those present recalled. 'She was really tired and not feeling very well.'

The prime minister was a Type 1 diabetic, meaning she had to monitor her blood sugar levels and inject herself in the stomach with insulin before every meal. Officials in Downing Street were secretly instructed in how to do the injections in case May became incapacitated on a foreign trip. But friends and foes alike in Number 10 say that has never happened. 'I think she manages it really well,' one civil servant said. 'She is very calm about it.'

When May flew to Bahrain for the Gulf Cooperation Council meeting in December 2016 it was suggested the prime minister get some rest rather than talk to journalists on the way out. Fiona Hill, hypersensitive to any suggestion that May was fragile, insisted that she do it. 'Are you mad?!' Hill said. 'As soon as you tell the press that she's unwell it will be a big story.'

One of May's aides, recognising that she was worn out, took to riding in the car with her to encourage the prime minister to take a nap. 'Occasionally I'd say, "Do you want to sleep?" If she wouldn't say "yes", I'd say, "I'm really tired today. Do you mind if I just close my eyes for five minutes, collect my thoughts?" She took it as her cue to do it herself.' Even this aide insists May never cried off work. 'I don't want anyone to read into that like she's not up for the job or well enough. I think she looks physically tired at times. She looks puffy. But I've never seen her when she doesn't want to do the work or says, "I'm too tired for that." She is relentless.'

As November became December the prime minister realised she needed to impose greater order on the Brexit process, which had been saddled with the uncertainty of her first weeks in the job. The cabinet debates of the autumn had allowed ministers to educate themselves about the challenges of Brexit but the time was arriving when the direction of travel laid out in the conference speech had to become firm policy. Those three months had bought Britain time, taking some of the sting out of the EU's anger and allowing the issues to be studied methodically as May preferred. A cabinet minister said, 'We had to make sure we'd exhausted all the options. Theresa wanted to show we'd tested everything. You can't govern based on assumptions.'

Yet the cabinet had decided no firm policy and May had not formalised the hints she had dropped at the party conference. She now faced a rainbow coalition of forces in the courts, Parliament and the wider political world determined to force her hand.

ENEMIES OF THE PEOPLE?

Anna Soubry was firm, that was her style. If Ken Clarke was the best-known Europhile on the Conservative benches, Soubry was the most outspoken. The MP for Broxtowe in Nottinghamshire had not won her marginal seat by apologising for who she was. During her days as a minister she had given an off-the-record quote to a journalist featuring the word 'chuffing'. When the hack had suggested that might identify her, Soubry had laughed and said, 'If I'd used "fucking" it would have identified me.' It had made her a favourite of lobby journalists, a divisive figure with her colleagues and a nuisance to the whips. It was December 2016 and Soubry was talking to the chief whip, Gavin Williamson, the man who had ensured enough votes for Theresa May in the leadership contest and was now charged with keeping her in power with a working majority of seventeen. The Labour Party had tabled a motion on an opposition day debate calling 'on the Prime Minister to commit to publishing the Government's plan for leaving the EU before Article 50 is invoked'.

On the face of it the motion was innocuous. May would surely have to spell out her plan at some point. It stopped short of demanding the government publish a white paper or hold a vote that would guarantee that Britain stayed in the single market, or even a second referendum. A vote on any one of those would be more problematic for the government if it was lost. But as soon as he read the motion Williamson knew it was a threat. It acknowledged that 'there should be no disclosure of material that could be reasonably judged to damage the UK in any negotiations'. The motion was entirely reasonable. Labour had designed it to garner the maximum parliamentary backing. Soubry confirmed that he had a problem on his hands. She said, 'I've read it and I have to say I can't see anything in it I don't approve of and could not support.'

Williamson was a slight figure with the demeanour of a trainee under-taker, but he was given to flashes of rage – the 'hair dryer treatment' they called it – if MPs were threatening to rebel. He played the role of chief whip with gothic glee, keeping on his desk a jar containing a tarantula called Cronos. Some said he saw himself as a real-life Francis Urquhart, the chief whip in *House of Cards*. Shouting was not going to work with Soubry – and she was just the tip of the iceberg. On this, he knew, she had twenty Conservative MPs behind her. For the first time, the govern-ment was in danger of losing a vote on Brexit in the House of Commons. It could not afford to do so. It had already been defeated in the courts.

When Theresa May announced, on 2 October, that she would trigger Article 50 by the end of March, the government was already facing legal action to prevent her from doing so. By 19 July, less than a month after the referendum, seven different plaintiffs had brought an action in the High Court arguing that only Parliament, and not the prime minister, had the authority to invoke Article 50. On that day, judges including Sir Brian Leveson decided that the lead claimant would be Gina Miller, a fifty-one-year-old Guyanese-born City fund manager who had voted Remain. Miller, a photogenic former model and mother of three, soon showed herself adept at garnering publicity for her cause. With the assis-tance of Lisa Tremble, a gifted PR who had once been David Miliband's special adviser, Miller had the backing of lawyers Mishcon de Reya and the heavyweight clout of QC Lord Pannick. Their claim was that, since the referendum had been advisory rather than legally binding, acting on it would require parliamentary approval. The government's case was that May could use the royal prerogative to trigger Article 50 since David Cameron had repeatedly made clear that he would respect the results of the referendum. The stage was set for a highly charged showdown over constitutional law.

Tensions were quickly inflamed. At the hearing on 19 July, Pannick complained that Mishcon de Reya had been subjected to 'racist and anti-Semitic abuse' by pro-Brexit protesters. Miller was soon the victim of online abuse. By January 2017 the police would be probing twen-ty-two cases of intimidation, including threats of beheading and rape and one offer of a £5,000 bounty to anyone who ran her over.

* * *

Tempers boiled over on 3 November, when a panel of three judges – the Lord Chief Justice, Lord Thomas of Cwmgiedd, Master of the Rolls Sir Terence Etherton and Lord Justice Sales – ruled, 'The Government does not have power under the Crown's prerogative to give notice pursuant to Article 50 for the UK to withdraw from the European Union.' David Davis had barely an hour's notice of the verdict and announced that, if it was upheld by the Supreme Court, an Act of Parliament would be required for Brexit to proceed – a process that allowed MPs or peers to table amendments that would enable them to dictate the terms of Brexit or even halt the process altogether.

The reaction of Eurosceptics was swift and brutal. Iain Duncan Smith accused the judges of sparking 'a constitutional crisis – literally pitting Parliament against the will of the people'. The *Daily Mail* delivered the most memorable rebuke, a front page with pictures of the three judges under the headline, 'ENEMIES OF THE PEOPLE', giving details of their links to Brussels and, in one case, their sexuality. If the verdict was not a constitutional crisis, the accusation that it was improper for the judiciary to involve themselves in Brexit now created one. For three days, debate raged over whether those who wanted to subvert the referendum result or those who wanted to silence an independent judiciary were the ones undermining democracy and the rule of law. On the evening of the verdict, Sajid Javid, the communities secretary, went on the BBC's *Question Time* programme and accused the judges of 'an attempt to frustrate the will of the British people'.

Caught in the middle was Elizabeth Truss, the justice secretary. The next morning, Truss wrote to her fellow ministers stressing that the judges were independent and urging them to desist from further attacks. However, Truss herself came under attack from the Law Society and one of her predecessors as Lord Chancellor, Labour's Charlie Falconer, who said that since the judges 'can't defend themselves' it was Truss's 'constitutional duty' to do so.

Truss spoke to Downing Street and to her aides, one of whom warned her, 'You've got two choices here and they are both really shit.' Condemning the *Mail* and supporting the judges and their ruling would be 'career ending' as long as May, Timothy and Hill occupied Downing Street. Failure to speak up would rupture relations with the judiciary. Truss's special adviser, Kirsty Buchanan, a former political editor of the *Sunday Express*, reinforced Truss's instincts that it was not her job to start telling newspapers what they could and couldn't write. Together they studied the Constitutional Reform Act, which showed she had a constitutional duty to uphold the independence of the judiciary. 'What it doesn't say is that you have to defend the judiciary by putting out a press statement within forty-five minutes of any critical headlines in newspapers,' a Ministry of Justice source said. At midday, an aide spoke to Downing Street about whether Truss should issue a statement and got a clear 'No way, Jose' response. A second call later in the day confirmed Number 10's position.

By the Saturday #whereisliztruss was trending on Twitter. Truss had lost her nerve and spoke to the chiefs of staff. They told her not to issue a statement. Truss sent them a bland quote defending the integrity of the Lord Chief Justice but going no further. 'Can't I even say this?' she asked. She phoned Lord Thomas himself and told him that she was going to make a statement supporting him. Again, the chiefs refused her permission to release it. Truss said she had told Thomas a statement was coming. They finally relented, changing a word or two and banning her from making any further comment. 'The lord chief justice is a man of great integrity and impartiality. Like all judges, he has sworn an oath to administer the law without fear or favour, affection or ill will,' the statement read. 'It was supposed to be enough, but without being too much,' an ally explained. It was too little too late for the lawyers and at least one minister, who said, 'I felt strongly that it was a matter for the Lord Chancellor to deal with – not a Lord Chancellor operating under Number 10. She should have got on with it.'

The row came at a time when ministers were encouraging the judiciary to be more accountable and explain their decisions better to the public. The High Court case was an example of where they might have done better, spelling out why the case mattered and making it harder to depict them as enemies of Brexit. But the incident not only proved the power of the chiefs of staff over cabinet ministers; it illustrated and unleashed the full range of venomous passions that the referendum campaign had both uncovered and kindled. Having embraced Brexit and the Brexiteers, Theresa May now felt under siege.

It was in that context that a cross-party group of MPs began to talk about how they might build on the High Court ruling to exert the power of Parliament and press the prime minister to reveal her hand. They included members of a Labour Party reeling from a second lead-

ership contest and a group of Conservatives who called themselves
Team 2019.

Team 2019 had formed when half a dozen former ministers and Remain-
backing Tory MPs met in the office of Alistair Burt, a former Foreign
Office minister and passionate pro-European, in September 2016. They
wanted to give the impression that they were looking forwards to the
date of Brexit, not harking back to the result of the referendum. But the
title created greater suspicion in the whips' office. The driving forces, in
addition to the short, balding and pathologically polite Burt, were Nicky
Morgan and Anna Soubry, close friends and former ministers who were
increasingly unwilling to bite their tongues. Dominic Grieve, the courtly
former attorney general; Neil Carmichael, the MP for Stroud; former
transport minister Claire Perry; and Ben Howlett, the MP for Bath. Sir
Nicholas Soames, who put grand in the word grandee, was soon attending their Monday meetings as well.

Gradually, numbers swelled to include Bob Neill, Jeremy Lefroy, Flick
Drummond, Alberto Costa and Stephen Hammond. 'There was a group
of twelve to fifteen that would meet regularly,' one MP said. Others, like
Alex Chalk, supported from afar but did not attend the meetings. The
group acquired their own researcher, Garvan Walshe, a former Tory
adviser now running his own consultancy, Brexit Analytics, which
helped businesses understand the risks of Brexit. His salary was paid by
Sir Tim Sainsbury, a former Conservative minister. Walshe penned an
article for ConservativeHome accusing May of making the same
mistakes on Brexit as George W. Bush during the invasion of Iraq,
comparing the government's aggression towards its critics to the shooting of 'peaceful demonstrators' in Iraq. He accused the Brexiteers of
'wielding the "will of the people" with the enthusiasm of French revolutionaries'.[1] Team 2019 now had to decide whether to behave like peaceful
demonstrators or Robespierre.

Nicky Morgan put her head above the parapet on the Sunday of the
Conservative Party conference, giving an interview to the *Observer* in
which she warned that pursuing a 'hard Brexit' would 'promote intoler-
ance and bigotry'. A tall and bustling figure with the air of a school
lacrosse captain, Morgan had been fired as education secretary in July as
part of May's cull of the Cameroons. To go to a centre-left newspaper on
the very day May was setting out her plans to trigger Article 50 in March,

was interpreted as an act of war by Downing Street and the whips' office. When Morgan spoke at an education event on the fringe, voicing her opposition to May's decision to allow new grammar schools, there were two whips – Julian Smith and David Evennett – in attendance to keep an eye on her.

The 'harshness' of May's party conference speech and Amber Rudd's announcement that companies should publish details of the number of foreign workers they employed persuaded the trainee rebels that they needed to become more proactive. Morgan and Soubry both took to the airwaves to denounce the Home Office plan. That week, Nick Herbert, who had led the Conservative Party's Remain campaign, also surfaced, telling the *Guardian* that Boris Johnson, David Davis and Liam Fox were 'the three blind mice' of Brexit, peddling 'Brexit fundamentalism'.[2]

Crucially, though, both Morgan and Herbert said Tory pro-Europeans should accept the result of the referendum. From that point on, the rows that consumed the Conservative Party were over the nature of Brexit, not its very existence. The moral core of the group, Alistair Burt, was not a natural rebel. A mild and modest man, he accepted that he had failed over forty years to persuade the British public of the benefits of Brussels. He did not want to spend his remaining years as a parliamentarian trying to reverse the referendum result. Instead, he told the group, they needed to make sure the new 'script is written as much by those who valued the EU, rather than by those who hated it'.

The first test of strength came in late October with the elections to fill the seats on a new select committee to shadow DExEU. Unusually it was comprised of twenty-one MPs, nearly double the usual number, something that appeared designed to neuter it at birth. One Conservative MP said, 'It's ridiculously large. It won't be able to agree anything.' The former shadow foreign secretary Hilary Benn was elected leader, beating off Brexiteer Kate Hoey. The election for the membership was a dogfight. By their own admission Team 2019 were late to get themselves organised and run a slate of candidates. Leavers ran a successful operation to secure spots for prominent Brexiteers like Michael Gove, John Whittingdale, Jacob Rees-Mogg and Peter Bone. 'We woke up to that quite late,' a Team 2019 member said. 'Everything was done at the last minute.' Belatedly, Nicky Morgan began to act as a whip, corralling supportive MPs, including George Osborne, to vote for the Team 2019 slate. They succeeded in getting Alistair Burt and Jeremy Lefroy elected, denying the Brexiteers a majority, but Anna Soubry failed by 'a handful of votes'.

Following the High Court ruling, Team 2019 was divided over strategy. Soubry was sick of watching Eurosceptics cause trouble and determined to give the whips something to think about. Burt did not want to vote against his own government and argued that the group should work privately on Downing Street. 'If we became the saboteurs who people like the *Mail* claim,' he told his colleagues, 'I think we'll lose influence.' Burt knew that he – and most of his colleagues – were not temperamentally the kind who could wage trench warfare against their own. He recognised that he might be too reasonable for his own good, telling his friends, 'We weren't built for this.' Burt resolved to keep lines of communication open to Gavin Williamson, the chief whip, and George Hollingbery, the prime minister's parliamentary private secretary. Williamson showed a close interest in their activities. He had appointed himself personal whip to Morgan, Soubry and George Osborne, though Soubry was soon passed to Julian Smith, who developed a reputation as a 'deeply dark force' with some MPs. Since party conference the mood music from Number 10 had been highly confrontational. 'If people asked questions about Brexit they were accused of thwarting the will of the people. That's the kind of language the PM was using,' a former minister said. 'She continually missed how that was interpreted by those of us who didn't embrace Brexit as she wanted.'

There was frustration that, beyond Williamson, the whips did not try to pretend they understood Team 2019's approach. 'It's a very, very Brexiteer whips' office,' one MP said. 'They have no sympathy or empathy with our concerns at all.' Burt and others sought to impress on May's envoys that principled demands about Brexit were not a plot. A former minister said, 'Alistair told them, "You've got to get Nick and Fiona to understand that putting contrary views is not the first step to unseating Theresa May and removing her as party leader."' What they did want was for Parliament to be allowed a say over Article 50 and any final deal struck with Brussels and for May to spell out her plans, preferably to Parliament in a white paper. They had the quiet support of Remain cabinet ministers like Amber Rudd. 'Amber said, "You've got to keep up the good fight, you've got to keep pushing," to which the response was, "You're in the bloody cabinet!"'

At first the Remainers had, pragmatically, conceded that Britain would leave the single market. As May remained tight-lipped about her plans their attitude hardened.

On 28 August, Britain Stronger in Europe – the Remain campaign from the referendum – was reconstituted as a new organisation, Open Britain, which was to become the umbrella under which all May's critics could find a voice. James McGrory and Joe Carberry would run it. They launched with an op-ed article by Anna Soubry, Pat McFadden and Norman Lamb – one MP from each of the main parties – and sought to buy themselves the right to be heard by admitting that the Remain campaign and their parties had got it wrong on immigration. 'Free movement of people cannot continue as it has done,' they wrote.

This consensual approach did not last long. Nick Clegg, McGrory's old boss, became the Liberal Democrat frontbench spokesman on Europe and began to demand single market membership. 'He genuinely thinks that has been the most catastrophic decision that has been taken in his lifetime,' a friend of Clegg said. By November, there was talk of the former Labour cabinet ministers Alan Milburn, John Hutton and Douglas Alexander, backed up by funding from insurance millionaire Sir Clive Cowdery, to push for a second referendum with the hope of overturning Brexit if public opinion cooled. Open Britain began to take a tougher line. In December another ghost of battles past resurfaced. Stephen Dorrell, the former Tory health secretary, became chairman of the European Movement with the explicit intention of blocking Brexit. 'Brexit is a mistake and we shall seek to build support for that point of view,' he said. 'The government has a mandate but I don't think the mandate it has reflects this country's interests, so I will seek to defeat it.'

The media was most interested in the activities of Tony Blair, who decided to use Brexit to effect his re-entry into domestic politics. In September 2016, Blair announced that he was winding up his opaque network of consultancy businesses – Windrush Ventures, Firerush Ventures and Tony Blair Associates – and would set up a non-profit outfit instead. In October Blair wrote in the *New European* newspaper (dubbed the 'Remoaner Gazette' by Brexiteers) that Remain supporters should 'mobilise and organise' an insurgency to make the public change its mind about leaving the EU.

From that point on, there were monthly meetings in Blair's offices on Grosvenor Square, bringing together Blair, Clegg, Dorrell, McGrory, former minister and EU commissioner Peter Mandelson and representatives of Best for Britain, a group set up by Alan Milburn and including Gina Miller, whose case was before the Supreme Court. Blair also met a range of politicians, including Liberal Democrat leader Tim Farron, 'to chat about the future'. In Parliament, Nicky Morgan and Anna Soubry had regular conversations to discuss parliamentary tactics with Clegg, and with Labour's Chuka Umunna and Chris Leslie, under the banner of Open Britain. A source who talked Brexit with Blair in November said, 'He's not impressed with Theresa May. He thinks she's a total lightweight. He thinks Jeremy Corbyn is a nutter and the Tories are screwing up Brexit. He thinks there's a massive hole in British politics that he can fill.' Another well-known figure approached by Blair said, 'He thinks Brexit is going to fail and Theresa May's going to fail.'

In Downing Street, the political team paid a close interest in this swirling cast of characters and the prospect that they might coalesce to form a new centre party. 'I think enough people are talking on these lines and enough people are making fairly public overtures that we have to take their intent seriously,' said a close May ally. 'Their intent is to at least operate a cross-party alliance.' In truth, there was only one figure in these conversations Downing Street was really concerned about – George Osborne.

The chiefs were alarmed to hear that, in the immediate aftermath of the referendum, a close ally of the former chancellor had held discussions with Tim Farron and a couple of Labour MPs in Westminster's Two Chairmen pub about setting up a new party called The Democrats. Osborne knew nothing of this encounter but, in private, he encouraged Team 2019 to argue for single market membership after Brexit as a way of putting pressure on May. 'George was saying, "The Eurosceptics have been making unreasonable demands for twenty years, it's time we did the same,"' one of those who talked to him that autumn revealed. Osborne did not attend any of the group's meetings but he was in touch with Nicky Morgan, Nick Clegg, Tony Blair and Peter Mandelson. 'He definitely talked to all of the protagonists, without a shadow of a doubt,' a source said. However, Osborne told friends Clegg and Blair's quest for a second referendum was 'hopeless', believing they should 'fight on the coming issues, immigration and trade, rather than the last issue'. Publicly, he called leaving the single market 'the biggest act of protectionism in history', because Britain was throwing away a deal with the market on its doorstep in search of deals further afield that he believed would be diffi- cult to deliver and demand choices – like offering more visas to Indian or Chinese visitors or accepting hormone-fed American beef – which the public would find unpalatable.

Team May were intrigued to the point of obsession by Osborne's activities and reports of his actions were sent regularly by the whips to Nick Timothy and Fiona Hill. In Downing Street they saw it as an embryonic vessel for the preservation of his leadership hopes. 'Team 2019? That's subtle,' one of May's aides said when told about the group by Gavin Williamson. 'They are obsessed and consumed by what he is up to,' a minister commented. 'They regard him as the real leader of the opposition.'

In fact, Osborne saw Team 2019 as half-hearted and badly organised and the people involved as ill-suited to rebellion. 'Trying to organise a rump opposition at the moment would be a waste of my time and effort and burn me out,' he told one ally. As a student of political history, Osborne knew that time rather than plotting was his best hope of becoming leader. Nonetheless, as a firm Remainer still, he provided encouragement and ideas about how to steer Brexit in the right direc- tion. 'There's been a smile here, a text there, an occasional comment in the corridor,' one Osborne ally said. 'It's unlikely that he is remonstrating with Nicky about her loyalty.' Knowing his Machiavellian reputation, Osborne joked with Gavin Williamson, 'You'll know when I'm organis- ing or rebelling, because we'll win.'

May had not just fired the chancellor of six years, she had patronised him in private, telling him to 'get to know your own party', and humili- ated him in public when her aides briefed details of the conversation to the media. After that the two did not exchange a single word for a year. A senior civil servant who worked with Osborne said, 'With George, the hatred goes quite deep, it's pretty personal. To start with he was predict- ing that she would not be sufficiently revolutionary for the Eurosceptics and that she'd be eaten by the revolutionaries. Then, presumably, the world would turn to George as the answer.'

To the chiefs, Osborne was both a threat to May and guilty of talking down Britain. To the consternation of some of his MP colleagues, Osborne had landed six highly paid jobs after leaving the cabinet. One was as a research fellow with the McCain Institute for International Leadership in Arizona. When Osborne spoke at a fundraising dinner for the Institute in London, one of those present texted Nick Timothy an account of his speech: 'Doom and gloom. Danger is coming. We need EU to provide peace and prosperity. He said he was going to research the origins of populism and how to restore proper politicians to government, like him.' The guest next to the spy described Osborne's view as 'a crock of shit'. A source close to May said, 'Some might say is unpatriotic.'

On 1 December, the assorted battalions of non-Tory Remainers secured a landmark victory, when Liberal Democrat Sarah Olney beat Zac Goldsmith to win the Richmond Park by-election. Goldsmith had stood down as Conservative MP to honour a promise to force a by-election if the government approved a third runway at Heathrow airport. He ran as an independent but fell nearly two thousand votes short. The Greens withdrew their candidate to improve Olney's chances following a hustings run by More United, a campaign set up that summer in memory of Jo Cox, the Labour MP slain by a far-right fanatic during the referendum campaign. Lance Price – a former spokesman for Tony Blair – was the group's mouthpiece and it became another forum where Remainers could compare notes. Downing Street insisted the vote would 'change nothing' of May's approach to Brexit, but said it had solidified her intention not to call a general election.

Labour lost their deposit in Richmond Park, but the party was ready – after four months of infighting triggered by the referendum – to play a leading role in the Brexit drama.

Jeremy Corbyn's problems had begun the day after the EU referendum, when he said in an interview that Article 50 should be triggered immediately. This enraged Labour MPs backing Remain and prompted an attempt to oust him. Corbyn's supporters believed he was misunderstood. One of his closest allies said, 'Jeremy came out and said Article 50 will have to be triggered. That's a statement of fact. That's what the referendum was about. He wasn't saying it needed to be triggered right now. It was a wilful misinterpretation. There was a period of mass hysteria after the referendum result.'

Corbyn was already under fire from Labour officials, who accused him of lacklustre effort for the Remain cause during the referendum and his closest aides of active sabotage. Corbyn, his chief adviser Seumas Milne and shadow chancellor John McDonnell were all longstanding critics of the single market, which they regarded as a capitalists' club that penalised workers. Another aide said, 'There are aspects of the EU we didn't like and we don't like, for example state aid and forced privatisation. That's why we campaign to "remain but reform". That's where we thought the public were.' But a senior official at Labour headquarters said, 'Had Jeremy campaigned during the referendum like he was to do during the general election, I don't think we'd be leaving the EU. I genuinely think he's to blame for this. It was absolutely shameful.'

The coup was triggered by the sacking of Hilary Benn, the shadow foreign secretary, the weekend after the referendum just as he was about to resign. More than sixty frontbenchers jumped ship and – in a stunning rebuke to Corbyn – 172 MPs voted to remove him in a no-confidence vote. Just forty wanted him as leader but Corbyn refused to go, citing his mandate from the party membership.

In the subsequent leadership election, however, Corbyn's upbeat campaigning persuaded more than one hundred thousand new members to join the party and propelled him to another victory, this time over Owen Smith. Europe became a feature of the leadership election, with Smith arguing that Labour should fight for a second referendum and seek to overturn Brexit. Had he won, Labour would have been in the simple position of battling for the 48 per cent and telling voters they were wrong. It might have finished the party but it would have had the benefit of simplicity. Instead, Corbyn immediately ruled out a second referendum. On the morning of the result he went for coffee with his closest aide, Seumas Milne, and two of his press spokesmen, Kevin Slocombe and Matt Zarb-Cousin. 'We straight away said you've got to respect the result of the referendum,' one explained.

Even once he had cemented his position, Corbyn's approach to Brexit was confused, but his equivocation perhaps reflected the ambiguities many voters felt towards the EU. His challenge was to show that he could mount a competent opposition to the government and reconcile the pro-Remain views of voters and party members in their metropolitan seats with the working-class supporters who backed Brexit in the Northern towns. After the party conference, Corbyn's team set up a Brexit subcommittee, chaired by the leader, which included John McDonnell, Diane Abbott, Emily Thornberry and Jon Trickett, plus the new shadow Brexit secretary, former director of public prosecutions Sir Keir Starmer. His appointment brought a forensic legal mind to the task and neutralised someone Corbyn's team saw as a threat. 'People were of the view that it was necessary to have Keir in the tent, that he was a potential future leadership candidate,' a source said. 'If you have him in the tent, locked into a difficult area, there's a lot to be said for that.'

For the next six months Labour pursued a twin approach. Corbyn and his closest aides sought to focus Brexit policy, not on the institutional arrangements which were obsessing the government, but on what choices made by the Tories would mean for ordinary workers. That allowed them to turn Brexit into just one more domestic political issue. A Corbyn aide said, 'For the leadership, it's not about the process, it's about different visions for the future. The government has the low-wage, low-growth economy, we've got the high-wage, high-growth, high-investment, high-skill economy with an interventionist state.' Labour warned that a chaotic – or sometimes 'shambolic' – Brexit would hurt the working poor. They demanded a 'Brexit that works for Britain and puts jobs, living standards and the economy first'.

Even as the leadership coup was still raging, John McDonnell gave a speech on 1 July laying out five Labour principles for Brexit. He called for existing workers' rights to be protected; for UK businesses to have the freedom to trade with the EU and EU businesses with the UK; for protection of residency rights for EU citizens living in the UK, and for UK citizens elsewhere in Europe; for the UK to stay part of the European Investment Bank; and for UK financial services to keep their access to the EU.

In parallel with this approach, Starmer and Emily Thornberry, the shadow foreign secretary, lawyers both, sought to find ways of tripping up the government and harassing them on the institutional details. On 11 October, Starmer and Thornberry issued 170 questions for the Tories on their Brexit plans. The effort was not focused but it was the right idea. In the weeks ahead, they began demanding a white paper and the right for Parliament to approve the Brexit plans. 'The first thing to do was to try to get government to move on from this position of "No running commentary",' a Corbyn aide said. That was how Labour came to devise its opposition day motion calling for the government to spell out its plan. Starmer said, 'Parliament and the public need to know the basic terms the Government is seeking to achieve from Brexit. This issue is too important to be left mired in uncertainty any longer.'

When the motion went down, the Tory Remainers were wary of being seen to form a cross-party alliance with the opposition, but the motion offered them a chance to show Downing Street that they were a force to be reckoned with. Briefings began to appear that up to forty Conservative MPs might back the motion.

Around the same time, Fiona Hill had reached out to Morgan and Burt and invited them in to Downing Street for two face-to-face meetings. She told them, 'I voted Remain as well, but believe me when I tell you it's all going to be okay because I'm in the middle of it. Britain will be better than ever.' The Remainers explained that they wanted a white paper. They believed, wrongly as it was to transpire, that there would come a time when May would need them and their votes to help face down the Eurosceptics. 'At that point we all expected that the prime minister would have to make compromises which would upset the Brexiteers,' a former minister said. 'We talked about, "How do we help her to make those compromises and be there to support her when she does?"'

Nicky Morgan, Anna Soubry, Alistair Burt, Dominic Grieve, Ben Howlett and Neil Carmichael all went to see chief whip Gavin Williamson and told him they were prepared to support the motion. 'We'd like to back this, there's nothing wrong with this amendment,' Morgan said. Williamson knew he needed a plan – and fast. Fortunately, Team 2019 weren't the only pressure group on the Conservative backbenches.

Steve Baker was looking at Twitter on his phone when he heard a cheer and looked up. 'What's happened?' he asked. 'You've just been made chairman of the ERG,' came the answer. The ERG was the European Research Group, once a group of Conservative MPs who had got together to fund a researcher, now the shock troops of the Eurosceptic right. During the referendum campaign Baker, a former RAF engineer and amateur military strategist, had masterminded a guerrilla campaign against his own government to boost the chances of the Brexiteers, most notably changing the wording of the referendum question in a way that experts said had boosted Leave's chances by four percentage points. In September 2016, Baker disbanded Conservatives for Britain, his old pressure group, and after May's conference speech, over breakfast in dining room A of the House of Commons, he had been elected by acclamation to repeat the trick with the ERG. This time, his goal was to keep his government on the track it had set, rather than knock it off course. By then two external Brexit groups had been set up. The businessmen Richard Tice and John Longworth led Leave Means Leave. Michael Gove and Boris Johnson lent their support to Change Britain, run by Gisela Stuart, the Labour MP they had worked with on the Vote Leave campaign.

Baker brought in a new MP, Michael Tomlinson, as his deputy while Suella Fernandes and Anne-Marie Trevelyan became vice chairmen. Every Monday Baker met with the 'steering group' of Paleosceptic veterans – Bill Cash, Bernard Jenkin, John Redwood, Peter Lilley and Iain Duncan Smith among them – who had led them into the battles over the Maastricht Treaty twenty-five years earlier. 'Without them nothing moves,' an ERG source said. 'With them everything starts shaking and quaking.' Soon, Baker had a WhatsApp group with eighty Tory MPs signed up and awaiting instructions.

On 20 November, Suella Fernandes fired the first shot, fronting a letter signed by sixty Tory MPs, including seven former cabinet ministers, which demanded that May pull Britain out of the single market and the customs union. Baker controlled which MPs did broadcast interviews for all the main Eurosceptic groups and fed in practical ideas to Stephen Parkinson, one of May's Downing Street political aides. Baker was also in close touch with Gavin Williamson, who told MPs, 'Steve's here to support the government now.' Williamson had a different name for the group of Eurosceptics, regarding them as less house-trained – The Taliban. They got special trips to Downing Street. Some MPs referred to Baker as 'the real deputy chief whip'. At the same time, Baker kept up the pressure for a hard Brexit. 'There was a real tension between rolling the pitch in a way which we knew was helpful and unhelpfully driving them forwards,' an MP recalled. 'It was loyal activism.'

When the day of the opposition debate arrived, Gavin Williamson feared amendments would be added to the Labour motion to impose greater obligations on the government. He did not want an embarrassing defeat. He contacted Team 2019 and informed them that he would be tabling an amendment of his own to the Labour motion accepting that the government would spell out its Brexit plans. Team 2019 were duty bound to vote for a government amendment that gave them what they wanted. Keir Starmer had been outmanoeuvred. The rebels had won – or so they thought.

Steve Baker was sitting in Williamson's office when the text of the government amendment was sent to the table office. It called on 'the Prime Minister to commit to publishing the Government's plan for leaving the EU before Article 50 is invoked', but there was a kicker. Williamson had added, 'this House should respect the wishes of the United Kingdom as expressed in the referendum on 23 June; and further calls on the Government to invoke Article 50 by 31 March 2017'. The chief whip had given ground where he needed to and was now bouncing the Remainers into supporting May's timetable for triggering Article 50. Williamson handed Baker the text of the amendment. Baker photographed it, tweeted the picture and texted a link to the entire parliamentary press lobby. A wry smile crossed Williamson's lips. With Cronos the tarantula looking on, he said, 'Steve, you're really quite organised, aren't you?' Baker replied, 'Yes chief, I am.' They both fell about laughing.

The motion was passed by 461 votes to 89. It was a non-binding vote, but through his manoeuvrings Williamson had ensured that, more than a month before the Supreme Court ruled definitively on whether Parliament should have to approve the triggering of Article 50, MPs had voted to support doing exactly that. 'His amendment completely spoiled their rebellion, and turned everything on its head,' a leading Eurosceptic MP said. 'It was a brilliant, brilliant piece of work by the government chief whip.'

It was also to contribute to one of the most spectacular rows of May's first year in power. Team 2019, particularly Anna Soubry, felt they had been misled. 'Anna was absolutely furious she was being asked to vote for something which accepted the triggering of Article 50,' a colleague recalled. 'She felt very betrayed. At that point the disillusionment started to set in. We realised that Downing Street were not interested in us, they were only into appeasing the Brexiteers.'

The incident which weaponised the relationship between Team 2019 and Downing Street became known as 'Trousergate'. It began in mid-November when Liz Sanderson, the Downing Street head of features, agreed that Theresa May would sit down with the *Sunday Times Magazine* for an interview and a glossy shoot with a portrait photographer. Sanderson was a former feature writer with the *Mail on Sunday* who had joined the Home Office as a special adviser after Hill was forced to resign. She put together a briefing note to May and the day before the interview, she and Katie Perrior, the director of communications, were called to see the prime minister. Knowing May would be expected to open up about herself for a long-form interview, they took her through a few obvious lines of questioning. When they had finished, Perrior asked the prime minister, 'Do you need a stylist?'

'No,' said May.

'Are you sure? I mean they're offering it, so if you want it go for it.'

'I don't want a stylist.'

'What about hair and make-up?'

Again May said 'No,' but there was hesitation in her voice. She changed her mind: 'I wouldn't mind.'

Perrior then asked if Sanderson could inspect the Mays' private flat above 11 Downing Street. 'I know it's your home but we might want to rearrange some things because we want the photos to look fab,' she explained. May readily agreed. Sanderson did a recce and was happy that everything looked smart.

At 7 p.m. that evening, the day before the shoot, Fiona Hill marched to the press office and began shouting at Sanderson. Minutes earlier she had demanded a list of British designers. 'I need that list now! How the fuck did this happen?'

Perrior emerged from her office to find out what was going on. 'Is everything all right?' she asked.

In front of the entire press office, Hill said, 'No, it fucking isn't all right. You have taken your eye off the ball again.' Perrior asked what the problem was. 'Where are the clothes?' Hill asked. Perrior explained that the prime minister had been fully briefed by Sanderson and 'the prime minister said she doesn't want a stylist and she wants to choose her own clothes'.

Hill was furious: 'First. Fucking. Mistake. Why on earth did you listen to that?'

'Because she's the prime minister. Anyway, her clothes are fantastic. She always looks good.'

'Big mistake. You need to realise that the PM does not know her own mind on this stuff and needs me to be the one making these decisions for her. First of all, it shows you're not in control of this, at all. Secondly, where are the fucking hydrangeas?' Perrior was lost for words, recalling a line from the film *The Devil Wears Prada* about a bullying boss in the fashion industry and her obsession with flowers. Hill continued, 'Flowers? Hydrangeas? You know, brighten up the flat a bit. Second big fail.'

Perrior suggested getting the *Sunday Times* people to bring some in the morning. 'I want hydrangeas now!' said Hill. Perrior dispatched her PA, armed with Perrior's credit card, to locate hydrangeas at seven o'clock in the evening. While that was happening, Hill had picked up the phone to May's favourite fashion designer, Amanda Wakeley: 'I'm really sorry to do this, but could we have a van full of clothes for Theresa's size tomorrow morning at 7 a.m. at Downing Street. I'm afraid the team here have fucked up.'

The following morning Hill was in work by seven, dressed in a designer leopard-print skirt with Gucci heels, when the journalists arrived. Perrior looked in briefly on the interview but, feeling surplus to requirements for the pictures, retreated to her office. A couple of hours later a pale-faced Sanderson sought her out. 'How did it go?' Perrior asked.

'Theresa looked really good.' Sanderson paused. 'But there might be an issue. She was in £2,000 worth of clothes. We will need a line to take.' The clothes Hill had helped May to select included a pair of brown leather trousers costing £995, a jumper worth £495 and a pair of spotless Burberry trainers which retailed at £295. For a politician who claimed to be working for people who were 'just about managing' it was a public relations disaster in the making. Perrior inspected the pictures and thought that May did not even look natural. Her languid pose was that of an ageing starlet rather than a no-nonsense national leader. Another of the Number 10 heads of department said, 'I remember looking at that photograph thinking, "It is not the leather trousers that are odd, it is that the plimsolls she was wearing had never been out of the house." They were virgin white. It all looked completely artificial.'

When the magazine dropped, on 27 November, journalists from other publications began phoning up, firing off awkward questions. 'Are they her clothes? Did she borrow them? Did she keep them? Did she pay for them? Does she have a stylist? Is Fiona her stylist?' There were no good answers. All Perrior and her colleagues in the press office could think about was: why did the prime minister allow herself to be kitted out in two grand's worth of clobber? That night even Perrior's mother told her May had gone down in her estimation. At the end of the week she went home to watch *Have I Got News For You*. All they could talk about was May's leather trousers. Then she watched *Gogglebox* and was confronted with the same images.

There was more to come, though. The following week Nicky Morgan told *The Times* that May's extravagant trousers had been 'noticed and discussed' in local Tory circles. 'My barometer is always, "How am I going to explain this in Loughborough market?" I don't have leather trousers,' she said. 'I don't think I've ever spent that much on anything apart from my wedding dress.'

Team 2019 had been due to go into Downing Street for a third time, this time to see the prime minister. Morgan was taken aside by George Hollingbery, May's parliamentary bag carrier, and told, 'I'm sorry, you can't come to that meeting.' Morgan said, 'I know exactly where this has come from. If they want to play it that way, okay.'

Three days earlier Alistair Burt had received a text from Fiona Hill saying, 'Don't bring that woman to Downing Street again.' Incensed, Morgan texted the chief of staff, 'If you don't like something I have said or done, please tell me directly. No man brings me to any meeting. Your team invites me. If you don't want my views in future meetings you need to tell them.' Hill, apparently responding to the part of the message about Burt, replied, 'Well, he just did. So there!'[3]

Morgan was furious. She felt Downing Street should have laughed off her comments. Instead they were intent on signalling that anyone who ever voiced criticism would be shot down. The week that Gavin Williamson fixed the amendment, turning the tables on Team 2019, someone briefed the *Guardian* that Morgan had been banned from Downing Street. She thought to herself, 'I'm not having this,' and passed the texts to the *Mail on Sunday*, which splashed the story on 11 December. Hill told colleagues, 'I will never speak to Nicky Morgan again. There's no point. It's nothing to do with the trousers. I fundamentally think it's wrong to share private text messages.'

The story included a quote from Adam Stares, deputy chairman of Morgan's Loughborough constituency association, who said, 'There's a lot of people who think she is taking sideswipes at the government and at Theresa May.' Morgan knew that Stares was friends with the whip

Julian Smith from their days in Yorkshire politics. She confronted Gavin Williamson, accusing Smith of getting her own association to denounce her. Smith did not admit that he had encouraged Stares, but he admitted speaking to him. Morgan confided in a friend, 'You know it's really lonely at the moment. I'm standing up for what I believe in but I'm getting killed right now.'

Fiona Hill's behaviour during that fortnight became a talking point around Downing Street. Many would have sympathised with her more if they had known that a month earlier she had separated from her partner Charles Farr, the chairman of the Joint Intelligence Committee. It was a stark reminder of the pressures real life and political life sometimes place on each other. But Hill did not seek sympathy by revealing the break-up.

The Commons motion meant the time was fast approaching when the prime minister needed to spell out her Brexit plan. Having seen off the two most awkward female backbenchers, Morgan and Soubry, she now had to deal with the two men who, in their very different ways, had become the biggest headaches in her government: Boris Johnson and Ivan Rogers.

5

HOW DO YOU SOLVE A PROBLEM LIKE BORIS?

Open with a joke, they say. Theresa May's gag certainly got a big laugh when she began her party conference speech. It was the perfect way to break the ice with the party faithful. In retrospect it might have been better not to choose as her joke the foreign secretary, Boris Johnson. Clearly revelling in her big moment, May strode to the mark and said, 'When we came to Birmingham this week, some big questions were hanging in the air. Do we have a plan for Brexit? We do. Are we ready for the effort it will take to see it through? We are.' May paused, taking her audience by the hand towards the punchline: 'Can Boris Johnson stay on message for a full four days?'

The audience laughed. Near the front of the stalls, Johnson waved. 'Just about,' said May, rotating her palm as if the verdict hung in the balance. The foreign secretary staked his claim to loyalty. 'Slavishly … religiously,' he shouted out.

Behind the smiles, though, Johnson's ability to carry himself in one of the great offices of state was already in question. His appointment – shortly after his career appeared to have imploded – was a surprise, not least to him. As one of the front men for Brexit he was not popular in the European capitals. But in the Whitehall reorganisation that followed, the Foreign Office was not in the box seats when it came to Brexit. His allies celebrated the fact that Britain's most mercurial politician finally had the chance to prove himself a serious contender for even higher office.

Yet throughout the autumn, controversy and gaffes appeared to follow Johnson as if he were the Pied Piper of political problems. First came the cabinet wars over Chevening, the grand country pile in Kent which is traditionally the grace and favour home of the foreign secretary or the deputy prime minister. In a sign that May had a warped sense of humour, she decreed that 'The Three Brexiteers' – Johnson, David Davis and Liam Fox – should share the mansion, a move that prompted newspaper articles about which of them should be 'the keyholder'. 'Boris cared enormously about Chevening. DD couldn't give a fuck,' one senior government figure recalled. 'Boris was insisting that "They can use it but they have to get my permission."' Davis, never one to miss an opportunity for devilment, engaged heartily in debates with Johnson about which of them was the senior minister before announcing to officials, 'Just tell them I'm not going to use it. Boris can do whatever he wants.'

May had given Johnson the job because she wanted him to shake things up, but also because she felt he was the wronged party after Michael Gove's betrayal in the 2016 leadership election. 'We wanted a big brain in there to reassess whether our policies in those regions are stale or need rethinking,' said one of May's aides. 'She wanted to give him a good job.' But by October there was widespread irritation that Johnson was learning on the job so publicly. 'Theresa was clear with him that he had to show his serious side,' a Downing Street source said. 'He took his time to settle.'

Others in Number 10 say May's team set Johnson up to fail. 'They thought Boris was a threat,' a Downing Street official said. 'Part of the plan of appointing him to that position was to let him discredit himself. He has done it a bit. You tame him that way.'

If that was indeed May's plan, it worked a treat. As he began to travel, the foreign secretary discovered that his colourful way of expressing himself was a world away from the nuanced niceties of the diplomatic world. Searching for a purpose, he seemed at times like a child in a sweet shop, latching on to each passing international crisis with his customary brand of dangerously quotable insight. He enthusiastically backed a 'no bombing zone' in Syria that had no prospect of support from the White House and consequently no hope of success. Disgusted by Russian backing for the Assad regime, he called on 11 October for 'demonstrations outside the Russian embassy', a move that was widely ridiculed. Two days later, at a select committee hearing, he admitted he did not know what the Commonwealth flag looked like. When an official drew it for him, he said, 'That's a lovely flag.'

With the cabinet on the verge of backing the expansion of Heathrow airport, which he had bitterly opposed, Johnson had to find a way around his ancient pledge, made while Mayor of London, to lie down in front of the bulldozers. 'I'm going to construct a sarcophagus that will allow me to be suspended under the bulldozers,' he said. 'Once they roll over me I will emerge like Houdini in order to fulfil my pledge.'

The ridicule might have been greater had Johnson not been stopped by his senior aide Will Walden from announcing his latest wheeze to boost Brexit Britain – a new Channel Tunnel for cars. In private conversations at the Tory Party conference he said, 'If you wanted to show your commitment to Europe, is it not time for us to have further and better economic integration with a road tunnel? That's what we need.' Johnson argued that such a plan had been ruled out in the 1980s 'on the basis that you could not clean the fumes out of the tunnel'. But he said, 'That's all changed. They now have the technology. You could come out of the EU but join Europe in the most fundamental way.' The plan was even more grandiose than the 'Boris Island' Thames Estuary airport he had advocated as London mayor and appealed to Johnson's sense of history. 'You undo the damage done at the end of the ice age,' he explained. 'The Channel is really a river whose tributaries used to be the Seine and the Thames. It became bigger and bigger and bigger as the ice melted until it separated Britain from France.' Reversing it would be 'a great symbol of European commitment'.

Johnson was weakened in mid-October by the departure of Walden to the private sector. Johnson had wanted him to be made chief of staff but he fell foul of a crackdown on the number of special advisers and their remuneration. Walden offered to take a pay cut and forget the grander title but then received a message from Sue Gray, in the Cabinet Office, saying Downing Street would not approve his appointment. His name, it seemed, was on a 'banned list' drawn up by Team May, which included special advisers who had worked for former ministers they did not like, such as Michael Gove, some civil servants, and people close to David Cameron. It was further evidence that May's allies did not want Johnson to build a strong team that could become a rival power centre. The foreign secretary recruited Liam Parker, Mark Carney's spin doctor at the Bank of England, to handle his media but he was still learning the ropes when the briefing wars began.

Two weeks after the party conference Johnson was embarrassed by the publication, in the *Sunday Times*, of an article he had written arguing for a Remain vote, just two days before he declared for Leave. The article had been dashed off to demonstrate the weakness of the Remain cause but its publication fuelled the views of some voters and MPs that Johnson had backed Leave to further his own ambitions. The vociferousness with which he pursued the Brexit cause can only have been fuelled by the need to prove that he had made the right decision. Some cabinet colleagues still felt he was too ready to approach Brexit as if he was part of the Leave campaign, rather than as a minister in a government that had to get to grips with the potential problems. 'We all call him Borisgloss, like he's Panglossian,' one cabinet minister said. 'All of us want this to work, even those who were passionate Remainers. That means that you have to engage in the difficulties.' Allies of Johnson said he was acutely aware that, having led the Leave campaign, he would be personally blamed for any problems with Brexit. Protests outside his front door in Islington by irate Remainers had already driven Johnson to move his family to the more protected surroundings of the foreign secretary's official residence in Carlton Gardens. A special adviser said, 'Bojo knows he's going to be drummed out of the country if this is a disaster. He already hardly shows his face in London, the city he used to run.'

Ivan Rogers, believing Johnson had an overly optimistic view of how easy it would be to reach a deal, invited him to Brussels for dinner with David McAllister, the German MEP with a Scottish father who was tipped by some as a successor to Angela Merkel, and some other Anglophile MEPs. Both sides were shocked by what they heard. McAllister gave Johnson an 'unvarnished' view of how Britain was seen for leaving the EU and warned that the final deal 'will take much longer than you think'. He said Britain would need a transitional agreement and would get no special privileges beyond what other third-party countries enjoyed. Johnson was aggressive in return, telling his fellow guests, 'This is why we've got to exit and this is why this venture isn't going anywhere.' McAllister 'went white' according to one account and declared later, 'I can't believe that is the British foreign secretary.'

Rogers also put Johnson in front of Anthony Gardner, Barack Obama's ambassador to the European Union, who gave him a similarly blunt view of how the EU was seeing things. As he had with Hammond, Rogers stressed to Johnson that a transitional period would be necessary: 'I don't think we'll do an FTA [free trade agreement] in the space of two years.' But, he pointed out, 'We have to leave the customs union if we want to do our own trade policy – so that's a battle you're bound to win.' He compared the prospect of leaving via 'a cliff edge' a year before a general election to an outbreak of 'foot and mouth disease cubed' because there would be huge delays at the border. 'What kills governments is the public sense of chaos,' Rogers warned. 'Don't take this from me, go and talk to customs people.'

May's desire to put Johnson in his place was again evident at the start of November when both accepted awards at the *Spectator*'s Parliamentarian of the Year dinner, Johnson for best comeback. In his speech, Johnson compared himself to Michael Heseltine's dog, Kim, who the former cabinet minister had admitted to strangling to calm it down. (Heseltine denied killing the dog.) 'Like Kim the Alsatian I am absolutely thrilled to have had this reprieve,' Johnson joked. But when May took to the stage she delivered a joke with menace: 'Boris, the dog was put down … when its master decided it wasn't needed any more.'

Johnson's allies pushed back hard at Downing Street, making clear that if he was slapped down again in public he would respond in kind. In Number 10 Johnson had an ally in Katie Perrior, who had helped run his first mayoral campaign in 2008. He also got a call from Fiona Hill, who said May 'didn't mean it'. May called Johnson and said, 'Oh Boris, I hope you didn't take too much offence last night. It was a joke.' He replied, 'I don't. I've made a living out of jokes but the papers seem to think there is something there and it doesn't help.' He made the point that May knew what she was dealing with when she appointed him and it was agreed that the jokes would stop. An edict even went to ministers that they should start referring to Johnson as the foreign secretary, rather than 'Boris'. A source close to May said, 'I think he had created the idea that it was okay to have a joke about Boris because he joked about everything and everyone. But that was the last time we made a joke about him, because I think she knew herself the caravan had moved on. He was a bit upset about it.'

As the most prominent face of a hard Brexit, Johnson was also the focus of lingering anger among EU politicians. 'Around the world, they all regard the guy as a British Trump,' reported a former minister who travelled a lot. On 16 November, Johnson was accused of 'insulting' Italian economic development minister Carlo Calenda when Boris said Italy should back a good trade deal for Britain or they would lose 'prosecco exports' to the UK. With his trademark verbal gymnastics, Johnson had suggested controlling immigration while maintaining trade was 'pro-secco but by no means anti-pasto'. But his desire for Britain to have its cake and eat it rubbed his counterparts up the wrong way. Dutch finance minister Jeroen Dijsselbloem – the president of the eurozone's Eurogroup – accused him of 'saying things that are intellectually impossible, politically unavailable'.

There was resentment at Johnson's statements during the referendum campaign, which many saw as misleading. When the foreign secretary travelled to Turkey later that month and told President Erdogan that he supported Turkish EU entry, just months after the Leave campaign had played on fears of Turkey to drum up votes, Manfred Weber – the president of the conservative European People's Party (EPP) grouping in the European Parliament – accused him of an 'unbelievable provocation'. Johnson's suggestion in January 2017 that EU leaders should not be tempted to give the UK 'punishment beatings' for Brexit 'in the manner of some World War Two movie' would only confirm to many continentals that he was more intent on being interesting than being diplomatic.

European officials mounted their own briefing operation against Johnson. On the evening of 30 November, the *Guardian* and Sky News began to report that the foreign secretary had privately told a group of EU ambassadors that he was personally in favour of the free movement of people. Four of them had spoken to Sky. One said, 'He did say he was personally in favour of free movement, but he said it wasn't government policy.' Johnson had always been liberal on immigration, but the claim was toxic since it flew in the face of his stance at Vote Leave and Theresa May's decision to put control of immigration at the top of her list of priorities.

When Steve Baker heard the news, he detected 'a political operation designed to discomfort Eurosceptics'. The ambassadors had been introduced to the journalists by British Influence, a group run by Peter Wilding, an arch-Europhile who had first coined the term 'Brexit'. Baker texted Johnson to ask what the 'line to take was'. The foreign secretary replied that he was 'in favour of migration under control'. Determined to close down the story, Baker messaged all 170 MPs and peers on an old mailing list he had used to stage EU rebellions against David Cameron and said, 'This is an attack on Boris Johnson. Boris Johnson's view hasn't changed, he's in favour of migration under democratic control. Nothing has changed.' He sent the same message to the European Research Group WhatsApp group and then tweeted his support for Johnson, urging others to do the same. 'The result was that within fifteen minutes we'd destroyed that operation against Boris,' a leading Eurosceptic said. 'What they were hoping for was Eurosceptics turning on Boris Johnson and tearing him limb from limb.' Baker had turned his Eurosceptic shock troops from a guerrilla unit fighting his own government into a praetorian guard for hard Brexit.

Even so, Johnson's cabinet colleagues continued to undermine him. In his autumn statement speech to the Commons, Philip Hammond could not resist a dig at Boris's failed leadership bid and his reference a year earlier that he would seek the leadership 'if the ball came loose at the back of the scrum'. Incisors gleaming, the chancellor told MPs, 'I suspect that I will prove no more adept at pulling rabbits from hats than my successor as foreign secretary has been in retrieving balls from the back of scrums.' Johnson smiled ruefully. A special adviser said, 'Number 10 advised Hammond not to put that joke in his speech and he didn't listen to them.'

Some of Johnson's problems were the result of the uncontrollable circus that has always surrounded him. In late November, he was in Serbia and was invited to speak about press freedom at the oldest bookshop in Belgrade. But when the owner produced copies of his biography of Winston Churchill to sign, Johnson found himself in hot water, accused of profiting from a diplomatic trip.

Others appeared to be the result of hostile briefing from his cabinet colleagues. Priti Patel was fingered for briefing the *Sun* about the Foreign Office wasting aid money. 'She felt very uncomfortable that he was making headlines on Brexit and she was stuck in DfID,' a ministerial aide adduced. Other colleagues ridiculed his contributions to discussion. One stated, 'Boris has not said anything of consequence in cabinet. It is very high level tendentious piffle.' Cabinet ministers recounted how May's patience with Johnson wore thin, on one occasion holding up her hand with her eyes closed and sighing as if she was trying to mute him. 'There was a flash of anger,' a cabinet minister said. 'That was unusual for her.' One minister even made the extraordinary claim that Johnson 'got the number of Punic wars wrong' during one of his classical disquisitions in cabinet. Johnson saw the hand of May's acolytes too. He told friends, 'I think there were at least a couple of shots from our friends in Number 10.'

The most damaging story was traced to the Treasury. On 20 November, at the height of the rows over the customs union, the *Mail on Sunday* claimed Johnson had turned up at the Brexit committee with the wrong papers.[1] In the meeting, he had annoyed Hammond by making a point unconnected with the chancellor's presentation. Another cabinet minister said, 'It wasn't that he turned up with the wrong papers. He started talking about something that we had discussed at the last meeting. He had just forgotten that whole discussion.' The chancellor told friends Johnson was unprepared and the anecdote was passed to the press.

Cabinet colleagues continued to be frustrated by Johnson's controversialism – and his seeming ability to get away with things they could not. On a cabinet away day in early 2017, Johnson was walking with Andrea Leadsom and Ben Gummer while press photographers stalked them. Gummer referred to the controversy over the size of the crowds at Donald Trump's inauguration. Johnson, who had misheard said, 'The Krauts? What do you mean the Krauts?'

'No, no, no. Crowds, Boris.'

'What about the Krauts?'

'I said the crowds, the people there.'

Johnson bellowed, 'I thought you said Krauts! It wasn't Krauts at all! I thought you were talking about Krauts.'

Gummer said, 'For God's sake don't say that in front of the cameras because they'll be able to lip read what you're saying.'

One minister who heard the story said, 'It shows the layers of his mind, what comes first, what you hear.'

The moment that led to a full-blown crisis at the top of the government came in early December, shortly after the prime minister had made a trade trip to the Gulf. In the Bahraini capital, Manama, May had become the first woman ever to address the Gulf Cooperation Council, the regional political organisation for the energy-rich Gulf monarchies: Bahrain, Kuwait, Oman, Qatar, Saudi Arabia and the United Arab Emirates. In a speech and over dinner with the ageing potentates, May sealed a strategic security partnership and agreement to unblock barriers to free trade, saying that in challenging times Britain wanted to be 'partner of choice' with its 'oldest and most dependable friends'. The warmth of the welcome impressed May and Fiona Hill, who was travelling with her. 'They just fell in love with her,' Hill told colleagues.

May and Hill were both livid when it emerged that, at a conference in Rome the following week, Johnson had criticised her new Saudi friends.

'There are politicians who are twisting and abusing religion and different strains of the same religion in order to further their own political objectives,' Johnson claimed. Referring to the conflicts in Syria and Yemen, he added, 'You've got the Saudis, Iran, everybody, moving in and puppeteering and playing proxy wars.' The comments were a flagrant breach of the diplomatic *omertà* on criticising allies in public.

In Downing Street, Helen Bower – May's official spokeswoman – needed a line to give to the morning briefing with lobby journalists. Hill issued her with an incendiary quote: 'Those are the foreign secretary's views, they are not the government's position on Saudi Arabia and its role in the region.' Instead of calming the situation, the quote was guaranteed to be seen as another slap-down for Johnson from Team May. Suggesting the foreign secretary did not speak for the government was hugely damaging. According to several sources, Bower queried the line and Hill ordered her to use it. Hill says only that she cleared it.

The resulting row was the worst to date. Katie Perrior was returning from a meeting outside Downing Street when the news dropped. The Downing Street slap-down to their best-known minister was leading every news bulletin. She received a call from Johnson, who was 'very cross' and hurt. 'I cannot believe you've issued that line,' he said. 'Why would you do that to me?' When Perrior returned to Downing Street, her phone still buzzing with calls from journalists, she saw Bower, who said, 'I told her that would happen.' Perrior went to see Hill. The chief of staff said, 'It serves him right, it's happened twice now.' But Perrior thought she was putting on a brave face. Hill looked like someone thinking, 'Oh my God, what have I done?'

Johnson went for a long walk. There was briefly concern that he might resign. A close friend said, 'He was in a really bad way that week. It really really affected him. It made him think, "What the fuck am I doing in this fucking job."' Perrior visited him in Carlton Gardens. Over a glass of wine she told him to calm down. 'It's not you, the prime minister doesn't hate you.' She recalled later, 'Every cabinet minister thought at one point it was just them, that the guns were on them from Nick and Fi and no one liked them or rated them. I had to tell them, "It's not just you who gets treated like that. I do as well, the foreign secretary does, the chancellor does."' In Downing Street she made the case that it was better to hug Johnson close than slap him down. 'When Boris is upset and angry, he says things, it causes World War Three. He just does his own thing, he does media interviews, he goes on the road. We don't need that.'

At the Prime Minister's Questions that followed, Peter Dowd, an enterprising Labour MP, got to his feet and asked May, 'In the light of the foreign secretary's display of chronic foot-in-mouth disease, when deciding on cabinet positions, does the prime minister now regret that pencilling "FO" against his name should have been an instruction not a job offer?' May replied with the grin of one who has prepared her own gag. 'I have to say that the foreign secretary is doing an absolutely excellent job,' she began. But there was a sting in the tail. She added, 'He is, in short, an FFS – a fine foreign secretary.' No one could be in any doubt that May was miffed. In text speak 'FFS' also meant 'for fuck's sake'.

Having seen the wisdom of offering an olive branch, Hill agreed to go for an early evening drink with Johnson at a central London hotel to restore friendly relations. The meeting was brokered by Ben Wallace, the security minister who had run Johnson's leadership campaign and was an old friend of Hill's. Jojo Penn, the deputy chief of staff, also attended. Johnson and Hill discussed how they did not properly communicate when there was a crisis. 'I wish you would take my calls,' the foreign secretary said. Hill hit back, 'I wish you'd bloody ring me up.'

It was not to be the last time Downing Street would have to deal with a Johnsonian eruption. The biggest beast in Theresa May's cabinet did not resign, in part because she did not want him to. Her ambassador to Brussels was about to quit, in part because she did.

6

IVAN THE TERRIBLE

A civil service mandarin who worked with Ivan Rogers for two decades said of the UK's permanent representative in Brussels, 'Ivan's problem was that while he was knowledgeable, he'd never say in a word what he could say in one hundred. He was bloody irritating, but he did speak truth unto power.' It was with an email of close to 1,400 words, sent on 3 January 2017, that Rogers signalled that he had tired of offering his counsel to politicians who did not like what he had to say and he would be resigning.

The news detonated in Westminster like a battlefield nuclear weapon – a deadly blast with unpredictable fallout that consumed its author as much as its targets. As head of UKREP, Britain's diplomatic post in Brussels, Rogers had not operated quietly, and the email – which leaked within hours, as he must have known it would – took few prisoners. After four months of cabinet deliberations, it claimed, Theresa May had not yet even set the 'negotiating objectives for the UK's relationship with the EU after exit'; Rogers urged his colleagues to 'continue to challenge' the 'ill-founded arguments and muddled thinking' of ministers. 'I hope that you will support each other in those difficult moments where you have to deliver messages that are disagreeable to those who need to hear them,' he wrote. 'Senior ministers, who will decide on our positions, issue by issue, also need from you detailed, unvarnished – even where this is uncomfortable – and nuanced understanding of the views, interests and incentives of the other 27.'

Rogers' style was more than familiar to the aides of David Cameron who had been on the receiving end of his missives during their renegotiation with Brussels ahead of the EU referendum. Daniel Korski, whose inbox contained several threats of resignation and expletive-laden missives from Rogers, remarked to a friend that day, 'It seemed quite mild compared with the emails we used to get.'

The explosion had been long in the coming, pitching as it did the irresistible force of one of the most headstrong officials in the British government against the immovable objects of Nick Timothy and Fiona Hill.

In the early days of the May government, the prime minister and Rogers had been on good terms. 'They actually got on really well when she was home secretary,' a Number 10 official said. When May travelled to Brussels to negotiate the justice and home affairs opt-outs, it was Rogers who had sat next to her. They shared an occasional gin and tonic at his residence. As a grammar-school boy, Rogers also had a strong fellow feeling with May socially, telling friends the Cameron regime had 'treated her pretty shittily'.

It was not long before Rogers began to rub May and her team up the wrong way. Glasses perched on the end of his nose like a disapproving schoolmaster, he spoke bluntly and fast. Words were not minced, meanings not finessed. He told May – as he had Cameron, Tony Blair and Gordon Brown – that he owed her his 'best assessment of where we're at'. With Rogers, that meant warts and all. He did not see the point of operating any other way. An ally said, 'Whatever else he is – and obviously he's driven people mad under numerous regimes – he does know a lot about how the budget works and how the single market works and how the customs union works.' Rogers' personal creed was that he would tell his political masters where the game was going and what he thought they should do about it. But, as he explained to colleagues, 'If they then say, "Interesting point of view but fuck off," then that's okay. The best civil servants get on and implement the wishes of the boss.' The problem was that May's team began to think he was doing too much of the advising and not enough of the implementing.

May first asked Rogers to see her in her Commons office the weekend before she became prime minister, at the start of what she assumed would be an eight-week leadership battle. 'Tell me how this really works and what you really think,' she said. Rogers briefed her on the technicalities of the Article 50 process and the dynamics in Brussels. When she entered Downing Street, he told Hill and Timothy, 'I'm totally committed to making Brexit work.' Having seen David Cameron's difficulties up close, his advice was that May needed to learn from her predecessor's mistakes, to 'start at the outset from where you want to end' and work her way backwards. 'Set an objective. Where do you want the country to be by 2025, what's our route to getting there?'

Contrary to the widespread view after he resigned, Rogers was not doing the work of the vanquished Remainers by steering May towards a soft Brexit. He believed from the start that a soft Brexit was never viable and that Britain was destined to go 'further out' than many initially assumed. In an appearance before the Brexit select committee in February 2017 – after his resignation – Rogers revealed that he had told May, 'If control of your own borders and no jurisdiction by the ECJ are your desiderata, the answer to that is to leave the customs union, leave the single market and strike as comprehensive an FTA with the EU as you can get.'[1] He told the prime minister she would get a better hearing in Brussels if fellow leaders did not think she was simply trying to emulate Boris Johnson's doctrine of having cake while simultaneously eating it. That meant moving on from claims of British exceptionalism inside the European institutions of which, in Rogers' view, Cameron's renegotiation was the failed last hurrah. It meant accepting that the single market came with the four freedoms and that the UK did want to hold on to 'the best bits' while ditching free movement of people. Rogers' concern was that May's team should adopt a pragmatic enough approach to Brussels that all this could be accomplished without 'massive disorder'. Tensions arose because, in explaining where the obstacles in Brussels lay, Rogers all too often seemed like the voice of Brussels in Whitehall, rather than the voice of Downing Street in Brussels.

Rogers' friends, including journalists in Brussels who dealt with him regularly, felt it was unfair to characterise him as a Europhile. 'I'm a deeply unenthusiastic European,' he told them. 'I experience co-decision making, I experience the European Parliament, I think the project has taken various turns for the worse.' Rogers had thought Cameron's referendum risky precisely because he was frustrated that the EU would not reform and believed that the referendum would be lost before it dawned on most of Cameron's political staff. He told Downing Street that political leaders on the continent would 'make absolutely heroic efforts which seem to us to be ludicrous' to preserve the integrity of the EU because 'the consequences of it falling over are too dark to contemplate'. That meant putting the political integrity of the EU before mutual economic benefit when negotiating Brexit. His position put him at odds with the Brexiteers and made him a Cassandra-like figure to Team May.

Rogers told colleagues – including Jeremy Heywood and Oliver Robbins – that May was embarking on 'the negotiation from hell' and none of them would be doing her a favour by not telling her where the opposition was coming from in Brussels. A Rogers ally said, 'Ivan's view was that she was going to find that out after she invoked Article 50 and then she'll come along and say, "Why the hell didn't you tell me that?" His job was to deliver bluntness from Brussels. He thought there was too much punch pulling which evaded telling her uncomfortable things. His style is to tell people uncomfortable stuff.'

The way he did so, however, left May's team with the impression he considered himself a professional in a team of amateurs. Rogers had been present at fifty or more European Council meetings, more than any other Briton alive. He saw May as 'the new girl' who had to learn at warp speed who to trust.

On 14 October, Rogers sent May a long 'scene setter' for her first European Council meeting, summarising what he had been hearing from the Commission officials and fellow ambassadors. Two months later it was to leak, with disastrous consequences for Rogers. He told May everyone he spoke to believed now that Britain would leave the single market and the customs union and that the negotiation would be about a deep and comprehensive free trade agreement. He told her, 'Most of them think that will take three or four years to negotiate, a couple of years to ratify, therefore nothing will be in place before the mid-2020s.' Rogers did not in fact say – as was later claimed – that he thought it would take ten years; he was communicating the views of his contacts. But it was hardly what May wanted to hear. He also warned Hill and Timothy that if they wanted a good trade agreement they would have to fight the hardline Eurosceptics, who he believed did not want Britain to sign any arrangement that would keep the UK in close regulatory alignment with the rest of the EU.

Before May's first Council meeting, Rogers briefed the reporters that the prime minister would tell her fellow leaders over dinner that the UK wanted to keep good relations with Europe and was not a 'wrecker' trying to bring down their project. He insisted later that he had 'stuck absolutely rigidly to the script' agreed by Number 10. He should perhaps have been more cautious in handling a new prime minister and a team of spin doctors who were under pressure not to give the media too much. When discussions between the leaders on the Syrian civil war overran, May never delivered the lines he had briefed, but the prime minister awoke to find them in the morning newspapers. 'It was not cool,' one source close to May said. Rogers was quizzed by Katie Perrior about whether he was responsible for the briefing because the line was not the one they wanted in the papers. Rogers pointed out it was in the pre-conference script. She asked him to clear what he would say to the Brussels press pack in future so they could agree on the best line to brief. 'If you're about to go into a negotiation it's tight lips and observation,' a Downing Street aide said. 'It's not like the old days when you can just freewheel.'

In July, Rogers had told May he was happy to move jobs if she wanted him to. Now he did so again. May demurred. But the briefing row dented his morale, coming as it did shortly after – against Rogers' advice – she set the March deadline for triggering Article 50 at party conference. May's team were also beginning to tire of him explaining why their approach was wrong before deploying his favourite line: 'I speak truth to power.' As one of them explained later, 'He says that all the time. Yes, you should tell truth to power, that's what all advisers do, but you also have a job to do, which is setting up our pillars for the negotiation. He wasn't moving at the pace that our thinking was moving at. Which is why he didn't see our thinking when we set our timetable at conference.'

To the civil servants it seemed as if Number 10 was not interested in their, and Rogers', knowledge of the workings of Brussels. 'One of the things they were starting to feel in the autumn was: are we really wanted? Are we contaminated by expertise?' one official said. 'People felt compromised by knowing their stuff.'

In meetings, Rogers' approach would 'visibly irritate Nick and Fi', according to another official present. 'They were pretty sharp exchanges.' When Rogers put across the views of his contacts in Brussels, he would receive a primer in practical politics from the chiefs. Rogers stressed the need for a long period of transition after Brexit and for the need to accept the sequencing for the talks agreed by the other twenty-seven member states. 'If we do that we'll be eaten alive by the Tory Party,' one of the chiefs replied. Another Downing Street source said, 'They would be openly rude to him in front of Theresa in those meetings. They didn't actually sack people. They made it so they know that they don't want you and they're not giving you what you need to do your job.'

May would also show her displeasure. 'The PM just cuts across him: "Well, this is my position and I'm afraid you need to think about it a bit more,"' the official recalled. Rogers was heard in Brussels bemoaning the 'control freak Home Office approach' of May's team, and had branded Hill and Timothy 'children' – a phrase that found its way back to the chiefs. Another Downing Street aide who watched the three of them together compared it to being stuck next to a couple about to divorce: 'No one wanted to be in a room with them.'

Some in government called Hill and Timothy 'the terrible twins'. It did not take long for 'Ivan the Terrible' to be coined by one minister in return. Frustrated that his advice was not being taken, political sources say, Rogers became difficult to work with. 'He is very rude about everybody. He just didn't seem happy with anything,' a Number 10 source said. 'It wasn't that Theresa wasn't happy with him, he just wasn't happy and it made it difficult to work with him.'

By autumn, Rogers was also frustrated that May was taking an age to firm up the decision to leave the single market and the customs union that had been implicit in her conference speech. A senior cabinet minister said, 'Ivan wanted clarity and he felt the machine wasn't deciding. He would keep coming to me and saying, "You must get to Number 10 to make their minds up about this." He felt he didn't know what message to give. Nobody knew what we were doing.'

Rogers' greatest fear, though, was that the government was not doing enough work to analyse the risks or prepare for the possibility of crashing out of the EU without a new deal, falling back on World Trade Organisation tariff rules. He told colleagues the prospect needed to be treated like 'a national emergency'. Privately he warned of 'mutually assured destruction'. Rogers had been arguing since 2012 that an exit contingency cell should have been set up in the Cabinet Office, but Cameron and Heywood had vetoed the suggestion. Without that work, May could not credibly threaten to walk away from negotiations, a card she needed to hold in her hand. 'My advice inside the Government is that you have to work through every area of British economic life, and work through what the default to WTO option really means and really entails, and where it really takes you,' he told MPs later.[2]

Friends of David Cameron say Rogers shared some of these concerns with the former prime minister when they had breakfast together that autumn. Cameron wanted to talk about the memoir he was writing, for which HarperCollins were reputed to have paid £1 million.

Allies of May say Rogers resented that it was May, not him, making the important calls. 'These are the biggest decisions that any government will take, probably in our lifetime, and they were always going to be taken by a PM, not an official,' said one senior figure in Downing Street. 'I think Ivan struggled with that. I don't know how it worked under the last regime but if Ivan didn't like that then it was his job to serve the PM like all of us. There's a hierarchy and she's at the top of it and he isn't.'

Ahead of the December Council meeting, Rogers had a meeting with Nick Timothy, at which he said he would write to Downing Street outlining the stories he thought would emerge from the meeting so that a press handling strategy could be worked out. He agreed not to brief on Brexit itself. Then on the evening of 14 December, Rogers began getting calls warning him that the memo he had written for May in October was about to be released. The following day the BBC's Laura Kuenssberg reported his warning that Brexit could take a decade – something that provoked an immediate backlash from pro-Brexit Tories.

When his face appeared on the evening news a colleague said, 'You've just been stabbed, haven't you?' Rogers could not prove that it was Downing Street who had knifed him, but where there might have been statements of support, instead there was a deafening silence. Senior Eurosceptics even took to the airwaves claiming that Rogers himself had leaked the contents of his memo. That night he spoke to his wife and told her he did not think he could carry on after Christmas. 'Once you're the story, you can't in my view do the job.'

Despite the tensions, some around May insist Rogers was not forced out. 'We genuinely were not saying, "This guy's got to go,"' one said. Fiona Hill told friends she had found out about Rogers' resignation from Sky News. Yet there is plentiful evidence that Rogers had been told it would make sense for him to start looking for his next job. Nick Timothy did not understand why Rogers had even stayed in post once the referendum was lost and it was clear he would have to implement Brexit. 'Nick's view was that Ivan didn't really believe in it and didn't really think it could be done and he genuinely didn't know why he stayed around,' said one confidant. Another source close to May said her Lancaster House speech, now scheduled for early January, 'was held up because people were waiting for Ivan to resign. There was talk of getting rid of him anyway. Had he not resigned he'd probably have been moved at some point anyway.' The source said the chiefs 'saw him as very close to Cameron, a person who failed at a renegotiation in the past, but also someone who would come along to those weekly meetings and just didn't contribute in a way that was seen as helpful. He was just relentlessly negative. There was definitely a sense that we just needed some fresh blood. He had a different point of view and it was never the kind of view that was going to find favour with the PM or her team.'

The foreign secretary had also tired of Rogers. 'Boris thought: how can we have this doom monger representing us at an EU level?' a source close to Johnson said. 'Boris was a bit pissed off with how he did things.'

In the week before Christmas, six days after the memo was leaked, Rogers was seen by two Foreign Office officials having breakfast with Jeremy Heywood in Villandry, an upmarket eatery in St James's which specialises in brunch for businessmen spending their employers' money. The exact details of the conversation are known only to its two participants, but based on their exchanges with others it is understood that they talked about Rogers' future and the way Whitehall was handling Brexit. 'Heywood said to him, "Think about how you handle this and get out,"' a Foreign Office source said. 'The view was: "He's got to go and go before the Lancaster House speech." Heywood was aware the writing was on the wall. The message was, "Why don't you do it your own way?"'

Heywood and Rogers had known each other for twenty-five years and could speak frankly to one another. Whitehall sources say Rogers was concerned that his relationship with Oliver Robbins was not as open and free-flowing as it had been with Robbins' predecessor Tom Scholar during Cameron's renegotiation, or before with Jon Cunliffe when he was at UKREP and Rogers in London. Rogers felt he and Robbins needed to be speaking several times a day, and they were not.

Under Cameron, Cunliffe, Rogers and Scholar had all deliberately argued in front of the prime minister so he could hear each side of a case being put – but May did not like to work that way. Neither were Rogers and Heywood on the same page. Rogers thought the system Heywood had set up, with DExEU as player and referee and Robbins servicing both DExEU and Downing Street, was flawed. On occasion, departments reported their position on an issue to Rogers and UKREP, but not to David Davis and DExEU.

Rogers also complained that Whitehall departments, swamped by the future of Brexit, were failing to stay on top of evolving policy in Brussels, where damaging regulations still had to be fought because they would impact Britain outside as well as inside the EU. When he gave evidence to the European Scrutiny Committee the following February, Rogers said, 'We were getting a diminishing quality and quantity of instructions through to UKREP. I said repeatedly at mandarin level, "That is not good enough. You have to be able to walk and chew gum at the same time."'[3]

Heywood and Robbins saw Rogers as a boat rocker, and viewed his growing demands for Downing Street to announce their plans as counterproductive. 'Ivan thought they were pussyfooting around while he was fending off foreigners who were asking what the policy was,' said another mandarin. 'I think he felt that he was being left to deliver all the negative assessments.'

More importantly, Rogers believed Robbins was reluctant to tell May the truth about the difficulties ahead, a view shared by other senior civil servants. 'Olly's more inclined to tell people what they want to hear than how it is,' a senior mandarin said. Another commented, 'He sees his job mainly as giving the PM what she wants.' In one crunch meeting that December, Rogers urged Robbins and Heywood to join him in being franker. Seeing that Rogers was on his way out, they declined. When Rogers saw Philip Hammond that week he told the chancellor that he had the support of neither Heywood nor Robbins. After their breakfast meeting the cabinet secretary suggested to other officials that if Rogers were to leave, Tim Barrow – the political director at the Foreign Office – was the right man to take over.

Once he had discussed it again with his wife over Christmas, Rogers decided to quit. Having heard that May might make her big speech in the first few days of January – and not wanting his resignation to be seen as a response to the substance of the speech – he pressed send on the email announcing his departure on 3 January from his holiday cottage in Dorset. The furore dominated the news for a week. Rogers told friends he had intended the email to be a morale-boosting call to arms for the embattled staff in Brussels, urging them to stick with Brexit and do the best they could. But his tone was interpreted as an assault on ministerial incompetence. 'Serious multilateral negotiating experience is in short supply in Whitehall,' he warned. One minister complained, 'It was spiteful. His heart wasn't in it and he had to go, but it's a shame he went the way he did.'

On the verge of laying out her plans, May might have been badly wounded, but she faced a weak opposition leader whose equivocation on Europe left him ill-equipped to capitalise. Eurosceptic MPs quickly rallied too, seizing on passages in the present author's first book *All Out War* – in which Cameron's aides had blamed Rogers for the failure of Cameron's renegotiation – to say, 'Goodbye and good riddance.' Downing Street spin doctors were quick to tell journalists about the dim view taken of his briefing gaffe in October and accuse him of pessimism towards Brexit. 'He forgot what he was supposed to be doing and was freelancing with his own views,' a cabinet minister said. 'I've never seen a photograph of Ivan Rogers smiling,' commented another minister.

In Downing Street, the incident was seen as a necessary clearing of the decks. 'Jeremy Heywood played a blinder and had Tim Barrow in the job within hours,' a Number 10 source said. 'Jeremy himself felt quite personally betrayed by Ivan.' May and her team had met Barrow. They did not know him well but were quickly impressed. 'We were really clear he was the right person. Jeremy definitely thought that. DD thought that. Fox thought that and so did Boris.'

As Barrow's name was put forward, Oliver Robbins made a power play. He argued that Rogers should not be replaced and that the new permanent representative should become a role that reported directly to him. 'He did not want a direct replacement because he wanted more control over that operation,' a Downing Street source said. Barrow, a Russian expert who had done the hard yards in Moscow, had vastly more foreign policy experience than Rogers but lacked his predecessor's budget, trade, financial services and single market expertise. What he did have, in the words of one of May's aides, was a reputation for 'giving good independent analysis and advice in the manner we'd expect senior diplomats to behave'. The contrast with their view of Rogers was obvious. In the Foreign Office, the admiration was distilled into one phrase: 'There is a saying, "Don't fuck with Tim Barrow,"' one official said. Barrow refused to see his new role downgraded into a Robbins satrapy and the power play was rebuffed. 'If you have done the dark arts in Russia you know how to play the game,' said an admirer.

Boris Johnson phoned Steve Baker, the Eurosceptics' shop steward, and briefed him on Barrow, asking for a public endorsement. The Eurosceptic MPs quickly offered their support.

David Davis received a text from Rogers after he had jumped overboard, which revealed how bruised he had been by being depicted as a bulwark of the Brussels and Whitehall establishment. 'I'm not a member of the establishment, I'm a grammar school boy from middle England, the son of a grammar school teacher and a school secretary.' A minister said, 'He saw himself on one level as very ordinary, on the other not very ordinary at all.'

Rogers was prepared to stay in the civil service, but over the next forty-eight hours a succession of ministers told Downing Street they could not trust him and would not work with him. Realising the game was up, he quit the civil service altogether on 5 January. May's aides were relieved by his departure. 'The number of stories emanating from Brussels correspondents from "senior diplomatic sources" reduced,' one said.

Yet gone too was a vast stock of European knowledge, institutional memory and the most capacious address book in Brussels. Looking back, it is possible to judge that David Cameron's negotiation with Brussels was hamstrung by listening too much to Rogers and his calls for caution over what could be achieved. Yet, as it became clear that the government might have been better to delay the triggering of Article 50, would have to pay a sizeable bill, would need a transition deal, and would be confronted by Eurosceptics pushing for a no-deal departure for which Whitehall was not prepared, it was possible to conclude that Theresa May's negotiation with Brussels was damaged by not listening to Ivan Rogers nearly enough.

Nonetheless, with the most difficult official out of the way, the prime minister now had to square her cabinet so she could make the big speech spelling out how she was planning to conduct the Brexit negotiations.

7

LANCASTER HOUSE

On 17 January, more than one hundred days after Theresa May gave her speech on Brexit at the Conservative Party conference, the prime minister got to her feet in Lancaster House and finally confirmed in public that she wanted a 'clean break' from the European Union by leaving the single market and abandoning full membership of the customs union. She announced that Britain would seek a 'new partnership', not 'partial membership, associate membership or anything that leaves us half-in, half-out' of the EU. Seeking to learn from David Cameron, she threatened to walk if the terms were not good enough, declaring, 'No deal for Britain is better than a bad deal for Britain.'

Those with a perverse sense of history might have recalled that Lancaster House, one of London's great neoclassical Georgian buildings, was the venue where Margaret Thatcher in 1988 had declared her ambition to take Britain into the single market. Here now was Britain's second woman prime minister declaring an intention to leave. It was a measure of the importance that she attached to the occasion that May took to the stage in the green and blue tartan Vivienne Westwood suit she had worn to her leadership campaign launch six months earlier. Before a canvas of King George III, the monarch who lost the American colonies, May delivered her case for British independence. The ambassadors of the twenty-seven other member states applauded, grateful at least for some clarity.

The Lancaster House speech had taken shape over the Christmas break, when Nick Timothy sat down with May to agree the main points. 'This is what I want the speech to be,' she said, explaining her priorities. Timothy worked her thoughts into twelve statements of intent, or 'pillars', some of them momentous, others peripheral. 'How does this structure work for you?' he asked. 'I like it,' May replied. It says much about May that she did not boil the points down to a media-friendly list of ten. When he had the skeleton of a text, Timothy brought in Chris Wilkins to help with the second draft. As the speech was refined, May 'commented on the arguments and the substance more than the language and sound-bites'. Since so much of the substance had been months in the planning, Timothy told colleagues, he found it 'one of the easiest speeches I've ever written'.

Before the Christmas break, the chiefs had taken soundings from a range of Conservatives who would have liked to think they would be consulted about the substance of such a momentous speech. However, as at conference, the decision-making circle was extremely small. Accompanied by Michael Tomlinson, another Eurosceptic MP, Steve Baker, the chairman of the European Research Group, went into Downing Street on 19 December to see Timothy and Hill. 'We were on transmit, they were on receive,' Baker told a friend. Baker was clear that May must stick to her three red lines: no single market, no customs union, and no ECJ oversight. The chiefs took all this in but gave nothing away. 'They were very cool operators,' Baker reported back to the other Eurosceptics.

May herself had played host to a group of a dozen Remain MPs, led by the former minister Alistair Burt, in her House of Commons office just before Christmas, at the meeting from which Nicky Morgan had been banned. They pressed the case they had been making publicly that the government's plans should be converted into a white paper, so they had legislative weight and could be properly scrutinised, and that Parliament should be granted a vote on the final deal.

The chiefs also talked to 'DD, Hammond and Boris', as well as Damian Green and Amber Rudd. 'The consultation was not wide,' a Downing Street official said. Unlike Cameron, who had toured the capitals of Europe before revealing his negotiating demands the previous February, the prime minister did not consult foreign diplomats, let alone foreign leaders, about her intentions.

The key development that helped May to achieve a cabinet consensus ahead of the speech was the emergence of an alliance between David Davis and Philip Hammond. Despite initial 'mutual suspicion', the Brexit secretary and the chancellor had come to see each other as the 'grown-ups' around the table. Davis's chief of staff, James Chapman, and Hammond's special adviser, Poppy Trowbridge, plotted to bring the two big beasts together like zookeepers encouraging reluctant pandas to mate. 'James constantly impressed on DD the importance of Hammond because Hammond needed a friend,' a source said. 'They influenced each other.' The two men agreed to meet once a week. 'They went for drinks in Hammond's flat, quite often.'

Hammond was beginning to understand that his defence of membership of the customs union was a lost cause. Davis, now better read in the detail, had begun to appreciate the complexities which concerned the Treasury. Cabinet sources say that he resorted less often to the old Brexiteer argument that 'German car makers and French knicker manufacturers' would ride to Britain's rescue and insist on a good trade deal with Britain. A government source who sympathised with the Treasury said, 'Davis made a lot of progress. It was painful at times. But DD did want to work with Big Phil. He did recognise it was vastly more difficult than he first thought.' Davis himself told MPs, 'This is likely to be the most complicated negotiation of modern times, and maybe the most complicated negotiation of all time.'

The rapprochement between Davis and Hammond was evident to cabinet ministers in meetings of the Brexit subcommittee. 'They would snigger together,' a minister said, at some of the contributions from Boris Johnson and Liam Fox. This created suspicion among some Leave-voting ministers, who wondered if DD was backing away from his belief that the UK could not stay in the customs union. 'There was a period when we all thought DD was wobbling,' said a leading minister.

They were more suspicious on 1 December, when the Brexit secretary told the Commons, in response to a question, that the government would 'consider' paying to 'get the best possible access for goods and services to the European market'. Hammond backed him up, saying Davis was 'right not to rule out the possibility that we might want to contribute in some way'. The Eurosceptics smelt 'an establishment betrayal'. Steve Baker, as convener of the backbench sceptics, phoned Davis and asked what the position was. Davis clarified that Britain would not be paying large sums to Brussels indefinitely but would settle its outstanding obligations. Baker messaged the MPs on his WhatsApp group, urging them to remain calm. But one veteran Paleosceptic urged him to break off links with Downing Street. 'Go radio silent,' the MP said. 'Just let them sweat, because they're betraying us.' Baker was concerned. 'This is people gearing up for civil war,' he thought.

Nonetheless, under the influence of Hammond, Davis began to say Britain would 'meet our obligations' on the exit bill, an acknowledgement of the political reality that billions would have to be paid to Brussels if Britain wanted a trade deal. 'Anyone who tells you any different is a fantasist,' a DExEU source said at the time. That put Davis and Hammond at odds with Boris Johnson, who continued to insist that Britain had no legal obligation to pay anything. 'Phil was trying to keep open the option of spending money to access the single market,' a Tory adviser recalled. 'Boris was very concerned to close that down.' In private, Johnson told colleagues, 'It needs to be nothing. Zero. There is no case at all for continuing to spend British taxpayers' money to trade with the rest of the EU. If the argument is you should pay for access to markets, they should pay us.'

Significantly, after Davis's hint that Britain might pay up, there was not a peep of contradiction from Downing Street. While Johnson and Fox had frequently had their freelancing interventions shot down by Number 10, May's aides remained silent. 'The most significant thing that happened that day is what didn't happen,' a special adviser said. 'DD talked about paying money into the EU budget and no one from Downing Street machine-gunned him in the street.' An MP close to Davis said he had been pressing the case to Number 10 that ministers – not the media – should start doing more to define Brexit publicly, a coded rebuke to May's insistence that there should be 'no running commentary'. Another source made clear that budget contributions were a centrepiece of government plans: 'The money is where they will try to compromise.'

Four days later, on 5 December, Hammond and Davis met ten influential City bosses at the Shard, Britain's tallest building. Both agreed that they needed to calm the fears of the City, which were beginning to percolate into the media and, Davis feared, hand Barnier a stick with which to beat them. 'If people in Britain panic and the press are saying, "The City's going to evacuate to Frankfurt," then that instantly becomes a lever for the other side,' Davis warned. Barnier had already shown himself an assiduous reader of the British newspapers, quoting back stories about the prospect of queues at the border in his conversations with British officials. The Shard event resolved very little, but it allowed

Davis and Hammond to be pictured together. 'What mattered more was the photo,' a minister said. 'Because everyone was trying to do their Kremlinology and saying, "Davis is in one corner and Hammond is in the other." And they weren't.'

Davis's support emboldened Hammond to push things further. On 12 December, in front of the Treasury select committee, the chancellor announced that a transitional arrangement would be necessary after Brexit because there was not time to secure a full deal in the two-year period of negotiations. It was a view, he said, that was shared by 'businesses, among regulators, among thoughtful politicians, as well as a universal view among civil servants'. It was not, at that stage, a view shared by Boris Johnson, Liam Fox or Steve Baker's Eurosceptics. On 29 November the prime minister had hinted to the CBI's annual conference that she would consider a transitional period. 'People don't want a cliff-edge; they want to know with some certainty how things are going to go forward,' she said. But May's 'cliff-edge' comment had not been pre-planned. It came about, in part, because she had only done three minutes of prep for her appearance. There was nothing unplanned about Hammond's intervention. Encouraged by Ivan Rogers, he was pushing for a transitional period to be agreed straight away. 'Phil would have liked to have a two- or three-year transition period, agreed at the beginning of the negotiation,' a fellow cabinet minister said.

Davis was prepared to countenance a transitional deal, but only if there was a fixed end point to transition to – and if it was not called a transition period. He believed the term encouraged Barnier to get the wrong end of the stick. 'His idea of a transition arrangement, is that you spend two years doing a divorce and then spend the next ten years doing the transition,' Davis warned his colleagues. 'In which time we're still under the ECJ, we're still paying out bills and all the rest of it.' Davis regarded Hammond's plan as dangerously open-ended and wanted the destination to be clear. 'How do you build a bridge when you don't know where the shore is?' he asked aides. Davis did not want to spend his political capital seeking a transition deal – but crucially he did not oppose it in principle. Within DExEU, George Bridges – the minister in the Lords – had joined Hammond in arguing for a transition period.

The chancellor was still on his own in arguing for Britain to stay in the customs union. In early January, when they returned from the Christmas break, Hammond met Boris Johnson for more than an hour.

The chancellor made one last bid to persuade the foreign secretary. 'Can we at least agree something on the customs union even if we can't have the single market?' Johnson replied, 'We can't do it.' Afterwards Johnson told Foreign Office officials, 'It was him saying to me that he is losing the battle with the prime minister. He's got to do it. If you're out, you're out.'

When Boris Johnson heard that May was planning to make the speech in January he decided he 'had to be useful'. He spent the Christmas break writing a 3,000-word paper on what he thought she should say. Johnson's allies call it a 'draft', though they concede that not many of his actual words (or jokes) found their way into the final speech. May's aides referred to it as 'a letter'. Johnson advised May to make a clear statement that Britain was going to leave the customs union and would be taking back control of its laws. He also urged her to explain to the rest of the EU that Brexit was about Britain making a positive decision for itself, not against them – the mantra of 'leaving the EU but not leaving Europe'.

Johnson was pushing at an open door when he asked the PM to adopt the positive vision of the UK unleashed as 'Global Britain', a brand he had developed as London mayor and made the centrepiece of a speech to Foreign Office staff in July. His allies briefed journalists that Boris was feeding into the speechwriting process. One even claimed, 'Her speech was 70 per cent his content – leaving the single market, leaving the customs union, agitating for free trade, not pulling up the drawbridge, an open and dynamic economy that people come to visit, global Britain – you could hear so much of him in it.' May's speechwriting team certainly read Johnson's thoughts, but most of them already appeared in the speech. 'There was basically no involvement in the speech,' a source close to May said. Her team did not mind Johnson's grandstanding because they were keen for senior ministers to feel they had 'buy in' to the process, and Boris's input showed that he was on the same page as the prime minister.

If Johnson can be said to have contributed anything it was an attitude of positivity, which Chris Wilkins was also keen to incorporate following criticism of the 'citizens of nowhere' line in the conference speech. He had worked for Nicky Morgan, one of the most outspoken Remainers, and wanted to bridge the gap between his old boss and his new one. 'Chris was concerned that the speech should be very optimistic and outward looking because we needed to bring in the 48 per cent and particularly the kind of people who might have been irritated by the citizens of nowhere thing,' a Number 10 official said. 'That was what he brought to it.' May's trip to the Gulf Cooperation Council in Bahrain in December, and the positive welcome she had received there about trading with the UK, helped crystallise the prime minister's view that she needed to use her big Brexit speech not just to outline the basics of her negotiating position but also to speak much more about the future and delineate Britain's global position.

Jeremy Heywood also pressed for an upbeat tone that would build bridges with those who had voted Remain. The cabinet secretary, who acted as the 'voice of the business community' in Downing Street discussions, told May she should offer an olive branch on immigration. 'Jeremy Heywood wanted a really firm commitment to continuing to attract the brightest and the best,' a senior aide said. 'He really, really was concerned that we maintain immigration for the best talent.' The phrase 'brightest and the best' made it into the final draft.

The most important political argument May planned to make – since it was not widely expected – concerned what would happen if there was no deal. In order to impress on the EU that May was prepared to cut and run if she did not get what she wanted, Nick Timothy came up with the line 'no deal is better than a bad deal'. Internally, the chief of staff had argued the point vigorously. 'There are some people on the European side who say the only acceptable deal is one which punishes Britain – that's not a good deal,' he said. 'There are some on our side who are so eager to do a deal that they'll want to sign up to all the bad bits of EU membership and none of the good bits. That's not a good deal either.'

In the aftermath of the speech, this approach was characterised as evidence of the prime minister's cavalier approach to Brexit and her total capitulation to the brinkmanship of the hardline Eurosceptics. But in private May was far from sanguine about the prospect of resorting to WTO rules, judging that scenario 'very sub-optimal'. Her view had formed in early September, when Oliver Robbins drafted a paper on the implications of moving to WTO rules for different sectors of the economy. May's response was to say, 'I really don't like the look of that and I don't want to go for WTO. I don't want to go there, I do want a preferential agreement.' The prime minister was convinced enough that, unusually, she did not ask for a more detailed paper to be prepared. A source familiar with the discussions said, 'She was very clear she wanted some sort of preferential economic and trade agreement and the WTO was unpalatable.'

David Davis believed Britain would survive a no-deal scenario 'perfectly well' but he also approved of May deploying the gambit, telling colleagues it was a strategy of 'mutually assured scaring the shit out of each other'. To Remainers who told him it was irresponsible to flirt with a no-deal Brexit, Davis said, 'The more people squawk about a WTO option being so terrible, the more likely it is to happen because it will persuade either side we don't mean it. And we bloody well do.' Another cabinet minister said, 'David Cameron's mistake when he was negotiating before the referendum was that the Europeans never thought we would walk away. This time we will.'

It was the chancellor, of all people, who raised the 'no deal' issue to Defcon One. On 15 January, the German newspaper *Welt am Sonntag* ran an interview with Hammond in which he suggested Britain could transform its economic model into that of a corporate tax haven if the EU failed to do a deal on market access. 'If we are forced to be something different, then we will have to become something different,' he said. Asked to clarify, he added, 'We could be forced to change our economic model to regain competitiveness. You can be sure we will do whatever we have to do. The British people are not going to lie down and say, "Too bad, we've been wounded". We will change our model and we will come back, and we will be competitively engaged.' Jeremy Corbyn dismissed this vision of the UK as Singapore-on-Sea as a 'bargain basement tax haven'. But Hammond had been concerned that May's speech would cause the pound to fall and he wanted them to see the government had a plan. His colleagues were grateful. Davis felt the threat would stop the Commission thinking it could push Britain around as it had Greece during the eurozone crisis. A fellow cabinet minister said, 'That was Phil being a team player even though he was not entirely comfortable with the strategy.' Hammond would back away from his comments when he talked to *Le Monde* in July but his intervention in January helped ensure that when May spoke, the pound actually rose.

Privately, Hammond was less supportive of his prime minister. That week the *Economist* had run a cover story on May under the headline 'Theresa Maybe'. 'After six months, what the new prime minister stands for is still unclear – perhaps even to her,' it said. The article was curiously timed since May was finally making her strategy public, but Hammond let it be known to a journalist at the magazine that he was amused by the article.

The final details of the speech were thrashed out during a breakfast meeting in Hammond's office in Number 11 Downing Street the same weekend. The dysfunctionality of the cabinet committee system had driven decision makers into ever smaller groups. 'It leaked like a sieve,' a cabinet minister said. 'We started having bilaterals, trilaterals and quadrilaterals with Theresa.' For the crunch meeting Boris Johnson was not invited. 'The civil service worked out that the only way that they could get any decisions on anything was with DD, Hammond and May in the room,' a DExEU official recalled.

Over two hours, the prime minister, the chancellor and the Brexit secretary – and their closest aides – went over each of the twelve pillars of the speech to 'stress test' them. One of those present said, 'It was one of the best meetings a group of politicians making big decisions have had in the time I've been there. They chewed the fat on everything and then came to the decision.'

The purpose of the meeting was to win Hammond's support for May's proposals. Davis was invited because it was felt he could help the chancellor over the line. 'DD can talk to him probably in ways that others can't,' a cabinet source said. The meeting was the moment Hammond finally accepted the inevitable, that Britain was leaving the customs union. The chancellor remained 'appalled' by the idea, but when the time came to fall into line he did so with a whimper rather than a bang. A source present said, 'I went in expecting there to be quite a big debate. In truth it was quite mild. It was not quite a shrug of the shoulders but he said, "Yes, okay." And that was that.'

A cabinet minister said, 'Phil knew this was the speech that mattered. The party conference speech was basically telling Europe "Brexit is actually going to happen." Up until that point, European governments kept on asking us, "How are you going to get out of this?" But the substantive policy was in the Lancaster House speech. Phil realised he had to make the best of a bad job, from his point of view.' A close ally of Hammond added, 'He saw the value in Theresa clarifying the situation. She basically bought off the Brexiteers wholesale. Philip still saw the problems but he realised that politically it was the only way to stop their being a leakage to Ukip.'

Sitting at the back of the room, Fiona Hill breathed a sigh of relief. 'That meeting was one of the single most important meetings because it meant Theresa could stand up and say that she had DD and Philip not just behind her but utterly intellectually in the same place as her,' a source close to May said. A cabinet minister agreed: 'In any economic project – and for God's sake this is the biggest economic project – you absolutely have to take a chancellor with you.' Hammond did not have much choice, as a cabinet source observed. 'The ship was already gone. Phil's only option was to jump onto the back of the lifeboat or into the sea. He jumped into the lifeboat.'

Once again, the most important decisions on Brexit in May's first year in power had been taken by a group of people who could have fitted into a telephone box. The fear of leaks was such that most cabinet ministers were only shown the text of the speech minutes before May delivered it.

When the Treasury got their hard copy of the final draft the day before, Hammond and his officials made one final effort to change the approach to the customs union. May's aides had worded that section carefully to maintain a degree of ambiguity. 'Full Customs Union membership prevents us from negotiating our own comprehensive trade deals,' it said, but 'I do want us to have a customs agreement with the EU. Whether that means we must reach a completely new customs agreement, become an associate member of the Customs Union in some way, or remain a signatory to some elements of it, I hold no preconceived position. I have an open mind on how we do it. It is not the means that matter, but the ends.' A Downing Street official said, 'That language was already a concession to the Treasury. When the chancellor's comments came back on the draft they were incredibly limited but he did want the language on the customs union watered down more and we pushed back on it. We retained the original language.' A special adviser added, 'Hammond mishandled it because she had made up her mind.'

In May's forty-two-minute speech the headlines came thick and fast. 'I want to be clear that what I am proposing cannot mean membership of the single market,' the prime minister said, since that would mean accepting the EU's four freedoms – free movement of goods, services, capital and people – and 'complying with the EU's rules and regulations that regulate those freedoms'. That, May argued, would mean 'not leaving the EU at all'. Instead of membership of the single market, Britain would seek 'the greatest possible access to it through a new, comprehensive, bold and ambitious free trade agreement'.

The plan Nick Timothy had devised in September was made flesh. His and May's greatest achievement was to make seem inevitable what after the referendum had only been logical. Having moved fast to put Britain on this path they had set a course from which the government could not be diverted. By waiting four months to make it explicit, much of the heat that might have led to the plan being contested had dissipated.

May repeated her priority to 'get control over the number of people coming to Britain from the EU' and ducked the chance to make a unilateral offer to EU citizens living in the UK. On the money, she said 'vast contributions' to the EU budget 'will end', but left open the prospect that Britain might pay to remain in 'specific European programmes'. Significantly, she also announced that she wanted a phased 'implementation period' because it was 'in no one's interests to have a cliff-edge', but made clear this would not mean the 'permanent political purgatory' of an indefinite interim deal. Hammond had his transition period, though under another name. May struck a far warmer tone than at the party conference, telling her fellow EU leaders, 'It remains overwhelmingly and compellingly in Britain's national interest that the EU should succeed.'

The speech was generally well received at home and abroad. Whatever their differences, it was a text the whole cabinet felt able to support. A source close to May said, 'Some of the divides between Leave and Remain camps were healing because ministers from both sides of the campaign were very happy with that speech and thought it was the right concept.'

Boris Johnson could be seen nodding vigorously while May spoke. At the cabinet that followed he declared it 'a great day'. Even Hammond seemed happy, pronouncing it 'a seminal moment' and 'an excellent speech'. 'He was so sycophantic,' a witness recalled. 'There were many rolled eyes.' While Remainers like Nicky Morgan were unhappy that May had confirmed hard Brexit, there was relief that the position was now clear. The Eurosceptics were delighted. Nick Timothy received supportive messages from Iain Duncan Smith and John Redwood. Steve Baker wrote in his diary, 'Amazing speech, joy abounds.' A Downing Street source recalled, 'We were incredibly pleased with how well it landed. For a short time, it looked like we had managed to unite all sides of the Conservative Party around this issue.'

There was just one dark cloud on the horizon in Number 10. Nick Timothy and Fiona Hill had asked Katie Perrior to organise a series of op-ed articles in European newspapers. A Downing Street aide said, 'The op-eds didn't happen. It was the press office's job to make it happen. They would say that Katie had not delivered on that.' The tensions between Hill and Perrior, which had exploded over 'Trousergate', would not be long in coming to the boil.

Nonetheless the reaction from the rest of the EU was calm. The other countries recognised that May had respected the integrity of the single market by acknowledging that the four freedoms were not something from which Britain could pick and choose. A cabinet minister said, 'A lot of them thought we wanted to stay in the single market but leave the EU. For a lot of them that redressed their fear that we wanted to be there having it all.' Another minister, who walked out of Lancaster House with several EU ambassadors, said, 'They liked the clarity. They didn't like what she was saying, they liked the fact that it has set the course and they knew what Britain wanted. Lancaster House was her finest hour.'

The experience of dealing with a group of outside egos arguing over populist policies stood May in good stead for her next assignment. On 27 January, ten days after the Lancaster House speech, she was due in Washington, the first foreign leader to visit the forty-fifth president of the United States, Donald J. Trump.

8

THE WHITE HOUSE

One minute before midnight a huge cheer rang out from the packed auditorium of the US embassy in London's Grosvenor Square. The giant screen flashed with the news that the Associated Press were calling the state of Vermont for Hillary Clinton, with its three electoral votes. The cream of political London and liberal high society let out a sigh of relief. It was presidential election night and the Democrat frontrunner finally had a state on the board. London was five hours ahead of the US and drink had been taken. In the foyer outside and in a large party area downstairs, thousands of well-dressed Londoners congratulated themselves on having the best invite in town, rubbing shoulders with cabinet ministers and veterans of past Washington administrations. Even the lead singer of the rock band Muse was there.

To those following things more closely on the big screen, the Vermont cheer would be as significant as the 'Sunderland roar' on Brexit night, the first symbol of a world turned upside down. Talking together against the far wall of the auditorium, several journalists, a minister of the crown and a special adviser smiled at the naïvety of the other guests. 'Forget Vermont,' said one. 'Look at Florida.' In the Sunshine State Clinton was closing on Trump, but not fast enough. Elsewhere Trump was heading for victory in the rust-belt states of Michigan and Wisconsin, the latter of which Clinton had never even bothered to visit. As it became clear that Trump was on course for the most unlikely victory in presidential history, the crowd thinned out, leaving just the hardcore hacks and US political nerds while the man from Muse posed for selfies. The Vermont roar was symbolic of a liberal establishment that had again got it wrong.

As dawn broke over London, Sir Kim Darroch, the UK's ambassador to the United States, sat down to write a memo, explaining what had happened and what Britain should now do to cash in. He wrote, 'At 6 p.m. this evening, Donald Trump was perhaps the only person in America who still believed he had a chance … The Trump team, some of whom we were with early in the evening, were sure they had lost; the Clinton campaign was celebrating. By 7 p.m., Fox News was privately telling the campaign that they were going to call the race for Clinton before 10 p.m. … then the results started to come in.' He said the 'electoral earthquake' which had propelled Trump to power had led to 'fear and loathing' in Washington. However, he suggested, Trump was 'an outsider and unknown quantity', who 'will surely evolve and, particularly, be open to outside influence if pitched right. Having, we believe, built better relationships with his team than have the rest of the Washington diplomatic corps, we should be well placed to do this.'[1]

Darroch – a bright, smooth operator who had held the most prestigious diplomatic posts in Brussels, Downing Street and the Foreign Office under four prime ministers – had engaged with Trump surrogates like Senator Jeff Sessions over a period of months, as had Foreign Office minister Alan Duncan. But Darroch had a problem. Bright and smooth did not get you very far with Donald Trump himself. The ambassador was already behind a self-appointed British envoy to the court of The Donald: Nigel Farage.

Theresa May was on her way home from a trade trip to India as America was voting. Tom Swarbrick, the prime minister's head of broadcast, attended the embassy party. He left at 4 a.m. and went straight to Downing Street. Around 7 a.m., with Hillary Clinton conceding defeat, Swarbrick was slumped dishevelled in his chair when there was a knock on the door. 'Morning, Tom,' said a very breezy voice. Swarbrick leapt to his feet and said, 'Good morning, Prime Minister.' May looked perfectly refreshed. 'So, what's your plan?' Katie Perrior was in her office curling her hair with hot irons a little later when the prime minister walked in – another rare foray into the world of the press office – to agree the quote they would issue to reporters. 'If my friends from Erith School could have seen me, they would have choked on their toast,' she told a friend later.

May recorded a clip for the broadcasters congratulating Trump on his victory, in which she said, 'We have a longstanding and enduring special relationship which is built on our shared values, of freedom, of democracy and enterprise. I look forward to working with president-elect Trump to ensure we can maintain the security and prosperity of our two nations in the future.' In the months ahead that relationship was to experience unusual strains, and efforts to get it to work for Brexit Britain would stall.

After May had said her piece, members of the press office – Perrior, Swarbrick, Lizzie Loudon and Tim Smith – reflected on Trump's populist campaign, coming hot on the heels of Brexit, and what it meant for British politics. A source observed, 'We collectively said to each other, "This is why you cannot underestimate Corbyn. If he campaigns on the basis of emotion, he can win. The government does facts, but we don't live in facts any more. We have to explain facts through emotional stories. You have to tell stories."' It was an analysis they would have done well to remember when May called her own election.

Trump's victory sent shockwaves through Whitehall and prompted hasty assessments of the damage he might do. Concern focused on his declaration that NATO was 'obsolete'. Trump's aide Steve Bannon, the alt-right theorist who ran Breitbart News before revitalising Trump's campaign, was a vociferous opponent of the EU and had professed the hope that it would break up. EU foreign ministers called an immediate 'panic meeting' as if a war had broken out rather than democratic elections in a close ally. It was boycotted by Boris Johnson, who told his counterparts, 'I think it's time we snapped out of the collective whinge-o-rama,' turning an attempt to curry favour with the new administration into an insult to Britain's negotiating partners.

In what seemed to be a snub to the UK – but was probably an early sign of chaos over protocol in the Trump White House – May was only the tenth foreign leader to be called by Trump. The Australian premier Malcolm Turnbull jumped the queue by getting the new president's mobile number from Greg Norman, the golfer. In recompense, Boris Johnson was the first foreign politician on vice president Mike Pence's call list. The media wondered if Britain's lowly place in the queue was anything to do with a tweet by Fiona Hill saying 'Trump is a chump', and one by Nick Timothy in May, which read, 'As a Tory I don't want any "reaching out" to Trump.' Yet May's team now began a systematic wooing operation to get the prime minister to the front of the queue for a White House visit.

On Saturday 12 November, Darroch was just digesting the fact that his election night memo had been leaked to the *Sunday Times* when things got worse. On Twitter there appeared pictures of Farage posing with Trump in front of the golden doors of his apartment at the top of Trump Tower in New York. The president was in the middle of picking his senior staff but still had time to sit down for nearly an hour with Farage, the businessman Arron Banks, who had funded the Leave cause to the tune of £6 million, and Gerry Gunster, the US political consultant who had brought some order to their anarchic campaign. They were accompanied by Banks' sidekick and spokesman Andy Wigmore, a part-time diplomat, and Raheem Kassam, Farage's former spokesman, who worked for the British end of Bannon's Breitbart operation.

Farage had attended a rally to support Trump in the final weeks of the campaign and was on Fox News most nights predicting that he would win. Now the favour was returned. Trump believed he would not have won without the example of Brexit and saw Farage as the *sine qua non* of the Leave campaign. The president-elect's opening question was, 'Nigel, do you think Brexit was bigger or was my election bigger?' Farage deferred to Trump, calling Trump's win 'Brexit plus, plus plus'. Banks explained, 'What Trump clearly recognises is that it's all part of the same anti-establishment movement that's been spreading like wildfire. In his own mind, he sees the connection between the two. He sees Nigel as the architect of Brexit.' The president made warm noises about a free trade deal with Britain, and Farage also got Trump to agree to the return to the Oval Office of the bust of Winston Churchill which had been removed by Barack Obama.

The meeting was embarrassing for the government, more so when Farage began offering himself as an informal envoy to the White House, an idea closed down fast. A Downing Street aide said, 'I think the UK brings enough to the special relationship for it to be special without Nigel Farage.' By the time Farage met Trump, the government had already dangled the prospect of a state visit to Britain, using the queen as their 'secret weapon' to woo the president. Trump gushed to Farage and Banks, 'My late mother, Mary, loved the Queen. I'm going to meet her, too. I can't wait to come over to England. My mum would be chuffed to bits when I meet the Queen.'

That did not stop Trump making mischief. On 21 November, he tweeted, 'Many people would like to see @Nigel_Farage represent Great Britain as their Ambassador to the United States. He would do a great job!' Downing Street said there was 'no vacancy', but for Darroch it was another setback. It was ten more days before May received a second call from Trump to help cement their relationship.

Boris Johnson also had some ground to make up. In 2015, after Trump had suggested there were 'no go areas' of London where the British police feared to tread, Johnson publicly accused him of 'betraying a quite stupefying ignorance that makes him, frankly, unfit to hold the office of president of the United States'. In early October the foreign secretary had told a friend, 'This is an election that is going to expose America's primal psyche as never before. If it is Trump, it will be a victory of really base daytime TV Redneck America.'

Now the foreign secretary and his advisers had emerged as key contacts for Mike Pence and the ideological end of team Trump – Stephen Miller and chief strategist Steve Bannon – while Hill and Timothy dealt with Reince Priebus, the chief of staff, and Katie Perrior talked to Sean Spicer, her opposite number in the White House. Johnson's advisers were keen to go to the US to meet the people they had been speaking to on the phone, but it was decreed they could not travel before Hill and Timothy. The decision would lead to mounting frustration.

The chiefs finally flew to Washington in secret in mid-December to meet Priebus and around ten other key Trump World contacts at a series of hastily arranged meetings in hotels, restaurants and coffee shops. To the rage of one colleague, the chiefs – who were accompanied by Johnny Hall, a private secretary, and Richard 'Tricky' Jackson, May's head of operations – flew business class. 'That's one of those things nobody does,' the source said. 'It is taxpayers' money. They should have just phoned ahead and got an upgrade.' The chiefs did not apologise for their comments on Twitter, which were not raised by the Americans either. Hill and Timothy met business associates of Trump and reported back to May, 'He's not a politician and he doesn't behave like a politician and if you want to understand the administration and influence it then the best thing you can do is a build a relationship with him on those terms.' The reward came on 8 January when Trump announced – via Twitter, of course – 'I look very much forward to meeting Prime Minister Theresa May in Washington in the Spring. Britain, a longtime U.S. ally, is very special!'

* * *

The same day Trump announced May's visit, the prime minister was due to do her first broadcast interview of the year, the launch show for Sky News's new Sunday political presenter Sophy Ridge. With Trump at the top of the news, Katie Perrior expected the young host would put her boss on the spot about a tape that had emerged during the presidential election campaign in which Trump boasted about groping women, saying he could 'grab them by the pussy' because of his celebrity status.

On the way to the studio in her armoured Jaguar, Perrior embarked on one of the most awkward conversations that can ever have been had with a British prime minister. To the snorts of the police protection officer, Perrior told May she would probably be asked what she thought of Trump's 'pussy' comments, and warned her the cameras would zoom in tight on her face, expecting her jaw to fall into the grimace that seized her at moments of unease. 'I don't do that,' May said, denying the evidence of a thousand press photographs. 'You do,' said Perrior. 'Keep completely and utterly still – poker face.'[2]

When Ridge asked May how the comments made her feel as a woman, the prime minister kept her composure and replied, 'I think that's unacceptable.'

The chiefs' trip had released Boris Johnson to make his own connections with team Trump. That night, 8 January, the foreign secretary was in New York for the first face-to-face meetings at Trump Tower. 'The Number 10 view was, "Boris, you speak to Bannon",' a Foreign Office source said. 'They're both agitators and disruptors. Bannon was blowing up the realm. Boris is the same.' In the boardroom on the twentieth floor of Trump's empire, Johnson and his team met Bannon and Jared Kushner, husband of the president-elect's daughter Ivanka and a key power broker. Bannon pointed to the ceiling and said, 'He's only three floors up,' as if Trump were a godlike presence gazing down on proceedings.

The exchanges were frank. One of those present said, 'It wasn't jovial. It was a very serious meeting.' Conversation roamed from the Middle East peace process to NATO, the Syrian civil war and Russia. 'Kushner went in quite hard, they weren't able to push him around. Boris pushed back.' The main issue for the British was to ascertain how Trump would approach global affairs and whether he was planning to tear up the international order to affect a new partnership with Vladimir Putin's Russia.

There were jaw-on-the-floor moments. When one of the Brits asked, 'What do you give Russia to get them to the table?' the reply astonished

Johnson. 'Steve Bannon being mischievous said if they want to move into some Baltic state, "We're relaxed,"' a source present said. To suggest that Russia be given *carte blanche* to march into a NATO state that both countries were sworn to defend on the pretext of protecting the Russian population was astonishing. Johnson leapt in, 'What? Like the Sudeten Germans?' comparing such a move to Hitler's march into Czechoslovakia in 1938. 'They recoiled,' the source said. 'Boris's grasp of history outflanked them on a bunch of things. I don't think they were serious.'

After three hours the meeting broke up. Thereafter Johnson and Bannon spoke most weeks. Kushner also kept in touch with Johnson and spoke to his aide Liam Parker about the Middle East peace process. Parker and Stephen Miller, Trump's speechwriter and senior policy adviser, also conversed weekly.

The choreography continued a week later when Trump used an interview with Michael Gove, in his new guise as a *Times* journalist, to praise Britain as 'smart' for backing Brexit, and called Barack Obama's statement during the EU referendum campaign that Britain was at the 'back of the queue' for a trade deal a 'bad statement'. He said, 'We're gonna work very hard to get it done quickly.'[3]

British officials were left open-mouthed and concerned by Trump's uncompromising inauguration speech, which appropriated the 'America First' slogan of isolationists before the Second World War, pledged to 'end the carnage' on America's streets and 'make America great again' – an oration even George W. Bush dismissed as 'some weird shit'. However, they were encouraged that Trump did not show his face at a party the night before thrown by the self-styled 'Bad boys of Brexit', Farage, Banks and co., who had taken over the top floor of the Hay Adams hotel.

Word spread that Trump was already calling the prime minister 'my Maggie' in an attempt to recreate the chemistry of Ronald Reagan and Margaret Thatcher. The president had also expressed his hopes for a 'Full Monty' state visit, with nine holes of golf at Balmoral, a personal tour of the Churchill War Rooms with Boris Johnson and dinner with the Duke and Duchess of Cambridge. British officials had put on the table the idea of a financial services passporting deal with the US as the precursor to a trade deal. There was, however, friction over the prospect of Trump seeing Prince Charles. The president's aides made clear that, as a climate change sceptic, he did not wish to be lectured by the heir to the throne about global warming.

Trump was also angry at the publication of a dossier by a former MI6 spy, Christopher Steele, which had been prepared for his political opponents, alleging that Russia held compromising material on him, including videos of him being urinated on by Muscovite prostitutes. Denouncing the story as 'fake news', Trump said, 'I'm also very much of a germaphobe, by the way, believe me.' The admission was about to impact on May's visit.

May saw the Trump visit as key to her Brexit strategy. She wanted a close relationship with the US and the prospect of a preferential trade deal. But she also sought to use the visit to ensure that Trump was engaged in Europe and NATO. May first used a speech to Republican congressmen in Philadelphia – the first by a British prime minister to a party retreat – to talk about American leadership and support for the post-war institutions. Calling NATO 'the cornerstone of the West's defence', she admitted that 'some of these organisations are in need of reform' but said Britain and America should 'recommit ourselves to the responsibility of leadership in the modern world'. Tackling Bannon's views head on, May added, 'It remains overwhelmingly in our interests – and in those of the wider world – that the EU should succeed.'

Diplomatic channels quickly detected approval from the EU27. One of May's aides said, 'The Europeans were anxious about the fact we were invited so early. Trump saying he wanted to break up NATO made them feel defensive and threatened. They were relieved we were defending European values.' Behind the scenes in Philadelphia, May had conversations with Paul Ryan, the speaker of the House of Representatives, and Mitch McConnell, the Senate majority leader, about how to deal with and rein in Trump. 'They were saying, "We can restrain this crazy man. We're all scared but if we work together in this network we can achieve things."'

On 27 January, a week to the day after Trump's inauguration, Theresa May became the first foreign leader to stride into the White House under its new ownership. She did so accompanied by a trio of female aides – Fiona Hill, Katie Perrior and Lizzie Loudon. Tom Swarbrick, head of broadcast, and Chris Brannigan, head of government relations, who had both hoped to attend, were told they were staying at home. This was Hill's answer to the Pussygate controversy. 'It was Fi's decision that we were going to have this all-female presentation, because that was a way to challenge Donald Trump.'

The two delegations held a closed meeting with a small number of aides, a joint press conference in the East Room of the White House and then a working lunch with a larger cast. In the closed session, Trump repeated his view that Brexit was 'really good for the UK' and added, 'I'm really struck by the number of meetings I've had in which people say they feel they've got the UK back again. That really pleases me'. They agreed that Jeremy Heywood would be the point man on trade discussions with Gary Cohn, the director of Trump's economic council. May happily unveiled the Churchill bust, which had been returned to a side table in the Oval Office.

May had already spoken to Trump about the importance of NATO in both her prior telephone conversations. Now she raised it again, addressing him as 'Mr President' but giving him 'a very hard time' until Trump relented. He said, 'I don't want to be a problem for NATO, I'm 100 per cent for NATO, you can say that'. In the press conference May did just that, using her opening statement to force Trump into repeating his statement publicly. She said, 'We've reaffirmed our unshakeable commitment to this alliance. Mr President, I think you said, you confirmed that you're 100 per cent behind NATO'. As May fixed him with a steely glare, Trump nodded and mouthed, 'True'.

The mood music was good as Trump showed his serious side in the closed meeting. A Downing Street source said, 'He was on top of any number of quite complex briefs and he'd only been president for a week. That impressed Theresa because she's a details girl'. Over lunch Trump also turned on the charm, addressing May as 'Theresa'. 'When I come to England I want to see you first on arrival,' he told her. 'I always keep menu cards for significant moments'. He promptly handed his to a staff member, saying: 'Keep that safe. I had lunch with the British prime minister'.

As they walked down the White House colonnade after the press conference, Trump took May's hand while the pair went down a ramp, providing all the world's press with the Kodak moment they wanted. Yet this was not quite the act of chivalry it appeared. The footage showed a man slightly unsteady on his feet. Word quickly spread through the White House press corps and May's aides that Trump had a phobia of stairs and slopes – a condition called bathmophobia. 'You see his hand go out almost instinctively for help,' said a British official. One American reporter pointed out sardonically, 'Trump tells people he hates stairs and ramps and hates germs, so when he gets to a staircase with a dirty hand-rail he doesn't know what to do.'

If that incident highlighted the oddities of dealing with Trump, May was quickly appraised about the controversies as well. In their meetings Trump had mentioned his plans to restrict arrivals to the US from six predominantly Muslim countries. May left Washington and was in the air to Ankara, where she was due to sign a defence deal with Turkish president Recep Tayyip Erdogan, when news broke that Trump had just signed an executive order imposing the ban, prompting the claim May had gone from visiting 'a crackpot to a despot'. Refugees in the air would arrive at US immigration to be told they were no longer allowed into the country. The move, a campaign pledge of Trump's, caused an outcry that left May looking flat-footed. At a joint press conference with Binali Yildirim, the Turkish prime minister, she refused three times to say what she thought about Trump's decision until she was heckled by reporters shouting, 'Answer the question.' Even then she managed only, 'The United States is responsible for the United States' policy on refugees.' Her desire to parade her new relationship with Trump, her own tough line on immigration and her disdain for danc-ing to the tune of twenty-four-hour news combined to create a public relations disaster.

It was left to Boris Johnson to sort out the mess and ensure British citizens were exempted from the ban. Downing Street arranged a confer-ence call between May, Johnson and Amber Rudd, the home secretary. 'Talk to your opposite numbers,' she said. 'We've got to try and fix this.' Nick Timothy liaised with the foreign secretary, who spoke to Rex Tillerson, Trump's secretary of state, and then the White House. A Downing Street aide said, 'Boris ended up on the phone to Steve Miller and hammered out an agreement. Boris said, "Can I get that in writing?" Miller sat at his computer, Kushner banged it over to us. We checked it with Number 10. Katie Perrior ran it past Sean Spicer, who took it to the president. You might say it's a bit strange that the British foreign secre-tary is on the phone to a White House staffer but this is an unusual administration.'

Unusual or not, the senior figures in the British government had now aligned themselves indelibly with the most controversial figure ever to occupy his office. It is hard to fault the desire to put Britain at the front of the queue to influence the new president and secure a post-Brexit trade deal, but in the coming months such eagerness began to look like an error.

The idea of a state visit by Trump attracted the threat of mass protests at home. On 6 February, the Speaker of the Commons, John Bercow, announced that he would be 'strongly opposed' to Trump giving an address in Parliament's Westminster Hall, an honour accorded to Barack Obama but one that had not been offered to Trump.

In March a fresh row erupted when Sean Spicer, the president's press secretary, repeated a claim made by an analyst on Fox News that GCHQ – the British intelligence listening station – had been used by the Obama administration to spy on Trump Tower. In a break from the tradition that the government does not comment on intelligence matters, GCHQ – with Boris Johnson's backing – issued a furious response calling the allegations 'nonsense – they are utterly ridiculous and should be ignored'. General H. R. McMaster, Trump's national security adviser, contacted his opposite number Mark Lyall Grant to apologise and Spicer conveyed his regrets to Kim Darroch.

The following week, Johnson visited the White House to meet Reince Priebus, Steve Bannon and Stephen Miller, and had McMaster over for dinner at Darroch's residence. It was a trip that coincided with the Westminster terror attack, in which an Islamist mowed down pedestri- ans on Westminster bridge before stabbing a policeman to death. Miller told Johnson, 'In twenty or thirty years' time everyone's going to look at Britain and think Brexit was the best thing you ever did.'

That spring, with the backlash against Trump's continually erratic behaviour gathering pace in Britain, the president and May held another conversation in which Trump indicated he did not wish the state visit to go ahead if it meant he would face mass protests in The Mall. 'I haven't had great coverage out there lately, Theresa,' he complained. May, perhaps with the sympathies of a fellow sufferer, replied, 'Well, you know what the British press are like.'

Apparently hoping the prime minister could arrange better coverage, Trump said, 'I still want to come, but I'm in no rush. So, if you can fix it for me, it would make things a lot easier. When I know I'm going to get a better reception, I'll come and not before.'[4]

To those who listened in, Trump's prickliness was not even the main feature of the call. More serious, to them, was the way he bamboozled

May, throwing her off her talking points to the degree that she was unable to make the policy interventions civil servants had planned for her. 'He's totally disarming,' a Downing Street aide said. 'Normally when she goes into a meeting and she has two delivery points, she will deliver them. She'll get a sheet saying, "You need to raise this issue. We want to move things in that direction. These are our two objectives for the call. You might also want to raise these points." With Trump he'll start with, "Theresa I love you, I've missed you." She can't speak to that. It's not the way you are supposed to speak to each other in these telephone calls. Her deliverable gets totally shot out of the water and she just can't grapple with it.' The aide said May's calls with Trump were 'the only example I saw of her in work not delivering when she set out to deliver … It shows you something about his power. He's a crazy person but there is a charisma and an effectiveness there. In speaking like that he prevents all sorts of conversations. He's completely in control. It's deeply worrying.'

By March, the prime minister had other problems. Having dealt with the international consequences of the world created by Brexit, May got back to work on the domestic issues. While she had been seeing Trump the Supreme Court had ruled on whether she could trigger Article 50 without parliamentary approval.

TRIGGERED

David Davis had thought they were going to lose from the start, but he still believed the government should fight the case. In mid-October 2016, two weeks before the High Court verdict against the government, the Brexit secretary sent the prime minister a letter outlining her options. He knew that Theresa May liked thinking over decisions, rather than having them sprung upon her. 'I think we're going to lose, whatever our lawyers say,' he wrote. The plaintiffs, led by Gina Miller, wanted the court to rule that only Parliament, not the government, had the right to trigger Article 50. Davis outlined three options if the government lost: appeal the case; give MPs a vote; or appeal the decision while offering some concessions, like a debate or a white paper outlining the government's Brexit plans.

Davis supported the third option. He believed it was desirable for the highest court in the land to rule on the constitutional principles involved to prevent further legal disputes that could disrupt Brexit later. 'I want an authoritative outcome that cannot be challenged,' he told colleagues. In an article for ConservativeHome, written in July before he got the job, Davis had recommended that the government publish a 'pre-negotiation white paper'. But that was a card best kept in May's back pocket until the Supreme Court had delivered its verdict.

Meanwhile, in preparation for the expected defeat, Davis took personal charge of drafting a bill, with just two clauses, to trigger Article 50. 'David had a "clean bill strategy",' a DExEU source said. 'He wanted it to be simple and do nothing else.' That was the best hope of getting it on the statute book unamended. May agreed with her minister's analysis and after the High Court verdict they engaged in two months of shadow boxing, knowing that they would have to make further concessions.

Davis told MPs it would be inconceivable to deny MPs a vote on the final Brexit deal since the European Parliament would get one, but he gave no ground on who had the right to trigger Article 50. May remained equivocal even about that, refusing to commit to a vote in Parliament on the final deal when she appeared in front of the Commons liaison committee five days before Christmas.

After their defeat in the High Court, some in Downing Street could not understand why they struggled on. 'I queried why we were continuing to fight the court case,' one senior aide said. 'It was clear we weren't going to win it. Basically, politics dictated that we should and so we saw it through.' May and her team concluded that the Eurosceptics would never forgive her if they were seen to give up.

The politics contributed to the government losing in court. Fear of the Eurosceptics prevented the attorney general, Jeremy Wright, and the government's chief counsel, James Eadie QC, from making an argument that would have boosted their chances of success. At issue was the nature and effect of the 1972 European Communities Act, the legislation that had taken Britain into the European Economic Community and formalised how EU law took effect in Britain. The government's argument was that the royal prerogative applied because Article 50 was an issue of 'treaty making and unmaking' and treaties were the sole preserve of the executive. The plaintiffs, represented by David Pannick, argued that it was the 1972 Act which gave effect to the treaty of accession and that another Act of Parliament would be required to reverse it – since the legislation conveyed rights on the British people that could not be removed at the stroke of a pen by the executive.

On 24 January, the president of the Supreme Court, Lord Neuberger of Abbotsbury, announced, 'By a majority of eight to three, the Supreme Court rules that the government cannot trigger Article 50 without an Act of Parliament authorising it to do so.' There were predictable fulminations from the Eurosceptics, largely calmed when Davis made a Commons statement announcing that he would publish a bill in the coming days, declaring that Britain was 'past the point of no return' on Brexit.

There would have been considerably more angst had they known the argument the law officers would have liked to make in court: that Article 50 was revocable. Pannick's case was that, once triggered, Article 50 was 'like firing a gun – the bullet will reach its target' and Britain would leave the EU. A minister said, 'We could have said to Pannick, "You're talking rubbish, it's not like firing a gun, because at any time the British government can stop this." Legally, that would have been a great argument and I think it would have really undermined Pannick's argument. But politically it would have been disastrous.' If Wright and Eadie had made that case, the Supreme Court would have ruled on whether or not the Brexit negotiations could be stopped and abandoned. 'The nightmare scenario would have been a delay while the European Court of Justice would have then had to decide,' the minister said. The reaction of Eurosceptics to the prospect of the Luxembourg court ruling on the rights and wrongs of Brexit can be imagined. Fiona Hill told friends the case was 'a pain in the head'.

May and Davis were now confronted with the challenge of passing a Brexit bill quickly enough to hit the prime minister's 31 March deadline to trigger Article 50. They did not doubt that the plaintiffs had brought the case to put a spanner in the works. 'Gina Miller really wanted to stop Brexit, it was nothing to do with giving Parliament its say,' a DExEU minister said. The Supreme Court loss bred a team spirit at the top of government. 'What brought the cabinet together was a sense of us having enemies everywhere,' another minister said. 'We were all in this together. If it went wrong, we would all go down.'

The day after the Supreme Court ruling, 25 January, Davis's original plan began to unfold as May sought to dissuade the Team 2019 rebels from amending or opposing the bill. In response to a question from Anna Soubry at Prime Minister's Questions, May announced that she would publish a white paper after all. The following day, continuing the choreography, Davis published the European Union (Notification of Withdrawal) Bill. It was just two clauses and fifty words long.

The following week, on 2 February, the government produced its long-awaited white paper. This did little more than turn May's Lancaster House speech into a formal document. One of the seminal rows of the autumn was proved pointless. 'We were always going to do it,' a source close to May said. 'We couldn't give a monkey's about the white paper.' The prime minister was amused to receive a call from Angela Merkel, who praised her political craft. 'Merkel congratulated Theresa for the white paper being identical to the speech,' a senior Downing Street official revealed.

There was a last-minute panic over the bill when officials pointed out that, under the EU treaties, leaving the European Union would also entail

Britain leaving Euratom, the atomic energy community which regulated nuclear security. Desperate to keep the wording of the bill to a minimum, DExEU and Downing Street felt bounced into a situation where they might have to add another clause, handing their opponents a greater chance of tabling successful amendments. Fiona Hill told friends it was one of the biggest 'Fuck! moments' of the whole process. 'Euratom was the most complicated decision we've had to take,' a source close to May added. 'It resulted in a late night meeting that went on for hours where there was a collective head banging. It was like one of those brain teasers, literally contorting the innermost parts of your brain matter.' In the end, senior figures in the nuclear industry were reassured that while Britain had to leave it would negotiate its way back into a parallel arrangement with Euratom. To avoid creating a rod for their own backs with Parliament, May's team decided to add that plan to the notes accompanying the bill. It was an elegant way of fulfilling her instructions. A cabinet minister said, 'One of the points that the PM makes constantly is, "Everyone is concerned about process, I am concerned about ends." Whether or not you are in the customs union or Euratom is less important than: have you got nuclear safety or near frictionless trade?'

The Tory rebels did not wish to be labelled as Brexit deniers, so they voted with the government on 1 February, at the second reading of the bill – the crunch moment at which legislation lives or dies. The narrow drawing of the bill put the Labour Party on the spot. Europe was seen by Jeremy Corbyn's senior aides as being 'in the "too difficult" box', one said. Now the leader of the opposition had to make a decision.

Ever since the High Court ruling in November, passions had run hot in the Labour Party. 'You had passionately pro-EU MPs,' a frontbencher said. 'You had those who always wanted to leave, you had a group in the middle who genuinely didn't want to leave but thought we had to accept the result and move forward. That became genuinely difficult to manage. It was a real conscience issue for people.' MPs were divided by their seats as well as their views. 'In one ear people were saying, "I represent a heavily Leave area, if you don't back Article 50 fully I'm a goner." And then lots of people saying, "I'm in a heavily Remain area and if you do back Article 50, I'm a goner."'

Some wanted Labour to abstain, but both Corbyn and Keir Starmer thought that would make the party look ridiculous. 'For the opposition to abstain on an issue as important as this would not be right,' a front-bencher said. 'The danger was we would be neither appealing to the 52 per cent nor the 48 per cent, Labour would have been the party of the 0 per cent.'

At a shadow cabinet meeting in late January, Corbyn argued that Labour had to vote for Article 50 and that he would impose a three-line whip compelling his party to do so. 'Jeremy argued for it as did the majority of people,' a Corbyn aide recalled. 'There were dissenting voices. Clive Lewis, Dawn Butler.' Those subject to the collective responsibility of the shadow cabinet were told they would have to resign if they disobeyed.

At the second reading, the bill passed by 498 votes to 114. Apart from Ken Clarke, every Conservative MP voted to trigger Article 50, but forty-seven Labour MPs defied their three-line whip. Dawn Butler, the shadow minister for diverse communities, and Rachael Maskell, the shadow environment secretary, both resigned their frontbench jobs. When the third reading of the bill was voted on, eight days later, the bill passed its Commons stages by 494 to 122. Fifty-two Labour MPs dissented, including Clive Lewis, the shadow business secretary, who also quit the shadow cabinet. Frontbenchers who were not part of the collective decision-making meeting were sent a letter of reprimand but allowed to keep their jobs.

Corbyn's three-line whip was presented as a principled respect for the referendum result, but there was another reason for it. 'If we didn't support Article 50, then the Tories would have called a general election there and then,' a source in the leader's office said. 'Labour would've been wiped out.' A shadow cabinet minister added, 'I think they were itching for us to vote against. That would have been the Brexit election.' When Theresa May came to call an election, she would find it far harder to convince the electorate that it was about Brexit.

The high drama on the Conservative benches came on 7 February, with a vote on amendment 110, tabled by the Labour MP Chris Leslie, which called for 'any new deal or treaty' with the EU to be put to a vote before both Houses of Parliament. Gavin Williamson and May's parliamentary aide, George Hollingbery, found themselves negotiating hard. Up to twenty Tory MPs were threatening to back the amendment. Alistair Burt, Dominic Grieve and Nicky Morgan – her Trousergate ban now rescinded – went in to Downing Street to see May and Nick

Timothy. A government lawyer was also waiting for them. After a discussion, May pushed a sheet of paper across the glass-topped table in her inner sanctum for the three former ministers to read. On it was a form of words. 'This is what David Jones will say in the House,' May explained.

Grieve, a former attorney general, had drawn up a proposal for a deal and fed it to May via Williamson. It had been changed, but the paper sitting in front of the rebels committed the government to a vote in Parliament. It said, 'We intend that the vote will cover not only the withdrawal arrangements but also the future relationship with the European Union. Furthermore, I can confirm that the Government will bring forward a motion on the final agreement, to be approved by both Houses of Parliament before it is concluded. We expect and intend that this will happen before the European Parliament debates and votes on the final agreement.' Morgan read the paragraph and said, 'The words are fine but they don't go far enough, they don't cover the no-deal scenario.'

There was a further discussion. May and her advisers argued that the word 'agreement' covered both scenarios, that Britain might agree not to agree with the EU. The prime minister was concerned that she should be able to use the threat of no deal as leverage in negotiations. Giving Parliament an explicit veto would remove that card from her hand. Morgan was not happy; she felt it left too much wiggle room. But Grieve and Burt were satisfied.

In the chamber, David Jones intervened on Keir Starmer to announce the decision and kept reading from his sheet each time he was probed further. In response to one question, Morgan felt he had rowed back slightly on what had been agreed. Downing Street spin doctors were also briefing that they had given no ground, when they obviously had, a modus operandi that was to come back to bite Theresa May during the general election. Morgan was seen in a heated exchange with Williamson at the back of the chamber. She tweeted, 'Govt did make a concession but for No 10 to then brief there was no change & Minister to undermine it makes no sense.'

In the end, amendment 110 was defeated with a government majority of thirty-three. Burt and Grieve opposed it, Morgan abstained and just seven Tories – including Anna Soubry and Bob Neill – defied their party whip. It was Neill's first ever vote against his own government. George Osborne, who the chiefs believed was fomenting rebellion by inviting colleagues into his office for private chats (claims he denied), was absent.

Davis got his bill through the Commons with no amendments, but the government still faced a rebellion in the House of Lords, where that old Europhile warrior Michael Heseltine, now eighty-three, had returned to the saddle for one last battle. In a week of drama, the Lords defeated the government on an amendment to guarantee the rights of EU citizens. Five days later, on 7 March, Heseltine led a rebellion of thirteen Conservative peers to pass a second amendment demanding a 'meaningful' parliamentary vote on the deal. During the debate – the best attended in the Lords since 1831 – the former deputy prime minister announced that he had been sacked 'from the five jobs with which I have been helping the government', including a post promoting regional growth. He insisted, 'It's the duty of Parliament to assert its sovereignty in determining the legacy we leave to new generations of young people.' One senior government source claimed that Heseltine 'cried' when he was dismissed. More surprising, perhaps, Heseltine said that when he left the government's employ he had never yet spoken to Theresa May.

After another week of to-ing and fro-ing, the Commons stripped out the amendments. The Lords backed down on 13 March and the bill received royal assent the following week. For Steve Baker it was a moment of great satisfaction. 'The thing for me that was joyful about it was that the Eurosceptic movement was actually united and had done something together,' he said. 'And it united with the government.' David Davis said, 'We are now on the threshold of the most important negotiation for our country in a generation.'

Having voted for Article 50 and backed Brexit, Keir Starmer drew a line in the sand and made clear that Labour would now fight the government over the sort of Brexit they were pursuing. On 27 March, he spelt out six tests that any deal must fulfil. Some, like a 'fair migration system', retaining a 'strong, collaborative relationship with the EU' and 'protecting national security', were uncontroversial. Two of them – 'delivering for all nations and regions of the UK' and 'protecting workers' rights and employment protections' – allowed Labour to make Brexit a domestic political issue, defining itself against a 'Tory Brexit'. Starmer's masterstroke was to demand that Britain keep 'the exact same benefits' she enjoyed within the single market and the customs union. Cleverly, the wording of this demand was taken from a comment made by David Davis months earlier. It was a stick with which Labour were to beat the Brexit secretary for months. 'It was a political device to hold them to account,' a senior Labour Party official said. 'It set the bar so high for the Tories that we could always disagree with them. Here's the bar, jump that high.' Starmer, a super-smooth operator fond of jargon, told colleagues it gave Labour 'grip' in the process. 'I think the phrase "grip" is ridiculous but Jeremy is and most people are more polite than I am,' one of Corbyn's aides said. The six tests were a success. When the general election was called, three weeks later, Starmer's plan meant enough things to enough people that it avoided a damaging split. However, another Labour bigwig was beginning to argue that Brexit could be stopped altogether.

Tony Blair's quest to transform himself from yesterday's man into tomorrow's political visionary – a role in which he had once excelled – took flight on 17 February. In a speech made under the banner of Open Europe, the former prime minister spoke with pseudo-religious intensity of his 'mission' to persuade Britons to 'rise up' and change their minds on Brexit, calling for 'a way out from the present rush over the cliff's edge'. Blair claimed people had voted in the referendum 'without knowledge of the true terms of Brexit' and argued that the consequences would be 'painful' and the benefits 'largely illusory'.

Blair suggested that a second referendum was on the cards if the public changed their views. 'If a significant part of that 52 per cent show real change of mind, however you measure it, we should have the opportunity to reconsider this decision,' he said. 'This issue is the single most important decision this country has taken since the Second World War and debate can't now be shut down about it.' Privately, he told friends opposition to Brexit would need to be running at 60 per cent for there to be any chance of stopping it.

The Brexiteers dismissed Blair as an out-of-touch elitist. Reworking Blair's riff, Boris Johnson said, 'I urge the British people to rise up and turn off the TV next time Blair comes on with his condescending campaign.' Nigel Farage compared him to a 'former heavyweight champion coming out of retirement' who would 'end up on the canvas'. Yet no one else trying to make the revanchist argument on Brexit succeeded in getting anything like the same coverage.

Blair's intervention gave new energy to the monthly meetings in his office and gave rise to fresh speculation that he might be about to set up a new political party. Between February and June 2017, senior Labour moderates – both past and serving – would have conversations about how to proceed. Blair told the author that his goal was to stake out a new policy agenda for the political centre, which he felt both main parties had vacated. 'What I'm doing is putting together a team of people who will try and articulate what a radical centre policy agenda looks like, because I think one of the problems is that both Labour and the Tories are really offering us two competing visions of the sixties.'

Behind the scenes he was a key player in conversations between moderates. A former cabinet minister said, 'They've not decided whether to recapture the leadership of the Labour Party or create some new movement. Tony's up for both. He's very involved, talking to Labour MPs, talking to union leaders' about turning around Labour. 'That's the focus of their efforts. But they accept it may not work and then they'll have to create a new movement.'

Joe Haines, Harold Wilson's old spin doctor, suggested that moderates in the Parliamentary Labour Party, at least two-thirds of the PLP, should make a universal declaration of independence and sit as a new grouping, electing their own leader to supplant Corbyn as leader of the opposition. There was talk of Dan Jarvis, a former major in the Parachute Regiment who was MP for Barnsley Central, emerging as the front man. Blair, friends said, tried 'frequently' to persuade David Miliband, a former foreign secretary, to return from New York, where he was running the charity International Rescue Committee. Miliband had warned in September 2016 that Labour was 'unelectable' and had not been further from power since the 1930s, but he was in a good job, with his sons settled in schools, and did not want to take a gamble that could end in humiliation. 'In the end David will want to come back to the UK,' a close friend said. 'But he remains very unsure as to whether or not he really wants to devote his life to this battle.'

Since the previous autumn there had been overtures from the Liberal Democrats. At the party's conference in September 2016, the leader Tim Farron praised Blair for introducing the minimum wage and investing in public services. Referencing the Iraq War, which the Lib Dems had opposed, he quipped, 'I see Tony Blair the way I see the Stone Roses, I preferred the early work.' Farron commissioned polling research which showed that his party's brand was badly damaged with voters, and allies made clear he would have been prepared to countenance a name change.

Nick Clegg, who said he agreed with 'every word' of Blair's speech, went further down this path than Farron. He and Blair were in regular contact. 'They met at Open Reason, which is Nick's organisation in central London,' a source said. 'They spoke a lot more on the phone. At one point they were meeting weekly.' Ostensibly these talks were about getting Blair to persuade Labour pro-Europeans to work with the Lib Dems. Two sources, a friend of Clegg and a senior Lib Dem, both claimed that Clegg told Blair the quickest way to set up a new centre party would be to flood the Lib Dems with membership applications by Labour moderates and take over the party. 'There are more of you than there are of us,' he said, according to one account. 'There was a little bit of a worry that it was a reverse takeover of the Lib Dems,' a source close to Farron confided.

Open Britain was a useful forum, because it also got Tory Remainers in the room as well. In an interview with the *New Statesman* which hit the streets on 31 March, Anna Soubry stunned her Tory colleagues by declaring that she would consider joining a new party. 'If it could somehow be the voice of a moderate, sensible, forward-thinking, visionary middle way, with open minds – actually things which I've believed in all my life – better get on with it.'

The ruminating about a new party gathered urgency after May called the general election and gained a patron saint on 7 May when the centrist Emmanuel Macron, who had set up a new movement, won a remarkable victory in the French presidential election. To Blair, this was proof that it was possible in a time of populist politics to win from the centre. To Peter Mandelson, the 'simple truth of Macron's victory is that he won by leaving his party, not despite doing so'.[1] Encouraged by Mandelson and others, leading donors who had ceased to give money to Labour since Blair's departure indicated that they would be prepared to fund a new movement or party. A close associate of Blair said, 'People will look at Labour's results and say, "Is this horse a dead horse or can it still be revived?" Some people have already come to the conclusion that it can't and therefore something else is going to have to be born out of all of this. If something did happen the money would be there. The unthinkable is being thought.'

Gina Miller put her name to a tactical voting campaign run by Best for Britain – whose chief executive Eloise Todd was a regular at Blair's monthly gatherings – to give funds, polling and campaigning help to anti-Brexit candidates. In June she was to claim in an interview that a new party would have been launched within days of the election if

Labour had done worse. One source who was in close contact with Miller said, 'I was pretty sure they were going to go the week after the election.' But others who worked with Miller say that is not correct. A friend of Blair said his priority was to help the moderates regain control of Labour, a view echoed by a senior Labour Party official. Friends of Blair and Mandelson said David Sainsbury, the peer who had funded the pressure group Progress, was prepared to fund 'a Tony-and-Peter-backed pressure group that would bring together all the moderate groups. That would've been the vehicle to be a new party, should it be necessary. If there was a leadership election after the general election and Corbyn won, there would have to be a new party. If he lost, it would just have been a moderate momentum' to support a new leader. Blair believed that anything he was forced to front would fail and that a new movement had to develop from the grassroots up. He told people, 'You can't just have a group of people with money coming together and doing something. I don't think this is going to happen through political leaders clubbing together. I think you're going to find it starts in the country.' Privately, he believed that if the two main parties did not respond better to the views of the electorate and those voters who felt homeless, a new party was likely.

Others involved in the conversations saw all this talk as futile. 'There is so much money on the pro-European side of the argument that people want to give,' one said, 'but they don't want to give it to another failed shitshow. The idea that they were setting up a new party – that was never what was being discussed. What they were obsessed with was this idea of building a movement that can challenge hard Brexit as a gateway to challenging Brexit itself.'

As Theresa May prepared that March to send her letter triggering Article 50, and as the complexities became clearer, a growing number of people inside the Department for Exiting the European Union were beginning to have their doubts about how their own government was handling things.

By March, with the Article 50 bill passed, DExEU under David Davis was drawing up the Great Repeal Bill, devising ways of turning European law into British law, while the Cabinet Office under Ben Gummer worked out how to make it function with the devolved administrations in Scotland, Wales and Northern Ireland. 'DD brought the laws back from Brussels and Ben made them work in the UK,' a cabinet source said. The task was far more complex than the ministers had realised. One said, 'I was wrung out every day with the intensity of the intellectual heavy lifting we were having to do. More than half of our statute book was intertwined with European law.'

For Gummer the work was also an emotional challenge as a die-hard Remainer, but one who passionately wanted to make Brexit work with the minimum of damage to his constituents in Ipswich, who had voted overwhelmingly for Brexit. 'It does take a degree of emotional resilience to be going in every day to make what is clearly a disaster less disastrous,' a close confidant said.

New problems kept flaring up. With Nicola Sturgeon, the Scottish first minister, increasingly threatening a second independence referendum and concerns about the prospect of a 'hard border' between Northern Ireland and the Republic, the cabinet held a meeting on 21 February at which Gummer was charged with finding ways of ensuring Brexit did not threaten the Union. Ministers were warned that any return to border posts in Ulster would lead to a campaign of violence by dissident Republican terrorists, while a trade arrangement with different tariffs either side of the border would lead to smuggling and complicated rules of origin on imports – and that was before ministers considered how EU migrants could enter the rest of the UK via Belfast. 'You can't wish these problems away,' a senior civil servant said. The Irish situation also removed a key argument Tory ministers might have used to dissuade the Scots from voting for independence. 'You can't say that we're not going to have a border with Ireland but we are going to have a hard border with Scotland,' an official said. This did not make for a quiet life. 'The default position with the devolved administrations is complaint,' a Cabinet Office source said. 'Whatever you do, however much you consult them, however much you pay attention to them, it's never enough.'

The amount of legislation being drawn up was mounting. By mid-March it was clear that, in order to keep the Repeal Bill to a manageable size, there would need to be at least another seven bills to prepare for life outside the EU, covering immigration, tax, agriculture, trade and customs regimes, fisheries, data protection and sanctions – any one of which could be challenged and amended by MPs and peers.[2]

Theresa May charged Sajid Javid, the communities secretary, with designing a new system for replacing EU structural funds, worth £8.5

billion over a seven-year period for the poorer parts of the country. During the referendum campaign, Boris Johnson had told voters in Cornwall, the only area of England defined by the EU as a 'less-developed region', that they would get the same amount of money after Brexit. But was this still viable? 'Cornwall gets three or four times the rest of England,' a source said.

David Davis approached the deal like a game of chess. In late spring he began thinking about war-gaming the final talks, and conducting a 'backwards analysis of the endgame', working out the steps necessary to get in a good position. He believed the deal would ultimately be influenced by special interests in each country and sought to work out which of them might help Britain. 'DD was looking at the Flems, who were desperate to do a deal, and wondering how much of a problem the Wallonians would be. What do the Bavarian car makers really want, or the French farmers? He wanted to know what final squeeze plays they might use. What might Spain want on Gibraltar?' Davis told colleagues, 'We'll have to bully, cajole, coerce and bribe our way through. That's the nature of this. It makes the Congress of Vienna look like a walk in the park.'

Davis and his minister in the Lords, George Bridges, clashed over preparations for a new customs regime. Davis told officials they were 'making it all far too complicated'. He said, 'We already have non-EU customs processes, we just increase the capacity.' Much of it, he argued, could be pre-notified so customs officers had only to use a barcode reader to know what was in each container, allowing most consignments to be nodded through. Nonetheless, Bridges was concerned that a lot needed to change at ports and airports if even a minimal level of inspections were needed for EU goods. A DExEU source said, 'We didn't have space for checking French cheeses or French livestock. There were potentially technical issues with the IT. Sometimes when David was confronted with these issues, his reaction was, "Don't tell me this." Sometimes he didn't want to hear tricky news.'

There were also divisions over the role of the European Court of Justice, which the prime minister had made a red line the previous year. Bridges and Davis's chief of staff, James Chapman, were concerned that the implications of ruling out ECJ involvement in any deal had not been thought through and would make it difficult to arbitrate a trade deal or continue as members of justice and home affairs initiatives. 'It's difficult to do that if you insist that the letters "ECJ" don't appear anywhere in the new treaty,' a source said. Davis and David Jones, his minister of state, were adamant that there would have to be a new arrangement, in which oversight of future deals would involve a hybrid panel including judges from Britain and the EU with an independent member.

As the legal complications were examined, DExEU officials grew frustrated that the prime minister was taking independent legal advice from lawyers she had brought into Downing Street from the Home Office. One official said, 'They're not the experts on the EU. You don't use your family lawyer to conduct a trade deal.'

The Brexit department itself was not settled. 'DExEU staff were tearing their hair out. There was a lot of discontent. They didn't think they had clear instructions. They didn't see DD as a good leader,' one official said. They also had, in Oliver Robbins, a permanent secretary who was rarely in the building. 'Olly was always on the road,' a minister recalled. 'Every other department I've worked in you had ministerial "prayers" where everyone goes around the table saying what they're doing and what they're concerned about. We just didn't have that. Olly wasn't there. It's very difficult to see how you can be running a machine that big and that important while also on the road.' In March, Davis hired Philip Rycroft to become Robbins' deputy and take day-to-day charge of the civil service team.

Far more serious was the impact of Robbins' dual role as permanent secretary at DExEU and May's EU 'sherpa'. It led to the prime minister and Robbins commissioning work from officials in the department which was sent to Downing Street, leaving Davis and the other ministers oblivious that it had even been commissioned and unable to read the resulting reports. A DExEU source said, 'There would be papers going into Number 10 whose existence DD was not aware of.' It put civil servants in a difficult position when they were banned from showing their work to their own ministers. Robbins was not secretive about it, but he told Davis, 'I have two responsibilities: to you, as your permanent secretary, but also to her, as her sherpa, and there will be times that I want to put information to her and she'll want to discuss it with me and I won't want to show you.'

One minister said Robbins often did not pass on to Davis intelligence from his trips around the EU. 'There wasn't really a great sense of what Olly was picking up on the grapevine,' he said. 'There were meetings going on quite often with the prime minister, Olly and the chiefs of staff, about policy positions that we were never part of. We never had had meetings on a formal systematic basis with the EU policy unit in Number 10.' That group, which included Denzil Davidson and Peter Storr, was also 'frozen out' by Robbins and the chiefs. Davidson and George Bridges 'formed an alliance' to keep each other informed.

It became clear to Davis's team that Robbins, as a career civil servant, put his sherpa duties first. DExEU ministers were constantly frustrated that they did not know the prime minister's intentions and had never seen an overarching plan for Brexit written down. They did not know if that was because none existed or because May was pathologically secretive. 'We were shut out of the loop because either she doesn't trust people, or she doesn't know what she's doing,' one minister said. There was also suspicion that Robbins did not always share bad news with May. 'Olly saw the way that Ivan [Rogers] went and acted accordingly,' said a source.

Similarly, officials in DExEU put their loyalty to Robbins above their loyalty to the secretary of state. On one occasion James Chapman asked officials where their work on automatic number-plate recognition systems had got to. The systems were expected to be employed at customs and would be used to monitor the Irish border. 'We asked for this three months ago,' he said. 'Where is it?' After a year at the Treasury, Chapman was used to officials working fast to tight deadlines. This time he was told, 'We've done a bit of work on customs for Olly. It's gone to Nick [Timothy] in Number 10 because they commissioned it.' When Davis heard this he 'erupted' and threatened, 'If this carries on, I'm going to resign.'

After months of being kept in the dark, Davis confronted Robbins and May. A fellow minister said, 'David Davis had a very forthright discussion with [Robbins] and he also spoke to the prime minister about it.' Davis was placated by Fiona Hill, who told him at these moments, 'Listen DD, you're the most important member of the cabinet, you're our favourite.'

George Bridges was also growing increasingly disillusioned. His main concern after the Lancaster House speech and throughout the spring was that not enough work was being done to prepare for Britain leaving the EU without a deal. He raised his fears with John Manzoni, the chief executive of the civil service: 'It's the no-deal side of this that we have to really grip.' A DExEU source said, 'George thought it was just taking far too long. We have DExEU cabinet committees taking place once every three weeks, but sometimes they got cancelled.' When Bridges had pushed, in January 2017, for the creation of a task force to make policy decisions around contingencies, Jeremy Heywood told him it was too soon. In September 2017, Bridges said publicly, 'We need to move up several gears to make sure we are fully ready,' warning that failure to prepare would mean 'we will be captured at the negotiating table'.

Having worked in Number 10 under John Major, Bridges disliked the ponderous pace of decision-making under May. 'George used to get very cross that things were not working like clockwork in Number 10 as they used to. He thought we could do Brexit if it was done properly but he didn't think we were doing it properly.' Bridges believed that May needed to run Brexit as if it was a wartime situation, with a very small group of ministers meeting on a daily basis to check on progress on all the key issues. 'None of that happened,' a minister said. Bridges also thought there should have been much more focus on the kind of Britain May wanted to build after Brexit, to show Remainers and young people that the country had a bright future. Instead, the rather churlish Brexit speech she had unveiled at conference, with its denunciation of citizens of the world, had broadcast, tonally, that Britain was a closed place slamming down the shutters. Bridges, like others in the department, was also hearing from ambassadors that, because May had floated the idea of no deal at Lancaster House, some mistakenly thought it was her desired outcome. 'Everyone thought we wanted to go in and kick the table over,' a DExEU source said.

The cabinet leaks in the autumn of 2016 had led May to create a new, much smaller, EU Exit and Trade (Negotiations) cabinet subcommittee, consisting of just herself, Davis, Boris Johnson, Philip Hammond, Amber Rudd and Damian Green. Liam Fox, who had been suspected of leaking by May's aides, was not included. But Downing Street officials said even that was not where the real decisions were made on Brexit. According to Number 10 staff, the crucial meeting took place once a week in the prime minister's Downing Street office with the chiefs, Jeremy Heywood and Oliver Robbins in attendance. 'Once I figured out that those were the key meetings, I quickly got myself invited to them,' said an aide.

The greater demand for secrecy led to a ludicrous situation where George Bridges had to defend the government's position on Article 50 under forensic questioning in the Lords while not being allowed to see papers that had gone to the cabinet committee. 'George very nearly resigned during the passage of the Article 50 bill, on the prime minister's insistence that no one other than the DExEU cabinet committee members were allowed to see papers that did not emanate from their department,' a minister said. 'The papers going to those departments were about policy issues that he was being asked about on the floor of the House. He was being trusted to take through one of the most contentious bills that's ever gone through and he wasn't trusted to see the papers.'

Davis went in to bat for Bridges with Downing Street, but 'he was just told "No".' An official said, 'The message was passed back from Fiona to the effect that they did not care if he resigned. In desperation, DD would show George his copies of the cabinet papers because he thought it was so absurd.'

In an entire year as a key minister on the issue that would define her premiership, Bridges had just one ten-minute conversation with Theresa May on Article 50. 'He never saw her other than that,' a source said. This same, distant behaviour was a feature of May's entire time in Number 10 and would cost her dearly in the general election.

The mounting complexities of Brexit, their belief that the government was failing to prepare properly for a no-deal scenario and growing concerns that difficult issues were being brushed under the mat began to take its toll on both Bridges and James Chapman. They found themselves lying awake, exchanging emails at 4 a.m. about thorny Brexit issues. 'Nobody at the department could sleep,' another official said. 'I've never worked so hard in my life.' The endless travel also took its toll on Robbins. 'He lost an incredible amount of weight because like everyone else in the department he was not sleeping or eating properly,' a source said.

It was in the midst of this mess of competing egos, growing concerns about the pace of work and the stress of a major national project in crisis that May sought to write her letter to Donald Tusk triggering Article 50 and starting the two-year countdown to Brexit.

The Article 50 letter was written in Downing Street by Nick Timothy and only shown to David Davis the day before it was delivered to Brussels. 'DD couldn't tolerate that he didn't know exactly what was in it or when it was going to be,' a Downing Street official recalled. A DExEU source said, 'Nobody saw the Article 50 letter until twenty-four hours before it was sent. DD kept asking. Bridges kept asking. We knew Hammond wouldn't be shown it. He kept asking as well.'

James Chapman and Katie Perrior were put in charge of a cross-Whitehall communications group to prepare a media plan for the delivery of the letter – but neither of them had a clue what was in it, leading to farcical scenes. Chapman sought to draw up a news grid, as he once would have done ahead of a budget, laying out a series of stories that could be trailed, along with a defensive media plan for difficult issues likely to arise – but it was all guesswork. Perrior wanted to target outlets like *First News*, the paper for teenagers, since it was their future that was being decided, as well as the usual newspapers and broadcasters. 'Forty people would turn up to this weekly meeting,' said one of those attending. 'There were people down the line from Brussels, comms people from the Foreign Office, someone from Number 10, and it was painfully obvious Katie and James didn't know what was in it.' This was more than just an inconvenience. In these meetings, James Roscoe from the Foreign Office would say, 'Our ambassadors across Europe are asking, "What's in this letter?" They need to prepare the ground with their counterparts so that this lands properly.'

For Chapman it was 'the last straw'. He told Davis that he had an offer to join the public affairs firm Bell Pottinger and that he wished to leave government. His wife was Greek and he had never been a Brexit true believer, but he had begun the job hoping to make the best of it. Seeing papers which suggested that EU migrants like his wife would be finger-printed (a plan later dropped), being accused of leaking and then being frozen out by the chiefs dulled his enthusiasm for the job, while his expo-sure to some of the problems convinced him Brexit would be a disaster. 'It was the worst year of my life,' he told one friend.

One of the reasons for the secrecy was that Downing Street wanted to use the letter to make a controversial coded threat to maximise leverage with the EU. Britain's intelligence agencies were the best in Europe and the UK, with France, was one of the two major military powers. At a cabinet meeting on 7 March, ministers studied a paper prepared by the Ministry of Defence and the Foreign Office and agreed they could play on EU fears that British withdrawal would leave Europe more vulnerable to 'increased Russian aggression' under Vladimir Putin. Leaked minutes of the meeting showed that Boris Johnson argued Britain had a 'strong hand' while Michael Fallon, the defence secretary, said the government had 'high cards' to play because 'the EU needs our capabilities'. David Davis agreed that the UK should not 'underplay' this strength when seeking a new deal with Brussels. Summing up the conversation, the prime minister said Britain was in a 'strong position' on what was a 'defining issue for the EU'.[3]

Despite this, ministers were in the dark that Timothy was planning to make the implied threat to withdraw cooperation so explicit until it appeared in the letter. 'Security' appeared eleven times in the six-page document. While the final version read, 'In security terms a failure to reach agreement would mean our cooperation in the fight against crime and terrorism would be weakened,' senior sources say that was dramatically diluted from the original draft. 'You should have seen the original version of the letter,' commented a senior government official. 'DD immediately said, "This security thing is dreadful." It read like an explicit threat to cease cooperation on security and terrorism if we don't get a trade deal. DD stormed into Number 10 and insisted it was changed and it was watered down significantly.' Amber Rudd, the home secretary, also demanded changes. A source close to Timothy denied that there was an explicit threat. 'Amber wanted it changed because she thought it could have been read that way. We changed the wording.' Despite the changes, the security issue was still the main headline when the letter was published, leading to accusations that Britain was guilty of 'blackmail'. When the row blew up, Downing Street said no threat was intended.

The letter was finally released on 29 March, a day that could have been calculated to annoy pro-Europeans – it was John Major's birthday and Tony Blair's wedding anniversary. The signing and delivery of the letter descended into low farce. At 4.40 p.m. May had still not physically signed it. The early evening news and the newspaper deadlines were fast approaching. Katie Perrior wanted a picture to mark the historic moment. 'There aren't many photos in politics where you need no words,' she said. The picture *was* the story. A Downing Street official recalled, 'Katie was pacing the room. There was an argument over whether the PM should do it in a black pen or a blue pen.'

Perrior advised, 'You always sign an official document with a black pen.'

'Well, what pen? What are we going to do with the pen afterwards?'

'Fuck me! Just get a fucking pen and sign it now,' Perrior shouted. 'We need a photograph now. Sign the fucking letter!'

The shot of May signing the letter made the front page of every national newspaper. Even then, a Number 10 source said, 'No one had thought about how the hell they were going to get this letter to Brussels.' Downing Street had briefed that Tim Barrow, the UK's permanent representative in Brussels, would be delivering the letter in person the next morning. When it became clear that media organisations were planning to follow him on Eurostar there was a fear that a journalist or prankster might try to steal the letter. It was decided to send it ahead with a junior civil servant, so 'when Tim Barrow does his morning activities he doesn't have to worry because he didn't have it on him – no one could stop that'.

It was a day of jubilation for Eurosceptics. After his role in Conservatives for Britain and the ERG, Steve Baker became a focus for colleagues wanting to say 'Well done' to somebody. Fellow MPs patted him on the back and said, 'Happy independence day.'

After the letter was delivered, a diplomatic incident erupted over Gibraltar, a problem which may have been spotted had the text been circulated earlier. The Article 50 letter made no mention of the Rock, despite requests by Fabian Picardo, the first minister of Gibraltar. By contrast, after a sustained campaign of lobbying by the Spanish government, the EU's draft negotiating guidelines, issued shortly afterwards, said explicitly, 'After the UK leaves the Union, no agreement between the EU and the UK may apply to the territory of Gibraltar without agreement between Spain and the UK.' Spain, like all member states, already had power of veto over a new deal with Britain but to expressly link this to Gibraltar caused uproar. 'It was unnecessary and provocative,' a minister said. Residents of the Rock feared Brexit would mean the return of border checks between Spain and Gibraltar, choking the vital flow of 13,000 Spanish and EU workers who commuted there each day.

The letter also caused a row between DExEU and the Foreign Office. A minister said, 'Gibraltar lobbied very hard to have them specifically mentioned in our letter and it was rejected by DExEU, to the annoyance of the Foreign Office. The Gibraltarian government is feeling very let down.' More than that, officials in Gibraltar were quick to brief the press that they had received no assurances from ministers that they would be treated the same as other British citizens. A senior figure told the *Sunday Times*, 'The issue is not sovereignty, it is whether Gibraltar gets the same benefits as the UK. That's where Theresa May, David Davis and Boris Johnson have been silent.' Picardo jumped on a plane and flew in to do an interview with the BBC's Andrew Marr on Sunday morning. 'Picardo was extremely cross,' a minister recalled.

May was now facing a crisis. That morning Michael Howard suggested she might be prepared to go to war over Gibraltar as Margaret Thatcher had over the Falklands in 1982: 'Thirty-five years ago this week, another woman prime minister sent a task force halfway across the world to defend the freedom of another small group of British people against another Spanish-speaking country, and I'm absolutely certain that our current prime minister will show the same resolve in standing by the people of Gibraltar.' Few in Downing Street doubted that Picardo had briefed the papers or that he intended to start his own war of words with the government as chief whipping boy live on air.

The prime minister phoned Picardo on Sunday morning to placate him, and Number 10 put out a statement saying she had reassured him that the government would never 'enter into arrangements' on Gibraltar against 'their freely and democratically expressed wishes'. The reality of the call was very different. An enraged Picardo lectured May about how he had been ignored by Nick Timothy and Fiona Hill. 'I get no engagement with your team whatsoever,' he complained. 'They don't pick up the phone to me, they don't return my calls. I don't really know if they know who I am. I could have told you this would have happened if we didn't have Gibraltar in the letter, but I couldn't get anywhere near.' Those listening in to the call could barely believe what they were hearing. After months of dealing with the aggression of the chiefs, it had taken the chief minister of Gibraltar to complain to May about their behaviour. 'They treated him the way they treated us,' a Number 10 official said.

May 'ummed and ahhed her way through' the call and said, 'We will rectify that immediately. I'll make sure my team contact you by the end of the day.' It was not Timothy or Hill who phoned Picardo back. It was Boris Johnson. 'We'll make it good. It's going to be fine,' the foreign secretary assured the first minister. When Picardo appeared on television he was placated and said he was satisfied that Gibraltar had been mentioned in the white paper earlier that month. 'Boris saved our ass on that,' a Downing Street official admitted.

A source close to May blamed ministers for failing to draw the issue to Timothy's attention. 'It was not in the letter because nobody suggested it should be in the letter.' In fact, there had been good reasons not to include Gibraltar, along with other controversial issues. Including them would have forced the EU to develop a formal negotiating position on them, which might have made it more difficult to get what Britain wanted. 'If we'd started putting everything in it would have allowed the Europeans to start countering absolutely everything,' the aide said. 'That's why we didn't put things in like ECJ restrictions and free movement.'

There was a final act in the comedy of errors. David Davis did a ring-round of his EU counterparts but made an embarrassing mistake. 'When we triggered Article 50 he rang people from every country and was told the next person he was going to speak to was Michel Barnier,' a source said, 'but he had the wrong briefing note and he thought it was the Finnish foreign minister. So for the first few minutes of the conversation he was on the phone to Michel Barnier talking about fishing and Finland. Barnier couldn't understand why he was talking to him about fish in Finland.' Officials who had begun to doubt Davis's ability to deliver Brexit dined out on the story.

In his early months Davis had overcome the initial scepticism of DExEU staff and won their respect, having knuckled down and made an effort to get across the detail, but as 2017 wore on, civil servants began to fear that his upbeat approach masked a lack of attention to detail. There were claims that he did not work a full week. Officials regarded his view that a deal could be done in two years as wildly optimistic, though one admitted, 'Candidly, we do need the politicians to have a slightly more ambitious view of the world than officials.' But a senior Tory said that summer, 'DD started his job in DExEU and the officials thought he was a joke. Then you got to Christmas time, New Year they thought he was OK. Now they think he's a clown again. Officials think he is lazy.'

The Article 50 letter had begun the countdown to Brexit. After May's announcement of the timetable six months earlier, there was no serious debate at the top of the government about whether it was a good idea to adhere to the March deadline. A change would have created a political storm and required powers of persuasion with the Eurosceptics that May had not proven she possessed. Yet May's optimism that she could do a deal in two years was to prove false within six months. Ivan Rogers told MPs he had warned May she should delay if she wanted to 'avoid being screwed' by Brussels. Dominic Cummings, the mastermind of the Leave campaign, was to call the triggering of Article 50 before the government had finalised its blueprint for Brexit or its contingency work for a no-deal scenario a 'historic, unforgivable blunder' akin to 'putting a gun in your mouth' and pulling the trigger. 'Kaboom,' he added.

Fears that the government was not prepared to leave convinced George Bridges that he should resign as a minister, a decision he would keep to himself until after the general election. When he resigned Bridges kept his counsel. Months later he said he had quit because he wanted to spend time with his children. Yet friends say he was also deeply disillusioned. 'George felt he wasn't making any difference, in a nutshell. He felt it was chaos and decisions that needed taking were not being taken. He didn't feel there was enough intellectual honesty with the prime minister about some of these issues.'

Nick Timothy and Fiona Hill were not concerned. They already had a plan to deliver Theresa May a far stronger hand in the negotiations by calling a general election. Twenty days after May sent her Article 50 letter, the prime minister announced that she was going to the country. The running of that campaign and May's performance during it would be heavily shaped by her relationship with the two chiefs of staff. As the telephone call with Fabian Picardo had revealed, their methods were not always designed to win friends.

PART TWO

HUBRIS

THE CHIEFS

September 2016 to March 2017

10

'ECONOMICALLY ILLITERATE'

Those waiting in the room outside Theresa May's office will never forget the look on Philip Hammond's face when he emerged on the morning of 15 March 2017. The chancellor was a tall, proud man but his head was held a little less high than usual. His face was the colour of a fashionable off-white paint colour with a pretentious name, chalky grey with a hint of pink at the top of his cheeks. A slight tremor was visible as he gripped his papers. He strode out, flanked by his economic adviser Karen Ward, a former HSBC banker, and his principal private secretary Stuart Glassborow. 'He looked as sick as a parrot,' a cabinet minister who witnessed the scene recalled. That morning Hammond had been summoned to May's office and told to ditch the flagship announcement in his budget – the fastest major budget U-turn in modern political history.

Seven days earlier the chancellor had announced that he was increasing National Insurance contributions for the self-employed from 9 per cent to 10 per cent, with another one-point rise slated for 2019, a measure which raised £2 billion. The money would be ploughed into social care. Since then, the Tory Party in Parliament had suffered one of its periodic losses of confidence. Fifty backbenchers had told the whips they were prepared to rebel. May ordered her chancellor to ditch the pledge and do it fast, before she stood up to take Prime Minister's Questions in the Commons. 'He was just told, "This is what we're doing" and "We told you this would happen,"' a Downing Street official said. 'We reversed the position.'

It was all a far cry from Hammond's confidence at the despatch box a week earlier when he announced that, in future, the main budget of the year would be in the autumn. The grey man of Westminster even risked a joke: 'The Treasury has helpfully reminded me that I am not the first chancellor to announce the last spring budget. Twenty-four years ago, Norman Lamont also presented what was billed then as the last spring budget ... What they failed to remind me of, Mr Speaker, was that ten weeks later, he was sacked.'

In the event, Hammond nearly beat that record by nine weeks. The bonhomie concealed a bitter row between 10 and 11 Downing Street that had been raging behind the scenes over the shape of the budget. It brought to a head deep differences of economic philosophy and a toxic clash of personalities between Hammond and Nick Timothy that had been rocking the government for months.

Hammond did not share May and Timothy's economic philosophy. Indeed, with the possible exception of Sajid Javid, no one in the cabinet shared it less. When the prime minister used her party conference speech in 2016 to declare that 'government can and should be a force for good ... supporting free markets, but stepping in to repair them when they aren't working', Hammond bit his tongue. His primary concern as chancellor was to ensure the government had fiscal wriggle room for Brexit. That meant keeping control of the purse strings. When he got the job, George Osborne delighted in telling friends, 'If you think I'm dry on the economy, you should see this guy.' Hammond lacked Osborne's sure touch with political tactics. Unlike Osborne, who made tackling the deficit a common-sense issue, Hammond talked about 'austerity' as if it was a virtue in itself.

In the run-up to the autumn statement, Hammond refused to fund schemes designed to attract the 'just about managing' working poor – JAMs in Whitehall speak – who Team May had identified as their target audience. 'Philip made it very clear that every pound in spending would have to be accounted for with cuts,' said one ally. Distracted by Brexit, Hammond's quiet victory over Timothy was little noticed but it fuelled the chiefs' view that the chancellor was an impediment to May achieving the goals she had set herself that first day in Downing Street. A Number 10 colleague said, 'Nick wanted to drive an ambitious agenda of social reform and the chancellor was seen as a roadblock to that.' Timothy confided to his friend that it would have been better if May had appointed a different chancellor: 'Nick has said to me that one of his greatest regrets was the speed with which they appointed the original cabinet and some of the roles that they then put people into, because it did stifle the reform agenda.'

Downing Street had tried to flesh out May's vision in a 'modern Industrial Strategy' on 21 January 2017, outlining government support for apprenticeships and plans to achieve parity of esteem between academic study at university and technical and vocational qualifications. But the detailed measures – introducing T-Levels as an alternative to A-Levels – would take years to enact or were a long way from the trans-formational agenda which had been promised. Greg Clark, the business secretary, was more *simpatico* with May and Timothy's embrace of the proactive state, but he also disappointed the chiefs with his caution. 'Greg ended up in a key role for the reform agenda and has just not been as radical or dynamic as Nick would have wanted someone in that role to be,' the Downing Street official said. Justine Greening, the education secretary, who was queasy about the push for new grammar schools, was also seen as too cautious.

When it came to housing, the boot was on the other foot, with Downing Street blocking radical proposals drawn up by Sajid Javid and the housing minister, Gavin Barwell. 'Every time we sent a draft of the white paper something would be taken out of it,' a source in the commu-nities department said. 'You can't have a housing policy that doesn't lead to more homes being built.' George Osborne told a friend that spring, 'They haven't actually done anything apart from Brexit.'

The pattern was repeated with measures May announced at the Birmingham party conference to crack down on fat cat businessmen. A threat to put workers on company boards to control executive pay irri-tated the chancellor and the business community but was then quietly dropped. A Hammond confidant said, 'They clashed over the workers on boards and the rather bunkum way of doing industrial strategy with lots of silly interventions.'

Hammond had some sympathy for Timothy's goals, but not the poli-cies he was drawing up to achieve them. 'Philip genuinely understood where Nick was coming from, and where the boss was coming from,' a fellow cabinet minister said. 'He does believe, rightly, that she has a good feeling for how a man on the Clapham omnibus feels about the rights and wrongs of the world.' But the chancellor would say, 'I can see what you're trying to achieve, but the means by which you're trying to do it aren't going to work, and might have perverse results that you've not thought about'. This was just the kind of Eeyoreish approach the chiefs could not stand. He was often supported in cabinet by Sajid Javid, who thought the assaults on business ridiculous. After one intervention, Fiona Hill phoned one of Javid's special advisers and said, 'You've got to tell your minister to calm down. He can't be going around saying this stuff, the PM won't be happy.'

Timothy regarded Hammond as lacking vision. One minister with whom he discussed the chancellor said, 'Nick will tell you Philip doesn't have an economic policy. It is in the nature of free marketeer liberals. They just want to let the market work.'

The Treasury and Hammond's continuing attempts to soften Brexit further soured relations with Timothy, the architect of clean Brexit. A special adviser said, 'The senior Treasury people had spent seven years doing controversial, difficult things in order to turn the economy around, and they could see that the course that the PM or Nick Timothy had chosen was going to drive it, at a stroke, off a cliff. They kept saying this and they never backed down.'

Hammond infuriated Timothy with his approach in meetings in the prime minister's Downing Street office. 'They were the worst meetings I've ever been in,' said one of those present. The prime minister made her displeasure clear. 'She wouldn't say anything,' the official said. 'She'd sit there mute, shaking her head imperiously, but not actually saying anything. DD was saying, "Oh come on, Phil, you're being a bit of a nervous ninny, this is all going to be all right on the night. Stop being so negative." Then Nick Timothy would just erupt from the back of the room. He'd tell the chancellor he was being totally negative and captured by the Treasury and wasn't interested in what he had to say. They were hideous meetings. Fiona Hill made it clear they weren't interested in hearing from these officials.'

Timothy did little to disguise his dislike of Hammond. 'Nick would roll his eyes every time Philip Hammond opened his mouth,' a witness said. 'It was appalling. Nick would saunter in and out ostentatiously as though he had more important things to be doing. Hammond was treated in front of his senior officials with utter contempt.' Another said, 'He would talk down to him like he was a subordinate rather than the chancellor of the exchequer.' A Hammond ally added, 'The Terrible Twins were ridiculous. Philip was just trying to have a dialogue but he was accused of being negative.'

After Hammond made his feelings known over Brexit, he told cabinet colleagues he would receive abusive text messages from Hill. 'Treasury people said they would tell him to "shut the fuck up"', an official claimed. Hill's allies say 'she did send him text messages in frustration to try to stop him briefing things and work in a collegiate fashion'. The chancellor urged colleagues and Number 10 staff to keep records of messages they received. Boris Johnson also showed aggressive texts to colleagues. Timothy denies that he ever sent abusive texts: 'I was quite often testy with Philip but I certainly never swore at him.' However, he cannot recall, but does not deny, swearing about Hammond behind his back.

When Hammond was not in the room, political aides and civil servants both say Hill and Timothy were vituperative about him in front of officials, knowing their views would be reported back. 'They called him "The Cunt"', one said. 'That was around the office in front of people like Will Macfarlane, our point man with the Treasury, who used to work in the Treasury,' another said. 'He knew it would get back to Hammond.' Hill denies using that term of abuse. When she had first joined the Conservative Party, she had worked for Hammond but became disappointed the chancellor was 'not a team player'.

The stories spread, in part, because the chiefs seemed keen for others to know about their treatment of the chancellor. 'Nick used to relate them with delight,' said a Downing Street official. 'Nick would say, "We've told you what the policy is, fuck off and follow it."' Those were not the words Timothy used to Hammond's face but a version of events he apparently wanted circulated. A source said, 'Nick would quite like the idea that he was abusing the chancellor. He relished those fights.'

After one bruising episode Hammond quizzed one of May's aides about the intelligence which had filtered back to Number 11. 'I heard Nick Timothy called me the C-word this morning,' he said. The official gave a non-committal answer. 'So you're not telling me he doesn't.'

'I'm not commenting, I've got nothing to say. They're difficult people to deal with, chancellor.'

Hammond seemed shocked and remarked quietly, 'That's nice, isn't it?'

The aide said, 'Chancellor, you've got more power than I do, so why don't you do something about it?'

Hammond appeared unconvinced. 'I don't have any more power than you do,' he said. 'We're both stuck in this hell hole together.'

On one occasion, several sources allege, Hammond complained to May that Hill had been rude to him. Shortly afterwards Hill confronted Hammond and said to him, 'Theresa and I always wanted you to be our chancellor, but if you think you're going to get between me and Theresa, you've got another think coming.' Hill has told friends she had several conversations with Hammond in his office in 11 Downing Street where she would say, 'Philip, we've known each other a long time. I don't know what's going on here. We're trying to get through a difficult period in the country's history, I don't see the logic for some of your behaviour.' Each time she left thinking the issue was resolved, 'then he would renege on the deal,' a source said. Hill even took Hammond's wife, Susan, for a drink at the Goring Hotel to try to persuade the chancellor to be more cooperative. 'He just didn't want to be part of the team,' the source said.

Hammond could be his own worst enemy. Some in meetings found him condescending and claim that, in moments of tension with Timothy, he would address the chief of staff as if he were a junior official. 'At times Nick pushed him so far that he would respond in ways which suggested that was what he thought,' one colleague of Timothy said. Hammond was also 'quite grand' with his own officials. 'They don't like him,' a Treasury source said. 'He's very us and them. They're servants to him. They are terrified of his little list. Every morning he has five things on his list and they won't be able to brief him on a meeting with the Prime Minister because he wants to talk to the head of VAT about something obscure. They're tearing their hair out, having to work through Philip's list. He doesn't really listen to anyone.' This was to be a trait that would cost him dear.

Hammond's special advisers were no match for the chiefs. Hayden Allan had worked for him at both the Ministry of Defence and the Foreign Office but did not have an economics background. The previous August, Hammond had recruited Poppy Trowbridge, the consumer affairs correspondent of Sky News, to handle his press. She was still finding her feet when the most difficult month of their working lives unfolded.

When budget preparations began in February, Timothy pressed for the government to start delivering on its domestic social agenda. Hammond was equally clear that he was not going to turn on the spending taps. 'Nick and the PM really wanted some radical ideas,' a Downing Street colleague recalled. 'Both from the Treasury but from across government – things we might do for JAMs. But the ideas weren't forthcoming. The whole conversation was, from the PM's point of view, quite unsatisfactory.'

May, Timothy and Will Tanner were frustrated that the prime minister was tied to the Cameron government's austerity agenda. Tanner proposed a change to the economic approach. Instead of aiming for a budget surplus, as Osborne had done, he suggested a target of getting everyday spending into balance by 2019. That would mean excluding debt interest payments of around 2.5 per cent of GDP from the calculations, freeing up £16 billion a year to increase public sector pay or invest in infrastructure. 'Within Number 10, Will, Nick to some extent and the PM herself thought, "We've lashed ourselves to something which is going to really punish us,"' a Number 10 official said. The cabinet secretary backed the Tanner plan. 'It was Jeremy Heywood's view as well as the PM's that the fiscal situation was such that actually you could loosen some things up a bit and borrow some more,' an aide to May said. 'Jeremy pushed that quite strongly. But the chancellor was not even prepared to entertain it.'

Timothy was also infuriated by briefings emanating from the Treasury that Hammond was building up a 'Brexit war chest', which he could use to stimulate the economy in the event of a downturn, since it implied that Brexit might be a disaster. 'That irritated Nick massively,' a friend said. 'He felt it was bad politics because you're going into a budget where you say, "We want to help the JAMs but we haven't got much to give you," and now you're saying, "Actually, we've got all this money but we're just holding it back."'

To Hammond's irritation, Timothy was pushing for funding for more free schools but did not suggest where the money could be found. An aide to May said, 'The chancellor's view was that if you want to spend money, you had to think where you were going to get it from. Nick didn't give a fuck where we were going to get the money from. Nick just loves spending money.' According to one account he told Hammond, 'You're the chancellor, you work it out.' Hammond actually had less control over spending than his predecessors since he had taken a decision not to micromanage the rest of Whitehall, as George Osborne and Gordon Brown had done. The chancellor would tell aides, 'I've given them their pot and it's up to them what they do with it.'

Hammond's personal manner inflamed the rows. Tory MPs were demanding changes to the funding formula for schools which they felt discriminated against those in rural constituencies. During a meeting in May's office Hammond dug in against unfunded increases in school budgets. Timothy argued that they could fund an initial investment. As for future years, 'We can worry about that later,' he said.

Hammond hit back, 'You don't just fund the first phase. We can't agree to something you don't have the money for. I need to know we can pay for that.'

After some back and forth May's team backed off. Yet at the moment of his victory, Hammond continued lecturing Timothy about the need to fully fund pledges. Another aide present said, 'I'd think to myself, "Don't say that, stop digging. You've just won! Shut up!" I felt like kicking him under the table. I was thinking, "You've not read this moment at all. You're pissing them off." He'd just carry on labouring his point. And he'd open up the row again.' A Downing Street official confirmed, 'Nick and Phil hate each other. You've got the chiefs with no social skills who can't get the best out of people. And you've got Phil, who can't read a social situation because he's socially autistic.'

The failure to find any big ideas to help the JAMs and Hammond's unwillingness to compromise on austerity meant the budget conversations soon got bogged down in technical discussions. Having dodged the issue of the growing crisis in social care at the autumn statement both sides agreed a substantial cash injection was needed while a Whitehall review run from the Cabinet Office devised a long-term solution. To pay for it, Hammond alighted on the longstanding anomaly which meant the self-employed paid substantially lower National Insurance contributions (NICs). He vowed to raise them. It was a classic tax rationalisation exercise beloved of Treasury officials and fraught with political peril. Nigel Lawson and George Osborne had both rejected the idea when it was presented to them but it appealed to Hammond's technocratic mind. 'He was obsessed with the equalisation of self-employed and employed people when it comes to tax,' a Downing Street official said. 'That was something the PM pushed back on and said "no" to.'

May and her closest aides argued that decisions were best left until a review of modern working practices, by former Blair adviser Matthew Taylor, finished its work in the autumn. 'We told him every time he raised it, "This is mental and you can't do it,"' a source close to May said.

'He persisted and persisted and persisted. He was absolutely adamant he had to do it.'

In a sign of Hammond's political naïvety, the chancellor seemed unconcerned that the 2015 manifesto had stated in black and white that a Conservative government would 'commit to no increases in VAT, National Insurance contributions or Income Tax'. When the issue was raised in Treasury meetings David Gauke, Hammond's deputy, pointed out that the legislation enshrining the tax lock in law had only covered Class 1 NICs, paid by normal employees, leaving Hammond free to raise Class 4 contributions for the self-employed. 'We dealt with that,' Gauke said. Yet the manifesto commitment made no such distinction. 'Philip was blindsided by Gauke,' a minister close to Hammond said. 'The spads should have picked it up too.'

The issue of the manifesto commitment barely seems to have been raised in the meetings to thrash out the final details of the budget. Hammond, accompanied by Karen Ward and his permanent secretary Tom Scholar, would face off against May, Timothy, Hill, Heywood, Wilkins and Penn, plus the prime minister's private secretary Will Macfarlane, over the details of the 'scorecard', the part of the budget red book which lays out the official costings of every tax and spending decision. 'We had a lot of meetings without resolution,' recalled one exasperated aide. 'The difficult issues on the scorecard were at the bottom but you'd always start at the top. You'd spend forty minutes talking about things which were relatively uncontroversial. Then you'd get to the difficult bits and the meeting would break up.'

After weeks of argument, the Treasury performed what May's team regarded as 'a stunt', altering one aspect of the 'scorecard', which had to be submitted to the Office of Budget Responsibility (OBR) to be audited several days before the budget. A Number 10 official said, 'The Treasury changed the scorecard then submitted it to the OBR and then came to us and said, "We had to make this change at the last minute, consequently there's a hole in the numbers and we need to find something to fill it, so we're going to have to do the NICs thing."'

In the final meeting, May and Timothy both made clear to Hammond that he would carry the can if there was a problem. The message was delivered with cold clarity by May: 'You're the chancellor, so on your head be it.' A Treasury official said, 'Most chancellors when they get that from their prime minister think, "Do I really need to do this?" He could have just had a slightly fiscally loose budget.' Yet Hammond stuck to his guns. The prime minister, technically the First Lord of the Treasury, did not overrule him. Both would pay a high price.

In the days before the budget, Downing Street stole the positive headlines – including the £320 million Hammond had finally approved for 140 new free schools and grammar schools, the first state-funded selective schools in a generation. There was a £500 million fund for technical education and the same amount to help develop electric vehicles, robots and artificial intelligence. All of which meant that when Hammond got to his feet in a packed House of Commons on 8 March, the only big-ticket item left for the media to chew on was the National Insurance rise. Having failed to 'roll the pitch' by explaining the issue to MPs and the media in the weeks beforehand, he told the House, 'Employed and self-employed alike use our public services in the same way, but they are not paying for them in the same way. The lower National Insurance paid by the self-employed is forecast to cost our public finances over £5 billion this year alone. That is not fair to the 85 per cent of workers who are employees.'

The reaction was swift and brutal. In the briefing for political journalists after Hammond had sat down, Poppy Trowbridge had a tough time. The media pointed out that the policy would cost 2.5 million people £240 a year. Within hours, Downing Street was briefing that the decision would be delayed until the autumn, when the Taylor Report was published. But that did not placate Conservative MPs, who were demanding to know why the chancellor was hammering strivers and entrepreneurs. Remembering George Osborne's 'omnishambles budget' of 2012 – where Hammond's predecessor had stupidly agreed to iron out tax anomalies on static caravans and Cornish pasties – Paul Butters of the Liberal Democrats labelled it the 'omNICshambles budget'.

On budget day Osborne's former special adviser Rupert Harrison tweeted, 'Think we can rule out a snap election.' In fact, the shambles had made it more likely, since it brought home to both Hammond and May that they were shackled to Cameron's manifesto pledges until they called one. Indeed, in a column for the *Daily Telegraph* the day before the budget, William Hague had urged May to go to the country, arguing that she needed a 'large and decisive majority' to help her navigate the troubles that lay ahead. Her chancellor had now added to them.

On Thursday the 9th, the day after the budget, one of May's senior aides briefed City contacts against the chancellor, revealing that the prime minister had opposed the NI hike. That weekend the blue-on-blue blame game was as vicious as anything from the Blair–Brown civil war a decade earlier. May and Hammond's inner circles traded insults over who was to blame for the fiasco. Cabinet ministers revealed that, astonishingly, the chancellor had failed to warn his colleagues when he briefed them on the morning of the budget that raising NICs might be seen as a breach of the Conservative manifesto. 'Philip did not mention the manifesto issue in cabinet and nor did Ben Gummer, one of whose jobs is to enforce manifesto commitments,' said one cabinet minister. A minister close to May denounced the NICs rise as 'a sneaky accounting trick' and added, 'Hammond has no appeal to the public, but he won't listen to anybody because he thinks he's the cleverest person on earth. We need to kill it now.'

Explosively, one of Hammond's closest allies launched a toxic attack on Timothy in the *Sunday Times*, complaining that May had left her chancellor with 'nothing but bad news to announce on the day'. The chancellor's ally said, 'Number 10 were pressing for more money. They have all these pet projects and they are very relaxed about raising tax. Theresa's instincts are clearly to tax and spend. There's an economic illiteracy in Number 10. There's no one there who knows much about economics.'

The words 'economically illiterate' exploded in May's court like a nuclear bomb going off. Timothy and Hill wondered if Hammond himself was responsible for the briefing. Their spies told them that the chancellor was fond of using the phrase. 'He did say they were economically illiterate quite liberally,' a Hammond ally admitted later. 'Frankly I think that was a reasonable thing to say. You can't pick and mix capitalism. Philip gets that you need proper capitalism, where you actually deliver growth, which raises revenue, which creates the opportunity to cut tax, which makes people feel better. But that was portrayed as unreconstructed and not savvy' by May's team.

That the phrase had made its way to a national newspaper was a declaration of war.

After a desperate forty-eight hours in which more than twenty MPs broke cover to condemn the budget, Hammond was summoned to May's office the following Wednesday morning and told, 'You will be U-turning on this today. We're going to do it at PMQs. I suggest you write to all our MPs beforehand, so Tory MPs are notified before the House.'

Hammond argued his point but the prime minister was in no mood to listen. She said it was vital that the public could trust the word of the Conservative manifesto. Those who were around May's office that morning say the meeting was a dressing down designed to humiliate Hammond. 'Nick was gloating while he was doing it,' one said. When Hammond rushed back to Number 11 to salvage his reputation, a Downing Street official remarked, 'He looked absolutely broken.'

While the chancellor scrambled to write his letter to MPs, Katie Perrior and Tom Swarbrick had a sensitive situation to manage. A dramatic U-turn was pending but Rory Stewart, the international development minister, was shortly due to appear on the BBC's *Daily Politics* show. 'We're going to have to speed this up,' Perrior said, 'because I'm not leaving a minister hanging out to dry.' Perrior called Rob Oxley, the DfID spad who was with Stewart, and said, 'We're doing a U-turn on National Insurance contributions. There's a letter in Rory Stewart's private email.' Oxley got Stewart to call Perrior, who gave the minister three points to make on air. Perrior was aghast when Stewart went on air and repeated the talking points he had learned the night before as if nothing had changed. He explained afterwards, 'I'd really learnt those lines yesterday and I just didn't feel that I could peel away from them.' Ten minutes later the policy was binned. When, months later, Stewart began positioning himself as a future leadership contender, a senior government source said, 'I'd be seriously worried if Rory Stewart went anywhere near the job. He was incapable of delivering three lines.'

Hammond was grateful for the support of the Number 10 press team and called May to thank her. The prime minister called Perrior on her mobile and said, 'I wanted to let you know the chancellor personally wanted to thank you and your team for all the hard work.' It was the first time Perrior could ever remember being thanked for anything in Downing Street.

To May's loyalists, the National Insurance debacle was proof that neither Hammond's judgement nor his team could be trusted. The chiefs blamed Trowbridge for the briefings, even though she had been flying to Africa for a break when the 'economically illiterate' briefing occurred. Timothy told friends that Hammond 'thinks he's a lot of cleverer than he is. He's not a very good politician.'

The 'economically illiterate' briefing led to a breakdown in relations between Timothy and Hammond which reverberated throughout the subsequent election campaign. 'Nick is user-friendly, but once you've crossed him big time, that is it,' one minister said. 'That was the terminal moment.' Timothy liked 'robust discussion' in private but could not forgive the fact that Hammond's team had broken the code of *omertà* by talking to the media. 'What absolutely infuriated them was that people were talking about the team,' the minister said. 'That's where the well was poisoned. There was loss of trust. That briefing in the press had a destructive, cancerous effect.'

The lesson of the budget for some around May was that they should trust their own judgement and get back to her stated mission. 'The biggest mistakes actually came when Nick and Fi let go of stuff,' one colleague said. A week after the NICs U-turn, May used the Conservative spring conference to unveil what she called the Plan for Britain, a programme that Chris Wilkins and Nick Timothy had been working on for months. It was supposed to be a blueprint for Britain after Brexit to coincide with the triggering of Article 50 but also a skeleton outline of the 2020 manifesto. Downing Street saw it as the direct descendant of the Downing Street and conference speeches the previous autumn but did a poor job of explaining its significance to journalists, who saw it as a platitudinous reheat of previous announcements. A Conservative Party official recalled, 'We did a lot of polling, a lot of focus groups for something that in the end turned out to be pointless. It was meant to be the governing document for the next year. Then they called an election and it all went out the window.'

May's Plan for Britain was overshadowed by other news. With delicious timing, a few hours before she stood up to speak at the spring conference, it was announced that George Osborne was to become editor of the London *Evening Standard*. The appointment stunned Westminster. For an MP representing Tatton in Cheshire to take charge of the capital's leading newspaper was audacious. To do so while holding down six jobs in addition to Osborne's parliamentary duties was too much for some of his colleagues. Osborne had already trousered – in Westminster parlance

– more than £700,000 from public speaking; secured a £650,000 stipend for four days' work a month from BlackRock, the world's biggest investment firm; been granted a £120,000 fellowship at the McCain Institute for International Leadership in Arizona; and would now take home more than £220,000 for a four-day week at the *Standard* – on top of his £75,000 salary as an MP. A senior civil servant said, 'He likes money. He's got Blair and Mandelson disease.' But an old friend called Osborne and told him to stick to his guns: 'The cuntocracy of jealous journalists and jealous colleagues will be out to get you.' He was not wrong.

On a WhatsApp group shared by Eurosceptic MPs, Sir Gerald Howarth wrote with withering sarcasm, 'A man of his immense ability can surely speak for Cheshire and London before lunch, advise BlackRock over lunch and tender his invaluable advice to the House after lunch before holding a dinner party for the *bien pensant* remainians of Notting Hill in the evening. Sorted.' Iain Duncan Smith posted a picture of Michael Douglas's character from the film *Wall Street*, the celluloid monument to eighties excess: 'Hmmm ... why do I keep thinking of Gordon Gekko ... greed is good.'

Osborne's reputation for ruthlessness was confirmed when it emerged that he had recommended the political journalist Matthew d'Ancona to Evgeny Lebedev, the owner of the *Standard*. D'Ancona was on the verge of getting the job when Osborne decided he fancied it himself.[1] Seeing the benefit of having a big name in the post, Lebedev was 'immediately sold on the idea'.

The prime minister's official spokesman, James Slack, was rendered speechless when the news was broken to him in his regular morning briefing. Nick Timothy and Fiona Hill were on a trip to Scotland to see Ruth Davidson when the message came through. Timothy thought the appointment inappropriate. How could Osborne attend the 1922 Committee as an MP when he was also a journalist? 'There are conflicts of interest in loads of different directions,' he told a friend. MPs contacted the chief whip, Gavin Williamson, to make the same point.

In Osborne's circle there was irritation that May seemed to have expected him to sit mutely on the sidelines despite the brutality of his sacking. Pronouncing himself a 'Londoner', Osborne declared, 'We will judge what the government ... against this simple test: is it good for our readers and good for London? If it is, we'll support them. If it isn't, we'll be quick to say so.' Lebedev was blunter: 'Frankly, George Osborne will provide more effective opposition to the government than the current Labour Party.' A minister close to May presciently concluded, 'It looks like a platform for vengeance.'

Yet, if the Timothy–Osborne and Timothy–Hammond feuds were toxic, they had nothing on the relationship between the two most senior women in Theresa May's team.

11

THE SNARLING
DUDS OF MAY?

Katie Perrior first threatened to resign in November 2016 when she was summoned to Waiting Room B in Downing Street. Nick Timothy and Fiona Hill had christened it 'the bollocking room' when they were on the end of dressings down there in the Cameron years. Now they were the ones administering the bollockings. Perrior sat down with Nick Timothy, who asked, 'How's it going?' Timothy knew the answer already. In the five months they had been working together, the relationship between May's director of communications and Fiona Hill had descended into open warfare.

'Not very well,' said Perrior. 'There have been incidents recently. I will not be spoken to like that in front of my team. I have been intimidated internally and externally humiliated. I will not put up with it. I'm thinking about moving on at Christmas.'

When she signed up to work for May – abandoning a public relations company she had sweated blood to build up with her business partner Jo Tanner – Perrior had imagined she would have the kind of relationship with May that her predecessor Craig Oliver had enjoyed with David Cameron – as a trusted adviser and sounding board present in the key meetings. Without that access a communications chief was next to useless because they could not predict the coming crises or speak with any confidence to journalists about the prime minister's intentions. Yet that was not how Hill and Timothy operated. The chiefs were May's only senior advisers. They had quickly established a fearsome reputation across Whitehall – where ministers, special advisers and civil servants knew them as 'the terrible twins' and 'the gruesome twosome' – for the levels of control they exerted and the uncompromising way in which they made clear who was in charge.

Perrior and Hill clashed because their expertise overlapped. Hill had not wanted to be comms director, but to Perrior it was clear that Hill did not want anyone else to do the job either. To Hill, Perrior was simply not up to the job. 'We had to scramble a team together and inevitably not everyone worked out,' she told a friend. Perrior felt she had tried to work with Hill but had been greeted with obstruction, abuse or the cold shoulder. Perrior was not invited to many of the key meetings. 'I'm not getting nearly enough time with the prime minister,' she told Timothy. 'I've been promised a meeting every week. It's constantly being taken out of my diary.'

Timothy asked Perrior not to leave and said of Hill, 'We can sort it.'

Perrior listened but was sceptical. 'I've told her if there's stuff I'm doing wrong and you're not happy with it, let's address it,' Perrior said. 'I'm trying.'

'I know.' Timothy appeared wearily perplexed. 'On paper, you should get on. You're both doers,' he said. 'She's really, really brilliant, you need to understand that.'

Perrior said, 'You need to understand, this is a job I've wanted since I was sixteen years old. I don't know what I've done wrong. I've worked in some tough teams but I've never experienced an environment like this.'

Timothy said, 'We can sort it. I want you to stay.'

Politics, they say, is 'showbusiness for ugly people', and the personal feuding behind the scenes in Theresa May's Downing Street would not have been out of place in a Christmas episode of *EastEnders* or the *Godfather* movies. The long-running clash with Perrior was just the most high-profile and debilitating of the feuds that Fiona Hill engaged in during her eleven months in Number 10, one of several that colleagues say affected her own happiness and productivity but also the smooth functioning of government itself. It did so under the nose of a prime minister who seldom ever challenged Hill or Timothy, and contributed to a feeling among ministers, aides and officials that the chiefs had been given *carte blanche* to behave as they pleased.

Hill fiercely guarded the chiefs' role as May's only serious advisers in the manner of a tightly-knit family resentful of a new arrival. 'I think they felt I wanted there to be three in that relationship,' Perrior told friends. 'But I never did because I don't live the Westminster life.' While Hill and Timothy had devoted themselves to May's advancement for a decade, Perrior went home to her family. She had no interest in 'hanging out with Theresa and Philip on a Sunday'. What she did want was the access and seniority to do her job properly. It was denied to her.

Perrior's relationship with Timothy, while not as toxic, was still strained. A special adviser recalled, 'He would tell everybody, including Katie, "You don't understand hierarchies. There are three people in this government. It's me, Fiona and the PM." It was a case of: what we say goes.' To many of the staff, the chiefs spent too much time seeking to show who was boss and not enough time using their power effectively. 'In Cameron's day there was a little sofa in the private secretaries' room. They had that taken away as they didn't want people sitting outside the prime minister's room. They had to stand in the corridor outside. It was little things like that.'

The arena for these power plays was usually May's Downing Street office, where the senior staff met every morning at 8.30. In addition to Hill, Timothy and Jojo Penn, the meetings would be attended by chief whip Gavin Williamson, George Hollingbery, May's parliamentary bag carrier, her principal private secretary Simon Case, the cabinet secretary Jeremy Heywood and Cabinet Office minister Ben Gummer. Perrior would take them through the morning media while other directors like Chris Wilkins, Chris Brannigan and John Godfrey watched, along with a revolving cast from the political section, including Alex Dawson and Stephen Parkinson.

To many, Hill, not the prime minister, was the dominant presence in the room. 'Those morning meetings were probably the best opportunities where you would get some reveal of who the PM was or what she was thinking,' one official said. 'But her contributions were never decisive.' By contrast, Hill played 'mind games'. 'When you've got power in that way, Fiona used it to control people, to remind people she's a top dog,' a colleague said. 'She would regularly say that other people were shit.' Perversely, the chiefs sometimes demonstrated their power by not turning up at all and going out for breakfasts with businessmen or journalists. On other occasions one of them would ostentatiously munch on a bacon sandwich while others spoke. Another aide said, 'I wouldn't bring my bacon sandwich into the PM's morning meeting and think it was perfectly acceptable to chomp away when everyone else was on their best behaviour.'

In a piece for *The Times* after she left Downing Street, Perrior described the chiefs as 'great street fighters but poor political leaders'. She wrote, 'Great leaders lead by bringing people with them, not alienating them before having even digested breakfast. The chiefs treated cabinet members exactly the same – rude, abusive, childish behaviour. For two people who have never achieved elected office, I was staggered at the disrespect they showed on a daily basis. I felt sorry for them and how they measured success by how many enemies they had clocked up.'[1]

This approach angered and frightened ministers, who saw that years of careful career-building could come to a juddering halt at the whim of the chiefs. 'Nick clearly believed in his own publicity about being the latter-day Rasputin,' a cabinet source said. A Number 10 official added, 'Nick was rude to officials and civil servants, to show that he doesn't give a fuck. He did it to show he was the big boy.' Ministers say Hill was very quick to fire off text messages when they had done something of which she disapproved. 'Cabinet ministers were treated appallingly,' a Downing Street source said. 'It was like a domestic violence relationship. Even when Number 10 said they could do interviews they didn't want to because they would get a bollocking the next day. They got slapped time and time again and every now and then they called the police, which Boris did a couple of times.' Hill's allies say she regularly took cabinet ministers to dinner to show them 'her door was always open'.

Political aides were not so lucky, often facing reprimands on email. 'She would never say, "I don't really like the sound of that, why don't we do this …"' said another of May's aides. 'It always came back to, "This is shit, where the fuck did you think this up?" It would come at a distance in an email – she'd never say it face to face.' This pressure from Number 10 drove some special advisers into a state of anxiety. 'There were spads who wouldn't answer the phone if they thought it was Number 10 calling,' a Downing Street official said. 'One had to have an almost daily trip to see their psychiatrist and another one displayed all of the signs of self-harm. We are talking about totally fucking up people's actual lives.'

Civil servants were not spared either. They were 'shitting themselves all the time', a Downing Street official said. 'They were in mourning for the Cameron years. There was a decency about his team.' In email correspondence with Cabinet Office, officials claimed Hill attacked those peddling 'bad news'. One said, 'You'd get messages like, "It is a fucking catastrophe that you work for the civil service" and "How the fuck do you work here?"' Hill flatly denied swearing in emails. Few officials wanted to work in the prime minister's private office since they would be sharing an office with the chiefs. 'Civil servants hated it,' a Downing Street official said. 'They had to listen to opinions like, "So and so is a fucking idiot."'

Timothy could also be brusque to the point of rudeness. A Tory donor who sat as a non-executive director on one of the Whitehall departmental boards emailed him about recruiting a senior civil servant, saying, 'Tell me what you're looking for and I'll make sure we get the right sort of person.' Timothy ignored several messages and then replied, 'Please do not email me on this address again.'

10 Downing Street is a small house, not a modern office space. Word of Hill's outbursts spread quickly around the building, damaged morale and contributed to a bunker mentality. 'The physical layout of the house has parallels with a medieval court,' according to one official who worked for May in both the Home Office and Number 10. 'We'd gone from an open-plan modern PFI-built department to a charming Georgian townhouse with Nick and Fi next to the PM and everyone else dotted around. The Home Office was a lot more collaborative. That changed.'

The sense of a medieval court was reinforced by a view that all staff were either 'Nick people or Fiona people'. Hill cultivated loyalty from those, like Tom Swarbrick, whom she had appointed, and was sometimes contemptuous of those Timothy had brought in. When Chris Brannigan, a Timothy appointment, encountered Hill for the first time he was met with a look that radiated hostility. Brannigan asked Hill, 'Is there anything you want to know about me?' Hill studied him carefully and then said, 'No, Nick is a good judge of character. If Nick says you are all right then you are all right.' From that point on, though, Brannigan was to complain to colleagues, Hill obstructed much of what he was doing.

Both Hill and Timothy sought to run the key departments using proxies. Timothy installed John Godfrey as director of the policy unit but used Godfrey's deputy Will Tanner, who Timothy had talent-spotted years before, to drive the work of the unit. 'Nick owned the policy unit in the same way Fiona was trying to run the comms department,' a source said. 'You watched this contagion take hold. Fi liked to work round the building, not by having an engagement with the directors, but by having a relationship with someone else within the team.' Hill recruited Lizzie Loudon, Iain Duncan Smith's former special adviser, as

ABOVE: Fiona Hill and Nick Timothy were like siblings together but their casual assumption of huge power left others in fear.

BELOW LEFT: Hill, one of May's two chiefs of staff, had a gut instinct for politics and was right about election strategy, but her behaviour in Downing Street alienated her subordinates.

CENTRE: Timothy, the other 'chief', was known as 'Theresa's brain' and helped her to a twenty-point lead in the polls, but wrote the manifesto that sunk her majority.

RIGHT: Katie Perrior, May's director of communications, had dreamed of working in Number 10 since she was a girl, but left after clashing with Hill.

ABOVE: Theresa May in her £995 leather trousers next to the 'f***ing hydrangeas' demanded for the photoshoot by Fiona Hill.

LEFT: May becomes the first foreign leader to visit Donald Trump at the White House. The president, who has a phobia about slopes and stairs, grabbed her hand for balance.

ABOVE: 29 March 2017. Theresa May signs the Article 50 declaration kickstarting two years of Brexit talks. Aides argued about whether she should use a black or blue pen.

RIGHT: May received EU Commission president Jean-Claude Juncker in Downing Street in April 2017. Details of their dinner soon leaked.

BELOW: 'Spreadsheet' Philip Hammond, May's chancellor, botched his budget and fought a rearguard action for a 'soft Brexit'.

TOP: Theresa May with Oliver Robbins, her Brexit 'sherpa' whose second job running DExEU confused officials.

ABOVE: Martin Selmayr, Jean-Claude Juncker's chief of staff. The 'Rasputin of Brussels' was accused of leaking details of his dinners with May.

RIGHT: David Davis and Michel Barnier. DD and the Commission's negotiator engaged in five rounds of largely fruitless talks in the summer of 2017 before May's Florence speech on 22 September.

LEFT: Nicky Morgan and Anna Soubry, former ministers under David Cameron, became May's most outspoken critics on Brexit.

RIGHT: Ivan Rogers, Britain's permanent representative in Brussels, warned May to delay triggering Article 50, but was ignored and resigned in January 2017.

BELOW: Gina Miller won her case at the High Court and Supreme Court to give Parliament a say, but she was branded a 'Remoaner' and received death threats.

ABOVE: Jim Messina, Lynton Crosby and Mark Textor were hired at the last minute to run the Conservative campaign, but they clashed with the chiefs and got little access to May.

BOTTOM LEFT: Patrick Heneghan ran five election campaigns for Labour, but Corbyn's team felt his choice of target seats was too defensive.

CENTRE: Tory veteran Stephen Gilbert was titular campaign director but often deferred to Crosby.

RIGHT: James Kanagasooriam, Populus's head of analytics, was the data wizard behind Ruth Davidson's success in Scotland.

ABOVE: Jeremy Corbyn with his gatekeeper, Karie Murphy. She bought a new outfit, believing he would become prime minister.

BELOW: Corbyn's chief adviser Seumas Milne encouraged him to make a controversial speech about the causes of terrorism.

**Daily Mail**

JUNE 8TH

WEDNESDAY, APRIL 19, 2017   www.dailymail.co.uk   NEWSPAPER OF THE YEAR   65p

In a stunning move, Mrs May calls bluff of the 'game-playing' Remoaners (including 'unelected' Lords) with a snap election and vows to . . .

CRUSH THE SABOTEURS

REPORTS AND ANALYSIS: PAGES 4–19

Theresa May said she had called the election because of opposition to Brexit. Not all her allies felt the *Daily Mail*'s treatment of the story was helpful to her.

press secretary. But when Loudon realised she was being told things by Hill of which Perrior remained ignorant she felt uncomfortable and passed the information to Perrior. Her relationship with Hill cooled.

When Loudon began a relationship with Will Tanner she was frozen out altogether. Tanner had previously been dating Jojo Penn, Hill's protégée and holiday companion, who had once spent a meeting practising her future signature: 'Jojo Tanner'. This bed hopping was par for the course. On one foreign trip a senior Number 10 aide got carried away on the plane with a more junior official in full view of the prime minister. A colleague observed, 'Downing Street was literally a shag fest, with people drunk on power and living on the edge.'

To some Downing Street staff Penn, the deputy chief of staff, was like a caring sister. But to those Hill did not like, Penn mimicked the same aggressive behaviour. She became known as 'Mini Me' after Dr Evil's sidekick in the *Austin Powers* films. 'Jojo went around the building acting like an arsehole to be like them,' a colleague recalled. 'She worked directly from Fiona's playbook.'

At the 2016 Downing Street staff Christmas party, in the pillared room upstairs, the sense of a medieval court was apparent to many. 'Nick was sitting on a sofa, and there were these adoring acolytes all around him,' one official recalled. A senior figure went over to Timothy, placed a hand on his knee and said, 'I didn't realise I had to come and pay homage to the master.' Timothy glared. 'If you lose a sense of humour in this business you are in trouble,' the official said. The Christmas card list was another opportunity for a Hill power-play. Fewer than usual were signed by the prime minister herself. 'The Christmas cards were signed by the autopen, but that was because Fi had struck off the names of people she didn't like,' a Number 10 source said.

The desire to control everything was not just damaging to the atmosphere in Downing Street, but also to Hill's own effectiveness. 'People admire her and say, "She's so feisty, she's so up for it," but it's not very productive,' a senior Downing Street official said. 'Fiona's in-tray was overflowing. If you're so powerful, run the fucking country, don't spend 70 per cent of your day on massive rows with people.'

Within a few weeks of May's arrival in Number 10, there was a steady drumbeat of complaint across Whitehall that decisions were stalled. Only the chiefs were allowed to make them. Another director in Number

10 said he submitted six papers to May that 'never reappeared'. He did not know whether the prime minister ever saw them. Traditionally, ministers could have papers added for the prime minister's evening and weekend red box. The chiefs demanded that they clear everything first, a demand that gummed up decision-making. A cabinet minister said, 'It was a closed shop, unless you were the three people that made all the key decisions. You couldn't get anything in the PM's box, unless Nick or Fi agreed. You never knew if Theresa had seen it. It was very different to the Cameron period. We went from sofa government with ten people to an armchair with two people in it. Your access to the PM was completely shut off. They didn't trust anyone. It was an environment where loyalty came before talent.'

Ministers never knew if May had made decisions or whether the chiefs had done so on her behalf. The chiefs even appeared to overrule May. On one occasion May told a cabinet minister he could publish a document. Then, an official recalled, 'We got a call from her private secretary, who had obviously gone through Nick and Fi, saying what she actually meant to say was, "This is never going to happen." There was always the question of who was pulling the strings.' A cabinet minister added, 'Whenever Fi told you something, it was always "*We* have decided this, *we* think this," it was never the PM. Fi actually thought she was the PM. Nick thought he was the PM. It was an unhealthy relationship.' Months later, Timothy admitted, 'We probably didn't communicate as well as we could have done, directly with the public and the media, and probably to a certain extent around Whitehall.'[2]

Part of Hill's objection to Perrior was that she had wanted to return the role of communications director to the civil service, where it had been when Sir Bernard Ingham was spinning for Margaret Thatcher. Joey Jones, the former deputy political editor of Sky News who had become May's press secretary at the Home Office, got texts from Hill offering him the job, but when he suggested that Lizzie Loudon would deal with the lobby while he talked to editors and columnists, Hill shot back, 'Nick and I will deal with editors.'

Perrior might have initially seemed less threatening. When she helped out during the leadership election she worked just a few hours a day, while continuing with her business. Another campaign staffer said, 'This is a fairly appalling thing to say but I thought she was just a mum that we knew who could help out a bit, sending out press releases. She didn't seem like a particularly powerful figure or someone who was going to rock the boat. She was just going to do what Fi said. That was Fi's experience of working with her. Fi didn't know her.'

Understandably, having decided to abandon her business for Number 10, Perrior wanted to do the job properly, but she immediately fell out with Hill. 'Fundamentally, there was a personality clash and it was never going to work,' said one insider who remained on good terms with both women. 'Katie took the view that as director of comms she'd do some interesting strategic stuff for the PM. Fi's view was very much that the director of comms job is solely to look after the lobby.' Perrior claimed Hill made it difficult for her to do even that. A junior official would call, shaking at the end of the line, to tell her that her meetings with the PM had been pulled. Perrior's computer settings were changed so she could no longer see the prime minister's diary. But the chiefs had forgotten to remove the access of her PA. Perrior would spot a gap in the schedule and just turn up to talk to May as her predecessors Alastair Campbell and Craig Oliver often did. 'We don't do that here,' she was told.

When Helen Bower, the prime minister's official spokeswoman, was seen having a drink with Tom Newton-Dunn, the political editor of the *Sun*, Simon Case, May's principal private secretary, questioned her. Since Newton-Dunn was the chairman of the lobby, the Westminster journalists' point man with Downing Street, the meeting was entirely appropriate. When Ed Balls, the former shadow chancellor, left *Strictly Come Dancing* after a run of flamboyant performances, Robin Gordon-Farleigh, a civil servant who worked on the grid, tweeted, 'Alas it's over. Well done Ed Balls for getting this far & entertaining us.' Nick Timothy spoke to Simon Case and told him to remind Gordon-Farleigh – who had worked for Gordon Brown – about the need for civil service neutrality. 'Be careful, they're watching everything you do,' he was told. Timothy told colleagues Gordon-Farleigh's real crime had been to be spotted with a group of lobby journalists a few days earlier.[3] Gordon-Farleigh left Downing Street shortly afterwards.

Hill and Timothy kept a tight control over the prime minister's activities. 'We had these excruciating weekly spad meetings,' a special adviser recalled. 'No one knew what the fuck was going on. Katie would be chairing them without knowing what was in the grid, running through the week and asking everybody what was going on. She would have no idea what the PM was doing because Nick and Fi hadn't decided whether they were going to tell her.'

Ministers were told not to commit news. One special adviser with a garrulous minister was told by Hill, 'Don't say anything, I don't want a story.' He recalled, 'You'd send him into TV interviews, with the aim of not creating any news. It was totally bonkers. Every interview your heart was in your mouth because of the Number 10 attitude.' This approach drove ministers mad. Many of them had a legal requirement to release information at certain times, only to find that their announcement had been pulled. 'Fiona pulled everything out of the grid all the time and then told Katie that it was a shit grid,' one Downing Street official said. One day, Hill would say, 'We don't feed the beast Katie, we do not feed the beast, when are you going to learn? That's how we survived in the Home Office, that's how she's always done it. We do not feed the beast.' Then, two weeks later, she would be enraged because there was nothing to brief to the journalists. 'There's nothing in this fucking grid!'

In reality, the entire news-planning process was subject to Hill's whims. 'It didn't work because Fi would change her mind all the time,' a senior official said. 'Either she'd ask why the hell we're doing something when she had approved it a week earlier, or suddenly she'd have a brain-wave about something she wanted to do now. Katie is right about that. That was pretty dysfunctional unfortunately.'

For many people who worked under her in Downing Street, Fiona Hill's mood swings defined their working day. 'Fi can be a difficult character,' said one colleague who had worked with her for several years. 'She can be totally lovely and charming and then she can be capricious. That's the reason why lots of people don't really like her, because they don't see her as consistent. I think that she's at heart a nice person but she lashes out. She was one of the reasons that Number 10 was not that nice a place.'

Hill's abrupt changes of mind and mood did not just affect the communications department. An official working in another corner of Number 10 said, 'Nick could be grumpy but it was Fi balling people out that would upset most because she's very volatile. She'll turn on a sixpence and she'll shout at you for doing something and then shout at you twenty minutes later for the exact opposite. People who hadn't worked with her before found that very difficult.' Hill's allies say this was evidence she was 'nimble' when events changed the game. But an MP who was fond of Hill said, 'I love Fi, but my advice to people was, "Don't put your head in the tiger's mouth," because you never knew when it would snap shut.'

This was not just uncomfortable, it hindered good policy-making. 'Most of us in the next rank down didn't float an idea because you were shouted down, so we just kept our heads down,' a middle-ranking Number 10 aide said. 'That was my strategy.' A departmental head in Downing Street said, 'Even when you thought you had landed something you never knew how long it was going to last.' May might approve something in a meeting, and then 'Fi would undo that when you weren't there. She would lose the paper, give Theresa contradictory advice or come up with some other plan that was half-baked. You were always running up against the brick wall Fi put up all the time.'

Chris Brannigan was repeatedly thwarted when he tried to organise events for business leaders to meet the prime minister. Hill's dithering over the guest list meant that some guests for the first dinner, in September 2016, were only invited the day before. 'Fi would always insist on attending these dinners and then never turn up,' an aide said. Hill's allies point out that the dinners were her idea and she was often too busy to attend. After the government had to placate Nissan, Brannigan tried to get a slot in the prime minister's diary so May could see other Japanese business leaders investing in the UK. When he left Downing Street in June 2017, eight months later, the meeting had still not taken place. Hill did not rate Brannigan, and did a lot of breakfasts and lunches with business people herself. 'Chris is a nice guy,' said a close ally of the chiefs, 'but there aren't many City people or business folk who I've met who thought he was a good interlocutor.'

For her colleagues, Hill's regular wining and dining made it even more difficult to get a decision from her. One said, 'We dealt with less and less activity in the house in the mornings, because she was out wining and dining. Then there were afternoon absences.' On a trip to the Far East Perrior stopped Hill joining a group of political journalists at the back of the plane 'dressed head to toe in flannelette pyjamas and two bottles of red wine down. In hindsight, I should have bloody well let her go.'[4] A senior official said, 'More often than not when I went down to their office at 7 p.m. – there must have been a dozen or more times where I went to check things with Nick and Fi – they had always gone to the pub.'

* * *

Perrior and Brannigan both used visits, at home and abroad, as a means
of getting alongside the prime minister without the chiefs controlling
their access. If Perrior could see from May's electronic diary that she was
out of town, she would jump in the back of the prime minister's Jaguar
herself. 'It's interesting to see you on this trip,' May would say, smiling
slightly.

'Yeah, only time I get you to myself. I've got a list. Can we start from
the top?'

Foreign visits provided even more face time, and Hill used access to
the trips as another means of control. When May returned from a trip to
New York, where Brannigan had made productive contacts with the
business community, Hill said to him, 'How did you get on the trip? I
can't see how we justified it.' When May flew to India to talk trade, Hill
announced that Brannigan and his team could only have one seat on the
aircraft. He had been planning to take Jimmy McLoughlin – son of the
party chairman – and an official called Chris Hopkins with him.
Brannigan complained to Timothy, 'There are hundreds of millions of
pounds in trade going here, and we're pissing about over ego.' In the end
he was allowed to take Hopkins but McLoughlin had to stay behind. On
May's trip to the Gulf Cooperation Council, there were no seats on the
plane for the government relations team. Hopkins eventually went
because Xavier Rolet, the boss of the London Stock Exchange Group,
which was doing a deal, paid for him to travel on a commercial aircraft.
Hill says she assigned seats on the basis of who was 'necessary' on each
trip.

One of the most memorable images of May's first year in office was a
picture of her arriving at the White House in January 2017 with a team
of female aides: Fiona Hill, Jojo Penn, Katie Perrior and Lizzie Loudon.
There was a striking omission: the official civil service spokeswoman she
had inherited from David Cameron – Helen Bower. Bower was highly
respected by Westminster journalists, but regarded with suspicion by the
chiefs, who said she should not expect to enjoy the same relationship
with May that she had with Cameron, who consulted her on policy as
well as communications. Bower's other black mark was that she had been
given a CBE in Cameron's resignation honours list. That made her a
'Cameron crony' in the eyes of the chiefs.

In a grid meeting before the G20 summit in China, Hill criticised the
spokeswoman in front of her whole team and questioned why the lobby

would want to hear from her at all. On the trip, Perrior and Bower angered Hill by preparing May for a tough press conference with a searching prep session. Hill was fond of telling Perrior, 'She was home secretary for seven years, she doesn't need to prepare.' But Perrior sensed the travelling lobby were preparing to cause trouble on Brexit at the end of summit press conference. 'We need to go in for the kill,' Perrior told Loudon and Bower. They began hurling aggressive questions at May, asking her to have another go when her answers were poor. The session lasted thirty minutes and Hill sat at the back, just staring at Perrior, her face like thunder.

When it came to the press conference, May gave what the three women in the comms team believed was her best ever performance. In the corridor outside, Perrior and Bower exchanged high fives. Allies of Perrior say Hill pulled her aside in front of the others and said, 'Don't you ever fucking talk to the prime minister like that again.' Hill does not 'recognise' this exchange. Later, May thanked her team and said how calm she had felt because she was well prepared.

On another foreign trip, a junior official asked the prime minister to spare five minutes to flick through a portfolio of pictures compiled by her official photographer, who was at the end of a six-month secondment from the Ministry of Defence. Hill said, 'That's not appropriate. No.' May said, 'I'd happily do that,' but the chief of staff persisted: 'I just don't think it's appropriate. We can do it back in the office,' and told the PM that she should get some sleep instead. 'It really doesn't matter, Fiona,' May said. 'I'm happy to do that.' What should have been a nice moment was rendered momentarily awkward, but May flicked happily through the pictures, commenting enthusiastically on them. Afterwards Hill sought out the official and said, 'Don't you ever approach the prime minister like that again.'

After the G20 summit, Bower was invited in for a private chat with the prime minister, a gesture which only emphasised how differently this leader operated. After seeing Cameron three or four times daily, the person expected to speak for the prime minister in lobby briefings twice a day could go an entire week without seeing her. It was an astonishing indication of how little May concerned herself with the media.

Hill wanted Bower out, and when her name appeared in media reports about the women going to Washington, the chief of staff took umbrage. She waited until Bower had moved her honours investiture at

Buckingham Palace to accommodate the trip before announcing, twenty-four hours before take-off, that there was 'no need' for her to go at all because 'we had an enormous team'. Ludicrously, Bower was told to tell journalists she 'had a bad cough'. She refused.

In Downing Street, May seldom visited the rest of the house to drop in on staff, to thank them for their efforts or boost morale. 'She is lacking emotional intelligence,' one aide said. At Christmas, Perrior suggested that May visit the press team for mince pies and prosecco. Her request was declined. The prime minister was too busy, the chiefs said. Eventually Perrior was offered a date in May.

Perrior took it upon herself to pass on praise, telling those who had done well, 'The prime minister asked me to personally thank you for the work you did yesterday.' When the Colombian president paid a state visit, Perrior gave up her seat at a lunch to Jessica Seldon, a press officer and the daughter of historian Anthony Seldon, since she had done much of the hard work for the event. May readily agreed, and Perrior told Seldon it was the prime minister's idea, handing her a signed copy of May's speech.

On another occasion, Perrior saw a press officer with a nice pen. 'David Cameron gave this to me on a trip,' the young woman said. 'He signed an accord and on the way back he said all that hard work was down to me and he gave me the pen. I carry it everywhere I go. It really means a lot to me.' When Perrior suggested to Hill, 'We should do much more of this,' the chief replied, 'Who the fuck gets off on a fucking pen?' Another Number 10 official said, 'Fiona and Nick thought the officials were their slaves.'

If this paints a bleak picture of May's Downing Street, things were different for those who had worked for her at the Home Office. Another Number 10 aide said, 'She's not a warm person but she's unbelievably kind and loyal. Every year that I worked for her, I got a Christmas card and a present from Theresa. It was usually thoughtful – a book or a nice bottle of wine, usually related to a conversation we'd had. She took time and effort.' To many of her colleagues, Hill seemed to want, if anything, to suppress these instincts.

When Perrior warned Timothy she might walk away in November 2016, it had an immediate effect. An hour later she was stopped in the corridor by Hill, who said, 'We can work out a plan. I'm sorry that you felt this way. It's all been rushed, getting in here, doing conference. The prime minister has said to me we need to do everything we can to sort this out.' This surprised Perrior, since she had made a point of not burdening May with her concerns. 'How does the prime minister know that I want to leave?' she asked. 'I never spoke to her about this. Indeed, she shouldn't know anything about it. She's running the country.'

That evening, a senior mandarin rang Perrior and said the chiefs had been told in front of witnesses, 'Do whatever it takes to make Katie stick around.' The civil servant made sure she understood what this meant. 'You have power the rest of us don't have. You should use it and spend it wisely and ask for some things that will benefit us all.' The image of a senior official encouraging a political appointee to neuter the chiefs is a striking one.

Perrior made her demands. She had been knocked off the distribution list for the prime minister's 'box notes', the papers going into May's red box. She confronted Jojo Penn and said, 'Does the prime minister trust me? I'm going to go in there now and ask that, because for some reason I'm not trusted enough to get box notes this week.' Half an hour later an email from Hill to the private secretaries instructed, 'It is imperative that Katie gets all the box notes, sort it out.' Perrior also urged the chiefs to take a more collaborative approach and hold a weekly Monday meeting after the 8.30 at which the senior staff could all talk about what they were working on, to encourage joined-up thinking. 'There's no sense of team in this place,' she told Timothy.

For two weeks the resignation threat seemed to work. The chiefs even started passing on details of their conversations with newspaper editors, outlining the stories they were interested in. At the end of the morning meeting, when Perrior would usually leave the room, she was encouraged to stay. The after meetings concerned political issues, like the chief whip reporting on an MP caught with his trousers down – issues a director of communications should know about to prepare a damage-limitation plan.

After a fortnight, Perrior was removed from the box notes distribution list again and the chiefs retreated to secrecy mode. The new Monday meeting was a disaster. After three of them, Perrior announced, 'I'm not coming any more.' The meeting had turned into an occasion for the chiefs to interrogate each of the directors. 'It was just an opportunity to scream and shout at people in the Cabinet Room,' one of those invited said.

The breakdown in trust was dramatised when Theresa May had her second telephone conversation with Donald Trump on 29 November 2016. Perrior took a call from the Huffington Post journalist Paul Waugh asking for more details. It was the first that she had heard of it. 'I'm in a meeting, I'll call you back,' she improvised. No one in the press office knew what was happening, because the chiefs had not wanted them to know. Perrior confronted Hill and said, 'If you want to be the comms director, do it.'

Hill replied, 'Read my lips. I don't want to do comms.'

Perrior became so frustrated that she briefly considered flushing Hill's head down the loo. Later she was to discover that Hill had made an oblique approach to Francis Elliott, the political editor of *The Times*, which could have led to him replacing her. Elliott consulted his old friend James Chapman, who told him, 'Don't touch it with a bargepole.'

By February, Perrior had had enough. In conversations with her friend Jo Tanner, she contemplated buying a dog and naming it 'NiFi' after the chiefs, 'so I could call it to heel'. But she knew in her heart that her days were numbered.

Perrior had another catch-up with Timothy. As she left her office, she turned to her PA and said, 'I might get fired. When I come back, if I give you a look, start getting boxes.'

It was a Friday. They drank tea in May's office, since the prime minister was in her constituency. This time Hill was there as well. Perrior said, 'I'd like to know what you want me to focus on. I've still got some of the problems that I had in November. They went away a bit, then they came back and I'm deeply unhappy. I'm desperate to make this work, this is the job I've wanted all my life.'

Three months earlier, Timothy had been concerned. Now he looked uninterested. He did not think the situation was sustainable. Hill went on the attack, telling Perrior that she was not up to the job. 'What's your fucking problem? You don't have any gravitas, any authority. We thought we were hiring somebody who had a bit of balls. We've seen nothing of that.' Her voice rising to a volume that was clearly audible in the private office, where Simon Case was working, Hill complained, 'You continually undermine me. Journalists who I've been friends with for fifteen years tell me what you're up to. You're just embarrassing yourself and me while you're at it.'

Perrior was furious. She spent most of her time denying rumours that she was threatening to quit. 'If we can't work together, don't be surprised when stories appear about splits. I am doing my best to cover up all this shit, but I can't do it on my own.' Perrior complained that Hill had a meeting with Robert Peston, the political editor of *ITV News*.

'You're telling me I can't speak to journalists!' Hill screamed. 'Nick has meetings with journalists all the time and you don't complain about that.'

'What I can't stand is the backstabbing going on,' said Perrior. 'We're meant to be on the same side. It's not just me – you can't work with Helen, you can't work with Lizzie, you can't work with anyone. In fact, if you're a woman, you're fucking done for!'

Back and forth they went. 'This is totally your fault, Katie,' Hill went on. 'This is your attitude towards work. Your news management is poor.'

'You keep taking stuff out of the grid. And then you have a go at me in front of all my colleagues about the grid being empty. It wasn't empty before you got your hands on it.'

At that Hill 'went nuts' and left the room. Perrior sat still and, to her eternal shame, felt a solitary tear slide down her cheek. She wiped it away. She challenged Timothy, 'I don't deserve this and you know it. You don't do anything about it.'

They talked for a while. Timothy explained, 'I've given up trying to broker between you two. I can't make it work.' He suggested that Perrior focus her efforts on influencing five key opinion columnists. 'Just do that. And drive stories out of the departments, because they're all lazy. And we'll see you in a month or two. Thanks very much.'

Just as they were finishing, Hill came bounding back into the room. Ignoring Perrior, she told Timothy, 'I can't believe it, I'm so excited I might cry.' To Perrior she resembled an eight-year-old child about to wet herself. Timothy looked uncomfortable at Hill's dramatic change of mood. 'I just found out. Rod Stewart said yes to coming to Downing Street,' continued Hill. 'I can't wait to call my mum. Oh my God!' In fact, Hill – a massive Rod Stewart fan – had misread the email. Stewart had not accepted the invitation.

Perrior picked up her stuff and walked out. She vowed to stay until July, so she would have done a year, and then to look for chances to leave by Christmas. If there was a general election, she could walk away quicker than that. 'I didn't really want to be there, but I didn't have the guts to leave,' she said.

Perrior was already being marginalised. Helen Bower had left to become director of communications at the Foreign Office. May's new official spokesman was James Slack, the former political editor of the *Daily Mail*, who had been Hill's favourite journalist for years. 'They had Slacky in mind all the time,' an official said. In the 8.30 a.m. meeting it was now Slack, not Perrior, who did the media summary. 'Nick and Fi tried in that meeting to give her steers about how to do the job,' a senior source said. 'She didn't want to accept that she wasn't doing the job very well.'

There are two sides to every story, of course. Many of Perrior's complaints about the chiefs were shared by colleagues, but it is only fair to put their side of things too. When Slack, who had seen the operation from the other side as a journalist, arrived in Number 10, Hill professed shock on learning that Perrior did not answer the phone to some lobby correspondents. She also expressed surprise that Perrior told journalists the chiefs had blocked interview requests which she herself had rejected. 'Katie used Fiona's name to get herself out of doing things,' a source said. 'Nick didn't have any faith in her ability to come up with a media strategy. We never, ever saw one.' The chiefs were suspicious that Perrior too readily shared her disenchantment with ministers. One colleague who was no friend of Hill said, 'Katie would say, "I know you're frustrated, I'm frustrated every day." She did that a little too much. She did it to Boris. She did it to journalists. You have to keep the front up.'

Timothy told a friend, 'I don't know how she filled her days, to be frank.' Perrior's penchant for downplaying her own intelligence did not impress him either. Officials say she would complain that some policy was too complicated, telling the chiefs, 'How am I supposed to explain it to voters if I don't understand it myself?' Timothy remarked to a friend, 'That's exactly what her job was – to understand it and work out how to sell it.' Hill was so concerned about the media operation that she hired a former Number 10 spokesman to conduct a review of Downing Street communications. Colleagues think the review would have been used to force Perrior out, but it had not been completed by the time she left government.

A Downing Street official summarised the chiefs' view like this: 'She was stupid, out of her depth and incompetent, and now she's lashing out to cover those things up. Her media slots at the 8.30 morning meeting were excruciating, with everybody present exchanging embarrassed looks. She was unable to articulate what stories were. She never gave a political account of why things were being written or reported. She misunderstood policy. She turned up on days when the main story in town was Scotland without any idea of what was in the Scottish press.'

Yet witness after witness said Hill was out of control. Many who worked under her thought it astonishing that the senior mandarins Jeremy Heywood, Sue Gray and Simon Case allowed what some described as her 'reign of terror' to continue unchecked. 'Heywood is a complete snake,' one special adviser said. 'He was asleep on the job. His priority was keeping his own job.' A senior Downing Street official said, 'He signed a Faustian pact with Nick and Fi. He is our modern version of Thomas Cromwell: there to sell his soul for whatever his preferment may be. He either didn't know about it, in which case he is incompetent, or he did know about it, in which case he is a coward and does not deserve that position.' A former senior mandarin who knows Heywood well said, 'Jeremy is a great survivor. I think he's more courageous on policy issues than he was on people. They reached a point when the ranting became just circus noise. They got used to people putting up with it.'

Simon Case, May's principal private secretary, was no keener on the chiefs than the others in the private office. One Downing Street aide remembered, 'He realised it was all going to end in tears at some stage – it had to. He didn't want to be associated with it.' But career civil servants who had hoped Case would protect them found that he wanted to keep his head down and plot his own exit rather than help them. 'He looked after himself,' one said. 'He regularly took the line, "I have got to have a way to work with these guys and so you have to trust the way I am handling it." I felt he regularly threw a whole load of us under a bus. Jeremy was completely absent.' Case himself experienced the chiefs' Janus-faced approach to personnel relations as he lined up a new job as director general for the EU–UK partnership in Brussels, the point man on thrashing out a new partnership. 'He had a terrible time,' said a Number 10 official. 'The minute they found out he wanted to move on they completely changed tack, were really nice to him. That fucked the civil servants off even more. When he was having a shit time, they felt that he was on their side. The minute he was having a nice time, they felt betrayed.'

* * *

The bigger question concerns May's knowledge of Hill and Timothy's activities, and why she did so little to rein them in. They were hardly the first Downing Street advisers to behave in an aggressive fashion. The examples of Damian McBride and Alastair Campbell, the spin doctors to Gordon Brown and Tony Blair, loom large in the recent past. The difference with May was that many of the prime minister's other aides believe she was so in thrall to them that she could not have controlled them even if she wished to.

'What I could never work out was whether Mrs May condoned their behaviour and turned a blind eye or didn't understand how destructive they were,' Perrior wrote after she had left.[5] Another senior figure said, 'You come to this extraordinary paradox: our quite moral, sincere, pious PM let that happen. That upsets me.' A cabinet minister added, 'In any other leadership role, of a big company or a corporation, Nick and Fi would never have survived. You wouldn't have made profit in that company, because they were being such a negative force.'

Some Downing Street officials have claimed that May did not see the worst behaviour because the chiefs were careful not to swear in front of her. An incident early in their time in Number 10 explodes that myth. 'I was sitting in the PM's office and there was something that had come up about George Osborne,' one official recalled. 'Nick said, "This is probably the very place where Cameron and Osborne would josh each other about who was posher." He said they would say things like, "You're a posh cunt," and "No, you're a posher cunt." "Who is the poshest cunt of the lot?" This is a conversation between Nick and Fi, and I looked across at the prime minister, thinking, "Do you think this is all right?" There was not a glimmer. She heard blasphemies and obscenities that would make a trooper blush. It wouldn't have been out of place in the boiler room of a ship.'

Several sources interviewed for this book described May as a 'captive' or 'prisoner' of the chiefs. Early in 2017, Boris Johnson returned to the Foreign Office after a meeting with May in which the chiefs had been particularly assertive and made a reference to Hill's signature policy: 'That's modern slavery, right there.'[6] Others compared them to a dysfunctional family. One senior figure in Number 10 said, 'I feel disloyal saying this, but she was made to feel she couldn't do without them. She genuinely loves them. I think they're the children she didn't have. When you love your child, you ignore their flaws.' To several of

her colleagues, Hill spoke occasionally about having an unhappy childhood and some believe that made May want to protect her. 'Theresa
May is an only child and saw that Fiona was vulnerable and felt protective to her,' said a friend of Hill's. 'Fiona's protection of Theresa was
about her fear that the bullies would get to her if Nick and Fi didn't
protect her.' But others felt the set-up odd and childhood experiences
were no excuse for bad behaviour. 'Lots of us had difficult bits of our
childhood,' said one colleague.

Alasdair Palmer, who worked for May as a Home Office speechwriter,
was struck by how different she was from the duo she employed: 'She is
thoughtful and polite; they are breathtakingly rude. They are certain they
are right about everything; she is much more tentative and willing to
listen to other views. They fashioned her public image and created her
persona as a "difficult woman", partly just by being difficult themselves
… They were dominating, high-handed and contemptuous of everyone
who did not agree with them … The puzzle is why May made them so
central to her political operation.'[7]

Palmer concluded that the reasons were a lack of trust and a lack of
personal confidence on May's part. 'Timothy and Hill had two great
attributes as far as May was concerned: they seemed to have all the
answers on the issues about which she felt uncertain; and they made it
clear that they were utterly loyal to her. May often feels there are plots
and conspiracies against her. Her reluctance to place her trust in people
means that when she finds people she thinks deserve it – such as Timothy
and Hill – she places excessive confidence in them and is too willing to
allow them to substitute their judgement for her own.'[8] May, officials say,
seemed to need the chiefs' advice and also sometimes to resent that she
felt compelled to follow it. 'I've seen them properly say "no" to her, and
you can see an underlying anger in her.'

Perrior said that in her ten months in Number 10 she saw May stand
up to Hill 'only a handful of times'. She recounted how the prime minister would more usually 'sit there while Fiona would raise some batshit
crazy idea and not say a word'. The one time May admonished Hill
publicly came on the day of the Copeland by-election, when Stephen
Parkinson was explaining the ground operation during the 8.30 a.m.
meeting in May's office. From the back of the room, Hill heckled aggressively, 'Well, what are we doing there today? Where's the pizzazz? Why
the hell haven't you got Boris up there today? Get him up there now!'

Parkinson explained that it was a get-out-the-vote operation, which meant knocking on the doors of supporters, not diverting resources into an event that would be too late to swing votes. May intervened and said, 'Fiona, I'd like to know what the point of all this is. If Boris goes up there today, he will be in tomorrow's papers and that will be too late. Anyone who knows anything about campaigning knows that.' One of those present said, 'Fi looked a complete idiot. That was the one and only occasion.' Perrior 'wanted the floor to swallow me up'. She wrote, 'The prime minister had, for once, dared to raise her voice, a rare moment.'[9] Hill told friends later that she 'felt really bad' about the episode.

An incident in 2011 when May was home secretary, which nearly cost the chiefs their jobs in government, vividly illustrated that she knew about their worst behaviour and openly condoned it. The affair began in July of that year when May signed off a pilot scheme reducing the number of compulsory border checks in favour of more intelligence-led stops for those deemed high-risk. Brodie Clark, the head of the border force, had detailed conversations about it with Damian Green, the immigration minister. Border officials were told they could stop automatically checking the biometric chips on passports belonging to UK and EEA nationals. However, with weeks to go, Clark was warned by a senior Home Office official that May did not understand the reasons behind the scheme. 'You'd better make sure the home secretary knows what's going on,' the official said.

On a Eurostar train back from Lille to King's Cross-St Pancras following a tour of French border facilities, Clark took the opportunity to discuss the matter with May. A civil servant who was on the train and watched the episode unfold says their conversation 'started and finished in a matter of minutes'. May refused to have the discussion without Fiona Hill and Nick Timothy by her side. 'This wasn't a case of Theresa hinting she would not have the discussion without her advisers,' the source said. 'She explicitly said she would not discuss the policy without them there.' Clark was left to send a written explanation to the home secretary. Whether or not she ever read it herself remains unclear.

During the summer, as three-hour queues developed at immigration desks at Heathrow airport, Clark authorised immigration officials to abandon fingerprint verification in visas for non-EEA nationals as well, and to stop watch-list checks at Calais, to speed up the proceedings. He used rules in place from 2007 that gave border staff permission to relax the rules on grounds of health and safety. But when details of the lowering of security were revealed, May threw Clark to the wolves, pointing out that she had explicitly ruled out any suspension of fingerprint checks in the new pilot scheme. The allegation was that Clark had overreached. The 2007 rules did not permit the relaxation of fingerprint checks or a relaxation for non-EEA nationals. But Clark explained that he had been under ministerial pressure to cut waiting times, and had not compromised security. He believed ministers knew what had been happening.

The affair was a perilous time for May, who was accused of misleading Parliament. She went on the attack. Clark was first suspended and then quit, saying he planned to sue for constructive dismissal. In an appearance before the home affairs select committee he said he was 'no rogue officer'. He accused May of blaming him for 'political convenience'.

Leading the charge against Clark was the *Daily Mail*. On 16 November 2011, the paper's home affairs editor James Slack – Fiona Hill's favourite outlet – ran a story based on a leaked draft report of the disciplinary inquiry into Clark. It revealed that he had relaxed biometric checks on non-EEA nationals on 164 occasions. Slack claimed the document was proof that 'the civil service threw open the UK's borders'.

Gus O'Donnell, then the cabinet secretary, was furious about the leak, which he assumed had been provided to the *Mail* by Hill and Timothy, ordering an inquiry and a trawl of their emails. According to a senior figure in the government, 'They didn't find anything, but Gus didn't believe it, and he went into the servers and had their emails rebuilt. There were a whole load of emails to the *Daily Mail* saying, "Here's all the shit on Brodie Clark." In one of the emails it also said, "We've got to make sure we delete all this stuff properly."' The leaks were direct from Hill to Slack, someone she would employ six years later. 'Most of the leaking came from Fiona but there were emails that showed that Nick was well aware of it,' the source said. May was presented with evidence of her team's attempts to smear a public servant of forty years' standing, and she dug in to defend them. 'They were saved by Theresa May,' a senior government official said. 'Clark was just completely shit-bagged. People like Gus O'Donnell tried to raise the alarm bell but Theresa protected them.'

The affair had other sinister overtones. Members of Clark's team bought 'burner' phones from Boots the chemist so they could contact him incognito. 'They went through every one of his expenses claims for three years to see if they could find something there that they could add to the story,' said one friend of Clark. 'He is a man of integrity. They couldn't find anything.'

A senior source in the border force at that time said May allowed the smear campaign and attacked Clark in Parliament because she was fighting for her own career. 'She got into a position that she couldn't get out of,' the official said. 'There was no point when Brodie was called up and told to account for his actions. They went public immediately. They went straight for the big gun. The *Daily Mail* were getting selective parts of the report before Brodie was even interviewed.' Hill and Timothy's leaks effectively denied Clark due process and any right of reply. Both special advisers were summoned to Downing Street for 'a bollocking' by David Cameron. A senior government figure revealed, 'Jeremy Heywood wanted them fired. He felt a civil servant had been treated very badly. He felt there was a pattern of behaviour there that was already well established. Cameron gave them a final warning. By any standards Brodie Clark was pretty shabbily treated.' Clark's case for constructive dismissal was settled out of court in 2012 with no admission of wrongdoing on either side. The Home Office annual report showed he was paid £225,000. Clark had only asked for £135,000. A senior government official said, 'Fiona and Nick's behaviour contributed to the size of the payoff.'

The leak inquiry was covered up. Hill and Timothy's actions have not been revealed until now. Years on, Timothy did not seek to hide his role in the affair, expressing the view that 'Brodie Clark should be in jail.'

The Brodie Clark affair showed May that her two closest aides were prepared to go to any lengths to help her. Yet it would be wrong to suggest that their influence was only malign. Timothy was a fiercely intelligent strategist of rare gifts, who helped May develop a political philosophy which had contributed to her easing into a twenty-point lead in the polls. Hill was a loyal aide who was more at home with policy than most communications experts and who had an instinct for politics that cannot be taught. As a cabinet minister said of Hill, 'You can feel these whistling Siberian winds around you, but she has many considerable qualities. She has a brilliant political touch, she knows things instinctively in her stomach. Some of the burning injustices were from her and some of them were from Nick. She's particularly passionate about modern slavery and about domestic violence. She brought rigour to those subjects which would otherwise have got lost.'

The policy and personality conflicts they engaged in were hardly unknown under previous administrations. 'All of us do things that irritate and upset others,' a minister said. 'At the centre of any organisation like this, in the White House or the Elysée Palace, it's a court. It is a series of very, very close human interactions. Relationships are very immediate and emotional.' The problem was that both chiefs were driven to pursue goals with the absolutism of zealots. As one colleague put it, 'I think the problem with the two of them is that you have someone who is really ideologically driven in Nick and then someone who is really emotionally driven in Fi, and then the combination of the two of them is utter chaos.'

Many of Hill's faults could be attributed to caring too much, and many did not work out how to handle her, perhaps women most of all. 'She's a fragile person in lots of ways, and she has complete loyalty to Theresa, so she threw herself into it,' a senior figure in government said. 'But I definitely don't think she's a bad person at all. I think the opposite – I think once you learn how to manage her, and also to stand up to her, then that was fine.' Another colleague said, 'I think there is a danger that Fiona is painted as utterly one-dimensional.' With those they liked and trusted, both chiefs could be charming company. There was also more than a hint of sexism in some of the commentary about Hill. James Kirkup, who worked with her during her time as a journalist in Scotland, was right to challenge the media orthodoxy that 'Mr Timothy is the thoughtful chap who does the intellectual stuff for Mrs May. Ms Hill is a shouty, shallow woman who does shoes and emotion.'[10] If it was true that Timothy did more to develop Mayism, 'it was Fi that gave her confidence in that political judgement', a cabinet minister said. 'She'd test her political judgement against Fi's instincts.' A friend of Hill said, 'Fiona gave jobs to lots of people like Katie Perrior that they wouldn't otherwise have had and she got no thanks for it.'

Timothy also had his defenders. Lauren McEvatt, a former special adviser at the Wales Office, recalled how he rode to her rescue. 'This idea that Nick is some sort of villain is complete rubbish,' she said. 'He's not a bully at all. The mark of an honourable person, and a decent leader, is how you treat the least among you. When I worked for one of, if not the lowest-ranking department on the Whitehall totem pole, Nick never made me feel as though I was unworthy of making a contribution, in stark contrast to how some of our other colleagues treated lower-ranking spads. When I was at my very lowest professional ebb, after I had been on the receiving end of an unbelievably bruising cross-Whitehall past-ing, it was Nick who picked me up and put me back together again. He's a tremendously supportive mentor, and a kind and loyal friend.'

The stresses of high office cannot be overestimated. One MP who saw both the Cameron and the May regimes up close said, 'Number 10 can turn you into a lunatic. I remember some hapless civil servant bringing in a briefing and Steve Hilton tearing it into pieces and jumping up and down on it, screaming and shouting. Someone who's not worked in there cannot know how relentless it is. It never stops flowing at you. Shit rises. All the difficult decisions come up to the top. You see mind-boggling incompetence at every level. For the people that are a proxy for the PM, it is balls-achingly, grindingly exhausting.'

If both of the chiefs were guilty of overconfidence and hubris, they still had good reason to be satisfied by April 2017. They had helped May traverse treacherous waters without major political error. One long-standing colleague said, 'Their judgement was good and it provided the sustained poll lead for ten months.' Hill and Timothy's skills had put them in a position where it was now thinkable to call an election. Yet when they did so, the tensions in Tory world that had built up on their watch were to sabotage the project they had created.

PART THREE

NEMESIS

THE GENERAL ELECTION

February to June 2017

BOLT FROM THE BLUE

For Liam Fox, 18 April 2017 was just another quiet Tuesday morning. After cabinet he was due to chair a brief meeting with his fellow ministers in the Department for International Trade. The first item on the agenda: updating his colleagues on what Theresa May had to say that morning. The note circulated to ministers read, 'Light cabinet agenda. Probably not much to discuss.'

Fox was one of nearly twenty cabinet ministers who were jolted in their seats when the prime minister sat down at the famous coffin-shaped table and opened the meeting with the words, 'I think the time is right to go to the country.' One of those present said, 'There was some laughing around the table, but everyone knew the moment it left her mouth that we have to do this.' At 11.06 a.m. May emerged into Downing Street and dropped her bombshell on a stunned Westminster.

From the moment she took power, the prime minister had told the public she opposed a general election. When she ran for leader, she had promised MPs in marginal seats that she would not put them at risk for five years. Now, after an Easter walking holiday with her husband Philip, she had changed her mind. It was the biggest gamble of her career, though in truth it did not seem like it at the time. The Conservatives enjoyed a poll lead of more than twenty points over Labour, while May's personal ratings were further still ahead of Jeremy Corbyn's.

The driving force, as in so much else, was Nick Timothy. He had first quizzed May on her approach the previous summer. She told him, 'I don't want an election because the country needs stability and certainty.' Timothy's own instinct was to avoid closing down May's options, and in the months ahead he discussed with colleagues whether to press the case. Another senior figure in Number 10 said, 'It was talked about in hushed voices from time to time, from the very beginning. The boss was very against doing it. I think Nick, at points, was keen.' At the back of all their minds was the 'Gordon Brown parallel' – a new prime minister with no personal mandate who vacillated too long over calling an election in the autumn of 2007, and whose premiership never recovered. Timothy recognised that the lesson it was essential to learn from Brown was not to discuss their calculations in public.

When the Tories won the Copeland by-election on 23 February, seizing the Cumbrian seat which Labour had held uninterrupted since 1935, the stars seemed to be aligning. It was the first by-election gain by a governing party since 1982, and the largest increase in vote share since 1966. May's lead had held steady for seven months. 'It was pretty clear there was a solid vote out there,' said a Downing Street staffer involved in the discussions.

By then, May was also being lobbied hard to call an election by two of her most senior ministers, Philip Hammond and David Davis. 'It was a pincer move,' a ministerial aide recalled. The chancellor urged May to take the plunge as early as January, complaining that the 'fiscal straitjacket' left behind by the Cameron government, which banned him from raising income tax, National Insurance and VAT, had left him too little room for manoeuvre if Brexit led to a downturn – a view reinforced by the chaos of the budget. Hammond told her, 'You can't get tax changes through, you've got no flexibility, until we've got a bigger majority. You've killed Ukip, so why don't you do it?' A source close to May said, 'Her approach was, "No, I don't think so, I said there should be certainty." At that point she didn't see on balance why she should do it.'

Tory high command was preparing for an election, but not one in 2016. On 16 February, a week before the Copeland triumph, May's most senior aides met at her official country retreat, Chequers, to draw up a blueprint for victory in 2020. Timothy and Hill were joined by Chris Wilkins, the director of strategy, Jojo Penn, Alex Dawson, Stephen Parkinson and the campaign professionals led by Sir Lynton Crosby, the Australian who had masterminded David Cameron's surprise 2015 election victory, both of Boris Johnson's wins in the London mayoral elections of 2008 and 2012, and numerous other wins for centre-right candidates around the world. He was accompanied by Stephen Gilbert, a stalwart of

Conservative campaigns for two decades who was contracted to the party, and Crosby's business partner Mark Fullbrook, who had overseen Zac Goldsmith's failed bid for London mayor.

Over 'a rather odd chicken lasagne' served, bizarrely, with boiled potatoes, Wilkins outlined the plan he had been developing with Timothy to position the prime minister for victory. It was the first campaign-planning meeting May had ever sanctioned. The central argument of Wilkins' paper was that 'we must unapologetically and clearly present ourselves as the change candidate'. It said, 'The public, particularly that key electoral group – the Working Class Strugglers – are now looking for someone to deliver wider, comprehensive change to how our country works … We must prove that we can – to quote a favoured phrase – "change to conserve".' This was straight from Timothy's reading of Edmund Burke, the eighteenth-century political philosopher, whose 'great revelation was that if we value something, we must be prepared to reform it in order to keep it'.[1] Timothy said, 'The entire political strategy of Theresa's leadership campaign and of the government from July 2016 to April 2017 was based on the kind of insight that Theresa had about the country and about the referendum campaign, that yes it was a vote to leave the European Union but it was also a vote for serious change. The message we were conveying all the time was "We get the anger, we get the need to change, we're on the side of change."'[2]

The paper also gave research weight to May's submarine media strategy. Wilkins' paper said, 'The prime minister is more popular than the party with the public … but one of the very things people like about her approach is that it is businesslike, and that she is quietly getting on with the job, and not always in the public spotlight.' Wilkins recommended that the 'visibility' of the PM should be controlled. 'The very power of the PM's presence is that she is not always present – we must continue to emphasise and harness that strength,' he wrote.

The fieldwork for the paper was conducted by Populus Data Solutions (PDS), which immediately made Crosby suspicious. 'Oh, so Populus have done it,' he said. PDS is an offshoot of Populus, a polling firm run by Andrew Cooper, who Crosby had supplanted as David Cameron's pollster and whose data putting the Remain campaign ahead in the EU referendum had been blamed for Cameron's defeat and resignation. Wilkins explained that all the analysis had been done by his in-house team in Downing Street, but Crosby 'instantly dismissed the strategy that Chris had just outlined and then went into a whole presentation himself about how they'd won 2015', one of those present said.

Crosby said later that Wilkins' presentation was 'classic populist woolly bullshit'.[3] On the day he said, 'Prime ministers can never be the change candidate. It's not about being the change, it's about doing what people want.' One source said, 'He dismissed it. There was no angriness but it was clear at that meeting that there was a difference in strategies.' When the snap election was called, that difference of opinion hardened into a rift. Crosby also presented a 'values study' he had conducted for the 2015 election, identifying how different groups of voters thought and the values and emotions that drove them. The party commissioned him to do another study to inform their thinking about 2020.

Wilkins' paper contained a 'segmentation analysis', dividing voters into five groups. It suggested that May was in a strong position with 'Traditional Conservatives', which included Ukip-backing Leave voters returning to the Tory fold. It warned that any general election campaign faced a risk from 'Conservative Leaners', younger predominantly Remain voters who liked Cameron's efforts to modernise the party but needed reassurance that May wanted an open and optimistic Brexit. 'Our research showed they were soft and we had to make sure we responded to that,' a senior Tory said. 'And that's why things like Lancaster House were all about Global Britain.' The largely overlooked Plan for Britain had also been devised with an eye on this group. The research identified an opportunity to reach out to 'Working Class Strugglers', predominantly Leave voters outside Labour's inner-city strongholds – many in the Northern towns – who were prepared to consider a vote for May but wanted reassurance that she would not backtrack on Brexit and that she was a different kind of Conservative. A Mayite who attended the Chequers meeting said, 'Those were the three key segments, and we had to make sure we brought them together to have a winning coalition. We'd identified that that young, slightly more metropolitan remain-voting group was our soft underbelly.'

Crosby was not interested. 'We brought in Lynton and co. and they threw out that strategy and put together something entirely new and it all went wrong,' the source said.

* * *

The Chequers meeting and a series of subsequent gatherings chaired by
Patrick McLoughlin also concluded that Conservative Campaign
Headquarters, known to all in the party as CCHQ, 'wasn't quite at full
power'. The party's ability to fight a ground campaign had been hit hard
by two highly embarrassing cases arising from the 2015 election. More
than twenty Conservative MPs were under police investigation over
expenses returns after visits by battle buses crammed with eager volunteers were recorded as national spending, rather than against the tight
limits in each seat. The affair had not been well handled, with the MPs
affected accusing party bosses of 'covering their own arses'. On 16 March
the Electoral Commission fined the party £70,000 for 'knowingly or
recklessly' filing dishonest returns. One of the MPs with the threat of
prosecution hanging over him was Craig Mackinlay, who had beaten off
Nigel Farage's seventh attempt to enter Parliament in the Kent seat of
South Thanet. His plight was complicated by the fact that Nick Timothy
had played a central role in South Thanet, and some of the spending in
question concerned a £14,000 bill from the Ramsgate hotel where he had
lodged during the campaign.

'The battle-bus stuff had really left CCHQ depleted and soft-pedal-
ling,' a Downing Street aide said. 'Even during the by-elections there was
a timidity in Central Office because that style of campaigning was under
a lot of scrutiny and people didn't want to be seen to be throwing the
kitchen sink at everything any more.'

McLoughlin had also shelved two other battle-bus initiatives following the suicide in September 2015 of Elliott Johnson, a twenty-one-year-
old activist who had joined the party's 'RoadTrip2015' election campaign.
RoadTrip, which enticed young grassroots campaigners to marginal
seats with the promise of curry and alcohol, was run by Mark Clarke, a
former candidate known as 'the *Tatler* Tory' by the tabloid press because
he once appeared in a list of rising stars in the society magazine. When
Johnson took his life on a railway line and named Clarke as his tormen-
tor it unleashed a scandal that led to months of damaging headlines
about sexual shenanigans and bullying. A report commissioned by the
party, the conclusions of which were made public in August 2016, identified thirteen alleged victims of Clarke, including six allegations of
'sexually inappropriate behaviour'. Clarke denied all wrongdoing.
RoadTrip was scrapped and with it Team 2015, another initiative set up
by Grant Shapps, the former party chairman, to channel activists to up

to a hundred key seats, which was credited with a key role in winning the majority in 2015.

The other problem for CCHQ was that in the Northern towns, which had not been part of the Tory battleground for generations, there was very little grassroots infrastructure. The cadre of field staff hired for the 2015 election in the hundred target seats had left. A member of May's team said, 'We realised if we were going to be looking at seats like Bishop Auckland, Wrexham and Sedgefield, which haven't been competitive for a long time, we were going to have to invest time and money in building them up, recruiting members and finding candidates.' McLoughlin and his team thought they had time and planned accordingly. 'Every time I asked them, they'd said, "No, there's not going to be an election don't be stupid,"' the aide said.

Later, others accused McLoughlin of complacency and May of naïvety about CCHQ's readiness. A minister said, 'What she didn't do is see if the machine was ready, she just assumed it was match-ready. Patrick is absolutely useless. I mean, why don't they put someone who's got real passion in there, a bit of energy, real focus? Madness!' A campaign veteran said, 'She'd been party chairman but she'd never been party chairman during an election campaign, and I think there was just a misunderstanding of what was required to run a successful election campaign.'

In mid-March some backbenchers concluded that a general election was a good idea. Andrew Bridgen, the feisty MP for North-West Leicestershire, texted McLoughlin on the 15th, calling for 'a snap GE on the 4th of May', the same day as the local elections, predicting, 'we would win handsomely'. McLoughlin, who knew how unprepared CCHQ was, replied sourly, 'Not sure about your analysis.' Bridgen got a warmer response from his whip, Chris Heaton-Harris. George Hollingbery, May's parliamentary private secretary, made time for a chat, and Gavin Williamson, the chief whip, said he would 'be sure to pass on' Bridgen's views. Five days later Bridgen met Stephen Parkinson from the Downing Street political team, who said May still did not want an election because she had promised new-intake MPs that she would not hold one.

By then the gist of Bridgen's exchanges had found their way onto the front of the *Sunday Express*. With hares running and the fear of being seen to dither like Gordon Brown growing, Number 10 spin doctors briefed aggressively that there would be no election. Concerned that she was being asked to lie to the press, Katie Perrior sought reassurance that

May's mind was made up. 'It's from the prime minister's mouth,' she was assured. In one private conversation with a journalist, Fiona Hill said, 'There is no way to do it without it being a shitshow.' As prophecies go, it was not a bad one.

In retrospect, Bridgen was onto something. Had May called the election on the same day she triggered Article 50, she could have had a short campaign that coincided with the local government elections and would likely have secured the triumph she hoped for.

May's initial judgement against calling an election was shared by Crosby and his pollster Mark Textor, another Australian who combined a tough exterior with the easy humour common in his countrymen. Towards the end of March, Katie Perrior, who knew 'Tex' from Boris Johnson's first campaign, met him in a bar in St James's and asked, 'If you were the prime minister, would you call an election now?'

Textor was horrified: 'That's fucking crazy.' As a pollster, he had closely studied Brexit and the election of Donald Trump, and had concluded that voters were more fickle than ever. 'Having just seen the tide of people swept away, from Trump to Brexit, you would not touch this with a bargepole,' he said.

May's mind was changed by a combination of factors. The first was the sense that her opponents were ganging up on her to thwart domestic reforms. An article on the front of the *Observer* on 18 March revealed that Nicky Morgan, the former education secretary, was joining forces with Nick Clegg, the former Liberal Democrat leader, and Labour's Lucy Powell to block May's push for new grammar schools. The same day, at the Lib Dem spring conference, party spokesman Tom Brake opposed the inclusion of Henry VIII-like powers in the Great Repeal Bill. 'We will, if needed, grind the government's agenda to a standstill,' he said. Coming just a week after the budget U-turn, May's team were spooked.

The following day Chris Wilkins went to see Nick Timothy, and said that if they were to push their agenda through they would need an election. Timothy replied, 'I think she does need to do it. Fi thinks she needs to do it. The chancellor's pushing it. DD's pushing it heavily. Maybe we should actually have a proper conversation about it.' Timothy, Wilkins, Hill and Jojo Penn discussed the issue among themselves and then approached May to say, 'This is something you should really start to think about.' After work one night that week, munching on bowls of crisps, they urged her and Philip May to give the green light. May was nervous, and her husband worried that the public would dislike the fact that she was reneging on her word.

Sources close to May say that if Labour had voted down Article 50, that would have provided a *casus belli* for a snap election. A minister confirmed, 'We had a number of discussions about the prospects of an election. The only way we could deal with it was to go to the country.' The Brexit argument the prime minister wanted was ultimately provided by David Davis. During a one-on-one conversation in March, he warned that holding an election in the spring of 2020, just a year after the Brexit deadline, would leave Britain 'over a barrel' during the negotiations, since knowing the government needed a deal signed and sealed before the election would allow the EU to play hardball. 'We would have been concluding negotiations within a year, or less than a year even, of the general election, which would put us under great pressure,' Davis argued. 'On timing alone, it was worthwhile resetting the election time.'[4] Three weeks before Easter, Davis also called Crosby, telling him, 'No one is closer to Theresa May than I, and I, Philip Hammond and Theresa May really run the country. I'm urging her to have an election as early as possible. We're well ahead in the polls and we'll win.' The Australian urged caution but Davis insisted, 'I'm persuading her and I just wanted you to think about it.'[5]

In the first week of April, Timothy, Hill, Penn and Wilkins had another conversation in May's office in Downing Street. Seated around the round glass-topped table where the prime minister did her most serious business, the inner circle weighed the pros and cons. The French presidential election, due to conclude on 7 May, had created a window before the EU27 were due to finalise their negotiating strategy. Formal talks would not begin until June. There was a one-off window of opportunity in which the prime minister could strike before Brexit negotiations became all-consuming. If things went to plan she could enter the talks with a stronger hand.

May was still 'very cautious' because she did not like going back on her word and had taken a long time to make it to Downing Street. But she was 'very alive' to the logic of the Brexit timetable. Wilkins told her, 'You have the ability to be a transformative prime minister but you're not going to do that as it stands. You've just seen what happened with the budget where you're hamstrung by the previous manifesto. If you really want to achieve anything then you've got to have your mandate.' Hill made a different case, telling May, 'Sitting on a mandate that isn't yours and is so small and going into Brexit, then actually there's no guarantee you'll make it through to 2020 anyway.' They all warned that the parliamentary party could only get more fractious as time went on.

Inevitably, they talked about polling. The PDS polls for the political team were showing a narrower lead than public surveys, but it was consistent and healthy. More importantly, May led Corbyn in every age range and social class. That was not a clinching argument, but it bought May space to make a decision. 'Polls were obviously important but not in the way that people think,' said one aide. 'The polls gave us the licence to have the conversation. But the conversation was never, "If we do this we're going to smash the Labour Party and have a massive landslide." Our expectations were probably in the region of a majority of fifty to sixty if everything went according to plan.'

As the meeting drew to a close, Timothy, probably the firmest advocate, said, 'It's the right decision.' He had made the case that an election should be called for 'governmental politics, not electoral politics', and 'the security of the Brexit strategy'. May did not commit herself but concluded by saying, 'Go away and think about how you'd run a campaign and talk to Stephen Gilbert about it.'

On 5 April, May left for a five-day walking holiday in Snowdonia, North Wales. By the following evening she was staying in Dolgellau, where she bought a copy of *Walks in and Around Dolgellau Town* by Michael Burnett. 'During the walk,' it advises, 'there are a series of revelations. Those moments of discovery are mind-cleansing. They focus you, give you that moment of clarity you need to make those important decisions.'[6] It was there, in the hills above the town, that May talked to her husband Philip and decided she was ready to take the greatest gamble of her career.

When she returned on the 10th, May called Timothy and Hill and announced, 'Let's do this.'

Philip May, her 'rock' was widely seen as the prime minister's most influential counsellor, but she had effectively been manoeuvred there by her most influential aide. A cabinet source remarked later, 'The person who made the decision to call the general election was Nick. It didn't really matter to be honest what Theresa thought. It was Nick's decision.'

A cabinet minister said it was Davis's argument about the Brexit timetable that had carried the day: 'The core reason was that she had realised,
and this was very firmly Nick's view, that they would be up against it in
Brussels before the [2020] general election, it would weaken our hand.'

Even after the disaster that befell her seven weeks later, it is hard to
fault the decision to grasp a propitious moment to put the government
on a firmer footing. A source close to May said afterwards, 'I don't think
any of us look back and say, "We shouldn't have done that."'

Timothy called Gilbert to let him know it was game on, and asked him
to put together an election-winning team. Then they met over coffee.
'I've not run a national campaign. You have, Lynton has,' the chief of staff
said. 'It has to be you guys.' Gilbert thought this was odd, since Timothy
had been involved in numerous campaigns in senior roles, but he
accepted that he had no experience of building a campaign team. In the
time available there was just one option: 'reassemble the old band'.

Gilbert had been in Number 10 until the 2015 election, and had
promised his partner that campaign would be his last, but he was then
roped into the Remain campaign, an unhappy experience. He had made
the same promise again. Having been ennobled by Cameron as Baron
Gilbert of Panteg, he agreed with Timothy that getting Brexit legislation
through the Lords 'wasn't going to be pretty', and that an electoral
mandate that gave May more leverage was desirable. Now he thought,
'This really has to be my last campaign'.

The 'Wizard of Oz' was in Fiji, celebrating his wife Dawn's sixtieth
birthday, when he received a call from a number he did not recognise on
the Thursday before Easter. He ignored it. The holiday had long been
promised and was due to last for several weeks. Nothing was going to get
in the way of that. Only later did he pick up a voicemail message from
Theresa May asking him to call Gilbert. Crosby, who did not have the
prime minister's number programmed into his Australian mobile phone,
told Gilbert he did not want to run another national campaign. The 2015
campaign 'almost killed him', a senior Tory remembered. 'His pacemaker
was literally pumping out of his chest.'[7] Crosby told Gilbert, 'I'm not
going to be able to be up at 3.30 every morning and working until whatever time every night. I don't want to run it, but we'd like to be part of it.
Stephen, you be the campaign director and make clear that we're advisers.' An email agreeing the terms was sent to Timothy. He suspected that

Gilbert, a talented but low-key operator, would have preferred Crosby to take charge.

Crosby's modus operandi was to take total control of a campaign and have sole access to the leader. In 2011 he had been hired to spend four years preparing for 2015 with the agreement that David Cameron and George Osborne would do as he said. Cameron received regular and blunt text messages about his mistakes. This time Crosby could not join the campaign immediately, and he lacked the same rapport with May. 'He didn't know Theresa sufficiently well that that relationship was ever going to be there,' a senior Tory said. Nevertheless, Crosby said Textor would put research in the field immediately, and his business partner flew in the following week. Crosby would follow ten days into the campaign.

Having teed up Gilbert, Timothy approached the only cabinet minister who had become part of May's inner circle. Ben Gummer was in his Ipswich constituency when the text arrived asking him to come to London. On the Wednesday the pair met at Number 10. Timothy asked him, 'What are you doing on 8 June?' Gummer fumbled for his diary and read out a forgettable engagement. Enjoying himself, Timothy dropped his bombshell: 'Theresa wants to have a general election.' Gummer was surprised and somewhat put out. As minister for the Cabinet Office he had just spent six months analysing each of the 554 commitments in the 2015 election manifesto to work out how they could be adapted to May's programme, and which should be ditched. Now Timothy asked him to start writing a new manifesto. Gummer was also defending a marginal seat, and his heart sank. More cautious than many politicians, he told Timothy, 'If you have an advantage then don't risk it.'

Over the next three days Gummer and Timothy went for slow walks in St James's Park, turning over ideas about the manifesto. Each discussion began with the chief of staff enquiring, 'How do you feel about it now?' Gummer admitted he was 'distinctly uneasy' but said, 'I trust you on this.' He never shared his concerns with May. Later, he wished he had. During Thursday's stroll, Timothy had said, 'I cannot stress the secrecy of this enough,' but Gummer had a big ask. He had promised his wife Sarah Langford, an up-and-coming barrister, that they would spend Easter weekend together. 'I'd very much appreciate it if I could tell my wife why I will be working. I do not want her to find out on Tuesday that I have lied to her, because this might be a marriage-defining moment.'

Timothy gave his permission with a grin. 'As long as your wife is not the political editor of the *Sunday Times* ...' In fact, Timothy had been mulling over a plan to release the news of the election to that same newspaper, but thought better of it.

Gummer and Langford spent Easter weekend in Suffolk with Gummer's family, including his father, the former cabinet minister John Gummer, now Lord Deben. In one of the more surreal examples of life co-existing with politics, the couple revelled in watching the world carry on as normal around them, knowing that an 'amazing explosion' was about to change everything. Gummer spent most of the weekend on his laptop pondering what he wanted his children's future to look like.

By the time May returned from Wales, the wheels of the campaign were already grinding. Stephen Gilbert chaired 'hush-hush' meetings in the Trafalgar Room of the St Ermin's Hotel with Timothy, Hill, Wilkins and Alex Dawson plus key figures from CCHQ: Darren Mott, the head of campaigns and Alan Mabbutt, the party's director general. Gilbert stressed that the decision came with risks which the campaign would have to mitigate, the most acute being that calling an election after saying she would not might undermine May's reputation as a straight talker. 'The PM is highly regarded but not terribly well known by voters,' he said. 'They think she does the right thing, and calling an early election could put all that at risk.' The first priority was to explain why the election was in the national interest.

It is a measure of the discipline and secrecy that characterised May's team that not a whiff of the decision leaked out for eight days, ensuring the element of surprise necessary to land May's argument cleanly. By now Sir Jeremy Heywood, the cabinet secretary, chief whip Gavin Williamson and Gareth Fox, the head of candidate selection for the Conservative Party, were also in the loop. Before 18 April, the number of people in the know was to rise to nearly thirty.

Gilbert made two other key calls. One was to Jim Messina, the data expert whose demographic-modelling software had helped Barack Obama win re-election in 2012 and was credited with propelling the Tories to victory in 2015. His efforts had been less successful a year later for the Remain campaign, a defeat that traumatised him. Messina had also lost the Italian constitutional reform referendum, which cost prime minister Matteo Renzi his job, but he was regarded as a key part of the band. He was hiking on a volcano in Iceland when the call came.

On the Monday, Gilbert also got in touch with Tom Edmonds and Craig Elder, whose innovative social media campaign had been a key driver of votes in 2015. Neither wished to turn down the opportunity to work with Crosby again. Edmonds would work full-time on the campaign with two of his staff. Elder attended meetings at CCHQ in the mornings and kept their company ticking over in the afternoons. Both were shocked to discover that in their two-year absence from Tory headquarters the in-house digital team had been cut back to just five people and there was no designer. Their efforts had been championed and well funded by Andrew Feldman, Cameron's co-chairman, but had gone backwards under McLoughlin, an old-school politician. The party's Facebook and Twitter messages had dwindled to a trickle. 'Between elections CCHQ naturally gets shit because there's nothing to do, most of the good people leave and there's just not much money around,' a campaign official said. 'Labour had been in campaign mode for two years and were a fighting machine. When Tom and Craig walked back in there was nothing there.'

Over the weekend before the announcement, May brought her most senior ministers into the picture, summoning Philip Hammond to her flat on Sunday the 16th and David Davis the following day. Both were delighted that their advice had been heeded. The chancellor told one ally, 'Finally, I'm going to get the majority of seventy I need.' That same day, May made her most important call – to Buckingham Palace to alert the queen that she intended to force an election. James Brokenshire, the Northern Ireland minister, was alerted, since the election could have an impact on stalled power-sharing talks in Ulster. The leading Brexit officials Oliver Robbins and Sir Tim Barrow were also told. Both believed a bigger mandate would make their jobs easier.

Yet it was only on the Tuesday morning that many senior staff were entrusted with the secret. Just before cabinet, Timothy took aside Stephen Parkinson, Chris Brannigan, the director of government relations, and John Godfrey, the director of policy. The first clue Brannigan had was when he walked into Number 10 that morning. 'Both chiefs of staff were in and I walked past the prime minister in the corridor and she had had her hair done. That made me think, "Who gets their hair done over an Easter bank holiday?"'[8] He expressed shock that the election would disrupt planning for a trade trip to China.

As the holders of the other great offices of state, the home secretary, Amber Rudd, and Boris Johnson, the foreign secretary, were summoned to May's office to receive the news shortly before cabinet, while Gavin Williamson was deputed to tell Damian Green. 'Boris had to be told before everyone else, but also couldn't be told before anyone else because then the world would be told before anyone else,' a cabinet minister remarked wryly. Rudd took the news in her stride, but the cabinet was delayed for several minutes as Johnson sought to talk May out of her decision. 'Boris told her not to call it in January and again on the morning when she told him before cabinet,' an ally said. The foreign secretary told May, 'It's up to you but I think people are sick and tired of elections. We just have to get on and do Brexit.'

As the ministers in the know filed into the Cabinet Room, Rudd and Gummer, both in the circle of trust, exchanged meaningful looks and a power hug. Gummer, assuming that Natalie Evans, the leader of the Lords, had been told, said, 'Eventful weekend,' and was met with a blank look. Unusually, both Hill and Timothy were in attendance at the back of the room. Ministers were told to hand in their mobile phones. The first item on the agenda was a discussion about Iraq, but May cut straight to the chase: 'I've been thinking about the problems facing us as a nation.' One minister said, 'She talked about the difficulty of the Brexit negotiations with the parliamentary timetable we have.' May finished by saying, 'I've come to the conclusion, therefore, after a great deal of thought, I think it's the right time to go to the country. After this meeting you will see me go outside the door of Downing Street and announce that we are going to have an election on 8 June.'

A 'wonderful wry smile' broke out on the face of Greg Clark, the business secretary. Another minister said, 'He could not suppress what we were all thinking: "My God she's brave. This woman has got fantastic *cojones*."' The night before, Gavin Williamson, expecting more resistance, had asked loyalists like Gummer to step in to back up May, but it was quickly apparent that this was an unnecessary precaution. Beginning in order of seniority with Philip Hammond, each minister in turn voiced support for the decision, some in the most florid terms. 'I did not hear a single negative comment in the room,' Chris Brannigan recalled. It was all systems go.'[9] The post of chief toady was secured by Justine Greening, the education secretary, who told May, 'This is exactly why you're the right person to lead us, Prime Minister.'

The other notable contribution was from Johnson, who made a positive case but, according to one colleague, 'looked a bit green'. Some detected unease in the foreign secretary, whose leadership ambitions had only been dented by his flame-out in the contest the previous July. 'He looked sick,' a witness said. 'I think that's because he rather thought 2019 was going to be a mess and that's when he'd become prime minister. He did say something positive, but you could tell from his demeanour that he was a bit disappointed.' It seemed now as if no one had a chance of replacing May before 2022. Fiona Hill said later that Johnson's facial expression proved that 'he knew he was fucked'.

The niceties over, a television was wheeled into the Cabinet Room so ministers could watch as May delivered her speech to the nation. Timothy sat in his office and then, with Hill, handed out a copy of the statement and a messaging sheet for ministers stressing the key points to get across in broadcast interviews. One person displeased with the statement was Chris Wilkins, who had written the first draft as a way of vocalising the strategy he had outlined at Chequers. His version acknowledged the centrality of Brexit to the decision and claimed credit for triggering Article 50, but then had May go on to say, 'I've always said that the referendum result was about more than just leaving the EU, it was about changing Britain. That's what I want to deliver.' Wilkins and Timothy encapsulated the speech in a simple proposition: 'Strong leadership in the national interest.'

The speech, as delivered, opened with a long section on Brexit, in which the prime minister told voters she had brought 'stability and strong leadership' and promised 'there can be no turning back'. Explaining that she had 'only recently and reluctantly' come to her decision, she then outlined her reasons for calling the election: 'If we do not hold a general election now, the negotiations with the European Union will reach their most difficult stage in the run-up to the next scheduled election. In recent weeks Labour has threatened to vote against the final agreement we reach with the European Union. The Liberal Democrats have said they want to grind the business of government to a standstill. The Scottish National Party say they will vote against the legislation that formally repeals Britain's membership of the European Union. And unelected members of the House of Lords have vowed to fight us every step of the way ... Division in Westminster will risk our ability to make a success of Brexit.'

May framed the election as 'a choice between strong and stable leadership in the national interest, with me as your prime minister, or weak and unstable coalition government, led by Jeremy Corbyn'. Top of the 'key points to remember' handed to the cabinet and emailed to MPs was, 'We need this election now to secure the strong and stable leadership the country needs to see us through Brexit and beyond. Every vote cast for Theresa May and the Conservatives will count to strengthen Britain's hand in the Brexit negotiations.'

Of her vision for post-Brexit Britain or her wish to transform society for the benefit of those left behind there was not one word in either the speech or the briefing document. 'Strong leadership in the national interest', which implied some purpose to the strength, had become 'strong and stable leadership'. The proposition for change had become a slogan about continuity. A source said, 'When Lynton and Tex got involved in that draft statement it was all about Brexit, which all of our research showed us people didn't want us to talk about.'

For the consultants, however, the Brexit approach was the only one that would insulate May from the charge that she had changed her mind for narrow party advantage. 'If you're calling an early election you have to have a reason,' a CTF source said. 'If you try to call an election on "I need the endorsement for my plan to look after people who are down-trodden and not doing so well," punters would say, "That's no reason to call an election." The only legitimate reason was that you needed to back her to back Britain for Brexit.'

Since receiving the call from Gilbert, Textor had ordered two focus groups with undecided 'soft voters', one in London and the other in the North-West, plus a nationwide poll. CTF prepared three memos on the data, including a 'strategic note' outlining a preferred approach. They warned that holding the election at all was a gamble: 'The research shows there is clearly a lot of risk involved with holding an early election – and there is a real need to nail down the "why" for doing so now,' the paper explained. 'Voters are actively seeking to avoid uncertainty and maintain the status quo, and yet by calling an election the Conservatives are the ones who are creating uncertainty. Therefore, Theresa May must be able to show that by holding an election now she is minimising future uncertainty and instability ... Voters do not want the uncertainty that an election will cause.'

Crosby urged May to be 'very careful', but did not think it his place to advise explicitly against calling the election, since she had already made up her mind. But he and Textor were not at all confident that the Tories

would win a healthy majority. They warned that they might even lose
seats, though the risk they identified at this stage was a revival of the
Liberal Democrats rather than Labour – a blind spot which would dog
the Tories throughout the campaign. 'If an election was held today there
is a risk that the Conservative vote share would end up broadly similar
to that the party secured in 2015,' the memo warned. 'There is the potential for a significant number of seats won from the Liberal Democrats in
2015 to return to Tim Farron's party.' The Australians warned that 'exceptionally high expectations' that the Tories would triumph were 'leading
voters to believe that they can vote for the best local MP … while still
remaining secure in the knowledge that Jeremy Corbyn will not be prime
minister'.

In expressing his reservations, Textor deployed one of his favourite
analogies to describe Tory support, comparing it to Lake George, an
expanse of water near Canberra which is sixteen miles wide but just
three feet deep and evaporates every summer. 'It fills every winter but if
you get here in February the whole bloody thing's gone,' he told the
author. 'It looks magnificent and tourists go, "Wow, look at that!" Then
a couple of days of heat and it's gone. Everyone measures its width not
its depth. As a pollster you test vulnerability, not width. The published
pollsters say, "Here's how far it is," but we tend to go, "What's the softness
of the vote? Where does it come from? What are the structural weaknesses?" You're not there to say, "Gee, bloke, you look all right." You're
there to do the blood tests – and many of the first tests were not that
good.'

When Textor put May's arguments for holding the election to voters
they agreed with them – but there were also firm majorities for all the
arguments against an election. The proposition that 'Britain already faces
enough uncertainty' had a net agreement level of 55 per cent. 'Support
for the election dissipated to net zero,' Textor explained to May's team.
'It looked good on the surface, but it wasn't sustainable.' Not over a
seven-week campaign.

The CTF research also suggested that May, as 'the most favourably
viewed individual tested', should take centre stage in the campaign.
Corbyn was 'the least favourably viewed', but of the other senior Tories
tested, 'only Ruth Davidson has a net favourable rating'.

Crosby's memo concluded with five points summarising 'what the
Conservatives must do'. In her speech in Downing Street May had

successfully responded to points one and two: 'Be clear why this election is needed now – to prevent future uncertainty that would hamper Britain's ability to make a success of Brexit', and 'Frame the election as a choice between continuity and stability, or chaos and uncertainty'. The early part of the campaign would attempt to embed the other three: 'Demonstrate the only way to secure a better future is through strong leadership, backed up by a stable and united party', and that the only way to achieve this was 'by voting Conservative'. Most critical, in terms of the conduct of the campaign, was point five: 'Use Theresa May as the campaign's main communication vehicle – and take every opportunity to contrast her with Jeremy Corbyn'.

The chiefs needed very little persuading that May should be thrust front and centre. Timothy admitted later, 'To be perfectly honest I didn't really challenge that. I was in a position to change this and I didn't. With hindsight obviously we would have done it differently'.[10] Part of Hill and Timothy believed May was a uniquely talented leader who ought not to share her likely triumph with grandstanding colleagues. One of their close allies said, 'The idea of her being the main message-carrier is something Nick and Fi weren't against. They certainly didn't want Boris or anyone else being there that much'.

May's announcement was greeted with a rapturous reception in Westminster, where MPs and journalists who could remember Gordon Brown's pathological caution applauded her audacity. At an impromptu meeting of the 1922 Committee that afternoon the prime minister was met with cheers and cries of 'Five more years!' If many were cynical about her motives, the rolling news channels quickly adopted the Tory branding. Sky News's ticker declared it 'The Brexit Election'. The following day's *Daily Mail* went further, its front page emblazoned with a shot of a stern-looking May and the somewhat hysterical headline 'CRUSH THE SABOTEURS'. By Sunday, the pollster YouGov had found that voters backed May's decision to call the election by a margin of 48 per cent to 26 per cent. More than half of those with an opinion believed a Tory landslide would be good for the country.

And yet the seeds of May's downfall had already been sown. It was a measure of how unprepared CCHQ was for the campaign that Andrew Goodfellow, the head of the Conservative Research Department, had handed in his notice the week before. He landed back in the country after a holiday as May made her statement, and then agreed to return.

'The political party that was the least prepared was, of course, the Conservative Party,' Chris Brannigan realised.[11] David Davis agreed: 'One of the things nobody thought about, I certainly didn't, was the fact that we were calling an election out of the normal cycle, meant that all the things that normally happened before a general election at party headquarters ... none of that had happened. The whole party was caught by surprise.'[12]

Patrick McLoughlin's ire at the decision was clear when he came across Andrew Bridgen later that day in Portcullis House. 'I don't know what you're fucking smiling at,' the plain-speaking party chairman told the MP. 'This is all your fault. We haven't fucking won yet!' Afterwards, one Mayite thought the whole team of consultants was overconfident. In his early chats with staff, Stephen Gilbert told the troops they were part of the 'best campaigning machine in the world'. The Downing Street official said, 'It very quickly became clear that the world had moved on and the CCHQ machine had not.'

Looking back, Nick Timothy was to think that the 'big strategic error' of the campaign was abandoning the framing of May as an agent of change in favour of Crosby's mantra of 'strong and stable'. 'It was a reassurance and continuity campaign rather than a change campaign, and on reflection I think that was wrong,' he said.[13] Yet even his allies acknowledge that 'there was no big argument about it' as the campaign began. The chiefs were happy to take advice from their expensive advisers, and Timothy resolved to write a manifesto promoting his vision of the prime minister.

When Timothy, Wilkins and Hill had first discussed the election among themselves they envisaged an old-fashioned campaign in line with May's submarine strategy. Timothy recalled, 'Our early instincts when we were thinking about the election were to have a more traditional campaign, daily press conferences, more policy content, certainly not make it a semi-presidential campaign.'[14] Another Downing Street official said, 'Theresa was going to do a few set-piece speeches, but basically carry on being PM, because that's what people like about her. But I remember when Nick pitched this, Stephen Gilbert instantly dismissed it out of hand, wouldn't even talk about it.'

Crosby and Gilbert – correctly – believed leaders could not hide away during election campaigns. 'In a national campaign, how can the leader not do media?' a senior figure said. 'She was criticised for not engaging with people enough. Imagine if she'd done even less. The idea that they wanted a collegiate approach when they shut most ministers out is laughable.' Another campaign aide said, 'In this day and age you can't have a Potemkin candidate, someone you lock away in a room saying, "She's doing serious things. Here's Boris!"'

The main victim initially of the CTF strategy was the rival strategist. From having been one of May's four most influential aides, it was made clear that Chris Wilkins would not have a seat on the main hub at the centre of the CCHQ war room. A senior campaign source recalled, 'Chris spent the campaign sitting on the floor of CCHQ writing whatever Mark Textor told him to write. CTF basically didn't want another strategist in the room. They made sure he wasn't involved.'

Relations between the chiefs and Katie Perrior were such that the prime minister's director of communications only found out there was to be a general election shortly before it was called. Since her last major bust-up with Hill in February, she had told her friend Jo Tanner, 'I'm dead to them,' and had crossed her fingers for an election so she could leave. 'I pray for it every day,' she said. When Perrior arrived that morning she wondered where all the special advisers were. She called somebody, and the spad said, 'I shouldn't be telling you this, we're in a meeting saying an election's going to be called.'

Perrior was called to see the chiefs. Hill told her she planned to take the role of campaign communications chief herself. They then asked her not to leak the news. Perrior was furious. 'I haven't leaked in ten months, and I'm not about to start now,' she said. After May's speech, Perrior saw the prime minister, who made no attempt to persuade her to stay. A friend said, 'Theresa had been convinced by then that Katie was shit and a pain in the arse.' When Textor phoned Perrior to ask why she was not yet in CCHQ, she explained that she had left. A source close to Hill said, 'The election was done on an absolutely strictly need-to-know basis. But we were working on the basis that Katie wouldn't be working on the campaign. It wasn't really working. That's fairly undeniable.'

With Perrior out of the way, Hill recruited Rob Oxley as head of media and her de facto deputy. It was a big promotion for Oxley, who had been Priti Patel's spad at the lowly Department for International Development, but he was the media operator with the most campaign experience, having served in the same role for the victorious Vote Leave campaign a year earlier. Hill also brought into the press team two experienced former lobby journalists turned special advisers, Craig Woodhouse and Kirsty Buchanan, plus Jeremy Hunt's spad Paul Harrison. More surprising was the departure of Lizzie Loudon, May's press secretary, who had won the respect of political journalists. Loudon decided to walk when told, dismissively, that she would have to report to Oxley. She had grown sick of Hill's behaviour, while Hill said that she had been shocked to hear that Loudon was not assertive enough in her briefings for journalists after Prime Minister's Questions each Wednesday.

The power plays continued when Stephen Parkinson, Chris Brannigan and Alex Burghart, a member of the political section, were all encouraged to seek seats rather than join the campaign. Parkinson had a long-standing ambition to be an MP and had worked for May since the Home Office, but he had also fallen out of favour with Hill, who believed – ludicrously – that he was a leaker. Gilbert's appointment to oversee the campaign left Parkinson – who had run Vote Leave's ground game and May's by-election efforts – with nothing to do. Nevertheless, the sense that he was Downing Street's candidate cost him selection as the candidate in the safe seat of Saffron Walden. He went to campaign for friends instead. Patrick McLoughlin leaned on Brannigan, a veteran, to run in the army seat of Aldershot, but he lost the selection as a result of an anti-Downing Street backlash from the local association, which wanted the arch-Eurosceptic Daniel Hannan. Brannigan would spend the campaign working with CTF and then helping out candidates in London. Burghart would fight and win Brentwood and Ongar. 'They wanted us out, but didn't have the courage to come and say it,' one of those pushed aside said. 'The only common theme about those who left Number 10 is that we all dared to defy Fiona Hill.'

If the loss of her two leading media mouthpieces and the sidelining of other senior aides troubled May, she appears not to have shown it. 'There's a slight emotional gap there,' a Number 10 official said. 'If I was her and could see people leaving I would wonder why and ask questions. She's a smart woman. There's no way she didn't know what Fi was doing, but I don't think she cared.'

Allies of Hill and Timothy rightly pointed out that it was the discipline they had instilled which kept the election secret safe for eight days. 'We needed to get the announcement right, which we did,' one said. 'That was the single most important thing in that phase of the campaign. It would have got very messy if it had leaked.'

Under the terms of the Fixed Term Parliaments Act, two-thirds of MPs would need to vote for an election to make it happen. The day after May's announcement, MPs voted by 522 votes to thirteen to approve the election. Nine Labour MPs defied Jeremy Corbyn's edict to back the motion, while the SNP abstained. A secret Tory contingency plan – to pass a one-line Bill by simple majority mandating an election on 8 June – was not required. When May was interviewed by the *Today* programme that morning she admitted, 'Every election has a risk.' But none of her senior staff seriously believed it. Perrior said, 'They thought they were home and dry.'[15]

Despite the simmering tensions already evident in the Tory camp, Team May had every reason to hope their gamble would succeed, since they were up against a Labour opposition which was far more divided and just as unprepared for the fight ahead as they were.

LENINISTS AND LENNONISTS

Jeremy Corbyn was recording a segment for Victoria Derbyshire's BBC2 current affairs show when James Schneider's phone started buzzing with news that May was due to make a statement. Schneider, a product of Winchester school with a jawline as firm as his conviction that Corbyn was the answer to Britain's problems, had helped make the Momentum campaign group successful before joining LOTO – the leader of the opposition's office – the previous October. He signalled to Corbyn to wind up the conversation and guided him into a different room in the suite of offices occupied by LOTO in the Norman Shaw South building across the road from the House of Commons.

It says a lot about the air of mystery surrounding Theresa May that as Corbyn's team began to war-game their response, 'We worked out six different options,' a source said. 'We started writing six statements. Is she resigning from ill health? Is it something about the Brexit negotiations? Some people thought it was military action.' There was also speculation that a senior royal had died.

Karie Murphy, Corbyn's office manager, phoned her temperamental familiar in Downing Street, but Fiona Hill was not picking up. Murphy was furious. 'If it was an election, she understood the process would be that the leader of the opposition would be informed, but obviously they didn't do that,' a Labour official said. Patrick Heneghan knew better. When he heard the news, Labour's experienced executive director of elections emailed his old sparring partner Stephen Gilbert to ask whether it was a general election. Gilbert did not reply, and there is honour among election strategists, as among thieves. Heneghan told colleagues, 'I know Stephen. If it wasn't an election, he would have told me, and obviously he can't tell me, so he's not replying. Therefore, it's probably an election.' The matter was settled shortly afterwards when May's lectern was wheeled into the street outside the famous black door, shorn of the government crest which adorns it during official engagements. 'That meant it was party business, not government business,' a source close to Corbyn said.

Corbyn's team watched May's speech with concern as she framed the election around Brexit, an issue which could only expose the divisions in Labour between their metropolitan Remain supporters and the working-class voters who had backed Leave the year before. The party held twenty of the top twenty-five most Remain seats, and the same number of seats where Leave won biggest. As May finished, Corbyn turned to his aides and said, 'She's done that pretty well.' One recalled, 'It very effectively set out what they wanted the campaign to be.'

If Team Corbyn was grudgingly admiring of May's positioning, the media reaction to the speech fuelled LOTO's contempt for what Corbyn's followers called 'the mainstream media', or 'MSM' for short. 'They're all so fucking awful it's unbelievable. They completely swallowed it immediately,' the source said. 'Sky were calling it the Brexit election. The BBC did it in the same way. The next day the servile press was running with "Crush the Saboteurs", idiot commentators saying, "Oh what a brave move", "wow", "fearless". It's just pathetic.'

Morale was boosted by Barry Gardiner, the shadow international development secretary, whose upbeat performances under Corbyn had made him an unlikely media star. Gardiner told the leader's team, 'All right, we weren't planning for this, but now we do this.'

Corbyn had been scheduled to go to Birmingham to launch a new policy on increasing the carer's allowance, the last in a line of announcements that had allowed Labour to dominate the airwaves while May was in Snowdonia. Aides assumed that he would cancel, but the leader said, 'No, people have come to it. We've got an announcement. We get straight out, we're campaigning, that's how I want to do it.' An aide recalled, 'Jeremy was quite calm. He's always quite calm. That was the first of a litany of examples where his instincts were absolutely correct.'

Corbyn was no ordinary leader. After a career of principled obscurity lasting three decades, in which he had voted against his own front bench more than five hundred times, he had only run for the leadership in the first place because John McDonnell did not want to, and the younger

Labour MPs on the hard left insisted they must have a candidate. Corbyn had only made it onto the ballot because grandees like Margaret Beckett and Sadiq Khan loaned him their votes to 'widen the debate'. Yet he had swept to victory on a wave of revulsion at the compromises of the Blair and Brown years and the lacklustre performance of his rivals – Andy Burnham, Yvette Cooper and Liz Kendall – who offered only incremental change when party members wanted revolutionary transformation of the political and economic status quo. Corbyn united the 'Leninists' – hard-left activists dreaming of a Bennite revival – with the 'John Lennonists' – young, idealistic activists, brimming with hope and what Barack Obama called 'the fierce urgency of now'. Matt Zarb-Cousin, who worked for Corbyn, was typical: 'I didn't really have much of a home in the party, but then Jeremy stood for the leadership and I felt a sense of purpose in my politics that I had been searching for.'[1]

In his first year in charge Corbyn had swelled party membership to more than half a million – four times the size of the Conservative Party – but presided over a collapse in poll ratings as it became painfully obvious to his own MPs that running nothing more than a parliamentary office and an allotment for thirty years was no preparation for creating a government in waiting – a conclusion that compelled 172 of them to declare him unfit to lead in the no-confidence motion. Many suspected that the summit of Corbyn's ambitions was to change the Labour Party, to ensure it pursued socialism not centrism, rather than to win a general election. Yet those around him saw a potentially transformational leader who could challenge a political establishment and an economic system they believed was letting down large swathes of the population. Corbyn had proved himself a superlative campaigner in both leadership elections. His inner circle believed the same would be true on the national stage. 'He's got a pull like I've never seen before,' one said. 'I've always admired the ability he has got to talk to anyone and everyone. He is quite charismatic at a personal level.'

Corbyn had come to realise that he could do something with this talent. 'He was a reluctant leader,' a member of his core team said. 'He lives in a simple house. He'd be a monk if he wasn't a politician. He sees himself as the representative of the dispossessed. What changed in Jeremy was when he started doing the visits as a leader of the Labour Party. He saw that he could make a difference.' There were already signs of growing seriousness. Corbyn, who seldom removed his dog-eared brown jacket in the first eighteen months of his leadership, was more smartly dressed after David Cameron told him his mother would have told him to 'put on a proper suit and do up your tie'. One aide said, 'In the early days it was a real ball-ache to get the guy to wear a suit. In some ways David Cameron's mum was the best thing that happened to him because that cut through to him. His wife was hurt by that. He thought, "typical Tory", but when he went out and met people he realised it made a difference.'

In Westminster, where many MPs looked down on his two E grades at A-Level, Corbyn was regarded as rather dim. His team saw a man who read Shelley and African literature. They rejected the caricature of him as a modern Chauncey Gardiner – the simple man who shoots to national prominence in the Peter Sellers film *Being There* – a political marionette for the views of Seumas Milne and the ambitions of John McDonnell. 'Jeremy has the final say,' an aide said. 'He's very disarming, but woe betide you if you treat him like an idiot. He's very sharp.' Beyond a reputation for being pushed around by overbearing aides, Corbyn and Theresa May also shared a zeal for campaigning in their own constituencies. 'Doing his surgery every Friday is not necessary but he does it because it keeps him in touch with people,' an ally said. The difference between the two leaders was that Corbyn had already endured adversity during his nineteen months in charge, and his team knew he would not wilt under fire. 'He's got an inner steel,' a source said.

Corbyn was also a happy warrior. When his team gathered in the large corner meeting room in Norman Shaw South, which Ed Miliband had used as his office, the leader was upbeat: 'We're going to have a positive campaign. We're going to do this and win. It's going to be a victory for the people we need to support.' If not all of his aides believed it, they were ready to die in a ditch for him, and they applauded anyway.

A belief in the durability of your leader and the sanctity of your cause is not enough to win an election, though. What drove the Corbynistas as the campaign began was not data, strategy or tactics, but a political analysis. It had four strands: a belief that an interventionist state and socialist economics are morally and self-evidently right; the proposition that the 2008 economic crisis had provided an opportunity for their brand of radical-left politics to challenge the prevailing orthodoxies; an understanding that British broadcasting rules meant equal air time for the leader of the opposition during an election campaign, allowing them to avoid the refracting distortions of a partisan press; and a belief that Corbyn could entice people who do not usually vote into the polling booth.

Milne was the primary theorist and anchor of Team Corbyn. Zarb-Cousin said that if 'Jez is the marksman upfront, Seumas is like the Tony Adams, the sweeper'. One of the most divisive figures in politics, the former *Guardian* columnist had voiced sympathy with both Soviet and Putin's Russia, and was regarded by many MPs as an anguine figure, whose preternatural calm shrouded aggressively left-wing views. His internal critics said he was disorganised, a terrible time-keeper and 'doesn't like people who disagree with him'. Others praised his strategic judgement, politeness and calm. 'He gets portrayed like a vampire but he's got a great sense of humour and is a very easy person to work with,' one colleague said. 'I don't remember him making many wrong calls. He doesn't shout and swear. Sometimes people misinterpret that, they think it's because he doesn't care, but he does care, he's just very good at handling a high-pressure situation.' Milne told his friends when he took the job that he would not 'rise to' media criticism. 'My whole life I've been saying the Labour Party should be a socialist left-wing party,' he said. 'And then the opportunity comes along. How could I ever walk away?'

It was a strength of Corbyn's team that nearly two years of disastrous poll numbers had not dented these beliefs. 'We've been correct all the way along and it's not because we've had data to back it up,' a Corbyn confidant said. 'The theory was simple: if you put forward policies which challenge the way everything's been for the last forty years and are massively popular – and polling suggests that they are – and we get fair broadcast time and we ignore the print lobby, then we'd rise significantly in the polls.'

In their first huddle after the election was called LOTO collectively agreed that they would stand or fall on their beliefs, primarily that the programme of austerity that began in 2010 should be consigned to history. 'We had thirty years of extreme market liberalism or neoliberal-ism,' a Corbyn aide said. 'Almost every working-age group in society is worse off in terms of living standards and stagnant wages and cuts. Those in charge have lost control, as the Brexit referendum demonstrated. And we recognised there is an underlying volatility in British politics since the financial crisis with the rise of the Lib Dems, the rise of Ukip. So, there was a whole set of thinking from which you could derive your strategy that wasn't just, "We would like to do nice things, so we will say that we will do nice things and everybody will think that it's nice."'

The second campaign insight was that Corbyn had to embrace the status of the change candidate. Another source from his office said, 'When people are struggling, they don't want to vote for the status quo. To be fair to Theresa May, she recognised that as well, but she didn't follow through with a transformative programme. Our approach was, "They say that you have to play by these rules, but these rules benefit the system. We're going to break all the rules."' Unlike May's team they would stick to their guns.

These beliefs were not shared by the long-serving senior staff at Southside – Labour's headquarters on Victoria Street in Westminster – who looked with despair at the way Corbyn's supporters openly disparaged the achievements of the Blair and Brown governments, including many of the campaign techniques they had developed. Ever since Corbyn's election in September 2015 the twin power centres of LOTO and Southside had existed in conditions of uneasy collaboration veering at times towards outright hostility. Some of Corbyn's team dubbed Southside 'the dark side'. Zarb-Cousin said, 'It was very difficult to get Southside to work with us constructively. Leaks from private meetings would occur on a regular basis. Sometimes journalists would even find out before we did.'[2] To the Corbynistas, the Southsiders were patronising and disloyal 'red Tories', too ready to compromise with the failed politics of the past. To the Southsiders, Corbyn's team were at best incompetent ideologues who didn't know what they didn't know about running a modern political party or an election campaign, and at worst dangerous zealots whose politics owed as much to Marx and Militant as they did to the Labour movement.

Patrick Heneghan knew more than most how little prepared Labour was for the campaign, since he had already masterminded two of them. Dubbed the party's 'armchair general', his clever use of resources and targeted operations in key seats in 2010 was widely credited with denying David Cameron a majority. Bespectacled and intense but with a fast-flowing dry wit, Heneghan could talk at a hundred miles an hour about campaign strategy. He had been trying for months to get a plan in place for a snap election. To the staff at Southside, Heneghan was the model of a modern political professional. To Corbyn's inner circle he was the embodiment of the problem, an outspoken and – they assumed – disloyal throwback to the days of Blair, Brown and Miliband, when political technique, spin, triangulation and the quest for a chimerical centre ground appeared to trump ideological purity. He was also immovable. The permanent staff at Labour headquarters were appointed by Iain McNicol, the efficient but undemonstrative general secretary, and he could only be removed by the party's ruling National Executive Committee (NEC), a body on which Corbyn's allies had not secured a majority. Simon Jackson, Labour's head of policy, Emilie Oldknow, the formidable executive director who ruled Southside with a rod of iron, and Greg Cook, Labour's in-house pollster, completed the gang.

As soon as May called the election a staff meeting was held in the Southside kitchen. 'There was quite a lot of shock,' one of those present remembered. Addressing the group, McNicol warned, 'This is going to be tough,' but Heneghan reassured staff, 'There is a plan.' He had overseen the creation of a 'war book' for a snap election. It included a fifty-page document sent to all MPs and constituency Labour parties (CLPs) advising them on what to do and a checklist of two hundred actions to be taken at HQ on day one, including hiring new computers and signing service-level agreements for software. 'No one else anywhere in the organisation had done anything, so it was a bit of a scramble,' a Labour official said. 'There had been not one snap-election planning meeting, not one.'

In the autumn of 2016, Jon Trickett was appointed by Corbyn as national campaign coordinator. The MP for Hemsworth in West Yorkshire was a jovial sixty-six-year-old with a grey goatee beard that contrasted with his frequently deep tan. He had the distinction of being one of just thirty-six MPs to have nominated Corbyn for the leadership. During his few short months in the job, Trickett hired a polling company – BMG – and an advertising agency called Krow. He also instituted election planning meetings between Southside and the leader's office. 'That at least had the virtue of getting people in the same room, which is not often the case,' said a LOTO source. The meetings took place in the leader's office. 'They would never come over to us until the campaign actually happened,' a Southside official recalled. 'Psychologically that was quite difficult for them, thinking they actually had to come to the dark side.'

The problem was that those Wednesday meetings seldom made any concrete decisions. Every week Heneghan suggested they begin planning for a snap election, every week there was agreement, and every week nothing more was done by LOTO to move things forward. Trickett, regarded as one of the more strategic thinkers around Corbyn, commissioned explanatory notes from the directors at Southside but was forced out of his post in January 2017 after a spat with Karie Murphy, Corbyn's gatekeeper. He was replaced by the MPs Andrew Gwynne and Ian Lavery. When the election was called, Labour high command had no plan for allocating resources and no campaign slogan. Most seriously, there was no agreed target seats list. A Southside source claimed that during his time Trickett had actually agreed 'a defensive key seats list', meaning Labour would focus on defending those it held, 'but not told the leader's office. He didn't want to tell Jeremy, because he didn't want to upset him.'

Tensions between Southside and LOTO were exacerbated by a series of personnel changes in Corbyn's office in the year before the election, which emerged out of deep divisions between his staff. Those with a taste for Russian revolutionary history split the warring factions into the Bolsheviks and the Mensheviks. The Bolsheviks were the hardliners who preached an uncompromising ideological line and implacable opposition to party moderates. They included Milne, John McDonnell, Andrew Fisher and Karie Murphy. Their numbers were bolstered in February 2017 when Milne recruited an old friend, Steve Howell, to be his deputy. Both worked in the 1980s for Straight Left, a Stalinist-sympathising newspaper which emerged from the pro-Soviet wing that broke away from the Communist Party. Where Milne was smooth to the point of feline detachment, Howell was argumentative. 'I think he was brought in to be abrasive and to be everything that Seumas isn't,' a source said.

The more moderate Mensheviks – named after the faction that split from the Bolsheviks in 1903 – had been dwindling in number ever since January 2016 when Neale Coleman, Fisher's predecessor as policy director, walked out. Three months later the deputy chief of staff Anneliese Midgley left to become political director of Unite, Britain's biggest union, telling friends Corbyn's court needed to be 'less mean to people'. She had fallen out with Katy Clark, Corbyn's political director. Simon Fletcher, the campaigns director, was next to go in February 2017, complaining that decisions agreed by Corbyn in meetings were either not acted upon or unpicked afterwards by Murphy. In March the exodus continued, with media spokesman Matt Zarb-Cousin, 'head of stakeholder engagement' Jayne Fisher and Nancy Platts, the leader's trade union liaison manager, all departing, the first two for 'health reasons', Platts after falling foul of Karie Murphy. Fletcher and Midgley's departures were particularly significant in the LOTO–Southside standoff. Both had campaign experience working on Ken Livingstone's mayoral contests, where in 2012 they had got on well with and respected the professionalism of Heneghan and Simon Jackson. But both had clashed with Milne, and refused to take part in a fly-on-the-wall documentary made by Vice News, which painted an unflattering picture of Corbyn's office.

Fletcher, in particular, had sought to use the EU referendum campaign to get LOTO match-fit for a general election, penning a memo advising that Corbyn's key staff relocate from Parliament to Labour headquarters for the duration of the campaign. 'Simon was concerned that they would underestimate the level of resources that need to be applied to such a thing to get it right, but also you can learn for the future general election,' a Labour source said. In the end only Fletcher, Midgley and a few junior staff did move over.

The victory of the Bolsheviks was engineered by Karie Murphy, the flame-haired gatekeeper. A close confidante of Len McCluskey, the Unite general secretary, Murphy shot to public prominence when she sought to win selection as Labour candidate for Falkirk after Eric Joyce was kicked out of the party for boozing and brawling in a Commons bar. Union operatives were accused of attempting to rig the vote to install her as the candidate. While Murphy was cleared of wrongdoing, the resulting scandal led to a change in the way Labour picked its leaders, something that ultimately made Corbyn's election possible. To her friends and allies, she had begun to instil order and rigour in an operation characterised by chaos. 'The reason why Karie is so good is that she's a working-class woman who doesn't take shit,' a colleague said. 'She tells them to fuck off and they listen.' Another said she insisted on 'working-class whisky' like Teacher's if offered a more refined single malt.

To her enemies, who were numerous, Murphy's power meant she was able to block proposals – like general election planning – which she did not understand or could not control, often by announcing that her preferred course of action was 'what Jeremy wants', even when the leader had expressed a contrary view in a previous meeting. Jon Trickett left after Murphy was rude to him about a meeting that had been rearranged. But he also judged that she was making it impossible to do his job. 'Karie can get things done, but at the same time if she doesn't want to do it, even if it has been agreed, it won't happen,' a LOTO source said. 'If somebody knows more than her about something, she is threatened by that. You can't run an election campaign like that.' A senior Labour official added, 'Everybody who's left the leader's office has said the same thing – they've left because of Karie. She has this management style of divide and rule. She literally moves people around every few weeks so they can't form alliances or plot against her. People are really genuinely scared of her.' The parallels with Fiona Hill are striking.

By the time of the general election LOTO had spent months lurching from one self-inflicted crisis to another, which left Southside with little faith that they could execute a successful campaign. The 2016 party conference had been disrupted by a toxic row over the Trident nuclear deterrent which ended with defence spokesman Clive Lewis punching a wall. Corbyn's team had also given a faltering response to claims of anti-Semitism in the party which erupted when Ken Livingstone, an old friend of Corbyn, suggested Adolf Hitler was a Zionist 'before he went mad and started killing millions of people'. Corbyn's own speech to conference in 2016 attracted negative headlines after Milne sent Zarb-Cousin to brief reporters and he said Corbyn was 'relaxed' about high levels of immigration, a spectacular own-goal just three months after concerns about migration fuelled the referendum Leave vote. At Southside they felt shackled to a circus. 'Seumas has no idea how the press works,' a Labour official said. It was a perennial complaint at Westminster that Labour press releases were sent out late at night, hours after the first editions went to press. Milne's nickname for all journalists was 'hyenas'.

Once Corbyn had won his second election as leader, most moderates decided he could not be removed and vowed to make Corbyn 'own' what they expected to be an electoral catastrophe. Blairites like Jamie Reed and Tristram Hunt walked away. Things were not so easy for the Southsiders, whose reputations were also on the line in an election.

It was in an atmosphere of mutual suspicion and trepidation that they embarked on the election campaign. Shortly after May's announcement there was a shadow cabinet meeting, a gathering steeped in gloom. 'You could see in people's eyes that they thought we were going to get twatted,' one of those present said. 'There was panic on their faces.' Emily Thornberry, the shadow foreign secretary, recalled, 'There were people who seemed to be genuinely concerned that they were not coming back.'[3] With good reason. Andrew Gwynne and Ian Lavery briefed frontbenchers the following day that Labour's internal polling meant they could be down as low as 126 seats, an electoral massacre.

After shadow cabinet there was a meeting in the leader's office, where McNicol and Heneghan sat down with Corbyn's top team: Milne, McDonnell, Murphy, Fisher and the leader's son Seb Corbyn, who worked for McDonnell – an arrangement the Tories liked to poke fun at when Labour complained about nepotism. Together they discussed how they would structure campaign meetings, select the key seats, secure funding, and what Corbyn's tour would look like. During the EU referendum campaign, Corbyn's key aides had complained that meetings at 9 a.m. were too early – a stance that appalled the party directors – but this time they agreed to a 7 a.m. get-together and conference call for the most senior LOTO and Southside staff. Another was scheduled for 8 a.m. involving the press team and other section heads. Later in the campaign there would be another call about the grid at 9 a.m. 'Some of them still weren't good at turning up in the mornings,' a Southsider recalled. 'Seumas never turned up on time,' another Labour official said. 'It's remarkable how part-time that campaign was.' Some of those on the morning calls, which were led by either Heneghan or Corbyn's strategy chief Niall Sookoo, cringed at the exchanges. 'There was a division between people who had done a campaign before and those who hadn't,' a Corbyn ally said. 'It was like kids and their parents. There was tension you could cut with a knife.'

The divisions between LOTO and Southside were physical as well as metaphorical. On the eighth floor of the building, Labour officials tore out half of their kitchen area to fashion office space for the migrants from Parliament: Milne, Murphy, Fisher, Howell, Schneider, Sookoo, David Prescott and the politicians McDonnell, Gwynne and Lavery. Corbyn was given an office at the end of this open-plan area that had once been occupied by Trickett. Those who remembered previous elections were struck by the sheer ordinariness of their leader. 'With Blair and Brown you'd know when the leader of the Labour Party was in,' one said. 'You'd sort of sense their presence and their charisma and look up in awe. Jeremy just wanders around and makes people cups of tea and is just a normal person.'

The party directors – McNicol, Oldknow, Heneghan, Jackson, Greg Cook and John Stolliday, the head of compliance – sat on the same floor but on the other side of the building, separated by a courtyard. Labour officials could see when Corbyn's team held secret meetings without them. 'There were parallel operations within the building,' a party staffer said. 'It felt like twin power bases. You can look into each other's offices across this courtyard. When people pulled the blinds down there was something going on they didn't want you to see. It was quite a strange Cold War operation going on.'

Just occasionally the LOTO crew would call in Heneghan or Jackson to answer technical questions, but they also developed their own strategy which remained a mystery to the headquarters staff. A senior Labour official said, 'They never told us anything they were doing. They would just tell us they were doing a speech, they want a venue booked, so we'd go and set it all up for them. Patrick and Iain would often only find things out because the events team would tell them. It was a non-functioning relationship between the leader's office and senior campaign people.' To the Southsiders, the chain of command in LOTO was opaque. 'I couldn't tell you who ran that general election,' a party official said. 'John McDonnell was probably the person who ultimately had the most say, but it was not clear who had responsibility for what.'

The Labour directors felt they were compensating for the inexperience of the LOTO personnel. 'There was no professional operation,' one said. 'We polished a turd, basically. The permanent party staff spent those weeks polishing many turds. They were very shiny by the end of it.'

Two rival press teams added to the confusion. The party's head of press and broadcasting, Neil Fleming, sat with his team on the second floor parallel to an entirely separate bank of LOTO press officers, with desks for Milne and Schneider, Corbyn's spokeswoman Sian Jones, staff imported from Momentum and James Mills, McDonell's spin doctor.

As soon as the election was called, Corbyn's office drew up a grid for the next five weeks, detailing the events and policies they wanted to promote. 'It wasn't very good and they wouldn't share it all with Southside,' a party source said. 'Southside got pissed off because they could only get that week's grid.' Milne and his team did not trust the Southsiders to keep any plans to themselves. LOTO's approach was often to retrospectively decide what the main theme of the day was, rather than plan it in advance. 'After the story was decided, they would write on a piece of A4 and stick it to the wall: transport, childcare, Scotland, defence, leadership,' a party official said. This had the added benefit of covering a glass wall of their new office space. 'They papered over the wall so no one could see in – it was very weird,' a source sympathetic to Corbyn said. 'We are talking about people who were Tankies. They probably thought it would keep out MI5!' A third official said, 'There was no strategy, there was no grid, there was no message. There was no plan.'

The Southsiders were also unimpressed by the lack of focus on messaging in campaign adverts and speeches. Corbyn was so used to speaking his mind that little attention was given to drawing up a message book with phrases, tested with polling and focus groups, designed to maximise Labour's appeal to voters. 'Here are the three things we talk about, here are the two things we say about the Tories – that was never formulated,' a campaign official said. To the leader's office the campaign themes were clear enough: austerity and Tory cuts bad, Jeremy Corbyn good. To them, the constant demands for New Labour-style plans were evidence that Southside's veterans did not understand their leader.

The difference of approach bubbled to the surface early on when Simon Jackson, the head of policy at Southside, let rip, explaining that Corbyn's team were not doing what was necessary to translate their vision into votes. 'You have a set of policies and beliefs, but that is not the same as having a strategy, nor a plan for winning,' he said. 'There is no strategy.' He accused LOTO of failing to draw up or share their own war book, a list of target seats or a scientifically researched study of target voters. Karie Murphy went on the attack, rounding on Jackson and the other Southsiders: 'You don't believe in Jeremy's project. We want to change society. We believe in delivering for the working classes.' She was backed up by Steve Howell, who said, 'We believe in a broad arc of transformation.' The phrase was seen as meaningless by the party directors: 'There was a belief that we could turn out the young people and non-voters, but it was never voiced as a coherent plan. The levers weren't pulled. There was no mechanism for targeting those people. There was no discussion about what our message was to them. Seven weeks out from a general election, to sit in a strategy meeting and for people to talk about an arc is ludicrous.'

In fact, Milne and Steve Howell did draw up a strategy document. In the first week of the campaign Milne, as titular head of strategy, was told the National Executive Committee expected him to deliver a summary of his plans. He and Howell created a sixteen-page PowerPoint presentation which contained fewer than six hundred words. The document finally unveiled Labour's election strapline: 'For the many, not the few', which veterans delighted in recalling had been appropriated from Tony Blair. It said the 'core theme' could be summarised as: 'Instead of a country run for the rich, Labour wants a Britain where all of us can lead richer lives.' As a summary of the Corbynistas' world view it was effective, but some at the NEC meeting regarded the performance and the document as 'cringeingly embarrassing' because it bore little resemblance to the detailed offerings that NEC members like Margaret Beckett were used to. 'It was unbelievably flimsy,' one of those present said. 'They just made it up overnight.'

More telling was what was absent. 'There was no list of target seats, there was no list of twin seats. You always have twinning operations where you send people from a safe seat to a marginal seat.' In 2015, in their presentation to the NEC, Ed Miliband's strategy team – Greg Beales and Torsten Bell – had devised a series of 'message frames' with core offensive and defensive messages appended to maximise Labour's advantages on social-justice issues and minimise its weakness on economic matters. 'It was wanky bollocks that Torsten and Greg came up with, but at least it was a grown-up political strategy,' a Labour official said.

Interestingly, Milne and Howell's analysis was that the 'core attack' from the Tories would be that 'Corbyn would bankrupt Britain', with 'secondary attacks' on the 'spectre' of an SNP coalition, Labour being 'divided on leadership and Brexit' and being 'weak and extremist'. Many Tories would later come to wish that the economy had actually been so central to their campaign.

At this stage of the campaign, Corbyn's longstanding links with Sinn Féin-IRA and description of the Hamas terrorist group as 'friends' in one Middle East meeting were considered his greatest handicap – though voters eventually seemed less concerned than most journalists. NEC members watched incredulously as Milne and Howell revealed a slide detailing how the 'Tories are the real extremists', listing such things as giving 'tax handouts to the richest'. An NEC source said, 'You could see jaws dropping' that Corbyn's team would seek to draw attention to the Tory attack line. 'It was dire.' The extremist angle was quietly dropped a week later when Theresa May ridiculed it in Prime Minister's Questions. After Howell's presentation, Milne 'laconically' answered questions from the committee. They did not give him a hard time, but one who was there concluded, 'It looked like something a couple of A-Level kids knocked up in an evening, which is effectively what happened.'

One thing the Southsiders were very grateful to Corbyn for, however, was the party's almost uniquely buoyant finances. A surge in new members and affiliated members during the second leadership contest meant Labour entered the campaign with £3.5 million in the bank. Another £150,000 was raised from small donors in the first six hours after May's declaration. They would go on to raise £4 million during the campaign from donations averaging £19. The existing war chest meant the party could start spending on day one, rather than wait for the usual cheque from the trade unions. This was even more advantageous than it would usually have been, since the prime minister's decision to call a seven-week election meant the spending limits of £12,000 per constituency would not kick in for ten days. 'We could spend that money on candidate-facing material, on the ground, and not have it included in the local return,' a senior Labour official said. 'Nearly £2 million went into the campaign in the first ten days.'

Around 90 per cent of that cash was funnelled to 'defensive seats', those Labour already held. After the campaign this was to become another source of division between LOTO and Southside, with the Corbynistas claiming they could have formed a government if Patrick Heneghan had approached things more positively. 'The Southside strategy was based on the assumption that we would be down to 160 seats,' a shadow cabinet adviser said, 'whereas the LOTO people said, "No, let's go and target some seats." They were right.' However, even members of the leader's office acknowledge that the target seats list was drawn up collaboratively on 19 April, a day after May fired the starting gun. The three-hour meeting involved Karie Murphy, Jon Trickett, Andrew Gwynne and Ian Lavery from Camp Corbyn, plus Heneghan, Iain McNicol and Emilie Oldknow from Labour headquarters. Milne, who was more interested in broad strategy than individual seats, and Howell, the one most aggressively demanding an offensive list of target seats, did not attend. 'Steve's view wasn't based on data or anything other than a hunch, and he didn't have a wide amount of support,' one of those involved recalled.

That was to change, but it is easy to see, at that stage, how the decision was taken. 'We were twenty-five points behind,' a party source said. 'That was real. In the local elections two weeks later we had the worst performance of any opposition party in thirty or forty years. Everyone agreed we were miles behind, and the best thing to do was to secure our defensive seats.' Another Southside official said, 'They agreed that list. The idea that we did it behind their back is just nonsense.'

MPs in all but the seventy-five safest seats got something, however hopeless their prospects or however hostile they had been to the leadership. Even John Woodcock, the MP for Barrow-in-Furness who was defending a majority of just 795 – and who a day earlier had put up a video message declaring, 'I will not countenance ever voting to make Jeremy Corbyn Britain's prime minister' – got money. 'We didn't write anybody off,' a Southside source said. 'If money was being handed out, and a group of thirty to forty MPs found out they've not got any, there would have been panic.'

The other reason for not sending money to offensive seats was simple. At the time of the meeting the only offensive seat where Labour had a candidate was Manchester Gorton, where a by-election had been due to take place on 4 May following the death of Sir Gerald Kaufman. It would take ten more days to get four hundred others in place. 'This is day two of the campaign, we have no offensive candidates,' an ally of Heneghan said. 'There wasn't even a process as to how we might select them.'

Candidate selection became another trial of strength in which the trade unions successfully flexed their muscles and even contenders backed by the leader's office failed to secure seats. Corbyn personally demanded that Simon Danczuk, the rebellious Rochdale MP who had been suspended from the party amid claims of sexual impropriety, should not be allowed to stand again. All sitting MPs were automatically reselected. Candidates for constituencies regarded as unwinnable – euphemistically referred to as 'challenge seats' – were shortlisted by Labour officials and then picked by a panel of three NEC members. The biggest prizes were the thirteen seats where sitting MPs were standing down. 'That's where all the real arguments were,' a party source said. 'That's where the trade unions had their list of people they wanted. There were a lot of deals done. Unite would get two, Unison would get two, that sort of thing.' Contrary to some reporting at the time, Seb Corbyn did not apply for a single seat.

Katy Clark, Corbyn's political director, was the most high-profile victim of the union horse-trading, perhaps because she had fallen out with Karie Murphy. 'She wasn't going to get it because the trade unions had done a deal which didn't include her,' a Labour official recalled. Clark had 'bought a new suit' and 'done her hair' and 'was literally sitting outside the room where the interviews were happening' when she was informed she should pull out, according to a source who saw her. 'She looked pretty fraught and upset.'

Corbyn set out his stall for the campaign on Thursday, 20 April. He was introduced by Dawn Butler, who offered the optimistic prediction, 'June is always the end of May.' The Labour leader used his first set-piece speech to challenge already dangerous media preconceptions. 'We had to combat the two things which had been swallowed hook, line and sinker on the Tuesday, which were that the election was a foregone conclusion – it was the scale of the Tory victory that was of interest – and that it was about Brexit,' a member of Corbyn's team said. In the first of many rousing addresses, Corbyn reminded voters that he had defied odds of 200–1 to become Labour leader, and vowed to confound 'the media and establishment' who 'don't want us to win'. In words which might equally well have been aimed at Southside, he said, 'They think there are rules in politics, which if you don't follow ... then you can't win.'

For Team LOTO it was a message that delivered a jolt to demoralised Labour supporters. One said, 'That gave lots of people, especially lots of activists and members who were a bit scared when the election was called, a big boost. It said, "This doesn't have to be a coronation."' The positivity was reinforced by Karie Murphy. 'Karie thought we had to think and act like we were going to win regardless of what the polls said,' a source close to Corbyn said. 'That had an effect on Jeremy as well.'

Despite the enthusiasm, Labour officials were baffled by the approach of the leader's office to Corbyn's campaigning activity. In the first few weeks there appeared little pattern to his movements, popping up in rock-solid safe seats like Bethnal Green and Bow, and Hackney South, and Tory-held towns like Harlow, Leamington Spa and Peterborough which were seen by Southside staff to be wildly optimistic. Labour headquarters staff concluded that Corbyn's team were sending him to places with large constituency parties where his supporters in the Momentum pressure group could guarantee a large crowd. They believed his purpose was twofold: to begin drumming up internal support for a third leadership race, and to run up the vote in safe seats so he could surpass the 30.4 per cent of the vote secured by Ed Miliband two years earlier. A Labour official said, 'They never said it out loud, but I think for them the first phase was Jeremy's survival. That was to be achieved by vote share.' Labour moderates, like former advisers Tom Baldwin and David Mills, were sufficiently concerned that this would be seen as an acceptable benchmark for Corbyn's survival that they publicly demanded that he gain more seats, more votes and narrow the gap to the Tories, as Neil Kinnock did in 1987, before he was allowed to stay as leader.

Corbyn's staff saw this criticism of the seats he was visiting as flawed, since many of the ninety rallies he staged during the campaign were not necessarily in target seats themselves but in convenient city-centre loca-tions, which would attract voters from neighbouring marginals. 'It was a new form of campaigning,' one explained. 'You create a hub and drag people out of the surrounding areas.' To LOTO, the Southsiders simply did not understand the breadth of Corbyn's ambitions. The leader's visits were orchestrated solely by Karie Murphy. Many of the seats he visited were to fall into Labour's clutches on 8 June. 'It was seats where we thought we could win if we got to the position we needed to get to,' a close aide said. 'Look through the seats that we won and look at the seats Jeremy visited: Croydon Central, Cardiff North, Bristol North-East, Crewe and Nantwich, Warrington South, Bedford, Colne Valley, Reading East.' Taking a leaf from Tony Blair's pursuit of 'Worcester woman' and 'Mondeo man', Corbyn visited seats with large numbers of target voters aged thirty-five to forty-five with children and a car, hitting them with messages on the cost of living, stagnant wages, school class sizes, the NHS and tuition fees. 'We won that group by 50 to 30 per cent,' a Corbyn aide said. 'That was the group that swung most to us.'

To some in Labour HQ this makes it appear more organised than it seemed at the time, not least because Murphy had a habit of changing her mind at the last minute. 'She would rip up arranged meetings and bus tours and move them to other places, regardless of the advice the police had given,' a campaign source said. 'The police were getting upset because there were big crowds and nobody was organising properly.' Other visits were to seats where Corbyn had promised the local MP he would visit. 'Jeremy would never break a promise, so he was going to these seats regardless of whether they were priorities or not for the campaign,' another Labour official recalled.

There were not many stops in Labour-held marginals. MPs in such seats were not Corbynistas since they had spent their careers attracting floating voters and regarded their hard-left leader as a deadweight. Peter Kyle, the only Labour MP in the South-East outside London, who was defending a majority of 1,200 in Hove, recorded an interview early in the campaign for the BBC which was only shown after polling day. He said, 'There's no doubt that Jeremy has been a drag on this campaign. He's coming up on door after door after door. It's a really strange position to be in as a candidate because I'm proud of Labour but I realise if I associate myself with Jeremy then we're dead here.'[4]

It was a perennial complaint of Corbyn's team – particularly Steve Howell, who showed a close interest in party literature – that the leader did not feature on enough candidates' leaflets. For his fans it was an article of faith that greater exposure to Corbyn would cause voters to warm to him. Howell said, 'We were confident his warmth and wisdom would shine through once he got the obligatory fairer hearing on broadcast media and spoke at ever bigger events in an atmosphere of heightened interest in politics.'[5] In Derby North, Corbyn's friend Chris Williamson said, 'The love for Jeremy Corbyn is palpable.'[6] Yet, four weeks into the campaign, even Howell had to admit on a conference call for candidates that it was better for canvassers to talk about Labour's policies than about their leader. In a leaked tape of the call, Danny Hackett, Labour's candidate in Old Bexley and Sidcup, gave warning that 'lifelong Labour voters cannot support us with the leadership team we have'. Howell replied, 'This is obviously within the party a sensitive subject … I think the focus of the response to that should be on the manifesto and on the policies rather than individuals.' He urged grassroots campaigners to stress that a Labour government would have 'a collective leadership'.

That argument was hardly reassuring to voters either, after Diane Abbott, the shadow home secretary and once Corbyn's lover, came unstuck in a 'car crash' interview on police funding on 2 May. Promoting a new Labour policy to recruit 10,000 new police officers on LBC radio,

Abbott was unable to explain how it would be paid for. Quizzed by the host Nick Ferrari, she stumbled, 'Well, erm ... if we recruit the 10,000 policemen and women over a four-year period, we believe it will be about £300,000,' implying they would get £3,000 a year each.

An incredulous Ferrari snapped, '£300,000 for 10,000 police officers? What are you paying them?'

Abbott tried to clarify but suffered broadcasting brain fade. 'Haha, no. I mean ... sorry. They will cost ... They will, it will cost, erm, about ... about £80 million.'

At Labour HQ John McDonnell reacted with fury to Abbott's gaffe, telling colleagues, 'There is no way Diane is going on television ever again.' Karie Murphy was tasked with passing on the edict to Abbott, but the first black woman MP was not one to be pushed around. Egged on by Labour peer Shami Chakrabarti, she continued to bypass the party press machine and book herself onto shows without consulting party bosses – with decidedly mixed results.

The Tories seized on Abbott's performance, pumping out social media videos. MPs from both sides quickly reported back that the gaffe had achieved 'cut through' on the doorstep. In a complex political environment, a recognisable politician having a meltdown was easily understood. Conservative focus groups began 'proactively bringing up how shit she's been', just as they had two years earlier with fears about a Miliband government propped up by the SNP. 'That's when we decided we were going to make a thing of her,' a senior Tory said. In CCHQ, the walls were decorated with a cartoon of Corbyn and Abbott dancing like the lead characters in the film *La La Land*.

Theresa May's reaction was very different, though. She was first played the Abbott interview on an aide's smartphone in the back of a car between campaign stops. May watched closely, grimacing in the right places, but when the video was over, her instinct was not to crow. The prime minister said, 'Do you know what? It's such a shame, because she is such an intelligent woman.' Perhaps it was evidence of May's decency, perhaps it was empathy from a politician who was no fan of broadcast interviews herself. Perhaps the PM had experienced a premonition of what trouble Labour's focus on police numbers would cause her later in the campaign.

For now, though, it was Labour that was in trouble. Labour MPs with majorities under 8,000 quickly got wind of an estimate by BMG that their seats were at risk. The word from the doorsteps in previously safe seats was dispiriting. On 24 April, six days into the campaign, BMG provided data showing that Labour would lose the election by 47 per cent to 28 per cent. 'They were saying that the Tories were going to get a majority of potentially two hundred, depending on how the Ukip votes were squeezed,' a senior official said. 'That is soul-destroying.' Labour's 'only hope', the pollsters counselled, was to tell voters Theresa May should not be given a majority so large it would usher in an elective 'dictatorship'.

Ten days later, when real votes were cast, Labour suffered a disastrous set of local election results, finishing nine points behind the Conservatives on 27 per cent of the vote and losing 382 council seats, while the Tories gained 563. Labour lost seven councils, including control of Glasgow for the first time in forty years, while the Tories picked up eleven, admittedly in seats where Ed Miliband had done particularly well when they were last contested in 2013. To complete the humiliation, Ukip lost every single seat it had held, but still managed to gain one from Labour. BMG's estimate now was that Labour would win 147 seats in June. Andrew Gwynne gulped hard. He was predicted to be one of the casualties.

The Conservatives were thrilled to gain seats throughout the Tees Valley in the North-East, making inroads with working-class voters who had backed Brexit. A Downing Street official said, 'In Northumberland County Council there's a subdivision, South Blythe, where the candidate didn't even turn up at the count. He was at the local Tesco where he worked, because he was a paper candidate. He's now the county councillor.' If the Conservatives could repeat those results on 8 June it would be a massacre of historic proportions.

What appeared to be impending tragedy for Labour was also accompanied by farce. Also up for grabs on 4 May were six new metro city mayoral posts. Corbyn ally Steve Rotheram won in Liverpool and former leadership contender Andy Burnham romped home in Manchester, but the Tories won the rest, including the Tees Valley, once a Labour stronghold, and secured a nail-biting win for Andy Street, a former boss of the John Lewis department store chain, in Nick Timothy's home city of Birmingham.

Desperate to focus on one of the few bright spots of a difficult day, Corbyn jumped on a train to Manchester for a victory rally. Burnham, who felt he had won in spite of the leader rather than because of him, went to dinner with his family, having made clear to Corbyn's office that he was otherwise engaged. There ensued a fraught series of phone calls as Corbyn's team contacted friends of Burnham to urge him to turn up. 'Tell him Jeremy is on the train,' one said. 'Karie just assumed if Jeremy turned up Andy would turn up too.' Lucy Powell, a Corbyn critic whose constituency includes Manchester Central, where the victory rally was held, had not even been invited.

While the moderates predicted disaster in June, Corbyn's team privately felt encouraged by the local election results. Niall Sookoo, the head of strategy, studied them and realised that despite the hammering, Labour was actually closer to the Tories than the national polls were showing. James Schneider briefed the lobby that the party was 'advancing' despite losing nearly four hundred council seats. 'Everything was moving in our direction,' a LOTO staff member said. 'If you compare where we were at the start of the election – twenty-five points behind – the polls had us fifteen points behind and in the local elections we were nine points behind. If we carried on the same trajectory, we would get to a decent position.' To the Southsiders this was putting misplaced hope ahead of experience. To the Corbynistas, that had always been the point of their project.

Nevertheless, by May, Milne and his colleagues knew something needed to change. Len McCluskey claimed publicly that holding just two hundred of Labour's 229 seats would be a 'successful campaign'. The initial war chest had been spent and organisational coherence was still missing from the leadership team. To resolve both issues Corbyn turned to the trade unions. Just before the local elections, Steve Howell and Patrick Heneghan went to meet TULO – the Trade Union and Labour Party Liaison Organisation – which coordinates the activities of the fourteen unions formally affiliated to the party. Howell asked the unions for £7 million, a figure they regarded as wildly unrealistic, saying the money was needed for social media advertising. Heneghan made the point that since it would take several weeks for the money to come through, they needed to act immediately. 'The current narrative in this campaign is, we are going to get battered,' he said. 'If we don't change that narrative in the next two weeks, we are dead. We've got to come out, and by mid-May be back in the race, because if this carries on, we're finished. That's why we need your support now, to be able to plan, to build.' On

8 May, the Monday after the local elections, the executive of Unite agreed to an immediate £2 million cash injection with another £2.5 million to follow. They also agreed that the union's chief of staff Andrew Murray would be seconded to Corbyn's team for the duration of the election contest.

Murray's appointment set off a tabloid storm, since he had only left the Communist Party of Britain to join Labour the previous December. A former *Morning Star* journalist who had expressed 'solidarity' with the hermit dictatorship of North Korea, responsible for the deaths by starvation of millions of its people, he also cited with approval the statement of Joseph Stalin's successor Nikita Khrushchev that 'Against imperialists, we are all Stalinists.' As a former chairman of the Stop the War campaign he was a longstanding friend of Corbyn. More importantly, as the power behind the throne in Unite, he knew how to run large and fractious organisations. The catalyst had been a 7 a.m. meeting a week earlier when John McDonnell had lost his temper over the faltering campaign. 'He was furious, saying, "This is a disaster; there is no plan,"' a Labour source said. 'John McDonnell's way of dealing with problems is to throw people at them.' Among LOTO staff Murray's arrival was a 'game-change moment'. One said, 'They were all terrified of him. Seumas notoriously used to rock up at midday and no one could get him to sign stuff off. When Andrew Murray turned up he was there at nine o'clock like a good schoolboy.' Immediately, Murray 'had a very good impact', a union official said. 'Andrew is a very serious person and knows how to get things done. Jeremy's appearances improved. His speeches were much sharper, the interventions were better and it just seemed to become more disciplined.'

Murray also pressed the campaign to sharpen the attacks on the Tories as 'the nasty party' and to broaden the target list to include more Conservative seats. 'It was core vote stuff – they're evil, they're bad,' a Labour official said. Another Southside source said, 'He rapidly ensconced himself in the little room where Seumas and Karie would sit. I got the impression that he was there to institute a core-vote strategy to shore up Jeremy. It was part of their planning for when they lost.'

As Labour prepared to write its manifesto, defeat still seemed likely. Despite the cold war on the eighth floor at Southside, the political pros had set up a functioning campaign and the faith LOTO had shown in Corbyn was being rewarded with well-attended events and air time. Yet

Theresa May was still defying political gravity, and the European Commission had handed her on a plate the perfect opportunity to hammer her theme of the Brexit election.

14

'ANOTHER GALAXY'

An enigmatic smile danced across Sir Lynton Crosby's lips. The gruff Australian was seated at the central hub in the Tory war room watching the twenty-four-hour news channels. Most of the campaign staff were glued to the TVs as well. Some of them were watching him. Multiple Theresa Mays walked to multiple lecterns in Downing Street and began to speak. It was Wednesday, 3 May and the prime minister was about to snatch victory from the jaws of defeat.

Minutes earlier, May had returned from seeing the queen at Buckingham Palace. Parliament had been dissolved. The period of phony war which had existed for a fortnight was over. For three days Downing Street had been reeling from damaging revelations in the press that May's plans for Brexit were in tatters, and claims from senior Eurocrats who had dined in Downing Street the week before that the prime minister was 'in a different galaxy'. For three days an embarrassed silence from Number 10, not quite able to deny the details of the row, had let the story rumble on. Now, instead of hoping the confrontation would go away, May was about to embrace it.

Standing behind another bare lectern the prime minister was in her sternest schoolmistress mode. 'Britain's negotiating position in Europe has been misrepresented in the Continental press,' she said. 'The European Commission's negotiating stance has hardened. Threats against Britain have been issued by European politicians and officials.' Then, the killer line: 'All of these acts have been deliberately timed to affect the result of the general election that will take place on 8 June.'

At CCHQ, Crosby leaned back in his chair, quietly satisfied. The Australian said nothing. He often didn't. But the staffers who watched him on these occasions knew he got more nervous than he liked to let on. When Crosby relaxed, so too did they. One of them said, 'That'll do it.'

May had called the election claiming it was about Brexit. Now it was. Some regarded May's intervention as hyperbolic. Chris Wilkins, watching in horror from the fourth floor, was one of several Mayites who thought it made the prime minister seem 'divisive' with swing voters and undermined her brand as 'the only statesmanlike candidate on offer'. But the speech gave the Tories a boost in the polls – just as Crosby had said it would. The Australian later told colleagues, 'This is a bruise we need to keep kicking.'[1]

It had all begun the previous Wednesday evening when May hosted a dinner in Number 10 for Jean-Claude Juncker, the president of the European Commission, Michel Barnier, the Commission's chief Brexit negotiator, and Martin Selmayr, Juncker's German chief of staff. The 'Rasputin of Brussels' was about to confirm his nickname.

The meeting began with air kisses on the steps of Number 10 between May and Juncker but then descended into an awkward standoff. The Commission group were perturbed that neither Nick Timothy nor Fiona Hill was present at the talks, which they took to be a snub, little realising that the chiefs had been banned by the civil service from attending, since they had formally resigned their posts to join the election campaign. When May enjoined her guests, 'Let's make Brexit a success,' Juncker pointed to Britain's planned withdrawal from the single market and the customs union and said, 'Brexit cannot be a success.' When the Commission president pointed out that Britain would become a 'third country' state at the point of Brexit, further outside the customs union even than Turkey, May seemed surprised, giving rise to concerns that she was not fully briefed.

Another flashpoint came when May demanded that a 'detailed outline' of a future free-trade deal be in place before the UK agreed to pay any money to Brussels as part of the Brexit divorce deal. An EU diplomat said, 'This was a rather incredible demand. It seemed as if it came from a parallel reality.' The prime minister's stance that trade must come first was met with incredulity by EU officials, who said her chief EU sherpa, Oliver Robbins, had already agreed that the methodology for agreeing the Brexit bill would be ironed out first – along with the rights of EU citizens in Britain and the issue of the Irish border. 'She took a firm position against something we thought we had agreed,' an EU diplomat said. 'It was completely unreal.' There was renewed concern that Robbins had not told May of the deals he had done on the sequencing of the talks because he did not want to give her bad news. A European ambassador said later, 'We don't know whom to ring. We thought it was Robbins, but it is clear he has been cut out. We have no one to call.'

May ploughed on, saying Britain did not owe the EU any money under the treaties. Her guests said the EU was not a golf club where financial obligations ended upon leaving, and that failure to pay up would mean national parliaments getting involved, who would be more likely to block a trade deal than other EU governments, a warning that German officials had repeatedly made to Robbins – a further alarm bell that the nuances were not being passed on to May. The EU source said the prime minister's views on the financial settlement 'border on the delusional'. May's further suggestion that the reciprocal rights of EU citizens be resolved by June 'astonished' her guests, with Juncker pointing out the difficulty of resolving access to healthcare quickly. When the prime minister indicated that a trade deal could be concluded quickly, Juncker pulled out a copy of the EU–Canada trade deal, a 2,000-page document that took nearly a decade to negotiate, and recommended that the prime minister study its complexity.

By the halfway point of the meal, the Commission president had remarked, 'The more I hear, the more sceptical I become.' At the close of the meal, Juncker told May, 'I leave Downing Street ten times as sceptical as I was before.'

At seven o'clock the next morning, having concluded that the talks were as likely as not to fail, Juncker picked up the phone to the German chancellor, Angela Merkel, and declared, 'It went very badly. She is living in another galaxy. Based on the meeting, no deal is much more likely than finding agreement.' May, he said, was 'deluding herself' about the progress of the negotiations. Merkel tweaked a speech she was making that day to the Bundestag to deliver a public rebuke to May, complaining that 'some in Great Britain still have illusions' that the UK would retain most of the benefits of EU membership when it left.

Details of Juncker's exasperation appeared in the *Sunday Times*, with a more lengthy blow-by-blow account in the German newspaper *Frankfurter Allgemeine Sonntagszeitung*, by a reporter known to be close to Selmayr, who had not troubled to hide his tracks. The report even speculated that May was minded to sack David Davis after he three times joked about how he had once brought a human rights case against her as home secretary. In fact Davis had only raised the issue once, and May had seen the funny side, but that did not deter Selmayr's weapons-grade briefing. A veteran EU diplomat said, 'An entire confidential dinner with a head of government being broadcast in full Technicolor, undoubtedly with added spin, it's an attempt to blow up the negotiations.' A furious Davis later remarked that if he had revealed details of the dinner he would have been fired. Another cabinet minister with experience of dealing with Selmayr branded him a liar who had repeatedly poisoned the well of EU negotiations: 'Martin will say black is white and apparently believe that it is so.' A veteran Eurocrat added, 'Martin has a powerful vision of Europe, but as the saying goes, if you have visions, you need to see a doctor.'

The newspaper reports were embarrassing for May, since they were published on the morning of her first campaign set-piece interview, with Andrew Marr, the BBC's most high-profile political interviewer. Never comfortable in the limelight, May was forced to utter the phrase, 'I'm not in a different galaxy.'

The leak was greeted with fury in the capitals of Europe. Within twenty-four hours, Barnier contacted British diplomats and asked them to relay his dismay to Davis and to Downing Street. 'They were embarrassed,' a cabinet minister said. Donald Tusk, the president of the European Council, who chairs the EU leaders' meetings, issued a public statement demanding 'discretion' and 'mutual respect' from the negotiators, comments his aides said were intended as a slap-down of the over-mighty official. Merkel was said to be 'infuriated' by the leak.

Selmayr seemed to revel in his notoriety. When May irritated Brussels further by declaring that she would not be able to authorise changes in the EU budget because of the purdah rules on political activity before the election, Selmayr promptly took to Twitter to announce the suspension of Brexit talks for the same period: 'Now, we'll have to apply FULL PURDAH RECIPROCITY. Talks with UK, formal or informal, will start only after 8 June.' After a public event on the same day as May's speech, where officials, business leaders and journalists hung on his every word, Selmayr happily posed for selfies with a string of admirers. Later, clutching a beer, he continued to taunt May for failing to spell out her opening position: 'I think that we will get a deal, but only if the British figure out what they want. Surely they will manage that after the election?'

Juncker also thumbed his nose at Britain, ostentatiously speaking in French at a 'state of the union' conference, since 'English is losing importance'. Asked about the dinner he said, 'I have the impression sometimes that our British friends do underestimate the technical difficulties we have to face. But the dinner was excellent.' He then took a swipe at the Downing Street chefs: 'I'm not talking about the food.'

For three days May's team seethed, but they also realised Selmayr had presented them with a political opportunity. Struggling to persuade voters that Jeremy Corbyn had a credible chance of becoming prime minister, May and Crosby embraced the chance to find a new villain to drum up votes. A senior Tory said, 'It was a gift. It was like a dragon wandered into Downing Street and Theresa slew it. People see Corbyn as a harmless arse. They see Juncker as a dangerous arse.' Another campaign official added, 'Selmayr is a shit and everyone knows he is a shit. But he's our kind of bogeyman.' That Sunday, YouGov found that 51 per cent of voters agreed that Brussels was trying to influence the outcome of the election. Just 24 per cent disagreed. Davis used an appearance on the BBC's *Question Time* to accuse the Commission of 'trying to bully the British people' by demanding a hefty divorce bill.

On Monday, 22 May the EU27 finally agreed its negotiating stance and Barnier announced that talks with Davis would begin on 19 June, eleven days after the general election. In a sign of how difficult they were to be, Barnier said the EU wanted the same rights for EU citizens in the UK, and any who had ever lived there, as if Brexit had not occurred. What's more, he called for these rights to be 'directly enforceable' by the European Court of Justice, anathema to May.

Some Tories were concerned that the affair of the Downing Street dinner had damaged relationships and Britain's prospects of getting a good deal. One said, 'Lynton Crosby is very good at what he does. He knows how to take maximum political advantage to win elections, but some of those decisions don't make it easier to govern.' Yet to govern, May needed to win the election. After it was over, Crosby was convinced the Brexit speech was her finest hour. 'She was outstanding,' he told the chiefs. But the seeds of the toxic divisions that would tear the Conservative campaign team apart were already beginning to show themselves.

15

STRONG AND STABLE

The moment that summed up for many the splits opening up within the Conservative campaign came when Theresa May walked into the Tory election war room and was nearly shot by one of her own staff. The gun was not a real one, fortunately, but a child's Nerf gun, which fired foam pellets. Crosby had sought to raise morale in CCHQ by periodically shooting the pistol at a life-size cardboard cut-out of Jeremy Corbyn. His swagger had led to one-upmanship from Rob Oxley, the head of media, who had purchased a Nerf submachine gun from Argos and had taken to shooting colleagues across the office to lighten the mood. Some of them saw this as the kind of high-jinks that had characterised the victorious and anarchic Vote Leave campaign, where Oxley had earned his spurs a year earlier. Others saw it as 'macho' posturing. 'It was a *faux* attempt at joviality where none existed,' one spad recalled. When May walked into the war room and a pellet slammed into the wall beside her, no one was in any doubt what the prime minister thought. Oxley was greeted with May's trademark death stare and 'total silence'. 'Rob looked like he had shat himself,' a witness recalled.

It might have been a minor episode of levity in a long campaign, but for the fact that it seemed to signal a gulf between those who had bought into Crosby's swashbuckling approach to politics and the other factions in the office. One campaign official said, 'There was a complete lack of coherence between four different teams. You had CCHQ people, you had CTF, you had Edmonds Elder, and then you had the spads who were drafted in from Whitehall. We were never introduced to one another, never told what the others were doing. It was four groups of people left to sort themselves out – with no human touch.' Another said, 'The fact it wasn't clear who's in control – the consultant team or the people who've been working with her for years – was a disaster.'

Crosby may have lacked the dictatorial control he had enjoyed in 2015, but he did try to recreate some of the atmosphere of previous campaigns, handing out mini cardboard Corbyns and masks of Tim Farron and Nicola Sturgeon to the 'Tory of the day'. Some were grateful for 'the only morale-boosting that was going on'. But for those who had worked on the 2015 campaign, this felt different: 'I like Lynton. In 2015 he kept morale in that building really high. That didn't happen this time. It didn't feel the same inside.' The word most commonly used to describe the atmosphere in 2017 was 'joyless'. Resentment was fuelled by CTF's army of thirty staff and rumoured £4 million bill while special advisers were expected to work for free.

At first Conservative campaign staff said the relationship between the campaign professionals – Crosby, Textor and Gilbert – and the keepers of the leader's flame – Timothy and Hill – was 'surprisingly good', certainly better than the mutual suspicion that governed Labour's LOTO–Southside splits. The five main players, plus Jojo Penn, Tom Edmonds, Alan Mabbutt and a rotating member of the press team would gather at 6 a.m. to review the media coverage, the latest polling and plan the day. These meetings were chaired by Gilbert and, when Crosby arrived from Fiji ten days into the campaign, increasingly by the Australian. The prime minister joined a follow-up conference call at 7 a.m. with the most senior staff, with a round-up meeting at 6 p.m. to review the day and look ahead at the next week at which Isaac Levido, one of CTF's top operators, was also present.

May was seldom in CCHQ as she was out campaigning, but also Crosby decreed, 'Keep her out of Central Office, we don't want her with all these germs.' Crosby had his reasons: 'Lynton and Stephen both had really nasty bouts of something during the campaign,' a senior figure recalled. Crosby also ordered campaign staff to 'wash your hands when you go to the loo. I don't want you spreading germs in the war room and everyone getting sick. Particularly you CRD boys,' an edict received with amusement by the Conservative Research Department. But when news of Crosby's metamorphosis into Florence Nightingale leaked he went 'fucking ballistic' and demanded the leaker be found and fired.

To those in the war room, the question that was never answered was a simple one: who was actually in charge? Not one of the thirty campaign officials interviewed for this book gave a straight answer to the question.

As far as Nick Timothy was concerned, he and Hill had ceded power to the consultants. He said, 'The funny thing is Fi and I are criticised quite a lot – especially in light of the election – for being too tight. It may be fair that we were too tight in government, but the one thing you can't say about us during the election campaign is we were too tight because we basically said, "We've never run a national campaign before." Lynton, Tex, Messina and Stephen Gilbert were brought in and we basically said to them, "You're the campaign gurus, you're in charge."' A friend of Timothy said, 'Would it not be logical to suggest that the people leading the staff meetings were the people running the campaign? Nick never led one. Nor did Fi. They were all led by Stephen Gilbert and Lynton Crosby.' Hill told friends, 'I was given a huge amount of responsibility but absolutely no power.' Once the election had gone wrong, allies of Timothy and Hill said Crosby was top dog. 'After Lynton was back in the country for a week or two, he effectively became the campaign director because Lynton cannot *not* be the campaign director,' a senior figure said.

Yet when the election was called, Downing Street staff were instructed differently: 'Everyone was told that Lynton was merely a consultant to the people who are running this election, which is Nick and Fiona,' one aide said. Crosby told a former minister that he 'probably only ever exchanged five hundred words with Theresa May' throughout the campaign. The campaign chiefs met with the prime minister about once a week in Downing Street or her home in Sonning, near Maidenhead. A source close to May said, 'It's absolutely not the case that there was a lack of access of them to her.' But May's views were usually communicated to the Australians and Gilbert 'through Nick and Fi'. A special adviser said, 'They made it very clear: "We know how she operates. She operates very differently to David [Cameron]. You don't know her like you know David and Boris. You go through us."' This was an unwelcome departure from the 2015 campaign, where Cameron sometimes chaired the morning meetings himself if he was not on the road. 'Nick and Fi fenced her off a bit,' a campaign director said. 'Lynton and Tex did not have that direct relationship.' Another senior figure said, 'Her chiefs would give her a recommendation and she'd make a decision with them. They would call Stephen and tell them the decision and Stephen would tell Lynton and Jim.'

With Timothy concentrating on writing the manifesto, it was Hill who was deciding where to go, what to do and what to brief the media. It was natural that those who had transferred from Whitehall, who were used to the overweening power of the chiefs, saw them as the ultimate source of power. 'Nick and Fiona were the decision-makers. They held all the power,' said one department head. 'Any kind of decision needed to refer to them.' Another team leader said, 'It felt like the campaign was being run by a sort of trifecta of Fiona, Lynton and Stephen Gilbert. There were two parallel campaigns. There was the campaign that Nick and Fi wanted to run for the PM, then there were things Lynton wanted to do.'

Watching from outside, Grant Shapps, the party chairman in 2015, was exasperated that the lessons of Cameron's victory were being ignored. 'Every successful campaign seeks to learn lessons from the past,' he said. '2010 was famously disorganised, with Andy Coulson and Steve Hilton pulling in opposite directions, so in 2015 we made a conscious effort to have a single arbiter in Crosby. But in 2017 the campaign unlearned all the lessons of the past and no single decision-maker was established. The result was a weak and chaotic campaign.' The lack of an undisputed leader meant there was a lack of anger and urgency when mistakes were made. A source who worked on both the 2015 and 2017 campaigns said, 'There should have been a shouty person. In 2015 I would get shouted at every five minutes: "Why are you doing this? Why aren't you doing this?" This campaign, nobody really ever shouted at me.' Some feel this led to a degree of complacency. 'In 2015 if that campaign had fucked up, everyone would be all over Lynton: donors, his clients, the opposition parties, journos. Lynton's arse was on the line. This time everyone figured, "If this goes badly we'll still pick up twenty extra seats and it'll be right as rain."'

Hill's modus operandi divided opinion as it had in government. A large number of campaign staff complained later that she was often absent from the war room, did not reply to emails, and her instructions sometimes left them unsure what she wanted. A source in the research department said, 'She was there in the morning meeting. She'd be around in the morning, tapping away on her iPad, and then just vanish.' Some in her media team were frustrated that she did not empower them to make decisions but was frequently unavailable when they needed taking. 'She didn't offer any kind of strategic direction,' one said. 'There were a couple of times where her suggestions were total madness.' Another added, 'You were left making decisions too late, racing to get stuff done, looking

chaotic to the media.' To some it seemed as if Hill regarded the campaign
as an awkward hurdle to be cleared before returning to the important
business of government. 'I can't wait until this is over, this is just something we've got to get through,' she told one colleague. When one of
David Cameron's closest aides asked Hill if they could give any advice on
the campaign, she is said to have replied, 'We don't find it difficult
running the government. How hard can it be to run an election?'

Yet other colleagues speak highly of Hill, and say that when presented
with options she would make decisions quickly and without fuss. 'Having
come into it quite scared of Fi, I actually found her to be pretty straightforward to work with,' one adviser said. 'If you could put a physical piece
of paper in front of her and say, "This is my plan," it was instantaneous
decision-making.' Another spad said, 'I think Fiona got a very unfair rap
during this campaign. If I didn't know about all the stories and had met
her for the first time on the campaign, I'd have thought that she was the
nicest, calmest person on the planet.' Another spad agreed: 'God love Fi.
I take people as I find them, and she was nothing but kind and supportive to me. In seven weeks I never once heard her raise her voice to
anybody. Quixotic people can be complicated. I quite liked her. Was I
frightened of her? Of course I was.' Those who liked her say Hill
responded positively if treated well herself. 'With senior people like that,
people only ever bring them problems. No one ever asks them how their
day is. If you answer the phone with a smile on your face and say, "How
are you doing?" they welcome it, they reciprocate, and it's a lot easier
than dreading the call or dreading making the call. I found her really
nice to work with by the end.'

Yet Hill could also be vindictive to little purpose. Lee Davis, a former
special adviser to Nicky Morgan, had given up her job to work on the
visits team in Yorkshire. When Hill spotted her in CCHQ she asked who
she was. Later that day, Davis got a call telling her, 'Fiona says you can't
have anything to do with the campaign.' Davis cried at the news. A friend
said, 'I thought it was so nasty to do to someone who's just a loyal foot-
soldier for the party. The only reason was her association with Nicky.'
Hill told a friend she did not believe Davis had 'behaved honourably'
when she was a spad.

Hill also allowed personal animus with broadcasters and ministers to
distort her judgement. When Adam Boulton, Sky News's veteran political presenter, used the hour before May's announcement of the election

to speculate that she might be standing down due to ill health, Hill fired off an irate text message to Boulton's producer saying, 'You might want to tell Bunter that he should watch what he is saying about my boss's health, utterly unfounded and untrue.' She then threatened to lodge a formal complaint with John Ryley, the head of Sky News. Perhaps incautiously, Boulton read out the text on air. When Boulton's colleague Beth Rigby wrote a blog suggesting Boris Johnson was to be sidelined during the campaign, a highly sensitive subject, 'Fiona decided Sky just weren't going to get anything,' a colleague recalled. For three weeks Sky were granted no ministerial interviews, culminating on the day of the Tory manifesto launch when Boulton complained on air about the ban. When Ryley sought to discuss the issue with Hill, she ignored him. 'Fi knows how to freeze someone out,' the source added. Hill had worked at Sky in the nineties, and was determined to punish an organisation for which she had little time. 'Why do we care about these fucking guys? They've got fuck-all viewers,' she said.

Hill's views on which ministers were allowed on television were also arbitrary and unbending. At the start of the campaign she handed the broadcasting team a list of 'good communicators' she wanted to see on television, and those who could be used *in extremis* or when their expertise was timely. Amber Rudd, David Davis, Priti Patel and Michael Fallon were all in the top tier, but as one media team staffer said, 'There was no way we could run a seven-week campaign with five people.' Karen Bradley and James Brokenshire, who earned their spurs alongside May in the Home Office, Damian Green, Patrick McLoughlin and the campaign 'attack dog', the security minister Ben Wallace, who had been friends with Hill since his days in Scottish politics, were also in Hill's good books. Boris Johnson and David Gauke, Fallon's understudy as a 'safe pair of hands' in a crisis, were available for 'judicious use'.

Johnson's sidelining was a frustration to campaign staff. 'I don't care if he pitches up to a Sikh temple and makes a gaffe,' one said. 'He is the closest thing we have got to a rock star.' Textor believed the foreign secretary could provide much-needed 'colour and movement'. They sent him to the Brexit-backing South-West but Hill diverted Johnson to Enfield, which was packed with Remainers. 'What the fuck is he doing there?' Crosby asked.[1]

The press team found Hill's admiration for the geeky Brokenshire bizarre. 'They put Brokenshire in a gym,' one said. 'The guy wakes up for breakfast in a suit and is the size of a pencil, and they wanted him walking around a gym with broadcast. Then there was a third tier, who were never to be let out of the cupboard.'

Those on the 'never use' list in a so-called 'Brexit election' included Brexiteers like Liam Fox, Andrea Leadsom and Chris Grayling, who spent the campaign doing regional tours, described by one aide as 'trying to organise a bunch of cats in the middle of a firework display'. Others banished to media Siberia included Justine Greening, the education secretary; Liz Truss, the justice secretary; and David Lidington. Hill's sheet decreed that Jeremy Hunt, the health secretary, should be confined to 'canvassing'. It is curious that ministers responsible for the public services were banished from the airwaves in an election where Labour was fighting austerity cuts in schools and hospitals.

The most high-profile member of the black-mark club, though, was Philip Hammond. The chancellor did not help his cause in the first week of the election when, on a trip to Washington DC, he hinted that he wanted to scrap David Cameron's tax lock, the pledge not to raise income tax, National Insurance or VAT. Hammond wanted to keep his options open, but for the chiefs and the Australians it was further proof that he had a tin ear for politics. After repeated calls from Downing Street to Hammond's special adviser Hayden Allen, the chancellor was ordered to issue a clarification, saying the Tories would always be 'the low-tax party'. Allen resigned a few days later. Hammond was summoned to see the campaign chiefs. A senior Number 10 official said, 'When Hammond landed he then went in for a meeting with Tex and Stephen. Tex's view was that the problem was not just Hammond's instincts in terms of how to communicate, but he wouldn't really listen on how to communicate and he didn't really get elections. And that was really dangerous.'

Crosby and Textor labelled Hammond 'a fucking cheese dick' and told Hill and Timothy, 'We need to keep him away from everything from now on.' A colleague recalled, 'I'd never really heard "cheese dick" until that point.' But the phrase caught life, and soon Hill was using it about Hammond too. The debacle simply reinforced her judgement that the chancellor should be neither seen nor heard, a position reinforced by briefings, attributed to Hill, that he would be fired in a post-election reshuffle. In the early stages of the campaign the chancellor was only allowed out in public once, joining David Davis for the unveiling of a poster and a rather flimsy document denouncing Labour's spending commitments as 'the cost of chaos'. Davis did most of the talking.

Hammond's banishment meant the Tories downplayed the economy. But campaign officials are also adamant that Hill and Timothy regarded economic differentiation as part of the Cameron–Osborne playbook from which they were keen to distance themselves. That meant no letters from hundreds of businessmen saying the Tories could be trusted, a favourite Osborne tactic, which Hill felt had failed the Remain campaign in 2016. 'At the beginning of the campaign, the steer we got was: no dossiers or letters this time,' a research department source said. 'No one believes them any more.'

A senior official recalled, 'Fiona wanted a distinction between us and the 2015 campaign. The events team weren't allowed to choose venues that Cameron had been to.' This edict dramatically limited the number of businesses and accessible venues Richard 'Tricky' Jackson's team could use for May's campaign stops.

The area where Hill's loathing of the Cameroon playbook had most impact was the Mayites' belief that social media was a gimmick ill-matched to the prime minister's serious public image. The stance, which stopped May commenting on Twitter on every banal development in public life, had virtue in government but was a serious impediment to campaigning during an election where platforms like Facebook, Twitter, Instagram and Snapchat had long replaced party political broadcasts and billboards as the main means of conveying a message to voters. In 2015 the Tories had won the social media war with a better-funded and better-supported Facebook operation. Team May did not even try to compete with Jeremy Corbyn. 'It wasn't that they didn't want it,' a senior figure in the campaign said, 'it was worse than that – they hated it. They specifically said they wanted to be the opposite of Cameron.'

This made for an awkward conversation early on between Hill and Tom Edmonds about what the campaign was allowed to do on social media. Hill said Steve Back, a photographer hired by the Tories for the duration of the campaign, would be able to send them some pictures, but there was no appetite for May to emulate Cameron by recording short video clips on an iPhone which could be instantly posted online. Hill was also reluctant to 'sign off' on the use of photographs which showed May in a less than perfect light, meaning that even when the digital team was able to post images of the prime minister it was long after the event in question had finished. 'It's better to get it out quicker than to wait four hours and have a perfect shot,' said a campaign source. 'Theresa's team just weren't interested, so you'd lost that huge advantage, especially when you're trying to make it a leadership thing, about her. The sign-off process was incredibly tortuous.' Edmonds pumped out more through the Conservative Party's social media channels than May's personal feed because only Crosby had to approve the postings.

Since the existing digital team in CCHQ had not been trusted by Downing Street, they had been dissuaded from making much use of Twitter, and the prime minister did not even have an Instagram account, a basic tool of the modern politician. On all social media regular engagement with followers is key to building an audience and trust with that audience, but May's tweets were rare and stilted. Consequently, her Twitter account had just 300,000 followers, compared with 1.2 million for Jeremy Corbyn. By the end of the campaign, Corbyn's 120,000 Instagram followers approached ten times May's reach. Conservative campaigners looked with envy at Corbyn, eight years May's senior but light years ahead of her as a social media campaigner. 'They're good at it, he likes it,' a Tory official said. 'They're not afraid to take a few risks. They did a few good stunts.'

Corbyn's best coup came on 15 May, when he ambushed a 'Facebook live' interview with May conducted by ITV's political editor, Robert Peston. The Labour leader posted a question as 'Jeremy Corbyn of Islington', asking May, 'Do you not think the British people deserve to see us debate, live and on TV?' May's face darkened with the combination of irritation and terror with which the public were to become familiar as the campaign went on, and claimed that people would rather the leaders 'take questions directly from the voters'. A story about the PM doing her first ever Facebook interview became instead a headline about Corbyn's audacity and May dodging televised debates.

At the start of the campaign, Crosby, Textor and Gilbert identified eighty-six target seats. They numbered all seats from one to five, where one was a safe Tory seat, two was a Tory seat that needed to be defended, three was a Labour marginal at the mercy of the Tories, four was a Labour seat that might be in play if things went well, and five was an unwinnable 'fantasy land' Labour seat. 'Before the campaign started we had thirty-five seats that were full-on targets [groups two and three], and then we had a further fifty-one which we kept an eye on' with a view to looking at them again after the local elections.

Gilbert thought around half of the fifty-one seats in category four might be winnable, suggesting that a very good night for the Conservatives would be a haul of around sixty gains – a number that would increase May's majority to 137 if all the category two and three seats were won as well. The public polling at that time suggested that the Tories could come away with an even bigger margin of victory of between 150 and 180, but this created a crisis of expectation management. Hill, Oxley and Crosby all briefed the media that Textor was privately warning that the polls could be wrong, but journalists thought they were being spun. Leaks of Labour's polling putting the Tories two hundred seats ahead reinforced the narrative that May was going to win big. After the election, Katie Perrior said, 'The smart thing to do would have been to ensure that the internal predictions were "leaked" to let the air out of the balloon.'[2] In fact, the Tories had good reason to keep their internal data from the public. When Jim Messina completed his first model, a little after Crosby had arrived from Fiji, it put the Conservatives on 470 seats, a majority of 290, the largest for a single party in British electoral history. When the number was read out, Textor said, 'Shit, do not say that in front of other people.'

The problem for the Tories was that they had shackled themselves with a seven-week campaign in which the only way was down. Crosby told colleagues, 'Long campaigns damage incumbents, because you're the target.' Until the passage of the Fixed Term Parliaments Act in 2011, a government could call an election and dissolve Parliament a minimum of seventeen days before polling day. But the law passed by the coalition raised that to twenty-five days. When May's aides raised the issue of election timing with Sue Gray, after Jeremy Heywood the second most powerful mandarin in Whitehall, she pointed out that if Labour refused to vote for an election Number 10 would need to allow a fortnight to pass an Emergency Bill with further time for the parliamentary 'wash-up' of legislation already going through the House. 'In 1974,' the last time a prime minister called a snap election seeking a bigger mandate, 'there were twenty-one days from announcement to polling day. This time it was fifty-one,' a Number 10 official pointed out.

The snap election also presented logistical issues for the Conservatives. 'To do an election address to forty-six million electors you have to buy the paper in from overseas,' a Tory political aide explained. 'There's not enough paper in the country for all the parties to print what they want, so it's a bit of a scramble and there are only about five printing firms in the country that can physically do it.' Once May fired the starting gun, candidates made frantic tours of their constituencies 'taking photos, swapping their jackets and jumpers so it looks like they've done it over so many days'. The leaflets written in the first week of the campaign would be delivered in the final four or five days before polling day. For Conservative MPs this meant literature which featured Theresa May as much as themselves. By the time they appeared May was no longer an asset.

In the first fortnight, Textor and Gilbert conducted a series of briefings for ministers and campaign staff. The political cabinet met upstairs in Downing Street's pillared room. Textor – wearing 'hilarious glasses like he'd just been kind of DJing in Ibiza the night before' – outlined the basics of the strategy and May's 'stratospheric' personal approval ratings. May then informed ministers that Ben Gummer would be 'harvesting ideas' for the manifesto. So peripheral was Jeremy Corbyn to May's thoughts that ministers said afterwards it was the first discussion they had ever had in a political cabinet under May about how to defeat Labour. On 24 April, Textor told senior staff at CCHQ that the three goals of the campaign were: 'Protecting and enhancing the prime minister; infusing that into every issue we face; and making the point that the only way to get her is to vote for a local Conservative candidate.' Textor's numbers showed that voters thought 'Theresa May seems eminently fair and reasonable. She trusts people and they trust her without being all fucking Big Society.' By contrast, he added, 'The words that people associate with Corbyn are "floundering", "weak" and "nonsensical".' But Textor added, 'We need to raise the emotional expectation that Jeremy Corbyn can win.' The argument he told MPs to use was this: 'If these clowns fuck up Brexit it will hurt local jobs and businesses.' He concluded by saying, 'Putting Theresa May in everything delivers you a four-point difference over the Conservative brand.' One campaign director recalled, 'Tex said that at that stage Theresa May was the greatest electoral asset on the right of politics since [Ronald] Reagan.'

To start with, it worked. The message from the doorstep was that May had surprisingly broad appeal. One candidate in a working-class seat in the North-East described the prime minister as 'electoral crack'. Andrew Percy, a local government minister who represented Brigg and Goole, said, 'I've never experienced anything like this in over twenty years' canvassing in general elections. Remain-voting Tory voters trusted the PM and Labour voters who backed Brexit were not only downing tools but switching to us. It was incredible.' A CCHQ official canvassing in South London said, 'In the first few weeks of the campaign, it was better to say, "I'm here on behalf of Theresa May." It genuinely helped. They liked her.' When Lauren McEvatt, a former special adviser, did telephone canvassing in Stockport early in the campaign, every target voter she spoke to answered 'more' to the question: 'Does Theresa May being leader of the Conservative Party make you more or less likely to vote Conservative?'

These reports convinced Crosby that his strategy was right, and the chiefs that May was the transformational politician they had always believed. 'That was exactly what Number 10 wanted to hear,' a Downing Street aide said. 'Their natural instinct to make it all about Theresa was exacerbated by that.' Tory MPs, with the combination of submissive awe and slightly sinister familiarity that governed the party's attitude towards a female boss, took to referring to their leader as 'Mummy' in text and WhatsApp exchanges. George Freeman, the MP who led the prime minister's policy board, summed up her apotheosis: 'The British public looked at her and thought that she was the reluctant leader, summoned to office in an hour of national crisis, the accidental prime minister there to put the country before party. They liked her style, her tone, her quiet, unflashy, steely resolve, and I think they quite liked the fact that she had been a Remainer. Her instincts weren't tribal and partisan on Europe, but she was reconciled to the result, which I think spoke to the mood of the nation. I think they loved her speech on the steps of Number 10 and they thought, "Here's a daughter of the Church and of public service, steeped in the best British values." She has John Major's moderate and decent One Nation instincts with a touch of Maggie's steel, and it's a winning combination.'

To those who had seen May up close – the less star-struck MPs, a large proportion of special advisers and nearly all journalists – those first three weeks of the campaign were a time of mystery, where the laws of politics appeared to have been suspended. Matt Chorley of *The Times* spoke for many when he mocked the cult of the strong and stable leader on 6 May:

'The Tory leader is now on the list of things you cannot publicly admit to disliking, alongside *Star Wars*, Center Parcs and other people's children,' he wrote. 'While everyone else is cooing at the empress's new clothes, I just don't see it ... Except for calling a snap election, Mrs May has barely said or done anything interesting for eleven months and yet is the subject of fevered fan-worship usually reserved for One Direction and Kim Kardashian's bottom.'[3] One bemused minister described the enthusiasm for May as 'the cult of no personality'.

Theresa May was still largely unknown, and Britons were painting the pictures they wanted to see on the canvas which, by design or inaction, she had left publicly blank. A minister said, 'There is less there than meets the eye. Journalists look for ulterior motives. Her motives are very simple. She wants to do what's best for the country. She thinks she's the best person for the job. It's not complicated.' There were other Theresa Mays, though, and they were to reveal themselves as the campaign went on.

May revealed something of her simple virtues in an interview with BBC1's *The One Show* on 9 May, alongside her husband. The star of the show was Philip May, who displayed a fine line in dry wit. Asked whether his wife was a tough negotiator, he said, 'Well, there's give and take in every marriage. I get to decide when I take the bins out. Not if I take them out.' Slightly too eagerly, Theresa jumped in, 'There's boys' jobs and girls' jobs, you see.' The comment was received with almost Pooterish glee by the mid-market tabloids. The exchange reinforced May's reassuring provincialism.

Fiona Hill was delighted that the interview had passed off without incident. Philip May had 'taken some persuading' that it was a good idea, and had done well. May herself had not been polished or pitch perfect, but that was almost the point. 'She seemed like your next-door neighbour,' a special adviser said. Tom Swarbrick, the head of broadcasting, told colleagues he was delighted with the 'boys' and girls' jobs' comment, which May had ad-libbed. 'It was two fingers up to the 5 per cent of the country who still can't get their head around the fact that 95 per cent of people still think in terms of boys' jobs and girls' jobs,' he said.

Yet her aides had also seen how uncomfortable May had been preparing for the interview. They had negotiated with the BBC that presenter Matt Baker could ask her about the death of her father, but after one brief question that elicited the response that his death was 'awful' Baker inexplicably moved on, and May did nothing to extend her answer – as many politicians would have – into a memorable moment of television which might have insulated her from claims later in the campaign that she lacked empathy. Some of those watching in CCHQ found the experience 'excruciating': 'It confirmed to me that out in front, talking about herself, is not what she likes to do. She's not good at it.'

Even as her popularity soared, some loyalists worried that May was brittle if left out in the sun. When Chris Wilkins saw a backdrop prepared for an event with the words 'Theresa May's team' he put his head in his hands. Textor demanded yard signs for Conservative candidates reading: 'Standing with Theresa May'. On 12 May the PM travelled to the North-East to unveil the Tory battle bus. The word 'Conservatives' was written in tiny writing on the door. Emblazoned down the side was 'Theresa May: For Britain' and, slightly smaller, 'Strong, Stable Leadership in the National Interest'. Those looking for negative omens noted it was the same vehicle the Remain campaign had used a year before, in different livery. Wilkins confided to a friend, 'I just don't think these guys get her. This is a politician who's built her career on quiet confidence. You wonder why that politician is suddenly touring the country on a bus with her name on it. It just runs counter to everything she is and our research told us people liked about her.' George Freeman agreed: 'Sometimes Lynton's brash Aussie chuck-another-shrimp-on-the-barbie politics is quite raw. If Australia was a person it would be a twenty-eight-year-old bloke in Speedos. If Britain was a person it would be a little old lady in a cardigan in Barnsley.'

Those who had worked with Crosby and Textor before sought to reassure these doubters. 'They're pirates, but they're our pirates,' one remarked. Whenever Nick Timothy felt uncomfortable, he told himself, 'These guys know how to run elections.' Another senior figure in the campaign, close to neither CTF nor the chiefs, said they were both complicit in pushing May into the spotlight: 'Whether it was Lynton's idea or not, they all – Lynton, Nick and Fi – regurgitated the stuff about her polling numbers being far ahead. Fi in particular swallowed the bullshit just as much as Lynton did.'

And what of May herself, so often an enigma?

'She wasn't comfortable doing it,' a close confidant said. 'But she accepted it because she was willing to take advice from people who she'd appointed.' In 'more than one conversation' in the boardroom at CCHQ, May told the Australians she did not like carrying the campaign on her shoulders alone. But as prime minister she could have brought a halt to it, and she did not. 'It wasn't like she was saying, "We mustn't do this,"' the source said. 'She was saying, "This isn't very me. I don't like pushing myself forward in this way. It's not my team, it's the Conservative Party." Her instinct was that it wasn't her.'

On the first Sunday of the campaign, a senior figure leaked details of the Tories' first retail offer to the *Sunday Times*, a commitment to cap household energy bills for the seventeen million families on standard tariffs, for an estimated saving of £100 a year. In a different form this aped an Ed Miliband pledge from 2015 which the Cameroons had denounced as near-Marxist market intervention, but it was of a piece with May's conference speech promising a more activist state, as markets were failing to deliver for ordinary people. Those who thought it was going to be the first of a series of pledges to families who were 'just about managing' were to be disappointed, but YouGov's poll that weekend was remarkable. It gave the Tories a twenty-three-point lead, and revealed that voters trusted May even more than Corbyn to run the NHS, while a Panelbase survey put Ruth Davidson's party north of the border on course to win a dozen seats. Only one of these findings was to hold.

Throughout April and the first week of May, the Conservatives' enduring poll lead and the lack of policy stories left the media covering the subject it loves the best – itself. A narrative developed that May's team were exerting freakish control over media coverage. It was set on 2 May, when the prime minister travelled to Cornwall. Her team had given a local website, Cornwall Live, the chance to interview her, but refused to let it film her answers – a request that was routinely declined even though it would have brought her to a wider audience. While May visited a factory, Cornwall Live's journalist was confined to an office room with regional camera crews from the BBC and ITV. He began posting pictures of keys hanging from the door. They were on the inside, but the impression given was that the hacks had been locked in. Tom Swarbrick was driving to the next event when a social media storm blew up. He contacted the BBC, ITV and Sky to point out that Cornwall Live's claims were false – and later got a retraction – but by then it was too late, and Radio 4's *PM* programme was broadcasting as fact that the Tories had 'locked journalists in a cupboard'. 'From that moment, the tone of controlled and managed campaigning was set,' a member of the media team said. 'And it was set on a lie.' A colleague added, 'Cornwall Live got more hits on the row they caused than they ever would have doing a proper interview. But focus groups showed that stuff cut through, and that really pissed me off.'

The incident led Hill, Oxley and Craig Woodhouse to order a 'masochism strategy', where May would make a virtue of taking every question from journalists at her events – even those she knew would be hostile. Tory spin doctors briefed the papers that their leader had taken five times as many questions as Labour's. But, as one exasperated political editor put it, 'The problem was not that she didn't take any questions, the problem was that she didn't give any fucking answers.'

A senior campaign official said, 'She hated doing the media.' Another aide said, 'She would roll her eyes when Fiona said she had to do an interview.' On one occasion May was asked to do a brief pooled clip for the broadcasters on a major story that was impacting the campaign. She said, 'I don't see why I should have to do it just because the media want to do it.' This attitude was inexplicable to journalists, who could not understand why a woman who had wanted to be prime minister for four decades could not see the point of more positive engagement with people who could help her explain herself to the voters. Media irritation bled into the broadcast coverage, and then into focus groups. 'When journalists were having a go at her for not doing interviews, that was quite damaging in the numbers,' a campaign chief said. 'People said, "If she's not telling us now what she stands for, how do I know what she's going to do after the election?"'

May's refusal to do televised debates with Corbyn played into the same narrative, and made it difficult for the Tories to kill the 'hiding away' story. 'Corbyn was actually taking questions from almost nobody, and being far more controlled, but it was impossible to get that narrative across,' an aide complained.

It didn't help that May's events were often shambolic. The Tories were late to deliver 'op notes' detailing where campaign events were to take place, in part because Hill and Jojo Penn were slow to approve the details and constantly changed their minds. 'If there's one thing I'm looking forward to not dealing with post this campaign, it's ops,' Hill said. On one occasion May and Philip Hammond were scheduled to visit the

same factory a day apart. A week into the campaign, Conservative officials told journalists to travel to Norwich for a rally, before changing the
destination at the last minute and telling them to head to Enfield in West
London, two hours back from whence they had come. 'The problem was
that venues for events were not getting signed off until very late the night
before,' a campaign official admitted. A research department source said,
'The ops team would identify a set of locations, and it goes to CRD to vet
them to make sure it's not run by the local chairman of the BNP or the
company is not going out of business. We were literally getting things
sent in the middle of the night saying: "We're going to go there at 7 a.m.
tomorrow, unless you've got any objections." Locations were changed on
a whim.' May often set off for events unsure why she was going to certain
places and not properly briefed on how many speeches she was due to
give during the day.

Unused to the pace of a national election campaign, the prime minister complained when she had to memorise 'yet another fifteen-minute
speech', and was constantly nervous of performing. Towards the end of
the campaign one adviser went to collect her from the room where she
was preparing for a rally and found Philip May pacing around outside.
'I went to move towards the door and he looked at me and said, "No, no,
no, no. Even I'm not allowed in there right now." I was really surprised
that she had kicked him out of the room. That was the level of focus she
deemed necessary to have. It felt a bit odd to me.'

For her set-piece speeches like the manifesto launch May would never
use an autocue, because 'she doesn't want to be like David' Cameron, but
in other circumstances she still craved the security blanket. On one occasion a member of the digital team made a two-hour journey to record a
social media advert. On hearing that he had failed to bring an autocue,
the prime minister refused to do the clip. 'It was only two minutes,' said
a despairing Tory. 'Most politicians can do that sort of thing standing on
their heads.' But not Theresa May.

As manifesto season approached, the lines May *had* memorised were
the ones causing her trouble. In rallies and interviews she parroted
'strong and stable', 'coalition of chaos' and assorted bromides about
Brexit. When comedians began mocking her for the strong-and-stable
mantra, at first the CCHQ staff were happy – it proved the slogan had
'cut through' to the public. But after a while even senior Conservatives
were mocking the minimalist campaign. When David Cameron was

revealed to have paid £25,000 for a wooden shepherd's hut for his back garden, he told a charity fundraiser the following week, 'I just heard Theresa talk about strong and stable leadership, but I only heard the first part about getting a strong stable.' Ruth Davidson went further. Quoting George Orwell, she said, 'Politics gives solidity to pure wind. I don't know what he would make of the current election campaign: strong, stable.'

One source close to May claimed that she complained privately that she was now an object of ridicule: 'I look stupid.' For his part, Crosby was frustrated that the prime minister worked in her talking points so robotically – leading her to be dubbed 'the Maybot', a nickname adopted even by some junior campaign staff. A Crosby ally explained, 'The idea wasn't that she was strong and stable, it was that we needed to elect a government with a clear majority so that it can be strong and stable, because you're going to have to negotiate with a bunch of pricks in Europe. And it all got parodied.'

May was only really happy doing what she did every weekend – knocking on doors and talking to voters. When she visited Scotland at the start of the campaign, Fiona Hill only allowed her a few minutes' canvassing before flying back to London. An angry May rounded on her chief of staff and said, 'Stop trying to limit how much time I'm spending on the doorstep. I'm a doorstep campaigner, and from now on I want to spend proper time knocking on doors speaking to people.' This might have been admirable in a local MP, but it suggested May was not ready for the very different responsibilities of being the lead singer in the Tory band in a national campaign.

Despite clear signs that the Tory campaign was not operating at full capacity there existed at CCHQ a blithe assumption that the result would go their way. A close ally of Nick Timothy said, 'I had conversations with Nick and Fi, where they used phrases like, "We will win a load of seats we've never even won before." Bishop Auckland was always mentioned, and Bolsover. People were getting excited about the prospect of unseating Dennis Skinner.' At that point the Labour veteran had a majority of nearly 12,000. 'Fundamentally, people assumed it was in the bag and all decisions stemmed from that,' a senior figure said.

Overconfidence led Hill to block Crosby from pumping out negative stories about Corbyn. 'We didn't want a situation where he was doing so poorly that if we kicked too hard, the British public would rally round an underdog,' a campaign source said. This judgement was understandable, but it also had the effect of amplifying the onslaught when it did come, and of giving Corbyn the space to define himself with voters who were just beginning to pay attention to politics. It was also frustrating for the Conservative Research Department, which had gathered 'a *Raiders of the Lost Ark*-style warehouse of Corbyn stuff'. A CRD staffer said, 'There were all the greatest hits: IRA, Hamas, Hezbollah. Every day I was saying, "Here's all these good stories, can we start getting them out?" I complained to CTF people and they said Fiona was blocking them.'

For three weeks the Conservative campaign ground relentlessly on with a logic all its own. One senior figure compared it to an oil tanker, but one that had sprung a few leaks and had commanders on the bridge who disagreed about where to steer. 'It felt like this oil tanker would keep going in a straight line from point A to B,' the adviser said, 'But a genuinely agile, inventive, hostile opponent could defeat us if they harried us all along that route. What if the original course we'd plotted was wrong, and the captain wasn't quite as infallible as everyone had made out?'

Fortunately for the Tories, two of their three main opponents, who had often shown themselves the most agile, were busy shooting themselves in the foot.

16

FROM SHARKS TO MINNOWS

One of the dominant themes of the 2017 election was the way the Tory–Labour battle eclipsed Britain's minor parties. The fate of Ukip and the Liberal Democrats on 8 June 2017 was to hang in large part on 23 June 2016. The EU referendum was to help sink Ukip and fail to revive the Lib Dems. It did so, in both cases, because of poor leadership.

Ever since the referendum, Ukip, the once mighty protest party which had forced David Cameron to call a referendum, had been in a tragicomic freefall of its own creation. In the three months from September 2016 Ukip had four party leaders, two of whom were Nigel Farage. When the hero of the Leave campaign had first stood down, the election to succeed him had been won by Diane James, who then unexpectedly quit after eighteen days, having realised she had little stomach for the scrutiny the role would bring. This might have been evident earlier if James had turned up for any of the leadership debates during the campaign, but she did not.

James had won because the frontrunners did not stand. Paul Nuttall, Farage's old deputy, sat out the contest for family reasons, while Steven Woolfe, an MEP seen as the party's rising star, had farcically missed the deadline for applications by seventeen minutes. When the second contest took place both stood, but Woolfe got into a punch-up with the aptly named MEP Mike Hookem over claims that Woolfe was talking about defecting to the Tories, and was laid out prostrate on a walkway in the European Parliament building. Arron Banks, the insurance tycoon who had bankrolled the Leave.EU campaign and was backing Woolfe, took a call from Farage. 'He's dead,' Mr Brexit announced. 'Woolfe. He's dead. He's collapsed after a bust-up with Mike Hookem.' When Banks laughed, Farage insisted, 'It's not fucking funny – he's dead.'[1]

Woolfe, fortunately, was not dead, but he was finished as a leadership contender while his health recovered, leaving the prize for Nuttall, a Liverpudlian bruiser who seemed to be tailor-made to peel Brexit votes away from Labour in their Northern heartlands.

Under pressure from Farage, Nuttall ran in the Stoke-on-Trent Central by-election. There he became embroiled in a succession of controversies that sank his campaign. First, he declared that he was living in a house in Stoke which he had not moved into at the time his nomination papers were filed, potentially a breach of electoral law. Then he was forced to apologise for falsely claiming on his website that he had lost friends in the Hillsborough disaster of 1989, which claimed the lives of ninety-six Liverpool fans, while controversy raged about whether he had been present at the tragedy at all. Close to a national laughing stock, Nuttall finished a distant second just seventy-nine votes ahead of the Tory candidate, who was considered a no-hoper. Yet another chance of a Ukip breakthrough in Westminster foundered on the reef of incompetence.

At the end of March the party's only MP, Douglas Carswell, quit the party, declaring that Ukip had achieved its foundational goal and should now shut up shop: 'I switched to Ukip because I desperately wanted us to leave the EU. Now we can be certain that that is going to happen, I have decided that I will be leaving Ukip.' When the election was called he announced that he would be standing down and voting Conservative. Many other Ukip voters were expected to do the same. Having campaigned nationwide two years earlier, the party only fielded candidates in 377 of the 650 constituencies in 2017. In the local elections Ukip lost every seat they were defending, making one solitary gain from Labour in Bolton. Woolfe publicly declared that he would vote for May, not Nuttall, to be prime minister. 'I have no choice,' he said.

As chief rifleman in the circular firing squad, Banks rounded on Nuttall for opening his general election campaign with a push on Muslim issues rather than treating the election as 'a second Brexit referendum', pronounced Ukip dead and announced that he and Farage would start a new movement in the autumn. In an extraordinary statement emailed to political journalists, Banks said, 'Tory-leaning Ukip voters rightly concluded this is about delivering Brexit and the other issues just don't matter in this election. If we use the analogy of Ukip as a racing car, Nigel was a skilled driver who drove the car around the track faster and faster, knowing when to take risks, delighting the audience. The current leadership has crashed the car, at the first bend of the race, into the crowd, killing the driver and spectators.' As assessments of precipitous political collapse go, it was on point.

In 2014, Ukip had won the European elections. In 2015 they received nearly four million votes and 12.6 per cent of the national vote share. The EU referendum result made them perhaps the most effective pressure group in British political history. In 2017 they secured just 1.8 per cent of the vote.

While the Tories' fondest hopes that they could attract voters appeared to be materialising, their darkest fear – that the Liberal Democrats would stage a revival by setting themselves up as the only major anti-Brexit party – was fading fast. During his two years in charge Tim Farron, the Lib Dem leader, had doubled party membership to more than 100,000 and had overseen several encouraging wins in council by-elections, prompting initial media predictions that Remain voters would propel the party to twenty or thirty seats.

The Lib Dems had actually made more preparations for a snap election than either of the two main parties, selecting more than four hundred candidates by the end of 2016, with most in place as early as September in case Theresa May went to the country. That enabled them to get a commitment from Nick Clegg, the former leader and MP for Sheffield Hallam, to fight again before he had had time to start seeking a new job. Clegg had been 'a little bit' reluctant. 'He and Miriam probably wanted to go off and do other things,' a party official noted. By moving to pin down Clegg – and secure commitments to run again from other big names ousted in 2015 such as Sir Vince Cable and Sir Edward Davey – the Lib Dems avoided a candidate-selection psychodrama in April and were able to hit the ground running.

Former Clegg aide Phil Reilly returned as director of communications in August to draw up a campaign grid, and Lib Dem peer Dick Newby was drafted in to write a manifesto. As 2017 dawned, Farron's team worked on the assumption that May would call an election for 4 May – as MPs like Andrew Bridgen had urged her to. When that window passed they 'relaxed a bit'.

Farron knew he had a challenge. Research conducted when he took over showed that the Lib Dem brand had been badly damaged by joining

the Tories in coalition government in 2010, and then ditching their
opposition to a rise in university tuition fees. 'We realised we were in a
worse state than we thought we were,' an official recalled. 'There were a
whole group of people who were just impossible to reach now.'

The party's flirtation with the possibility of a new party since the EU
referendum had an ulterior motive. 'That whole third-party thing was
about showing those soft Labour Remainers who we were going to try to
go after in the election that we were a viable force,' a close aide explained.

When it was announced that May was going to make a statement in
Downing Street, Farron was en route to Cornwall for the party's local
election launch event. His spokesman Paul Butters armed him with three
statements, 'one for direct rule in Northern Ireland, one for the snap
election, and one for if they'd blown the shit out of [Abu Bakr]
al-Baghdadi', the boss of Isis, which had established a terrorist caliphate
in parts of Syria and Iraq. When the leadership realised May had gifted
them a chance to rebuild three years earlier than they had feared, there
was jubilation. Chief executive Tim Gordon emerged from his office at
Lib Dem headquarters in Great George Street and declared, 'We've been
waiting for this.'

The most important issue to settle was the party's stance on Brexit.
Norman Lamb, a centrist who Farron had beaten in the leadership
contest of July 2015, argued that the party should respect the result of the
referendum. This was a natural impulse for an MP defending a marginal
seat in North Norfolk, where six out of ten voters had backed the Leave
campaign. A compromise was thrashed out in which Farron agreed the
Lib Dems would not seek to oppose the triggering of Article 50, but
would fight for a second referendum to be held on the Brexit deal – effectively handing voters veto powers at a later date. 'Norman wanted to
accept the will of the people, and Tim said, "We can't do that, let's have a
referendum on the deal,"' a source said. 'It polled reasonably well,
actually.'

Farron announced the new position on 7 September 2016 on the
Today programme, arguing that 'voting for departure is not the same as
voting for a destination', and that 'none of us voted for whatever it is that
we might get from the deal arranged and negotiated by David Davis'.
When the government's bill to trigger Article 50 was voted on in
February, Farron marched six of his MPs through the No lobby against
it. Lamb and Greg Mulholland both abstained, saying they could not

defy the public will. 'For better or worse we all voted to hold the referendum. You can't now say we reject the result,' Lamb said.

When the election was called, the Lib Dems prepared to wheel out a
series of pre-planned announcements – ruling out any pacts or coali-
tions to insulate them from claims that they would prop up a Corbyn
government; adding 1p to income tax to inject funds into the NHS;
reversing school funding cuts; and accepting the recommendations of
the Dilnot Review into social care provision. The one sticking point was
the party's Brexit position. Farron's closest aide Paul Butters was among
those arguing, 'We should make this election a referendum on Brexit. If
you are voting for us you are voting for an anti-Brexit party.' Most of the
party's big guns agreed that they should make Brexit the centrepiece of
their campaign. On 24 April Farron told the *Independent* that the pledge
to hold a second referendum would be in the manifesto, giving voters the
chance to reverse Brexit. 'It is still possible for the British people to stop
a hard Brexit and keep us in the Single Market,' he said. 'If they want, it
will also be possible for the British people to choose to remain in the
European Union. Democracy didn't end on 23 June and the people must
have their say over what comes next.'

Having spread themselves too thinly in 2015 defending more than
forty seats – of which they won just eight – Farron's team concentrated
on seriously fighting thirty seats, with the hope that they might double
their contingent of eight MPs – or, on a good night, squeeze into the
twenties. It quickly became apparent that they were in contention in
strong Remain seats in South-West London like Twickenham and
Richmond, where former cabinet ministers Cable and Davey were
hoping for a return, but the hoped-for revival in much of the West
Country was stalled. There was a fundamental disconnect between the
party wanting to reverse Brexit and voters who had overwhelmingly
backed the Leave campaign.

When real votes were counted in the local elections the Lib Dem
performance was disappointing. They had managed 18 per cent of the
vote but lost forty-two council seats when psephologists had predicted
gains of a hundred – a haul that dented media interest in the third party
as an electoral force at a critical time in the campaign.

In retrospect, Lib Dem officials believe the election came too soon for
them to make a persuasive argument that Brexit was a disaster and
should be opposed. 'We put all of our chips on red and Brexit,' a senior

figure recalled. 'The most difficult conversation I've ever had was with a journalist when they said, "Point to one statistic that says that Brexit is bad, that proves your hypothesis right now." And that's actually quite difficult. Because you can point out that NHS staff workers are leaving, that costs are rising a little bit, that fuel is getting a little bit more expensive – but they're not killer. Yet. And so you are the doom-mongers when even Labour Remainers and others felt, "We need to make this work."' By focusing on Brexit, to the exclusion of almost everything else, the Lib Dems used up their 'political bandwidth' broadcasting a message to which even many Remain voters were unreceptive. 'Brexit worked really well for us in places like South London but it made things very difficult in the South-West,' a source said.

The biggest problem, however, was closer to home – their leader. Farron was unusual in British politics in having worn his evangelical Christianity on his sleeve. During the leadership contest with Lamb he had faced some awkward questions about his views on homosexuality and gay marriage, where his faith conflicted with his political liberalism. Some MPs and activists had been put off voting for him after an interview with *Channel 4 News*'s Cathy Newman in which he had struggled to answer whether he thought homosexuality was a sin. 'We are all sinners,' he said. When Farron won the leadership contest handsomely, he and his team thought the issue was closed. Newman had not forgotten, however, and when she interviewed Farron at the start of the election campaign the day after May's announcement, she asked him again. Once more he refused to be categorical, telling her, 'Just because I'm a Christian, it would be a bit boring for everybody if we spend the next six weeks asking me to make theological pronouncements.'

While it might be legitimate for a politician to keep their religious views to themselves, the media smelt blood, questioning Farron at every event about his views on homosexuality. Privately, one of Farron's MPs revealed that the leader had indeed once confided that he believed gay sex was a sin. Farron's position was that his votes had never been determined by his religious views. Yet because he failed to close down the issue it began to freeze out even Brexit as the dominant theme of his campaign.

Paul Butters made a snap decision, which he later came to see as a 'massive error', that Farron should keep dead-batting the question. 'We're not going to get drawn into religious chat,' he told his boss. 'There is a difference between your faith and you as a legislator, and as soon as you get drawn into it and say, "That's a sin," people will go, "Well all right, what about this? What about that?"' If Farron said more, that would mean a whole day of coverage for a policy position would be lost. Butters felt his judgement was justified when Farron's office got wind that a former Tory cabinet minister was priming journalists with other 'gotcha' questions to ask him. 'If you bat it away, at a certain point they will get bored and they will move on.'

The problem for Farron was that the media did not get bored. For nearly a week, when the party should have been showing voters it was relevant again, the Lib Dem element of the main news bulletins was dominated by his latest equivocal pronouncement on homosexuality. Other members of Farron's team tried to persuade him to act. Phil Reilly and Sam Barratt, the head honchos in the communications department, both argued that he should do a clip for the broadcasters clarifying his position. Others flipped day by day. The discussions in Farron's office at party headquarters, a spartan room decorated only with a Blackburn Rovers poster, became heated. 'People would storm out, there would be shouting matches,' a source recalled. 'One of the policy advisers went out crying at one point, it was that shouty.'

Farron's office was inundated with so many emails from irate Liberal voters that by the second week of the election his staff felt compelled to create a new folder in his inbox entitled, baldly, 'Gay Sex'. It filled up throughout the campaign at the rate of hundreds of emails a week. The leader began to cut a dispirited figure, and the issue also created tensions among his staff, described by one Lib Dem source as 'half Christian, half gay', a combination that fuelled a toxic blend of resentment and pity towards him.

Farron was also coming under pressure from celebrity gay rights campaigners like Sue Perkins and David Walliams, who both criticised his failure to answer the question. On the other side, religious leaders, including the Archbishop of York John Sentamu, told Farron 'to use his bully pulpit to talk about faith in politics', a source said.

The tide turned against Butters after a car-crash interview with LBC radio on 23 April, in which Farron refused eleven times to say whether he thought homosexuality was a sin. After six days Farron was sick of it, and turned to Butters and said, 'I've heard your advice. Thank you very much. I'm going to lance the boil now. I'm gonna tell people what I think.' In an interview with the BBC on 25 April he said, 'I don't believe that gay sex is a sin.'

Yet that did not close down the issue of his religious beliefs. On 16 May the *Guardian* unearthed an interview Farron had done with a Salvation Army magazine in 2007 in which he described abortion as 'wrong' and said, 'Personally I wish I could argue it away.' Again, Lib Dem high command made clear that Farron was pro-choice and had no plans to change abortion law, but the damage was done and another news cycle was lost.

The fuss about sex also deterred the Lib Dems from announcing another controversial policy. Three days before the publication of their manifesto they ditched plans to announce that they wanted to legalise and regulate prostitution so they could tax the proceeds – a policy which they hoped would raise £10 billion a year. The plan was ditched after a stress-test exercise in which Paul Butters played Sam Coates of *The Times*, regarded as one of the most awkward lobby correspondents. 'What's the tax on a blow job?' asked Butters, warming to his theme. 'How much for a hand job?' There were objections from MPs too. Sarah Olney, on the back foot in Richmond Park, said she would find it 'morally indefensible on the doorstep'.

In retrospect, the party might have been better off going ahead. The 'blow-job tax' would have been an effective 'dead-cat' policy from the Lynton Crosby playbook. The Australian's black book of electoral dark arts stipulated that when you're getting panned in the media, you should 'throw a dead cat on the table' to distract attention.

The gay sex issue may not have swung many votes. Party bosses insist the effect was 'tiny in terms of the canvass data'. But the issue did probably prevent the Lib Dems from making a serious attempt to win back young voters and students who had abandoned the party over tuition fees. The biggest problem, one strategist recalled, 'is it cost us that bandwidth. If I have to spend a day doing a clip or answering questions on gay sex, that's me not talking about my message.'

The collapse of Ukip and Farron's 'gaygate' distractions ensured that if protest voters were looking for a home, or if Theresa May faltered, Jeremy Corbyn had political space to offer working-class Brexiteers and metropolitan Liberals something different to believe in. It was an opportunity Labour was to seize with both hands.

17

MANIFESTO DESTINY

The general election of 2017 was turned on its head on the evening of Wednesday, 10 May, when James Schneider, one of Jeremy Corbyn's media spokesmen, took two calls that sent shockwaves through Westminster. The first was from Jack Blanchard, the political editor of the *Daily Mirror*, one of the few papers sympathetic to Labour. 'We've got the whole manifesto,' he told a dumbstruck Schneider. The document had not even been finalised, and was not due to be launched until the following week. Never before in British political history had an entire manifesto leaked. Schneider went onto autopilot: 'We don't comment on leaks.'

An incredulous Blanchard said, 'Is that really what you're saying?'

'Yes, for now. I'll call you back.'

LOTO went into crisis mode. Should they try to close down the story by pretending the document was a fake?

Shortly afterwards Kate McCann of the *Daily Telegraph* called to say she had the manifesto too. Schneider snorted, 'What, the whole thing?' but didn't challenge McCann to prove herself, something that made her suspicious that another paper had the document too. Blanchard's door on the press gallery corridor in the House of Commons had been closed since lunchtime, a signal that he was working on a big story. He had called his bosses at 11 a.m. to say he had the whole Labour manifesto.

The news that the *Telegraph*, a Conservative-leaning newspaper, had Labour's plan for government settled any arguments in Corbyn's office. There was no longer any need to deny the obvious. 'Rather than contain it, we go the other way,' Schneider said. He issued the same bland statement to both newspapers: 'We don't comment on leaks. Our policies will be laid out when we launch our manifesto, which is a plan to transform

Britain for the many, not the few'. It was agreed that the document would be leaked to the BBC to enable the leading broadcaster to cover the story properly.

The forty-three-page document was explosive. The *Mirror* highlighted 'eye-catching measures' to 'renationalise Britain's energy industry, railways and the Royal Mail', and spending pledges of '£6 billion a year extra for the NHS and £1.6 billion a year for social care'. Describing it as Labour's 'most left-wing election manifesto in a generation', the paper reported, 'University tuition fees will be abolished entirely, and town halls ordered to build 100,000 new council houses a year under a new Department for Housing'. The *Telegraph* characterised the policy platform as taking Britain 'back to the 1970s by nationalising industries, forcing wage caps on businesses and giving huge power to the unions'. Its front-page splash also highlighted plans to borrow £250 billion over the next decade.

The following morning, Team Corbyn sent out Andrew Gwynne, who had fast become their best media performer, to face the cameras. 'He did this incredible media round where he had to simultaneously not comment on any of the policies while arguing that they were exactly the transformative programme that the British people wanted,' a LOTO source said. 'He did an incredible job.'

A tiger was loose in the china shop. Labour had little choice left but to ride it. To understand how they were able to capitalise on their misfortune it is necessary to turn the clock back several months.

On 15 December 2016, five weeks after Donald Trump was elected the forty-fifth president of the United States, the *Guardian* ran a story announcing that Labour's strategists were 'planning to relaunch Jeremy Corbyn as a left-wing populist in the new year, as the party seeks to ride the anti-politics mood in Brexit Britain'. The story, which was based on a briefing by the election coordinator Jon Trickett, revealed that 'senior Labour figures believe his unpolished authenticity could help the party draw on the wave of anti-establishment feeling'.

Corbyn's team wanted the public to see their leader as they did. 'We saw the Brexit vote as an anti-establishment vote, and we know Jeremy is an anti-establishment candidate,' a leader's office aide said. But polling and focus groups in the autumn of 2016 showed 'that the public weren't seeing Jeremy in that way'. Corbyn had been an MP since 1983.

To many voters that made him a Westminster lifer, part of the problem, not the solution. Previous attempts to depict him as a crusading outsider went wrong, never more so than in August, when he recorded a video calling for renationalisation of the railways while sitting on the floor of a 'ram-packed' train from King's Cross to Newcastle. Virgin Trains retaliated by releasing footage showing Corbyn walking past empty seats.

Milne got together with his communications team – James Schneider, Matt Zarb-Cousin and Sian Jones – as well as Trickett to discuss a way forward. 'There was a conscious decision to make Jeremy more the populist leader. That was something that Jon Trickett was quite keen on,' a LOTO source said. Corbyn's team resolved to take a leaf from Trump's playbook and confront the media, believing that opposition from conservative newspapers would actually help convince voters Corbyn was an outsider committed to taking on the rich and powerful. 'Part of the strategy is to accept and sometimes encourage the opprobrium of those who are utterly discredited in the eyes of the public,' the source said. 'Trump wasn't getting the hearing in the mainstream media he wanted. That was the same challenge facing Jeremy. He's a socialist leader who wants to fundamentally change society so that wealth and power rest with the majority and not with the elite. Anyone who thinks that is always going to get shitcanned. I don't think you can have a conventional leadership strategy for an unconventional leader.'

Trickett's colleagues would have preferred him to brief the *Guardian* that Corbyn was seeking to emulate Bernie Sanders, the left-wing populist who ran Hillary Clinton close for the Democrat nomination, rather than Trump. They were also annoyed that Trickett had placed the notion of a relaunch in the public domain when the process had been intended to be gradual. 'There wasn't ever the idea for a full-blown relaunch, let alone a Donald Trump relaunch,' one colleague said. 'We discussed and agreed in late November a shift in strategy. There was an agreement to be clearer in calling out injustices and the power behind those injustices, to be more confrontational with the media and more radical in terms of policy. Jeremy was receptive to it.' But if the media was expecting a relaunch, that was what they would get. Schneider argued, 'You don't always get to choose when you're being looked at, but when you're being looked at you need to get cut-through. People are talking about a relaunch – let's play into it.'

At first it looked as if this might be the same mess as previous announcements. On the evening of 9 January, a week before Theresa May's Lancaster House speech, Milne's team briefed extracts from a speech the following morning in which Corbyn, who had always been a passionate defender of open borders, would say, 'Labour is not wedded to freedom of movement for EU citizens as a point of principle.' This created a raft of headlines about Corbyn taking a much tougher line on immigration, which spooked the leader. The speech was tweaked to clarify that Labour wanted to prioritise market access rather than a cap on numbers. 'It looked like a U-turn and like Jeremy was backtracking from what we'd briefed,' an aide recalled.

The 'relaunch' was saved when Team Corbyn decided to deploy their own 'dead cat' – a new policy on high pay. When Corbyn was interviewed by Radio 4's flagship *Today* programme he, apparently casually, dropped into conversation, 'I would like there to be some kind of high-earnings cap, quite honestly.' An aide recalled, 'We were looking for something to say on the *Today* programme to distract from immigration being the story of the day. What we came up with was the maximum wage.'

The reaction was immediate. Newspaper websites erupted with stories condemning this latest socialist pipedream, pointing out that Corbyn's football team, Arsenal, would have to sell all their highly-paid players if the policy was enforced. It was exactly what LOTO wanted. 'The point is to get some powerful voices to hate it, because it helps it to get cut-through,' an aide said. Later in the day, the Labour press office clarified that what Corbyn had in mind were restrictions on pay ratios between the highest and lowest paid in a company, but by then the media hype train was running. By mid-afternoon Schneider and his colleagues watched Sky News vox-pop voters in Peterborough on their views about the pay cap. 'Everybody knew that Jeremy had said something, it cut through in three hours,' one of the comms team said. 'People were talking about it, and were saying that it was a good idea.' After the speech, Corbyn did an interview on the maximum wage with Global Radio, which meant his announcement was top of the all-important drive-time bulletins on Heart, Capital, Classic FM, LBC and Smooth. An aide recalled, 'The headlines were, "Jeremy Corbyn cracks down on high pay, economists say it's mad". Perfect! That will mean millions of people will hear something they like and that some experts are opposed to it.' Polls soon showed the policy was popular.

Donald Trump could not have hijacked a news cycle better. LOTO's new strategy had worked. When the manifesto leaked, Corbyn's team remembered the relaunch and vowed to run towards the gunfire.

There was speculation in the aftermath of the leak of the Labour manifesto that it was shared with the media by Corbyn's team in order to seize control of the news agenda. In fact there was fury in LOTO. 'It was a hostile act. It was a malicious leak which we just rode very well,' a member of the core team said. 'Everyone in the leadership was very annoyed, because it made us look incompetent.'

In Tory Central Office they also had advance warning of the manifesto. 'We got it a couple of hours before the *Telegraph* and the *Mirror* published,' a source close to May said. 'Lynton had it from somebody at the *Telegraph*.' Crosby, Nick Timothy and the political team looked it over and agreed a response. They branded the leak 'a total shambles' and condemned 'Jeremy Corbyn's plans to unleash chaos on Britain'.

The following morning Corbyn announced that there would be a leak inquiry, and there was talk of bringing in a forensic intelligence company to go through emails and text messages to trace the source. There were plenty of candidates. Under Labour's constitution, the manifesto had to be signed off in a 'Clause V' meeting involving the shadow cabinet, the NEC and the affiliated trade unions. That Tuesday, 9 May, officials on TULO, the trade union and Labour Party liaison organisation, were brought in to read the manifesto in hard copy, but some were also sent copies electronically by Andrew Fisher, who also sent the document to the party in Scotland and Wales. 'There were loads of different versions swimming around,' a Southsider said. 'Fisher was none too careful.'

It is a measure of the fractious relationships at the top of the Labour Party that in the crisis meeting that first evening Corbyn's aides blamed party deputy leader Tom Watson for orchestrating the leak. A senior Labour official said, 'They all went: "It must be Tom."' Watson had received his own copy, which appeared to some to be the same as the version leaked to the *Mirror*. Blame for the *Telegraph*'s version of the leak was placed at the door of a moderate union political officer. 'They were the two people on the top of the "shoot" list,' said a leadership source involved in the discussions that night. 'The belief that the copy that was leaked was essentially Tom Watson's version and the other one was the

TULO copy. At the time people said, "We've got him, we can finally do Watson.'"

Watson had been all but frozen out of the election campaign, and was widely understood to want his 'name on the wall' as interim leader and kingmaker to Corbyn's successor. Suspecting the Corbynistas would try to frame Watson, his adviser James Robinson and Tom Hamilton, Watson's head of policy, frantically compared the version of the manifesto in the papers with the draft Watson had been sent, not knowing if they would be able to prove their innocence. They were relieved to discover that the version they had contained a different foreword, and other small but unmistakable changes. The page on industrial strategy and energy in the draft given to the papers featured plans for a national investment bank which were absent from Watson's copy. Watson, Robinson and the union political officer all categorically deny any involvement in the affair. Senior staff at party headquarters were also suspected. Matt Zarb-Cousin, who had left Corbyn's office in March, took to Twitter to condemn 'another leak from Southside', an outburst that prompted a letter from Iain McNicol threatening him with legal action 'if you say anything about my staff again'.

Months later, a senior figure at the *Mirror* revealed that the leak came from the unions. Labour's official verdict was delivered to the NEC on 19 September. Iain McNicol said that a 'stakeholder in one of our regions' was responsible. This was accepted by Corbyn, his office and the NEC without comment.

When frontbenchers and union officials turned up for the Clause V meeting on 11 May they were made to sign for numbered copies of the manifesto. 'This caused much internal amusement, given it was on the front page of all the newspapers at the time,' a Labour staffer recalled.

The Corbynistas were initially also angry because they had planned manifesto announcements through the weekend, culminating in the big reveal – the abolition of tuition fees – on the Sunday before the launch. 'It fucked up our grid,' a Corbyn aide said. The consequence of everything dropping at once was that some proposals – including the provision of free universal childcare – never got the attention LOTO desired.

The leak inquiry never resolved the issue, because very quickly Team Corbyn realised the leak was a Godsend. 'There's nothing like a document you're supposed not to read to make people read it,' a shadow cabinet member said. The huge raft of policies gave the broadcasters a field day. For the better part of a week Labour dominated the airwaves. 'People were debating for days whether nationalisation was a good thing,' a LOTO source said. 'Most people think it is. Young people don't look at nationalisation and think British Rail, they think, "I pay for the BBC and that is quite good. I like the NHS, that's quite good."' Another official in Corbyn's office said, 'Whoever leaked it, it backfired terribly for them.'

Just as the decision to embrace the leak followed from the lessons of the 'Trump relaunch', the decision to write a bold manifesto packed with expensive policies was fuelled by the success of a policy blitz Corbyn ran over the Easter break, while May was up a Welsh mountain. In the space of twelve days, Corbyn announced eight policies, the first time during his leadership that he had succeeded in dominating the news agenda. The proposals included giving free school meals to all primary school pupils, funded by putting VAT on private schools, and raising the minimum wage to £10 an hour by 2020. 'It was our best sustained period of coverage that we had had since Jeremy had been leader,' one of Corbyn's team said. Finally, Corbyn was being defined by his policy agenda, rather than Labour's internal disputes or LOTO's at times faltering grasp of the process of politics.

For much of Corbyn's tenure he and his closest aide Seumas Milne had seemed more interested in foreign affairs than domestic policy. One Labour official who watched their interventions on Trident and the conflict in Syria with bemusement said, 'They see everything through the reference of global imperialism: anti-Western, anti-American, anti-Israeli.' Karie Murphy's arrival in 2016 had given a sharper edge to work on the domestic front. 'Karie is more of an old-fashioned class warrior,' the official said. But beyond renationalisation of the railways, which Corbyn had unveiled at his first conference as leader in September 2015, there had been no eye-catching policies. A Corbyn admirer in the trade union movement said, 'One of my frustrations was Jeremy was elected as a very left-wing member of the Labour Party and yet it was very hard for most people to understand what a Jeremy government would do.'

The second leadership contest over the summer of 2016 forced Corbyn and his allies to provide more definition to his plans. In July of that year John McDonnell unveiled plans for a national investment bank and up to £500 billion of borrowing to pay for new infrastructure.

McDonnell had also laid the groundwork to firmly cost Labour's day-to-day spending, a move that helped lend some credibility to the manifesto.

McDonnell was one of the most intriguing and divisive people in the Labour Party. His entry in *Who's Who* listed among his hobbies 'fermenting [sic] the overthrow of capitalism'. During his first major foray at the despatch box he brandished a copy of Chairman Mao's Little Red Book. His advisers included 'economics consultant' James Meadway, a former member of the Trotskyist Socialist Workers Party. In the eighties even Ken Livingstone regarded McDonnell as too hardline when they worked together at the Greater London Council. In September 2016 footage emerged of him at a campaign event three years earlier describing the economic crash of 2008 as 'a classic capitalist crisis' and declaring, 'I've been waiting for this for a generation!' He said, 'Look, I'm straight, I'm honest with people: I'm a Marxist,' something he sought to play down in broadcast interviews.[1]

McDonnell's internal enemies saw an uncompromising hard man whose support for the IRA was even more overt than Corbyn's. In 2003 he said those involved in 'the armed struggle' should be honoured, arguing that 'it was the bombs and bullets' that 'brought Britain to the negotiating table'. One profile even claimed he was so well known in a working men's club in Camden, a hub of IRA activity, that he was given the nickname 'the quartermaster' by the Republicans who drank there.[2] McDonnell was also on the record praising rioters and calling for 'insurrection', a stance he appeared to echo after the general election was over, when he called for a million people to take to the streets to topple the government. A senior Labour official said, 'He has this Uncle John routine. He's your best mate. He understands where you're coming from. He does that on the radio a lot, he does it when he's speaking to journalists and when he's speaking to normal people. But I think he really does believe in calling for a million people to smash the state. He is more dangerous than the rest of them. He's not a student politics troll who's happened to find himself in the leadership.'

Under Corbyn, McDonnell chaired most of the Monday strategy meetings in LOTO. Colleagues describe an intense and short-tempered figure who was the most quickly agitated when LOTO failed to behave professionally or compete. 'John McDonnell wants to win the flip of a coin. If he's pissed off with you, you know about it,' an ally said. 'John and

Jeremy have been friends for years. They're like brothers.' Allies hinted at a softer side. In one of his first Treasury questions McDonnell slapped down a backbench Tory MP who had read a planted whip's question for not knowing what she was talking about, and was rewarded with laughter. The MP sat down, mortified. McDonnell bought her a box of Ferrero Rocher chocolates and wrote her a note apologising and urging her to bounce back. He also banned his aides from telling the story.

McDonnell's approach to the economy – and the Labour manifesto – was shaped by a humiliating setback in 1992 when he fell fifty-three votes short of winning the seat of Hayes and Harlington he was to seize in 1997, a loss he blamed on the controversy over Labour's 'shadow budget' that year.

McDonnell also employed the least left-wing spin doctor in the leadership team. James Mills was in his early thirties and sported a salt-and-pepper beard and just enough arrogance to get along. As a former staffer in Labour HQ and an aide to Yvette Cooper and Ed Balls, he was regarded as 'not the full shilling' by the hard left. Mills was also disliked by many at Southside, who regarded him as a 'sellout' for going to work with LOTO. McDonnell valued him, though, for his links to lobby journalists and his belief that Labour needed to find ways of appearing fiscally prudent.

When in October 2015 George Osborne sought to trip up McDonnell by proposing a bill to enshrine a 'fiscal responsibility charter' in law, mandating the government to put the public finances in surplus by 2019–20, the shadow chancellor's first instinct was to back it, before he changed his mind. Mills then wrote two papers arguing that Labour should draw up their own alternative charter and properly cost their spending pledges – a move that was opposed by others around Corbyn like Andrew Fisher, who believed Labour could find the funds needed for the public services by printing money. In April 2016, McDonnell unveiled his own fiscal rules, which owed much to the work of economist Simon Wren-Lewis, under which a Labour chancellor would have to show the independent Office of Budget Responsibility (OBR) at every budget that they could balance day-to-day spending within five years. This was limited to current spending, allowing Labour to borrow heavily for investment. The other major rule was that at the end of the Parliament, debt would have to be lower as a percentage of GDP than at the beginning.

When it came to writing the manifesto, two issues divided
McDonnell's team from some of those around Corbyn: whether or not
the pledges should be properly costed, and where tax rises should be
targeted. McDonnell, with Mills and Meadway's backing, was keen to
be transparent. A Southside source said, 'There was a big argument
internally about whether or not we would produce costings. The Labour
Party is haunted by the idea of alternative budgets, but John set a bar for
himself quite high early on when he said we would publish full details
of our plans.'

Milne was 'concerned' at the prospect of the huge costs being put in
the public domain, and Simon Jackson, the head of policy at Labour HQ,
also thought it a mistake. He sent Milne a long email outlining issues
with the costings, not least the spurious specificity of the numbers
produced by Meadway, where every penny of the £48.6 billion raised in
taxes was to be spent. The figures did not include the £500 billion of
capital spending or any costings for the nationalisation of Britain's thirty-
two water companies, which the industry later estimated at £69 billion.
The costings were only for the year 2018–19, and the price of some
policies would increase dramatically after that. One of the footnotes was
even drawn from Wikipedia. Nonetheless, the decision to cost the
pledges gave heart to Corbyn's army of online supporters and handed
them a stick with which to beat the Tories when they refused to publish
similar calculations.

Another row erupted over income tax. On the weekend before the
manifesto leak, Mills briefed the Sunday papers that Labour would guarantee not to raise the taxes of those earning less than £80,000 a year,
protecting 95 per cent of taxpayers from hikes in income tax, VAT and
personal National Insurance contributions. McDonnell and Mills
remembered how the Tory pledge not to raise taxes in 2015 had put Ed
Miliband in a difficult place, and with Philip Hammond apparently
intent on ditching that policy, vowed to steal a form of it for themselves.
For the Bolsheviks, protecting people from tax rises seemed like the
wrong priority. 'That was not a very popular idea because it was not seen
as left-wing,' a source said. 'People like Andrew Fisher were really
opposed to it.' Some around Corbyn wanted the threshold set at £50,000
or £60,000, but that would drag in too many voters. 'John Mac was never
going to stand on a platform of doing that,' a LOTO source said. 'He
remembered the 1992 election. That is burned in his memory.'

The man charged with 'holding the pen' on the manifesto was Andrew Fisher. A pasty-faced former operative with the Public and Commercial Services Union, Fisher was a member of the Trotskyist Socialist Action group. Only a year earlier he had been temporarily suspended from the Labour Party after it emerged that he had called for voters to back Class War rather than Labour at the 2015 election. That year he had also celebrated the defeat of Ed Balls, the 'architect of Labour's miserable austerity-lite economic policies', and described Ed Miliband's front bench as 'the most abject collection of complete shite'.

Shadow cabinet advisers and Simon Jackson's policy team at Southside fed in ideas to Fisher. Jackson's team had been preparing two plans since the autumn, one for an election in 2020, another in case of a snap poll. Permanent Labour staff found Fisher easier to deal with than Milne or Karie Murphy. 'His politics are a bit mad, but he's not an idiot,' one said. 'I think he knows when things are nuts.'

In went mass renationalisations, a policy pushed hard by Milne. In went the studiously ambiguous EU policy thrashed out by Keir Starmer earlier in the year. In went a whole raft of policies that were developed under Ed Miliband but were 'sitting on a shelf' because the previous leader had lacked the courage to embrace them. One example was Corbyn's decision to axe employment tribunal fees, a policy over which Miliband's team had agonised for months. One despairing party moderate, on reading the manifesto, complained that it was 'Ed Miliband's manifesto with hard-left hundreds and thousands sprinkled on top'. The trade unions also fed in a twenty-point plan on workers' rights and industrial strategy. Karie Murphy was clear that the party's paymasters should get what they wanted. 'I remember Karie said, "We have to change our approach to the trade unions. They are part of us and we should give them a policy programme that they can support,"' a Southside official recalled. In LOTO there was only admiration that Fisher had managed to finish it in two and a half weeks. 'He was the first to deliver a manifesto on time for the printers in six elections,' a Corbyn aide said.

Labour manifestos are usually a product of negotiation over several years, during which extravagant spending commitments are whittled down to an affordable plan for government through various 'national policy forums'. This time the process worked in reverse, with more and more policy thrown into the mix. 'You normally have four years to get rid of stuff,' a party official said. 'This was literally starting with everything. Andrew Fisher and the shadow ministers just put everything in. Trade unions put even more in at the Clause V meeting.' That suited Milne and Schneider, who wanted as many policies as possible to pump out to the broadcasters. This might be the only chance the hard left got to present their wish list to the electorate. They were determined to take it. There was little if any contemplation of which policies would attract which voters. 'We chose the policies since it is self-evident that they are right,' said one Corbyn aide, with customary certainty.

Those who gathered for the meeting to sign off the manifesto, at the Institute of Engineering and Technology on Savoy Place, said it was 'beyond insane'. Outside, the car carrying Jeremy Corbyn ran over the foot of BBC cameraman Giles Wooltorton. Inside, the room was stuffed with the entire shadow cabinet, the entire NEC, a dozen union officials and the parliamentary committee of MPs – around seventy people in total. They received a call to arms from Karie Murphy to back the plans: 'This is what we want. This is what we believe. Let's stand on it.'

Chapter by chapter they worked through the manifesto, with each shadow minister presenting on their own areas of responsibility. 'Then somebody from GMB will stand up and go, "Well this is all fine but we need a strong commitment on this because it means jobs in our factory here,"' one of those present said. 'Amendments were made, the shadow minister responsible might mention four of them and just ignore the other two, and then everyone would go, "Great, move on." We had the bizarre spectacle where Barry Gardiner presented his bit on the environment and then actually tried to make an amendment to his own chapter. The whole thing was mad.' Jonathan Ashworth, the shadow health secretary, dealt with his amendments by reading out a long list and saying, 'Yes, yes, yes, yes, yes.'

The meeting descended further into chaos as the push-button microphones were not working properly. 'People couldn't hear what other people were saying,' the official said. Corbyn, who was supposed to be co-chairing the meeting, chipped in occasionally on obscure issues: 'It was quite a bizarre afternoon.' At one point the meeting even agreed to reverse the Beeching Report of the 1950s and rebuild local branch railway lines across the country, though that was never added to the manifesto.

Tom Watson pushed for no major changes on the big spending commitments, only asking for a few pet policies to be included. 'There was a sense that if Jeremy was going to lose, which they assumed, they should let him have his manifesto,' a moderate in the room said. A LOTO source agreed: 'Watson was of the opinion: make them own it. As a result, we got the whole lot through.'

For one observer, it was the silence of one man that spoke the loudest. Throughout the meeting, which lasted just over an hour, Len McCluskey sat mute, 'not raising his hand at any stage, because he was completely happy with the manifesto'. The Unite boss said later, 'I was overjoyed that here was not only a manifesto but a leadership that believed in it and could passionately deliver it. We're not having five more years of austerity. We're going to give you an alternative. We're going to make your life better. We're on your side.'[3] Win or lose, Labour would be doing so from the far left.

The most expensive item in the manifesto, with a price tag of £9.5 billion, was the pledge to abolish university tuition fees, which cost students up to £9,000 a year. An interest rate rise from 4.6 per cent to 6.1 per cent – announced on 11 April, a week before May called the election – made the issue topical and toxic for the government. The decision pitched a determined John McDonnell against Andrew Fisher, who had been wary of Corbyn committing to the policy during his second leadership campaign. Fisher was allied with Angela Rayner, the shadow education secretary, who was pushing for more money to go into pre-school education and further education funding instead. The unions backed Rayner. A senior official in a major union said, 'We had an argument because our members were going to be more affected if Sure Starts were reopened. That was a bigger priority for us.'

'John Mac was the big advocate for tuition fees,' a leadership source said. 'He knew that Jeremy really wanted it, but Fisher wanted to spend more money on the NHS.' At one stage there was talk of matching the promise of Vote Leave a year earlier to spend £350 million a week extra on the NHS (the size of Britain's gross contributions to the EU budget). 'There was a time when we just wanted to put it on the side of a bus and send it round the country,' a party official said. 'For the life of me I still don't understand why it didn't happen.'

Others say the question was not whether tuition fees would be scrapped, but how it would be paid for. In the end McDonnell opted for raising income tax on high earners, but Labour also considered a windfall tax. To many commentators the policy was actually a regressive one, since it was, in effect, asking all taxpayers to subsidise university students, who tend to be middle-class. But that was not how Corbyn's team saw it. A source close to McDonnell said, 'They think it's a tax on working-class people who do well for themselves. They are ideologically opposed to it.' The shadow chancellor also had one eye on boosting support for Corbyn among the students in Momentum who would help protect him in the event of another leadership challenge. A former LOTO employee said, 'John understood in the first leadership campaign that we pulled a layer of young people around us and he didn't want it to dissipate. He was worried about it.'

In another sign of Labour's growing strategic acuity, Corbyn's team returned to the pledge on Monday, 21 May, saying they would include students starting university in England that autumn and that students partway through their courses would not have to pay for the remaining years. The timing was crucial. It was the last day on which people could register to vote. It spurred another wave of student registrations. 'That was an intelligent thing to do,' a former Corbyn employee said. It also raised some estimates of the cost to £11 billion.

Six days before the election, Corbyn gave an interview to the music magazine the *NME* hinting that he might write off student debts altogether, something that would have cost £100 billion: 'I don't see why those that had the historical misfortune to be at university during the £9,000 period should be burdened excessively compared to those that went before or those that come after. I will deal with it.' Several frontbenchers went further, claiming on Twitter that the debts would be scrapped, a position from which Corbyn distanced himself after the election.

While tuition fees inspired an army of students to rally to Corbyn's flag, there was also concern among many that the manifesto had little to say about the most crucial public policy area for the working poor – the Tory policy of freezing benefits. Corbyn's opposition to the freeze had been one of the issues which propelled him to the leadership in 2015. Debbie Abrahams, the shadow work and pensions secretary, wanted the cuts reversed and help given to the so-called WASPI women, those in their fifties whose retirement planning had been thrown into turmoil by rises in the state pension age. But McDonnell's insistence on costing the manifesto meant he was not willing to pledge to reverse them – though

it is not clear that Corbyn fully understood this. In two campaign interviews he claimed that Labour would reverse the cuts, only for the press
office to issue clarifications.

When McDonnell was pressed by officials in Southside he said he
would match any moves by the Tories on benefits, but would not
pre-empt them. Fisher remarked, 'I didn't think politically it was a big
deal.' In effect a judgement had been made that the working classes
would assume Labour was on their side without them having to commit
money to reinforce that notion. Corbyn's philosophical approach, an
aide explained, was to ease welfare spending by removing the need for
it, rather than throwing money at it: 'Our analysis of the welfare system
is that it is based on two enormous market failures: sky-high rents and
low pay.' Increasing the living wage to £10 an hour was the Corbynites'
way of helping. Nevertheless, the choice to subsidise students rather than
those on benefits enraged many MPs, who saw it as symbolic of a leadership mining votes from Corbyn's metropolitan supporters while leaving Labour's working-class heartlands open to Tory incursions.

The manifesto was printed in, appropriately, a little red book, entitled
'For the Many, Not the Few'. At the launch, Corbyn said, 'It's a blueprint
of what Britain could be and pledge of the difference a Labour government can and will make.' It was met with a rapturous reception by the
Corbynistas. Chris Williamson, the candidate in Derby North, who had
lost his seat in 2015 by just forty-one votes, proclaimed, 'This is the best
manifesto since 1945.'[4]

Westminster awaited the verdict of the Institute of Fiscal Studies, the
independent thinktank whose pronouncements on budgets and autumn
statements had become a biannual assault course for the political parties.
Their conclusion was that if Labour did raise £49 billion in tax, as
McDonnell was proposing, it could push tax receipts to the highest level
in seventy years; and if Labour did boost spending by £74 billion, public
expenditure could reach the highest level since the mid-1980s.

The IFS confirmed that if McDonnell's figures were right he would
keep to the fiscal rules he had set himself, but they questioned his sums.
Labour were planning to raise £6.4 billion by lowering the threshold at
which people paid the 45p rate of income tax from £150,000 to £80,000,
and to introduce a new 50p rate on earnings over £123,000. The biggest
tax haul was £19.4 billion from increasing the main rate of corporation

tax to 26 per cent by 2020–21, as well as £3.7 billion by reversing Conservative 'tax giveaways' on capital gains and inheritance tax. However, Paul Johnson, the IFS's director, warned that Labour might raise less than half what they hoped. He told the BBC, 'The chances of getting £50 billion are pretty small. You'd get £20 billion to £30 billion.' He added, 'A bigger state than the one we have been used to is perfectly feasible as many countries have demonstrated, but Labour should not pretend that such a step-change could be funded entirely by a small minority at the very top.' In elections past the IFS verdict might have been damning. But Corbyn's team had read the public's weariness with austerity measures well, and since the EU referendum experts seemed to have ever less influence on voters. 'No one thought the IFS mattered,' a LOTO aide said. 'That's Westminster bubble stuff.'

The changed landscape also made life difficult for the Tories, who had beaten Labour in 2010 and 2015 by warning that their spending plans would lead to excessive borrowing. A senior Conservative official said, 'There's not much point having an argument about costings when we say, "That policy will cost £10 billion," and Labour say, "Yeah, it will cost £10 billion." "How are you going to pay for it?" "By borrowing money." The last election was all about trying to trick Labour into admitting they were borrowing. This time, that was the policy.'

After banning dossiers, Fiona Hill suddenly announced that she wanted one, and CRD staff had to pull a thirty-six-hour shift to turn round a paper which identified a black hole of £59 billion in Labour's plans in 2020–21. The dossier, 'The Cost of Corbyn', was unveiled at the Tories' second press conference of the campaign. Theresa May took to the stage with Philip Hammond on 17 May, the day after Labour's launch. 'Any party which asks the British people to entrust to them the responsibility of forming the next government through the crucial years of our Brexit negotiations must demonstrate that it has the credible economic plan and the capable team,' she said. 'No one could look at what Jeremy Corbyn and his Labour Party offered yesterday and conclude that it passed that test.'

Sadly for May, she then failed the crucial campaign test of navigating a press conference successfully. The Tory dossier was barely newsworthy, and had obviously been knocked together quickly. Over at Southside, where Labour officials were set to publish their rebuttal of the Tory dossier, the view was that the Tories had actually missed huge areas of unfunded spending on renationalisation and infrastructure. 'I think you could probably get to a trillion pounds of spending commitments really easily if you were minded to do so,' a Labour source said. 'They botched it.'

All of which meant the journalists were looking for a story, and when May repeatedly refused to say that the chancellor would keep his job after the election, they had one. The prime minister's refusal to engage in what she regarded as media games had fuelled the psychodrama and knocked the preferred news line off the top of the bulletins.

May had actually refused to discuss a reshuffle with Nick Timothy and Fiona Hill, but both had the knives out for Hammond, and enough senior journalists knew that to make May's studied neutrality inflammatory. Even if she was not prepared to confirm Hammond in post, she ought to have found some words of praise for her chancellor. Instead, she made a grudging admission when pressed: 'As Philip says, we have worked together over the years, many years, longer than we would care to identify.' It was a perfect storm in which May's absence of news sense, her longstanding disdain for the media, hesitancy under fire, irritation with Hammond and stubbornness combined to court disaster. Press and broadcasters led with the story, and Hammond was banished once again to political exile.

If Tory spin doctors were hamstrung in making economic arguments by the blacklisting of Hammond, they were also wary about condemning Labour policies which their own polling told them were popular. A CRD source said, 'There's no point telling people they can't have nice things, and being the party of not having them.' This stance infuriated MPs. Anna Soubry said later, 'Jeremy Corbyn's campaign was all blue skies, magic money trees, buy a unicorn, everything's going to be marvellous. But it inspired people to believe in some sort of future. We failed pitifully to take on what he was putting forward, have the argument and put the economy at the heart of the campaign. We know every campaign is won on the economy.'[5]

The tidal wave of expensive policies distracted the Tories from digging deeper into the small print of Labour's manifesto. It was three days before they spotted that the costings required Labour to reverse the tax break for married couples brought in by Cameron – and even then the BBC seemed uninterested, an incident that led to furious rows between Rob Oxley and Laura Kuenssberg, the political editor, and her boss Katy

Searle. Sheridan Westlake, one of the party's most forensic brains, spotted Labour's admission that they might replace council tax with a 'land value tax', which he quickly dubbed a 'garden tax' because those with larger properties would be hit hard. Yet the Tories became so distracted by their own manifesto and the subsequent terrorist attacks that they made little use of Westlake's work until the final days of the campaign. One senior CCHQ official said, 'It's exactly the sort of thing that George Osborne would have picked up on.'

Labour officials were relieved that the Tories did not react quicker. 'The only attack they did which was quite smart and hurt us was the garden tax,' one said. A member of CRD concluded later, 'If we had listened to Sheridan two weeks earlier, we might have won a majority.' Another Labour adviser said he expected the Conservatives to make the point that higher corporation tax would be passed on to shoppers: 'I assumed they were going to get the biggest fifty consumer-goods companies in the UK, work out the impact of that tax increase and say that will add £20 a week to the cost of a basket for the average shopper – and they didn't.'

The other reason the Tories did not attack on economic matters was because they had got out of the habit of doing so, in part because the chiefs did not want to use the Cameron–Osborne election playbook. To most cabinet ministers it was a given that taxing and spending, borrowing billions, was the road to economic ruin, but they had stopped making the argument to voters at the very moment the public had begun to lose interest in deficit reduction. If anything, Nick Timothy's emphasis on tackling failing markets helped legitimise Labour's attacks on the system. Finally, Tory attacks on Labour had focused on process, the frequent insurrections against Corbyn, rather than his policies, which many Conservatives regarded as barely worthy of discussion. 'All we did was concentrate on them being divided,' a senior campaign official said. 'We hadn't made the economic argument against Corbyn for two years. We hadn't argued that nationalisation was bad, we just thought people who wanted that were nuts.'

The public did not think Labour were nuts, however. As one Labour official put it, 'People do like free stuff.'

The question remains: how radical was Labour's manifesto? As a prospectus for tax-and-spend social democracy it was certainly audacious, mapping out a shift towards Scandinavian levels of taxation and state spending, the like of which had not been seen in Britain for four decades. But these were not, yet, outside the European mainstream. A Corbyn aide said, 'It was only radical in a UK context. It's not Cuba or Venezuela. We would have had tax rates comparable with Canada. Are you telling me Justin Trudeau is a Marxist? We would have been in the mainstream of the G7. Our corporation tax rate would have been lower than Germany and France, lower than Gordon Brown's. Are you telling me he's a Marxist?'

McDonnell's insistence on a veneer of rigour over costings tempered what might have been an even more bracing platform. Commentators like the arch-Blairite John Rentoul teased the Corbynistas, arguing that the Lib Dem manifesto did more to redistribute income to the poor, while scrapping tuition fees and widening free childcare meant poor taxpayers subsidising the middle classes. He concluded, 'This is a funny kind of socialism.' As one LOTO source put it, 'This is more right-wing than Harold Wilson and Michael Foot, and it's written by the adoptive sons of Tony Benn.' Nonetheless, Labour had shown that it was viable to make a case for the end of austerity economics. Adam Klug, the national director of Momentum, said, 'I think that was a real turning point. People got so excited and galvanised behind that manifesto.'

On 11 May, the day of the manifesto leak, Labour's own pollsters BMG projected the likely Tory majority would be 158. At CCHQ, Mark Textor's numbers showed the salience of Brexit as a campaign issue 'drifting down', and Labour were 'now seen to be talking about the issues that mattered to voters', a senior Tory official said. But the headline poll numbers did not immediately shift. The Labour manifesto, with its optimism and handouts, was necessary but not sufficient to transform Corbyn's fortunes. For Theresa May's campaign to implode, the Conservatives would have to publish a disastrous document of their own.

Which is what they now did.

'NOTHING HAS CHANGED!'

Evening was creeping in on Sunday, 21 May when Sir Lynton Crosby turned to Jeremy Hunt and grimly uttered the words that signalled the greatest crisis in the Tory election campaign. Despite his reputation as a profane colonial, Crosby speaks softly, with a gentle Australian burr. He rarely raises his voice. He did not need to now. There was no mistaking his conviction. 'This could lose us the election,' he said.

The campaign strategist and the health secretary were in Conservative Campaign Headquarters, where an emergency meeting was about to take place. Just one subject was on the agenda: whether Theresa May should become the first major party leader to tear up the centrepiece of her general election manifesto in the middle of a campaign. Both Crosby and Hunt had thought from the start that it was a major risk to announce a potentially historic shake-up of the social care system before May had secured a good majority. Now they were both certain.

In the three days since the publication of the Conservative manifesto, both men had been bombarded with calls from MPs expressing dismay at the policy, which their opponents had branded the 'dementia tax'. On the doorstep the policy was toxic, and the widespread goodwill towards May had evaporated almost overnight. Something had to be done, but what? The situation was complicated by the fact that divisions over the policy had spread beyond the familiar tensions between May's chiefs of staff and the Australians. Fiona Hill, who felt politics deep in her bones, found herself pitched into opposition with Nick Timothy. She had a very bad feeling about the policy. It was to be the most important disagreement of their careers, one that led to a brief but painful rupture in their relationship and ultimately to their departure from government.

Crosby's objections were simple. He had not been kept in the loop or been given enough time to prepare the ground for a policy which was both radical and complicated. The media team awaited the outcome of the key meeting, knowing that whatever was decided it would be them who had to face a baying press corps. They all knew what was at stake: the fate of a serious but flawed policy, the relationship between the campaign leaders, the destiny of an election campaign, the credibility of a government, and the reputation of an enigmatic prime minister whose strength and stability were now in question.

The Conservative manifesto became a problem because the early differences over strategy at the top of the campaign were never resolved. Having decided to adopt Lynton Crosby's Brexit-focused campaign emphasising stability, Nick Timothy went away with Ben Gummer to write a manifesto built around Theresa May as a candidate for change. By contrast, Crosby went around telling people, 'I wouldn't have a manifesto at all.' A CTF source said, 'We made clear that this is not an election where the principal focus should be on policies and the manifesto, because if Brexit is the main focus then make it the focus.' When Crosby reported back on CTF's focus groups and polling he told the chiefs that voters had 'had enough of change' with Brexit, and 'don't want big policy ideas, they want to know that she has their back'. Textor's focus groups had revealed that a large number of working-class Brexiteers were considering voting Conservative for the first time in their lives because of May, but that they were concerned. A source familiar with the data said, 'The niggling doubt they had was, "If we give her this mandate, what is she going to do with it? Is she going to be like any other Tory and hit me, or is she going to be on my side?"'

The view that the Tories should barely bother with a manifesto was shared by much of the cabinet. In a briefing with Textor and Gilbert, several ministers suggested writing a document that would set out the direction of travel without going into unnecessary detail, as Margaret Thatcher's 1979 manifesto, long seen as a model of how to do things, had done. 'The prime minister summed up the discussions in that way,' one of those present said. Andrew Goodfellow, the head of the research department, went further, suggesting that the party should just issue a short document containing a statement of values and brief details of specific plans for which the government wanted a mandate. 'We could just press release it on the morning that Labour announce theirs,' he argued.

Yet Timothy and Gummer, ensconced in monk-like isolation on the fourth floor of Central Office, had other ideas – for two reasons. Manifestos perform an important constitutional role in Britain. Policies for which the government obtains a mandate cannot, under the Salisbury Convention, be blocked by the House of Lords. Part of the reason for calling the election was to insulate the government from defeats in the upper House. That meant detail on contentious policies in black and white. 'Every day we were thinking about the Lords,' Gummer told friends. When Thatcher wrote her spartan manifesto in 1979, she had a large majority in the Lords. May had none. What is more, senior backbenchers, like John Redwood, who contacted Gummer and Timothy urging them to 'write a manifesto of three words', also offered 'ninety-three suggestions about what to put in it', a source recalled.

Secondly, Timothy saw May as the figurehead of a mission to transform the positioning and appeal of the Conservative Party. He wanted to use the manifesto to crystallise that vision in a well-written statement combining philosophy and intent. Theresa May was fond of saying there was no such thing as Mayism, but Timothy wanted to define it for her anyway. 'If you're Nick and Fiona, you're probably only going to get one election where you get to put out a manifesto,' a CCHQ official noted. 'And if you're sincere about getting a mandate to shift the party, you're not going to miss that opportunity.' Another senior aide said, 'He has wanted to deliver the 2017 manifesto all his life.'[1]

When he tapped up Gummer, Timothy explained that he would frame the shape of the manifesto based on May's wishes – with the prime minister making the final call herself – but that Gummer would 'hold the pen' and bring the document together so it was stylistically consistent. They believed it was a paper that people would study closely, and making it read well with a polemical edge was important to both. They shared a Google document with John Godfrey, the Number 10 policy director, and his deputy Will Tanner a week after the election was called. Gummer began by revisiting the Plan for Britain, while Timothy worked up a series of position papers on issues that interested him, like corporate governance, takeovers of critical national infrastructure and the 'burning injustices' that May wished to tackle. Gummer put together language on other key areas, staying as close as possible to the 2015 manifesto so as to avoid unnecessary upheaval in Whitehall.

Timothy held discussions with May on her vision for the manifesto with Hill and Jojo Penn, and then talked to Gummer. Timothy alighted on the idea of framing the manifesto around five big challenges facing Britain: capitalising on Brexit; making the free-market economy work for everyone; combating the injustices which remained in society; tackling intergenerational unfairness; and the challenges posed by the digital world. He took the idea to May, and 'the boss really liked it'. The concept had a pleasing echo of the Beveridge Report of 1942, the blueprint for the welfare state, which identified five 'giant evils'. The prime minister agreed that the intergenerational fairness issue would mean being bold in curbing universal benefits for pensioners and reforming social care.

At that point Timothy penned an introductory chapter, which survived almost unchanged to the final draft, which was effectively a statement of who May was and what she stood for. When the chapter riffed on May's greatest hits, like her desire to build a 'Great Meritocracy', 'govern in the interests of the mainstream of the British public' and take decisions 'based on what works', while eschewing 'ideological crusades', it captured her practical provincialism to a tee. Yet in a section entitled 'Our Principles' Timothy penned an electrifying passage in which he attempted nothing less than to reshape the philosophical basis of Conservatism – forging a creed that transcended class, geographical and generational divides.

'Conservatism is not and never has been the philosophy described by caricaturists,' he wrote. 'We do not believe in untrammelled free markets. We reject the cult of selfish individualism. We abhor social division, injustice, unfairness and inequality. We see rigid dogma and ideology not just as needless but dangerous. True Conservatism means a commitment to country and community; a belief not just in society but in the good that government can do; a respect for the local and national institutions that bind us together; an insight that change is inevitable and change can be good, but that change should be shaped, through strong leadership and clear principles, for the common good. We know that our responsibility to one another is greater than the rights we hold as individuals ... We respect the fact that society is a contract between the generations: a partnership between those who are living, those who have lived before us, and those who are yet to be born.' As a summary of May's elusive 'ism' it is hard to top, a philosophy rooted in the belief that there should be no no-go areas for conservatives.

From the very beginning, though, Timothy and Gummer made a fatal assumption. 'This was not a prospectus for victory, this was a prospectus for government,' a minister said. Both men believed the only way to restore trust between the electorate and the political class was to be honest about the challenges ahead. Yet they were not honest with themselves that the first task of a manifesto is to win an election.

On the ground floor, campaign staff had no idea what was going on. A special adviser said, 'You didn't go and interrupt the fourth floor unless you were invited up.' Once the election was called, Gummer and his special adviser Rupert Yorke began collecting policy ideas from cabinet ministers. Some were more useful than others. The defence sections were largely unedited from submissions by Sir Michael Fallon, the defence secretary. Many of health secretary Jeremy Hunt's ideas survived, though a commitment to train 50 per cent more doctors and nurses was judged too expensive, and 'fiddly' changes on patient safety were seen as too granular for a manifesto. Sajid Javid, the communities secretary, successfully argued for measures to tackle homelessness to be included. Gummer worked closely with Matt Hancock, the digital economy minister, on the technology chapter, and Justine Greening, the education secretary, who was pressing for a £1.2 billion increase in school funding, 'was practically a member of the policy unit', another source said, though, perhaps unwisely given its resonance with parents, May's aides ruled school funding to be an issue for the next Whitehall spending review, not the manifesto. To Downing Street's surprise, Liam Fox also provided a 'some really good ideas' to recreate the old Board of Trade and appoint new trade commissioners to boost international business after Brexit, which reflected 'intellectual rigour and a really coherent plan'. However, May's team were unimpressed by Boris Johnson's Foreign Office submission, which was 'basically a speech' from the foreign secretary on Global Britain and the need to spend the aid budget more intelligently. 'It revealed the lack of profound thinking that had been happening, either at a ministerial or official level,' one said. 'There was nothing, other than a whole series of assertions.'

It is notable, given the importance that was to attach to it later, that not one minister raised the issue of increasing public sector pay.

In a process that was to create a great deal of ill-feeling, most ministers then heard nothing from the manifesto team for three weeks while each section was worked up by Gummer, Tanner and Godfrey, with help from key spads like Douglas McNeill, May's economics adviser. The work was kept very tightly restricted, both to prevent leaks and to avoid the 'cackhanded' process in 2015 when 'a whole load of lunatic policies' were added by special-interest groups at the last moment. 'It was like looking at the results of a raffle,' one spad shuddered. Boris Johnson's father, Stanley, had had more input than some cabinet ministers, persuading the Cameroons to include support for a ban on ivory sales.

The secrecy left Philip Hammond highly agitated and 'pushing very, very hard' to see the sections on the economy. 'He was profoundly frustrated and not a little humiliated by it,' a fellow minister who discussed the issue with the chancellor revealed. Not only was Hammond forced to negotiate with Timothy, with whom his relationship was dire, he had to do so using Gummer as an intermediary, while the more junior minister was unable to tell him what he wanted to know because the wording had not been signed off by May. Hammond's main demand was that Cameron and Osborne's tax lock be scrapped so he had more freedom of manoeuvre on income tax, VAT and National Insurance, a request with which May's team were happy to comply. Otherwise the Treasury's submission was regarded as 'a nugatory response'. 'That was all he wanted,' one May aide said. The original language in the manifesto simply referred to the Tories as the party of low taxes, without making any specific pledges. Hammond argued for it to be toughened slightly so that it said, 'It is our firm intention to reduce taxes on Britain's businesses and working families.' A source said, 'There were several times when the chancellor made a vigorous defence of the position and Nick accepted on the merits of the argument the points he was making.' Timothy and Hammond even shared one conversation in which they agreed to pull together: 'Let's do what we need to do. Let's win this election.'

Timothy and Gummer also had input from the backbenches, through the Downing Street policy board led by George Freeman, the MP for Mid Norfolk. Freeman was one of the more interesting, if sometimes eccentric, Tory MPs. A descendant of William Gladstone, the great nineteenth-century Liberal prime minister, his father Arthur Freeman had won the Grand National steeplechase in 1958. Elected in 2010, Freeman realised sooner than most after the financial crash that the Tories needed to take a tougher line with bankers and big business if they wanted to reflect the public will. In 2012 he was contacted by Nick Timothy, who had spotted a kindred spirit, and introduced to Theresa May, who named Freeman as one of the leading young Conservative thinkers in her party conference speech in 2013, a wide-ranging text crafted by Timothy to project May as a future leader. When Cameron resigned, Freeman briefly flirted with running for leader himself before backing May, but he was disappointed not to be offered a ministerial post. He secured instead the unpaid but grand title of chairman of the prime minister's policy board, with a desk in the Cabinet Office. Officials there unkindly claimed that Freeman had as many conversations 'about where his office should be, the nature of his letterhead, what he could call himself and whether he'd have a pass' as he did about policy.

For the manifesto, Freeman collated and sifted seventy different submissions from MPs, many of which found their way in. Rebecca Pow fed in ideas around 'blue belt' marine reserves. Lucy Frazer, a rising star, suggested that drug companies sponsor high-level apprenticeships for science and maths students. Freeman's own submisson to the manifesto was a 'messianic commitment to schools and skills' which would have allowed the top universities to raise their fees if they offered free bursaries to those on low incomes – all funded by philanthropists on the model of American universities. Given Labour's decision to scrap tuition fees altogether, it is perhaps fortunate that May did not offer universities the chance to raise fees, however beneficial that might have been to the less well-off.

Frozen out by Timothy and Gummer, Freeman was blamed for several stories about the contents of the manifesto, including a claim that the government might cancel HS2, the high-speed rail link. 'Every single story, more or less, that came out was George-related,' a campaign source said. 'None of them were rooted in reality because he had no idea what was going on.'

Over a period of three days between 11 and 13 May each secretary of state was called up to the fourth floor of CCHQ to see their sections of the manifesto and provide their comments. Many were content. Liam Fox glanced at his section, said 'Great,' and was gone. Hammond, happy that he had got his way on tax, 'didn't kick up very much of a fuss at all'. But others found the process humiliating. 'We were treated as if we were going in to MI5 to see top-secret documents,' said one minister. 'I was ushered into a sealed box, told I could read my bit while someone watched to make sure I didn't take notes, and then told to leave the paperwork behind. It was ridiculous.' A senior cabinet minister said later the process should never have been tolerated. 'We are all complicit. We were spineless.'

One of the most difficult conversations was with Andrea Leadsom, the environment secretary, who had been rebuffed by Downing Street for months over her wish to reform agricultural policy post Brexit. Gummer, convinced that agriculture would be the most complicated part of Brexit, said she should run a consultation on the future of farming for the lifetime of the next Parliament, with a view to drawing up concrete proposals for 2022. Leadsom had wanted to hold just a six-month consultation. In return, the manifesto team said they would guarantee to match EU levels of subsidy to the farming industry until 2022, rather than 2020, a move that delighted Leadsom. The commitment was even more expensive than it might have been, since during the manifesto-writing process it was discovered that the Treasury had previously only funded the pledge up to the start of 2020, rather than the end of the year. 'It was a wonderful Whitehall fuck-up,' a minister admitted.

While the final details were being thrashed out, Gummer worked hand-in-glove with David Gauke, the chief secretary to the Treasury, to cost every pledge. Down to the tens of millions – a rounding error in Treasury terms – the manifesto was cost-neutral. The figures were double-checked by Douglas McNeill. Gummer went home and proudly told his wife, 'The price is zero!' He and Gauke had 'sweated blood' to make the sums add up. Gummer wanted the costings published, but the rest of the team disagreed. Will Tanner argued that some of the savings were based on internal government figures which were difficult to publicly footnote. Tanner also feared that Labour would pick over every decimal point, creating 'a lot of noise' that would distract from the policies themselves and undermine the Tory reputation for economic credibility. Publishing would also set a precedent for the future. The 'risk judgement' was that it would be better for the IFS to pronounce that the plans were sensible.

It was a mistake. As one Tory put it later, 'We had a fully costed manifesto. It was completely fiscally neutral. And we didn't tell anyone.' On social media, Labour was left to crow that theirs was the only costed manifesto. The idea that the Conservatives had not published costings was seen as further proof that May liked to hide from public scrutiny. 'We got totally shat on for cutting free school meals and charging people with dementia, but we didn't even get the plus side of saying it was costed,' said a despairing campaign official.

When the manifesto was published, they had bigger problems.

The crisis in social care had been nudging its way to the top of the polit-ical agenda for a year. An ageing population – the number of people aged over eighty-five was expected to double by 2030 – combined with local authority budgets stretched to breaking point, had created a shortage of care beds and a ticking time bomb of worse to follow. For the elderly it was a lottery whether they would become incapacitated or contract dementia and need care. Anyone with capital and income in excess of £23,250 had to pay for their own residential care – meaning that many had to sell their homes to pay for it. To complicate matters, those requir-ing care at home also made a means-tested contribution, but their homes were not taken into account during the calculations.

Under the coalition government NHS spending was protected in real terms, but funding for local councils fell by 40 per cent, leading to cuts in funding for social care of around 17 per cent. By 2016 council leaders estimated that there was a £5 billion black hole in funding. A shortage of care beds had a knock-on effect on the health service, since elderly patients with nowhere to go suffered 'delayed discharge' and became 'bed blockers' on NHS wards instead. Plans floated to merge health and social care spending had come to nothing.

The autumn statement in November 2016 offered no extra money for social care. 'We didn't want to make cash available without linking it to wider reforms because cash is the all-important lever for getting people to change,' a source close to May said. To bridge the gap, Downing Street announced that local authorities would be able to bring forward increases in council tax to meet short-term needs. In the spring budget of 2017, Hammond found another £2 billion for social care. A long-term solution was needed, but what? A minister said, 'If you're going to pay for social care you have two choices: you either tax people who are working or you tax people who need the social care.'

Attempts to reform elderly care funding were littered with contro-versy. Labour's plans in 2010 to set up a National Care Service, funded partly from patients' estates after death, was branded a 'death tax' by the Conservatives. The coalition government bought time, handing the issue to economist Andrew Dilnot, a former director of the Institute for Fiscal Studies, who reported back in July 2011. The Dilnot Report recommended that residential care costs be capped so that no one would be expected to pay more than £35,000 over their lives towards the cost of their care. The rest of the bill, then estimated to be £1.7 billion a year, would be picked up by the state. The plan was greeted with dismay by the Treasury. By introducing the idea of a cap, Dilnot was effectively proposing a social insurance scheme, where financial risk was shared by citizens and state. Dilnot's expectation was that an insurance market would then develop in which people could pay a small premium to cover the costs of the care bills they would pay. From that point on, most political debate concerned the 'floor' in assets over which people would pay something (still set at £23,250) and level of the 'cap' over which people would pay no more.

The coalition passed a Care Act in 2014, raising the cap proposed by Dilnot to £72,000 and the floor to £118,000 – both of which were supposed to come into force in April 2016. But when the Tories won power in 2015 they said this would not kick in until 2020, after councils lobbied for money up front to deal with the immediate care beds crisis. When Theresa May became prime minister, despite the new legislation, those with more than £23,250 in assets, including their homes, were still expected to pay for residential care and there was no cap on costs.

For May the issue was emblematic of the tough questions she wanted to be seen to be dealing with. Katie Perrior recalled, 'Theresa May would say often, "Politicians have been ducking this problem for years."'[2] Ben Gummer had three different briefings with Fiona Hill in which the chief of staff made it clear that May regarded the issue as 'unfinished business' and 'important to her'. The manifesto team consequently believed it was 'something we had to produce the goods on'. They felt strongly that it would be 'dishonest' and would damage public trust in politics if they announced after the election plans they had clearly been working on before it. This was a good moral judgement but a poor political decision.

From the autumn onwards, May had received 'five or six submissions' from a civil service team under Cabinet Office official Paul Kissack. But beyond repeated briefings that it was a big issue, the prime minister's aides gave little clue publicly to her thinking. A PR campaign to explain the scope of the problem and prepare the public for the hard choices ahead did not fit with Hill's submarine strategy. Sir Michael Fallon, the defence secretary, was not alone later in wishing Number 10 had been more proactive: 'What we needed to explain better was that we were dealing with an unfairness, where some people were paying an awful lot and other people weren't paying at all.'[3]

A lot of the initial work was overseen by John Godfrey, the head of the policy unit. Godfrey was an old friend of Theresa and Philip May who made his money in the City with Lehman Brothers and Daiwa Capital markets before spending nine years with the insurance giant Legal & General. His insurance expertise was central to the government concluding that Dilnot's plans were flawed, since no insurance market for care costs had developed. 'The joke in the policy unit was that they were getting rid of the Dilnot plan and replacing it with the Godfrey plan,' a Number 10 official said. 'It was his thing!' Mild and unassuming, Godfrey was seen by most in Downing Street as 'a chairman rather than a chief executive' in the policy unit, setting a general direction while Will Tanner did most of the heavy lifting on the detail. By the time the manifesto came around Timothy had already concluded that Godfrey's appointment had not really worked.

After the election, Timothy's enemies suggested that he had removed the Dilnot cap in the forty-eight hours before the manifesto was printed. Those involved in writing it describe this as 'complete bollocks'. May, Timothy and Gummer all regarded Dilnot's plan for a cap as iniquitous because they saw it as asking taxpayers, many of them on modest incomes, to subsidise wealthy fifty-year-olds who had got lucky on the back of rising house prices. 'It's wrong to ask a young person trying to get on in life to stump up so that someone living in a million-pound house in the South of England can have that inheritance protected for their children,' a source familiar with May's thinking explained. 'She was absolutely explicit about this, and felt very strongly that we were not rewarding people for hard work, we were rewarding people for unearned income. The Dilnot cap was immensely regressive.' They were backed up by Philip Hammond, who 'always regarded Dilnot as unaffordable'. By the autumn of 2016 Dilnot's plan was dead in Whitehall; the public just did not realise it.

In seeking to devise an alternative, the policy experts looked at the system of free universal care in Scotland, but concluded that the standard of care was poor. 'What it's ended up doing is rationing care for people with dementia, so although they claim they got free care, actually it's bloody awful for the people who need it,' a senior source said. 'We didn't want to go down that route.' Gummer was supportive of a long-term savings plan where young people would pay £3 to £5 a week throughout their working lives to pay for their care in later life, but that was rejected as a 'tax on young people to pay for the cost of old people'. The other principle they regarded as paramount was 'that it needed to be fair to younger generations'.

The policy they devised was to set a floor of £100,000, so people would not begin paying for residential care until they had assets of that level. This effectively protected an inheritance of £100,000 for everyone. The level was more than four times the existing £23,325, but less than the £118,000 mandated by the Care Act which had never come into force. Crucially, there was no cap on care costs, which the middle classes had regarded as the most attractive aspect of Dilnot. One of those involved said, 'We had explicitly decided that a floor was the most aggressive intergenerationally fair way to do it. We knew that that was going to be controversial but we thought we could weather it.' Tanner joked with Godfrey, 'You should make sure no one historically remembers this as the Godfrey plan, because a load of people will be really pissed off.' Timothy admitted after the election that the plan was a mistake: 'With hindsight, I regret the absence of a cap.' He also regarded a cap as a con against voters, because it was 'incredibly rare' for patients to run up costs in excess of £100,000.

Secondly, Timothy and his team moved to end the anomaly which meant that a person's home would not be taken into consideration when means-testing domiciliary care provided in their home. Timothy regarded this anomaly as 'really weird'. In return, the rules would be changed so the costs of domiciliary care could be deferred until death, as was already possible for residential care, with the costs recoverable from a person's estate. The 'death tax' was back.

The manifesto team resolved to pay for long-term care for the elderly by scrapping winter fuel payments, worth up to £300, for the wealthiest pensioners and replacing it with a means test – though the manifesto did not specify which pensioners would keep it, a decision which provoked huge disquiet when it was announced. The team also examined whether to cut free bus passes as well, but concluded that free travel for the elderly was relatively cheap and a key factor in easing loneliness in old age.

In what came to be seen as a third strand of an assault on pensioners, the manifesto would also include an end to the 'triple lock' which guaranteed that the state pension rose each year in line with earnings, prices or 2.5 per cent, whichever was higher. Since the crash, pensioners had seen their incomes protected while working families had suffered a wage squeeze, but again, May did not pre-empt the decision with a sustained effort to build the case for a change.

The final measure that caused fury was a decision to end free school lunches for children in their first three years at primary school, regardless of their parents' wealth. Instead, the poorest pupils would get a free breakfast for every year of primary school. Child development experts said a free breakfast was more beneficial to those in poverty. The poorest pupils would also get a free lunch. But instead of spinning the move as 'two free meals' for the poorest pupils, the policy was depicted as an assault on middle-income families.

The plan did not have the support of Justine Greening, the education secretary, who advised May's team that the manifesto's plan for schools should focus on per pupil funding, an issue which MPs were reporting was controversial on the doorstep since the Tories had not yet pledged to keep it rising in real terms as Labour had. 'There was a decision taken to guarantee defence spending, which was not coming up on the doorstep compared to school funding,' a senior DfE source said. The number crunchers fell £500m short of the £1.2bn needed, yet to Greening's bemusement Timothy and Tanner inserted policies without telling her like free travel for apprentices and a national retraining scheme which cost hundreds of millions. A source close to Greening said, 'Justine felt per pupil funding was crucial, but they would not agree. It was a huge mistake. We should have had that election commitment. We ended up having to do it instantly after the election anyway. Perversely, a party that had actually delivered one of the most sustained rises in school standards for many years had an election with education as a big problem and a vote loser.' Greening's minister of state, Edward Timpson, paid a heavy price. He was to lose his Crewe and Nantwich seat by forty-eight votes.

While Timothy, Gummer and Tanner were at work, Crosby and Textor had grown concerned that they were not able to test the main policies in the manifesto in their private polling. Mick Davis, the chief executive of the Conservative Party, also sought reassurance that the document would not be anti-business. Crosby was fond of telling politicians, 'You can't fatten a pig on market day,' meaning that they had to lay the groundwork with the electorate.

It is not true, as some tried to claim later, that the Australians were kept totally in the dark. At lunchtime on 25 April, more than three weeks before the launch, Timothy sent Textor an email containing a list, drawn up by Tanner, of 'some of the slightly more controversial' measures likely to appear in the manifesto. It reveals that the Tories were, at that stage, thinking of outlawing strikes by key workers like doctors, nurses, teachers and prison officers where minimum service levels were not guaranteed during industrial action – a policy that was dropped but which might have alienated public sector employees enough to put Jeremy Corbyn into Downing Street. Top of the list of problem policies was 'Scrap the Winter Fuel Payment for all but the poorest of pensioners at risk of fuel poverty', followed by scrapping the pensions triple lock. On social care, the team was at that point only considering a floor of £50,000, half what it would become – and Gummer's plan for 'a social care insurance system' was also still in the mix. The email said, 'We will change the rules so people receiving care at home can defer the costs while they are alive, just as they can already for residential care and guarantee that, no matter how large the cost of care, people will never be left with less than £50,000 in savings and assets after paying for care costs.' In this exchange Timothy and Tanner did not point out that Dilnot's plan to cap care costs had been scrapped. 'It's not true to say that the specific policy initiatives as expressed in the manifesto were tested and researched,' a campaign official said.

'Lynton's approach is very simple,' a friend explained. 'You don't do anything until you've researched it. That works when you have time to research it. When somebody decides to call an election and then produces a manifesto that is unveiled internally a few days before it is unveiled externally you can't research anything. You can't test an eighty-four-page manifesto in a day.'

CTF's research found that there was support for the idea of intergenerational fairness but that voters were confused, not only by the new care policy, but by how the existing system worked. 'There were so many questions in the focus groups,' a CTF source said. 'People don't understand social care full stop,' Timothy told Gummer. This does not appear to have given them pause about making the plans a centrepiece of the manifesto.

Timothy and Crosby had conversations about the awkward policies, and so too did Hill and Gilbert: 'If anything we spent less time talking about social care than we did about winter fuel payments and free school meals and the triple lock.' Plans to give the green light to shale-gas extraction were also expected to be controversial, though the issue never became a feature of the election. Timothy reported back to Gummer that Textor had found widespread support for some of the tougher measures. 'Nick was always really surprised,' a source in the policy team said.

The weekend before the launch, Gilbert asked Crosby, 'Have you seen the manifesto? I'm a bit worried about it.' They sat down and read it, identifying areas of concern. Crosby's list of problem policies ran into double figures. When they saw the plan to remove free school meals, Gilbert said, 'My God, it's going to be "Margaret Thatcher milk-snatcher" all over again.' Crosby's concern was that the detail and framing of the manifesto 'came from nowhere'. May had never talked about the five big challenges it was supposed to address. There were also no positive retail offers. Mark Textor was concerned that the manifesto offered nothing at all on Brexit, which was supposed to be the *raison d'être* of the campaign. The consultants sat down with Timothy, who explained that he had May's backing: 'These are things she wants to do. She wants to change the Conservative Party. If we get this wrong you can all blame me.'

Crosby concluded that May had put her name on the ballot paper and deserved the right to be judged accordingly. The only item he asked to be changed was a minor tweak to the wording of the section on fox-hunting, which repeated a pledge of Cameron's to hold a free vote on whether to overturn the existing ban, another issue which later blindsided the Tories. 'That was the only feedback we ever had from him,' a source close to Timothy said. The chief of staff told colleagues he was surprised that the Australians did not want more watered down. 'We went into this thinking that we would write something that Lynton would then cut in half,' the source added. 'We were amazed that nothing was touched.'

The seeds of disaster had now grown roots.

Throughout the process there was poor coordination between Timothy, Gummer and Tanner writing the manifesto, Crosby and Textor testing some of the content, and Fiona Hill's communications team, who would have to sell it to the press and the public. At no point did all the campaign leaders sit down with May herself and work through the manifesto's themes to ensure they supported the campaign or how they might be sold to the electorate – something that happened as a matter of course under Cameron and Osborne, where communications were regarded as integral to policy-making. Asked what was happening with the comms strategy, Timothy told one colleague, 'I'm leaving that to them.'

On 14 May, the Sunday before the manifesto launch, Timothy, Hill, Gummer and Jojo Penn saw May to finalise the details at her constituency home in Sonning near Maidenhead. Gummer handed over a list of the most controversial items and they went through them one by one. The discussion took two and a half hours. When they had finished, Crosby and Gilbert had a separate meeting with the prime minister. Hill and Penn were by now 'nervous' about the social care plans, which they both regarded as 'complicated'. Hill was particularly worried. 'I think she thought it was a bit risky to bite that much off during a campaign,' a colleague said. Another claimed, 'She liked it even less than Lynton – and that's saying something.'

Gummer told them, 'If you want to fix this problem, this is the way to do it.' He admitted that there was a question over how much of the plan should be revealed ahead of the election, and admitted he was not an expert in communications, but told May, 'My own view is that if you are being consistent with your mantra of being honest and open and straightforward about problems facing us', it was better to 'do as much as we think is possible'.

Timothy and Hill's relationship had remained strong throughout the campaign. At one point that week, Timothy approached Hill and ruffled her hair from behind on one side before moving to the other side when she turned her head. They both laughed. 'They are just really good friends,' an observer said. 'It's obvious from the way they behave.'[4] Yet on what was to become the most important public policy decision of their time with May, the two chiefs of staff had irreconcilable differences. 'On social care she leaned with Lynton, not with Nick,' a Number 10 source said. If Timothy had the more developed political philosophy, Hill's strength was her feel for how the public would respond. A special adviser said, 'I thought her judgement was sharp, her political instincts were very, very strong.'

In the crunch meeting the prime minister sided with Timothy and Gummer, but Hill did not let the issue drop. The final tweaks to the manifesto were made on the Monday and the Tuesday morning, when the document had to go to the printers. That lunchtime, Hill cornered Timothy again and demanded that the care policy be removed. There were no eyewitnesses to the row that ensued, but a friend of one of the participants described it as 'a big argument'. The chiefs were used to disagreeing in private, but this was different. Hill felt they were on the verge of making a critical mistake, but Timothy informed her that it was 'physically impossible to take it out at that stage'. 'It was already gone and the PM had decided, she'd signed it off at that point,' the friend said. A close ally of both chiefs said Hill was so furious 'they barely spoke for forty-eight hours'.

Hill's job now was to sell a policy she did not believe in.

The rest of the press team only saw the manifesto on the Tuesday as it was going to the printers – two days before the launch. Rob Oxley went upstairs to the fourth floor and scanned the document. His chief concern was that there was no firm commitment on tax after Hammond's intervention. He sent Craig Woodhouse, Tim Smith and Kirsty Buchanan to read the document and work out which stories should be briefed to which media outlets, and where they would need a defensive plan. 'It was very much a "Can you check this for what the problems are going to be?", not "Then we can then change them," one of the team recalled. Woodhouse spotted one duplicate paragraph which Rupert Yorke phoned through to the printers in time, but all the policy stayed. 'Nick Timothy went out for lunch and had his beard trimmed,' one recalled.

The document Timothy had penned baffled the press team. One adviser saw it as an 'over-intellectualised' product of 'Red Tory' philosophising, rather than a series of sellable proposals: 'There was no flesh to any of it. I went upstairs thinking there would be some kind of road map to removing the public sector pay cap. Instead we got gruel yesterday, gruel today, and here's a bunch of gruel for tomorrow. I expected a rabbit out of a hat on housebuilding. All it said was "We're going to build some houses." Well fine, but how?'

The press team went to Hill and expressed concerns about the care policy. 'I know, I have had this row a lot,' she said. 'I fought this battle. I lost.' On the Wednesday morning Hill convened a news meeting at which the media plan for launch day was discussed. 'We'll lead on social care,' she said. The decision might seem perverse. Why draw attention to the policy you think is the most problematic? 'Policies like this need weeks of warming up journalists, charities and industry leaders,' Katie Perrior said later, 'not whacked out in a manifesto and briefed the night before.'[5] But Hill knew the social care policy was going to get wall-to-wall media coverage whether she liked it or not, and judged that it was better to brief it proactively, in the hope that it would land with the most positive gloss. 'You might as well get one day's good headlines out of it, which we did,' one of her team said. The policy would be given to the leading newspapers on the Wednesday afternoon for the first editions the next morning. The broadcasters could run it from six o'clock on the Thursday morning. Launch day.

Hill wanted the main story on the ten o'clock news on the Wednesday night to be tough new rules on immigration, which would see a doubling of the fee companies would have to pay for hiring a skilled worker from outside Europe from £1,000 to £2,000 – with the extra money invested in training British workers. This caused friction with her deputy Rob Oxley, who was trying to help finalise the media end of the manifesto launch. He was on a train to Yorkshire as Nick Timothy twice rewrote the briefing script, which was only finalised at nine o'clock, giving the spin doctor less than an hour to 'land' the story, which he duly did, and it led the evening news.

Colleagues had begun to notice that Hill and Oxley were not getting on at all. On the Vote Leave campaign, Oxley had enjoyed a strong relationship with the director of communications Paul Stephenson, who was always accessible, set a clear strategic direction and empowered him to make his own decisions. He felt he was getting none of this from Hill. The flip side was that some in the war room thought Oxley had grown too big for his boots, and saw the way he explained his decisions to Hill as 'talking down to her'. A fellow special adviser said, 'Rob pissed off a lot of people.'

The lateness of the manifesto meant there was no week-long rollout plan for the policies, still less a grid building a narrative up to the big day. May's five big challenges dropped from a clear blue sky, and were never heard of again afterwards. 'It was all so last-minute,' one official said. A source said, 'It was just, "How do we get through tomorrow?" The whole campaign was like that. There wasn't a strategy. It was a series of daily events.' On the Wednesday, Hill even tried to draw up a list of policies her team could brief on the Thursday, a decision that baffled her colleagues, since the manifesto would already be public by then. 'It didn't make any sense,' one said. 'Some of her decisions were batshit crazy.'

It was not Hill or Oxley's fault, though, that they lacked the one thing they really needed – a positive policy that could be guaranteed to knock the care plan off the top of the news bulletins. It was an accepted comms strategy, particularly in the build-up to budgets, to brief the bad news first, leaving the launch moment to unveil the killer policy to blow it out of the water. This did not happen, because Theresa May had blocked the one plan that might have saved the day.

During the manifesto brainstorming sessions, Timothy announced that he would like to scrap stamp duty – a levy on the purchase price of a house – for first-time buyers. 'One of the things we were trying to do was abolish stamp duty, or to significantly reduce stamp duty,' one of those involved in the conversations said. 'That would have played really well with young voters. To pay for it we would have potentially had to do something with capital gains tax, which would have hit high earners.' Timothy was keen to think radically, but May ruled out the plan: 'She decided that some of the tax rises that we'd have to do to pay for it were too much.' Timothy agreed that the idea was 'politically difficult within the constraints of Conservative politics'. Yet it was just the sort of eye-catching transformational idea that could have dramatised for voters that May was a different sort of Tory.

A wealth tax on high-value properties was also considered, which would have seen capital gains tax – usually only levied on second homes – slapped on first properties. 'It was denied publicly but it was very briefly considered,' a senior source said. 'We did the numbers, but it would have been quite punitive at the top end, especially for someone who's been sitting on a house for fifty years that's gone up in value from £300,000 in 1950 to £6 million now.' While the tax would have personally hit John Godfrey, the policy director was favourable to the plan.

In what might prove to be the most fateful judgement of her premiership, May reserved her political courage for social care. 'She was keen to be bold where there were clear challenges like social care, and she thought that the public understood the scale of the challenge, but she was less keen to be actively redistributive in a way that would have alien-ated the party, a Downing Street source explained.

Six months later, in the midst of another political crisis, the idea would be revived.

That the policy landed at all well in the morning papers was down to what several colleagues described as the 'heroic' efforts of Paul Harrison, Jeremy Hunt's special adviser, who was working in Oxley's press team. Hunt had been shown the health commitments in the manifesto by Gummer at the end of the previous week, and assumed that he had seen everything that was relevant to his portfolio. The first he knew about the social care policy was when he was handed a copy of the manifesto on the Wednesday, the day before the launch. He noticed with horror that there was no cap. By then Harrison was aware that Hill's plan was to lead the following day's news with social care. A press release had already been drawn up by Will Tanner and the press team were preparing to contact the papers. Tanner emailed the release to Harrison, who discussed it with Hunt, who was on a campaign visit in Oxford.

Hunt acknowledged that social care was an issue that desperately needed to be fixed, but when he had gathered his thoughts he emailed Harrison to say, 'This is a disaster.' In another email, to Tanner at 12.03 p.m., Hunt sought to sugar the pill: 'In a nutshell this is a great policy! Massive tribute to team for getting it through and PM for being true to her word.' But then he wrote, 'However I need some more details to stop a train crash tomorrow, not least because this will be the first time in living memory we have announced the people who will lose from our policies on the day of a manifesto launch.'

The first version of the press release, which Tanner had helped put together, made a virtue of ditching Dilnot's cap, a policy that was rela-tively well understood. The health secretary was also disturbed that there had been no 'pitch rolling' for such a dramatic shift. The changes to domiciliary care were also troubling, since Hunt knew many people did not understand that home care already had to be paid for. A member of the press team recalled, 'We were about to start briefing it and it went in front of Jeremy who went tonto. He had to be talked off the ledge.'

Hunt made the point that the press release contained no mention of the fact that the changes would raise money that could be ploughed back into funding elderly care. 'If we are announcing the losers we need to talk winners otherwise it will just look like a "state shrinking" measure,' his email said. 'Labour are promising [an] extra £2.1 billion for social care so we need to find a way of matching that ... We also need to quantify roughly how many extra care home packages will be funded.'

Harrison, a phlegmatic individual with a wiry beard running to ginger, had braved one of the toughest communications jobs in a Conservative government with steel and humour as Hunt found himself locked in a bitter dispute with striking junior doctors. But now he went to find Fiona Hill and said, 'I am really worried about this.'

Hill replied, 'I am really worried too.'

With the clock ticking towards 5 p.m., they went into crisis talks on the fourth floor with Timothy, Godfrey, Tanner and Douglas McNeill. After fifteen minutes Hunt, who had raced back to CCHQ, joined them. Timothy made it clear that he felt the policy was necessary, but was willing to listen to his more junior colleague about how to present it. Hunt and Harrison got the press release to spell out that the changes would raise £2.5 billion.

Most papers led the next morning with the idea that winter fuel payments were to be cut to pay for elderly care, the simplest aspect of the story. Thanks to Harrison's efforts, the friendly papers put as positive a gloss on the changes as they could, the *Daily Mail* stressing that the deferred payments scheme would mean that no one had to sell their home in their lifetime, rather than interpreting it as a death tax, as they might have for a Labour policy. 'People forget this – the front of the *Daily Mail* was "No one needs to sell their homes",' a colleague of Harrison's said. 'It unravelled faster than the omnishambles budget, but it landed all right.'

When Hunt was interviewed on the *Today* programme's flagship 8.10 a.m. slot he stressed that the party was prepared to make difficult choices but emphasised that the £100,000 'floor' meant that in future no one would be 'completely cleaned out'. By then, though, he had already been upstaged by Sir Andrew Dilnot. On Wednesday evening, the health secretary had phoned Dilnot to tell him what was due to be announced. It had not gone well. Gummer's team of civil servants in the Cabinet Office had been talking to Dilnot for months, and the economist had appeared to be relaxed about changes to his proposals. But when Hunt called him, Dilnot 'completely flipped his lid'. 'He behaved like a child who had had his toy taken away from him,' a senior government source said.

The next morning Dilnot denounced the new policy and complained that May had missed 'an open goal'. He said the new plans 'fail to tackle the central problem that scares most people' if they needed care. 'The analogy is a bit like saying to somebody: you can't insure your house against burning down. If it does burn down then you're completely on your own, you have to pay for all of it until you're down to the last £100,000.' He also attacked the changes to domiciliary care: 'The majority of people who are getting care not in a residential care home but in their own home will find themselves worse off.'

Dilnot's outburst incensed ministers. One said, 'He compared it to your house burning down, which of course is a chance of one in several million, whereas the chance of needing care is one in four. He was completely disingenuous about the way he represented it.' The minister blamed the quick change in coverage on 'a combination of him behaving like a toddler, and misexplanation by the mainstream media, which might have been attributable to our press department'.

With its centrepiece unravelling, the manifesto launch took place in an atmosphere of barely contained farce. At six o'clock the evening before there was still no venue, as Hill and Penn ruled out location after location, and campaign chiefs discussed whether they should just use CCHQ. 'There was so much going on with the manifesto that people said, "You sort it out," "No, you sort it out,"' a Downing Street aide recalled. Fifteen different venues were lined up and then abandoned. Timothy canned one – the Canadian memorial hangar at the Yorkshire Air Museum – pointing out that launching a general election on the eve of Brexit talks at a Bomber Command airfield surrounded by Second World War aircraft was a bad look. Crosby, characteristically, had been more bullish, emailing the other senior staff on 16 May to say, 'I don't think the Second World War issue is relevant or a problem ... and you won it. Nice contrast with the anti-defence Corbyn.'

Tom Swarbrick, the head of broadcasting, had BBC producers on the phone close to tears begging to be told where the launch would be, since they would normally set up their equipment the evening before a big event. Eventually CCHQ settled on an old mill in Halifax, a marginal seat the Tories expected to win. When the journalists arrived the next morning they were kept waiting outside. 'People were still building the set until five minutes before we let them in,' a special adviser recalled. Even then there were more people than seats. 'How the fuck can they not have counted the number of seats?' a member of the press team complained.

The cabinet travelled up to Halifax together by train and bus. It came to resemble a magical mystery tour as they finally got to see the whole manifesto. Justine Greening was shocked to discover the free school breakfasts policy had been included. 'The first thing she knew about universal free school breakfasts was when she saw a tweet from a journalist,' a senior source said. For his part, Ben Gummer felt sick, knowing the whole world was about to mark his homework. Light relief was provided by Boris Johnson, who returned from the restaurant car with sandwiches for his colleagues, bacon butties wedged under his chin and a vat of coffee swinging from his arm, chattering like a demented steward, 'Bacon and egg. Sausage and egg. You're a veggie? Veggie bacon and egg?'

Sajid Javid got the rudest shock. As minister for local government he oversaw the councils making tough calls on social care, yet he had no idea of the plans until Jeremy Hunt approached him on the train. Javid's allies say he had asked Gummer what the social care policy was when he was called in to see his section of the manifesto the previous week. According to this account, Gummer replied, 'We're working on that. We need to keep it really tight.' Javid told friends that repeated texts asking what was happening in the days ahead were ignored by Gummer. The manifesto team denied that Javid asked questions in that meeting, and claim he had expressed no view on how the policy should be constructed. Most importantly, he was regarded as 'completely untrustworthy' by Downing Street. 'Sajid didn't see the social care policy but he didn't ask to see it either,' a senior figure said. 'We had all got used over the last eight or nine months to not sharing anything with him because he was leaky. Why, in something that's this sensitive, when you've got to discuss options of all kinds and then discard most of them, would you include him when you'd find them all in the papers the next day?'

As the cabinet arrived at the launch venue, Javid discussed the care policy with other ministers. He was concerned his political antennae had failed, because he felt the decision to make care a centrepiece of the manifesto was 'weird'. 'This is going to be a disaster,' he told one colleague.

May's speech was notable for her referring to 'my manifesto', but it soon became a document for which she might have been better advised to share responsibility.

Both Labour and the Liberal Democrats claim to have coined the term 'dementia tax' to describe May's care plans, but the first mention of the phrase on social media was from a man called Phil Lewis. At Labour headquarters, James Mills got a tip-off about the care policy when it was briefed to the papers, and prepared a response. He focused on the plan as a backdoor inheritance tax. Labour's initial intention was to attack the care, winter fuel and pensions policies collectively as a 'pensioners' penalty'. But the following morning Andrew Fisher was reading a report warning that the number of deaths from dementia was set to quadruple by 2040, and suggested they refer to a 'dementia tax'. He mentioned the idea to James Schneider, who fed it to Corbyn for an appearance on Jeremy Vine's show on Radio 2 at noon. The Labour leader called the proposal 'a tax on dementia' (though it is not clear he even understood the policy, as the following day he claimed the Tories had 'put a £100,000 cap on social care' for each person – precisely what they had not done).

Separately Paul Butters, Tim Farron's spokesman, began pushing the dementia tax idea to journalists. The Lib Dems were soon printing leaflets with a picture of an old lady and the slogan, 'Your home confiscated to pay bills after death'. By 4.25 p.m. Will Heaven of the *Spectator* had written a blog pointing out the difference between two old ladies with assets of £322,000, one of whom contracts dementia and the other who doesn't. One would be able to pass on everything to her family, while the other would lose £222,000 in care costs.[6] Whoever was responsible, the concept was common currency in Westminster by 1.13 p.m., when Jim Pickard of the *FT* tweeted, 'I've no idea who coined the phrase "dementia tax" but it will stick, not least because it is accurate'. Stick, it did.

The Tories' refusal to say which pensioners would lose winter fuel allowance left most thinking they would lose out. Labour seized on a report hastily produced the day after the manifesto by the Resolution Foundation – run by a former Labour Treasury aide, Torsten Bell – which calculated that if the government restricted payments to the poorest pensioners on pension credit, ten million people would lose out. Had CCHQ said that only those on the higher rate tax would lose out the issue might have been contained, but Fiona Hill told her press team, 'Don't panic,' and the issue rumbled on. A suggestion by Rob Oxley that they turn the issue around and attack Labour for suggesting that rich pensioners like Jeremy Corbyn and Mick Jagger should keep the perk was rejected. David Davis said later, 'Basically what we did was have a manifesto that upset each sector of our own voter base. On winter fuel payments, we should have said what the level was. It is not just about the policies, it is about the clarity of the policies, because people will assume the worst.'[7]

The haste with which the manifesto was cobbled together also led to the free school meals policy unravelling, in a fashion that might have been scripted by Armando Iannucci. Mike Crowhurst, the Downing Street policy lead on education, had overseen a press briefing which claimed that the free breakfasts were going to cost just £60m, a drop in the ocean compared with the £600m that was due to be saved from scrapping universal free lunches. The problem was that Crowhurst had misread the details of the costs and take-up rate of a trial scheme. 'That trial had different costs because it had free food provided by the group that was doing it,' a source said. It meant the calculations were wrong by a factor of ten to fifteen. Greening had been told the government could not find the extra £500m they needed to guarantee a real terms rise in per pupil school funding but here they were, as one ally put it, 'accidentally announcing a policy that costs between £600m and £900m a year if it gets significant take-up, thereby completely eradicating any of the savings people had wanted to make by scrapping free school lunches'.

Not only had the botched calculations driven a coach and horses through the manifesto costings, the £60m price tag also appeared stingy. It led to the calculation that the Tories had only budgeted 7p each for the new breakfasts – a third of the bare minimum required to provide something nutritious. The error made it impossible to argue the case that poorer pupils would be better looked after with their two free meals a day. Crosby and Textor's insistence that all quotes sent to the media referred to Brexit also tied the hands of the press team. 'We weren't allowed to fight back on substance,' one said. 'Everything had to be "but they'll fuck up Brexit", which isn't really much use to you when you're trying to engage over 7p breakfasts.'

That the issue did not blow up into a catastrophe on the scale of the dementia tax was largely down to Greening. An accountant in a previous life, the education secretary did some frantic calculations and worked out how she could spare Number 10's blushes by contriving a way to justify the £60m figure – effectively arguing that was the amount of extra money needed once both policies were taken into account. 'She was like Carol Vorderman on *Countdown*,' one friend recalled. 'She started with the number and worked backwards.' Crowhurst sent a 'late night email' to one of Greening's special advisers saying how sorry he was.

Hill's dislike of social media campaigning meant little effort was made to promote the manifesto online. In 2015, Edmonds and Elder had created an interactive manifesto that allowed Facebook users to see exactly which policies were relevant to their lives. Timothy's philosophical manifesto to reinvent Conservatism was difficult to boil down to eye-catching adverts for Twitter. Even footage of May's speech at the launch was poor-quality, with a wobbling camera. 'That was because they only settled on the venue the night before,' a Tory official said. 'The lighting was shit. The camera was bouncing all over the place.' More importantly, there were very few policies 'worth shouting about' on social media.

Since Hill and her team were left largely to their own devices to devise the communications plan, the rationale for the care policy – that it was supposed to redress generational unfairness between the cash-poor young and the asset-rich elderly – was totally lost. 'The great irony of this election,' a minister said later, 'is that we produced a bloody brave manifesto which was designed to try and start the journey towards intergenerational justice, and we lost our majority on the basis of the youth vote because that argument was never made.' Such an argument would not have killed the negative stories, but months of ministers laying out the case that the elderly had done well at the expense of their grandchildren would have helped to land the policy. Those who wrote the manifesto believed the way it was briefed, with all the attention on the negative changes to care, winter fuel allowance and pensions, 'fed very clearly' into Labour's 'anti-austerity narrative' by fuelling the notion that the Conservatives were 'mean-spirited and nasty' – the very thing that Theresa May had warned about a decade earlier. Anna Soubry said, 'I'm afraid it confirmed that somehow we were the nasty party after all.'[8] Taking aim at Hill, a central campaign figure said, 'There are questions to be asked about the communication of those policies, I would say.' A special adviser agreed: 'If Nick writes a policy, Fiona is supposed to sell it.' But another of Hill's team defended her: 'Great comms is not a panacea for bad policy. All she could do was play the card she was dealt.'

Timothy and Gummer were also frustrated that other policies they saw as positive were completely ignored by the press team. 'We had loads of good stuff in there which we had deliberately designed for retail politics. We'd worked really hard on a discounted travel offer for apprentices,' one said. 'It never appeared. I know it frustrated Nick. We had a really good shipbuilding policy. The technical education bit was absolutely groundbreaking.' Timothy believed plans to revisit the principles of the NHS internal market could alter the public perception that the Tories were hell-bent on privatisation of the health service – but journalists were never told what that section of the manifesto meant. These were all worthy policies, but hardly game-changers from a media point of view.

The bigger problem was that in their initial briefing, and when they had to respond to attacks, the press team neither had the full details nor understood the policies they were defending. As a colleague of Timothy put it, 'There weren't that many people in the building who actually really understood the care policy – maybe three – and even some of them were a bit shaky.' On the Saturday morning, with a 'dementia tax' media storm in full flow, Lynton Crosby looked at the briefings on social care that had gone out to MPs explaining the policy and sought out Nick Hargrave from the research team. 'Mate,' he said, 'you need to rewrite this entirely, because at the moment I don't understand what the policy is, and I don't understand why it's a good thing. All we're doing is taking a lot more money off them, and potentially their house.' It was a good summary of the problem. The curiosity is that it had taken until a day after the launch for the Australian to put his foot down.

That morning Crosby, Gilbert, Hunt and the whips got calls from panicked and furious MPs and candidates. 'It was felt on the doorstep straight away,' a member of May's political team said. 'They'd heard it on the news and were confused about what it was. There weren't any leaflets to explain it, because what was in the manifesto hadn't been communicated to the team doing leaflets.' Michelle Lowe, the candidate in Coventry South, said, 'Voters who had worked hard all their lives to buy their own home to pass on to their children could not believe our social care policy. They saw us betraying their hard work by preventing them leaving money to their children. They were unsure whether they would still receive the winter fuel allowance, and kept asking where the cut-off point would be. The timing of the manifesto could scarcely have been worse, coming only days before postal votes dropped on doormats.'[9] Chris Brannigan, campaigning in a road of £800,000 houses in Twickenham, got a clear message from voters: 'To their view, that was losing £700,000 worth of family treasure.'[10] Others were told by elderly activists, 'I am no longer delivering your leaflets.' Hunt heard stories of people tearing up their Conservative Party membership cards and yard signs being thrown over. 'These were established Tory supporters,' another official said. 'There was genuine fury.'

MPs reported that some voters were horrified that their care costs would not be capped. Others had been shocked to discover that anyone with assets in excess of £23,325 currently had to pay at all. While the cabinet received a ninety-four-page briefing on the manifesto, MPs only got a thirty-five-page version. They bombarded CCHQ with email requests for clarification: 'What happens if you live with your brother or sister?' 'What if your spouse dies?' A special adviser said, 'If you're going to have complex policies, you have to provide complex briefing to candidates.'

'There was outright hostility everywhere,' a senior figure in the campaign recalled. One candidate in an urban seat phoned Gilbert to say that they had knocked on a door and the voter had torn down the Conservative Party poster in front of him. Nicola Blackwood, the public health minister, and James Berry, who was in a dogfight with the Lib Dems in Kingston and Surbiton, both complained.

Some MPs picked up the phone to journalists. 'All the manifesto offered was blood, sweat and tears. There was nothing good in it,' one said. There were already demands for the heads of Timothy and Hill. One veteran MP observed, 'It seemed like two people had got off their potties without wiping their botties and written a manifesto.' Another said, 'This is not the time for recriminations, but there will be a time for recriminations. There might have to be a couple of people shot.' Nigel Evans, the MP for Ribble Valley, compared the manifesto to the only voyage of the *Titanic*: 'We were steaming under blue skies and then we created our own iceberg and steered our own campaign towards it.'

Crosby believed the situation was becoming a mortal risk to the campaign, and said so in a series of emails to the senior staff. 'Lynton's a blunt guy – everything he says, in words or written down, is pretty direct,' an official working that weekend said. In a moment reminiscent of the television comedy *The Thick of It*, 'There was one point when Lynton forwarded the chain to John Godfrey and sent it to the wrong gmail address, so some random John Godfrey received an entire chain of Lynton Crosby emails about social care policy. There ensued several hours of trying to work out whether or not this John Godfrey was real. That was a hilarious speed bump.'

By Sunday, CCHQ was in full crisis mode. That morning the front page of the *Mail on Sunday* screamed 'DEMENTIA TAX BACKLASH', and featured a poll by Survation suggesting the Tory lead had shrunk to twelve points, down five in a week. The poll looked like an outlier that weekend, but Survation were to be the campaign's most accurate pollster.

More worrying for the Tories was what their internal data was showing. Jim Messina was carrying out fieldwork so he could refresh his model over that weekend. A senior campaign official said, 'It started on the day of the manifesto and finished on the Sunday.' When it was over, Messina told the Australians, 'It's just fallen off a fucking cliff.' Gilbert told colleagues he had never seen a fall so 'substantial and immediate'. On the first day of polling the Tories were doing well, slightly down on their performance at the start of the campaign, but with a ten-point lead consistent with the public polling. From Thursday through to Sunday responses began to swing to Labour, giving the Tories a lead of just 33 per cent to 30 among Conservative 'leaners'. By the fourth day it had fallen to 'hung Parliament territory'. The model that had once put the Tories on 470 seats now had them on 304, twenty-seven seats down. Theresa May was on course to lose her majority. A Messina Group source said, 'We advised the campaign they should go back to targeting the seats they deemed "safe" and that had been ignored at that point.' The fieldwork was so contradictory that it was decided to junk Messina's model. 'You never knew whether to take the first or third or an average of the days, whether the worst day was as bad as it was going to get,' a campaign source said. 'We decided to abandon it and do it again.'

Labour's internal polling had also given Corbyn cause for hope. For the first time, the large Conservative lead among the over-sixty-fives was narrowing, and Ukip supporters who had abandoned the party over Europe – the so-called 'Labour Leavers' – were returning home to their ancestral home.

Jeremy Hunt and Paul Harrison swapped messages on the Saturday morning, and both went in to CCHQ on the Sunday. They were both 'very worried', according to colleagues. That morning Fiona Hill messaged the WhatsApp group for special advisers and said, 'I'm having a think about a few mitigation ideas.' The media was awash with claims that cabinet ministers had been left in the dark. Hunt came into the office around 1 p.m. and sat down with Harrison and Douglas McNeill, May's economics adviser. There was one question on their minds: 'Do you U-turn or do you ride it out?' Hunt was 'forthright' that changes should be made. The only way to close the issue down was to give 'certainty about the maximum cost of social care'. That meant a cap.

Work began on modelling the options. It was suggested that costs might be capped at around £85,000. Civil service officials were consulted, a clear breach of the purdah rules during elections. Crosby and Gilbert became involved in the discussions. Crosby was clear about the risks of inaction. He turned to Hunt and said, 'This could lose us the election.' One of those who spoke to the Australian that Sunday said, 'His view was that we were making a values judgement against our own base.'

After six o'clock the big guns assembled in the chairman's office at CCHQ – Crosby, Hunt, Timothy, Hill and Gilbert – to contemplate the most dramatic manifesto U-turn in history. There was immediate agreement that something had to be done, but not about the timing. Members of the cabinet had been in touch demanding change. Gilbert wanted to wait a day and get focus-group evidence. There was an open discussion about whether a U-turn would damage May's personal brand. But others around the table were 'very ardent' – none more so than Nick Timothy, who could see that he had to help facilitate a solution to the problem he had created. 'Nick more than anyone else persuaded her to switch,' a campaign director said. 'He had the first conversation with her.' May was consulted by telephone, but it is another symbol of her detachment that she did not call the campaign chiefs together in Sonning or Number 10 so she could participate fully in the discussion. The prime minister was 'frustrated'. 'When she sets out her position she wants to stick to her position, and she did believe in the policy,' one of those present recalled. May initially felt she could 'ride it out', but 'By the end she also realised that something had to give.' Another present said, 'I don't think we were thinking about how unprecedented it was. We were thinking: our candidates are struggling to hold the line and we haven't really explained it very well and it feels like we've passed the point of explaining it better.'

The decision taken in principle, they agreed to finalise the details in the morning so May could adjust her position when she launched the Conservatives' manifesto in Wales. 'We were all left with quite pale skin from that Sunday,' one of the campaign commanders admitted afterwards. Timothy, Hill and Hunt had further calls that night with Ben Gummer, who voiced concerns that a U-turn would damage May's personal brand as a straight-talking politician, and would undermine the 'strong and stable' mantra: 'I think her brand is the most important thing here,' he warned. 'Hold on tight. Just give it a few days. We'll get through it.' After the election he regretted never having the same conversation with the prime minister herself. Timothy listened, but made it clear that the collective view was that the policy had to change. Gummer felt his friend had been weakened by the media onslaught and was feeling bruised. His parting shot was to advise, 'If you must do it, please do not put a number on the cap. Don't box us in. Make sure this cap is a good cap and not a regressive one.'

Gummer wanted flexibility because he and Timothy had been working on several different plans for a cap that achieved some of what Dilnot had envisaged but without the flat, regressive ceiling on costs which they regarded as bad policy for the poor. During the first part of 2017, and during the manifesto-drafting process, Timothy and Gummer had looked at a system which would have protected those – like patients with motor neurone disease or multiple sclerosis – who needed care from middle age, but they had not concluded how best to accomplish that by the time of the election. Another option under consideration would have seen people pay a sum on retirement, chargeable against their estate after death. That would have allowed people to effectively set their own cap, by deciding how much of their assets they wished to protect, with the wealthiest paying far more than those with modest means. 'We were really interested in various different insurance options which would allow people to be able to pay a premium on retirement, which we'd charge them against the estate, which would in effect be a cap,' an official familiar with the work said. 'People would be able to make a decision: if they don't have any assets to protect, or if they were very, very rich, they wouldn't really care. But those people who wished to protect their inheritance would be able to do so. It's the same as a cap. We had not sufficiently worked it out.' The manifesto authors also felt that revealing their hand at this stage would have added an extra level of complexity that would require too much explanation.

When the campaign commanders convened at the six o'clock meeting on the Monday morning, they mulled over the details again. May had three options. She could do a straight U-turn and introduce a cap at a fixed level. They could fudge the issue and indicate that they would deal with the problem, but only once they had won the election. Or the prime minister could say, 'I've listened to the public. You have my word that this consultation will produce the right outcome.' The consensus was that the situation had gone too far for that ploy to be successful. The device they chose – led by Fiona Hill – was to signal that the consultation and the green paper would contain a cap, without explaining exactly how it would work. Hill said, 'The manifesto says we're going to have a consultation, let's make sure this is part of the consultation. Don't say that you've changed your position.' No one else had any better ideas. 'There was no competing evidence and there was nobody arguing the contra-case,' one of those present said. The decision was made. The question now was how to communicate it.

The urgency was heightened when Rob Oxley learned that a group of Conservative backbenchers were going to break cover in the pages of the London *Evening Standard* that morning, and call for the care policy to be scrapped. Oxley went to Timothy and Hill and argued that they should pre-empt the story: 'I know we're doing a U-turn. Do we want it to be presented as we're doing a U-turn in response to backbench anger, or do we just want to admit that we got this wrong?' He suggested that they give the story to the *Standard*, and then asked the killer question: 'Do you want this to be a conversation at my level or do you want it to be higher up?'

Which is how the secretary of state for health, Jeremy Hunt, came to call the previous chancellor of the exchequer, George Osborne, to give his former colleague the biggest scoop of the campaign just three weeks into his new job. 'I got wind that there was going to be a U-turn on the social care policy which had been the centrepiece of the manifesto,' Osborne said. 'With just forty-five minutes to go until our first edition we got the story onto the front page.'[11]

Relations between CCHQ and Osborne had been dire throughout those three weeks, straining the relationship between Oxley and the paper's political editor, Joe Murphy. An early attack story worked up by CRD on Labour's plans to raise inheritance tax – a policy they calculated would affect half of all London households – was handed to the *Standard*, but only made a small inside piece, when it might have been a front-page splash. At the same time, Osborne delighted in giving great prominence to negative news about Brexit, which he announced to the world in tweets at 11.30 every morning, and in penning waspish leader columns, one of which claimed that not one cabinet minister backed May's policy of restricting net annual immigration to the tens of thousands. Tory high command thought Osborne was exacting revenge for the brutality of his sacking by May the previous July. The prime minister had fired Osborne as her first act in Number 10, and then advised him to 'get to know the party' better. Now she was reaping the whirlwind.

Osborne might have been done a favour, but he did not soft-pedal the U-turn. His splash headline read 'STRONG & STABLE? PM'S CARE U-TURN TURMOIL'. At CCHQ those who did not know about the change of policy looked aghast at Twitter. Officials who did know about the U-turn, but not about the briefing operation, turned to each other and said, 'How the fuck have they got that?' In the press team they wondered if the big beasts had made the right call. 'I'm not sure we thought enough about the crack we were putting in "strong and stable",' one said. Osborne understood: 'I think it destroyed the sense of momentum in the Tory campaign, the sense that this was going to be a coronation. It also undermined the central slogan: strong and stable. That basically disappeared then from the Tory campaign.'[12]

The occasion for the U-turn was the launch of the Conservatives' Welsh manifesto in Wrexham. May delivered her prepared lines well, attacking the 'fake claims, fear and scaremongering' peddled by Jeremy Corbyn, before pivoting into the main announcement: 'I want to make a further point clear. This manifesto says that we will come forward with a consultation paper, a government green paper. And that consultation will include an absolute limit on the amount people have to pay for their care costs.'

When it came to the questions, May faced a torrent of incoming fire over the size of the cap, with one reporter referring to a 'manifesto of chaos', and veteran broadcaster Michael Crick calling her 'weak and wobbly'. The prime minister was defensive and terse at the best of times. Now, with her back to the wall, she reverted to type – with disastrous effect. When the *Telegraph*'s terrier-like Chris Hope pressed her one more time, she glared at the journalists and declared, 'Nothing has changed!' spreading her palms wide like a revivalist preacher, a gesture she must have believed conveyed openness but which appeared defensive. This was greeted with the sound no politician wants to hear – mocking laughter from the journalists, summoned to witness a U-turn only to be confronted by a prime minister treating them and the public like fools. May's voice rose a pitch higher than usual, cracking a little as she plaintively repeated, 'Nothing ... has ... changed.' This time her hands chopped downwards like two machetes smashing a carcass. There was no admission that she had erred, or any detail about the new cap. 'We have not changed the principles we have set out in the manifesto,' she insisted. That was true as far as it went, but she had certainly added to them the key element of a cap. To journalists who had covered the war in Iraq, May was a new Comical Ali, the spin doctor for Saddam Hussein, who insisted the Americans were not in Baghdad when their tanks could be seen over his shoulder in the background.

In the audience at Wrexham was Gareth Baines, the Conservative election agent in the ultra-marginal seat Vale of Clwyd. He wrote later: 'An elderly couple behind me kept saying – audibly – "Yes you are" every time May said she absolutely definitely was not performing a U-turn (even though she was).'[13] Back at CCHQ, the war room watched in horror. 'Why the fuck's she said that?' one staffer asked. Another observed, 'The thing about having to say that nothing has changed is, you only have to say that when something definitely has.' It was a verbal tic, like May's habit of starting answers with the phrase 'I've been very clear' when she was at her most obfuscatory.

Timothy felt May had landed her explanation as well as could be expected. He put the terse exchanges after that down to 'lobby sport'. Others were not so sanguine. Another Mayite told friends later that he found it an 'excruciating experience'. One campaign chief said, 'When she was using the form of words that was agreed, it was OK. The backs-to-the-wall response was a problem.' Once again the prime minister's brittle temper and inability to think on her feet had cost her dear. Some pointed the finger at Fiona Hill for encouraging May not to concede that she had changed her mind. Crosby despaired. In situations like this, David Cameron had been at his best, not his worst. When Crosby tried to argue that week that May's change of heart was evidence that she was strong and would listen to alternative views he was asked the inevitable question: 'Then why on earth didn't she say that at the press conference?' He paused before replying, 'You'll have to ask *her* that, mate.'

Labour officials could not believe their luck that May's refusal to admit to her own U-turn had undermined her brand so comprehensively. One said, 'Cameron's genius, every time a U-turn happened, was to say, "I've made the decision, this has to stop and I'm stopping it." Someone else would be thrown to the wolves. The Tories' numbers would tick down, Cameron's numbers would tick up – it happened every time. People looked at May saying "Nothing has changed" and thought, "You're a vicar's daughter, why are you lying?"'

That evening May faced the BBC's most fearsome inquisitor, Andrew Neil, and in a performance that had campaign staff at Tory headquarters watching slack-jawed, continued to deny the obvious. She said the Tories had 'not rewritten' the manifesto, because 'nothing has changed from the principles'. When she insisted that the Conservatives' 'credibility is not in doubt', Neil snapped, 'Your ability to answer this question may be in doubt.' Even then Tory high command did not realise the long-term impact of May's performance. 'We saw it was a bump in the road, not something that would fatally wound us,' a senior official said.

Was the U-turn necessary? When the damage done to May's personal brand became clear, some MPs and strategists drew the conclusion that it would have been better to brazen things out. 'That night no one understood what the hell the cap meant, but they did know there had been a U-turn,' a cabinet minister said. 'Raising the bar from £23,000 to £100,000 was actually a very strong retail line, but it was never communicated properly, and the public have just got no idea how social care works unless they've got a relative who had been in care.' That was a very good reason not to include the care policy in the manifesto in the first place, but not necessarily the best reason to ditch it. Yet to everyone making the decision the U-turn had seemed necessary. The problem was that May's performance meant the usual benefits of changing course were lost. 'We did a hard handbrake turn and appeared to run over a whole bunch of people,' a Tory official said. 'We hadn't got any of the positives of the U-turn.'

The care policy was so damaging to May because, in an attempt to move the Tories onto new terrain, she appeared complacent about maintaining the support of her own base. 'If you're rock-climbing,' a

Downing Street aide said, 'before you reach out for the next handhold, you make sure you've a firm hold on the one below.' Coming at a time when postal votes – popular with elderly voters – were being issued, the policy could not have been much worse-timed. An MP close to Downing Street saw a bigger problem: 'It was one U-turn too many. It caused an ex-post-facto rationalisation of all the previous U-turns. Suddenly, she didn't just look weak on this, she looked weak on calling the election when she promised not to call the election. She looked weak on advocating hard Brexit when she had been a Remainer. The budget as well. It was like a pack of cards, and the whole thing came tumbling down.'

As the week went on, Crosby, Textor and Gilbert were faced with a dilemma. May was not the kind of in-your-face candidate constantly demanding the numbers, but they knew she was bound to ask at some point, and they did not know what to tell her. Textor's tracker was going the same way as Messina's model: downwards. Another of the campaign chiefs said, 'There was definitely a time that week when everyone was like, "Fuck. We are in some serious trouble." The CTF one, from the manifesto onwards, was down every single day.' Crosby, Textor, Gilbert, Messina and Tom Edmonds got together. 'What are we going to tell Theresa when she asks us?' one said. CTF did not like handing over the raw data. They wanted campaign staff and the candidate to do the best job they could, not obsess about the polls. But if May asked, they could not lie. Her numbers were way down, but Crosby also believed that 'polls were actors', meaning they could have an impact on the behaviour of voters and candidates. He did not want to panic May, who was already lacking confidence. 'She doesn't take pressure at all well,' one senior figure said. 'She just further retreats.' Another source said, 'They wanted to give her an honest answer, not an answer that would send her into convulsions.' The Australians concluded, 'We'll tell her, if the election happened today, then she might lose a few seats.'

Textor's greatest concern was about the leaching away of Ukip votes. His tracking poll had a question designed to monitor underlying sentiment in the electorate: 'In terms of your heart, not your mind, would you rather vote Tory, not at all, or Labour?' Before the manifesto 'the Tory answer was in majority on that question', a source said. Afterwards, 'It just died terminally – it didn't even swing up again.' Textor's numbers

showed the dementia tax had become a 'proof point' which convinced
these voters that May could not be trusted with a big majority.

The issue came to a head on 24 May, when the senior staff went into
10 Downing Street for a council of war with the prime minister. May did
not ask explicitly what the numbers were, but Textor felt it was the closest she had come. His allies claim he produced an A3 sheet summarising
his latest findings with a graph showing that Conservative support in the
so-called 'aided vote' – where the pollster mentions the names of the
candidates – 'had gone below the line', meaning a loss of majority. 'Tex
used that as an opportunity to show people the graph and show her that
we could lose,' a source said. 'He showed her not only the big decline but
the fact we were going below the red majority line. It really shocked her.
Everyone was dumbstruck and thought Tex was going nuts.'

The events of this meeting are hotly disputed. Timothy has said May
was never told she might lose her majority. Another campaign director
who was present says Textor's presentation did not have, as its central
prediction, a hung Parliament, though it was clear that May might not
gain any seats. Textor's tracker was not actually designed to produce an
accurate seat projection, but to monitor trends. 'Out of the polling you
can do a broad seat projection and assume that all seats of a similar
character behave the same way. That was giving a range. The worst-case
scenario was that we'd broadly be where we were, there'd be little change.'
But Team May cannot have been in any doubt that they had suffered a
serious setback. 'We were talking about the damage the manifesto had
done – that it could be quite severe. I don't recall it being discussed as
potentially a loss of majority.' The following day, May was en route to a
G7 meeting in Sicily when a YouGov poll in *The Times* dropped, showing
the Tory lead down to just five points.

The disputes were the first ripples in a feud which was to engulf Tory
world, pitching the two sides of the campaign into a bitter blame game.
Its first victim was Nick Timothy. In the aftermath of the U-turn, the
papers were packed with inaccurate briefings: that he had personally
pushed the care policy in defiance of his colleagues, and that he had
personally pulled the cap on costs in the final days before the manifesto
was printed. There were also claims that he had fled from CCHQ and not
been seen for a week. Timothy detected the hand of Crosby and his allies
in these briefings.

The publicity proved damaging because in some seats the perception of the chiefs of staff as over-mighty advisers even came up on the doorstep. A CCHQ official said, 'I had five or six instances where people said, "Why is this Nick Timothy running the country?"' A minister close to May said that week, 'I'm afraid Timothy has become the evil monster of the campaign. The trouble is the public now see the apparatus around her and they don't like it.'

A Downing Street aide on the campaign accused Crosby of peddling this narrative: 'Lynton got fucked off with Nick and Fi, and then was probably a bit naughty when the manifesto came out.' A special adviser added, 'Lynton positioned himself against the manifesto, still thinking it would be fine and he would get the credit when we won.' Timothy told one friend, 'It's not very nice knowing you're being set up to be the fall guy.' The suspicion was mutual. When Timothy took calls in the street outside the war room, another campaign aide remembered, 'You could see Lynton and Tex looking out of the windows wondering, "Who is he on the phone to?" They thought he was saying, "It's Lynton's fault, Lynton's fucked it. Why didn't Lynton spot it?"'

Fiona Hill had good reason to be furious with Timothy. He had persuaded May to ignore her objections to the care policy and given her twenty-four hours to devise a media plan, but Hill's fiercely protective instincts kicked in. 'I feel terrible for Nick,' she said. 'It's a terrible position to be in. This isn't right. I really think I should be with him.'

Timothy continued to show his face in the war room: 'He didn't hide away,' a colleague said. Those who had helped put the manifesto together felt particularly bad for him, because Timothy had proved a thoughtful boss. At lunchtime on the day before the launch, he had sat down for a solid hour in the midst of the chaos, writing a letter to each of the eight or nine members of the policy unit who had contributed, telling them that they'd done a sterling job. 'They were not one-liners. They were serious, thought-through, emotionally felt letters,' said one recipient. 'Every single one of the policy unit was chuffed to bits that he'd done that. Nick can be a hard taskmaster at times. He's not an easy man to argue with – but at heart he's a good, loyal, nice guy.'

Between Timothy and the Australians, though, 'the atmosphere was actually fairly poisonous'. One senior figure said relations never recovered: 'From the manifesto onwards it was all tits up. Lynton was frustrated they had ignored his advice. It's like tracing back through the history of a bitter divorce. There's one big moment of conflict, and after that every little thing the other person does just pisses you off.' To the campaign professionals, Timothy's exercise in 'intellectual masturbation' had derailed what had been a successful campaign. One senior strategist said, 'The approach was to demonstrate that getting a mandate for a good Brexit was important and to show that Theresa May was a different kind of Tory. The manifesto undermined both of those things.' In this account, Timothy was to blame for not listening to the pros. To the Mayites, the old hands had never understood Theresa May, and their churlish reaction to a brave and serious manifesto proved it.

Watching from afar, David Cameron 'couldn't believe the fuck-ups', one old friend said. 'He was incredulous at it. The manifesto came out and he said, "Every rule has been broken. No positivity, going after pensioners. Hello!" When you are ahead, you just keep it boring. It's so obvious.' Cameron could have offered his views, but he was not asked. A brief audience with May just before the campaign was described as 'very awkward' by a friend of the former prime minister: 'She was just going through the motions.'

Ultimately the responsibility for the manifesto mistakes lies not with Timothy but with May, who never chose between the competing campaign visions or forced the policy wonks, spin doctors and strategists to develop an integrated campaign. She herself was not a good enough political performer to sell either her policy or her U-turn to a confused public and a press corps tired of her stonewalling. A former minister said, 'Nick was right, intellectually, to want to take some of the huge QE-incubated asset wealth from the South-East to support a fairer social care system up North. But the fatal error was to forget that that has to be sold on the doorsteps. I think Nick and Fi allowed their almost religious belief in Theresa May's invincible personal brand to make them forget that it might not be so obvious to everyone else.'

Theresa May claimed nothing had changed. In fact, everything had changed. She had shown that in the eye of the storm she was a poor candidate. A day after the U-turn, terrible events were to engulf the election that would ensure she would now be tested as a prime minister as well.

MANCHESTER

Ariana Grande had not long completed her set when Salman Abedi detonated his suicide vest with what horrified witnesses remembered as 'a deafening bang'. It was 10.31 p.m. on Tuesday, 22 May, the day after May's U-turn, and more than 14,000 people were heading home from Manchester Arena. If this was a general election about young people it was never more so than at that moment. Grande, a wholesome American pop singer, was twenty-three, a year older than Abedi, a Sunni Muslim born in Manchester to Libyan refugees. Many of her fans were less than half that age. Abedi's bomb sent a murderous hail of nails and other shrapnel ripping through the foyer, packed with hundreds of fans and the parents who had come to pick them up. Twenty-three people were killed, including ten children, one as young as eight. Another 250 were injured, many of them in life-changing ways.

At the start of 2017 just one person – Gunner Lee Rigby – had been killed in Britain by Islamist terrorists since the 7 July attacks on the London transport network in 2005. Now, after the Westminster attacks, it had happened twice in the space of two months – on May's watch.

The prime minister and her team were up all night liaising with the police and the intelligence services. Sometime after 3 a.m. the Downing Street switchboard patched May through to Jeremy Corbyn. The Labour leader agreed immediately to her suggestion that the campaign be suspended. 'There wasn't that much advice getting to Jeremy at that point, it was just his decision,' an aide said.

The general election was on pause; the politics was not.

* * *

May was always comfortable 'getting on with the job'. After the catastrophe of the manifesto it was also the best advertisement for her to continue in Downing Street. The assumption of everyone in CCHQ, and not a few in Southside, was that the attack would help the Tories, not least because Corbyn's attitude to terrorists was seen as his Achilles heel. Yet there were still perils for May. Was the attacker known to the authorities? Could the attack have been prevented? Could government cuts be blamed?

In campaigning terms, the first question the prime minister faced, however, was whether to tweet about the attack. This caused heated exchanges between the campaign consultants and May's chiefs of staff. Timothy and Hill saw her prime ministerial duties as separate from those of the campaign. Crosby, Textor and Tom Edmonds were paid to see things differently. One of May's aides recalled, 'The only time I can remember any kind of friction between us and them was in response to the two terror attacks. They were getting really agitated.' The Australians and the digital director wanted May to issue a message on social media: 'We need to tweet from the campaign account.' They argued that the public would want reassurance from their leader that the authorities were on top of the issue. The chiefs refused. Timothy said, 'We never, ever use social media for this kind of thing and we're not about to change that now. She'll give a statement to the country from Downing Street at whatever time, and you'll just have to wait for that.' Once again, whatever power Hill and Timothy had ceded on paper over the campaign, their role as May's Praetorian Guard meant they always had the whip hand in any dispute if they wished to exercise it.

The chiefs felt engagement on social media was beneath May, the kind of gimmicky behaviour that David Cameron had engaged in. To someone like Edmonds, though, it was just a common-sense engagement with the modern world. A senior campaign official who sympathised with Edmonds said, 'The Number 10 people were sceptical about the PM using personal social media, and I think the Aussies would say it's a symptom of the ridiculous hostility to anything that David Cameron did.' One irritated consultant said, 'She had a very Home Office way of dealing with things, which is all tightened up. One of the secrets of crisis relations is just keep talking. You don't need a speech. People want to know what the hell is happening. Look like you're in the know. And you don't wait ten hours to do it.'

At six minutes past midnight, Jeremy Corbyn put out a tweet: 'Terrible incident in Manchester. My thoughts are with all those affected and our brilliant emergency services.' It was nothing profound, but it showed he was up and functioning and engaged with the issue. It got more than 19,000 retweets and more than 60,000 'likes', and helped him build his audience. 'Even if it's a platitude, you are saying what everyone else is feeling,' a Tory official said. 'Theresa leaves a huge gap. It's part of her job to show the nation you care and you're there.'

It would be more than two hours more before voters heard from the prime minister. At 2.13 a.m. the Downing Street press office emailed a statement to journalists which read: 'We are working to establish the full details of what is being treated by the police as an appalling terrorist attack. All our thoughts are with the victims and the families of those who have been affected.' The statement lacked any personal touch. May had been similarly slow to act publicly on the day of the Westminster attacks. That attack began at 2.41 p.m., but she did not speak in Downing Street until nearly 9 p.m. – more than six hours later. The only footage of her on the early-evening news was of her armoured Jaguar fleeing the scene. One special adviser observed at the time, 'The PM was not there to provide reassurance.'

The issue erupted again at the end of that week when May attended the G7 summit. Desperate to get the campaign back onto Brexit, Mark Textor suggested that the prime minister tweet from a session also attended by Jean-Claude Juncker and Donald Tusk, 'I hate sitting around with EU bureaucrats. Looking forward to getting back on the campaign trail.' A campaign official said the Australian was concerned that after weeks of presenting the EU as an adversary for electoral purposes, shots of May 'standing awkwardly next to a bunch of world leaders' would be all that voters remembered. Textor wanted May to show them she was 'jimming it to the Europeans'. This idea 'got very British silent looks', one of those present said. 'I was sitting looking at Nick and his eyebrows shot up. The idea that she'd tweet from a meeting surrounded by EU people slagging them off is so not her.'

May chaired a meeting of the COBRA emergency committee – named after the room in which it meets: Cabinet Office Briefing Room A – at nine o'clock on the morning of the Manchester attack, and then made a speech afterwards at a lectern in Downing Street. With the indignant stoicism she was expert at projecting, the prime minister accused the bomber of plotting with 'cold calculation' to carry out 'among the worst terrorist incidents we have ever experienced in the United Kingdom'. Condemning the attacker's 'appalling, sickening cowardice', she described her disgust at the 'warped and twisted mind that sees a room packed with young children ... as an opportunity for carnage'. It was a powerful performance – and not just for electoral effect.

At May's insistence, both chiefs of staff, who had resigned from the civil service in order to join the campaign, were given special dispensation by Sue Gray, the head of propriety and ethics in Whitehall, to return to Downing Street at this moment of crisis. This was understandable but underlined the prime minister's dependence on the chiefs. Amber Rudd, who arrived at the Home Office at 4 a.m. after the attack, was not allowed to consult her special advisers.

The home secretary, a mother of two, became 'quite emotional' about the details of the attack. The chiefs reported back to colleagues at Matthew Parker Street that they and the prime minister had also been badly affected. 'Hardened people, who'd been through rough politics, who had been through issues like this in government, were taken aback emotionally by the Manchester attack,' a senior campaign figure said. 'The PM, Fiona – they were all exposed to a lot more detail than we were, which was gruesome and horrible.' When Diane Abbott, the shadow home secretary, went in for a briefing, she had barely sat down before she complained that the families of the dead were being kept in the dark. 'She wanted to know why they hadn't been told their children were dead or alive,' a Whitehall official said. 'She had to have it explained to her that traumatised policemen were trying to piece together the body parts of young children.'

May travelled to Manchester to visit victims in hospital and confer with the chief constable, Ian Hopkins. The hospital visit was not a media event, but an official who was with her told colleagues the prime minister had been 'amazing with all those children' – a softer side she rarely revealed to the public.

At a second COBRA meeting, intelligence chiefs reported that Abedi had been known to the security services and the police, but was not regarded as a serious threat. In the days ahead it would emerge that he had been reported to the authorities for extremism by as many as five community leaders and family members, and had been banned from a mosque – claims that would prompt an internal inquiry by MI5, the domestic security service. More immediately pressing was the question of whether Abedi was part of a cell or had acted alone. Manchester police conducted raids across the city, carrying out a controlled explosion at the property in Fallowfield where Abedi had lived. His elder brother and three other men were arrested in connection with the attack. That evening the Islamic State of Iraq and the Levant claimed the attack was carried out by 'a soldier of the Khilafah' in response to Western 'transgressions against the lands of the Muslims'.

After the COBRA meeting May made another statement, announcing that the terror level was being raised from 'severe' to 'critical' for the first time since July 2007, meaning that 'a further attack may be imminent'. The decision had been taken by the independent Joint Terrorism Analysis Centre. May said she did not want to 'unduly alarm' people, but revealed that the government was sending up to 5,000 military personnel onto the streets – under police command – to protect public buildings. It was the first time the plan, codenamed Operation Temperer, had been activated. 'I think she handled that well,' an aide watching from CCHQ said. 'She's the right person when these kind of things happen.' The following morning soldiers were helping to protect Parliament. They would remain there through the weekend. The threat level was at 'critical' for four days.

By now May was locked in a major diplomatic war of words. Within hours of the attack, Abedi's name and other intelligence on the attack shared with the security services in the United States and France was leaked. That morning's *New York Times* even printed crime-scene pictures of the backpack bomb. May and Rudd hit the roof. 'The PM was fucking furious,' a Downing Street official said. She and the home secretary protested. May made clear that she would raise the matter with Donald Trump at the G7 summit later that week, telling reporters, 'Intelligence that has been shared must be made secure.' Trump said he would prosecute the leakers. On 25 May Greater Manchester Police said they had stopped sharing information on the attack with US intelligence.

Just when Tory officials thought nothing more could go wrong, one of the press team got an email asking, 'Why is the PM's home address in a picture on this website?' The spinner clicked on the link to a Huffington Post story and saw a photograph of the ballot paper in Maidenhead,

complete with the prime minister's full home address. He phoned the
website and the Press Association, and asked them both to remove the
image. Then he called the Metropolitan Police, whose response was laced
with profanity. 'The PM has always put her home address on it because
she thinks the electorate should know where she is,' a source said. 'A lot
of candidates list their agent's address. That's a huge credit to her.' In the
midst of a terrorism crisis it was also a security threat, and another
symbol of how awkward was the transition for May from brilliant local
campaigner to national leader.

Corbyn's team were frustrated that May was able to use her office to get
publicity while they were prevented from campaigning. 'The
Conservatives wanted to shut the campaign down for a long time,' a
source in Corbyn's office said. 'But obviously they didn't shut theirs
down, because Theresa May was on TV doing prime ministerial things.'
The practicalities of what a campaign suspension involved were complicated. Politicians stopped attending public events or knocking on doors.
Officials at Labour HQ sent out messages on all their WhatsApp groups,
to candidates and party officials, telling them to stop campaigning
immediately. The Conservatives had had tens of thousands of candidates' election addresses printed, and had to contact Royal Mail and ask
for them not to be delivered – a serious blow, since people were already
filling in their postal-vote ballots. 'There will be lots of people who voted
by post without getting their election address,' a member of May's political team said.

Corbyn addressed a gathering in the kitchen at Southside on the
Wednesday morning. He condemned the 'dreadful event' and said his
thoughts were with the families, and that democracy should not be
delayed by violence. He announced that he would make a speech the
following day. People nodded their approval. They were then taken aback
to see Karie Murphy come forward to speak. 'We're not going to be
cowed by them,' she said, her irritation at the campaign suspension clear.
'We've spoken to Number 10, we've spoken to Theresa May, but we're
going to get back to campaigning as soon as possible. We're not going to
let this stop our campaign.' A Southside official said, 'They were deeply
frustrated by the pause in campaigning, because they felt it was too long
and inappropriate.' Matt Zarb-Cousin agreed: 'I don't think terrorism
should interrupt a general election, a democratic process. That's the first

point. Secondly, the longer the campaign was suspended, the more it benefited the Conservatives.'

The terrorist attack might have led to a general election truce, but it did not quell Labour's infighting. Manchester's new mayor Andy Burnham arranged a vigil in the city's Albert Square on the Wednesday evening. Corbyn's team in London immediately sought to 'muscle in'. In a series of 'increasingly frantic' phone calls to Burnham's office, the Labour council leader Sir Richard Leese and local MPs like Lucy Powell, Seumas Milne and Karie Murphy sought to 'badger' them into securing Corbyn a prominent role in the vigil. 'From quite early on, their concern was, how can they get Jeremy involved in it, which just wasn't anyone else's concern at that moment,' a Manchester Labour source said. 'They were just making endless phone calls to anybody and everybody.'

The calls were regarded as a ridiculous distraction by Burnham's team, who were trying to reunite families and identify the dead. 'Richard and Andy were livid with Jeremy's office,' an insider said. Corbyn was advised to wait a day and then visit the injured in hospital. Ignoring the requests, Corbyn, Murphy and Lavery jumped on a train to Manchester. On arrival, the leader's aides made it clear that they wanted him to pose for pictures and film a television clip surrounded by Labour candidates and workers from the emergency services. 'There were quite a few things where we had to say, "No, that's not going to happen,"' a source said. 'There were so many bad ideas mooted, one of which was that Jeremy would do a clip with all the Labour candidates standing behind him.' Murphy wanted Ian Lavery, the campaign coordinator, whose seat was in Northumberland, to have a more prominent role than Manchester MPs.

The affair led to an extraordinary showdown at the Midland Hotel in the city centre. Lucy Powell told Corbyn he should sign the book of condolence, attend the vigil and go home. Corbyn was also warned not to wave at the crowds or agree to selfies. A senior source in the trade unions said, 'There was a very, very, very bad scene around it. Karie was shouting and screaming, saying that Lavery was going to lead the parade of candidates.' A Labour source said, 'I don't know why Ian Lavery was with him. He was the campaign coordinator. It would be like Theresa May arriving with Lynton Crosby.' Lavery pushed back, saying he was representing the shadow cabinet. Murphy said the idea of a clip with candidates 'has been agreed at our strategy group'. Powell hit back, 'I don't give a shit. We're not doing it.'

It was only when Leese broke down in tears as he described the scene of destruction that Corbyn's aides backed off. 'This is about this city, not you,' he said. 'In that meeting Richard was crying, not because of their ridiculous behaviour, but because he was so upset telling them what had happened – about the dismembered children's bodies and about how difficult a task it was going to be trying to identify everybody,' a witness said.

Earlier in the day, Corbyn's team had also suggested that he should visit the scene at Manchester Arena, a proposal that was only scrapped after police insisted it was a live crime scene and would disrupt the investigation. A party official said, 'They demanded that they do a site visit, and the police were saying, "You can't do that. We'd have to clear a huge area, because Jeremy's a protected person. We'd have to take active officers off an active investigation just to protect VIPs going around this place. You can't do it." Karie was absolutely insistent that we were going to do it. We all thought that was just a dreadful decision. It took active officers off a terrorist crime scene in order to facilitate a visit by Jeremy Corbyn – but he got good pictures out of it.'

Murphy's approach to the police was 'very tetchy' throughout the campaign. Armed officers were only assigned to Corbyn at the start of the campaign, against the wishes of many in LOTO, who thought they would cramp his style. 'At first his office said he wouldn't accept it,' a Labour official recalled. 'Very quickly after he had his first briefing they realised you do have to accept it. You can't move around the country if you're not a protected person. They realised the police wouldn't be able to guarantee visits. They're quite a useful barrier against photographers. When you're trying to get him out of a car it's handy to have a couple of big burly cops with guns around.' Murphy's attitude did not soften. 'The general attitude to the police all the way through actually was really bad,' a source said. 'They were really worried by the uncontrolled crowds. They kept telling us they couldn't protect him in this way. Karie rejected their advice.'

The Labour leader claimed his stance on terrorism was to support peace and dialogue in conflicts around the world, but his political opponents pointed out that all too often this involved talking to the representatives of terrorist groups that opposed Britain, America and Israel, which he saw as imperialist nations. Newspaper readers were already familiar with the fact that Corbyn had referred to Hamas and Hezbollah as 'friends' during a meeting in Parliament in 2009, and also with his longstanding association with Sinn Féin, which had brought him into contact with convicted IRA terrorists. Most notorious was the occasion in 1984, two weeks after the Brighton bombing – in which the Provisional IRA attempted to murder the entire British cabinet in their beds at the Conservative Party conference – when Corbyn invited convicted IRA volunteers Linda Quigley and Gerry MacLochlainn to the House of Commons. In the years after that he was frequently pressed to condemn IRA violence, but refused to do so without bracketing it with that of loyalist paramilitaries.

There were also doubts about his willingness to take action against terrorists. The previous November, days after the Paris attacks in which 130 people were killed by marauding gunmen, Corbyn declared that he was 'not happy' with the idea of Britain's security services having a 'shoot-to-kill policy'.

Corbyn's closest allies decided he should confront the issue rather than duck it. Steve Howell, the deputy communications director, said, 'We thought perceived weaknesses on … national security could actually be strengths – if we could reframe them.'[1]

Seumas Milne, with strong support from Andrew Murray and Howell, persuaded Corbyn that he should set out his view that Britain's foreign policy, with its history of overseas interventions, was responsible for fuelling terrorism. They knew it was a controversial stance, just days after children had been slaughtered by a suicide bomber, to suggest that Britain rather than Islamist ideology was responsible, but it was also a foundational belief of Corbyn's senior aides. After the 7/7 bombings in 2005, Milne, then a *Guardian* columnist, had contacted aides to Ken Livingstone and asked why they were not blaming the war in Iraq for the bombings.

'There was a bit of a debate about whether to do it,' a source in the leadership said. 'There were some late-night phone calls. There were heated discussions. Seumas was really pushing for it. Jeremy agreed. Andrew Fisher was ambivalent. Murray was all aboard the bus. They genuinely had a belief that the wider public would actually agree with Jeremy on this.' LOTO did not commission polling to back up their view: 'They believe that stuff.' Another Corbyn aide said, 'Ultimately all of the key strategic decisions are Seumas. We felt that actually on foreign policy,

we were where the overwhelming majority of people are.' Milne wanted
Corbyn to say what he thought, but he was also determined to change
the news agenda, which was focused on Theresa May's sober handling of
a national crisis. To do so they needed a speech that would be controversial. It was time to wheel out the Trump strategy again. 'They thought
suspending the campaign was to May's advantage,' a source close to
Corbyn's office said. 'They wanted to resume their campaigning, they
wanted to do so acknowledging what had happened and diagnosing why
it happened.'

Again, they concluded that the opposition of much of the press would
actually help them; and they believed the positioning would help
persuade some Muslim voters, who were leaning towards the Tories, to
come home. 'There was concern that we would get such a shellacking in
the press that it would be difficult for us to be heard,' an aide to Corbyn
said. 'The counter-argument to that was that the controversy makes sure
that people definitely hear our points.'

Milne, Murray and Howell holed up together for more than a day
writing the speech. Within LOTO there was a debate about whether to
trail the 'fluffier bits' or the heart of the speech with the Friday-morning
newspapers. They went with the most controversial line. 'Seumas wanted
to brief it that way,' a source said. The extracts stressed that Corbyn was
not attempting to 'reduce the guilt' of the bomber, but then sought to
explain why terrorists might want to attack Britain. 'The responsibility
of government is to minimise' the risk of terrorism, Corbyn said, and to
ensure 'that our foreign policy reduces rather than increases the threat
to this country'. He went on, 'Many experts, including professionals in
our intelligence and security services, have pointed to the connections
between wars our government has supported or fought in other countries and terrorism here at home ... We must be brave enough to admit
the "war on terror" is simply not working.' Corbyn was correct that security chiefs had said that the war in Iraq had increased the risk at home,
but to imply that this made terrorist attacks explicable – from a leader
who had never explained how he would tackle the threat, beyond an
undefined desire for peace – was breathtakingly bold four days after the
worst atrocity on home soil for twelve years.

When Labour officials saw the text of the briefing they were horrified.
Southside WhatsApp groups lit up with moderates repelled by the idea
that Britain had brought terrorism on itself when Islamists had launched

attacks across the West in countries that had played no role in Iraq, Syria or the war on Isis. One Labour official said that evening, 'The speech is totally insane.' Another explained, 'They want to get back into the agenda that matters to them – rail nationalisation, disability issues, the environment, industrial strategy. They have no understanding that leadership and security are the primary function of a PM in the eyes of the public. We just thought: "This is going to lose us the election."'

In Tory headquarters there was 'incredulity' that Corbyn had decided to focus on what the Conservatives regarded as his weakest suit. 'There was genuine anger that someone would say that,' a special adviser recalled.

Crosby deployed the cabinet's heaviest hitters to respond, including bringing Boris Johnson out of cold storage. The foreign secretary's main contribution to the campaign up to that point had been to refer to Corbyn as a 'mutton-headed old mugwump' at the end of April – which, depending on your stance, was either evidence of Johnson's fundamental lack of seriousness or a put-down perfectly calibrated to cut through with the public without seeming too rude to a Labour leader still considered, at that stage of the campaign, a bit of a no-hoper. It certainly had people looking up 'mugwump' (someone aloof from party politics who professes disinterested and superior views).

On the morning of Corbyn's speech, the foreign secretary was hosting Rex Tillerson, the US secretary of state. When Crosby heard this his face lit up as if to say: this is a gift. 'We've got to get Boris out.' Fiona Hill agreed. In his and Tillerson's joint press conference, Johnson branded Corbyn's speech 'absolutely monstrous'. He said he found it 'absolutely extraordinary and inexplicable in this week of all weeks that there should be any attempt to justify or to legitimate the actions of terrorists in this way'.

In Matthew Parker Street, Crosby and Textor both praised Johnson, and said he should play more of a role in the campaign. 'He was pointedly saying that Boris could inject some energy,' one staffer recalled. Amber Rudd, as home secretary, was already prominent in the response to Manchester. That morning they also wheeled out Sir Michael Fallon, their best 'fireman', to do a broadcast round.

From that point on Johnson got his own grid of events and was wheeled out for the spin room of debates. 'Get to the South-West, fight the Liberal Democrats,' Crosby ordered. 'Get to the North-East. This is

the message: Brexit, Brexit, Brexit.' Tom Edmonds began to feature
Johnson in Facebook adverts targeted at Labour Leave voters – the only
senior figure excluding May who was used that way. Two days before the
election, Johnson made a speech saying the prospect of Corbyn in
Number 10 made him 'shudder'.

Corbyn had a tough time on terrorism and foreign policy when he
was interviewed by the BBC's Andrew Neil on the Friday evening. He
said his speech was simply making an argument that had also been made
by 'Boris Johnson in 2005, two former heads of MI5, and of course the
foreign affairs select committee'. He did not challenge Neil's accusation
that he had never publicly condemned an IRA atrocity, but claimed, 'I
didn't support the IRA. I don't support the IRA. What I want everywhere
is a peace process.' He insisted that he backed NATO, but failed to explain
why in the past three years he had described the organisation as 'a danger
to world peace' and called for it to be wound up. Yet Corbyn looked less
defensive than May had done when interviewed by Neil, and emerged
relatively unscathed.

Diane Abbott did not when she booked herself on *The Andrew Marr
Show* that Sunday, against Milne's wishes. The shadow home secretary
was confronted by a comment she had made in 1984 that 'Every defeat
of the British state is a victory for all of us,' and her call, in 1989, for MI5
and Special Branch to be abolished. She took the novel approach of
comparing her past views to an old haircut: 'I had an afro. It was thirty-four years ago. The hairstyle has gone and some of the views have
gone.' Waiting in the wings, Amber Rudd had to put her hand across the
mouth of her special adviser Mo Hussain to stop him laughing out loud.
Asked what qualified her to be home secretary, Abbott said, 'I worked in
the Home Office for nearly three years as a graduate trainee.'

The Tory press operation began pumping out attack stories on
Corbyn's views, including a dossier of how he had boasted about 'opposing anti-terror legislation ever since I first went into Parliament in 1983'.
He had voted against seventeen major counter-terrorism bills, from the
Prevention of Terrorism (Temporary Provisions) Bill in 1984, which
outlawed Northern Irish terrorist groups, to more recent laws to permit
surveillance of suspects' mobile-phone activity. One of the hardest-
hitting stories, which made the front page of the *Sunday Times* and the
splash in the following day's *Telegraph*, revealed that in 2014 Corbyn had
attended a wreath-laying at the grave of Atef Bseiso, a PLO man who

helped orchestrate the massacre of eleven Israeli athletes at the 1972 Munich Olympics. Sir Michael Fallon said, 'We thought it right, given he wanted to be prime minister, to draw attention to his record and make sure that he was asked pretty searching questions about his past sympathy with various terrorist groups.'[2]

At Southside, though, Corbyn's aides felt the establishment media were overplaying their hands. James Schneider, who had done rebuttal on the attack stories during the leadership campaign, just copied and pasted his stock response.

Paradoxically, some Tories realised that the Manchester attacks had made it more difficult to paint Corbyn as a terrorist sympathiser. Voters had an emotional, not a political, reaction to the bombing. 'It always felt a bit odd once there were actual terrorist attacks happening,' a CRD source said. 'People were more concerned about security. But when kids were literally being blown up in Manchester, it's a lot harder to believe that Jeremy Corbyn thinks that terrorists are brilliant.'

Corbyn's views did hurt him with some voters. Labour parliamentary candidates began telephoning moderates at campaign headquarters to complain that the speech had gone down badly. One party adviser who had been knocking on doors for a month said working-class voters asked him, 'Why has he started to talk shit again?' Focus groups run by the Southside professionals also found some disquiet at the speech. When participants were asked if Britain's foreign policy was responsible for terrorism, they broadly agreed with Corbyn. A YouGov poll on Friday suggested that 53 per cent of voters backed Corbyn's analysis that it had made the country less safe. But when the focus groupers were asked if the Labour leader should make that case, respondents overwhelmingly said 'Absolutely not, you're giving succour to the enemy,' a source familiar with the findings said. Over at Matthew Parker Street, Lynton Crosby urged Tory staff to ignore the poll: 'They might think he has a point, but that doesn't mean they think he should be prime minister.'

Six million people watched a highly polished US-style attack ad put together by Tom Edmonds, which filleted Corbyn on defence and terrorism, culminating in audio of him hanging up during a Radio 5 interview when asked if he would condemn the IRA. It was Labour's most-watched video of the entire campaign, garnering more than ten million views on Facebook, YouTube and Twitter. 'That was the one piece where we knew it rattled them,' a Conservative official said. 'You had people bringing it up in focus groups.' However, among the young voters Corbyn was trying to attract, the video may have backfired. A former minister said, 'My children are teenagers, and a lot of their friends were showing it to me with horror. The tone of it was so relentlessly personally negative that I think it was a fusion of a message that would work with the pensioners, broadcast to the young. It was a disaster.'

To the generation of Corbynistas born in the 1990s, the IRA and the Troubles were as relevant as Vietnam or the Korean War. Matt Zarb-Cousin, a Corbyn ally in that age group, said, 'Most people know about Jeremy and John [McDonnell]'s past. They've either already factored it in or simply don't care.'[3] Adam Klug of Momentum said, 'We saw Jeremy's really principled approach to international peace really cut through. There was a common assumption that the terror attacks, which were obviously horrendous, would damage Jeremy politically, but I think we actually saw the opposite happen.' A Tory cabinet minister agreed: 'By the last few days we looked mean and ungenerous.' John McDonnell felt that 'It turned Jeremy into an underdog, and British people quite like underdogs.'[4]

Worse for the Tories, pro-Corbyn blogsites discovered that a Conservative councillor in Croydon, Maria Gatland, was a repentant former member of the IRA. She was small fry compared with Corbyn and McDonnell, but the Tories looked like hypocrites. The story was a viral hit on the left.

May's main problem was that she too had a record to defend. At Milne's instigation, Corbyn's speech on the Friday also highlighted Labour's pledge to pay for 10,000 more police following Tory cuts. During the period May was home secretary, the number of frontline officers had been cut from 144,000 to 124,000. The Tories pointed out, accurately, that the budget for those engaged in counter-terrorism had been increased, but Labour's stance on reversing austerity was now able to insulate Corbyn on security. 'Labour will reverse the cuts to our emergency services and police,' he said. 'Austerity has to stop at the A&E ward and at the police-station door. We cannot be protected and cared for on the cheap.' By the following week police cuts had become the dominant issue in the election.

The Conservatives seemed paralysed. Once again there was disagreement between Crosby and Hill over how to respond. 'Lynton argued that we needed to take it on, get out there, put out a counter story,' said one campaign official. 'Fi took the view that we should not, and that it would disappear sooner than it did.' Textor lost his temper: 'They won't listen to us on the police. They won't respond. They don't think it's a big deal. In the age of social media, you can't sit there for forty-eight fucking hours. You've got to respond instantly.'[5] Crosby said, 'OK, just tell them that Jim's numbers show they've gotta deal with it, and then Jim will you go see Fiona?'

Jim Messina's firm had a 'social listening' operation, which calculated which stories were being talked about online and who was dominating the conversation. It showed that the police-numbers issue was off the charts. 'You could see the numbers bounce,' a campaign aide said. 'It was all anyone was talking about.' Hill agreed to meet Messina that evening, Monday, 29 May. Messina waited for two hours at the Ham Yard Hotel, but Hill did not show up. She sent him an email apologising because she had run into someone else and gone for a drink. Messina called her and said, 'I really want to talk to you.' Hill agreed to swing by the office the following day after a trip with May, but again failed to appear. 'The online stuff was scaring the shit out of us,' the source said. 'Jim was trying to tell them they had to get their shit together. Fiona blew him off twice.' Messina told a colleague, 'If no one wants my opinion, then fine.'

When Hill did finally send out a minister to respond it was May loyalist Karen Bradley, the culture secretary, who was not fully across the issues and was hardly a heavy hitter. 'They put out a cabinet minister who reporters don't give a shit about,' one consultant seethed. 'We needed to change the conversation.'

The failure to deal with the issue in the week after the Manchester attack would come back to haunt the Tories when terrorists struck again in London on the weekend before the election. 'Labour focusing on police cuts was devastating,' a special adviser said. 'That hurt us more than social care. We had put more money into armed police, but armed police aren't those in the community. They destroyed us on that.' The intense media focus on the work of the emergency services reinforced Corbyn's campaign narrative rather than May's. George Freeman said, 'The terrorist attacks heightened our love of frontline public service – the heroic nurses and ambulance-drivers and fire crews and police. There was an assumption that this would be good for the Conservative Party because it will speak to security. In fact, the combination of the austerity on the front line and Jeremy Corbyn's intervention on the follies of Iraq being just as responsible for our insecurity – I think that struck a chord.' After the election one of the directors at Southside acknowledged that the Corbynistas had been right. 'To be fair to them, I think the leader's office were more perceptive, and more in touch with what people and voters were thinking, than we were. I find it abhorrent. His defence of terrorist organisations in the past and his views on defence and security are just hideous. But it seemed to strike a chord with the people that came to the Labour Party. What do we know?'

The other effect of the Manchester attack was to fossilise the main campaign where it had been before the bombing. The Tories had lost a clear week in which they might have recovered from the 'dementia tax'. 'The Manchester attack froze the campaign at exactly the wrong moment for us,' a senior Conservative official said. 'The manifesto had changed the campaign, so when the campaign restarted, it restarted from a fundamentally different place.'

That place was not where one of May's closest aides wanted to be at all.

20

'THIS ISN'T WORKING'

There were two weeks to go before polling day when Fiona Hill announced that she wanted to blow up the whole campaign. Nothing felt right to her. They had come into the campaign to bank the political capital the prime minister had spent ten months building up, and now Lynton Crosby was letting their account dwindle to nothing. Hill and Timothy's relationship had been strained by the manifesto launch, so she went to find Chris Wilkins, the Downing Street strategist whose vision of May as a change candidate had been ignored. Wilkins was kicking his heels in Matthew Parker Street, barely part of the campaign. 'We've just become the Remain campaign,' she said. 'It's all about fear, and no hope at all.' In one of the morning meetings Hill let rip with a *cri de coeur*: 'There just isn't enough fucking joy in this campaign. We need to make it lighter.' She also confided in Jojo Penn, Tom Swarbrick and Craig Woodhouse, telling them, 'This isn't working.'

Hill was not the only one concerned. Steve Baker, the convener of the Eurosceptic MPs, was also worried that the campaign would not deliver the mandate for a clean Brexit he was looking for. He complained to friends that the campaign had become a 'necessary drudge', and texted the chiefs, 'Can we please have some joy?'

In her discussions with colleagues, Hill talked about what May's Downing Street team had originally planned: an extension of what they did in government. The PM was supposed to make a few well-timed set-piece interventions – May, heavily prepped by Hill and Timothy, was good at those – while the rest of the cabinet would fill in the gaps with press conferences and television appearances. They could get back to that, couldn't they? Send May out with a big speech or two. There was still time. 'Fi was really pretty depressed and wanted to change it at that point, go back to what we originally planned,' a senior Tory who spoke to Hill that week recalled. Another colleague said, 'Fi was completely aware that it was a disaster. The original plan was that the PM would campaign in the way that she had governed. Fi wanted to reposition the whole thing. To go back to big set pieces, hammer the economic message, go home. Stop the "strong and stable" bollocks.' Wilkins was 'very supportive' of Hill's approach. He was keen to get his teeth into a meaty speech, to try to turn things around.

Nick Timothy agreed that there was a need for a more upbeat tone. Yet colleagues say Hill found her comrade in arms did not have the stomach for a fresh fight with Crosby. 'Because the manifesto had been so manifestly on him – he had been the guy who'd taken all ownership of it – as soon as something went wrong with it, it became very difficult for him to argue strategically,' one friend said. 'Nick lost faith in his own judgement,' another added. The other factor was that the numbers were improving slightly. The initial slump in Conservative support after the manifesto had corrected itself a little. Everyone in the campaign still expected to win.

Timothy was just as depressed as Hill by what the campaign was doing to May's reputation. 'By that stage I was having WhatsApp conversations with Nick and speaking to him on the phone every few days,' a cabinet minister said. 'He certainly felt that we started off with a campaign that everyone wanted, and it became progressively one which Lynton wanted, and was not one that he liked or Theresa liked.' May privately voiced the view that the Australians were 'so much more right-wing than we are'. But as far as Timothy was concerned, the Australians were guys who delivered votes. You didn't have to like the way they did it. Even David Cameron complained at times that their campaigns were limited, repetitive and negative, but they had got him over the line in an election when conventional opinion had judged a majority impossible. 'We've got to stick to what we're doing now,' Timothy told one ally. 'We need to stick tight to Lynton now because we've basically done the deal. We've just got to cling on.' After the election, Timothy explained, 'We knew the campaign wasn't going as well as we'd hoped, but actually on the basis of the research and data there was no urgent need to change the strategy because the projections still looked good.'[1]

Even this might have been wishful thinking. After the election, CTF sources made clear that Textor and Crosby were both warning that there were huge risks, but some colleagues think Timothy was looking for reassurance that the manifesto had not finished May's chances, and tended to remember only the good news. 'Post the manifesto, Nick was quite traumatised,' a senior figure said. 'He withdrew a lot, he spent all his time seeking reassurance. He'd go to Darren Mott, to Lynton, to the chief whip, to Stephen and Tex. What he was seeking, in hindsight, was someone to tell him that it was all OK. He heard what he wanted to hear.' A Downing Street colleague who had seen Timothy relish previous fights was struck by his passivity: 'That's why there was friction between him and Fiona. Normally he loves the fight. Normally he'd say, "Fuck you, I'm going to show that I'm right." He must have been wounded if he wasn't fighting for it.'

In the war room they could tell all was not well between the chiefs. 'The strange thing in the week after the manifesto,' a campaign official said, 'was that it went from Fiona agreeing with Lynton over the care policy to Nick aligning himself with Lynton over campaign strategy.' Another source confirmed, 'Nick sided with Lynton in the last week or so, against Fiona and the PM's wishes. Nick bottled it and backed Lynton.' The common theme was that Timothy got his way and was at odds with Hill, his closest friend and colleague. The ties that bound Team May grew strained again. 'They were totally allies until the general election campaign, and then it all began to fall apart,' a special adviser noted.

The Mayites vowed to ride out the campaign, but they were already looking ahead, thinking about how they could repair the damage. 'We certainly took the view all the way through that the campaign had ruined the PM's brand and everything that we'd worked to put together,' one of May's senior aides said. 'Its conduct and strategy had undermined everything we'd done. But as long as it delivered the numbers, which we were told it would, then we'd just have to work doubly hard to try to rebuild that afterwards.' The downbeat mood extended beyond the chiefs and Wilkins to other Downing Street staff. 'It was a countdown, not to election day, it was a countdown to the day the Australians were no longer in our lives,' a Number 10 official said. 'That was the way it was talked about.'

Without Crosby, though, campaign officials think the campaign might have fallen apart altogether, and delivered Jeremy Corbyn into Downing Street. The period after the U-turn was a dangerous one in Matthew

Parker Street. MPs and party donors were on edge. 'The manifesto unnerved the numbers, but the members too,' a senior figure said. 'You could have easily have had a situation, from a management point of view, where the campaign falls apart.' A close ally of Crosby said, 'If Lynton had not been there to hold it all together, wobbles like that turn into implosions.'

Crosby called for a return to the Brexit message which had been extensively tested by Textor. 'That's what all the research showed was the issue on which people were prepared to come back to us,' a Conservative source said. 'Lynton was relentless about getting them back on-message.' The placards and slogans changed, though in keeping with the chaos of the campaign this was initially due to a mistake, not a plan. The press got excited at one rally in the week campaigning recommenced when the Tories began to downplay 'strong and stable leadership', but the truth of the matter was, one campaign official said, 'There weren't enough placards, so they mixed them up with some older ones because they happened to be there.' By 30 May, the slogan on the prime minister's lectern and positioned on the backdrop behind her was 'For the best Brexit deal'. Another read, 'Theresa May and the Conservatives: a Brexit deal for a brighter future'.

Crosby closed down further policy announcements. 'After the social care U-turn, there was a decision to not talk about policy for two weeks. It came from Lynton and Tex,' an official said. The chiefs went along with the edict. After the Manchester attack, Rob Oxley, Will Tanner and Craig Woodhouse had planned to brief some positive stories on debt relief, mental health and the honours system, so that their output went beyond attack stories on Corbyn and terrorism. They were told, 'This isn't the kind of campaign we're running.' Fed up with being told they couldn't brief anything, Oxley and Woodhouse drew up their own 'dark grid' for the papers and began handing out stories without consulting Fiona Hill. They noticed other stories appearing which the research department had drawn up. Someone in CTF was operating their own back channel. One of Oxley's freelance operations further damaged his relationship with Hill. The head of media had got hold of a document drawn up by Labour policy adviser Lachlan Stuart, showing that Corbyn had been considering bringing back a visa scheme – the tier-three entry route scrapped by David Cameron in 2013 – which would have allowed unskilled foreign labourers to move to the UK and compete for jobs. After discussions with Woodhouse, Oxley gave it to his old flatmate Kate McCann at the *Telegraph*, and to the *Daily Mail*, both of which splashed the story on 30 May. Staff at the *Sun* were furious to have been frozen out, and Crosby was despatched to placate its editor, Tony Gallagher.

Oxley began to notice that his emails were returned even less often than usual by Hill, while Craig Woodhouse got responses. Woodhouse 'worked like a Trojan' on story ideas and press releases, and colleagues saw him grow in influence with the campaign commanders.

One effect of the Tory ban on policy stories was to cede the broadcast air war to Labour. It was not just that Corbyn's populist policies were popular; they also gave the broadcast media a seemingly endless series of announcements on which to focus, even after the Labour manifesto was published. 'We had a good model,' a Corbyn aide said. 'We briefed the story of the day beforehand, someone from the shadow cabinet would do the morning broadcasts. Jeremy would pick it up around mid-morning, and then images of the day would be Jeremy on the stump surrounded by people at rallies and the bits in his speech that relate to the announcement of the day.' They were never short of material. 'If you've got a manifesto which is where the overwhelming majority of good people are now – but these things are so outside what's been offered recently – you've got a huge wealth of stories that can sustain a very long period. There aren't fifty agenda-setting stories about Theresa May, I don't think ...'

The Conservatives believed Labour's announcements were too often taken at face value by the media. 'It felt like the broadcasters had decided fairly early on that Labour couldn't win and therefore Labour didn't get that much scrutiny for what were fantastical positions,' a senior campaign official said, before adding, 'There's no point just moaning about that, I don't think we did fully enough to expose the madness of their positions.'

Meanwhile, the Conservatives pumped out negative stories to the newspapers, but these were not likely to get traction with the BBC. 'I don't think we gave broadcasters broadcast-style stories,' Timothy was to admit to friends after the campaign. 'All we ever gave them was stuff slagging off Corbyn, which was half-arsed,' a press officer said. 'Had we had a manifesto written for two weeks, we could have absolutely dominated for a fortnight.' That ship had sailed. Beyond the energy price cap and a plan to build new council houses to help 'generation rent', briefed to the *Sunday Times* the weekend before the manifesto, there were few retail policies. 'She didn't make the manifesto live on a retail level,' said one consultant. '"What does it get me? Does it get me lower taxes?" The only retail thing they got from us was the bad stuff.' Timothy's view was that offering tax breaks or pledges of X number of hours of free child-care, as George Osborne had done at election time, did not fit with May's honest approach, since they were 'promises quite easily made and difficult to meet'.

At Southside they could see that the Tory manifesto had magnified the effect of Labour's own. 'That was a massive switch moment in the campaign,' said a source in the leader's office. Indeed, this was one of the more productive periods of cooperation between LOTO and the Labour lifers, as the research and media teams combined efforts to dissect the Conservative manifesto.

Labour's polling was still showing that support among working-class voters was soft. Milne and his team called Patrick Heneghan in to one of their Sunday strategy meetings and asked what they could do about it. Together they decided to target more direct mail containing attack messages – often on Tory NHS spending – at 'Labour Leave' voters. 'We knew from the polling company that we had a problem with the white working class,' a Southside source said. 'We knew it on the doorstep. We addressed that with our resource allocations and spending in the second part of the campaign.'

When it became clear that Tory support among the over-sixty-fives was easing, LOTO demanded action again. The message came out: 'We need to scare pensioners now. There's a segment of the electorate that has been closed to us, and we've got to get in there.' The digital team in Southside created videos highlighting the care, winter fuel and pensions policies for targeted Facebook adverts. 'We followed through with significant spend,' another source said. Corbyn's team were beginning to behave like a conventional campaigning organisation. A Labour official said, 'It's not a group of people they actually cared about, but they were aware it was causing them problems with the polling numbers. They seized the opportunity and acted on it.'

As the Tory lead over Labour narrowed, the party also got more adventurous with its target seats, to which it shifted funds from direct mailing and digital advertising. By now the £4.5 million from Unite was coming onstream. 'That money went into part defensive and part offensive,' a Labour official remembered. The money was allocated by both Patrick Heneghan and Steve Howell. The leader's office saw the target-seats list, added some and removed others, and then approved it. By that stage Labour had thirty offensive target seats. One of them was Canterbury, a university seat in Kent which Labour had never won. They were eventually to gain thirty-six seats (offset by six losses), which supports the contention that Southside made sensible use of resources once the upturn in the polls put more seats in play.

Having lost the argument about campaign strategy, Fiona Hill resolved to go where she could do most good, and took herself out of the office several days a week to travel with the prime minister. 'Theresa was not performing very well,' a source said. 'She needed her hype woman there.' May would need all the help she could get, because at just the moment her confidence had taken a knock, she had to carry the campaign in public in the televised interrogations that had replaced the leaders' debates.

21

I, MAYBOT

Jeremy Paxman was supposed to be the tough one, but it was the audience who landed the blows. It was the laughter that did it. Theresa May, under fire over cuts to school funding, said, 'In the Labour Party's manifesto we know the figures don't add up.' At that point the audience began laughing. The prime minister was momentarily frozen by panic. Then the heckling started. Someone in the audience yelled that Labour's plans were costed. Another shouted, 'You've clearly failed.' It was 29 May, and the first televised showdown of the campaign for the prime minister – a joint Sky News/Channel 4 production. Paxman went first. The veteran inquisitor was at his most sneering, asking the prime minister if her U-turns – National Insurance, social care and an early election – would lead EU negotiators to conclude that she was a 'blowhard who collapses at the first sign of gunfire'.

Corbyn dealt better with the incoming fire. He refused to say that he would back a drone strike against a terrorist plotting overseas to attack the UK, dismissing it as a 'hypothetical question'. Where May had been petrified before Paxman, Corbyn was playful. When the interviewer asked why, as a lifelong republican, his party's manifesto was not openly seeking to abolish the monarchy, Corbyn leaned forward and smiled. 'Look, there's nothing in there as we're not going to do it,' he said.

It was authentic Corbyn. Despite a tabloid furore about whether he would bow to the queen when he joined the Privy Council, Corbyn had got on rather well with her. 'When he went to see the queen for the first time he gave her his own home-made jam,' a leadership source said. 'It was blackcurrant jam. He refused to bow, but it turned out he didn't need to. He genuinely likes her. He would abolish the monarchy tomorrow if he had half a chance, but at a personal level he really, really liked her.'

Adam Klug of Momentum was cheered by the two performances. 'Their notion of leadership was that a supposedly strong and stable leader was someone who says they're strong and stable all the time. Whereas you've got Jeremy, who's so natural, and nothing is fake about his genuine interest in people. It was clear how much more popular Jeremy actually was.'

May's discomfort was clear. 'You could tell she didn't want to be there and she didn't know how to do it,' said a senior figure on the Tory campaign. Unexpected questions created a brief flicker in her eyes that combined fury and fear, something her aides called 'the flash'. May's nervousness undermined her election message. 'There you are running a campaign about being bold and talking to the Europeans and standing up to them,' a consultant said, 'but non-verbal communication is pretty powerful. Voters had this image in their head of a strong and forceful woman, and they saw a bit of a nervous one.'

She was also robotic, giving answers that seemed to have been churned out by a malfunctioning android programmed with a meagre diet of soundbites, something captured with devastating waspishness by the *Guardian*'s sketchwriter John Crace the previous November when he first labelled her 'The Maybot' ('Whirr. Clunk. Clang. The Maybot's eyes rotated into life...'),[1] a name that was to stick with devastating effect.

Under such intense personal scrutiny for the first time in her career, May's personal awkwardness and the nervous tic she exhibited, where she grimaced from the side of her mouth, pulling her chin back into her neck, suddenly became an issue. 'Theresa, not unlike George Osborne, could have done with speech and language therapy over her mouth,' one special adviser said. 'George always had that completely inadvertent sneer. It's just how his face landed. If he was a woman you'd say he had a "resting bitch face". Theresa has a "resting panicked face". She's awkward-looking.'

When the first programme was over, one Conservative staffer watching in the war room at Matthew Parker Street turned to the person next to him and said, 'Well, that's why we didn't do any proper debates.' Tory high command fell out over a lot of things during the 2017 campaign, but on one thing they were agreed: Theresa May should not be sent into a face-to-face debate with Corbyn. They remembered David Cameron coming unstuck as 'Cleggmania' catapulted an outsider to public prominence in 2010, and the media obsession that drowned out coverage of other campaign events. Nick Timothy recalled, 'We all just agreed debates would have been a mistake. Everyone looks back at 2010 and thinks the debates were not a good idea. They sucked all the structure out of the campaign in 2010, and I think they'd have been in danger of doing that again this time. We didn't spend loads of time talking about it. I think everyone was just of the view we shouldn't do it.' After the event some, including Timothy, believed it was wrong to pre-announce that May would not go head-to-head with Corbyn: 'I do think the non-participation then fuelled the feeling we didn't do scrutiny, which was not right given the number of interviews she did and the questions she took at press conferences.'

May's position was weakened because Labour took the opportunity to make her refusal to do the debates a campaign issue. Many voters thought the prime minister's failure to participate was evidence of weakness. 'People asked how she could negotiate a Brexit deal if she could not debate her opponents,' said Michelle Lowe, the Conservative candidate in Coventry South. 'People no longer liked her.'[2] The debates decision combined with the care U-turn to undermine May's campaign message. 'If you go into a campaign and you U-turn quickly, or you do not turn up to debates because you do not want to be shouted at, then your whole mantra of strong and stable starts to fall away,' Katie Perrior observed.[3]

Corbyn also declined an invitation to the first debate of the campaign, a fruitless face-off for ITV on 18 May between Liberal Democrat leader Tim Farron, Caroline Lucas for the Greens, Paul Nuttall of Ukip and the leaders of the two nationalist parties, Nicola Sturgeon and Leanne Wood. The exchanges degenerated into a free-for-all, with leaders talking over each other when they weren't piling in to attack Nuttall, who found himself in the role of proxy whipping-boy for the absent Tories.

For the second, seven-way, contest Labour had agreed to attend, and the Tories rostered Amber Rudd. The home secretary was May's chosen successor in her own department, and had performed well in broadcast interviews after the Manchester attack. She was already being talked about as the frontrunner to succeed Philip Hammond at the Treasury. She also had debate experience, having led the Remain campaign's effort to duff up Boris Johnson during one EU referendum debate the year before. The debate, in Cambridge University's Senate House, was scheduled for the evening of Wednesday, 31 May, two days after May's faltering performance. Apart from an hour of signing intelligence warrants each morning, Rudd's team blocked out Monday, Tuesday and the whole of the Wednesday for debate preparations on the fourth floor of CCHQ. She had known for more than a fortnight that she would be flying the Tory flag. 'She was obviously very excited,' a friend said.

Despite picking her for the role, Fiona Hill showed very little interest in the preparations. Timothy was also absent. 'Nick didn't come in once,' said one of those involved. 'I was surprised by that because she was representing the party.' Tom Swarbrick, the head of broadcasting, led Rudd's prep, assisted by Alex Dawson and a rotating cast of junior advisers playing the other leaders, including Karen Bradley's spad Aidan Corley as Farron, former Welsh Office spad Lauren McEvatt as Leanne Wood, Andrew Goodfellow as Nuttall, and Salma Shah, who had joined Swarbrick's team for the campaign, as Lucas. To those who had seen Rudd prepped a year earlier by a high-powered team of Craig Oliver and Alastair Campbell – communications directors to two prime ministers – it was a curiously low-key effort.

Mark Textor and Lynton Crosby briefly showed their faces on the Wednesday morning. The Australians warned Rudd not to let her Remain sympathies get the better of her in exchanges with Nuttall. 'Amber is on the more liberal side of the party, and her instinct would be to attack him, but Lynton said, "Don't do that, because we want to get Ukip votes."' Crosby urged Rudd to try to deliver the key 'strong and stable' message with more subtlety than May. 'He wanted "coalition of chaos" and "strong and stable leadership", but told her not to chant this line all the time, but use it as a theory – that you can only have a strong economy with strong Brexit. There was a lot of pivoting to strong Brexit.'

Rudd's special adviser, Mo Hussain, had shown her clips of the ITV debate. She studied Tim Farron's technique of attaching personal stories to his answers, such as his family's use of the NHS – a device that had been conspicuously lacking in May's television grilling. 'You are the government minister. This is going to be five or six on one,' Hussain warned Rudd. Another source present said, 'We prepped for questions along the lines of "My benefits have been cut," or "Someone has committed suicide in my family as a result."' The Tory team told Rudd not to get drawn into a free-for-all, but to stand back and let the other leaders squabble. That, they judged, would be the perfect moment to intervene and tell viewers, 'That is what a coalition of chaos looks like,' dramatising one of the key Conservative campaign messages. Swarbrick also suggested Rudd borrow a device from David Cameron, who had pointed at each of his rivals in turn and denounced them for their policy of 'more borrowing, more borrowing, more borrowing'. This time, Rudd was encouraged to stress that a vote for each of the minor parties would lead to Jeremy Corbyn becoming prime minister: 'Vote Lib Dem, get Corbyn; vote Green, get Corbyn; vote Ukip, get Corbyn …' At that stage, Rudd had no idea that she would be taking on the Labour leader as well, but Corbyn's team were again about to reveal their flair for the dramatic.

The day after May was heckled on television, Patrick Heneghan walked into Labour's morning campaign meeting and said, 'Jeremy should rock up to the Cambridge debate.' Labour had hitherto regarded the seven-way contest as a gathering of 'losers' which the leader should avoid. Heneghan pressed the case again at the 9 a.m. meeting. His argument was simple: 'May is on the back foot now. We can spin this as: she's not turning up because she's scared, because she was rubbish on Monday. She knows she can't go again.' Crucially, he added, 'We shouldn't tell anyone until the morning that he's doing it.'

Andrew Murray immediately saw the advantages of what Heneghan was proposing. Andrew Gwynne and Ian Lavery, the two campaign coordinators from Parliament, also liked the gambit. Andrew Fisher and Simon Jackson were opposed. The supporters saw a chance to wrongfoot the Tories. Slowly a plan developed to send out John McDonnell on a media round to make the announcement on the morning of the debate itself. 'They will be in a spin over there all day, they won't know whether to send her or not, and Jeremy will have won by the time he turns up.' Milne and Karie Murphy were despatched to talk to Corbyn. The leader was not enthusiastic. He envisaged a rerun of a debate in the 2015 election in which Cameron had not participated, and Ed Miliband found himself under fire from the minor parties. An aide said, 'Jeremy's view was that when Ed Miliband did it everyone attacked him, and he became the status-quo person.'

On the Wednesday morning, with the decision still not made, Corbyn and Jonathan Ashworth, the shadow health secretary, held a press conference on the NHS, designed to spearhead a week of campaigning on public services. 'It was ludicrous, because we couldn't make a decision,' a party official said. 'We went back to Southside after the press conference and Seumas was late to the meeting because he was meeting Jeremy about it. I think the decision was taken about half past ten.' By that stage even Andrew Murray was against the plan, because Corbyn had not had time to prepare properly. But having detected a groundswell of concern from the CLPs that Corbyn should not duck the challenge, Milne had come around. 'It was Seumas's call,' a LOTO source said. 'John Mac wasn't for it. Jeremy originally wasn't for it. Seumas listened to the activists.'

Once it was agreed that he would take part in the debate, Corbyn went on a marginal constituency visit rather than going through debate prep. The downside was that as soon as it was revealed that he was doing the debate, Ashworth's health announcement was overtaken. 'We killed our own story,' one Labour official said. Corbyn received some preparation from Milne and Andrew Fisher. He had also had media training from Marc Lopatin, a communications adviser who also worked as a dispute mediator, and Paul Mason, the former economics editor of *Newsnight* whose book *PostCapitalism: A Guide to Our Future* had made him a poster-boy for the Corbynistas.

The only question for Labour now was whether Theresa May would perform another U-turn. 'We honestly thought they would turn up,' a source in Corbyn's office said. Many Tories later wished that she had done so. It would have delighted the media for May to appear at the very last moment, walk on stage even as Rudd was being mic'ed up and say, 'I'll take it from here.' However, the prospect of a grand gesture was never seriously discussed that day in Tory Central Office. None of the campaign commanders believed the prime minister would have made a good fist of it, still less have consented to try. Nor had they seen Corbyn's curveball coming. 'We didn't contingency-plan for Corbyn turning up,' one admitted.

Corbyn's decision raised the stakes for Amber Rudd. The home secretary was already under huge pressure after the Manchester attack, and was having to spend large amounts of time in her constituency of Hastings, where she was defending a majority of less than 5,000. Also, unbeknownst to most people on the campaign, her father had died on the Monday evening. On the Tuesday morning she made clear, 'I want to continue,' but she made no mention of her bereavement in the debate prep that day. It was only six months since her ex-husband and the father of her two children, the journalist A.A. Gill, had died of cancer, but Rudd 'didn't want to make a big thing out of it'. One of the special advisers helping her prepare said, 'Amber is a fucking pro. There is no way that I would have been able to tell that she had had a bereavement that week. I only found out when I read it in the paper.'

When she found out that she was taking on Corbyn, Rudd's response was, 'OK, fine, let's get on with it. It could be fun.' She began practising new lines, pointing out that four out of five Labour MPs did not vote for Corbyn in the no-confidence vote: 'If your own people haven't got confidence in you on Europe, how are you going to go face-to-face with twenty-seven other leaders?'

The debate itself, in the words of one Tory adviser, was 'an absolute pie fight', a war of words over which the moderator Michal Husain frequently lost control. 'There were so many times you couldn't hear what anybody was saying because they were shouting at each other,' a source close to Rudd recalled. Corbyn landed a few blows on government cuts, but struggled to stand out from the pack of progressives attacking the Tories. The most memorable lines of the night were delivered by Farron and Lucas. The Green Party leader rounded on May's absence: 'The first rule of leadership is to show up.' In his closing statement, Farron delivered a brilliant set piece he had come up with during prep sessions at the Ministry of Sound nightclub. Knowing he would speak before Rudd, he urged voters to change channels before the home secretary's statement. 'Amber Rudd is up next. She's not the prime minister. The prime minister is not here tonight. She can't be bothered. So why should you? In fact, *Bake Off* is on BBC2 next. Why not make yourself a brew? You're not worth Theresa May's time. Don't give her yours.'

For Paul Butters, Farron's spin doctor, it was 'literally the high point of the campaign'. When his man had delivered the line, Butters left the spin room at the Cambridge Union, went outside for a cigarette, and 'did a little jump in the air'. He went to the bar, sank a pint and then returned to the spin room, where he said to the waiting hacks, 'I have to be honest, we smashed that. No spin required.'

Farron was arguably the best-prepared of all the leaders. His debate prep team included Downing Street coalition veterans Sean Kemp and James McGrory. The latter had been the chief spokesman for the Remain campaign, and delighted in delivering a pitch-perfect Paul Nuttall impersonation. 'James treated being Nuttall like it was therapy,' a witness said. 'He loved using all the arguments that he had had to rebut during the referendum campaign. He brought everything back to immigration or foreign aid – and I mean every possible topic. If Nuttall had been a tenth as good, it would have been alarming.' But it was the experience of Kemp, playing Corbyn, which was most instructive. 'It made me realise how the debates really played to his strengths,' Kemp said. 'He's totally unencumbered by self-doubt. Most opposition leaders worry about going too far or striking a balance. Corbyn just says, "X is terrible. People are suffering. That's why I want Y, which the rich will pay for." It's like being a Lib Dem used to be. If you don't want to agonise about what your policies mean in practice, you can hoover up applause lines.'

Rudd survived a tough night. She hit back at Corbyn's austerity attacks by accusing the Labour leader of funding his ambitious plans with a 'magic money tree', another of Crosby's favourite soundbites. Like May, she was laughed at by the audience – among which the left-wingers were very vocal – when she was confronted over the lack of costings in the Conservative manifesto. Yet she performed confidently, and allowed herself one moment where she appeared to be measuring the curtains in Downing Street, saying, 'Theresa May may not be here, but I hope to make a good fist of setting out Tory policy ... Part of being a good leader is having a good strong team around you.' Privately, Rudd was happy. She had landed the lines she had been asked to, and she had braved a difficult evening, under great personal strain, with greater aplomb than May would have managed. 'She was relieved when it was done,' a friend said. Fiona Hill called Rudd and said, 'You were great. Thank you.'

On the Friday it was Theresa May's turn back in the spotlight – this time to face a *Question Time* showdown with Corbyn. The programme, broadcast on 2 June, just six days before the election, gave Corbyn his toughest television experience of the campaign. It was the Labour leader's turn to be jeered and heckled as he ruled out 'first use' of nuclear weapons, saying he would deal with threats 'by negotiations and talks', and would press for 'disarmament'. Asked by the host, David Dimbleby, how he would react if this 'ideal' was not possible in a conflict situation, Corbyn seemed uncomfortable. An audience member in his fifties tore into the Labour leader, asking, 'Would you allow North Korea or some idiot in Iran to bomb us and then say, "Ooh, we'd better start talking"? You would be too late.' Another member of the audience called Labour's manifesto 'a letter to Santa Claus', and a third asked Corbyn, 'Why have you never regarded the IRA as terrorists?' When Corbyn again refused to condemn the IRA by name, saying merely that he 'deplored all acts of terrorism', the questioner hit back, 'They did kill a lot of people didn't they?'

In CCHQ they felt the public had managed to land blows in a way the Conservatives themselves had failed to do. 'I was incredibly buoyed,' a special adviser said. 'It felt quite significant. Perhaps we overstated the resonance.' In the spin room after the debate, a team of ministers and Oxley's media team were quickly out in force delivering strong attack lines as the newspaper reporters rushed to file their copy, while Labour's operation was slow to crank into action. One remarked later, 'The only time I really walked away thinking we'd properly done Labour in was after the York BBC *Question Time*. Corbyn had a bad night and we smashed the shit out of them in the spin room.'

Seumas Milne realised Labour had a problem. It was nearly midnight when he phoned Corbyn from his train back to London and told him, 'We need, without looking defensive, to seal down the Trident thing so it doesn't keep intruding in the next few days. We just need a form of words … to shut down the nuclear question.' That was the conclusion to a conversation in which Milne had said it would be 'completely off the wall' and 'bonkers' for Britain to ever respond to a nuclear attack with a strike of its own, describing the deterrent as 'a complete emperor's new clothes. If there has been a first strike, what is the point of the second strike?'

Milne was not aware that a regional Tory press officer, returning from his brother's wedding in the North-East, was sitting behind him recording everything he was saying. Rob Oxley, Craig Woodhouse and Kirsty Buchanan were having a drink at their hotel when the press team's WhatsApp group began to buzz with the news that Milne had been caught confirming that there were no circumstances in which Corbyn would ever use the deterrent, not even if Britain had already suffered a nuclear attack. Oxley ordered a total lockdown: 'No one tells anyone anything about this. This is a proper story. We save this.'

The recording was sent to an audio expert to boost its quality. Fiona Hill questioned whether the tape was real: 'Are you sure it's Seumas?' The press officer had taken an out-of-focus smartphone picture of Milne making the call. They compared his clothes, tie, watch and cufflinks with pictures from the debate before handing the tape to the *Mail on Sunday*, which splashed the story. Frustratingly for the Tories, the tape of another part of the conversation was of such poor quality that Milne's words were undecipherable. The press officer had heard him talking to Corbyn about how he would hold on to his job after losing the election. 'We couldn't quite get it off the tape, but the person had overheard it, and Seumas said, in essence, "If you lose you can just say they didn't let you run the campaign you wanted to run." There was a discussion about how they could keep the leadership.'

It was the only time during the campaign that a covert recording by Tory aides – usually a favourite election tactic – bore fruit. 'It wasn't that there was none of it going on,' a press officer said. 'But what could they say in private that was crazier than the stuff that they said in public?'

When the *Mail on Sunday* called Labour HQ that Saturday, it caused widespread mirth at Southside. 'It was comical,' a Labour official said. 'Seumas came in. He was so white. He was embarrassed. He knew he had fucked up massively and there was no one else to blame. Whenever he gets caught out he tries to blame someone else, and this time he had no get-out-of-jail-free card.'

The spin room in York was the venue for one of the most bizarre displays of the campaign, which saw Boris Johnson blowing kisses at Labour's Ian Lavery after he suggested that the foreign secretary had never visited a food bank. 'I actually started some when I was mayor of London. I think you should take that back, old boy,' said Johnson. 'Take it back.' The two then pointed at each other before Johnson pursed his lips and made kissing noises. If that was not strange enough, the foreign secretary then got into a wrestling match with Andrew Gwynne. When the Labour man muscled into shot during a solo interview by Johnson, complaining that Boris had refused to debate him, the foreign secretary put his arm around Gwynne and shoved him to the floor. 'Don't be a pillock,' Gwynne responded. Johnson called him 'a big girl's blouse'.

The explanation for Johnson's erratic behaviour was a story in *The Times* that morning suggesting that David Davis might replace him as foreign secretary, with Ben Gummer becoming Brexit secretary – a move that would never have been tolerated by the Eurosceptics. However, Johnson had begun to convince himself that May might sack him if she got a big majority, something he thought was on the cards. That very day he had told a journalist that he was going to have a bet on a majority of more than eighty. 'He was pouring his heart and soul into the campaign,' an ally said. 'Then all of a sudden you see this story. It left a really bad taste in his mouth. He was in a foul mood.' On the train to York, Johnson called Fiona Hill and asked where the story had come from. Hill gave him short shrift. She had enough on her plate without dealing with paranoid cabinet ministers. In the green room before the debate Davis wound Johnson up, saying, 'We were just talking about this *Times* piece.' Hill lost her temper. 'If one more person fucking mentions this, I'm going to lose my shit,' she said, before storming out.

The bigger issue for the Tories than Johnson's clowning around was May's performance. For the first fifteen minutes of her *Question Time* grilling, the prime minister seemed more confident. She dealt with the question of why she called the election with uncharacteristic bluntness: 'I could have stayed on doing that job for another couple of years ... I had the balls to call an election.' However, when she was confronted by a nurse called Victoria Davey about the squeezing of her pay, the Maybot returned. An empathetic politician like Bill Clinton would probably have walked towards the woman, asked more about her life or offered to meet her afterwards. May saw only a threat, and retreated to her talking points: 'I recognise the job that you do, but we have had to take some hard choices across the public sector in relation to public sector pay restraint. We will put more money into the NHS, but there isn't a magic money tree that we can shake that suddenly provides for everything that people want.' For many watching, it confirmed May's transformation from a different sort of Tory into a distant leader lacking the human touch.

May's aides were aware of her shortcomings, but could not agree on how to deal with them. According to one witness, when the prime minister was being briefed for one broadcast appearance Tom Swarbrick had suggested she acknowledge the sacrifice of public sector workers, only to be shot down by Nick Timothy, who argued, 'In an election campaign you cannot concede any ground.' Some felt this attitude had made May think she could not show empathy to public sector workers. 'People were worried about what the next day's headlines were going to be – "Prime minister admits NHS close to collapse". That was Nick's point. She does instinctively feel empathy and sympathy. I was surprised by the degree to which she allowed herself to hold back for fear of it being taken out of context and blown up.'

Crosby and Textor wanted May to show strength, not weakness. 'CTF's answer was always, "There's no more money. I'm the prime minister. Sorry,"' another aide said. 'It was very brash.' But ahead of the *Question Time* appearance, Textor had sought to strike a balance. 'Tex suggested, because it was perfectly clear that "the Maybot" was a thing, she was a bit more conciliatory on the feeling, but at the same time hard on the policy response.' May appears to have only taken in half the briefing. Worse, Textor's suggestion that she 'walk along the audience' was greeted with a familiar refrain: 'David Cameron did that, therefore we can't do that.'

For their part, the Australians thought May was prepped by the Downing Street team as if she was doing a turn in the Commons, rather than engaging with the public. 'Some of the media types around her thought it was like Prime Minister's Questions, where you can have a glib answer. But when you've got a live audience of real punters, they see through it,' a source said. 'What works in the chamber doesn't work out there.' May's encounter with the nurse lit up social media with claims that the prime minister was out of touch, cold and uncaring.

The accuracy of this depiction was a subject which divided even her Downing Street staff. 'I'm not having a go at her, but she's just a naturally very reserved person. She doesn't express much emotion,' one senior figure said. Katie Perrior, who had known May for a decade, believed she had been trained by Fiona Hill not to show her softer side. 'She sometimes comes across as too cold,' Perrior said. 'She's been trained to be afraid of the media.'[4]

In private, May could be understanding and considerate. One parent who got to know her because their child had diabetes described her as 'kind and considerate' to children with the condition. Yet stories like that contributed to a view in Westminster that May was good at empathising with people whose experiences she had shared, but less good at putting herself in the shoes of those whose lives did not touch on hers. During the campaign another CCHQ staffer said, 'The only time I ever saw her in a situation that was in her comfort zone was when we did the Bath and Wells show.' It was the kind of provincial English event with which May was familiar. The prime minister happily posed with children demanding selfies. 'It's probably the sort of thing she grew up with. She seemed to have had fun.'

May lacked the personal prima-donna characteristics of some politicians. On a campaign visit to Stockport she had tea in a café with volunteers from a local theatre. 'After that she needed to use the loo, which was at the end of this room,' an aide recalled. 'There was this little lady already using it. She just stood there and waited and fiddled about with her purse and her phone. When the other lady was finished she opened the door and squealed. "Oh, I'm sorry you were waiting!" The PM said, "No, no, it's not a problem, it's fine." She was so normal. If that had been David Cameron we'd have had to find him another toilet.'

Yet May's unwillingness to show more understanding of the nurse's situation, or to reveal anything to the media beyond her chosen sound-bites, was now an existential threat to her premiership. It also made her, in the words of one campaign aide who spent time on the road with her, 'absolutely miserable'. At an event on 29 May, the prime minister took a question from Quentin Letts, the waspish sketchwriter for the *Daily Mail*: 'I don't mean to be rude, but you seem to be a bit of a glumbucket. Are you enjoying the campaign?' Her face like thunder, May visibly flinched and gave a stock answer.

Misery gripped staff in Central Office, who could see their poll lead evaporating but had no faith in May's ability to turn the situation around. 'When Cameron was in the shit with his back to the wall, you knew he could pull it out of the bag,' said one former Downing Street aide who had worked closely with May during the coalition years. 'He had another gear. Theresa had no second gear.' When May appeared in CCHQ towards the end of the campaign, she struggled even to rally her own troops. To weary incredulity from campaign staff, who were tired of fighting for someone they did not rate, she simply repeated her standard stump speech while staff gazed at their phones.

As the poll lead closed and her performance became a focus of criticism, senior figures on the campaign are clear that this created a vicious circle in which May's confidence in herself took a hit, making her even more nervous and stilted. On 1 June, she pulled out of an interview with Radio 4's *Woman's Hour*, sending Justine Greening to replace her. Ed Miliband, discovering wit he had failed to show the electorate two years earlier, tweeted in mockery of government rules on JobSeeker's Allowance: 'Can I report someone who has failed to attend two job interviews in forty-eight hours. I know where she lives. What is the sanction?'

Those who admire May blame both CTF and the chiefs for making her shoulder the burdens of the campaign single-handedly: 'Did she perform badly? Yes. Was she always going to perform badly if set up in that particular context? Absolutely.' But in the age of twenty-four-hour news it is not possible to excuse May from being poor at public relations. Communicating who you are and what you stand for is at least a third of the job. May was not an innocent abroad – she had wanted to be prime minister since she was a teenager. It was incumbent on her to recognise her shortcomings and get help to correct them.

Jim Messina, the data expert who led Barack Obama's re-election effort, saw in May the echoes of another female politician who had not known what a campaign would entail and who shrank from the spotlight when an initial burst of public popularity led to uncomfortable scrutiny from the media – Sarah Palin, the Republican candidate for vice president in 2008. As May lost confidence, Messina told colleagues a story about Obama: 'In 2008 when they picked Sarah Palin everyone was saying, "Oh my God, she was brilliant on her announcement speech and she's gonna change the race." Obama said to me, "Jim, you know it took me a year to figure out how to run for president."' Messina told a colleague, 'You can't call an election that even your own political people don't know is coming, if you've never done it before. She and her chiefs just weren't ready for it.' He did not mention this to May herself. Amazingly, he had only two conversations with the prime minister in the entire campaign.

May's last major media appearance before the election, an interview with ITV's Julie Etchingham, was perhaps the most indelibly awful. Asked to recount the naughtiest thing she had ever done, the prime minister's face became a mask of horror. 'Oh goodness me,' she said, the chin reflex kicking in. 'But I suppose the ...' her voice trailed off. In the wings, three of her aides – Fiona Hill, Tom Swarbrick and Tricky Jackson – looked at each other, sensing danger, not knowing what she would say. May put on her best school governor's voice and said, 'Nobody's ever perfectly behaved, are they? I have to confess when me and my friends used to run through the fields of wheat, the farmers weren't too pleased about that.' What might have been seen as charmingly provincial at the beginning of the campaign became, in the harsher environment after the manifesto, a source of instant ridicule, further evidence that May was weird.

On several occasions May expressed concern about the course of the campaign and her place in it. 'Does it always have to be me?' she asked during one meeting. One of her closest aides said, 'Theresa's a party person, and she didn't feel that comfortable doing the whole "Vote for me" thing, and I think that came across.' Another aide said, 'I think Lynton ran a campaign she didn't really believe in. She doesn't like saying "strong and stable" a thousand times. They certainly had a meeting about halfway through the campaign where she said, "How many times do I have to keep saying this? You're making me sound stupid," and he said, "I'm sorry Prime Minister, but that's what the message of the campaign is."'

The difference between May and every other leader Crosby had ever worked for was that at no point during the campaign did she lose her temper and demand a rethink; at no point did she scream, 'This isn't working!' Those who had worked on the 2015 campaign vividly recalled the moment, two weeks from the end, when David Cameron told the Australians the campaign was 'lacking fizz' and he wanted to change tempo. After discussions he tore off his jacket, rolled up his sleeves and became much more aggressive on the stump. May never did so.

One seasoned campaign official said, 'A leader has to say, "Look, I'm getting frustrated." Being calm works when you're running the country. But the campaign actually needs some inner emotion. I've never been through a campaign before where someone has not expressed an opinion. You do need a leader to lose it occasionally.' Another campaign veteran said, 'Ultimately a leader decides the tenor of the campaign. She never expressed a view. She never amped up her performance like Cameron. What Boris Johnson calls "giving it a bit of welly". She doesn't express much emotion.' As one special adviser put it, 'Lynton was – unfortunate turn of phrase – polishing a turd. The manifesto didn't cost us the election, the person did. She didn't connect.'

With two weeks to go until election day, most Conservatives knew that the product they were selling was not as good as they had hoped. They only realised later that the way they were selling it was not working either.

THE CORBYN SURGE

(and Why Almost No One Spotted It)

It was barely audible at first, just a few voices in the crowd – how these things always start. Many a football crowd had used the song, but sometimes those chants began and were simply taken away on the breeze. Not this time. There was no music to help them, no bass guitar pumping out the unmistakable riff of the White Stripes' hit 'Seven Nation Army' – E, G, E, D, C, B. Dung, da, da, da, da, dung, dung – just a few enthusiasts. But as the chant spread it caught like a flame meeting dry leaves. Soon the whole crowd was chanting it in unison:

Oooooh, Je-rem-eeeee-Corrr-byn
Oooooh, Je-rem-eeeee-Corrr-byn
Oooooh, Je-rem-eeeee-Corrr-byn …

The location was Prenton Park in Birkenhead, home to Tranmere Rovers football club. The occasion was the Wirral Live Music Festival, and the Libertines were due to play before a crowd of 20,000. It was the evening of 20 May, and the Labour leader had dropped in to make a brief speech on sport and music. Now he was topping the bill. British politics had never seen anything like it. As he finished, Corbyn shouted, 'Thank you for giving me a few minutes. And remember, this election is … about … you!' That was when the crowd found its voice.

At first Corbyn did not know what the crowd was chanting. 'When you are on the stage, you can't actually hear everything that is going on,' he told the YouTube channel Copa90. 'Then I'm looking at these guys chanting and I realise they are smiling, so I paused and realised what they were chanting. I was quite moved, actually.'[1] At 8.09 p.m. Labour's former deputy leader John Prescott, who had previously been critical of

Corbyn, tweeted, 'Something is definitely happening.' Within days the Corbyn chant was his recognised anthem.

What was happening was what came to be known as 'the Corbyn surge' – yet many thought it was a mirage founded on the false hope that young people would vote. The British Election Study, the most authoritative source, found that just 47 per cent of under-twenty-fives voted in 2015, compared with 85 per cent of over-sixty-fives. The figures were comparable during the EU referendum.

Labour veterans remembered the 1983 general election, the last time the party had a leader from the hard left, when Michael Foot had been met with rapturous crowds at rallies, and gained the impression that he was winning an election he was to lose by a landslide. The Corbynistas felt this was a different scenario. 'Trade union membership was two or three times what it is today back then, so it was a lot easier to organise,' one said. John McDonnell recalled, 'All the old hands were saying, "Oh yeah, big crowds, but you're talking to the converted. And the young people, they'll never turn out." I thought: we've got a phenomenon here that people have never seen before.'[2] At one campaign event, supporters stood in a river to listen to Corbyn because the banks were packed with people. When Manuel Cortes, General Secretary of the Transport Salaried Staffs' Association (TSSA), helped organise a birthday party for Corbyn in the last week of May, he said, 'When he walked into the pub, it was almost like if a pop star had walked in. He was surrounded by people and everybody wanted to take selfies with him. Three weeks into the campaign he started to look like a prime minister in waiting.'[3]

Corbyn was a natural campaigner. Four decades of pressing the buttons of left-wing audiences at protest rallies stood him in good stead. While May seemed contorted by shyness and hauteur, in the words of one Labour aide, 'Jeremy just seemed happy on the television.' Corbyn's personal approval rating climbed from minus 42 to minus 2, and had even overtaken May's by the end of the campaign. But he remained less popular than his party, while May was more popular than hers.

Tory MPs noticed a change on the doorstep. One said, 'At the beginning of the campaign you'd say, "Look me in the eye and tell me you want Corbyn to be your PM," and they'd avert their eyes. At the end they were saying, "He's not as bad as you lot are making out."'

Corbyn also had a good campaign temperament. Where May was brittle and defensive, two leadership elections and two years of incoming fire had trained Corbyn not to look grumpy or irritated when under attack – traits which had disfigured his relations with broadcasters during his first year in charge. Emily Thornberry, the shadow foreign secretary, said, 'I thought it was ironic that Theresa May was going into the election as "strong and stable", because of all things that describes Jeremy extremely well. He is very strong and stable, some would say pig-headed, but he certainly knows what he wants, and he gets on with it.'[4] When he did get into trouble, notably in a *Woman's Hour* interview on 30 May, when he failed to recall the costings of his free childcare policy and frantically searched an iPad for the answers, a bumbling affability helped him weather the storm. Voters saw him as a human being, prone to lapses like them.

Nonetheless, when on 23 May Labour high command sat down with their pollsters BMG, one of those present made a note of their findings because he was so struck by them: 'I wrote down that they told us that the surge is not real.'

So, what made the Corbyn surge possible, and why did so many experts read it wrong? The leader's optimism and energy gave Labour an advantage over Theresa May in the 'air war', the headline battle which is most visible to the press and public. But election campaigns have three other important elements: the 'ground war' fought by activists on the doorsteps; the 'cyber war', which pits campaigners against each other on social media sites like Facebook; and the 'data war', where strategists use computer modelling to find voters for the cyber and ground warriors to target. In 2015 Labour had emphatically lost the ground and the cyber wars, but this time around the Conservative advantage was obliterated, with dramatic effect.

Corbyn may not have been able to rely on trade union mobilisation like Michael Foot, but he had something much better than that. It was called Momentum. The grassroots group that helped make Corbyn competitive emerged from his first leadership contest. It was the brainchild of Jon Lansman, an ageing Bennite who had spent three decades fighting for the Campaign for Labour Party Democracy (CLPD), a left-wing organisation that wanted members to control the party and introduce mandatory reselection of MPs as a device to purge those not committed to red-blooded socialism. Lansman established Momentum in October 2015 to control the email and supporter lists from Corbyn's campaign and mobilise the cohort of Corbynistas to support the new leader.

Lansman, along with John McDonnell, understood that the way to entrench something that would outlive Corbyn was to fight to change the Labour Party, rather than to change the country. Like many schooled on the hard left in the eighties, Lansman relished obscure procedural battles to elect delegates to bodies like the Conference Arrangements Committee (CAC), which decides what issues are debated at Labour's conference. 'Jon Lansman's view was, we can create a database of people that we can use to win CAC elections and CLP nominations and parliamentary selections and so on, and that is why Momentum exists,' a party source said. A senior trade unionist recalled that Lansman even left Corbyn's campaign to 'go and run the CAC election for him and Katy Clark, because he thought that being on the Conference Arrangement Committee was more important than Jeremy Corbyn being leader of the Labour Party'.

Yet if Momentum was established, to use the shorthand description of the Corbynistas, by an arch 'Leninist' fighting old battles, it drew its strength from the thousands of 'John Lennonists' inspired by Corbyn. To the younger generation of organisers radicalised by the Iraq War and the age of austerity that followed the 2008 economic crash, who included James Schneider, Momentum was a British incarnation of the Syriza protest movement in Greece, and Podemos in Spain. This difference of approach created some tensions. Activists like Schneider resented press claims that Momentum was being used as a Trojan horse by Trotskyite entryists, kicked out of the party in Neil Kinnock's expulsion of the Militant Tendency in the eighties. In February 2016 Momentum set up a formal membership structure under which members had to 'support the values and aims of the Labour Party', a move designed to prevent the Socialist Party – the successor to Militant – and the Socialist Workers Party from returning to Labour. From January 2017 Momentum members also had to join the Labour Party.

Real as these fears were, media attention on the Leninist agenda of some of the Momentum leadership hoodwinked the moderates and the Tories into underestimating the importance of the Lennonists. By the time of the general election Momentum had evolved into a movement of 150 local groups, 23,000 members and 200,000 supporters – all run from the offices of the TSSA union in Euston. After the election Patrick

Heneghan told a pollster friend, 'I was only aware of a third of Labour's campaign.' A Corbyn aide said, 'There was the traditional campaign, which allocated the financial resources on the basis that we were going to lose, and did traditional canvassing which told us we were going to lose. There was the Jeremy campaign at the top, which was transformative and thought we could win. Then there was a Momentum ground campaign, which was entirely aligned to the political approach of the leadership.'

The Conservatives dismissed this vast army as 'clicktivists', who confined themselves to waging war online for Corbyn. Yet the Momentum leadership, in line with LOTO, devised ways of getting them onto the streets, a task made easier because the election took place in university term time. Adam Klug, the group's national coordinator, said, 'We used social media and digital technology to mobilise large numbers of people to actually get out on the doorstep.' Klug and Momentum's fellow national organiser Emma Rees liaised with James Schneider in Corbyn's office to direct supporters to Corbyn's campaign events. A website – MyNearestMarginal.com – let activists locate campaign events in the five nearest marginal constituencies, and ElectionDayPledge.com signed people up to volunteer on 8 June. Adam Klug said, 'We had about six campaign days where we got people along to campaign for Labour in different marginals. On the final day just under 10,000 people pledged to take the day off work. We calculated that there were about 1.2 million doors knocked as a direct result of our website.' The Momentum army gave Labour a huge advantage over the fossilised Tory ground operation. 'Labour had more than three times as many people to call on as the Tories,' said Steve Howell.[5] Even where there was a functioning Conservative ground game, it was not enthused like Labour's grassroots. 'It's a lot easier to motivate people around a sense of hope, positivity and solidarity than it is around something that's negative,' Klug said. This enthusiasm also boosted Labour coffers: 'Online fund-raising alone raised more than £4 million in donations averaging £19,' Howell recalled.[6]

Momentum was essentially a force multiplier. Ed Miliband had vowed to cut tuition fees, but he did not have Momentum. By vowing to abolish fees altogether just as the interest rate was raised, Corbyn energised young activists. 'Miliband was offering a similar thing on student fees and yet it had a completely different effect,' a Tory cabinet minister reflected. 'The increase in the interest rate, no one had really clocked that in Westminster, and it really electrified the issue in young people's minds.'

The ranks of students were swelled by public sector workers feeling the pinch after seven years of pay restraint. Gavin Barwell, who was defending a majority of just 165 in Croydon Central, said, 'There was a conversation I particularly remember with a teacher, who had voted for me in 2010 and 2015, who said, "I understood the need for a pay freeze for a few years to deal with the deficit, but you're now asking that to go on potentially for ten or eleven years, and that's too much." That is something that Jeremy Corbyn was able to tap into.'[7] On election day, Barwell – one of the Conservatives' savviest marginal-seat candidates – had a hundred supporters helping him get out his vote. Momentum had, according to one estimate, a thousand people on the streets in South Croydon.

One other factor fuelled the ferocity of Labour's ground game – fear. 'We were told we were going to be destroyed, so we fought,' one aide said. 'Every single Labour MP fought. I've never seen people campaign like this. I had MPs from other parts of the country who literally rang and said, "I've never campaigned before. Can you teach my staff about campaigning?"' The result was that retention rates of Labour's 2015 voters rose from 75 per cent to 91 per cent during the campaign.

Corbyn travelled more than 7,000 miles during the campaign, appearing at ninety rallies. The formula meant that LOTO did not have to over-think his public appearances – a trend that had afflicted Ed Miliband's 2015 campaign, culminating in the leader unveiling the notorious 'Ed Stone', an eight-foot-tall slab engraved with his pledges. One of those who helped run Miliband's campaign observed, 'The rallies gave them a platform every day. They didn't have to think about the backdrop, the event, the crowd, or whose building it was, or one of the things we spent hours thinking about.'

At his final appearance, a raucous gathering at a church in his constituency, Corbyn claimed to have staked out a new centre ground in British politics. With hundreds outside unable to get into the packed church, he declared, 'Hope that it does not have to be like this, that inequities can be tackled, that austerity can be ended … This is the new mainstream, and we have staked it out and made it our own, together.' One of his aides said, 'We have hugely shifted the centre of gravity of politics in this country.'

The enthusiasm Corbyn generated was given more practical effect because Momentum arranged for organisers from Bernie Sanders' 2016 campaign for the US Democratic nomination to hold training sessions for volunteers, drafting in Bostonian Erika Uyterhoeven, Sanders' national director for outer-state organising, among others. 'The right can throw money at elections – we throw people,' Uyterhoeven said.[8] Adam Klug said, 'They delivered short talks and training on canvassing techniques. Roughly 70 per cent of people who went to these trainings had never canvassed before. It gave people confidence to go out and knock on doors.' Sanders' team put on sessions in London, Hull and Nuneaton, the town considered the bellwether of the 2015 Tory victory. They urged the volunteers to share personal stories about why they were fighting for Corbyn. 'When you get people talking to each other, it just creates a buzz and an energy in the room, especially when people are speaking from the heart and saying why they're there,' Klug recalled.

Another Sanders aide, Jeremy Parkin, taught the recruits a 'response cycle' for dealing with non-Labour voters. 'Start by acknowledging someone's concerns,' he said. 'Say, "I see where you're coming from."' He encouraged campaigners to tell their personal stories to voters too: 'If you change two people's minds, you've tripled your voting power.'[9] Using role-play scenarios, the trainees learned that when voters raised the subject of immigration they were often really concerned about services like the NHS becoming stretched, or a shortage of housing or jobs, allowing the canvasser to outline Corbyn's proposals in those areas. 'You use facts and figures and then you end up and ask, "Will you vote Labour?"' Klug said. 'You do that cycle twice. If you ask them and they're not convinced you go one more time round, and then if they're still not convinced you say, "That's fine, thank you."' When the training sessions were complete the newly confident doorknockers would go straight into a real canvassing session on the streets, to put into practice what they had just learned. The Sanders team also introduced Momentum to the idea of a carpool website so volunteers could share rides to campaign events, and 'peer-to-peer texting' to help recruit others.

While Momentum was the provisional wing of LOTO, it did not operate in isolation from the main party structures. Momentum supporters were summoned to Labour canvassing sessions using Southside's events-organising software. A Labour official explained, 'We allowed Momentum to link into our software. They were driving people to

Labour Party events. You can't go around canvassing with a copy of the electoral roll if you're not the Labour Party. If Momentum were doing that, that would be a criminal offence.' Adam Klug confirmed, 'Everything we did was in harmony with Labour's national campaign. We sent coaches from Birmingham, Leeds, Sheffield, London, out to canvass.'

Where Momentum could claim to have made a significant contribution was where they decided to put their resources. 'We targeted seats that regional Labour parties thought weren't winnable,' Klug said. 'Some of the candidates or sitting MPs were pessimistic. In Battersea, for example, the local party thought it wasn't worth putting resources into it. In Kensington there was a big Momentum presence.' Both were Labour gains on the night. Many moderate candidates had cause to thank Momentum afterwards. Yet even Klug admits that these deployments were based on belief and hunch, rather than a strategy derived from data: 'It was an optimism and a belief that we had a message that would win in many seats that seemed unwinnable. This politics is rooted deep in people's hearts and minds about the vision of society they want to live in. That motivates people to not just plod along but to commit everything they've got, and to persuade other people to go out and canvass.'

Momentum did not just recruit volunteers for the ground war, it also mobilised young people to register to vote, a campaign launched with the support of celebrities including the grime artist Stormzy and the Hollywood star Danny DeVito. 'In just over three weeks, more than two million people visited the Electoral Commission's website,' Steve Howell said, 'leading to an unprecedented number of successful registrations by young voters.'[10]

Faced with the sheer volume of Momentum activists, the Tories were overmatched. Some Conservative associations, even in seats classified as winnable, had as few as three members. 'One dose of botulism in the prawn sandwiches and we could be three associations down by dinner,' a special adviser joked. The one hundred paid organisers employed in 2015 had all left. In Brighton Kemptown, where the Tories trailed by just 690 votes before polling day, ministers visiting the seat were surprised to discover that the local association consisted of little more than the candidate and his family.

The scandal over the battle-bus expenses and the Rabelaisian culture of Road Trip, exposed by the death of Elliott Johnson, meant that there was little effort centrally to boost the firepower on the ground in key constituencies. Grant Shapps, the party chairman in 2015, bemoaned how his efforts had been maligned: 'Number 10 appeared to believe they could win 2017 entirely as an air war. But they'd forgotten that the unexpected win in 2015 saw 100,000 volunteers of Team 2015 knocking on doors. The same activists also did huge amounts of social media all over Facebook, using Snapchat filters and the like. It was Momentum before Momentum was even invented. Yet by 2017 the campaign seemed to believe they could do away with activists on the ground and replace them with even more Theresa May – and forgo activists tweeting and replace them with centrally-purchased social media. The result wasn't authentic, and failed to bring the campaign to life. We must never again try to campaign without campaigners on the ground.'

The evolution of the Conservative campaign also meant Tory literature, devised and sent for printing while May was riding high, was quickly obsolete after the publication of the manifesto. A Tory official said, 'It was just the "strong and stable" messaging from seven weeks previously, which by that point just didn't feel sufficient.'

Theresa May's events were visually uninspiring compared with the mass rallies of enthusiastic young supporters who flocked to see Corbyn. 'We certainly always struggled for numbers at events,' a campaign official said. 'All these events looked exactly the same on TV: a tight shot of a little room with a bunch of placards.' The just-in-time planning meant local activists often felt frozen out. Hamish McFall, a former Tory candidate, said, 'May visited the marginal constituency in which I and many others were campaigning. Nobody much was told about her visit, and only the candidate and two others were allowed to meet her. Contrast that with the – however false and deluded – throngs of supporters at Corbyn's rallies.'[11] David Cameron's team had always matched events to locations, so that an announcement was relevant to the host business, but because decisions were taken so late, May's events usually had no connection to their surroundings. On the day of the local elections the Tories won across the country, but inexplicably staged an event in West London, where there weren't even any elections. 'We could have gone anywhere, but we didn't,' said an exasperated member of the media team. 'It was baffling.' The nadir came during a visit to a Dunelm factory near Nottingham, when May did not even visit the shop floor but was ushered instead into an unphotogenic back office to meet three staff next to a pile of boxes.

The ops team frequently had to prevent even worse visuals. On a visit to London's Smithfield meat market first thing in the morning towards the end of the campaign, the press pack was about to arrive when a special adviser spotted that one of the butchers' cabinets contained an entire pig's head. Coming after a biography had claimed that David Cameron once put his genitals in a pig's mouth as part of a university ritual, the risks of a porcine picture were acute. 'We had to deploy a junior volunteer to stand in front of this cabinet,' the spad recalled. When the rolling maul of journalists swept through, 'this poor young chap got slightly buffeted, but firmly stood his ground'.

Labour had always had a strong ground game. Their supremacy in the social media war – after being comprehensively outmanoeuvred in 2015 – was more surprising, and arguably more significant. Tom Edmonds, the Conservative head of digital, pumped out professionally-made content, but was limited to paid-for advertising on Facebook, by far the most important platform, since six out of ten people in Britain used the site. During the campaign the Tories spent around £2 million on paid-for advertising, up from £1.3 million in 2015. That compared with £1.2 million for Labour. Three-quarters of the spend went on Facebook adverts.

Labour's great advantage was that their army of young supporters, inspired by Corbyn, were far more willing to share campaign materials with their friends via Facebook, Twitter and Instagram. One of the most remarkable statistics of the entire campaign is that one in three Facebook users saw Momentum content during the campaign, yet Momentum spent just £2,000 on Facebook adverts, because they could rely on their supporters to distribute campaign materials for free. 'The content was so accessible,' said Klug. 'It resonated, it was creative and it was clever.' Among the successful videos was a satirical take on austerity, with a young daughter asking her father why she got no free school meal, her class sizes were larger and she couldn't afford to go to university. He replies, 'Because I voted for Theresa May.' The daughter asks, 'Do you hate me, Dad?' 'Obviously,' he replies.

Jim Waterson, the political correspondent of Buzzfeed, who has done most to chronicle the rise of social media campaigning in Britain, says Corbyn's message was well suited to social media. 'In 2015 if you said on Facebook, "I'm a moderate socialist who doesn't believe it's electable, so I'm voting for Andy Burnham," you would get ten likes and a load of people having a go at you. If you say, "I believe in full-fat socialism with Jeremy Corbyn," then everyone goes, "Yeah! Me too!" It's quite hard to argue a moderate position, because it does terribly online. Corbyn produced a message that did really well online. If you were the average twenty-year-old, your social media was just swamped with everyone saying the only cool, possible thing to do was vote Labour.'

It helped that Corbyn enjoyed a huge lead over May in terms of his personal social media following. 'By the end of the campaign his Twitter following had grown 32 per cent, to 1.2 million,' Steve Howell recalled. 'His video posts on both channels were watched by millions, with one attracting 8.35 million views.'[12] Corbyn had three times as many Twitter followers as May. Momentum's Facebook page reached 23.7 million views, and videos were watched by 12.7 million unique users. Ben Soffa, who ran Corbyn's groundbreaking leadership digital operation and married Corbynite MP Cat Smith, was now Labour's head of digital campaigning. Marsha-Jane Thompson, Momentum's social media manager, ran affiliated social media accounts like JC4PM, which was able to churn out campaign videos far quicker than Labour HQ. Jack Bond managed the leader's own social media profiles. If Corbyn was on a news programme his appearance would be clipped and put on social media, while the Tory digital team had to go through a laborious approval process to run anything featuring Theresa May.

In Sheffield Hallam, where Labour was hoping to oust Nick Clegg, Adam Klug said, 'Sixty-nine per cent of eighteen-to-twenty-four-year-olds saw one of Momentum's videos,' the most for any constituency targeted by the group. One Corbyn rally in Birmingham was viewed 1.5 million times on Labour's Facebook page. 'That's the same as the ITV leaders' debate,' an aide observed. The grime music star JME recorded an interview with Corbyn which got more than 300,000 views on YouTube. Rapper Lowkey got more than 100,000 views for his video backing Corbyn.

Individual MPs like Angela Eagle created their own content, filming adverts with local people to champion her cause. One featured an SAS veteran, which helped neutralise anti-Corbyn feeling from armed forces voters. For £200 Eagle was able to get the video in the Facebook feeds of 45,000 voters in her Wallasey constituency.

Labour also ran a clever advertising campaign in marginal seats. Voters who raised concerns about the NHS on the doorstep would find their details fed into the party's central voter database. The party's digital team then used software called Promote, developed in-house, which linked voters in the database to their Facebook profiles. Within twenty-four hours they got Facebook adverts about the state of the health service.[13] Labour also devised a phone-banking app where an activist could dial in from home, be connected to a potential Labour voter and make their case from a prepared script.

The apogee of Labour's online audacity came on the Monday of election week, when the party paid £100,000 to place an advert with all seven million users of Snapchat, the most popular app with young voters. More than one million clicked on the link provided which told them where their polling station was. 'It was just a turnout mechanism. We've never spent that money before on a single thing aimed at young voters,' a Southside source said. 'It really worked.'

Both Labour's in-house digital team and Momentum concentrated on producing high-quality videos on key issues like rail nationalisation, leaving their supporters to spread them. 'We would see something going viral and put a professional spin on that,' a source in the leadership said. A Labour source said, 'People are more likely to engage with something if their friend has shared it and if it's interesting, not if it just says "Sponsored by the Conservative Party".'

A senior Tory campaign official said, 'One of the things that surprised me when I went back into CCHQ was that the social media machine had been dismantled. Labour had the unions, Momentum and lots of kids in their bedrooms. The only thing that we were able to do was mount a fairly traditional but highly corporate, paid campaign.' Prior to the 2015 campaign, Tom Edmonds and Craig Elder had spent two years getting Facebook 'likes' in the target seats, so that when they posted paid-for adverts, they were then shared by Conservative supporters for free. 'You can cover up some of the cracks with paid advertising but it's still far better to have organic followers,' another official said.

When Edmonds and Elder left CCHQ in 2015 the party's email mailing list contained 1.4 million names, but the lack of proactive messaging sanctioned by May's team meant that that had dwindled to 1.2 million by the time they returned. 'Because people change emails you get natural attrition,' a source explained. 'You need to stop sending things to dead email addresses.' When programmes like gmail detect that an email has not been opened by the vast majority of its recipients, it will mark that message as spam and filter it from inboxes, adding several hours to delivery time while the message and its sender are assessed. The result was that on election day, an email sent at 1 p.m. targeted at those likely to vote after work arrived in some inboxes at four o'clock the next morning, six hours after polling stations had closed. Here was a direct example of Team May's neglect of social media costing them votes.

For their part, the Mayites thought the consultants were too ready to rerun the 2015 campaign. Chris Wilkins had a young colleague from his digital comms agency who volunteered for the Tories. He warned Wilkins early in the campaign, 'Labour are killing us on social media and our digital output is making some basic mistakes.' When Wilkins suggested his colleague join the digital team he was ignored.

The Tory campaign in 2017 was actually more sophisticated than the more successful effort two years earlier. In 2015, Edmonds Elder ran 350 different Facebook adverts targeted at four basic voter types. This time there were more than 4,000 adverts tailored to dozens of different voter blocs depending on their stance on Brexit, which part of the country and the type of seat they lived in, and who they had voted for before. 'It was far more sophisticated,' a member of the digital team said. Their video detailing Corbyn's views on terrorism got 8.2 million views on Facebook, 1.3 million on YouTube, and 600,000 on Twitter, making it the Tories' most-viewed video of the campaign.

The Conservative digital team also exploited a loophole in electoral law to maximise the impact of their advertising. Edmonds realised he could target adverts at key areas of marginal seats, tailor national messages to local issues, and even mention the constituency – as long as he did not refer to the names of the candidates – and still charge the bill to the national campaign rather than the heavily restricted expenditure in each seat. 'You can say, "The gardens tax is going to hit families like you in Richmond," or "A vote for Jeremy Corbyn's candidate will mean you get hit with a garden tax,"' a source explained. 'But you can't then name the candidate.'

The moment when Edmonds realised what he was up against came after the Manchester bombings when Stephen Gilbert told him, 'We're suspending the campaign.'

Edmonds replied, 'OK. Are Labour doing it as well? Are all the third-party organisations doing it?'

'That's a good point,' Gilbert said. 'Do you know how many there are?'

A few hours later the two men were staring at a list of more than forty organisations that were helping Labour, from the trade unions, through single-issue pressure groups like Hope Not Hate and the People's Assembly Against Austerity, to larger left-wing campaigns like 38 Degrees which boasted mailing lists of ten million people. 'All these organisations could spend £700,000 during the campaign, and they could target it at whatever constituency they like,' a campaign official said. 'We, on the other hand, didn't have anyone to do that. Even groups that should support you, like Taxpayers Alliance, spend all their time campaigning against HS2 and government policies.'

Labour's other advantage was that it could leave its allies to do the negative campaigning, while the official party feeds pumped out positive material on Corbyn and his policies. Edmonds had to use the official Tory social media accounts to do both. 'Because we didn't have any third-party channels we had to deliver our own negatives,' one of his colleagues said.

Finally, while many Labour candidates knocking on doors were reassuring older voters unsure about Corbyn that it was safe to vote for them because he would not end up as prime minister, the social media campaign was energising youth voters with the opposite proposition, enabling Labour to conduct a Janus-faced campaign to maximise its returns. Dan Watkins, who fought Tooting for the Tories, said, 'While the Labour candidate was distancing herself from Corbyn in her leaflets, on the doorstep, and in public, below the radar on social media she took a very different line and played up her leader to younger voters.'[14]

Corbyn's digital outriders included keyboard warriors like Zarb-Cousin, Aaron Bastani of Novara Media, The Canary, Sqwawkbox, and Thomas Clark of Another Angry Voice. Some were members of a WhatsApp group called Digital Fightback. Their points of contact included James Schneider and Karie Murphy. Most simply did their own thing. Clark was just a thirty-something from Nottinghamshire who posted 163 articles in seven weeks from his home, with headlines such as 'How many of Jeremy Corbyn's policies do you actually disagree with?', but nonetheless had the same reach online as the *Sun* newspaper. Zarb-Cousin said, 'I think this election is the first where social media played a pivotal role. The top ten links shared on Facebook during the general election campaign were either pro-Labour or anti-Tory, achieving roughly half a million shares each.'[15]

These articles prove that the social media war was not just an internet extension of the main campaign, but operated in an entirely different dimension. When Nick Timothy and Ben Gummer were writing the Tory manifesto, they barely paused to think about the inclusion of a renewed commitment to hold a vote on reversing the fox-hunting ban. 'There were no red lights flashing,' a campaign source admitted. However, when May was questioned about her own views she said she had 'always supported fox-hunting', a policy opposed by eight out of ten voters. Watching from afar, Katie Perrior despaired: 'If she had ever mentioned the words "fox-hunting" on my watch, I think I would have leant across the table and had words.'[16]

Fox-hunting never became an issue in the air war. Online, it was a major driver of Labour votes in urban seats and among working-class voters who were open to voting for May but equated fox-hunting with 'Tory toffs'. Jim Waterson of Buzzfeed explained, 'Strong moral messages go viral. Enough people hated fox-hunting that it made them share content about it. It made others feel they were not a good person if they didn't share the stories. A picture of Theresa May next to a fox cub going "What do you prefer?" has more effect than an exclusive news story.' In an election called to discuss Brexit, more fox-hunting stories went viral than Brexit ones. The effect was devastating for the Tories. Michelle Lowe, the candidate in Coventry South, said, 'The biggest topic of conversation by far amongst these Labour-background urban voters was fox-hunting, often preceded with the comment: "We never thought she would be in favour of fox-hunting." Potential urban switchers began to think that the prime minister was the same as any other Tory, and began doubting her.'[17] Waterson added, 'I genuinely think that fox-hunting cost the Tories seats.'

While the fox-hunting problem was caused by adhering too closely to one David Cameron policy, another social media buzz issue emerged from abandoning another. Timothy and Gummer were keen to strip out the endless minor policies hung on the 2015 manifesto like so many Christmas baubles. Among those ditched was support for 'a total ban on ivory sales'. Timothy thought the policy disrupted the antiques market, and that there were better ways of saving elephants from poachers. To many voters, the exclusion of the ivory ban meant May endorsed slaughter for tusks. An article on the pro-Corbyn website Evolve Politics was shared more than 70,000 times and read by more than a million people.

Kevin Pietersen, the England cricketer who campaigned to save the rhino in his native South Africa, tweeted at May, 'We're on for a Twitter war!!!!!!!!' when he heard. A Tory official said, 'The Cameron manifesto went into insane detail. Because it was so recent, every pledge that wasn't explicitly referenced in the 2017 manifesto became "You're dropping your pledge to do this ..." The manifesto never had the proper political checks or a defensive media plan for issues like this.'

For weeks, stories were going viral, being widely shared on social media platforms and moving votes, and the Tory press and digital operations did nothing to rebut them. 'CCHQ needs a unit in elections to track stories,' a special adviser said. 'We need a rebuttal unit killing them, but we didn't even have eyes on this problem.'

The growing prominence of social media has its dark side. During the election campaign it was an outlet for bullying, harassment and sexist, racist, homophobic, Islamophobic and anti-Semitic abuse, directed at candidates and MPs. Many kept their heads down at the time, lest they be labelled oversensitive. But afterwards the vast extent of the horror prompted the prime minister to commission an inquiry by the Committee on Standards in Public Life.

The first to break cover was Tory Sheryll Murray, who used a question at PMQs to reveal, 'I've had swastikas carved into posters, social media posts like "Burn the witch" ... people putting Labour Party posters over my home.' Her colleague Andrew Percy, a convert to Judaism, was called 'Zionist scum' and his staff were spat at while canvassing. Ameet Jogia, who stood against Barry Gardiner in Brent North, found a voting booth smeared with graffiti stating 'Vote Labour Barry, not Jogia. Keep Pakis out of politics.' Female candidates were subjected to repeated rape and death threats. Diane Abbott was targeted with racist and sexist abuse that went far beyond criticism of her campaign brain-fades. She told a parliamentary debate, 'I've had death threats, I've had people tweeting that I should be hung if "they could find a tree big enough to take the fat bitch's weight". There was an EDL-affiliated Twitter account BurnDianeAbbott. I've had rape threats, been described as a pathetic, useless, fat, black piece of shit, ugly, fat black bitch.' Her colleague Paula Sherriff, a Labour MP, called the election 'the most brutal', and said she could not remember a single day in the previous two years when she had not received abuse, 'whether that be death threats or a picture of me mocked up as a used sanitary towel'.

Many of the Corbynistas directed most of their fire at moderates in their own party, labelling former Blairites 'red Tories' and devising a dialect of their own in which non-lefties were branded 'absolute melts', 'slugs' or 'centrist dads', while Jeremy Corbyn was 'the absolute boy'. In this language, attacking an opponent online was known as 'salting', and vanquished enemies were 'seen off' or referred to with sarcastic deference as 'skipper'.

At times hatred of the Conservatives was promoted as an explicit strategy. Early in the campaign the Tories got hold of a recording of a group of Corbynista academics at a Momentum event saying they wanted to launch a campaign of hate against Philip May, the prime minister's husband. The session was during an event called 'Take Back Control' in Shoreditch on Saturday, 22 April, the first weekend after May called the election. It was part of Momentum's politics festival 'The World Transformed'.

Asked what the left should be doing during the election, panellist Paolo Gerbaudo, director of the Centre for Digital Culture at King's College London, said, 'My answer is hate … Make the left hate again … I'm full of hate these days. Maybe it's just because I'm a hateful person.' Gerbaudo complained that the hate in society was taken out on the wrong people, before suggesting that Philip May was a legitimate target: 'There's so many right people to take it out against. I don't know if it was fake news or real news, I think it was real news, that the husband of Theresa May works for a £1 trillion hedge fund that is profiting from tax avoidance. So let's take loads of hate against that man … Let's be personal. Let's be visceral! Let's hate!' He also suggested that to take power the left needed to 'take the media' and storm the headquarters of NewsCorp, owners of the *Sun*, *The Times* and the *Sunday Times*: 'I'd love to do that but I'd probably go to jail.' When Gerbaudo suggested that the left should be 'not as nasty, but almost as nasty' as their political opponents, fellow speaker Ash Sarkar – a senior editor at Novara Media whose Twitter profile demanded 'Luxury communism now!' – interjected to urge activists to actually be 'nastier', adding, 'I'm on Team Hate.' Sarkar went on to make repeated calls for the hard left to 'arm the mandem', street slang for a group of men or boys.

To the regret of some Conservative campaign officials the recording was never passed to a newspaper and the story never saw the light of day. 'We had that right at the beginning, and it was pretty vile,' a special adviser said. The fear was that releasing it would unleash the very personal hatred threatened against the Mays. While it was a Momentum event, Paolo Gerbaudo had no role in either the Labour Party or Momentum. But he was a lecturer at one of the UK's best universities, responsible for influencing young adults at a formative stage of their lives – and this was not an isolated example. After the election, younger Tories thought it was evidence of a phenomenon that affected the election result. 'Say the phrase "left-wing bias" to a Tory over the age of thirty-five and they'll instantly start going off on one about the BBC,' one campaign aide said. 'Say "left-wing bias" to anyone who's been to university in the last decade and they'll tell you about left-wing bias at universities. It's a huge problem for us.'

Arguably the biggest problem for both main parties was knowing which data to trust. It was a dilemma shared by the pollsters themselves, whose reputations were on the line after a 2015 election which they had collectively botched by missing the Tory majority. Most got the EU referendum wrong as well.

After the debacle two years earlier, the UK Polling Council held an investigation and discovered that pollsters had underestimated the number of Tory voters by failing to reach enough over-seventies and including in their models too many young people who were interested in politics. Anthony Wells of YouGov said, 'The sort of people taking part in polls were too engaged, too interested, too likely to vote. 2015 was wrong because the turnout differential wasn't right – old people turned out, young people didn't, but the young people who took part in polls did go out and vote.' That meant the pollsters either had to find and monitor the kind of young people who did not vote in 2015, or adjust their turnout models to downplay the influence of political junkies. 'ICM and ComRes had a fancy turnout model based mainly on social class,' said Wells, 'while we spent lots of money trying to get young people who were less interested in politics – and then weighted it based on how interested people said they were in politics.'

The EU referendum was also a disaster for some pollsters, but not everyone got it wrong in the same way. Andrew Cooper of Populus had a bruising time, being blamed by some in the Remain campaign for wrongly telling David Cameron that he was ahead. Cooper said, 'We studied carefully the reasons for that poll error, and came to the conclusion that the underlying problems of deep, persistent sample bias and of turnout modelling are very clear and very significant, but impossible properly to fix. So we resolved to stop doing traditional voting-intention polls.' Populus turned instead to private client research based on a demographic model and data analytics rather than traditional polling.

In Corbyn's team there was widespread mistrust of the public polling, since the headline numbers were so dependent on the preconceptions of the pollster. 'If you drill down into raw numbers from all polling that you can get your hands on from the last two weeks of the campaign,' a Corbyn aide said, 'it broadly shows the same thing: Labour one to three points ahead. Then they apply what you think is going to happen. We had a heavy scepticism of politically accepted wisdom. That's different from saying "The polls don't know anything." It's the way in which they're interpreted which is wrong.'

On 25 May, a week after the Tory manifesto was published, YouGov put out a poll showing a lead of just five points for the Conservatives. Most other pollsters were showing leads of eight to ten points. The poll added to jitters at CCHQ. Six days later YouGov released the first election prediction drawn from a new model which had been devised by Doug Rivers, YouGov's chief scientist in the US, along with Jack Blumenau and Ben Lauderdale of the London School of Economics. In 2015 an earlier iteration of the model had predicted the Liberal Democrat wipeout, but not the Tory majority. Then it successfully predicted Donald Trump's victory in the US.

For their general election version, they first did a survey of more than 70,000 people, acquiring demographic information and voting intention. They then performed a 'regression analysis' to work out which factors drove voting intention, and built a predictive model. 'Your voting intention is a function of how you voted last time, your social grade, your education, your age, where you live, and your interest in politics,' Wells explained. 'It's an extremely complex model, and it takes account of how each factor interacts with each other – for example, you might be a Remain voter who lives in a constituency where the MP is a supporter of Leave. It goes down to granular things like that, and the interaction between them.' Once the model was built it was applied to each constituency in turn, utilising census data, the voting history of the 2015 election and the EU referendum to predict the election result. That process was so complicated it took a high-powered computer nine hours to complete.

The Times splashed on the findings the following morning, 31 May. The model was predicting a hung Parliament. At CCHQ there was a combination of disbelief leavened with mild panic. There were eight days to go. Anthony Wells called the Tory MP Nadhim Zahawi, one of YouGov's founders, to tell him the news. Zahawi shared the alarming prognosis with David Davis. 'Are you sure?' the Brexit secretary said. 'No I'm not sure,' Zahawi replied. 'I didn't design the model.'

The Conservative campaign consultants were more than irritated, they were concerned. Their own data had been up and down, but Lynton Crosby was trying to hold together a faltering campaign, and he could not afford the party grandees, donors and CCHQ staff to believe the wheels were falling off. When *The Times* front page dropped, sterling began to fall. At 4 Matthew Parker Street, Mark Textor was withering about YouGov's efforts, telling one meeting, 'In thirty years of campaigns I've never seen a polling industry as shit as the UK polling industry. Ninety per cent of the time it's just wrong.' One of those present said, 'We all laughed ... erroneously.' Jim Messina took to Twitter to ridicule the pollster: 'Spent the day laughing at yet another stupid poll from @ yougov.' Messina's intervention was retweeted by Mark Textor. Tory ministers referred to the pollster as 'YouGuess'. Messina had been asked by someone in the press office to send the tweet, and later regarded it as 'a mistake'. Later, Textor told friends the tweet was 'a bit of a diversion'. One said, 'There was a lot of nervousness, particularly from donors, about the manifesto. We didn't want senior party grandees going "Shit!"'

Among those who were losing their seats on the model was Amber Rudd, the home secretary. The message from CCHQ was to remain calm. 'She was told by people like Darren Mott that it was all fine, that there was nothing to worry about,' a source close to Rudd said.

This was not a rogue result. On YouGov's model, the Tories had dipped below the threshold needed for a majority on 22 May, nine days earlier. They were never to move back above the line. In the six days after the publication of the Conservative manifesto, their expected tally of seats fell from around 350 to around 312, the difference between a majority of fifty and fourteen seats short. As the campaign went on, 7,000 people were surveyed each day, allowing adjustments to be made. Each YouGov model used the previous week's data.

The company knew their reputation was on the line, having got it wrong in 2015. Company bosses were told that Crosby was going around saying, 'I put Populus out of business last time. I'm going to put YouGov out of business this time.' Zahawi phoned Stefan Shakespeare, YouGov's chief executive, and said, 'They'll be queuing up to close you down if you're wrong on this. You've just moved the currency by one and a half per cent. I'm going to spare you the agony: I'm going to call for your resignation when you're wrong.' He later had to tweet a public apology.

YouGov were not alone, though. On 27 May Survation had put the Tories just six points ahead. On 3 June, five days before the election, they gave the Tories a lead of just one point. What's more, they did so in two separate polls, one for the *Mail on Sunday* and another for *Good Morning Britain*. In their final poll, on 7 June, Survation got the same result again – the Tories on 41 per cent, a solitary point ahead of Labour. In 2015, Survation's boss Damian Lyons Lowe had come closest to the election result with a final poll putting David Cameron six points up and heading for a majority. Not believing his own data, he had refused to publish it. This time he was prepared to go down with the ship – and YouGov were lashed to the mast with him. Their final model put the Tories on 42 per cent, four points ahead of Labour, which translated into 302 seats for the Conservatives, twenty-four short of a majority, with Labour on 269. Anthony Wells was nervous: 'I was personally full of doubt. Until you've actually done it in a general election you don't really know for sure if it's going to work. We did all get it wrong in 2015, and we had all come up with different experimental methods, and there was no way of knowing which of us were correct.' His doubts were fuelled by Labour friends saying it was 'awful on the ground'. Wells recalled, 'All the information we were getting tended to suggest that we were the ones that were going to be wrong, and that Martin [Boon] at ICM and ComRes were the ones that were going to be right.' He believed the Tory lead was around nine or ten points. His colleague Joe Twyman was also nervous: 'On election night I was pretty sure that one of two politics graduates from Sheffield University was going to have to resign, and I assumed it would be me.' The other was Nick Timothy.

In the final public poll, Wells allocated votes to those who said they would definitely vote but had offered 'don't know' as their preferred party. In the 2015 election those people predominantly voted Conservative. After the reallocation YouGov's poll had the Tories seven points ahead. In the end it was YouGov's model and Survation's polling that most closely mirrored the final result.

The polling mistakes in 2017 were less serious than in 2015 because they resulted from clearly underestimating youth turnout, rather than because pollsters had found it impossible to build a representative sample of voters. In short, their data was right but the tweaks they made to it were wrong. In 2015 both had been wrong. 'The problem in 2015 was sample,' Wells explained. 'The problem in 2017 was people trying to solve sample through turnout.'

Whatever their model or methodology, every pollster showed a decline in Conservative support and a significant rise in Labour support during the campaign, most of it after the manifestos. YouGov used a panel of voters, so they could ask people they polled at the beginning why they changed their minds by the end. When Wells asked voters what they remembered from the Labour campaign, they cited 'saleable things like tuition fees, increasing taxes on the rich and renationalising railways'. The memorable parts of the Conservative campaign were all negatives: 'the dementia tax, taking benefits away from old people, taking away kids' school dinners'. For that, the other Sheffield graduate was responsible.

Different problems afflicted the data teams in CCHQ and Southside in spotting the Corbyn surge. Both parties were so focused on a narrow sector of the electorate that they missed what was happening elsewhere. By choosing to measure the switchers from Ukip and the retention of traditional Tory votes, CCHQ was not seeking to monitor what happened with Labour's younger voters. Sir Julian Brazier, who was to lose Canterbury, recalled afterwards, 'When we were knocking on doors, Mum comes to the door and says, "Yes, we're right behind you," and then you say, "The whole household?" and she says, "Well, my husband." They never knew what their children were doing – their children were never in. The canvass returns we were getting looked very promising, but they were misleading us.'[18] More than one Tory cabinet minister later confessed that their own children voted Labour.

Belief that the Tories would make good gains was fuelled by sitting Tory MPs in Leave-backing constituencies in the North, who reported back to CCHQ that their vote was going to rise thanks to direct switchers from Labour, often in working-class areas where the Conservatives did not usually get a look-in. Andrew Bridgen, the MP for North-West Leicestershire, said, 'Everywhere I went our vote was getting bigger, but in some places the Labour vote was getting even bigger.'

Conservative high command placed a lot of faith in Jim Messina's model to tell them where they were competitive. They were paying a reputed £100,000 a week plus expenses for the privilege. Messina told colleagues he had a thousand pieces of data on every voter, purchased from data sets compiled by credit-checking agencies like Experian. That told the campaign where people shopped, what they bought, how they travelled to work and the best way of contacting them, be it an email, text, phone call or a knock on the door, and allowed targeted advertising to be sent. However, the Tories' strong leads in the first model completed by Messina did not help them, since they caused advertising spend to be pumped into seats which were ultimately out of reach. 'As the campaign goes on you suddenly realise, when you get more honest polling come through, you wasted a quarter of your budget on these seats because they're never going to be in play,' a campaign director said. 'We had models based on Theresa being God, and that then changed the type of people we were targeting.' For a period in the middle of the campaign, CCHQ even stopped canvassing Ukip voters. 'Early on it was pretty clear that Ukip voters were splitting very heavily for us, and we took them out of the target-voter-type data,' a Tory ground-game expert said. 'We should have probably kept them in. That slipped back.'

Following May's plunge in popularity after the manifesto, the digital team suddenly had to pump advertising into places like Hastings and Putney, which they had thought were in the bag. MPs in what were thought to be safe seats were told to move their teams of supporters into Labour-held target seats instead. Gareth Baines, the election agent in Vale of Clwyd, a Tory–Labour marginal in Wales, recalled, 'The talk was of CCHQ viewing any seat with a Labour majority of around 8,000 as a target – such optimism within the party I can never remember.'[19] 'Candidates in seats with majorities under 5,000 were told they were safe and sent to campaign in Labour-held marginals,' said one MP. 'Some people told CCHQ to "piss off", and it's just as well they did, or they'd be out of jobs now. People were told far too late in the day that the polls were turning against us.' Many, like James Davies, who had only won Vale of Clwyd in 2015 by 237 votes, and James Wharton in Stockton, were swept away.

In target seats, CCHQ data-crunchers produced lists of 10,000 target voters who grassroots campaigners were supposed to speak to – to the exclusion of all others. In the early part of the campaign they were told to ignore local issues and concentrate on the national message – Theresa May's strong and stable leadership – leaving local candidates discredited when her popularity plummeted. Gareth Baines said, 'My candidate became Theresa May's personal chattel, all literature from CCHQ referred to "Theresa May's candidate" – any local connection was lost … Then came the manifesto, and the tide turned. There was real anger at the "dementia tax".[20]

The 'national only' orders continued long after they should have been abandoned. As late as ten days before polling day CCHQ sent staff in Brentford and Isleworth, where Mary Macleod was to lose to Labour's Ruth Cadbury, an email saying, 'Research has shown that in this seat any mention of local issues will push voters to Labour. I know it is tempting to discuss local issues as this is Labour's approach, but we must not be tempted. If we once discuss local issues on literature, social media or the doorsteps, we risk losing this seat.' Macleod's team were told they would be cut off if they disobeyed: 'If these points are not followed then the DM [direct mail] support from CCHQ for this seat will be pulled.' One local official said afterwards, 'We were being bullied. CCHQ were arrogant, incompetent and misguided.'[21] Macleod was to lose by more than 12,000 votes.

Ten days out, Crosby knew Putney, Battersea, Kensington and Wimbledon were all at risk, and they got new directed mail shots. One (male) candidate burst into tears when told by the Australian that he was in danger. In another seat, an MP who was complaining about being in trouble was more insouciant. When he was tracked down 'he was at the queen's fucking garden party', a senior source recalled.

Selecting which seats to target was not Messina's responsibility, but his data provided a guide, along with Textor's national polling. The field team under Darren Mott was also contributing intelligence, but his team did not have time to build up a comprehensive database of voting intentions from doorknocking, particularly not in seats, like those in the North-East, where voters had only thought about voting Tory since May came to power. A senior campaign official said, 'You've got modelling, polling, you've got canvass returns, reports from the field, published polling, what journalists are saying – all of that information is what you base your judgement on, not just on what the model says this morning.' Yet some thought it strange that Chris Scott, the director of voter communications, who was link man between Messina's team and others in CCHQ, was not a data expert.

The snap poll also meant Messina had other commitments, and he was only present for five of the seven weeks of the campaign – though his London director Tara Corrigan, who had also worked for Barack Obama, was present throughout. 'There were a lot of delays where we were waiting on Messina for data, waiting for his guys to crunch stuff,' another campaign staffer complained. The lack of one dominant campaign chief, coupled with Crosby's belief that Messina was the world's best data man, meant that he, like other campaign directors, was never under much pressure from above. 'Nobody was kicking him,' a colleague said. One Conservative data expert said, 'The Tories would have won if they had an understanding of where the battleground was. In this campaign targeting was the emperor's new clothes.'

Two weeks out from the election, Downing Street officials were seriously worried. One of May's aides, who was from Gloucestershire, received half a dozen emails saying the data was 'terrible'. 'Some of the emails were incredibly bullish, and one was pretty rude about the Prime Minister, saying "She needs to pull her finger out,"' the aide said. 'We were sending people to knock on doors of people who were lifelong Labour voters. My lesson from that was that the data wasn't very good.' In Alyn and Deeside (Labour majority 3,343), activists were ordered to knock on the doors of 'hardcore socialists' in Connah's Quay, an area that housed the Labour constituency office.

In the final week of the campaign, which is usually devoted to GOTV – getting out the vote you have already identified – 'We were doing persuasion audiences,' still talking to voters who might support the Conservatives. That meant that people were knocking on the doors, even on polling day, of people who did not support them, something that unnerved the ground troops, who were used to ferrying confirmed supporters to the polling stations. In other seats, perverse decisions were based on inaccurate data. Activists from Kensington, where the Tories eventually lost by just twenty votes, were ordered to go to Ealing Central and Acton, where Labour won by nearly 14,000. Zac Goldsmith's team, who were to scrape home by forty-five votes in Richmond Park, were told to help in Twickenham, which the Lib Dem Sir Vince Cable reclaimed with a majority of nearly 10,000. Michelle Lowe, the candidate in Coventry South, added, 'Only 50 per cent of the targeted people we were talking to were actually planning to vote Conservative. We were knocking up Corbynites.'[22] Another MP blamed the chief whip, Gavin Williamson, for misleading candidates: 'There were two target seats next to each other. They were each told by Gavin that they were the real target, and the other one was going to help them on polling day. They all sat there waiting for the reinforcements that never came.'

In a campaign where there had been little time to prepare, and in seats where the Conservatives had no grassroots organisation, the influence of the data was magnified. Messina's role in winning the 2015 election also caused some to override their natural instincts. 'Candidates who had newly arrived in their seat took it on trust,' a campaign official said.

MPs were also reporting back to CCHQ on the preliminary postal-voting returns, which showed them heavily outperforming 2015. Stephen Gilbert remembered 2015, when the field reports put the Tories on 325 seats, closer to the final result than either Crosby or Messina had predicted. 'People were saying by the final weekend that we were back in a strong position,' a senior figure recalled. In Ipswich, Ben Gummer was conscious of a growing number of Tory voters complaining about the national campaign. But his canvassing confirmed that Labour and Ukip voters were switching to him. Nick Timothy called him and said, 'The postal-vote returns are amazing and the focus groups are good.'

Yet the data and some of the feedback from the ground was wrong. When the Corbyn surge occurred, the Tories were fighting on the wrong battlefield. 'Something clearly went massively wrong with the data,' said one of the campaign directors. A source close to May said, 'Political parties have got so hollowed out, if you've made the wrong assumptions then you're not going to notice the surge.' Just as Hillary Clinton lost the presidency to Donald Trump without ever visiting Wisconsin, the state that gave him victory, the Tories couldn't even see what they couldn't see. Another Downing Street aide said, 'Because you're not blanket canvassing, you don't see what's happening on the rear flank. We were across the country sending people into unlikely territory for us, tough council estates, and they were saying right until the end they were planning on voting Tory this time, "because of Brexit" or "because I like her". But there were 2010 and 2015 Tory voters who were saying, "Hmmm, not sure this time."'

Theresa May's visits told the story eloquently. Of the forty-three marginal seats the prime minister went to during the campaign, the Tories won just five.

Labour headquarters was just as blind.

Unite campaigning teams who were sent into Yorkshire and the North-East in the final two weeks did not detect Corbyn gaining ground either. 'We didn't see a surge,' a senior union official said. 'In Batley and Spen the door was being shut in our faces. The surge was voters that we didn't know and young people, but it wasn't detected from our core vote.'

The same picture emerged in Labour's focus groups in towns like Stevenage, a seat they would eventually fall short in by more than 3,000 votes. 'The focus groups were all in Labour targets that we should have been picking up in 2015,' a Southsider recalled. 'They were all with former Labour voters and they were consistently showing nine out of twelve participants going over to the Conservatives, all the way through the campaign.' Labour was detecting the rise in working-class Brexiteer support for the Tories, but not their own surge with the young and grad-uates. 'It turns out that we were talking to the wrong people. Those people did go to the Conservatives, it was just a whole load of new people came to Labour. Those focus groups weren't wrong, they just didn't capture what was actually happening.'

Labour MPs, who could see households that had voted for them in 2015 turning away, reported back that they were haemorrhaging votes. Several moderate MPs began keeping detailed canvassing records, ready to present to the NEC after the election, showing how Corbyn had personally cost them votes. A Southside official said, 'All the way through the campaign we were hearing from sitting MPs that Labour voter after Labour voter was saying they would not vote for Labour while Jeremy was there. I heard it myself when I did doorknocking.' Just as at CCHQ, Labour's internal polling data and doorstep canvassing was all pointing in the same direction. 'Everything that we were being told, from our MPs to people on the doorstep, our pollsters – who continued to tell us that the bounce wasn't real – suggested that we were going to lose,' another party employee said. The doubts extended to the leader's office. 'Being in control of the party, being able to get people to turn up to a rally, being able to shout about the Tories, is all they've ever wanted,' an aide said. 'But they still didn't think they could win.'

Yet just as the Corbynistas did not trust the pollsters, they did not trust Southside's canvass information either. 'Labour's data is extremely good at telling you how someone who hasn't moved in the last twenty years, and also frequently opens their door on a Saturday morning, is going to vote,' a Corbyn aide said. 'That means you will over-represent people who are retired or owner-occupiers, and hugely under-represent young families, sharers, private-sector tenants, shift-workers and so on, groups that are moving dramatically towards us.' LOTO also believed that voters who once backed Tony Blair but disliked Corbyn were over-represented in the groups canvassed. Once again, the Corbynistas relied on hunch: 'We didn't have better data to know, but we understood that the analysis of that data was structurally flawed, and therefore not to be believed in the way that it was being presented.'

They were right to be sceptical.

What they did have was a profound belief that the crowds flocking to Corbyn's events were indicative of something. 'Those sort of things don't happen randomly,' said a leadership source. 'We were getting a lot of anecdotal stuff on the ground. It was a silent earthquake. The tremors were coming through. The machine didn't know what was going on, but the activist base did – but no one trusted the activist base.'

In England and Wales, despite cutting-edge data operations and grassroots canvassing, both main parties failed to accurately measure the Corbyn surge. But there was a corner of the kingdom where the Conservatives ran a highly successful campaign which combined a strong female leader arguing for compassionate Conservatism, backed up by a data operation that ruthlessly identified both their opponent's greatest weakness and the battleground seats.

Scotland.

23

POLITICAL ALCHEMY

The location was an inauspicious one for such an important meeting: the Blythswood Room of Edinburgh's Best Western Bruntsfield Hotel, a grey-flock-wallpaper and Formica monument to middle-management chic remembered by one participant as 'very grotty'. The personnel were a little more august: the great and the good of Scottish Conservative politics, led by Ruth Davidson, the pugnacious 'kickboxing lesbian' of many a tabloid profile who had injected authenticity and energy into the Tory cause north of the border. She was joined by Mark McInnes, the director of the Scottish Conservatives and the best unknown political organiser in Britain; Kevin Ancell Davidson's spin doctor Eddie Barnes; and David Mundell, the Scottish secretary.

It was Friday, 16 October 2015, and the Scottish Tory high command was meeting to discuss why they had failed to achieve the breakthrough they had hoped for at the general election. Mundell had won their only seat in an SNP landslide, and the old joke held true: there were still more pandas in Scotland than Conservative MPs. The only consolation was that the same was true of Labour and the Liberal Democrats, both of which clung grimly to a solitary seat, tiny islands threatened by a rising nationalist tide. Even a once-in-a-generation political talent like Davidson had failed to make much headway.

The key to the meeting that would lead to the historic Conservative breakthrough of 2017 came not from one of the veterans, but when a previously unknown twenty-seven-year-old data analyst of Sri Lankan extraction got to his feet. James Kanagasooriam was introduced by Andrew Cooper, the experienced Conservative pollster who was known to the Scottish Tories from his work on the Better Together campaign during the Scottish independence referendum in 2014. As the grandees picked at their bowls of 'lukewarm and tasteless' carrot soup, garnished with ready-salted crisps, his young colleague boldly declared, 'You're going to become the second party. One day you'll win twenty seats.'

There was laughter. They looked at him wondering if he was mad. Davidson's response was firm. 'No way,' she said. There may even have been a swearword – there usually was. Kanagasooriam was an affable chap, a bit inexperienced, but he spoke with clarity and conviction, always a persuasive attribute in politics. Better than that, he had evidence.

Kanagasooriam's nascent political career had begun a year or two earlier, with some work with the thinktank Policy Exchange. He then made it to the final two after applying to be David Cameron's speechwriter. Not bad for someone who had never written a speech. That was how he met Andrew Cooper, Cameron's pollster. When Cooper went to work for Better Together he remembered Kanagasooriam, by then working at Rothschild's Bank, and asked him to become head of analytics at Populus. Both were bystanders during the 2015 election, since Crosby and Textor were brought in to run the Tory campaign and polling, and the Australians were no fans of Cooper. But, seeing that the pollsters had got the numbers so wrong, Kanagasooriam sought to approach politics in a different way, using statistical techniques he had learned in the City.

He discovered a pattern that allowed him to devise two new measures to describe and analyse the political landscape which provided 'structural mathematical underpinnings to how people vote'. A source familiar with the work said, 'The two components were made up of thousands of different things, but they show there are two things that matter in life.' The exact details of the model are shrouded in commercial confidentiality, but Andrew Cooper publicly described the two measures as 'security' – a concept which includes levels of affluence, education and employment – and 'diversity', which encompasses the politics of identity and measurements of how urban is the area in question. Plotted against each other they create a pattern that explains how both people and individual constituencies are likely to vote. Kanagasooriam discovered a 'latent line' which separated richer, more secure and less diverse Conservatives from poorer, less secure, more diverse, more urban Labour supporters. People and places whose balance of security and diversity is on or close to the magic line are floating voters or marginal constituencies.

When he applied the model to Scotland, Kanagasooriam had a crucial insight. 'Areas that looked like Conservative areas in England and Wales were shared between four parties: the SNP, Labour, Lib Dems and Tories,' a Scottish Conservative source said. That was a frustration for the Scottish Tories, since it meant their vote was scattered. It was also an opportunity, since many seats could be in play if they could find the right way of appealing to these voters. When he analysed the results of the independence referendum, Kanagasooriam realised that the temperamentally Tory voters in Scotland overlapped with large numbers of voters who backed the Union. The logical conclusion was that rather than run on bread-and-butter political issues, Davidson should perform 'political arbitrage' by attempting to reconstitute the Tories as 'the Unionist party', and effectively refight the referendum in order to bring all the potential Tory supporters back under one roof.

As Kanagasooriam laid out his findings, David Mundell sat quietly watching him, saying nothing, wondering if the party had found the key to its revival. Davidson – a rare politician who is both literate and numerate – immediately grasped the significance of what she was being shown. The Tories were not even winning a majority of their own base, but they were being shown the way back. 'We need to be the constitutional party, the Unionist party,' she declared. She also realised that the demographic overlap between Labour and the SNP meant they were engaged in a death-match for the same voters. 'Oh my God, the SNP are going to take out Labour at the next Holyrood elections,' she said.

With his audience convinced, Kanagasooriam showed how the model would let the Tories drill down into constituencies and pinpoint individual roads, so that they could target voters who best fitted the profile of Conservatives in seats held by the SNP. In 2015 Cooper and Kanagasooriam had blind-tested their mathematics on the streets of Scotland. 'They were able to go to a postcode, walk up a road and say, "This person should be a Tory,"' a campaign source said. 'They discovered that these voters wanted all the same things. What they needed was the permission to vote for the party they were existentially inclined to vote for anyway. The key to unlocking a natural voter was the constitution.'

The SNP's dominant wins in the last two Holyrood elections had disguised another key fact: only thirteen of Scotland's fifty-nine Westminster seats had backed their call for independence. That left forty-six where a Unionist message could be dominant.

The model was first deployed in the Holyrood elections of May 2016. By microtargeting voters who 'looked like Tories', Davidson asked them to 'Lend me your votes.' Her main campaign proposition was constitutional – that while the SNP would win, 'Scotland needs an opposition,' and Davidson, not Labour, was best-placed to take on Nicola Sturgeon. Having hoped to win twenty to twenty-five seats, the Conservatives more than doubled their holding in the Scottish Parliament to thirty-one seats. To her campaign team, 'Ruth was a gateway drug into voting Tory.' Populus examined the results. 'The people who would have voted Tory in England and Wales were now voting in Scotland, but not to the same level,' a source said. 'There was a hell of a long way to go.'

Six weeks later, the day after the EU referendum, Nicola Sturgeon declared that a second independence referendum was 'highly likely' following the UK's vote to leave, claiming it was 'democratically unacceptable' for Scotland to be taken out of the EU against its will. The SNP had now lost two referendums, and was projecting a message that it respected the outcome of neither. On 13 March 2017 Sturgeon finally ended the speculation and announced that she would ask for permission to hold a second referendum on Scottish independence between the autumn of 2018 and the spring of the following year. The Conservatives knew they could not refuse her out of hand, but argued that it was too soon after the previous referendum, the result of which the SNP had said would stand for a generation. Davidson pushed a 'not never, but not now' line, while Theresa May accused Sturgeon of playing games. 'Politics is not a game,' she said gravely. Privately, Davidson was ecstatic. She had the opening she had been waiting for.

Without a good candidate, no amount of data will win you an election. Taken together, you have a perfect storm. Six months after the meeting in the Bruntsfield Hotel, Populus conducted polling which proved what they already believed, that Davidson's diverse characteristics made her popular with voters and in areas that were close to the magic 'latent line'. 'Her personality is such that she naturally owns the line,' a source said. 'She is a very strong advocate of LGBT rights, but she's also a Church of Scotland Christian and an army reservist. She's a strong Remainer and quite economically driven. She's political alchemy, in the sense that she's able to demographically hold different groups together.'

The other key to an electoral advance was to offer enough policy meat to different groups along the magic line, rather than devising a platform that appealed to just one section of the electorate. 'There needs to be cake for everyone,' one of the team said. By backing the Union, tax cuts and Trident, Davidson tickled temperamental Tories. Her cosmopolitan outlook attracted some Green and Lib Dem voters. When the SNP campaigned to stay in the EU in 2016, that gave Davidson the opportunity to reach out to the 36 per cent of SNP supporters who voted Leave in Westminster seats where the Tories were in second place.

Kanagasooriam's model was not used during the EU referendum because while Cooper had overseen the Remain campaign's polling, the modelling had been done by Jim Messina. When Kanagasooriam plotted the EU referendum results he found another latent line, this time running in the opposite direction, separating Leave's poor, insecure and non-diverse vote from Remain's secure and diverse heartlands, with the waverers along the line. He then applied the model to the US election, where the interaction between Republicans and Democrats mirrored that of Leave and Remain. The Populus model showed that US pollsters were underestimating Donald Trump's strength. He also discovered that its predictive power worked in Germany, successfully calculating blind whether a place was in the former West or East Germany.

On 18 April, Theresa May phoned Ruth Davidson an hour before she told the rest of the cabinet that she was calling a general election. When the prime minister had hung up, Davidson 'did a little bit of air-punching up and down the corridor of the Scottish Parliament', according to one of those present. She then called Eddie Barnes and Mark McInnes and gave them the good news.

Unlike in England, the Scottish local government elections were contested in every council, making them a dry-run national election. Davidson had put the party on a full war footing the previous December and ensured Westminster candidates were in place. Consequently, the Scottish Conservatives were more battle-ready than CCHQ. Davidson took the strategic decision to keep all the resources concentrated on the council campaign until 4 May, to get the maximum momentum from the local elections. She needed to overtake Labour for her general election strategy to work. 'We're going to demonstrate that we are the party to back if you want to stuff it to the Nats,' she told staff. The local election campaign cemented the trust between Davidson and Populus. Kanagasooriam had predicted the Scottish Tories would win 280 seats. They took 276, having gained 164, and Populus correctly identified nearly every ward they would win.

Davidson could again not believe her luck when, on 1 May, Sturgeon said, 'The issue at the heart of this election is, whether you support independence or oppose independence.' A senior Scottish Conservative said, 'We knew that we'd do better if we made it a referendum on Nicola Sturgeon trying to drag Brexit back to independence, rather than if we ran it as a referendum on the UK government's performance.'

Davidson had just one big decision to make: whether to try for a Westminster seat herself. One of May's chiefs of staff asked her to run. 'I think that was a close decision,' a friend said. 'She would have stood in the South-West. Almost everyone was trying to get her to do it. I think she seriously considered it, but the [Scottish] party needs her. She feels loyalty.' Davidson had already moved from Glasgow to Edinburgh because her partner was based there. She could not move again. 'You only get to carpetbag once,' she told aides. She also had other priorities. 'I'm thirty-eight and I want to start a family,' she told friends. Her medium-term political goal was to become first minister in Scotland. That meant fighting the 2021 Scottish elections.

The stakes were high. In order to burst the SNP's bubble and derail a second independence referendum, Davidson knew the Unionist parties together needed to take ten to twelve seats from the nationalists. 'If they lost in single figures they were still riding high,' a leading Tory said. 'There was still the inevitability of another referendum.'

As the general election campaign began, Davidson had a strategy that successfully blended her own strengths with cutting-edge political modelling. The only problem was that she had to fight the campaign chiefs in London, who did not want to leave her to fight her own battle. Davidson was much more popular in Scotland than Theresa May, but she came under pressure to accept the national 'strong and stable' campaign message focused on the prime minister.

Davidson had deployed May on leaflets as a strong leader who had already rebuffed Sturgeon's quest for a new independence referendum and argued that Corbyn and his Scottish Labour leader Kezia Dugdale were too weak to stand up to the nationalists. But in CCHQ this was not enough. Darren Mott complained to Davidson that a leaflet sent to a quarter of a million homes, paid for by London, did not put May front and centre. 'There was a concern that there wasn't enough Theresa May and there was too much of individual candidates and a bit too much Davidson,' a Scottish source said. The standoff led to paralysis. 'Well into the campaign, they had a load of Theresa May leaflets, no polling had happened in Scotland,' a campaign official said. 'CCHQ thought they could only win three to eight seats.'

The other problem was that the involvement of the data whizzkid had not been signed off by London. Kanagasooriam was in despair. He knew every road in Scotland to target, but had no role in a campaign in which he believed the Tories might win twenty seats. He got in touch with Mark McInnes. The party director was an Edinburgh councillor and organisational 'genius' who had seen the Scottish Tories through their worst times. Kanagasooriam forwarded McInnes his spreadsheet showing that the model had calculated that Lanark and Hamilton East, where the Tories had finished more than 18,000 votes in arrears in third place in 2015, was going to be a three-way marginal in 2017. McInnes said, 'Holy shit!'

In CCHQ, Crosby and Textor were no fans of Populus, since they disliked Andrew Cooper. More significantly, Fiona Hill had grown up in Greenock, and wanted a say in the Scottish campaign. 'She thought that they should have complete control, and that this was a Brexit election and Theresa May was the leader, and I think she may have felt that given her background she had permission to override Ruth Davidson,' a Scottish Tory source said. 'She summoned them down to London to discuss the message.' Five weeks before polling day, Davidson and McInnes travelled south for a showdown. When they arrived, there was no sign of Hill. 'Having called this meeting, Fiona didn't turn up,' a Scottish Tory said. It was a familiar pattern. Davidson was irritated that she had had to take a day out of her own campaign, but found it useful to talk things through with Crosby and Textor instead.

She used the meeting to argue that Populus had to be involved. 'Ruth said, "We need to work with the guys that we've been working with for the past two years, we've done really well with them,"' a source familiar with the exchanges said. She told Crosby, 'We've got really good data because we've had a national campaign every year for the last five years, apart from the years where we had two national campaigns. We know where our people are, and we know where people who might listen to us and vote tactically might be as well.' A Scottish Tory recalled, 'It was actually a really good meeting, and everything was fine after that. There were no issues at all. They knew what we were doing and we could back it up with all the numbers. Ruth did not feel slighted.'

Afterwards they summoned Kanagasooriam to Scotland. He began to draw up a formal list of target seats. The only one for which CTF had done polling was Berwickshire, Roxburgh and Selkirk, a Borders seat which the SNP held by just 328 votes in 2015 but which the Tories were set to grab easily. Given that there were so many gains to be made in Scotland, Textor's lack of interest is curious. There was every chance that as many seats could be gained in Scotland as in England and Wales combined.

Populus extrapolated the 2016 Holyrood results onto the Westminster boundaries to come up with the list of twenty targets, the last of which was Argyll and Bute in the West Highlands. In 2015 the Conservatives were third there, more than 15,000 votes behind the SNP. In some target seats the Tories had come fourth, but Kanagasooriam believed that there were voters out there who were existentially inclined to back them. All they needed was a little encouragement.

When Davidson returned with the funds she needed, the campaign cranked up its Facebook advertising and sent new direct-mail leaflets – shorn of May – to the different target voters: SNP Leavers plus Lib-Dem-voting 'cultural Tories' and Labour Unionists who could be persuaded that the Conservatives were best-placed to beat the SNP. Every day Tory canvassing data was fed into the Populus model. They found that the Labour vote was holding up better than many expected in Edinburgh and the Lothian regions. The Tories were gaining disgruntled Leave voters from the SNP while leaking some Remain voters to Labour. In the North and Ayrshire in particular there was excitement. The Tories were coming from a long way behind, but expecting huge swings.

The model gave Davidson and McInnes confidence that the Borders seats were in the bag, allowing them to divert resources to the twenty three-way marginals across the Central Belt. They were bemused to see the SNP campaigning in Berwickshire. 'We knew straight away that the SNP hadn't quite cottoned on to the scale of the Tory surge,' a campaign source said. McInnes 'absolutely poured' people into Moray and Gordon, where the Conservatives were mounting their most audacious challenges, seeking to oust Angus Robertson, the SNP leader in Westminster, and Alex Salmond, the party's greatest panjandrum. Here the local election result was crucial, since it put the Tories in second place above the Lib Dems, who had held the seat until 2015. 'Lots of Tories had been voting Lib Dem because it had previously been held by Malcolm Bruce, but the Lib Dems knew it was us versus Salmond,' a campaign source said. 'We got all of the Tories that had previously voted Lib Dem to give Salmond a bloody nose.'

When the Conservative manifesto was published on 18 May, Davidson was presented with another potential clash with London. She had more warning of the social care policy than most ministers, since the policy director for the Scottish Tories, a Slovakian political scientist called Marek Zemanik, was in close touch with Ben Gummer and his special adviser Rupert Yorke. When Davidson saw the final draft she said, 'We've got decisions to make.'

In Scotland there was free social care for the elderly in their own homes, but when they went into residential care only £26,000 of their savings was protected, and their homes were included in the means test. 'The deal that the party down south was offering, to keep £100,000, was infinitely more generous than what currently exists in Scotland,' a Scottish Tory said. But Davidson's political instincts led her to the decision that May should have taken, to ditch the plans. She told her team, 'You can't sell a policy that nobody ever heard of, that takes a paragraph to explain, three weeks before a vote. And you don't fuck off pensioners.' The Scottish Tories stuck to the line 'It's different in Scotland.' They got a free pass from Labour and the SNP, who did not want to have to explain that May's policy was actually more generous than what was currently in place in Scotland.

The Scottish Tories had already ruled out any change to fox-hunting rules in Scotland, so Davidson ripped that out of her manifesto too. She also exploited a grey area over which welfare policies were devolved to ditch the cuts to the winter fuel allowance as well. Again, she said, 'We just decided we don't fuck off pensioners during a general election campaign, we need their votes. We don't take stuff off people, that's not how it works.' Her campaign argued that since they were not imposing the dementia tax, they did not need to cut the winter fuel allowance to pay for it. 'The three worst issues, we just made dead issues,' a campaign source said, 'because we saw in advance that they might be problematic for us.'

Davidson's team were amazed that Sturgeon did not use her bully pulpit as first minister to dominate the air war. 'We were astonished that Nicola, with the biggest microphone and the ability to control the news agenda, didn't just pick a decision a day of the UK government that they hated and just hammer us on it,' a senior campaign source said. 'They allowed us to keep on the constitution for a long period of time.' Sturgeon's problem was that the coalition the SNP had built in 2015, between people who voted Yes to independence and those who had voted tactically for the nationalists because they hated Labour, was falling apart. What had once been an insurgency was now a party of government – in a world that favoured insurgents, not the establishment. 'They couldn't talk about their record and they didn't want to,' a senior Tory said. In 2015 the SNP army of fifty-six MPs had vowed to shake up Westminster. 'They stopped English people shopping on a Sunday and they stopped a change to fox-hunting – in England,' said an amused Tory. 'Well whoopdee-fucking-doo. What did you do for Scotland? Fuck-all.'

As election day approached, Labour were beginning to gain ground in Scotland on the back of the Corbyn surge. Sturgeon changed tack, arguing that the two parties should work together to evict the Tories. But this was greeted with a snub from Corbyn, who said he would not agree to a coalition with the SNP. The nationalists were now shipping votes to both of the main English parties. The Tories were not monitoring hard-left voters who backed independence, but the SNP were, and they knew those votes were returning to Labour. 'The SNP saw it coming,' a Conservative campaign source said, 'because three days before the poll they started running the argument, "If you want to support Jeremy Corbyn, the SNP are more Corbyn than the Labour Party in Scotland." They didn't have enough time to sell it.'

Sturgeon's final, desperate throw of the dice came in a televised debate two days before polling day. The first minister claimed that Kezia Dugdale, the Scottish Labour leader, had told her in a private telephone conversation that she would consider voting for independence because of Brexit, and might agree to a new indy referendum. The gambit backfired, because it looked as if she could not be trusted with a private conversation. Davidson used the debate to hammer home her message: that only the Tories, not Labour, could be trusted to be guardians of the Union.

With good data and good judgement, Ruth Davidson had got the Tories in a position to make big gains in Scotland. In London, Theresa May was about to find herself on the back foot again.

24

LONDON BRIDGE

There were ten days to go when Karie Murphy bought the new outfit she planned to wear to Buckingham Palace. In the morning meeting Jeremy Corbyn's office manager and gatekeeper announced, 'We are going to win. I'm going to the palace.' Wiser heads tried to explain that even if Corbyn won he would probably take his wife, Laura Alvarez, with him to see the queen. Murphy was not dissuaded: 'I'm demanding to go to the palace.' By the time of the election, the story was already spreading like wildfire. Within a month it had taken on the quality of holy writ, proof either of the supreme and justified confidence of the Corbynistas about their ultimate electability, or of their misguided optimism – depending on who was telling the story. 'She was absolutely convinced they were going to win,' a Southsider said. 'She had been going around for ages saying that. She went out and purchased her dress, which was a moment of intense self-confidence. It was ludicrous.'

Murphy's confidence did not stop there. She also produced a seating plan for the new war room she was planning to build in 10 Downing Street, complete with seats for some of Corbyn's favourite bloggers. When one version of it leaked during the campaign, moderates and the leader's office dismissed it as a fake, but a seating plan did exist. A Labour official had taken a picture of the computer screen on which Murphy was planning the first socialist government in a generation. 'Karie was always confident of going to Downing Street,' a LOTO aide said.

From the Conservative perspective, events were beginning to make it seem as if Murphy might be right. On 2 June, the Friday before polling day, the Crown Prosecution Service announced that Craig Mackinlay, the Tory MP for South Thanet, was being charged under the Representation of the People Act with offences of making false election expenses claims over his campaign against Nigel Farage two years earlier. At CCHQ there was 'genuine anger' at the decision. The CPS had until 11 June, three days after the election, to decide whether to charge Mackinlay. 'That really took us by surprise. We couldn't believe that they'd decided to do that,' a campaign official said. Tory spin doctors briefed the media that the decision was politically motivated.

With their backs to the wall and the polls tightening, senior Conservatives reached out to newspaper proprietors and editors, asking for their help in a final-week push. They received a counterblast of irritation asking why the Tories had done so little to challenge Labour's economic credentials throughout the campaign. Craig Woodhouse cranked Sheridan Westlake and the Conservative Research Department into action. Among the calls asking for more support, the most difficult were those to the editor of the London *Evening Standard*, George Osborne. Needle with the former chancellor had been evident from the day May announced the election, forcing Osborne to choose whether to surrender his parliamentary career. When one journalist suggested that 5 per cent of the decision was based on wanting to put Osborne in a difficult position, a May aide said, 'You think only 5 per cent?' and smiled.

As the race tightened, Osborne had not let up publishing excoriating leader columns on May's policies and performance. On 27 May he went on the *Today* programme and said he would not be 'pulling my punches', dismissing the Tory manifesto pledges on care as 'clearly badly thought-through because the prime minister herself decided to rethink them'. Four days later he went further, printing a blistering editorial which said, 'The Conservative campaign has meandered from an abortive attempt to launch a personality cult around Mrs May to the self-inflicted wound of the most disastrous manifesto in recent history and, after the atrocity in Manchester, shrill attacks on Mr Corbyn's appeasement of terrorism. Their campaign seems to have gone out of its way to avoid the very issue – Brexit – that was supposed to be the very reason we were having an election in the first place. The result can be summed up by what we imagine to be the conversation around the breakfast table in Downing Street: "Honey, I shrunk the poll lead."' One of Osborne's allies recalled that before he did interviews as chancellor, aides would let him vent in private, 'getting out all the things that he wanted to say that he couldn't say – draining the dams so the pressure was not too high. At the *Evening*

Standard, there's no one there to let the pressure off a bit.' A profile of Osborne said he had told colleagues he would not rest until May was 'chopped up in bags in my freezer'.[1]

At CCHQ the view was 'Enough is enough.' Crosby was one of several senior figures, who included former aides, to call Osborne. The message was simple: 'You've had your fun, but steady on in the last week.' The *Evening Standard* duly printed an editorial backing the Conservatives, but for many the damage was already done. A cabinet minister said, 'I think it's not very honourable. People feel betrayed. When you have the privilege of holding high office like that, I think you need to act with a sense of decorum.'

The Tory push on the economy bore fruit quickly. On Friday, 2 June the *Daily Mail* splashed on 'CORBYN'S SLY DEATH TAX TRAP', highlighting Labour's plans to scrap Osborne's cuts in inheritance tax, and claiming that it would drag an extra 1.2 million families into paying the tax. The *Sun*'s front page was emblazoned with a mocked-up image of Corbyn's 'magic money tree', hanging with Labour's spending pledges – all under the headline 'LEAF IT OUT' and the strapline 'HE MUST BE BARK-ING'. The story returned to claims of a £300 billion black hole in Labour's spending plans, which would cost families an average of £3,500. For the *Sunday Times* on 4 June, CRD had prepared what amounted to be a greatest-hits list from the ghost of campaigns past. The Tories accused Corbyn of plotting a 'triple tax whammy' that would cost home-owners £5,000 a year, and sent out Boris Johnson to deliver the attack lines. The briefing combined fears that Labour's extra borrowing would drive up interest rates and mortgages, with Sheridan Westlake's garden-tax research and the inheritance-tax warnings to create a larger headline number. Even Philip Hammond was let out to speak to the *Sunday Telegraph*.

At Southside, John McDonnell's adviser James Mills had been expecting a 'tax whammy' story, a hardy perennial of Conservative campaigns since 1992, when the successful rubbishing of John Smith's shadow budget helped secure John Major another five years in Downing Street. Mills devised his own final-weekend economy special, briefing the *Observer* that Labour would cut VAT during the next Parliament.

The brief prominence of economic matters was swept aside at 10.07 p.m. on Saturday, 3 June, when the emergency services received the first calls to inform them that another terrorist attack was under way in the capital. Three men wearing fake suicide-bomb vests mowed down pedestrians on London Bridge with a seven-ton truck before running amok in the Borough Market area, stabbing revellers with twelve-inch-long ceramic blades. In their brief rampage, eight people were killed – three of them on the bridge – and another forty-eight were injured, including four off-duty police officers who risked their lives to confront the terrorists. In one pub members of the public threw bottles and chairs at their assailants, who were yelling, 'This is for Allah.' Eight minutes after the first 999 calls were made, armed police shot all three terrorists dead in the street. It was six days since the terror threat level had been reduced from 'critical' to 'severe'.

Theresa May, along with Fiona Hill and Nick Timothy, rushed back to Downing Street and chaired a COBRA meeting on the Sunday morning, while police made twelve arrests and carried out controlled explosions in the Barking area of East London. The chiefs quickly found themselves in another confrontation with Lynton Crosby, who urged them not to call another halt to electioneering: 'Don't suspend the campaign, just keep going.' The chiefs overruled him, Timothy saying, 'Hang on a second, she's not just the figurehead of the campaign, she's the prime minister. And there's just been a horrific terror attack and people have been killed, so she's got to be the prime minister first.'

Through the night, though, the consultants could not get a straight answer about what was going to happen, because May and the chiefs were dealing with the fallout from the attack. 'Stephen Gilbert and others in the party were really unhappy about the lack of information they were getting from Nick and Fi about what was happening, whether we were suspending or not,' a campaign source said. 'It was like drawing blood from a stone to get that confirmation from them.' Eventually the Tories, Labour, the Liberal Democrats and the SNP agreed a one-day suspension, but Ukip refused to comply, Paul Nuttall saying it was 'what the extremists would want'.

The prime minister was facing a serious crisis. This time the culprits were better known to the security services. The ringleader, Khuram Butt, was a twenty-seven-year-old Pakistani-born British citizen who had been reported to the police for trying to radicalise children and was a member of the banned extremist group al-Muhajiroun. He also had links to jailed hate preacher Anjem Choudary and worked for Sajeel Shahid, a contact of Mohammed Siddique Khan, who led the 7/7 attacks in 2005. In 2015 Butt had sought to intimidate Muslims into not voting in the general election. The Italian branch of al-Muhajiroun introduced him to one of the other attackers, Youssef Zaghba, a Moroccan-born employee of a London-based Islamic television channel. In 2016 an Italian prosecutor had informed the British authorities that Zaghba had Isis-related material on his mobile phone when he was detained at Bologna airport en route to Syria and told officials, 'I am going to be a terrorist.' He had been kept under surveillance throughout his time in Italy. The third attacker was Rachid Redouane, a failed asylum-seeker from either Morocco or Libya who was not known to the police.

Most embarrassing for the government, in 2015 Butt had been the subject of an active investigation by MI5. When no evidence that he was planning an attack was detected he was moved from a pool of 3,000 terrorist suspects into a 'low-priority' group of 20,000 extremists on MI5's radar. He remained there despite appearing prominently in a 2016 Channel 4 documentary called *The Jihadis Next Door*, in which he was shown arguing with police in Regent's Park after praying in front of a black Isis flag celebrating the terrorist caliphate. When these facts were emblazoned on the front pages, May and her team went into meltdown. Officers in the security service were told that an enraged Fiona Hill was demanding that 'heads must roll'. Word reached MI5 officers that their director general, Andrew Parker, was going to be fired by May after the election because Butt had slipped through their fingers. 'There were some fingers being pointed in Andrew's direction, with some saying he should go,' an intelligence source said. Once tempers had calmed, the prime minister announced that there would be a review by the police and intelligence agencies to see if the attack could have been prevented.

May used an address in Downing Street after the COBRA meeting to announce that the campaign was suspended for one day, but the general election would go ahead as planned on the following Thursday. After the customary praise for the 'professionalism and bravery' of the police, the prime minister went on to reveal that five terror plots had been thwarted since the Westminster attack, and then struck a defiant note: 'We cannot and must not pretend that things can continue as they are. Things need to change.' She then mapped out a blueprint for tackling 'the single evil ideology of Islamist extremism'. The government, she announced, was prepared to 'extend the length of custodial sentences for terrorism-related offences. 'It is time to say, "Enough is enough."'

The prime minister's speech was more than seven minutes long, and Tom Edmonds' digital team wanted to run a much shorter clip on social media. They identified the most important thirty seconds, but May's team would not let them use the edited version, insisting that the campaign Twitter feed, like May's Downing Street account, should run the whole speech, on a platform better suited to videos of a few seconds. Another opportunity was missed to spread May's message on social media. 'That would really have flown online,' a campaign source complained later.

Politically, the thorniest issue for May was that the exemplary performance of the police catapulted the issue of resources into the headlines once more. In a speech in Carlisle on the Sunday, Jeremy Corbyn highlighted May's own cuts. 'You cannot protect the public on the cheap,' he said. 'The police and security services must get the resources they need, not 20,000 police cuts.' He said that he would hire new staff for the security services, and stated unequivocally that he would authorise the use of deadly force in a situation like the London Bridge attacks. The following day he used a brief interview with ITV to call on May to resign, a move that earned him headlines and some ridicule, given that voters would be able to dispense with the prime minister's services just three days later if they chose.

Corbyn's speech after the second attack bore little resemblance to his intervention after Manchester. Some Labour moderates think he consciously rowed back. 'They had a moment of panic and realised they had gone too far,' a Labour adviser said. 'He was basically saying that if MI5 asked for the power to waterboard Diane Abbott, he'd give it to them.' All Corbyn was guilty of, in truth, was seizing an opportunity. He had perhaps learned more from Tony Blair than he liked to let on.

Labour's call for more police resources had been given momentum by Cressida Dick, the new commissioner of the Metropolitan Police, who told ITV's *Good Morning Britain*, 'In the face of this changing and changed threat, absolutely I will be seeking for London and for policing generally more resourcing, obviously.' At CCHQ they sighed. 'We ended up having a week-long row about police numbers, not a week-long row about the economy, which was the plan,' a Tory adviser said. 'The problem with that was Theresa May's police cuts, and there was no positive way to spin those numbers.'

* * *

Crosby and Textor could see Tory support softening. 'Ukip voters started moving back to Ukip because they saw people who they saw as immigrants involved in these attacks,' a campaign director said. 'The police numbers thing was a dead weight we couldn't lift off the campaign.' On 31 May Textor told staff in CCHQ that they had to act to 'bring back the Ukip bleeders'. Knowing they needed a more robust response, Timothy wrote May another speech for the Tuesday morning, in which she threatened to tear up human rights law in order to deport foreign terror suspects and place restrictions on those suspected of posing a terror threat, but against whom there was not enough evidence to bring a prosecution. 'If human rights laws stop us from doing it, we will change those laws so we can do it,' she said. The pledge made the front pages of most of Tuesday's newspapers, and led the broadcast news. 'That was one of the few times we got given a proper story to brief,' a member of May's media team said. 'That was the one time where there was a shitty story – police numbers – and there was a conscious effort by the campaign to shift it and we did shift it.' The speech also 'flew' on social media.

The same day Diane Abbott gave an excruciating interview to Dermot Murnaghan of Sky News, in which she claimed to have read a report on security and resilience, but could not recall any of its recommendations. For Corbyn's other senior aides it was the last straw. On the morning of Wednesday the 7th, the day before the election, minutes before she was due to give an interview to *Woman's Hour*, it was announced that Abbott was standing down as shadow home secretary. She was replaced on Radio 4 by Emily Thornberry, while Lyn Brown took over her frontbench brief 'temporarily'. As Corbyn's former girlfriend and political soulmate Abbott was unsackable, but she could be sidelined. Corbyn's spinners told journalists she had been failing to cope with diabetes. Abbott's friends told the BBC 'she was moved without consultation – not at her request'.[2]

The proof that Abbott's health was just an excuse was quick in coming. An email prankster impersonating Seumas Milne emailed her suggesting that she 'add some colour to the illness that prevented you from appearing on *Woman's Hour* this morning', and that she 'mention some medication which might be retrospectively seen as a mitigating reason for the Murnaghan interview'. Abbott, believing she was replying to Milne, wrote back, 'I'm not sure what colour I can add. I have always enjoyed good health until the last few years. And diabetes, in itself, would not stop me doing *Woman's Hour*. I am worried about telling untruths about my health which are easily disproved.'

Nonetheless, Corbyn had successfully turned his biggest political weakness into a stick with which to beat the government. A coda to the row came on the Wednesday night, the eve of polling. Adam Klug of Momentum attended Corbyn's last rally at Union Chapel in his Islington constituency, the culmination of a nationwide tour which had begun at dawn in Glasgow and taken in six rallies across the country. 'There were thousands of people queuing up around the block who weren't able to get in because it was absolutely packed,' Klug recalled. 'The police were doing their job and making sure everyone was safe, but everyone was chanting "No more police cuts, no more police cuts," so there was a positive rapport.' That same evening, Karie Murphy gave a valedictory eve-of-polls speech to the war room at Southside, culminating with the battle cry, 'Prepare for Downing Street!' Reactions divided along traditional lines. 'LOTO people thought they had a chance,' a Labour official recalled, 'while everyone else thought they were going to hell in a handcart.'

It was finally time to find out who was right.

25

MAYDAY!

It was around 9.30 in the evening on election day when Jim Messina entered the war room at Conservative Campaign Headquarters. The American data expert was in ebullient spirits, high-fiving his colleagues. He was nervous, but he was a glass-half-full kind of guy in a room of repressed English people, and he liked to keep spirits up. It was a reassuring sight to Tory campaign staff. If Jim was high-fiving people, everything was going to be fine. 'Someone had to be the nice guy when they were walking the donors through,' a Messina ally said. 'Jim's wife accuses him of being happy at funerals.' Messina had spoken to an adviser to Barack Obama – not, as some Tories inferred, to Obama himself – who was working with Labour, who told him Jeremy Corbyn was on course to lose twenty or thirty seats.

On the ground floor of 4 Matthew Parker Street there was a sense of anticipation. 'It was very much an atmosphere of beginning to locate where the bottles of vino were,' a Downing Street official said. 'Darren Mott was saying, "It's all looking good," and we were getting messages through saying Labour MPs were despondent.' On the fourth floor, the party was already in full swing by 9 p.m. In order to maintain a veneer of professionalism in the war room downstairs, Tory staff were given wristbands – white for the war room, pink for the party. 'If you wanted a drink you were supposed to go upstairs,' a Number 10 official said.

Reconstructing those final hours before the exit poll dropped has something of the quality of imagining England on the eve of war in 1914. It is to glimpse a world we no longer recognise, inhabited by a political class overconfident of their achievements, marching optimistically towards events they did not understand which would leave their careers in ruins and their country changed forever.

At 9.25 p.m. Lynton Crosby texted Nick Timothy and asked, 'How you holding up?' The chief of staff replied, 'I feel good thanks. What do you reckon?' Crosby responded, 'We should do well,' but admitted, 'My hesitation is any Labour ground effort we are not picking up the impact of.' He was concerned that Labour had sent out a blitz of up to four direct-mail letters the day before. 'People outside of London even got letters from Sadiq Khan!' Crosby's allies described it as a 'lengthy caveat'. Timothy's said it in no way suggested the Tories would lose ground.

In the final days of the campaign, Timothy had several heart-to-hearts with his closest confidants. He told Will Tanner a week before the election that he envisaged three scenarios. The first was a 'stonking majority', the second a majority of thirty or forty, which would provoke a debate within the party 'about whether or not the election was the right thing to do'. In this scenario, Timothy believed May would be 'probably finished in the medium term'. Timothy's worst-case scenario was a small majority very similar to what May had already. 'In that case, I'm finished, Theresa's finished, Fi's finished,' he said. 'Nick was very honest,' one friend said. 'He knew he was being set up as the fall guy.' But Timothy undoubtedly expected to win comfortably. In the final week he told a cabinet minister, 'When it's done and dusted we will be able to turn around and say, "We ran a fantastically disciplined campaign, and the result we have got is a good working majority to do all these things to make Britain better."' He was proud that the Mayites had had the discipline to bite their tongues even though they disliked Crosby's approach. Another campaign official confirmed, 'On the final day Nick Timothy complained that they hadn't actually had time to start planning for the following days back in government. For me it is that complacency which cost us.'

Much of Timothy's confidence came from a document he had been sent by accident, a spreadsheet prepared by Jim Messina's data operation which showed the Conservatives winning 371 seats, enough for a Commons majority of ninety-two. Timothy believed that to be Messina's final model. 'The idea that they were projecting anything other than that is a lie,' a source familiar with Timothy's thinking said.

In fact, the spreadsheet passed to Timothy was more than a week old. Messina actually completed a final model on Tuesday, 6 May – two days before the election – which showed a very different picture. Tara

Corrigan, the head of Messina's London office, sent an email to Chris Scott, the director of voter communications at the Conservative Party, at 5.02 p.m. that day showing the Tories on course to win just 329 seats, enough for a majority of only eight – nine fewer than May had inherited. What is more, 329 was only the average result. The model showed a likely range of outcomes from a high of 354 seats, a majority of fifty-eight, to 303, which would have left May twenty-three seats short.

This data was passed to the Australians, but appears never to have been shown to the chiefs. It is one of Crosby and Textor's business practices not to show clients raw polling data. Amazing as it seems, 'Jim and Nick did not have a conversation in the final two weeks of that campaign,' a friend of Messina said. 'There was no email, there was no conversation.' In 2015, Messina had presented his numbers directly to Cameron. Throughout the 2017 campaign, he told a colleague, he had spent 'less than ten minutes total' with May. He privately pronounced it 'insanely weird'.

Mark Textor's mood had been on a rollercoaster all week. On the Tuesday his tracker poll had shown that the Tories had bounced back from the manifesto disaster. 'The roll-up to Tuesday night had us recovering strongly, and that's what basically led them to their conclusion that we'd have a majority of forty to sixty, maybe seventy,' a senior colleague said. 'That was definitely the CTF worldview at that point. We were fine in the seats we were defending.' However, the day before the election, Textor's poll of fifty marginal seats showed the Tories tied with Labour. Since two-thirds of these were seats the Conservatives hoped to gain, even a dead heat implied that they would make gains, but it was not the firm lead they were hoping for. On the night before polling, Crosby called Messina and said, 'Boy, our numbers tonight just took a big hit and I'm nervous about it.' Textor's nervousness grew further on election morning, when the new data from his final poll 'Track 30' showed the Tories on course for a hung Parliament. 'It was like someone recovering from an illness. We'd picked up for a couple of days, but then we just died,' a source said. 'It was terrible.' Since Textor's polls were compiled as a rolling average of small samples over three or four days, one day's bad results would not dramatically change the headline numbers – but it was cause for concern. After the election CTF would not release their precise numbers because they had signed a confidentiality agreement with the Conservative Party, but the author has confirmed the details of Textor's polling with two other senior figures on the campaign who were not employed by CTF.

Those who had fought national campaigns before felt Timothy heard what he wanted to hear, and only comprehended what was actually happening when the exit poll dropped. 'At university three weeks out, you know rationally that you haven't studied enough, but it's really that night before the election – or walking into that exam room – that you emotionally understand it,' one veteran said. 'Before that you kind of know it, but you don't emotionally accept it. When you actually see the numbers, then you emotionally accept what you were rationally told before. But only then.'

The Australians and Messina were not the only ones with an uneasy feeling in their stomachs. Alex Dawson and Nick Hargrave on the political team were most in tune with the intelligence from the ground. One of their Downing Street colleagues was alarmed when Hargrave said, 'I think we're going to lose Ipswich and we might lose Hastings.' Even before the exit poll dropped, Ben Gummer and Amber Rudd, two of May's closest cabinet allies, were on life support. Nadhim Zahawi had been campaigning in Birmingham Erdington, Timothy's home seat, and found one in three houses he was knocking up were voting for Corbyn. He texted Stefan Shakespeare at YouGov to say, 'Mate, I think you're onto something.'

The civil service was also hedging its bets. On the Friday before the election, Sir Jeremy Heywood ordered mandarins to prepare plans for a Labour victory. 'Before that there was literally a plan A and a plan B – a plan for a Conservative majority and the secretary of state coming back, and a plan for the secretary of state not coming back,' a civil servant said. 'That was it. It was extraordinary complacency.' Some shadow secretaries of state only met officials the day before the election.

One person who certainly doubted that May was on course for a landslide was her predecessor. David Cameron had heard the campaign talk, and knew his approach to elections was openly trashed by May's team. He had wanted to help – but the phone never rang. 'DC was furious during the campaign because CCHQ didn't get in touch with him,' a former aide said. 'He didn't get a phone call from the prime minister.' Cameron told one friend, 'I'm angry they're not using me.' To another he seemed baffled and hurt that May had not bothered to consult him. Cameron had made a point of involving John Major, and believed that respecting those who had previously held the highest office was 'the done thing'. 'He was absolutely crushed,' that close ally said.

Two days before the election Cameron asked a former aide with good links to Central Office, 'What do they think they are going to get?' On being told that May expected a majority of sixty to seventy, Cameron probed further: 'What seats do they think they're going to get?'

'Seats in the North-East especially. Darlington, Tynemouth ...'

'They're not getting those seats!' Cameron said, remembering how hard they had been to crack. The world had changed since Brexit, but Cameron refused to believe it had changed that much. 'The Ukip vote is collapsing, but those are Labour seats,' he said. 'Ukip voters are not Tory voters. If that's their strategy, what the hell are they doing? This seems ridiculous to me.' Cameron had also been canvassing in London, and had not liked what he found. 'Every door I knock on they say, "I'm a Tory voter but I'm not voting Tory this time because of Brexit,"' he told his friend. 'I think we've got a London problem as well.'

On the Labour side people were preparing too. In Birmingham, Tom Watson, Labour's deputy leader, contemplated the speech he might have to make if things went as he expected. Yvette Cooper and Chuka Umunna, moderates in self-imposed exile, wondered whether they would be launching leadership bids early the following morning. Cooper's former adviser Amy Richards had resigned from her job at Portland Communications a few weeks earlier to join what she expected to be another fight for the soul of the Labour Party. Cooper had already lined up a launch venue. Umunna had secretly recruited Will Straw, the campaign director for Britain Stronger in Europe, to run his own leadership effort. Clive Lewis and Keir Starmer were also considering their options.

In Southside, Patrick Heneghan contemplated Labour's internal polling and what he was hearing from MPs on the ground, and concluded that Labour would be down to between 180 and 200 seats, perhaps 210 on a good night. He told colleagues BMG had Labour thirteen points behind – at the upper end of the published pollsters – and were predicting a Conservative majority of eighty to a hundred. 'We knew it was all down to the youth vote,' a party official said. Across the office Andrew Murray also believed the Tories were on course for a good win. Another leadership aide said, 'I thought on election night we were going for a fucking hammering.'

The poor bloody infantry in CCHQ and the press team did not know what was about to hit them. When the special advisers were forced to resign from government to work on the campaign they were given three months' severance pay. One Downing Street special adviser had bet £8,000 of his payoff on a Conservative majority in the hope of winning £1,000. Other spads had bets on marginal seats they thought the party would gain. They were confident of victory as they had heard privately about two polls conducted by City financiers, both of which gave the Tories a majority of sixty or more. One of the press team recalled, 'There was no impression from anyone that anything was wrong.'

Then, at 9.56 p.m. they saw Fiona Hill take a phone call and the world changed.

The exit poll had never leaked before. Labour got the first tip-off. At 9.45 p.m. Katy Dillon, the head of broadcasting, got a call which she shared with the war room. 'The exit poll is shocking,' she told Heneghan, who was exasperated by the lack of more concrete information. 'Katy, go and find out what kind of shock. What the fuck does "shocking" mean?' In fifteen minutes they would find out.

Around that time Nick Timothy, Fiona Hill and Jojo Penn returned to CCHQ after having dinner with Darren Mott and a few others at the nearby Caxton Grill. In one of those moments of low farce that characterises so much politics, the most powerful man in the British government then realised that he had left his laptop and papers in the restaurant, and returned to get them. Hill arrived with her sister, family members having been invited to join the expected victory party.

Timothy was back in the war room when, at 9.56 p.m., staff saw Hill come into the room, phone in hand, 'not looking very happy' and searching for her fellow chief. When she finally spotted him she beckoned him into a small office off the main war room called the Derby Room: 'You just noticed in the corner of the room Fi dragging Nick into one of the side rooms.'

'I just got the exit poll result,' Hill told Timothy. 'They're saying it's a hung Parliament.'

'Are you joking?' asked a shocked Timothy.

'I'm not fucking joking about this.'

They beckoned Alex Dawson to join them so they could agree the 'lines' they would give to the press team and ministers. The exit poll might not be right. It did not accord with what Timothy understood about the data. They walked through the war room, a hundred pairs of eyes on them, down a corridor past the CCHQ kitchenette to an area by the Thatcher Boardroom with sofas and televisions where the top team were planning to watch the results come in. There they found Crosby, Textor, Gilbert and the others. By now it was one minute to ten. 'I'm told it's a hung Parliament,' said Hill. Crosby thought, 'Ah, shit.'

Just before the top of the hour Hill had taken a call from the BBC's Andrew Marr. 'I got the impression she knew already,' said Marr. 'It was very shortly before ten, because I was frustrated I had heard late, and thought I wouldn't have enough time to get reaction, my job.' But a friend of Hill suggested Marr was her source: 'She only took one call.' Since Marr's intention was to elicit a reaction, not to impart information, it is hard to fault him for doing what he did.

In any case, there were other leaks. Fifteen minutes earlier, at about the time Katy Dillon had taken her call, a leading political blogger was also rung by someone with inside information, telling him to shift his betting position while he still could. 'It's all gone wrong,' the source said. Even earlier, at 8 p.m., one of the members of the exit poll team rang a Conservative special adviser who he knew had put down a lot of bets on Tory gains, to advise him to bail out. The spad did not hear his phone ring, and only spotted the missed call after the exit poll had been released. By the time he rang back to ask if the exit poll was right, it was too late. 'It's real,' his contact said. 'That's what I was trying to tell you earlier.' The spad ended up losing money on all but one of his fifteen bets.

When the bongs of Big Ben signalled that it was ten o'clock, the screens flashed up with 'Exit poll: Conservatives largest party.' Intoning like a hanging judge, David Dimbleby said, 'And what we are saying is the Conservatives are the largest party. Note they don't have an overall majority at this stage. Three hundred and fourteen for the Conservatives, that's down seventeen.' Labour were forecast to win 266 seats, with the SNP down to thirty-four and the Lib Dems up to fourteen. 'The prime minister called this election because she wanted, as she put it, certainty and stability. This doesn't seem at this stage to look like certainty and stability.'

In the Tory war room there was incredulity. 'It was just basically dead silent for ten minutes, and nobody moved an inch,' a Downing Street official said. Shortly afterwards the deathly stillness was broken by the sound of retching. 'It sounded like someone being sick,' a special adviser recalled.

Timothy asked Gilbert what he thought. 'It could be right,' he said. An exit poll was not a poll, but a survey of more than 30,000 actual voters. The margin of error was much smaller than an opinion poll. Crosby was outwardly more bullish, reminding those present that the exit poll in 2015 had underestimated the number of Tory seats by fourteen, the difference between having a majority and not. 'Tex was quieter,' one of those present recalled.

Timothy and Hill spoke to May by telephone. 'We all just agreed we just needed to stay calm and see what the actual results were going to be,' a senior figure remembered. 'Lynton and Messina were saying, "This is wrong, stay calm."' But to those who saw him, Timothy was 'clearly distressed'. On air Andrew Marr relayed what Hill had told him: 'The reaction of senior Conservatives – and I've talked to a few – is that they flatly don't believe it.'

Rob Oxley visited the back room to check the lines to take. Crosby repeated that exit polls had been wrong before. At 10.04 p.m., political journalists received a message saying, 'Early days. This is a projection, not a result. Last time the exit poll said we would get 314 and we got more than that.' The same message reached Katie Perrior, who was due to do broadcast interviews. 'Inside CCHQ the staff were saying the exit poll was wrong,' she said. 'I was asking what they had to base that on. They said, "Crosby said it was wrong."'

At 10.45 p.m. the Australian paid a visit to the main war room to try to raise the morale of the shellshocked troops. He gave a pep talk to the press team including Oxley, Tom Swarbrick and Tim Smith: 'It's bullshit. We'll be all right. These numbers are wrong. The swing in Newcastle won't be as much as they're expecting. They'll have to revise it. Keep going. We'll know by 3 a.m.' Some felt it 'spoke volumes about Lynton that he came out and tried to cheer people up'. But to one of the Downing Street staff, Crosby's behaviour was jarring: 'He started going around the office sort of joking and play-fighting with people, saying, "The BBC haven't got anything right in their life. Don't worry." It was really unconvincing. It was quite bizarre.' Even if the exit poll was wrong by twenty seats, 'it was still nowhere near where we wanted to be'.

Fiona Hill also made a point of talking to some of the special advisers: 'Hold your nerve. It will be fine, but it will be a shit three hours. Make sure the kids don't panic, make sure that you cheer them up.' Paul Harrison, Craig Woodhouse and Oxley, all grizzled pros, sought out those in their first campaigns. 'Rob Oxley came around and did a sort of hilarious pep talk,' a CRD source recalled. '"Guys, I know it doesn't look good now but have a drink, relax a bit, I promise you it'll all look different at two o'clock," Oxley said. "We thought we'd lost it on the Leave campaign."'

Theresa May was at home in Sonning with her husband. 'I didn't actually watch the exit poll myself, I have a bit of a superstition about things like that,' she said later. When he broke the news, Philip May took the prime minister in his arms. As the realisation hit her that her gamble had gone disastrously wrong, May was first stunned, and then began to cry. 'My husband watched it for me and came and told me, and I was shocked at the result,' she said. 'It took a few moments for it to sink in, what was really going on. My husband gave me a hug.' She let slip 'a little tear at that moment'.[1]

May felt an overwhelming sense of loss, and 'a responsibility' to others. 'I felt, I suppose, devastated really. I knew the campaign wasn't going perfectly. But still the messages I was getting from people I was speaking to … were that we were going to get a better result than the one we did.' She added, 'You're a human being: you've been through that experience. But I was there as leader of the party and prime minister, and I had a responsibility, as we went through the night, to determine what we would do the next day … I got on the phone to CCHQ.'[2]

Jeremy Corbyn was at home in his modest Victorian terraced house in Islington with his wife Laura and his closest aides, Seumas Milne and Karie Murphy. When the exit poll dropped the leader gave a slight nod of recognition. 'Jeremy doesn't do fist-pumping,' one staffer said. He had believed what he had believed for forty years. Corbyn had privately predicted that he would win 37 per cent of the vote. It looked now as if he might do rather better than that. He went back to sipping his cup of tea.[3]

The rest of Team LOTO were at party headquarters in Victoria, which had also been divided into a working floor on the eighth level and a party room on the second floor, where cans of 'Trade Union' pale ale were consumed in volume. The atmosphere in the war room was 'nervous'.

Corbyn's aides had mapped out four different scenarios and devised media 'lines to take' for each one. They were: a widening gap between the two main parties, which was the outcome expected by most party officials; a large increase in Labour's vote share but a loss of seats; a stalemate where both big parties took seats from each other; and a 'clear shift in our direction'. Win or lose, Milne and Schneider prepared to brief the media that this was 'the largest increase in support for a political party during an election campaign in British history, where the terms of the debate have been drastically shifted, where we've shown the viability of policies that unambiguously benefit the majority'.

In the side of the office occupied by the leader's team people punched the air and screamed with delight when the exit poll dropped. 'There was a sharp excited intake of breath, hands on mouths,' said a Corbyn aide. 'People were in shock.' Someone said, 'Fucking hell,' someone else, 'My God, that's winning lots of seats.' David Prescott exclaimed, 'Yes, yes, yes!' A party staffer said, 'They were all jumping up and down, just celebrating wildly. And we were just sort of standing around going, "There's no way that's right, that doesn't tally with anything we've seen."'

The exit poll suggested the result would be in line with the most optimistic of Labour's four scenarios, and worse than any of Nick Timothy's three predicted outcomes. Milne and Schneider spoke by telephone and agreed a line for the media: 'If this exit poll is correct, Theresa May has lost her mandate and lost her authority to govern. She went into this election saying, "If I lose seats then Jeremy Corbyn will be PM." Well, she's lost her mandate.'

The eighth floor of Southside was alcohol-free, but the staffers present tucked into takeaway pizza with gusto. One staff member joked, 'We're having pizza and having elections every year. We really are turning into Italy.'[4]

John McDonnell and James Mills were in the green room at Elstree studios with Conservative cabinet minister Sir Michael Fallon and Ross Reid, a special adviser, waiting to go on the BBC coverage when the exit poll dropped. McDonnell was stunned, and had to hold in his excitement according to one witness, while Fallon 'looked as if he had been kicked in the balls'. Reid sat with his head in his hands. McDonnell was to be the main face of the leadership on television that night, and he was determined not to get carried away to start with. He remembered 2015, when it had looked as if David Cameron would fall short but had ended up with a majority. He remembered 1992, when his own dream of a seat in Parliament had been dashed by fifty-four votes.

At Momentum's headquarters in Euston, Adam Klug was watching with around twenty colleagues. 'A lot of us thought we were going to lose thirty seats. Before ten you do suddenly get those doubts. I remember just standing near the door as if I was going to run away. I was thinking, "You'll see a hundred seats for Jeremy and then you could just walk out the door." But then the results came through and I felt incredibly vindicated and validated.' The crowd of twenty quickly became sixty.

There was nearly as much joy on the sofa of ITV's election coverage, where George Osborne and Ed Balls were becoming the must-watch double-act of the night. With acidic relish Osborne said of May, 'The worst thing she's done in her life is no longer running through a wheatfield.' One viewer took to Twitter to declare the former chancellor duly elected as the new MP for 'Schadenfreude Central'.

It was very different for Tony Blair. It is said that when the exit poll flashed up, the former prime minister put his head in his hands and said, 'I don't understand this country any more.' The months of talking about how moderates could wrest back control of the levers of power in the Labour Party were at an end.

For election night the Corbynistas and the Southsiders had come together physically as well as metaphorically. Andrew Fisher, the architect of the manifesto, sat in a small room off the main campaign hub with Patrick Heneghan, the party's chief election brain, and other party directors Simon Jackson and Neil Fleming. Fisher was impassive when the exit poll dropped. 'On a personal level, we all got on well,' one source said. 'There were no fights, no tetchiness. We were sat in the same offices for fifty days. You learn to get on.'

Heneghan had built up an efficient reporting network from party officials on the ground at the counts, who monitored each ballot box and reported back to Southside. This gave him a more accurate and much quicker assessment of the race than the BBC was reporting. Information added by those at the counts went straight to Heneghan's computer, which gave him real-time statistics, colour-coded on the size of the samples. He posted the key figures on a whiteboard on the wall. 'We were getting information an hour ahead of the Tories,' one official said. 'Faster than anybody else.'

* * *

When the first actual result came in at 11.02 p.m., both Crosby and Heneghan believed the exit poll was wrong after all. Labour's Chi Onwurah had increased her majority in Newcastle Central, but the Tory vote was nearly six points higher too, and the swing to Labour was just 2 per cent, not the 7 per cent predicted by the exit poll. The trend was similar in both seats in Sunderland, which had been a bellwether in the EU referendum campaign, where there was a swing towards the Tories. In the command space Crosby and Messina 'mouthed reassurance' at Timothy. A senior Tory said, 'When the first two or three results came in, and we were outperforming the exit poll, we were starting to get an "It's not over until the fat lady sings" feeling – but then it got bleaker and bleaker.'

At 11.55 p.m. the result in North Swindon showed the Tories losing ground further south. Justin Tomlinson, the Conservative MP, saw his majority slashed by more than 3,000, with Labour's vote soaring by over 10 per cent. A source close to Corbyn said, 'When North Swindon came in and you could see the massive swing to us and the fact that the Ukip vote wasn't breaking to them, we knew we were onto something.'

Around that time Darren Mott, the head of the Conservatives' ground operation, collapsed and an ambulance was called. Happily, Mott, who had been ill during the campaign, recovered and did not need to go to hospital, but the symbolism was bleak. 'It was pretty dramatic when you think the guy running your ground operation might have had a heart attack,' a colleague said. 'It was a moment of drama in a weird night.'

Things were so febrile that Steve Baker, who was defending a Conservative majority of nearly 15,000 in Wycombe, was told at 10.30 p.m. that he would lose. In the event he hung on with a majority slashed to less than 7,000. In a trend that was to be repeated across the country, his vote had gone up since 2015, but he saw Labour support soar on the backs of students and previous non-voters turning out.

At 12.51 a.m. any lingering hopes of a healthy Conservative majority were extinguished when Labour held Darlington – number thirty-six on the Tory target list – a seat that had been held by Michael Fallon until 1992. Jenny Chapman, the sitting MP, and her Conservative challenger both boosted their vote by around 8 per cent. Ukip support had collapsed, as the Tories had hoped, but – in the first sign that David Cameron had been right – it appeared to have split almost equally between the two main parties. It was to be a theme of the night. *Match of the Day* presenter

Gary Lineker remarked on Twitter, 'I think Theresa May has won own goal of the season.'

Labour also increased their majority in Wrexham, scene of May's U-turn on social care. The prime minister's imprecations to the press that day had proved prescient. In Wrexham, nothing had changed. By 1.13 a.m. Labour were on the march in Scotland as well, grabbing Rutherglen and Hamilton West from the SNP, the first of six gains north of the border.

By 2 a.m. the Tories had lost Battersea in South London, costing Treasury minister Jane Ellison her seat. George Osborne called the result 'the revenge of the young'. It was also evidence of a pro-Remain backlash. By the small hours it was clear that May could be forced into changes. Even David Davis suggested on air that the government might have lost their mandate to exit the single market and the customs union: 'That's what we put in front of the people. We'll see by tomorrow whether they've accepted that or not.' In Hove, where Labour's Peter Kyle had feared his leader was a liability, a majority of 1,200 had become 18,000. Feeling more generous after the results were in, he said, 'We could have saved our country from a hard Brexit, and that is something history will thank Jeremy Corbyn for.'[5]

The dire results quickly began to endanger some of May's key allies. Ben Gummer was at his constituency chairman's house in Ipswich when he got a call from a close friend at his count telling him he was going to lose by around a thousand votes. He was 'astounded'. One of the manifesto's main authors was out of a job. The other would not be far behind him. Another six ministers were to lose their seats that night, including Nicola Blackwood in Oxford West and Abingdon, and Rob Wilson in Reading East, both swept away on a wave of student votes. James Wharton, who had been told to leave his Stockton South seat and campaign in neighbouring offensive seats, was another victim of the Tory campaign, along with Edward Timpson, David Mowat and the City minister Simon Kirby.

The moment most Conservatives abandoned hope even of a majority came at 2.17 a.m., when Labour seized Bury North on a 5 per cent swing. Like many Tory MPs who lost that night, David Nuttall had seen his vote go up but was swamped by Labour, who added 12.5 per cent to their vote share in 2015. 'Darlington not coming to us was bad,' a Tory aide said. 'Losing Bury North was curtains.'

The terror attack at Manchester Arena on 22 May 2017 killed twenty-three fans of Ariana Grande (above left) and led to a suspension of campaigning. Jeremy Corbyn (below) was accused of trying to hijack the vigil afterwards.

ABOVE: Jeremy Corbyn launching Labour's manifesto. The little red book was called 'the star of the show' in Labour's campaign.

BELOW: Shadow chancellor John McDonnell was the most outspoken supporter of abolishing tuition fees and insisted on costing Labour's manifesto, giving the party a key edge over the Tories.

INSET: Shadow home secretary Diane Abbott gaffed during the election and became a focus of Tory attack ads; she also suffered horrendous abuse from internet trolls.

ABOVE AND LEFT: When the Labour leader addressed a Libertines gig at the ground of Tranmere Rovers, the chant 'Oh, Je-rem-y Cor-byn' was born.

RIGHT: Jeremy Corbyn suffered a meltdown on air when he struggled to remember details of his own childcare policy but his calm persona meant he could ride out the campaign bumps.

ABOVE: Ian Lavery, Labour's campaign coordinator, clashes with Boris Johnson. His attempts to 'muscle in' after the Manchester terror attack were seen off by local officials.

BELOW: Ruth Davidson, leader of the Scottish Conservatives, led her party to twelve gains and is tipped as a future prime minister.

ABOVE: It was a sign of May's weakness after the election that she felt compelled to bring back Michael Gove (far left) as environment secretary.

BELOW: Sajid Javid (left), the communities secretary, warned May that she would be ousted unless she sacked the chiefs, then launched an outspoken attack on them in cabinet.

The Grenfell Tower disaster on 14 June 2017 was seen as a monument to government failure and Theresa May's lack of empathy. The prime minister visited the emergency services while Jeremy Corbyn hugged the victims' families.

ABOVE: As MPs moved against May, Peter Brookes of *The Times* captured what many saw as the growing futility of her premiership.

TOP LEFT: Grant Shapps clashed with Nick Timothy when he was David Cameron's party chairman, and led an attempted coup to oust May after the election.

TOP RIGHT: Andrew Mitchell, a close ally of David Davis, told a Tory dinner that May should resign.

BELOW: Theresa and Philip May with Alex Jones and Matt Baker from *The One Show*. May revealed that she and her husband have 'boy jobs and girl jobs' around the house.

BELOW: Boris Johnson with Andrew Gwynne. The main parties' most ebullient media spokesmen clashed frequently in spin rooms.

RIGHT: Theresa May's 2017 party conference speech became a nightmare as she suffered a coughing fit, was presented with a P45, and her set fell apart.

BELOW: 4.30 a.m. on 8 December 2017. Theresa May and her aide 'Tricky' Jackson board her plane at Brize Norton to fly to Brussels to secure 'sufficient progress' and finalise the first phase of Brexit talks.

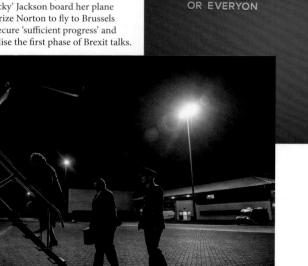

The atmosphere in 4 Matthew Parker Street was now 'a stunned quiet mess'. Rob Oxley stared blankly at a nation-building game on his laptop. 'He was building a civilisation as one was crumbling about him,' a colleague recalled. Even the people on the ground floor began to drink, fortifying themselves with cheap supermarket quiche, wine and beer. Someone produced a bottle of whisky. Others went to the Blue Boar bar nearby, where they drowned their sorrows with 'Theresa's Kitten Heel Fizz' cocktails. One adviser said, 'It was horrible. People were just leaving to get drunk.' There was gallows humour. When Alan Mak, a noted thruster from the 2015 intake, won Havant after 3 a.m., three members of the press team were dancing upstairs. One began shouting, 'Alan Mak for leader!' The others joined in. 'The Mak campaign starts here and starts now!' An older campaigner urged them to stop: 'You make a joke here and it gets tweeted out in the next five minutes – this is really irresponsible.'

Watching the mess unfold, David Cameron messaged one of his friends, 'I didn't do so badly then!' In gatherings around the country, Cameron's aides watched with incredulity, amusement and then anger as the seats they had sweated blood to win two years earlier were handed meekly back to Labour. Many Cameroons were enjoying an alcohol-fuelled evening in Ireland at the holiday home of Henry Macrory, a legend of the Tory press office. At least one former special adviser present had not even voted Conservative: 'I spoiled my ballot paper. I couldn't bring myself to vote for her.' Emily Poole, a former adviser to Stephen Crabb when he was Welsh secretary, penned a blog post saying she had voted Labour because her values had been 'flushed down the drain' by May.

The biggest scalp of the night was not even a Tory. Nick Clegg had survived the Liberal Democrat massacre of 2015 brought about in part by the decision he made to join the coalition government in 2010. Yet even as his party was making gains, Clegg was cast out in Sheffield Hallam, an apparent victim of cosmic payback for dropping the Lib Dem pledge to abolish tuition fees, as another tidal wave of students swept him away. It was the nearest thing to a 'Portillo moment' in the 2017 election. Clegg gave a dignified statement, which prompted his former spin doctor James McGrory to tweet, 'If you want to see what we've lost take a look at that defeat speech from Nick Clegg. Classy as fuck. What a man.'[6] Seven minutes later, Sir Vince Cable, the man who had repeatedly plotted against Clegg, won back the Twickenham seat he had lost in 2015, paving the way for him to seize the party leadership he had long coveted.

At ten minutes past one, bolstered by the information on his computer and whiteboard, which had not yet filtered through to the broadcasters, Heneghan felt confident enough to call Corbyn, Milne and Murphy in Islington and tell them, 'There's absolutely no way the Tories are keeping their majority. We are 100 per cent confident.' Corbyn was 'delighted', but the result was still on a knife-edge. At that point Labour's data model was predicting a maximum of 320 seats for the Conservatives. If they lost a handful more there was an outside chance that Corbyn could be prime minister if he struck a deal with the SNP. Heneghan spoke to Steve Howell, who phoned the BBC to complain that their coverage was still speculating about an outright Tory win. 'There was a moment in the night where one of the field ops team suggested to us that we were going to be the largest party,' a senior Labour official recalled. 'That lasted for about twenty minutes.' Hopes that Labour might grab Shipley from the ardent Eurosceptic Philip Davies proved wide of the mark.

Some of Corbyn's aides joined trade union officials at Unite's party at the International Transport Federation headquarters in Borough Market, a short distance from the scene of the terror attack five days earlier. Holding court, a jubilant Len McCluskey purred over the revival: 'It is seismic and it will be recorded as such in history as a moment when, in a sense, Labour found its heart and its soul again, and I see it as being the first step; one more step to government.'[7]

At Southside, moderates and Corbynistas alike cheered Labour gains. 'We all genetically hate the Tories,' a moderate adviser said. 'We are Labour. We campaigned as a family.' The loudest celebrations on the eighth floor were for Corbyn's closest allies, such as Cat Smith, who turned a majority of 1,265 in Lancaster and Fleetwood, a seat she was expected to lose, into one of 6,661. The comedian Mark Steel led the celebrations with Karie Murphy, who was now at HQ. 'Karie was leading it all, drinking lager,' an aide said. 'There was a euphoric mood. Iain McNicol even sat down next to Karie, drinking.' The crowd sang 'Oh, Je-re-my Cor-byn …' When Shami Chakrabarti, the shadow attorney general, returned from a shift on television she was greeted with chants of 'Shami! Shami! Shamii!'

Not all the Southsiders were enjoying the show, as each gain tightened the stranglehold of the hard left on their party. 'The reaction to what is supposed to be good news was weird,' one moderate said. 'Lots of people were like, "I feel sick." In many ways it's the worst result possible.' Corbynistas singled out Simon Jackson and Katy Dillon for criticism. 'A handful looked like you had invited them to the cinema to watch a video of themselves naked as youngsters,' a LOTO source said. 'They had a wet-weekend look on their faces. I don't think they wanted a Tory land-slide, but they didn't want Jeremy to do well.' Dillon told friends later, 'I was upset we had lost the election.'

For their part, the Corbynistas booed the re-election of John Woodcock, the MP for Barrow in Furness, who had begun the campaign posting a video of why he would never support Corbyn to be prime minister. They also refused to applaud the return of Jess Phillips, another vocal Corbyn critic.

After 2 a.m. Corbyn took a call from a friend at his count who told him that his own result in Islington North would be his best ever. Two years earlier, Corbyn had won just under 30,000 votes. This time he would secure over 40,000, and a majority of more than 33,000 on a swing of 8.7 per cent. Aides said he was visibly touched as he left to hear the result at the nearby Sobell leisure centre. 'That'll be my fifth consecutive rise in the vote,' he said. 'I owe everything to my Islington supporters.'[8]

At his count, Corbyn attempted to high-five Emily Thornberry, but at the key moment the shadow foreign secretary moved her hand and the leader of the opposition's palm slapped into his colleague's ample bosom. Corbyn grimaced momentarily, but quickly recovered his composure; Thornberry took it all in her stride. It was 3.07 a.m. when Corbyn, notes scribbled in a black notebook, took to the stage and called for Theresa May to resign. 'We changed the face of British politics,' he said. 'What's happened is people have said they have had quite enough of austerity politics ... and not giving our young people the chance they deserve in our society.' He concluded by saying, 'The prime minister called the elec-tion because she wanted a mandate. Well the mandate she has got is lost Conservative seats, lost votes, lost support and lost confidence. I would have thought that's enough to go, actually, and make way for a govern-ment that will be truly representative of all the people of this country.' Behind him the Ukip candidate, Keith Fraser, mouthed 'Terrorist sympa-thiser' at the banks of television cameras.

Just as Corbyn was finishing his speech the BBC reported that Labour had taken Canterbury, a seat that had been in Conservative hands since 1874, again on the back of student votes. Four hours later they would grab once-true-blue Kensington as well, by the princely margin of twenty votes.

Few victories gave the Corbynistas more pleasure than Chris Williamson's in Derby North, where Williamson, one of Corbyn's closest friends in Parliament, had lost his seat in 2015 by forty-one votes. At 5 a.m. Williamson went to his constituency office and tore down the black binliners he had stuck over the sign reading 'Chris Williamson MP' two years earlier. 'New Labour's dead,' he said. 'No doubt about that. It's dead, buried and finished. It's a regrettable chapter in our history. Historians will think, "My God, what were they doing?!"'[9] To which the moderate reply would be: winning three elections.

Once it was clear that Theresa May had put the party into retreat, the chiefs withdrew from the sofa area. Fiona Hill decided to head to Maidenhead to talk to May, who they knew was in a bad way. Hill was her emotional support and wanted to be with her – perhaps also to head off any thought of resignation.

Before she departed, Hill spoke to the dwindling remnants of her media team – Oxley, Swarbrick and Woodhouse – encouraging them to start telling journalists what had gone wrong in the campaign: 'It's over. Brief your heads off.' Her audience took that as licence to attack Crosby and Textor.

Timothy retreated to the boardroom to talk over his options with Chris Wilkins. When Swindon North swung to Labour just before midnight, he said, 'Oh fuck!' Several of the results had been symbolically wounding for him. When Labour's Jack Dromey held Birmingham Erdington – Timothy's ancestral seat – the defeat for his brand of blue-collar Conservatism was complete. 'It is still counter-cultural for the working classes to vote Tory,' a friend observed. 'It's a disaster for the modernisation project.' Around 4.30 a.m. Labour held Halifax, where the disastrous Tory manifesto was launched, Holly Lynch increasing her majority from under five hundred to more than 5,000.

At 4.36 a.m. Anna Soubry was one of the first MPs to break cover and publicly criticise the leadership. 'We ran a dreadful campaign,' she said. 'That's me being generous.' Another well-known Conservative said,

'Nick Timothy will have to shave off his beard and go into a witness protection programme.'

Timothy was aware before election day that, whatever the outcome, he and Hill would find themselves in the firing line, and had held confessional conversations with Wilkins, Ben Gummer, Stephen Gilbert and Will Tanner. One confidant said, 'Nick had said to me in the later stages of the campaign, when he still thought we were going to win handsomely, "We are going to have to change after this." They had realised how unpopular they were personally. They knew there was a big job to do to repair party relations.' Now Timothy was extremely bruised and despondent, mulling over what he should do. From midnight onwards, he had concluded that he would have to resign. 'He realised straight away that that was it for him and that he'd have to go,' a close ally said. Timothy confirmed later, 'Nobody told me I had to go, but it became inevitable. The exit poll was a shock, and when it became clear that it was right, it was obvious that I would have to go.'[10]

Timothy's first instinct was that the prime minister would have to resign as well. In the scenarios he had mapped out a week earlier, the chief of staff had concluded that even simply holding the seats the Conservatives had already would lead to her being forced out. 'He was concerned that if she stayed on then she'd have a horrible time at PMQs,' a source said. 'He felt that he'd inadvertently put her in this position that was going to be horrible for her.' Timothy wanted to see the final numbers, but his fear was that the result 'could be brutal' for May. He wondered, 'Is it worth it?' During their hour-long conversation he and Wilkins even considered May's successors. 'Oh my God, we're hours away from prime minister Boris,' they joked. Timothy's view was that the party would not accept a coronation.

Timothy was racked by guilt over the manifesto, and rehearsed once again with Wilkins his regret that he had not included a cap on care costs. He was also in WhatsApp contact with Ben Gummer, his co-author, whose loss brought home the human cost of his mistakes. By deciding to quit he hoped to insulate May. Wilkins urged him not to do anything rash, but Timothy was adamant: 'There's only one way it's going to go for me.' Another Downing Street official said of Timothy and Hill, 'I think they both knew that night they would have to go. They're self-aware and their instincts are good. They knew immediately.'

*   *   *

When May was interviewed by Radio 5 Live after the election she said, 'I didn't consider stepping down because I felt there was a responsibility there to be sure that the country still had a government.'[11] That is not how some of her aides and friends recall it. Afterwards, ministers and others who discussed the events that night with the prime minister and her closest allies said Philip May had to talk the prime minister out of quitting. He himself briefly wondered whether she would have to go, but then sought to boost her confidence. 'Philip May was probably more important than anyone else that night,' said one senior figure. 'He was instrumental in making sure that she was in a better place.' Another Conservative suggested that Philip May played as vital a role in persuading his wife to stay on as Denis Thatcher had in urging Britain's first woman prime minister to resign in 1990. While Thatcher saw his wife's best chance of preserving her political legacy as getting out of a leadership contest she might have lost, May saw it as vital for his wife to stick around if she was to construct a political legacy at all. The prime minister was also in touch with her chief whip Gavin Williamson, who told her she owed it to the party to fight on and form a government. Philip May was encouraged by Chris Grayling, the transport secretary, who texted him saying, 'She can't go.'

An MP who is close to May said, 'She swung violently afterwards towards thinking it was over. There was a crisis of confidence. The wobble was stilled by a sense of duty. Philip was quite significant in that. Once the reality had set in and the processing started, she didn't go over it for a long period of time. Duty was the thing that did it for her. People gave her a sense of, "You can fight on, and it's your duty to do so." Gavin and Philip were very influential.'

Williamson was a key figure because May credited him with having delivered her the votes to seize the Tory crown the previous July. 'She knows that she would not have got the leadership but for him,' an MP close to the prime minister said. 'He was the person who delivered the numbers of MPs, more so than anyone else. Ever since then he has been her principal adviser on the parliamentary side.'

Fiona Hill met the couple at their home in Sonning and reinforced the message. She appears to have been less convinced than Timothy that May should resign. 'She wanted to stay on,' the MP said. Hill took the Mays to the count at a leisure centre in Maidenhead. The prime minister was taken to a gym where Tricky Jackson had set up a green room. In among the weights she waited with Liz Sanderson, Tim Smith and Mo Hussain, Amber Rudd's spad who had been running the media operation on May's battle bus.

Philip May and the prime minister's election agent Philip Dumville sought to fill the dead air, keeping up a commentary on the results, seeking to vocalise what they were seeing on television: 'What's happening next? That's good, we won that. Angus Robertson is gone. Oh, OK, we've lost this.' May was quiet, contemplating the blank walls, but appeared more engaged than Hill, who seemed mentally detached from what was going on, 'staring into the abyss'. When one bad result came in she reached out, gripped the hand of the person sitting next to her and squeezed hard; the grip of a child clinging to its mother on a roll-ercoaster ride. Eventually May decided she could stand the atmosphere no longer and said, 'OK, let's just go. Let's get on with it and go out there.'

As well as acting as Nick Timothy's confessor, Chris Wilkins was also working on a speech for May's count in Maidenhead. By the time Jeremy Corbyn was calling on her to resign, the prime minister was already at her count, dressed incongruously in the red outfit she had worn to meet Donald Trump at the White House. She appeared drained and listless, moving with a hunched gait, her face caked in more make-up than usual. Wilkins had to write blind, since he had not been able to talk to May and had no idea whether she was thinking of resigning. He began tapping out a speech that would talk about the Conservative Party doing its duty to the British public, studiously avoiding mentions of May herself. 'Chris had to keep the options open,' a source said. Parts of the speech he cut and pasted from a 'lines to take' document that had been circulated to all MPs. As the prime minister prepared to speak to the nation that had refused to embrace her, she had precisely zero input into the words she would say. When the speech was written, Wilkins simply emailed it to May. He never heard anything back.

May's speech was almost word for word what Wilkins had sent. With comedy candidate Lord Buckethead (249 votes) gazing on, the prime minister said, 'At this time, more than anything else, what this country needs is a period of stability. If the Conservative Party has won the most seats and probably the most votes then it will be incumbent on us to ensure that we have that period of stability – and that is exactly what we will do … Whatever the results are, the Conservative Party will ensure

that we fulfil our duty.' By investing the Tory Party with that responsibility, it was far from clear that May was planning to continue.

When MPs saw her address the cameras they were amazed by the
inclusion of phrases from the spin document on 'getting the Brexit deal
right' and 'doing what is in the national interest', which now rang hollow.
'None of us read out that stuff,' one said. 'It's fairly amazing that she did
at a moment like that.' May was never proactive about her media messaging, but it is astonishing that she did not choose her own words at such
a moment.

At CCHQ staff watched sick with dread. As May drew to a close, Craig
Woodhouse turned to Tom Swarbrick and said, 'If there's one thing we
can do here, it's when she finishes we just have to clap.' They were the
only two who applauded. Shortly afterwards, Crosby showed himself in
the war room. 'He was totally white,' one witness said. 'That bubbly,
fun-guy persona had just totally gone. All he kept saying was, "It's just
one of those things. Just one of those things." He must have said it five
times.'

May's demeanour convinced some MPs watching her on television
that she might be on the verge of throwing in the towel. 'A lot of us were
concerned having seen her when she was making her speech at her count,'
one prominent figure said. 'There was a perceived danger that she might
have thought it was necessary to throw in the towel.' Graham Brady, the
chairman of the 1922 Committee, the shop steward for Conservative
backbenchers, texted May to say, 'Don't do anything precipitate.'

May and the staff with her got in a two-car convoy back to London,
flanked by police motorcycles, their every move shadowed by a Sky
News helicopter for a thirty-minute journey that seemed to last a
hundred years. The prime minister rode with her husband. Hill sat in the
car behind with Jackson, Hussain, Sanderson, Smith and Steve Back, the
photographer who had been signed up by the Tories for the duration of
the campaign. Hill asked Hussain, Amber Rudd's special adviser, whether
the home secretary was OK, but otherwise said nothing. The others
listened in silence to the radio recounting the disaster. The fate of Rudd
was now the main drama.

The home secretary had endured a campaign as tough as anyone apart
from May. As one of the few cabinet talking heads and the minister in
the eye of the storm following two terrorist attacks, as the Tory standard-
bearer in the main debate two days after the death of her father, Rudd

had been through the mill, and had not been able to devote as much time as she would have liked to her constituency, Hastings and Rye. With the broadcasters reporting that she was in trouble, Hussain had to watch helpless as the cameras showed his boss pacing up and down at her count as the returning officer ordered a full recount of the votes, which is only done when an election is too close to call. It was not until 4.54 a.m. that Rudd was declared the victor. She had scraped in by 346 votes. In the Tory war room there was euphoria. Throughout the bleak evening staff had become emotionally invested in Rudd's fate. One special adviser said, 'That was the brightest moment of last night. If she had lost, that would have been the moment at which I would have cried. It was really nice in a really fucking dark evening.' Some remained clear-eyed: 'When you're cheering your home secretary winning by three hundred votes in an election you're expecting to walk, it's not the sign of a good night.'

The only other results that elicited cheers were those coming from Scotland. As dawn broke it was becoming clear that Theresa May was clinging to Downing Street thanks to Ruth Davidson's stellar performance. North of the border the Scottish Tories were on course to pick up twelve seats, bringing their tally to thirteen, their best showing since 1979. They even claimed the scalps of Angus Robertson, the SNP's leader in Westminster, and most dramatically, Alex Salmond, the former first minister, the latter on a swing of more than 20 per cent. It might have been even better. In the seat of Perth and North Perthshire they lost out to the SNP by just twenty-one votes. In all, Davidson's Tartan Tories secured nearly 29 per cent of the vote.

Without the Scottish revival the Conservatives might not have been able to continue in government. Since the speaker and Sinn Féin, which won seven seats, do not vote in the House of Commons, Jeremy Corbyn would have needed to construct an alliance of 322 MPs to stop May retaining power. If you assumed the DUP would side with the Tories, May had 326 seats, while the other parties together had 317. A senior Labour official said, 'Five more seats, and Jeremy would probably be PM. If the SNP hadn't lost those seats to them in Scotland, Jeremy would be PM. It was on a knife-edge.' Put another way, if Ruth Davidson's team had won only eight seats, Theresa May would have been out of Downing Street. James Kanagasooriam's model had saved the day.

The Scottish Tories might actually have done better. 'I was disappointed with the UK campaign; it cost the Scottish Tories five seats,' a source said. If those five seats had fallen, there would have been no need for May to go to the DUP for support.

When May got to CCHQ at around 4.30 a.m. she went into the board-room with her husband, Hill, Timothy, Penn and Wilkins, now part of the inner circle again. They were all bewildered by events. The conversation was 'quite general'. Hanging in the air was the ultimate question: would she resign? May said, 'Obviously we need to see what the final numbers are. But we are clearly still going to have the most seats and the most votes.' She was conscious that she could not continue if she lacked the support of the big hitters in the cabinet.

Gavin Williamson had fed in intelligence that MPs were ringing round sounding out MPs on behalf of both Boris Johnson and David Davis. 'We need to speak to DD,' May said. Davis assured her of his loyalty. Johnson then sent the prime minister a text, urging her to keep her 'chin up'. 'We are with you and behind you,' he said. The prime minister showed the message to her aides. The strong impression May gave was that 'she had already decided she was definitely staying. By the time she turned up that wasn't much of a conversation. She'd concluded she'd still got the most seats and was qualified for it and should carry on.'

The aides asked May if she wanted to get the field team in. 'Well, OK,' she replied. Darren Mott had gone home after being taken unwell, so they sent for Stephen Gilbert. 'Do you want Lynton and Tex as well?' someone asked. 'We might as well,' May replied, unenthusiastically. 'The consultants were just pretty shocked,' a Downing Street official said. Lynton and Tex were looking white. They sat at the end of the table and mumbled, "I'm sorry." Then there was a frosty conversation.'

May quizzed the consultants, on whom the Conservative Party had spent around £4 million. 'How come you never saw this coming?' she asked. 'You've been sending me round all these seats and I've just been doing what you told me to do. And we didn't come anywhere close to winning, so what's been going on? Explain how this has happened.' One May ally said, 'It was not "Explain how you've failed," but "Where are these voters going, how does this make sense?"'

The Australians looked sheepish. They 'talked about the surge in the youth vote and how there'd been a lot of churn, but there was no clear explanation of what had happened', one campaign official recalled later. May pressed again: 'Why were my MPs so wrong about all the feedback they've been getting from their canvassing? I just don't understand it.' The Australians muttered that most MPs were not in swing seats. 'She asked the questions and nobody had any answers,' one of those present said. 'She wasn't shouting or anything but she was quite cold. There was quite a chill in the room.'

The meeting broke up. The consultants and Wilkins left. The crunch meeting about May's future now took place with a smaller group – May, Hill and Timothy. It was 5 a.m. The chiefs had not coordinated what they would say, but Timothy believed they would have to resign. He told friends later, 'We both knew it. It had reached us that some people were planning to call for our heads if the result was less than adequate.' While Hill had been with May in Maidenhead, Timothy had spoken to her by phone and made it clear that he felt he would have to resign. 'We think there's going to be pressure for us to go. We think we should probably go,' he told May. When the prime minister did not commit herself to accepting his view, Timothy pressed the point: 'If there are people who are out to get Fiona and me and they're going to use us against you, then you don't want us seen around you, so we need to let you have these conversations with people without us being there.' Other senior Tories say Hill knew she would have to resign as chief of staff, but the prospect of her staying on as a personal aide to the prime minister remained live for another thirty-six hours. May agreed there would be pressure for the chiefs to quit, but indicated that she did not want them to go. One of the closest teams in Downing Street history was disintegrating.

The subject of May's resignation was raised in a neutral fashion: 'What do you think?'

May responded, 'The worst thing that could happen for the country right now is an absence of leadership, and the Conservatives need to make sure that Jeremy Corbyn can't become prime minister, so it's out of the question.' She was visibly 'quite shocked' by events, but remained 'businesslike'.

Once it was decided, Timothy texted Wilkins to say, 'She's going to fight on.' Wilkins replied, 'Good, I think that's the right thing to do.' It had been only the briefest of conversations but it had confirmed May's resolve.

If she had been aware of what her cabinet ministers were up to at the time, she might have felt differently.

While his wife's future was being decided, Philip May was in the war room, a sight which one aide found unbelievably poignant: 'There was a moment where Laura Kuenssberg was talking on TV about how terrible this was for the PM. Laura was not being horrible, but Philip May came over and was watching it and his face as his wife was being beaten up on live television was not great.'

At 5.19 a.m. May went into the war room, which now resembled a scene from the end of a conflict – empty bottles and discarded food wrappers competing for attention with the sense of despair. 'It looked like someone had shat in the meringue – just glum all round,' said one Downing Street official. The staff applauded, and May had to calm them. She seemed 'shellshocked', on the verge of tears. 'I thought she was going to break down in the middle of it,' one staffer said. May spoke about how the party must go on. In the press team, two aides caught each other's eye. 'Our initial reaction was she was going to resign,' one said. 'You don't speak in that way unless you're thinking about it. She was very, very close to crying. Her voice was quivering. She was holding a lot in.'

May told the staff, 'This is a disappointing result. There have been extraordinary shifts in British politics, but this is still the best political party in the world. This result is not down to lack of effort on your part. Everyone here has worked incredibly long hours, and I'm thankful for all the work people have put in. We live to fight another day.' She even found time for a joke: 'And I'm sorry for all the cheesy pasta you've had to eat.' Theresa May was made of strong stuff. She needed to be to have got this far, but now she was in meltdown. 'Her voice was really breaking and crackly, and didn't inspire one with confidence,' a special adviser said. 'I very viscerally felt that it was a difficult speech for her to give.'

Hill briefed what was left of the press team. It was important to ensure that the public knew May's intentions. 'She's not resigning. Make sure everyone knows we're going to form a government.'

Two moments symbolised the transformation from campaign to government. At 5.49 a.m., according to a source who kept detailed notes of the evening, the Australians departed. 'Lynton and Tex just left,' one witness said. 'They'd been in the chairman's office and they just marched out, didn't say goodbye to anyone, tails between their legs.'

One minute earlier, Laura Kuenssberg had tweeted, 'Source says Crosby "ran a campaign against our instincts – we were told 'no' to changes + when we said 'strong + stable' had become a joke."' There was no one in Tory high command who did not think Fiona Hill was Kuenssberg's source.

Five minutes later, at 5.53 a.m., the Tories failed to oust Labour's Alan Whitehead in Southampton Test, meaning it was numerically impossible for them to secure a majority.

Later that morning Crosby, who had helped elect both John Howard and Tony Abbott, got a text from 'a former Australian prime minister' which read, 'Bad luck, you had a crap candidate.'

The blame game had begun. The battle for May's reputation would have to wait. Her battle for survival was only just beginning.

PART FOUR

CATHARSIS

THE FALL OUT

June to October 2017

SHELLSHOCK

David Davis arrived by helicopter, but his was not the mercy dash that he later implied. The Brexit secretary had been booked to do the main morning round of broadcast interviews. The price of his agreement had been that he arrive in style from his Haltemprice and Howden seat in East Yorkshire. 'His one demand for the campaign was the helicopter into London,' a Conservative official said. Another official observed, 'There are certain admirable qualities to this level of self-absorption.'

Party officials were irritated but not surprised when Davis decided not to take to the television studios after all. Theresa May's fate was unclear and he was certain to be asked about his own leadership ambitions. At 6 a.m. one of his aides received a call saying, 'He might be prime minister later today.' Davis had lost to David Cameron in 2005, and had felt his frontline political career was at an end when he left the shadow cabinet in 2008. He was grateful to May for giving him a big job. Privately he was very supportive of the prime minister, urging her to stay. Yet he did not want to say so in public – at least not yet. 'He didn't know what to say,' a Tory adviser said. 'He wanted to talk to her and tell everyone else that she can continue, that Brexit must go on,' said a source close to Davis.

When he arrived at Downing Street, Davis found May in a state of distress. He thought she had been crying. If the prime minister had earlier resolved to stay in Number 10, now she needed her resolve stiffening. 'Do you want to stay?' he asked. 'I'll fight for you to stay.' Davis made clear that May had to stick around to negotiate the opening stages of the Brexit talks. 'They had a face-to-face meeting and that went very well,' a May aide said. 'Clearly that was a conversation that went well.'

Around 8 a.m. May began a cabinet ring-round to solidify her position. She called Boris Johnson and formally asked, 'Do you intend to stand against me?' Johnson was in his kitchen when the call arrived. He said he would remain with her. 'We've won, we've got to form a government and we've got to get Brexit done.'

Johnson also refused to do a media round at eight o'clock that morning, despite the best efforts of the broadcasting team. The silence from May's cabinet was deafening. Johnson said to a CCHQ official, 'The train was running along very nicely. And we just smashed it into the buffers.' Despite his text message to May, Johnson was a politician given to changes of mind when the circumstances shifted. Many half-expected to see him pop up on the BBC making an announcement of his own that he was running for leader. 'I came off the phone call thinking, "This is it, he's going for it,"' said one special adviser who talked to the foreign secretary that morning, 'and if he goes for it, we are fucked.'

In the Uxbridge Conservative Club the previous evening, Johnson had just finished a plate of burger and chips and was halfway down a pint of Young's ale when the exit poll dropped. He was seated conspicuously at the front of the room with his wife, the QC Marina Wheeler, his special advisers Ben Gascoigne and Liam Parker and the local council leader, Ray Puddifoot. Johnson's reaction to the exit poll was a pithy, 'What the fuck!' His second reaction was to fear for the future of the EU negotiations: 'Christ, Brexit. This is going to cause massive problems. We've fucked Brexit. We've fucked Brexit.'

Johnson felt people would be watching his reaction and told his team, 'Look, guys, we're going to start getting texts. There's going to be a lot of stuff on social media. Don't talk to anyone.'

The embargo did not last long for some members of Johnson's circle. As early as 12.35 a.m., Jim Waterson of Buzzfeed was reporting on Twitter, 'Boris Johnson is "already on manoeuvres" claims Tory MP, who says the foreign secretary is "sounding out" a few colleagues about leadership.' Sir Alan Duncan, the minister for Europe and Johnson's deputy at the Foreign Office, called one of Boris's aides around 1 a.m. trying to sound them out about his intentions. Duncan, an experienced operator with a delight for the Westminster game, declared gleefully, 'I imagine you are now on manoeuvres.' Appropriating a favourite phrase of Johnson's, they agreed the election result was a 'goat fuck'.

Johnson had his own concerns. His team were getting regular updates from the count at the Uxbridge civic centre. To their consternation Labour was leading in what they had thought were safe Tory wards.

Rumours that Amber Rudd and Anna Soubry were both in trouble contributed to their nervousness. Johnson's majority was pushing 11,000 but word came back that it was likely to be cut to 7,000 on a night when he had hoped to increase his lead. Updates came in every half hour and the news was not good. 'The numbers went from seven to six, to five and then it was three thousand,' an aide said. Johnson's team drove to the count slipstreaming behind a police car in his special adviser Ben Gascoigne's VW Golf. When they arrived, they counted the boxes of ballot papers and could see he was only two ahead of his Labour rival. It was ten to three in the morning when Johnson was finally re-elected with a majority just over 5,000.

Johnson thought about his remarks in detail. He knew everything he said would be pored over by the media looking for evidence of disloyalty to May. Liam Parker advised him, 'Talk about the people of Uxbridge, not the people of Great Britain.' Johnson spoke about Hillingdon and London and said, 'We've got to listen to our constituents.' But he made no comment on the national results. Johnson was depressed about the election, which he had twice told May not to call. 'He was seriously down about it,' a friend said. 'There was a lot of, "What the fuck? How has this happened? What the hell! What the hell!"'

Between 2 a.m. and 5 a.m. that morning, May's future as prime minister hung in the balance as cabinet ministers contacted each other and senior figures in Matthew Parker Street to try to ascertain whether she was going to resign or anyone was going to move against her. 'There was a lot of manoeuvring at cabinet level,' a leading member of the war room said. 'Senior figures in the cabinet were phoning up trying to understand what the PM was doing.' Those who were with Johnson into the small hours of the morning say that he had his phone in full view at all times, and that he made no calls to MPs to sound them out about his prospects or whether he should challenge May. By dawn he had texted May to say he would back her. After his count, Johnson and his aides retreated to his official residence in Carlton Gardens to watch the results. Johnson kept saying, 'Poor Theresa, I hope she is okay.'

However, it is clear that several of those around him, and some of the MPs supporting him, were testing the waters on his behalf. MPs say Amanda Milling, an MP from the 2015 intake who had been one of Johnson's four principal parliamentary supporters a year earlier, was one of those canvassing the views of colleagues. 'Amanda Milling was texting people to ask what they thought,' one MP said. One of Johnson's inner circle also spoke to a special adviser who was in CCHQ that night and offered him a post in Downing Street. 'If we win there will be a job for you,' he said. The recipient of the call was in no doubt that Johnson's team expected to be walking through the doors of Number 10 in short order. A special adviser took a similar call at lunchtime on Friday and a Boris aide said, 'I just want you to know that if anything happens there is a place for you in Downing Street.' Ben Gascoigne had decided to leave government and sat out the election. Johnson now asked him to stay. 'Boris was hot on getting his team together,' another friend said. 'Ben had decided it was time to walk. He had agreed his payoff. Boris would not have done that unless he needed him for something quite quickly. They were on standby.'

By 6 a.m. members of the 1922 Committee were calling staff at central office asking whether the cabinet would move against May. 'They were in information gathering mode,' a special adviser said. 'No one was revealing their hand but they were desperate to find out what other people's hands were. At that point there was zero command and control. Nick and Fi had gone.'

One of the MPs phoning around on Johnson's behalf was Nadine Dorries, who had been pictured in tears at the public event where he revealed that he was dropping out of the leadership contest after Michael Gove, his campaign manager, announced that Johnson was not ready to be prime minister and he was running himself. One of those she called was Gove. Dorries said, 'Michael, you need to back Boris and revive the "dream team".' Gove said he was not sure, but he texted Johnson anyway and said, 'We should talk.' The next Gove heard of the matter was when he was contacted the following day by a journalist from the *Mail on Sunday* who said he understood that Gove had reached out to Johnson. Gove reflected that if that was the level of discipline with which a second Johnson leadership campaign was to be conducted, he might be better off holding his fire. Yet he told a friend over dinner, 'I suppose I'll have to support him.'

Two other key players were in action that day. Dominic Cummings, the director of Vote Leave, who had disappeared from frontline politics since referendum day, saw his chance to reconstitute the Johnson–Gove team which had so spectacularly fallen apart a year earlier. At 5 p.m. on Friday, he called Steve Baker, a key ally from Vote Leave. A source present said, 'Dom called up and said, "You need to back Boris." Steve wouldn't back Boris.' The source said Johnson had been in touch with both Cummings and Lynton Crosby earlier in the day. 'Boris was trying to get Dom to try to help him and he had Lynton trying to help him on the Friday. But, classic Boris, none of them was speaking to each other. You had different people trying to set up rival operations ringing round to drum up support.' Cummings had long wanted to shake up Downing Street. 'He wants to take over Number 10,' a friend said. 'That's the only thing he's interested in. He saw his opportunity.' It was not to be the last that was heard of Cummings in the months ahead.

The *Mail on Sunday* splash that weekend began, 'Boris Johnson is preparing a new bid to become Prime Minister', and quoted a 'close ally' as saying it was 'go-go-go' for Johnson. The *Sunday Times* revealed how five cabinet ministers had offered to support the foreign secretary if he ran and quoted one of Johnson's close confidants, the economist Gerard Lyons, attacking May. 'I thought the campaign was appalling,' he said. Both papers carried polls showing that a clear majority of voters wanted May to resign immediately.

It was around 4 a.m. on election night when Johnson began receiving messages from his colleagues. Intriguingly, one of those who contacted him was the minister with whom he had frequently clashed on Brexit, Philip Hammond. The chancellor was cagey in his approach, but it was taken by Johnson to mean that if he decided to run for leader, Hammond was prepared to support him. Johnson told his aides, 'Philip's just texted me. He's 100 per cent behind me if I go for it.' Then he pulled a face. 'Clearly he wants to remain as chancellor.' In fact, Hammond had left a voicemail, which had been converted into a text urging him to call back. Johnson was 'circumspect' in his response. 'He didn't say anything back to encourage it,' one source said. They did not discuss ousting May but both men knew that there might be a vacancy. If details of this exchange had emerged only from Johnson's camp it would be reasonable to question their veracity, since it would have been extraordinary for the leading Remainer in cabinet to back its most prominent Brexiteer, but the main thrust of the offer exchange was also confirmed by a close ally of Hammond's.

When it became clear that the result was not going as the Tories had wished, Hammond consulted colleagues and asked, 'What are we going to do now?' One ally said, 'I know in that first day he thought Boris could be the answer because he'd have this reach and appeal.' In one conversation Hammond said, 'If we can get Boris to move on a few things, immigration and stuff, maybe he's got the reach. He's shown he can campaign.' In a move that would have appealed to Johnson's fascination with ancient Rome, Hammond believed the foreign secretary could head a triumvirate at the top of government alongside himself and David Davis – an arrangement which would immediately have seen Johnson cast as Julius Caesar, with Davis in the role of Pompey and Hammond, the Treasury man with personal wealth in excess of £10 million, playing Crassus. 'DD's now in a better place on Brexit and the three of us could do it,' the chancellor suggested. 'He thought DD could run Brexit, he could run the economy and Boris could run the shop,' said a source familiar with the conversations.

Hammond felt himself 'too grey' for the top job. 'I don't think he particularly wants it and [the triumvirate was] what he saw as the solution,' the friend said. Hammond's backing for Johnson was 'predicated on Theresa going'. The chancellor did not wish to join a coup, but since he had expected to be fired if May had been returned with a healthy majority it seems Hammond was prepared to move quickly to cement his position with a new leader. 'I don't think he urged Boris to do it,' the Hammond ally said. 'He said, "Well, what are you going to do?" Boris just sort of bungled it. It was all very fluid and there wasn't a clarity over what Theresa was going to do.'

The triumvirate plan was a non-starter because Davis was not interested in joining the undercard. 'DD was very unhappy with that proposition,' a cabinet source said. 'It all unravelled.' An MP who called Davis to ask whether he was prepared to support Johnson that morning was given short shrift. 'I pleaded that the party and the country would need a compelling top team.' Davis was unmoved.

The case for Johnson was clear enough. After 'Glumbucket' May, his supporters could argue that he was best placed to make the optimistic case for Britain's role in a post-Brexit world. At home, his name recognition and 'Heineken candidate' credentials – as the advert had it, refreshing the parts other Tories 'cannot reach' – had long been part of his appeal. Twice he had taken on the hard left in London, in the form of Ken Livingstone (a figure whose operation was regarded as better organised than Corbyn's), and vanquished them on both occasions. Yet memories of his shambolic leadership campaign the year before, and more recent experience of his erratic behaviour when unleashed in election spin rooms, prompted caution.

Johnson also heard from Priti Patel and Amber Rudd, though neither was as forward as Hammond. 'He got a number of texts that he thought were unusual,' a Johnson ally said. 'It was very, very clear that there were people looking to him at that moment. The general feeling at that time – and spads were texting each other – was: "This is a disaster. She can't survive."' There was even a text from David Davis, who MPs believed would be Johnson's main rival for the leadership if May were to fall on her sword. 'DD was just trying to test the water to see where Boris was and work out what he was potentially facing.'

Later that weekend, Johnson also got a call from Michael Fallon, the defence secretary. His message 'was similar' to Hammond's, a source said, offering conditional support. The following weekend the pair were seen having a beer together on a bench outside the Bricklayers' Arms in Chipstead, Kent, a watering hole close to the foreign secretary's grace and favour home Chevening and Fallon's Sevenoaks seat. Andrea Leadsom, the runner-up in the previous contest, also had a conversation with Johnson. 'They all asked, "What are you thinking?" They reached out to him saying, "We need leadership and if she can't provide it, you're the man,"' a source close to Johnson said. 'Boris was the one who could connect back with the people and explain the party's vision to normal human beings.'

Yet when Johnson saw the splash headline in the *Mail on Sunday* – 'BORIS SET TO LAUNCH BID TO BE PM AS MAY CLINGS ON' – he went 'absolutely apoplectic' and called the editor, Geordie Greig, to complain before taking to Twitter to brand the report 'tripe'. The situation was also awkward for his sister, Rachel Johnson, a columnist at the paper, who confronted Greig in turn saying Boris had been 'stitched up'. Johnson did not contest the *Sunday Times* report. The furore delighted Johnson's old rival, George Osborne, who was reviewing the papers on the *Andrew Marr Show* that weekend. 'It's a permanent leadership campaign for my friend Boris,' he said.

In a series of WhatsApp messages sent to Tory MPs, clearly designed to leak, Johnson sought to calm the situation, while guaranteeing he would be the subject of a second day of headlines. They read:

Folks we need to calm down and get behind the prime minister

1 she won more votes than anyone since margaret thatcher
2 I can't remember us having anything like 43 per cent of the
   vote
3 we have got to stop the narrative that Corbyn somehow won this
   thing – he barely did better than Gordon useless brown when we
   beat him in 2010
4 we must get on and deliver for the people of this country –
   including a great Brexit deal
5 we must not allow the media to spread mischief not least because
   the public are fed up to the back teeth of politics and politicians
   and they certainly DO NOT want another election
6 yes of course we need to think about the lessons of this election
   but not in the papers
7 the pm is a woman of extraordinary qualities and frankly the
   public are looking to us to get behind her with discipline and
   determination
8 on with the job!

The first person to respond was Michael Gove, who said, 'Boris is right.'
Conor Burns, Johnson's parliamentary aide, added, 'Spot on Boris.' Many
of his fellow MPs reflected that had Johnson been more au fait with
Twitter eleven months earlier – when his leadership bid collapsed in part
because he had failed to tweet that he was offering Andrea Leadsom a
senior job – he might never have been in such a position.

In the days ahead, Johnson felt unfairly punished for the incautious
enthusiasm of his supporters as the finger of blame was pointed at Parker
and his MP backers. 'He's done the right thing but has been burnt by
others,' an aide said that week. MPs who wanted to see Davis or Rudd
replace May were equally adamant that Johnson backed off because he
realised he did not have enough support in Parliament. 'He would have
run if he could have won,' a source familiar with the conversations said.
'They couldn't get the numbers.' Among those delighted that the foreign
secretary had not taken over were some of Britain's EU partners. On the
morning after the general election, a senior official in Angela Merkel's
office texted a British contact to say, 'Anyone but Boris.' Ministers shared
the view that Johnson would make getting a Brexit deal more difficult.

'If Boris is made PM by acclamation, he will walk into Brussels and they'll laugh and spit at him,' one cabinet minister said.

Around 8 a.m. May began calling her senior colleagues to ensure that she had their backing. The prime minister had by then despatched her chief whip, Gavin Williamson, to Belfast to seek a deal with the Democratic Unionist Party (DUP). That left deputy chief whip Julian Smith and May's parliamentary private secretary, George Hollingbery, orchestrating a ring-round of MPs to gauge support in the parliamentary party. Those who spoke to May that week say her resolve to continue was fragile. 'I think if the men in suits had come to her and said she was hurting the party, I think she would have stood down,' an adviser said. Having been silenced during the campaign, most members of her cabinet remained silent after it, refusing to rush to her defence. In private they put her against a wall and threatened to bring her down unless she got rid of Nick Timothy and Fiona Hill.

That morning one minister told the author, 'The headline is fuckety, fuck, fuck with knobs on. The chemical composition of the government has to change. The party will not swallow Nick and Fi any more. Serious people are saying, in numbers, that they have to go. The problem is that she is nothing without them.'

In conversations with May, Philip Hammond, Michael Fallon and Chris Grayling all emphasised that they wanted to see the back of the chiefs. Fallon even confirmed it publicly that Sunday: 'I and other colleagues have made that clear to her. She absolutely understands that a minority government requires a different approach, a more collective approach.'[1] Sajid Javid sent an uncompromising message to May via an intermediary. 'He made it absolutely clear that if she didn't get rid of them, it wasn't just that he wouldn't serve in her cabinet, there would be serious trouble. She couldn't possibly have survived, if she hadn't got rid of them.' Another cabinet minister warned that May's position was precarious, comparing her with Edward Heath, who was forced to resign after calling a snap election in 1974 and watching a winning position evaporate. 'She's got to reach out and widen her circle or end up like Ted Heath. He called an election and lost it and thought he could survive but the anger was much worse on Sunday than it was on Friday. By Monday they were throwing things at his window. You can't go on ruling the country with three people.'

The revolt against the chiefs was not just a reaction to the election result. On the final weekend of the campaign several ministers had contacted the *Sunday Times* to say that, win or lose, Hill and Timothy should have their wings clipped. Upon learning this, a senior figure close to May texted the journalist writing the story to say, 'You should write that Boris, Amber and DD are part of our inner circle.' The message was a calculated snub to Hammond. Instead of focusing on calls for the power of the chiefs to be curtailed, the story fuelled speculation that the chancellor would be sacked in a post-election reshuffle.

Hammond, according to those close to him, had resigned himself to his fate. 'I think he was expecting to get the bullet,' a friend said. 'He's one of these stiff upper lip type people. Doesn't want to show any vulnerability.' In one conversation, the chancellor said, 'Well, I'll leave, I'll go and earn some money.' When a close ally spoke to him the night before the election, the chancellor said wistfully, 'We'll just have to wait and see, won't we?'

Afterwards, Nick Timothy said these reports were overdone. 'Theresa refused to even talk about post-election reshuffles because she thought it was inappropriate, it took things for granted, she wanted to concentrate on the campaign, so that was just never on the cards.'[2] But ministers kept reading that they were going to be sacked and regarded Hill, in particular, as drunk on power. A Downing Street source said that week, 'They slag off Liam Fox. They don't want Justine [Greening] there. They want to move Liz [Truss].' In story after story, Hammond read that he was to be replaced by Amber Rudd.

Colleagues say Timothy had also entertained the idea of breaking up the Treasury and replacing Tom Scholar, the permanent secretary. 'Nick had big plans,' one said. 'They had a longstanding belief that the Treasury had too much control, ever since Theresa was in the Home Office with George [Osborne] announcing policies in her area.' Hammond had heard all these rumours and was determined to put a stop to them. That morning he confronted May. 'He asserted he was bloody fed up of being briefed against by them,' a friend said.

May said, 'It wasn't me. I didn't brief against you,' denying responsibility for the behaviour of the chiefs.

Hammond put her on the spot: 'You were going to sack me, weren't you?' The prime minister implied she had not been about to fire him. Hammond did not explicitly call for Timothy and Hill to be fired but he made clear he was no longer prepared to work with them. May had to choose him or them. The chancellor's main goal, however, was to move the dial on Brexit. He told May that she needed to put jobs first in her Brexit negotiations – a coded rebuke to her pledge to put controls on immigration at the top of her list of priorities. Allies say he made his agreement to stay on at the Treasury 'conditional' on May giving ground. 'We've got to realise that the City is absolutely apoplectic about what's going on,' Hammond said. May could not afford to lose her chancellor, a fatal blow while so weakened, so she agreed. A source close to Hammond said later that week, 'Philip is very keen that these negotiations start on the right foot and that we will put British businesses and jobs first. We can't lose sight of the fact that the economy is the most important thing for people's lives.'

Under extreme stress, May was suffering what people who saw her that Friday describe as a 'personal crisis of confidence'. Timothy and Hill did not appear in Number 10, leaving May alone without political advice. 'There was zero command and control,' a special adviser observed.

Hill's last act before disappearing was to call Craig Woodhouse and say, 'I'm going to ground, can you call the prime minister and sort out some lines, I'm leaving you in charge.' When she made the call, Rob Oxley had gone home to sleep for a couple of hours. When he awoke he found a text from Woodhouse explaining what had happened. Oxley had felt himself frozen out by Hill over the previous week. There was only room for one of them in Number 10 and it was not going to be him. A colleague who saw him shortly afterwards said, 'He looked like Skeletor.' Woodhouse went into Downing Street by the back door, was given a pass and a desk and told to get on with it. Seven weeks earlier he had been a lowly special adviser in the Department of Culture. He was now the senior political spin doctor in the government. Even failed campaigns have winners. When he saw Jojo Penn, who had become a good friend, she confided that the chiefs were sleeping but she was not expecting to see them again in Downing Street.

Into the political vacuum stepped the cabinet secretary, Sir Jeremy Heywood. 'On that Friday morning after the election, the political oper-ation basically disintegrated,' a Number 10 aide said. 'Nick and Fi had gone. At one stage on the Friday there was not a political person in Number 10.' First Jojo Penn and then Chris Wilkins arrived, but they quickly realised they were not running the show. 'What was quite evident at that point was that the civil service had taken over.' Wilkins arrived to find that May was in a meeting with Heywood, Sue Gray, May's new principal private secretary Peter Hill and her official spokesman, James Slack. Wilkins was the head of strategy but he was not invited to join the meeting. 'They'd closed ranks around the PM,' a source said.

One Conservative compared May that day to a recently bereaved relative in a daze, being steered into doing things at the suggestion of others. 'It was a case of sign here, do this, say that. Make a statement, do a deal with the DUP, visit the palace, even though there is no longer any constitutional reason to do so.'

Heywood and the other mandarins regarded it as their duty to ensure the continuity of government. The parliamentary arithmetic meant that only a deal between the Tories and the DUP could deliver a majority in the Commons. From their point of view propping up May was their only viable course of action, even if she was incapable of thinking clearly for herself. At 10.10 a.m. it was announced that the prime minister would visit Buckingham Palace to see the queen at 12.30 p.m. Ten minutes later Downing Street announced that May had secured an agreement with the DUP. In truth, the deal was not finalised, but Gavin Williamson had received indications from the DUP that they were prepared to back the Conservatives in a confidence motion and, equally clearly, the reassurance that Democratic Unionists would never allow Jeremy Corbyn into Downing Street. The Labour leader's IRA sympathies might have done him little harm with much of the electorate, but now they denied him a chance to become prime minister.

The DUP link-up was necessary but hardly desirable for the Tories. Attention quickly focused on the Northern Irish party's opposition to abortion and gay marriage, and the support of some party representatives for creationism. Their links to loyalist paramilitaries were also a gift for Corbyn's supporters. Liam Young, a former Labour parliamentary adviser, tweeted, 'To be fair Theresa May warned of coalition of chaos propped up by extremist terrorist sympathisers. She just didn't say she'd be leading it.' More than 72,000 people 'liked' the tweet.

Strictly speaking, under the terms of the Fixed Term Parliaments Act, May did not need to go to Buckingham Palace at all. She remained prime minister until she resigned or was forced out after a vote of no confidence. But her advisers recognised that half the battle in moments of constitutional tension was to look and behave like a prime minister. Driving to the palace in her official Jaguar, stalked by news helicopters, was what prime ministers did. The only problem was that May was not looking at all like a prime minister. Shortly before she left for the palace, May once more broke down in tears. The make-up artist who had been called in to help her prepare for her audience had to do May's face again.

The audience cannot have been easy for May, who was returning to her monarch in rather less pomp than when she had last visited the palace to call the election. Royal sources say their encounters were no more enjoyable for the queen. 'It would seem to be the case that in the private audiences between the queen and Mrs May, I don't think the queen finds Mrs May any easier company than anyone else,' confided a source who has discussed the issue with a senior figure in the royal household.

In accounts of the fifteen-minute meeting which reached Whitehall officials, the queen asked May about her deal with the DUP and the prime minister confirmed that she had an arrangement in place. The precise wording of her assurance is not known, but it was delivered bluntly enough to cause irritation later among some courtiers when it took May nearly another three weeks to get the DUP to sign on the dotted line.

As soon as she returned to Downing Street, May marched to the lectern, which had become her security blanket in times of turmoil, to deliver another speech. Her problems began with the opening sentence: 'I have just been to see Her Majesty the Queen and I will now form a government.' The words raised hackles with some in the royal house-hold. A Tory peer commented, 'She said, "I've formed a government," not "the queen has asked me to form a government",' adding that one palace flunky 'was alarmed by her formulation of words'. In fact, the wording had been agreed between Number 10 and royal officials, but not everyone at Buckingham Palace was aware of that.

May's more immediate problem was the tone of the rest of her speech, in which she sought to show that she was back in charge. Wearing a Thatcheresque bright blue two-piece suit, May pledged to move straight to Brexit talks and protect the country after the terror attacks. There was a brief nod to her speech eleven months earlier, optimistically vowing 'over the next five years' to 'build a country in which no one and no community is left behind'. But this was a speech designed to show strength not compassion. 'What the country needs more than ever is certainty, and having secured the largest number of votes and the greatest number of seats in the general election it is clear that only the Conservative and Unionist party has the legitimacy and ability to provide that certainty by commanding a majority in the House of Commons,' she said, before concluding, 'Now, let's get to work.' The speech contained no acknowledgement that the prime minister had called an election in search of an enhanced mandate and received a startling rebuke from the electorate, and certainly no expression of contrition. Of the thirty-three Conservative colleagues who her campaign had condemned to defeat there was not one mention. Watching in Downing Street, one official said, 'My jaw hit the floor because I thought, "She missed it, she forgot to mention the result or the party." I thought: "Fuck!" It was a massive failure.'

The fury of MPs was immediate and pronounced. That afternoon a senior Tory MP told ITV's Robert Peston, 'We all fucking hate her. But there is nothing we can do. She has totally fucked us.'[3] A senior backbencher added, 'Most colleagues want her to go but I think she should dangle – from a rope.' The speech embodied the toxic cocktail of overconfidence and tone-deaf delivery that had cost May her hard-won majority. She appeared to have learned nothing. Garvan Walshe, the researcher hired by the Tory Remainers, spoke for many when he said, 'May's speech [was] utterly tone deaf. Reminds me of Middle Eastern dictators denying street protests outside their palaces.'[4]

In the offices of the *Evening Standard*, George Osborne was having the time of his life. The paper went through four different editions with disparaging headlines about his old foe: 'MAY HUNG OUT TO DRY', 'MAY'S RIGHT ROYAL MESS' after she had visited the palace, 'QUEEN OF DENIAL' after her speech in Downing Street and, finally, 'MAY'S IRISH BAILOUT' when it became clear she was aiming to strike a deal with the DUP. Osborne said, 'I was expecting, like a lot of Conservatives were, a speech in which she acknowledged the election had not gone the way she had hoped, good Conservative colleagues had lost their seats and that she was going to try harder and work together to provide stable government. We heard none of that.'[5]

Afterwards it was claimed that May's speech was the same one she would have delivered in victory, with the addition of two paragraphs on the DUP. In fact, it was written from scratch that morning. While it was typed up by Chris Wilkins, it had been drafted under civil service orders. Wilkins had sat in his office all morning waiting to be called. He was eventually presented with handwritten notes by Peter Hill and James Slack and told to craft a two-minute speech. 'It was a statement basically written by the civil service,' said one Number 10 source. 'They said, "All that matters is that Europe needs to hear a strong message from a strong PM. This is basically not a message to the country. This is a message saying, "We've got a government, we've got a PM."' May had only a short read through of the speech before she delivered it. As ever, she made no changes, apparently unable to see that what was put in front of her was wholly inadequate for the occasion.

Skilled operators elsewhere in Whitehall watched aghast. 'She's not terribly well served,' a special adviser said that day. 'What the fuck was that speech on the doorstep? No contrition, no humility, nothing. Why didn't she challenge that? Why didn't she say, "This is crap"? If I turned in something like that my boss would have gone fucking bonkers. This is why the "Maybot" is so wounding. She just reads out what she's given to read. She has no judgement of her own.'

May's lack of emotional intelligence was reinforced when Stewart Jackson, who lost his seat in Peterborough, revealed that he had received a 'lovely text' from David Cameron – a prime minister to whom he had often been a thorn in the side – but not May. 'I've had nothing from her or the chairman of the Conservative Party, and I think that's quite poor to be honest,' he told Radio 5 Live, before condemning the 'hubris and the arrogance and the bunker mentality' of the May regime. 'You can't really run a government from an ivory tower.'

Seeing the tidal wave of negative reaction, Craig Woodhouse and Tom Swarbrick decided May would have to give another statement to the broadcasters. The collapse of political hierarchy meant they were allowed in to see the prime minister themselves.

The most significant intervention was that of Graham Brady, the chairman of the 1922 Committee. A committed Brexiteer, Brady believed it was better to keep May in place rather than risk a leadership election which might unpick the Lancaster House approach to negotiations. By the time he saw May in her Downing Street office, around 2.30 p.m., Brady had been inundated with messages from MPs urging him to convey their disgust at May's lack of penitence and use his influence to demand the heads of Timothy and Hill.

Brady told May, 'It's important that you stay. I think colleagues will support you,' but urged her to apologise to the party and make 'personnel changes', stressing that it was a 'universal view' that the chiefs had behaved badly. According to another member of the 1922 executive, the chairman made clear that May's scheduled appearance in front of backbenchers the following Monday would be 'a bloodbath' if the chiefs were still in post then. May said, 'As it happens, I'm doing another interview.' She also indicated that the issue with her aides would be resolved.

Shortly after May's meeting with Brady she received a call from Nick Timothy, who said that he was going to leave Downing Street. He told the prime minister that both he and Hill should go. 'I said to Theresa in Conservative Central Office on the Friday morning that I thought it was probable I would have to resign, then I did so over the phone that afternoon,' he said. 'She understood why.'[6] Technically both had already resigned from government to fight the campaign, so there was no need for him to submit a formal resignation letter. They agreed to wait for a day to make the announcement, not least because Hill did not want to leave.

It was 4.30 p.m. when a tired-looking May, her eyes red-rimmed and puffy, recorded a clip for the cameras in the Cabinet Room, saying she would 'reflect on the results' and finally apologising. 'I'm sorry for all those candidates and hardworking party workers who weren't successful, but also particularly sorry for those colleagues who were MPs and ministers who contributed so much to our country and who lost their seats and didn't deserve to lose their seats.'

The last order of business in Downing Street on Theresa May's longest day was to begin a cabinet reshuffle. She called her most senior ministers, starting with Philip Hammond and Amber Rudd, then Boris Johnson, David Davis and Michael Fallon. Johnson pressed for more money for the Foreign Office and more control over aid money. At 5.18 p.m. Downing Street issued another press release saying the big five were all keeping their posts.

It had been a brutal day for the prime minister, but she was still in post. The shock result had scuppered the plans of many. While the Tories began the blame game over a victory that seemed like a defeat, Labour were consumed with recriminations over why a defeat that tasted like victory had not been the real thing.

*   *   *

After a brief nap at home, Jeremy Corbyn went to Labour headquarters at 7.45 a.m. on the Friday morning, where he was greeted by a small crowd of supporters. The leader had a spring in his step. In the war room, LOTO staff on one side of the horseshoe office in their red Jeremy Corbyn T-shirts, Southsiders in dishevelled suits on the other, Corbyn addressed the assembled staff, making a gracious speech about their efforts in the campaign. 'Nobody expected us to do well,' he said. 'We've not quite got there but it was an amazing achievement.'

Iain McNicol, as general secretary, would usually have given a response but he was not there. Karie Murphy stepped in and addressed the permanent party staff: 'You've all seen the result, and you now understand that the country's with us, not with you. It's about time that you all learnt that people really support a champion of equality and social progress.' To the Southsiders 'it came across as a threat'. Corbyn did not step in to call for unity because at that moment his team began chanting, 'Oh Jer-em-eee-Cor-byn.' The Southsiders studied the floor or their smartphones. 'We all found emails we needed to respond to,' one said.

Another incident that soured the atmosphere occurred later that morning when David Prescott confronted John Stolliday and said, 'Thank you for applauding Marsha de Cordova in Battersea.'

Stolliday replied, 'David, I applauded every Labour gain.'

'No you didn't,' Prescott charged. 'I was watching you.'

Another party official said Niall Sookoo was 'boasting' about Corbyn's success in a manner that jarred with some. The campaign had begun with Labour on course for its worst result since 1935 and ended with it increasing its share of the vote by 9.6 per cent, the biggest uptick during a campaign since 1945. Corbyn secured a higher vote share than at any time since Tony Blair's second landslide in 2001. Crucially, Labour was now second in more than fifty seats with majorities of less than 6 per cent, which left the Tories looking over their shoulders and keen to avoid another election. Labour had made net gains of thirty seats and picked up nearly 12.9 million votes. Yet Corbyn's return of 262 seats was the fourth worst in Labour's history, just four more than Gordon Brown had managed in 2010. 'For the professional Southside staff who'd been there for ages, we had lost,' a party official said. 'It was as bad as Gordon Brown. The sense that people were celebrating a defeat was quite hard for a lot of people to take. But it didn't bubble over as I feared it might do because we were expecting much worse. A lot of people going into that night thinking there would be fisticuffs and raised voices and there would be lots of people who you wouldn't have to ever see again.' Sadly for the moderates, the Corbynistas were there to stay.

On social media, Corbyn's followers declared that he had actually won the election and began referring to him as the 'real prime minister', an approach that invited ridicule but reflected the enthusiasm he had generated and the sense of momentum he now enjoyed.

By exceeding expectations, Corbyn's supporters did not need to trigger the 'Save Jeremy' campaign they had been plotting for weeks. Plans for a rally on the Friday at which his young supporters would have demanded he stay were canned. Those who had quietly been drawing up dossiers on Corbyn's greatest opponents in the PLP, like John Woodcock and Jess Phillips, filed them away for the time being. The plan had been to blame a catastrophic defeat on the enemy within, the moderates. 'There was an assumption that it might be negative and we had to plan for the worst,' a source in the leadership said. 'Momentum had a plan ready to go in that eventuality. Unite had a plan ready. It would have made a lot of use of videos of Woodcock and co. They'd have said, "You can't fight with one hand tied behind your back."'

On the other side, Tom Watson parked any intention he might have had of making another speech calling for Corbyn to quit. The trade unions who doubted the leader felt relieved they had not lost their nerve and made their concerns public. Had things turned out differently, the second anti-Corbyn coup would have been under way by lunchtime. 'If the election had gone badly, Watson was going to talk Jeremy down and say "resign" but he wasn't going to stand,' a leading plotter said. 'Unite would have stayed loyal but Watson is close to the GMB,' said a LOTO source. 'It would have been a toss-up over Unison. The general secretary is not Jeremy's biggest fan but a majority of his members are. USDAW and Community would have been against him.' The potential Labour leadership candidates abandoned their launch venues and their speeches calling for a change of direction, while their campaign staff returned to their day jobs. 'They were all ready to go,' said one Southside official. 'When you try to recruit from head office, it's transparent.'

The moderates had what appeared to be a revenge of sorts on Corbyn's team. 'After we all left they axed all the cards for people working on the campaign,' a source in the leadership team said. 'You need a security card to get into Southside. They deactivated them all, including Seumas and Andrew Fisher's. The order came down from Emilie Oldknow that people who don't work there had to clear their desks and go back to LOTO. Milne had to knock to get into Southside.' The Corbynistas believed this was part of the moderate plot to take total control of party headquarters, the equivalent of coup plotters seizing the radio station before ousting the president of a banana republic. In fact, it seems to have been a decision taken by a junior official at an office outside London, who turned off the authorisation of those no longer needing access to Southside.

Corbyn stayed out of these confrontations. That afternoon – no longer encumbered with police protection officers – he walked, as usual, through the Andover estate in Islington to his constituency office. He was followed, Pied Piper-like, by a group of black primary school children shouting, 'Vote Labour!'[7]

Labour's internal squabbles perhaps distracted attention from a concerted effort to stop May being confirmed as prime minister. Emily Thornberry took to the television studios and said that Labour was prepared to put forward its own Queen's Speech and accused May of 'squatting in Downing Street' – a taunt that had been used against Gordon Brown in 2010. But there was little follow-through which could have put Buckingham Palace in a difficult position until a formal deal was secured with the DUP. 'There were no leader's office staff around to talk to about it,' a Labour official said. 'Karie had been drinking in the evening. Seumas wasn't about. There was no one there. At that moment of intense danger for the prime minister, where we could have applied some constitutional pressure, we didn't. Emily went out off her own bat. There was no central thinking about our tactics.'

Labour quickly descended into infighting. Karie Murphy attacked the party directors for adopting a negative outlook at the start of the campaign, without which she claimed the election could have been won. The argument took another turn when demographic data was published that first weekend which showed where the votes were won and lost.

The assertion in the small hours of election night by arch-Blairite John McTernan that the result was 'the young turning out to oppose Brexit a year late' was largely borne out by two huge post-election surveys of more than 50,000 people conducted by YouGov and Lord Ashcroft.

Some 60 per cent of Leave voters backed the Tories while 51 per cent of Remain voters went with Labour, according to Ashcroft's results. Yet while the Tories secured a small swing in seats which backed Leave in the EU referendum, Labour's vote share soared by up to 12 per cent in Remain strongholds – most notably in London. Tory gains in Leave areas were often cancelled out by the nationwide swing to Labour, allowing embattled Labour MPs like Ian Austin in Dudley North and Gloria de Piero in Ashfield to cling on. The Liberal Democrats, despite losing vote share overall, also saw double-digit rises in the most rabidly Remain areas, a factor in four of their five gains from the Conservatives.

Labour's greatest successes came in seats with large volumes of young voters, particularly in university towns like Canterbury, which returned a Labour MP for the first time in two centuries. A House of Commons Library report found that Labour support among the under-thirty-fives had risen by twenty points compared to 2015. YouGov found that age was the single most important determinant of voting intention. Labour led by forty-seven points among first-time voters, while the Tories won the over-seventies by fifty percentage points. For every ten years older a voter was, their chances of voting Conservative rose by nine points. The 'tipping point' age at which someone was more likely to vote Tory was forty-seven. At the start of the campaign this had been thirty-four, a strong indicator of the effectiveness of Corbyn's campaign. The Tories survived thanks to differential turnout. While 57 per cent of eligible teenagers voted, the figure was 84 per cent for the over-seventies.

The power of Labour's pledge to scrap tuition fees turbocharged a deepening educational and cultural divide between liberals with a university education and more conservative school leavers that had been evident after the election two years earlier. Labour won among voters with a degree by seventeen points, while the Tories won by a 22 per cent margin with those who left school at sixteen. It was not just students voting for Corbyn, but their university-educated parents as well. Similarly stark divisions were evident in levels of home ownership. An Ipsos MORI study found that the Tories had won among mortgage holders by twenty-five points, while Labour was ahead by twenty-three points for those renting a home.

The figures which ignited debate in the Labour Party were those showing that class had largely been eliminated as a determinant of voting intention. Neither main party had less than 38 per cent in any social category in YouGov's poll. Labour gained ground with middle-class AB voters but trailed the Conservatives by seven points among C2 skilled manual workers, suggesting Corbyn's popularity with metropolitan liberals did not always translate to traditional Labour voters. Conor McGinn, the MP for St Helens South, was one of the moderate MPs concerned by the lack of focus in the manifesto on the working poor. 'The lesson New Labour taught us was that you can't win elections with just the white working class,' he said. 'This election taught us that you can't win without them either.' Michael Dugher, who stood down in Barnsley East, went further, condemning the triumphalism of the Corbynistas. 'They were like the generals of Dunkirk, presenting a self-evident military catastrophe as a PR victory. The last time Labour won an election in 2005, Jeremy Corbyn claimed it was a damning indictment of Tony Blair and his illegal foreign war. Blair got ninety-six seats more than the greatest victory for socialism since the war.'

The Tories had their own frustrations with the white working class. Ashcroft's poll showed May winning 57 per cent of Ukip's 2015 votes, ten points lower than most Conservative strategists had hoped for. A Tory official said, 'The ex-Labour Ukip voters we thought would vote Conservative because of Brexit. Actually, Brexit wasn't about Brexit for them, and Jeremy Corbyn was saying Old Labour things that they liked, and it was enough for them to vote Labour again.'

Quantitatively, May's performance was far from disastrous. She added more than 5 per cent to David Cameron's vote share in 2015, which had given him a surprise majority. But it was only the Tories' performance in Scotland that prevented the party losing the keys to Downing Street.

At the same time there was concern, from George Osborne and others, that May and Timothy had turned the Tories' backs on liberal metropolitan voters. A former minister said, 'Having promised a fundamental realignment to the north, we ended up losing the south, not winning the north and alienating the young, the professional classes, teachers, public servants, the retired and pensioners, and business. Other than that, it was brilliant.'

Nevertheless, it was an election of fine margins. If the Tories had won 533 more votes in nine marginal constituencies Theresa May would have had a majority. Equally, if Corbyn had gained a little over two thousand votes in five seats he might have been able to keep her out of Downing Street altogether.

If both the Tories and Labour had fallen short of their desired outcomes, they had obliterated their smaller rivals. Collectively, the two main parties seized 82.3 per cent of the vote, the highest figure since 1970. It was a factor that was to put the leaders of Ukip and the Liberal Democrats out of business.

Paul Nuttall resigned his disastrous leadership of Ukip at 10.45 a.m. on Friday morning, declaring, 'The new rebranded Ukip must be launched and a new era must begin with a new leader.' During his six months and twelve days in charge, Nuttall had presided over three by-election losses and the collapse of public support. Ukip secured just 1.8 per cent of the vote, more than ten points down and its worst perfor-mance in sixteen years. In 337 of the 378 seats where it fielded a candi-date, the party lost its deposit.

The way was clear for the third leadership contest in the space of a year. Gawain Towler, the party's long-suffering head of press, said, 'I have served under nine UKIP leaders, four of whom were Nigel Farage.'[8]

Tim Farron had steadied the Liberal Democrat ship, presiding over four gains which lifted his party back to twelve seats, though vote share had dipped a little. Farron, though, had had enough. On the Wednesday after the election he announced that he was resigning as well, saying he felt 'remaining faithful to Christ' was incompatible with leading his party. 'To be a political leader – especially of a progressive, liberal party in 2017 – and to live as a committed Christian, to hold faithfully to the Bible's teaching, has felt impossible for me,' he said.

Farron claimed later that he had decided to stand down two weeks before the election but kept the decision to himself. But he also came under pressure to quit from Lib Dems in the House of Lords. 'Some of the peers were a little bit unhappy with our election performance. Tim went to a meeting and the peers had a bit of a moan.' Farron was criti-cised by Liz Barker and Sally Hamwee. Farron emerged from the meet-ing and told his aide Paul Butters, 'Fuck, I don't want to do this any more. I don't need this.' It was just the third time in a decade of working for Farron that Butters had heard him swear. As word spread that the leader was going to resign, Brian Paddick, the party's 'shadow home secretary', who had been told that his job would go to an MP now there were enough of them to fill the major posts, took to Twitter and announced that he was resigning. Paddick, who had once been Britain's most senior gay police officer, said he was quitting because of 'concerns about the leader's views on various issues that were highlighted during the campaign'.

Theresa May spent the weekend telephoning MPs who had lost their seats. 'She was tired,' said one aide. 'She'd stayed up for thirty-six hours. She felt the loss of colleagues' seats personally, she felt personally responsible for that.' This was a common refrain from May's staff, that privately she could show she cared. The lack of empathy was a political problem not a personal one. Some of the calls were difficult. May had helped get Nicola Blackwood elected in Oxford when she was first a candidate. 'It's a target seat that the Maidenhead Association have helped with over the years,' the aide said. 'She was sad for them all.' Edward Timpson, a thoughtful and able minister, lost Crewe and Nantwich by just forty-eight votes. James Wharton lost Stockton South by 888 votes after being ordered by CCHQ to campaign in neighbouring seats where the Tories were trounced. Ben Gummer might have been about to become May's justice secretary had he not lost Ipswich.

One of those rung by May recalled, 'She is not someone who overly emotes, but she was very conscious of the impact that this had personally.'

At 5.14 p.m. on Saturday 10 June, Nick Timothy's resignation became public when the joint chief posted an explanation for his departure on the ConservativeHome website. In it, Timothy acknowledged his regrets over the care policy and his role in the manifesto. But his primary purpose was to open a briefing war with Lynton Crosby over who was to blame for the campaign. 'The reason for the disappointing result was not the absence of support for Theresa May and the Conservatives but an unexpected surge in support for Labour,' Timothy wrote, identifying how some voters were 'tired of austerity' and 'younger people feel they lack the opportunities enjoyed by their parents' generation'. But defending their political project, he went on, 'Ironically, the Prime Minister is the one political leader who understands this division, and who has been working to address it since she became Prime Minister last July. The Conservative election campaign, however, failed to get this and Theresa's positive plan for the future across.' This was an arrow aimed squarely at Crosby. He also took a pot shot at Jim Messina: 'It also failed to notice the surge in Labour support, because modern campaigning techniques require ever-narrower targeting of specific voters, and we were not talking to the people who decided to vote for Labour.'

Fiona Hill's resignation was not announced until a little later. When Timothy called her that morning to say he was going and they should make a joint announcement, Hill said she wasn't ready. Throughout the day there were rumours in Downing Street that she wanted to resign as chief of staff but stay on as May's personal aide. A cabinet minister said, 'The idea was that anyone associated with the manifesto had to go. Nick realised that but Fi wasn't involved with that. In the end I think her capacity to tell people to "fuck off" may have come back to bite her.' Hill eventually released a terse statement to the effect that she was quitting altogether, saying it had been a pleasure to serve in government and work for a such an 'excellent prime minister'. She added, 'I have no doubt at all that Theresa May will continue to serve and work hard as prime minister – and do it brilliantly.' Hill felt she had left May at the mercy of the party's chauvinist snobs who had never rated her. 'It won't be long before the bullies start circulating,' she told a friend.

Martin Selmayr, the Rasputin of Brussels, reacted to the departure of the Rasputin of Downing Street by tweeting a single word, '*Bauernopfer*', a German chess term for a pawn sacrifice. A former cabinet minister predicted that defenestrating the chiefs would not save May: 'King Charles I's adviser Strafford was his most effective lieutenant but he had to be sacrificed and that left him defenceless. Theresa will be less effective without them.'

Hill fled to Switzerland and then New York to decompress, telling friends the only way she could cope with what had happened to her was not to talk about it. Timothy wrote a longer piece for the *Spectator* on what had gone wrong, which concluded, 'At times like these, you find out who your true friends are … The biggest lesson … has been a reminder of the importance of friends, family and love.' Timothy had separated from his fiancée Nike before the election but had a new relationship to sustain him with Georgia Berry, the energy adviser in the Number 10 policy unit.

With one author of the manifesto cast out, May contemplated bringing back the other to replace him. When MPs got wind of the possibility that Ben Gummer might become chief of staff, there was a revolt. 'A load of us texted and said, "Over our dead bodies …"' stated an MP. A minister added, 'She wanted Gummer – totally politically oblivious. There's no way he could have come in after the manifesto.'

May turned instead to another minister who had lost his seat. Gavin Barwell, who had been tipped for the cabinet, was steeped in Tory politics having held a range of posts in the party and Parliament. Having fought a marginal seat he also knew about hard work. 'He's there at five in the morning,' a Downing Street colleague said. 'He literally has done every job and he's done it really well. He can look anybody in the party in the eye: councillor, whip, adviser, marginal candidate, chief executive, and say, "I know how you feel."'

Barwell's first move was to gather all the special advisers from across Whitehall in Number 10 at 8 a.m. on Monday morning. He said, 'The people in this room did a good job because we went into the general election with a sustained poll lead for ten months. So you can't have got everything wrong. I'm here to learn from you about what worked well and what didn't.' The contrast with his predecessors did not need stating. 'He's been very collaborative from the beginning and it's hugely appreciated,' a colleague said.

While Barwell was finding his feet, the civil service effectively ran Theresa May's reshuffle. Some of the political staff felt that the prime minister should still conduct wide-ranging changes in the middle ranks of the cabinet, but the same mandarins who had sent her into the street with an ill-judged speech counselled caution. 'Over the course of that weekend it was the civil service which decided what the cabinet reshuffle was going to be,' a political aide said. 'The message was stability. She was away with civil servants all the time.' On this occasion their advice not to antagonise an already enraged cabinet was probably sound.

The degree of civil service control became apparent when Chris Wilkins was called in on Sunday to help May plan for her meeting with the 1922 Committee the following day. When Wilkins went to May's office he found Peter Hill, Sue Gray and the other private secretaries gathered around a whiteboard on which the reshuffle was being drawn up. He was ushered out and the door was closed. For Wilkins, this was the final straw. He had seen his election strategy ignored and been frozen out of the campaign. He was no longer prepared to see decisions made without him. Drained and emotional, he stormed out, agreeing to take a few days off to think about his future. Another official in Number 10 that weekend said, 'The machine has done its impressive machine-ness. It's taken complete control as it does in these situations.'

Many of May's promotions would have delighted the civil service. She briefly considered asking William Hague to return as deputy prime minister but then gave Damian Green, the work and pensions secretary, Ben Gummer's job in the Cabinet Office with the added title of 'first secretary of state', a post which Hague had held under David Cameron. Green had been at Oxford with May. His wife, Alicia Collinson, had been May's tutorial partner. The prime minister was circling the wagons with people she trusted. There were promotions too for David Gauke, who replaced Green, and David Lidington, who took over as justice secretary from Liz Truss, who in turn replaced Gauke as chief secretary to the Treasury. Green, Gauke and Lidington were all sober, intelligent, low-key Remainers. More importantly, none of them had designs on May's job.

To placate the Eurosceptics, May played the only ace in her back pocket. With almost all the changes made, the call went out to Surrey Heath where Michael Gove had just finished lunch with friends. It was 4.45 p.m. when the Downing Street switchboard connected May's diary secretary to the former secretary of state for justice she had fired eleven months earlier, with the instruction that he should demonstrate 'loyalty' if he hoped to return. Gove's *Times* column had steered clear of criticising May and in recent months he had been in touch with the chiefs about ways that he might be helpful. Now he jumped in the car and headed for Westminster.

'As I started to drive I thought, "There's no vacancy. Maybe this is a wind-up,"' Gove recalled. 'The phone went once more. It was switch. The prime minister's diary secretary came on and said, "I'm afraid there's been a cycle race around Downing Street so you can't park near here. Could you please drive to a tube station then get the Underground and you will be met in the underpass between Westminster tube and Whitehall on the Treasury side by a civil servant who will then take you into 70 Whitehall." I thought this was a massive wind-up. Dom Joly has been rehired to do *Trigger Happy TV* and I will walk through the underpass and there will be a giant inflatable red box and they will say, "Gotcha." When I did come out of the underpass and saw this very nice assistant private secretary from Downing Street with the two official phones I thought, "Maybe it is real."'

As he was entering the Cabinet Office, Gove was spotted by Kate McCann of the *Telegraph*, who tweeted the news. Gove's wife, Sarah

Vine, saw the tweet and called him to say, 'Where are you, are you in Chobham?'

'No,' came the reply, 'I'm in Number 10 Downing Street and I'm due to see the prime minister shortly.'

Before the election, there had been no great hope among Gove's allies that he would be offered a lifeline. A senior backbencher said, 'We're not expecting her to give Michael a job because she's got everything else wrong. Why would she get that right?' With few options, May asked Gove to become environment secretary, a job with endless Brexit complexities. Part of the delay had been trying to shift Andrea Leadsom to Lidington's old post as leader of the Commons, but without full cabinet rank. David Davis's former special adviser James Chapman was to call her 'the dimmest bulb in the cabinet'. Nonetheless Leadsom held out for several hours, threatening to resign unless she was promoted to home secretary or foreign secretary. Fearful that her former rival might spark a leadership challenge, May placated her with offers of a more prominent media role.[9]

Social media erupted with glee that Gove would now be the minister responsible for protecting fields of wheat from marauding vicars' daughters. If Boris Johnson was bruised by the return of his old foe he didn't show it, quickly taking to Twitter to proclaim, 'It's a GOVErnment of all the talents. Welcome back to Michael!'

May's other gambit was to bring in Steve Baker as minister of state at DExEU, replacing David Jones. Other members of the European Research Group, including Anne-Marie Trevelyan, were made parliamentary private secretaries. It looked like an attempt to silence some of the most prominent sceptics.

The changes at DExEU were among the most controversial. George Bridges, concerned at the slow progress of preparations, had resigned the weekend before the election. Crucially, David Davis had no idea that Jones was being fired and the Welshman was given no explanation when he was summoned to May's Commons office. Jones thanked May for the opportunity to serve and then there was a long pause. 'Well, is that it?' Jones asked, the condemned man politely enquiring of the firing squad.

'Yes, yes, that's it really,' May said, features drawn, her body visibly sagging.

On the way out, Gavin Barwell told Jones, 'I thought you handled that very well. It's very difficult for her, you know.'

Jones, who felt the process had been difficult for him too, immediately rang Davis, who was stunned: 'I don't believe it! I've lost half the department.' Davis had been deprived of two of his four ministers less than two weeks before he was due to start formal negotiations. 'It was a very odd decision,' another minister said. 'David Jones had cultivated a massive number of personal relationships in Europe. I don't think Theresa understands the extent to which personal relationships are vitally important in this process.' It was not the first time that charge had been laid.

Knowing that her leadership was on the line, May faced two further ordeals – a grilling by her MPs and first by her cabinet. Freed from what some had seen as a tyrannical regime under 'the terrible twins', cabinet ministers used their first meeting since the election as a truth and reconciliation commission.

'Sajid Javid was the first to stick a knife in,' one of those present said. The communities secretary confronted May, telling her, 'Prime Minister, your problems didn't begin when we called the election. They began the day you became prime minister and you appointed these two people. Your chiefs of staff and their behaviour cost us this election.' Javid wagged his finger while May sat, downcast, contemplating the table, her arms crossed in front of her as if she was hugging herself. 'When you should have broadened contributions, you narrowed things because of them.' Javid then rounded on Nick Timothy's economic agenda. 'One of the abiding lessons of this election result, is that we didn't talk about our fundamental strength, which is the economy. Now is an opportunity to dump all those anti-business policies that we had in our manifesto.'

Two months earlier, Javid's intervention would have been tantamount to political suicide, but now his colleagues saw it as brave. 'There was this intake of breath with people thinking, "How the fuck is he going to get away with all that?"' a witness recalled. 'But then it is about throwing the first stone. Once they see that it has landed the rest of them all got involved.' Afterwards Javid was inundated with texts praising him for speaking out.

Philip Hammond weighed in, criticising the failure to project a coherent economic message – and by implication the failure to use himself. He made the point, 'We can never outspend Labour and we shouldn't try.' The chancellor provided a 'forensic analysis' without emotion, analysing what had gone wrong and what processes needed to change to make the cabinet function better. 'It was like getting a view from McKinsey or PWC,' a source present said.

Andrea Leadsom, who did not usually say much but perhaps sensed that another leadership election might be around the corner, asserted herself, complaining that while May had repeatedly claimed it was a Brexit election, she had never said what Brexit was actually for. At least that is what her colleagues thought she was saying. One confided, 'The only person who said anything that was nonsensical was Andrea Leadsom, who never says anything that makes any sense ever.' Damian Green made the same point: 'We called an election about a single subject and had nothing new to say on it.'

May apologised for the election result but her loss of authority was palpable as every single minister spoke, a trend that would be repeated in the weeks ahead. On this occasion Boris Johnson was muted and Patrick McLoughlin, who had defied all logic to remain as party chairman, made an upbeat intervention, hailing the seats where the party had done unexpectedly well. At his first meeting back, Michael Gove sought to make a joke: 'I can't believe England is having a Conservative government foisted upon it by Scottish Conservative MPs.' It would normally have brought the house down but it was too soon. Gove's gag was greeted with silence. 'He turned up like a naughty schoolboy and no one would talk to him,' a witness recalled.

May and her political team consulted the two Gavins, Barwell and Williamson, as well as her PPS George Hollingbery, ahead of the 1922 Committee meeting on Monday evening. When May entered committee room 14 she was greeted with the muted banging of desks and what one correspondent listening at the door outside likened to 'a low rumble of approval ... akin to a herd of elephants running from an ivory trader'.[10] Barely looking at her hand-scribbled notes, she said, 'I have been a servant of the Conservative Party since I was stuffing envelopes as a child,' vowing to do what was best for the party.

The prime minister offered her MPs both an apology and a contract: 'I am the one who got us into this mess and I'm going to get us out of it. I will serve as long as you want me.' When the questions went on, Graham Brady intervened to ask if May had time to answer more and she replied, 'Don't worry, I told you I had changed.' It defused a lot of the tension. Most MPs left impressed that May was contrite and had agreed to take a more consensual approach than before. Heidi Allen, the MP for

South Cambridgeshire, said, 'I saw an incredibly humble woman who knows what she has to do, and that is be who she is and not what this job had turned her into. She has lost her armadillo shell and we have got a leader back.'

After the meeting David Davis had an approach from four of the MPs who had been urging him to run for leader over the weekend, telling him he was right to urge caution. He had gone public to call the plotting 'self-indulgent' because he feared it would lead to an election the Tories would lose. 'Destabilising the party at this time is madness,' he said. By the end of the week, some of them were plotting against May.

With Corbyn's allies predicting an election by Christmas, Tory MPs had effectively concluded that a bad prime minister was better than no prime minister. As one MP put it, 'Theresa has finally entered into coalition with her own party.'

Having come under fire for the election campaign, May now faced a second pincer movement – this time from ministers who wanted to exploit her weakness to reopen the approach to Brexit. On that Monday, the prime minister received Ruth Davidson in Downing Street. The leader of the Scottish Tories explained that she saw the election result as a repudiation of the hard Brexit position outlined by May in the Lancaster House speech. Afterwards she said she was pushing for an 'open Brexit', and 'I do think that there can be changes in the offer of Brexit as we go forward.'

Davidson, like Hammond before her, found May unwilling to admit that her Brexit stance had cost her seats. 'There was no acknowledgement from the top that that was the case,' a senior Conservative said. 'There was just no idea in the very early days post-election that anything was different and that failure to show a bit of movement would not only leave the country judging us, but would also leave the party vulnerable to a split.'

May had felt under fire for three days from the most prominent Remain campaigners in the Conservative Party. Nicky Morgan, who she had fired as education secretary, was already predicting her demise: 'It's fairly clear that Theresa May cannot lead us into another general election.'

George Osborne was also to the fore. The leader column in Friday's *Evening Standard* had branded May 'in office but not in power', the same devastating charge that Norman Lamont had once levelled at John

Major. It also called for May to 'rethink the hard Brexit' and remain in the single market and the customs union. 'Out of the chaos of last night, some sanity might emerge.' That Sunday, Osborne put in one of the most memorable performances ever seen on a televised newspaper review. 'Theresa May is a dead woman walking,' he said. 'It's just a case of how long she is going to remain on death row. We could easily get to the middle of next week and it all collapses for her … You've got the prime minister, who's supposed to have won the election, in hiding.'

Behind the scenes a powerful group of liberal Conservatives were working together, including the two previous Conservative prime ministers, David Cameron and Sir John Major. Cameron had privately become an advocate of the 'Norway plus' option, keeping the UK in the single market via membership of the European Economic Area (EEA) for the duration of any transition period. The circle included Osborne, Davidson, Amber Rudd and Andrew Feldman, who had been Cameron's party chairman. 'There were lots of conversations that were flying around involving not just current members of cabinet and political cabinet but also people who had been involved in the recent past and previous leaders, plural,' said one source involved in the talks.

The conversations were not confined to EU affairs. The party liberals also wanted a leadership candidate lined up in case May threw in the towel. 'In the first few days, when it wasn't clear whether Theresa would stay or go, there were a lot of conversations that they were all involved in,' the source said. One thing they were all agreed on was that a candidate must be found to take on Boris Johnson and David Davis. 'It was the stop Boris show,' a former Number 10 official said. That weekend Osborne told political friends, 'Boris Johnson will never be leader of the Conservative Party.'

Cameron was also 'having conversations about what comes next'. He and Osborne regarded Davidson and Amber Rudd – both of whom had been handed big roles in the televised debates during the referendum – as protégés best placed to lead the party in future.

An effort was made by former ministers and MPs to see if Davidson was prepared to run. She was the one success story of election night, and with her pugnacious wit and playful aggression with the media was strong in all the areas May was weak. On the downside, she was not in Parliament and had never been in government. One figure who knew her well said Davidson changed her mind about whether she wanted to be leader 'every other day'. And there were moments after 8 June when she wished she had stood for Parliament. Later that month, a close ally said, 'If she'd won a seat I think she would already be prime minister and part of her thinks that too.' The same might also have been true of Osborne if he had kept his seat, but in a friend's words, 'He stepped off the rollercoaster.'

Davidson was cold-eyed about the prospect of making the move, which would have required her to fight and win a by-election against the thunderous noise of Eurosceptics convinced she was coming to overturn the EU referendum result. 'It won't be David [Davis] and it won't be Boris but it won't be me either,' she told one Westminster figure who urged her to throw her hat in the ring. 'It's not just that I don't want it. It's that it can't be done. You can't have someone who's not in the House of Commons and you can't have someone who's never been in the House of Commons being PM. You can't have somebody who's not done a big job take over at a time of national crisis. It's preposterous.' A friend of Davidson said, 'Can you imagine the by-election? Nigel Farage standing against her to stop Brexit being watered down, half the parliamentary party in revolt, then the actual leadership election.'

There was calculation, too, in Davidson's coyness. One source familiar with her approach said, 'Why would she want to come down and be the leader that splits the party and didn't have the parliamentary party behind her and had to do the hard yards to demonstrate that she had something about her? Why would she want to do that whilst having a by-election at the tail end of a fag-end government that is diving south anyway?' A cabinet minister said, 'Ruth will be prime minister. Her time will come. If she were an MP she absolutely would be the game-changing leader we need.'

The group came to the conclusion that Amber Rudd would be their candidate, despite her wafer-thin majority. A former cabinet minister said, 'I had a conversation with Amber to say, "Is this something you have been thinking about? Are you interested?" This was at the time when we thought something would happen pretty quickly. She was clearly eyeing the top job but trying to do it in a way that didn't attract any attention. She said, "I'm definitely interested in doing it and let's have a chat about it."'

A well-connected Cameroon said that Feldman would put his fund-raising machine at Rudd's disposal when the time came. Kate Fall,

Cameron's deputy chief of staff, was also said to be supportive. 'Feldman will get her the money when she needs it,' the source said. They concluded that the tiny majority should not terminate her hopes. There was even the suggestion that Lynton Crosby might be prepared to abandon his longstanding support for Boris Johnson to help Rudd. One of Rudd's former parliamentary staff had gone to work for CTF Partners, Crosby's firm, and the home secretary had hired him to do some polling in Hastings.

Stephen Gilbert, who had fought more campaigns than almost anyone else, told one of the plotters that Rudd would actually be likely to increase her majority if she was prime minister. Another senior figure in CCHQ said, 'On this Westminster decision that it can't be Amber because she's got a narrow majority – we kept hearing Corbyn can't win. We've got to start challenging these Westminster logical assumptions. She was highly convincing during the campaign.'

The liberal Tories agreed they would fight for a softer Brexit and make sure they were ready to run Rudd if May stumbled. 'The grey suits aren't just on the 1922 Committee,' one said. It soon looked as if they would need to be ready fast. If May stayed, Rudd was determined to support her. She did not think any Remainer would be elected by the Tory grass-roots prior to Brexit.

On Wednesday 14 June, the prime minister's leadership was engulfed in a crisis that – at her moment of maximum weakness – cruelly exposed again her personal shortcomings and the poor political judgement of the civil servants who had filled the vacuum caused by the disintegration of the Downing Street political operation.

At fourteen minutes after midnight the London Fire Brigade was called to Grenfell Tower, a residential block in Kensington, West London, to attend a fridge fire on the fourth floor. Firefighters thought they had put out the fire but then the flames caught on the exterior cladding of the block and spread with frightening speed up the outside of the building. Within half an hour the entire tower was engulfed in flames and a thick shroud of black smoke, punctuated by the sound of exposed gas pipes exploding. In scenes like those from a horror film, more than two hundred and fifty firefighters and seventy fire engines battled the blaze, fire crews in breathing equipment being driven back from the upper floors by the intense heat and falling debris. Residents, who were told to remain in their flats, dialled their loved ones to say goodbye. Two mothers threw their children from the windows to people waiting below. Three others jumped to their deaths rather than be burned alive. Only at 4.14 a.m. did the Metropolitan Police urge the crowd waiting below to tell their friends to evacuate by any means possible. For many it was too late. At least eighty people were presumed dead.

The inferno was more than an avoidable tragedy. It was also a perfect political storm in the febrile atmosphere after the general election. The combination of dozens of impoverished people, many of them immigrants, dead in a council tower in London's richest borough while a clueless Conservative council lost control of its own streets was catnip for the Corbynistas. There was much for the protesters who stormed Kensington Town Hall the following afternoon to protest about.

It soon emerged that a residents' group, the Grenfell Action Group, had repeatedly written blogs highlighting safety concerns – the fire extinguishers with 'condemned' written on them, the lack of sprinklers, the single entrance and exit, the corridors clogged with old mattresses – and the refusal of Kensington and Chelsea Tenant Management Organisation (KCTMO) to engage. In November 2016, the group had warned, 'only a catastrophic event will expose the ineptitude and incompetence' of KCTMO. After the fire, the new cladding and insulation on the building – which residents claimed was to make it look nicer for those in the more expensive parts of the borough – was shown to be flammable and liable to emit toxic fumes.

In the midst of Britain's worst ever fire disaster, the response from Kensington Council and the government was equal parts defensive and sluggish. It was two days before Downing Street announced a £5 million fund for those who had lost their homes, four before a new disaster management team was despatched to West London to replace the overwhelmed local authority. The finger of blame also pointed to Downing Street. A review into fire safety had been delayed for four years by the previous housing minister – Gavin Barwell, May's new chief of staff.

In normal circumstances it would have been difficult for a prime minister to perfectly calibrate a response to such events. Exhausted and lacking confidence, May allowed herself to be guided down what seemed like a path that would protect her from the political fallout. Instead it would put her premiership in its greatest peril. When the prime minister visited the scene, she met police and firefighters but did not go to see the victims or the residents of the community affected and blocked any media access. The Maybot was back at the worst possible moment. Jeremy Corbyn was accompanied by the cameras as he hugged people affected at a makeshift refuge centre set up in a church. One woman he met said, 'Theresa May was here but she didn't speak to any of us. She was shit.' Had the general election been held a week later, there seems little doubt Corbyn would have won it. Only the Conservative press complained when the Labour leader reverted to type by calling for properties to be 'requisitioned' in the rich areas of the borough to house the homeless.

The police had told Number 10 there would be security issues if May met the residents. The safety-first approach was endorsed by her private office civil servants. The prime minister and her staff should have overruled them all. An aide recalled, 'She did not meet anyone who survived because the civil service said, "You've got to go, but the least risky thing to do is to go and meet the emergency services." It was the lack of any real political input to that process that led to what happened.' David Cameron's aides, so often vilified by May's team, watched unbelieving that May could be so inept. 'The police always tell you not to do stuff,' one said. 'Sometimes you have to do it anyway.' May looked scared, callous and incompetent. 'There's such a vacuum at the heart of Number 10 with Nick and Fi gone,' a special adviser said that week. 'Everyone there is knackered, new or under-resourced.'

To make matters worse, Andrea Leadsom visited the scene and, in a television clip, claimed she was representing Parliament in her new role as leader of the Commons. She asserted that Number 10 were aware of her plans. To that, a Downing Street press officer said simply, 'That is a total lie.' Leadsom's friends said she was actively contemplating running for leader again.

For many Tory MPs Grenfell was the final straw. A minister who had backed May for the leadership said, 'She can't handle human adversity very well because she doesn't really do people. This is our Dunblane. We're despised. We look like a bunch of puny shits at the moment.'

Just as bad was the sense that problems were following May around. 'It's feeling a bit Gordon Brown, where everything is just going wrong,' a prominent backbencher complained. 'I think this inferno could be the fuse that lights a political tinder keg that will burn all summer,' a lapsed loyalist said. 'I've seen the end of Thatcher, I've seen the end of Major,

I've seen the end of Blair. When people start to look at plane crashes, terrorist attacks and burning towers as symptomatic of governmental failure, you're in real trouble.'

Tory grassroots members began bombarding their MPs with criticism of the prime minister. They remembered when she had warned them they were seen as 'the nasty party'; now she was the one making them appear nasty. 'I've got moderate, serious members texting me saying you've got to get rid of her quickly because every time she appears she's making the party more toxic,' a Midlands MP said.

'Grenfell was a critical moment,' a ministerial aide added. 'She had got rid of Nick and Fiona, which was a good thing, but could she make decisions on her own? It showed she couldn't. She was Home Office to the core. She took the advice of officials rather than follow her gut. Cabinet ministers were frustrated and very angry and said, "We can't give her too many more lives."' A sober member of the 2010 intake added, 'It's reaching a stage where one more mistake like this and people will say this can't carry on. She just wants to be behind the door of Number 10 and not talk to anyone.'

Gavin Williamson, Julian Smith and the other whips began a frantic ring-round of MPs, reminding them that any move against the prime minister would lead to chaos, an election and a Corbyn government. But May's authority was in freefall, fuelled by concerns sweeping Parliament that she was no longer in the right frame of mind to lead.

Downing Street staff worried that Philip May was much more in evidence than usual that first week, hovering like a concerned carer in the background. 'He would come down to the office with her in the morning,' an aide said. 'He is one of those few people that she trusts and has any sort of feel for. She looked fucked, she looked tired and I don't think she was thinking straight.'

That Wednesday, May addressed all the staff in the pillared room on the first floor of 10 Downing Street. 'I just want to thank you all for looking after me for a year at Number 10,' she said. 'I really wanted to say how much Philip and I have appreciated it. And when I came back through the door Friday morning when you all greeted me …' That was when her voice caught. One of those watching said, 'I thought, "Fucking hell, are we going to get the PM blubbing in front of the entire Downing Street staff – from the chief of staff down to the custodians, everybody is going to see this." She pulled herself back.'

Some of those watching believed the prime minister was in no fit state to carry on. 'If anything comes along that has got any weight to it at all it will finish her off,' a Number 10 official said that week. 'She has not got the physical resilience to be able to do it. Which means we aren't going to get anyone who is able to make a straight decision. As we saw in the campaign, when she doesn't know what to do she only relies upon those two people.'

By the end of the week, a senior political appointee had decided enough was enough and sought to get help for May. 'By Friday, she was absolutely beaten, grey skinned. There was no brightness in her eye and there normally is, even if she is having a really hard time. I've seen people with shellshock and she looked worse than that.' A still-loyal cabinet minister agreed. 'She was shellshocked but determined – less bouncy, less in your face, not as completely in control as she normally is.'

The Number 10 official began phoning friends and even former Downing Street colleagues trying to devise a psychological support plan for the prime minister. 'This is cruel, this will break her in two. People who have had that amount of bruising find it really difficult to recover themselves,' he warned. The aide suggested to Gavin Barwell that he could get a member of the SAS to speak to her about 'resilience'. He said, 'I can get you former special forces commanders, I can get you people who have really been in crunching encounters who can give the boss some advice to keep her on track – because they will realise it is in the national interest to keep her on track and keep her going.' The offer was not taken up.

May was still haemorrhaging staff. On Monday 19 June, first John Godfrey and then Chris Brannigan were summoned to see the prime minister. Brannigan sat down, expecting to talk about how they could salvage the China trade trip, preparations for which had been derailed by the election, and said, 'Prime Minister, I am delighted that you are looking better today.' May looked nonplussed. 'Chris, you know your contract ends when the election is called, and I have decided not to renew it.'

Minutes earlier John Godfrey had been dismissed as head of the policy unit. May's aides had concluded that 'it didn't really work' and that he had been 'a bit overwhelmed by it'. The same day Will Tanner, Godfrey's deputy, who remained close to Timothy, decided he was leaving too.

Brannigan was stunned. He told colleagues that May did not even thank him for his service. When he queried the decision with Gavin Barwell he was told, 'The truth is the decisions to replace you all were made before I arrived, they were made before the election.' The chiefs had struck from beyond their own political graves.

With May undergoing a personal crisis and Downing Street apparently falling apart, there now began a concerted plot to force May out and install a caretaker prime minister.

THE FOUR HORSEMEN

To the target of the approach it probably appeared like an innocent encounter. The Conservative MP bumped into a colleague in the corridor in one of the darker corners of the Palace of Westminster. After a few well-chosen platitudes designed to put the 'mark' at ease, the MP raised the subject of the prime minister. 'She's got to fight on, hasn't she? The alternative is far worse. The last thing we need is a leadership election.' The MP waited for the response, nerves jangling. There was a pause. The target of the enquiry looked over their shoulder. The MP's pulse quickened. His friend seemed to shrink back into the shadows. Confident they were not being watched, the second MP said, 'She's lost all authority. I don't see how we can go on like this for much longer. There's no way she can fight the next election.'

'How interesting,' said the MP who had initiated the conversation, before remembering an urgent appointment. When he was out of sight, he phoned a former cabinet minister, said, 'You should talk to him,' and gave the name of the MP who was wavering.

The whole chat was an example of 'false coat trailing', a tactic developed in Cold War spy recruitment operations. The first MP was testing the loyalties of the second by pretending to back May. The target was thought to be sympathetic to the cause of removing May but the plotters had to be sure. You can't be too careful when you are trying to bring down a prime minister. Some MPs had a habit of telling people what they thought they wanted to hear. Others were thought to be offering themselves as co-conspirators so they could report back to the whips' office on what the plotters were planning.

The plot began in the aftermath of the Grenfell Tower tragedy. Four former cabinet ministers started to have conversations. They did not all meet together, that would be too provocative. But they all talked and agreed that May was finished and could not fight the 2022 election. The only thing to be determined was the time and manner of her departure. They agreed they would sound out MPs about whether they were prepared to sign a joint letter calling on the prime minister to quit.

The lead plotter – who was flushed out three months later as Grant Shapps, David Cameron's party chairman – outlined a plan to his colleagues which would see them recruit more than forty backbenchers and then gather a party of 'men and women in grey suits' to visit May ahead of the party conference in October. The core plotters had all served in the cabinet and saw no route back to preferment while May remained in Downing Street. Shapps had long been at daggers drawn with the Mayites. He had banned Nick Timothy and Stephen Parkinson from the candidates' list. May had dismissed him as international development minister in her great cull of the Cameroons. Shapps believed that if he had not done so, Timothy would have been an MP and unavailable as chief of staff. He told one friend, 'I feel slightly responsible for the mess the country has got itself in. He couldn't have written that appalling manifesto and presumably wouldn't have fucked up the election.' Downing Street later named David Jones, Cameron's Welsh secretary and a Brexit minister fired by May, as one of the conspirators.[1] He was a devoted ally of David Davis. Shapps also talked to George Osborne and discussed the plan with Andrew Mitchell, who had run Davis's 2005 leadership campaign. Mitchell hated 'the Westminster mob', having been forced to resign as chief whip in 2012 after apparently referring to a Downing Street policeman as a 'fucking pleb'. Mitchell said he was 'not a letter writer', but according to MPs he funnelled potential conspirators to Shapps, who employed five 'runners' to drum up support in the tea rooms and bars.

'After the election, she did the minimum, which was to sack her chiefs of staff,' one of those involved said. 'I gave her a bit of space. Grenfell then happened, and the follow-up was so poor that I reached the point of feeling that it may well be untenable for her to try to struggle through to Brexit in 2019. That she may need to go sooner. The challenge then was to see what kind of support there was, for doing something sooner rather than later.'

After a few days of sidling up to colleagues and having coffees in Portcullis House, the four former cabinet ministers compared notes. The

mood music was encouraging. MPs had been shocked by May's disastrous performance over the Grenfell inferno. 'The support for a change
was almost universal,' one MP said. 'Any common-sense person would
look at the results of the election and say there's a price for massively
underperforming, leading us into this mess and having our colleagues
lose their seats. The vast majority – three-quarters – of the backbenchers
believe that. But it's one thing, to say and believe that, and the next thing
is: are you prepared to do anything about it?'

Under Conservative Party rules, the only way to oust a reluctant
leader by force was for 15 per cent of the parliamentary party to send a
letter demanding a vote of no confidence to the chairman of the 1922
Committee, Graham Brady. After the election that meant forty-eight
MPs would have to agree. The plotters did not want to pursue the formal
route. It would lead to a bloody confrontation for May. Better to show
the strength of the rebels in private and offer her a way out.

'A less formal route would be perhaps to have twenty-five people,
perhaps the former cabinet ministers, go to see the leader and say, "Time
is up, and here are another twenty people who believe the same thing.
You can't really not listen to us, and we would like to give you space to
have the dignity of naming the process for your departure."' If May
refused to stand down, 'we would need to go to the newspapers, with
perhaps a joint letter or article,' one conspirator explained.

One of those approached to join the conspiracy said, 'They wanted
people to start thinking about writing letters and giving interviews
saying, "Things have to change." They wanted to create a rolling campaign
where one person went public and then another person would go public.'

Some of those involved did not trust the executive of the 1922
Committee. Brady had made clear publicly that he wanted May to stay
on. His executive was dominated by hard Brexiteers, who saw the prime
minister as the guarantee that the Remainers in cabinet could not water
down the proposals outlined at Lancaster House. 'Graham gave every
impression of accepting letters from anyone plotting against Cameron
with great alacrity,' one MP explained. 'But I think if we'd written to him
demanding the end of May those letters might have been filed in the
nearest waste paper basket.'

The plotters were determined to run a professional operation. They
remembered Boris Johnson's leadership campaign the year before, where
campaign chiefs belatedly discovered that some MPs thought to be

committed to Johnson had not been properly nailed down. 'With Tory MPs you don't need to double check, you need to triple check. Unlike the Boris list, which was a random conversation in the tea room, everyone was checked, cross-checked, approached in different ways to check that's what they really believe,' one former minister said. When Mitchell suggested that fifty MPs wanted May out, Shapps concluded he was too quick to 'tick a yes'.[2]

Another of the four former cabinet ministers was employed as 'the convincer', to go in and push the wavering MPs over the line to join the rebellion. 'People need leadership and to be led, and so there is also a role for one of our number who says, "I think your perspective is wrong. We do need to act now." You have to take a combination of approaches.' Most of the conversations took place in Portcullis House, in MPs' offices and the Despatch Box coffee bar in the atrium below. 'Those tables saw a lot of business done,' the source said. 'You kind of can ask people the same question from different angles, or present the polar opposite perspective, just lightly, and see what they come back with.'

It was a highly time-consuming enterprise. MPs had to be taken on a journey, like an espionage agent being wooed, from disillusionment to recruitment. There was something of the psychiatrist–patient relationship. 'You need to have that conversation in enormous detail,' a former minister said. 'You need to have a conversation where people come to you and say, "You know what, I don't think there is any future here." That is not a two-second thing. Usually that's an hour-long coffee. It's quite a detailed process where they're telling you rather than the other way around.'

After each conversation the conspirators reported back to Shapps, the sole keeper of The List. Some of those involved supported the claims to the crown of David Davis, others of Boris Johnson. Shapps kept an open mind. The important thing, from his perspective, was to gain a consensus on the need to move on from May. One MP compared the effort to 'gathering support for the EU referendum' by getting the support of both Remainers and Brexiteers, Davisites and Johnsonians. 'You need to sign people up on the basis of: Theresa is definitely not the person, there are better people out there.'

Nonetheless, one of the four former cabinet ministers at the heart of the signature gathering was adamant that Davis was aware of his activities and did not seek to urge him to stop. The MP claimed that Davis's

closest allies in Parliament suggested names of those who might be interested. The Brexit secretary was not plotting to bring down May, but he
was aware that others were testing the waters and if the job was to
become free he was determined to ensure that it was his. 'His concern
was to make sure there would be a serious alternative available, as well
as this possibly being his last opportunity to do the job,' a senior plotter
said. 'All I know is that if the opportunity arose for a leadership election,
he would be one of the candidates. He's not spoken to me about reining
it in or not reining it in.' Davis was not informed about the numbers or
the identity of those who were prepared to sign the letter. Another of the
former cabinet ministers said, 'He was careful never to have his finger-
prints anywhere near it but he has kept in touch with what was going on.'

The conspiracy ran for more than a month and Davis did little to shut
it down. The Brexit secretary was monitored closely by the chief whip,
Gavin Williamson, who warned May that he was not to be trusted.
'Maybe DD's early loyalty was all part of his game, because he thought
she was going to be brought down anyway,' said a source close to the
prime minister. 'That's what the chief whip thought. But he sees the
worst in everyone.'

While attention on election night had been focused on the activities
of Johnson's acolytes, Davis had also been behaving like a man keeping
his options open. At 9.30 p.m., half an hour before the polls closed, he
phoned Anna Soubry for a chat. Soubry was a Remainer and no great
friend of Davis. He had never phoned her for a chat before. She later
assumed he had got wind of the exit poll early and wanted to sound out
colleagues.

On the evening of 15 June, Nicky Morgan and Soubry met for drinks.
'Okay Miss Smartypants, you were right and I was wrong,' Soubry
declared. Morgan had always been sceptical of May's secretive and
aggressive-defensive approach to politics, judging her unsuitable to lead.
Grenfell seemed to have made her case. But when they were both
approached to sign the letter they claim to have refused. 'Nicky wasn't
part of the gang,' a friend said. 'She was asked if she was interested in
being so and she said, "Now is not the time. Count me out."' As public
advocates for May to go, both were on Shapps' list, though.

It was clear to the gang of four that Davis was the most likely beneficiary of their actions. But he would not have a clear run at the leadership,
not least because many blamed him for talking May into calling the

disastrous election. One minister said, 'He always likes these big, swanky-wanky gestures and the bravado does not convert into good practical politics.'

The rebels had decided there would have to be an election, since MPs believed the lack of a contest in 2016 had allowed May to hide her deficiencies as a public performer. 'There can't be a coronation,' one plotter said. 'It needs to be an open competition, it needs to go to the party members.' To those who feared that a leadership contest would spark a general election, the plotters said that by running a high-profile campaign the winner would gain legitimacy with the public as a democratically elected figure, in the same way that Jeremy Corbyn would cite his mandate from Labour's leadership elections. 'Going to the membership and having a bit of a thing in the country and possibly even televised debates, is a proxy for going to the country for a general election,' one former minister said. 'As Corbyn showed, you can get away with a lot if you do that properly.'

As they sounded out MPs, they realised there would need to be a fresh trigger to tip many of them into the regicide camp. The next test of May's ability to govern would be the votes on the Queen's Speech, now scheduled for 28 and 29 June. 'Labour will try to amend it,' one of the plotters said. 'That's when we'll know if it's going to hold or not. If the vote's lost there will be a vote of no confidence and at that point you have to strike.' In that scenario a leadership contest could be held over the summer, with a new prime minister in place in time for the party's annual conference in Manchester in October.

But before the government could hold a Queen's Speech, they needed a formal deal with the DUP.

The sense of a government blundering around in the dark was reinforced the weekend after the election when Downing Street emailed journalists a statement saying, 'We can confirm that the Democratic Unionist Party have agreed to the principles of an outline agreement to support the Conservative Government on a Confidence and Supply basis when Parliament returns next week. The details will be put forward for discussion and agreement at a Cabinet meeting on Monday.' At midnight Downing Street was forced to admit they had jumped the gun after the DUP issued a statement of its own: 'discussions will continue next week to work on the details'.

May was also under pressure from Tory MPs, who wanted it written into the agreement that the DUP – which did not support gay marriage – would have no sway on social policy outside Northern Ireland. The issue was raised by Ruth Davidson in her call with May on the day after the election and by several ministers at political cabinet the following week. 'I don't think it had dawned on her that she needed a formal position on it,' one of those present said. MPs complained that they were being harangued for aligning themselves with bigots. A former minister said: 'We don't need a deal with the bloody DUP. The DUP doesn't want a general election any more than we do. They don't want the slightest threat of Jeremy Corbyn in Number 10. Call their bluff.'

May had ignored advice from Ulster experts in the House of Lords to finalise the deal herself with DUP leader Arlene Foster and despatched Gavin Williamson to talk to the DUP's chief whip, Jeffrey Donaldson, and their Westminster leader, Nigel Dodds. Williamson and Donaldson had been working hand in glove for more than a year, but the frontline politicians would need more persuading. Immediately after the election, Williamson met Donaldson and Dodds in Stormont, then they went somewhere quieter. The expedition resembled a spy thriller. A Number 10 source said, 'When Gavin asked where he was going, he was sent a message saying, "Go into one village, drive out of the village, keep going, turn left, go into the lay-by, we'll meet you there and take you somewhere else."' The final destination was Gill Hall, a seventeenth-century house in the Lagan Valley, Donaldson's constituency. Having thrashed out the broad principles of a deal, they celebrated with sausage rolls and Northern Irish gin and tonic. 'We had a broad agreement fairly early,' a Downing Street official said, 'but it was never going to be signed until a lot closer to the deadline.'

After the Grenfell fire, the deal then 'stuttered' over money. 'Treasury bean counters got to work,' one source familiar with the talks said, agonising over the consequences for Scotland and Wales of sending more money to Northern Ireland outside the parameters of the Barnett Formula, which determines spending in the nations of the UK. The delay also meant that the Belfast end of the DUP became more involved. 'It slightly engorged their appetite,' a source familiar with the discussions said. 'A degree of provincial greediness kicked in. These people feel shafted by the government for forty years. They're small-time grifters. The advice from SW1 was, "Don't be small-time grifters, be big-time grifters."'

The eventual deal would see the British government hand over £1 billion of taxpayers' money to Northern Ireland, in exchange for the votes of ten DUP MPs on Brexit, budgets, confidence votes and terrorism matters. It led to accusations that the Tories had now grown their own 'magic money tree'. The sensitive negotiations even survived a fire alarm going off in the middle of the night at the Royal Horseguards Hotel, which saw the DUP delegation turfed onto the street just hours before the signing ceremony. The deal was signed on 26 June by Williamson and Donaldson, since it was an agreement between two parliamentary parties, rather than two leaders, but the sight of May standing to the rear emphasised for many Tory MPs the degree to which she was reliant on others, particularly her chief whip. Significantly, the deal was time-limited until 2019, the date not only of Brexit but the assumed date of May's own departure – 'Mayxit'. Arlene Foster was flown home on an RAF plane, for which the Conservative Party reimbursed the government £20,000, when flights were available that day for £41.

The deal was unpopular enough that May took the unusual action of phoning David Cameron to ask for his support on the weekend before the announcement. The result was that Cameron offered to tweet in support of the deal: 'ask facing PM, given the circs, is to deliver the most stable govt possible – today's DUP deal helps achieve that. All Cons should support.' His old ally George Osborne produced a front-page graphic of May as Mini-Me to Arlene Foster's Dr Evil. A source close to Cameron expressed bafflement: 'Doesn't Theresa realise what this looks like? She trashed him in the campaign, has barely spoken to him since becoming prime minister and now has to go cap in hand for his support. It's shameless.'[3]

The seventeen days of negotiations after May first claimed to have secured her government led to renewed tensions between Downing Street and Buckingham Palace when the Queen's Speech was delayed forcing a clash with Royal Ascot, a staple of the queen's calendar. Senior courtiers were unable to get answers from Number 10 in the days that followed about the status of the DUP deal or about rumours that May was on the verge of resigning.

A source close to the palace said, 'There was a high degree of uncertainty about whether Theresa May would survive. They were getting a lot of silence about what Mrs May's plans might be. They didn't have anybody except the private secretary in Number 10 to talk to. The private secretary didn't know what was happening because Timothy and Hill were out. It is certainly true that the palace was being given a greater sense of certainty about the deal than was accurate because the truth is that the DUP buggered Mrs May about longer than she thought.' A Tory adviser added, 'The palace was irritated. They felt that the deal with the DUP hadn't been done. She sent Gavin. Gavin thought he had assurances that he didn't have.'

While the affair did not lead to a formal complaint from the palace, the queen's officials repeatedly made clear their irritation at the silence from Number 10. 'They were getting more frustrated with it because they were running into Ascot and the state opening of Parliament,' a source who has discussed the events with a senior figure in the royal household said. 'Because the queen and the Duke of Edinburgh are so old, it's quite difficult to have them sitting about. Basically, the palace was pissed off about the complete lack of communication.'

The delay irritated both the queen and Prince Charles, who was determined to sit at his mother's side during the Queen's Speech in place of the Duke of Edinburgh, who was suffering from a virus. 'It is certainly true that with the queen and the Duke of Edinburgh there was a bit of, "Oh for God's sake", at what they saw as a lack of courtesy. There was also quite a bit of irritation coming from the Prince of Wales, who was being more petulant.'

A minister who was involved with scheduling of the Queen's Speech said they were made aware of the palace's anger by civil servants but thought it unreasonable: 'I think the formation of a government is a bit more important than a trip to the races.'

When it came, two days late, May used the Queen's Speech debate to apologise for failing victims in the wake of the Grenfell fire, declaring that she would 'put things right'. The prime minister told MPs, 'The support on the ground for families in the initial hours was not good enough ... That was a failure of the state, local and national, to help people when they needed it most. As prime minister, I apologise for that failure.'

The Queen's Speech itself was a slimmed-down affair, which junked much of the Conservative manifesto. At its heart were no fewer than eight Brexit bills, including the great repeal bill, now renamed the European Union (Withdrawal) Bill.

* * *

May was not out of the woods yet. That evening, at a drinks party organised by the former cabinet minister Owen Paterson, Davis was urged to stand for leader. The Brexit secretary gave more than forty MPs an update on the status of the negotiations with Brussels. Then Sir Desmond Swayne, a former aide to David Cameron, got to his feet and said, 'The Prime Minister's time is clearly limited. It's quite clear we will have to think of a successor and I cannot think of a better leader than the person we have just heard speaking.' The words were greeted with applause. Davis responded, 'Thank you, but this is my last job in politics.'[4] The following day Boris Johnson, pinned down by Channel 4 News, said he would not run for leader until after Brexit in March 2019.

On 26 June the members of the One Nation group of Conservative MPs met in a dining room in the House of Commons overlooking the Thames. There, Andrew Mitchell broke cover and declared to a room of twenty-five MPs that May had lost all authority and should resign. For five minutes the former international development secretary held court. One MP present said his remarks 'were clearly prepared'. One of the organisers said, 'He wanted to know the dinner was definitely happening and who was going to be there. He knew what he was going to say.' Another present recalled, 'Mitchell effectively said she was dead in the water. He said she was weak, had lost her authority, couldn't go on and we needed a new leader. Some of us were very surprised and disagreed with him.'[5] The outburst put Damian Green, the de facto deputy prime minister, who was also present, 'in a very awkward position'.

Nicky Morgan did not go as far but she said, 'There is a big, big problem with Theresa May. She cannot fight the next election. I think she's got to go sooner rather than later.' Loyalists like Damian Hinds asked, 'What's the alternative? We've got to stick with her.'

Two weeks later Mitchell's comments were emblazoned on the front page of the *Mail on Sunday*. That same weekend, Downing Street spin doctors were forced to deny that the prime minister was on the verge of resigning for health reasons. The *Sunday Times* carried quotes the same day from a close friend of Davis saying there was a groundswell of support developing for him to take over in the autumn. 'What a lot of colleagues have realised is that David is clearly the man. He can do Brexit and take on Jeremy Corbyn. If she doesn't want two years of the most abject misery, she should read the tea leaves and take action at conference.' While Mitchell's call for May to resign was on the front of the *Mail* on 9 July, *Sun* readers were treated to a piece by Grant Shapps warning that May needed to face 'the reality that an unforced snap election has reduced her reach and power'.

Mitchell's intervention irritated some plotters. Others said it was necessary to destabilise May with a steady drip feed of stories questioning her position, an echo of the tactics used to bring down Iain Duncan Smith in 2003. 'Leadership battles require MP headcount,' said one of the plotters. 'However, in this case to get the race going you need a lot of press stirring to push her out because we would rather have a resignation than a vote of no confidence.'

The following weekend, 16 July, a Davis ally quoted in the *Sunday Times* claimed that Philip May was urging the prime minister to resign. 'She's completely shot,' the friend said. 'I know there are people talking to her about how it would be better for her to take the initiative rather than to be done in. She looks so wounded that it isn't her enemies that are saying that, it is people who love her.'[6]

This was the final straw for Davis, who phoned the author that night and demanded to know who he had talked to. 'It's not bloody helpful,' he declared. The Brexit secretary then told MPs, 'I've read the riot act to Mitchell. I've told my friends to shut up.'

Davis was not the only possible caretaker leader if May were to stand down. By the end of June Philip Hammond's name was also in the frame. Even some Brexit supporters saw the chancellor as a possible placeholder, provided he vowed to stand down after two years so that someone else could lead the Conservatives into the next election.

A serving minister said, 'I think Philip is the only plausible candidate for a couple of years, with DD running Brexit. He is a more credible caretaker than the current prime minister. The PM's brand is so damaged it is painful. The calculation that people are beginning to make is that she is so inadequate we can't wait two years with her in place.' In the belief that Hammond wished to put the brakes on Brexit, even Peter Mandelson suggested to the chancellor in an email that he was 'the only hope'. An adviser who saw Hammond as just as lacking in the human touch as May, pronounced, 'Theresa May is Philip Hammond with a fanny, and the inverse is also true.'

The prospect of Hammond usurping Boris Johnson sent the foreign secretary's circle into uproar, one ally declaring Hammond 'a "can't do" politician when the public wants a "can do" figure'. A shrewd minister observed that the infighting between Johnson, Davis and Hammond was strengthening May: 'They're all in perpetual check, the three of them.'

Hammond found himself in the firing line at cabinet on 11 July. In the midst of a row over whether to lift the public sector pay cap, which limited rises to 1 per cent annually, the chancellor declared that public sector workers were 'overpaid' when their generous pensions were factored in. Hammond then declared train drivers 'ludicrously overpaid' and launched into an ill-judged disquisition on how it was so easy to drive a newly automated train these days that caused Amber Rudd to intervene and say, 'What, even a woman could do it?' When other ministers 'piled in', May remarked, 'Chancellor, I'm going to take your shovel away.'

Hammond was under pressure from Justine Greening, Jeremy Hunt, Karen Bradley, James Brokenshire and Michael Fallon to ease controls on austerity. Michael Gove and Boris Johnson also voiced support for an end to seven years of pay restraint. When the full details of his double gaffe – which left him looking callous and sexist – were briefed to the weekend papers, Hammond was quick to claim that it was his Brexit stance that had prompted the leaks. In fact, it was as much about his manner with his colleagues.

The papers that weekend were also rich with reports from the *Spectator*'s summer party, the jewel in the crown of Westminster parties. Johnson and Davis faced off like the US and Russian armies coming together on the Elbe in 1945 – erstwhile allies who knew they were now political rivals. Davis flirted with Johnson's sister Rachel and pronounced the foreign secretary 'a failure' for letting her defect to the Lib Dems. 'You're too toxic for your own sister,' he crowed. 'They were like a pair of rutting stags locking antlers,' one witness attested. To cap it all, one of Johnson's aides confronted Davis over glasses of Pol Roger champagne about briefings that he would demote Johnson if he became prime minister. The aide told Davis that if the briefings didn't stop, 'I'll kick you in the bollocks.' His opponent, equally refreshed, replied, 'Well, I'll kick you in the bollocks.' *West Wing*-quality dialogue it was not.

The free-for-all showed that May had totally lost control of her cabinet. But it also saved her from an immediate challenge, since it reinforced a growing view among younger Tory MPs that none of the leading contenders should be entrusted with the job. One cabinet minister accused Davis and Johnson of 'willy waving' and said, 'Boris and his

people, quite frankly, need to put a fucking sock in it.' Another minister
said: 'Their ambitions should only be allowed to express themselves post
Brexit or we're in a complete fucking mess.'

May sought to instil some discipline by announcing that 'no minister
is unsackable' and then ordering her ministers to stop leaking from cabinet. In one of the most significant meetings since the election, the executive of the 1922 Committee went to see May in her Commons office on
the Monday after the Hammond leaks and made clear the prime minister would have their support if she wanted to sack any of the members
of her cabinet. Brady was circling the wagons again. 'We said that she
had our support in ensuring that the cabinet behave with the necessary
discipline,' an MP present said.

As for the future leadership sweepstakes, the call went up to 'skip a
generation'. Ministers like Sajid Javid, Justine Greening, Dominic Raab
and Rory Stewart, and rising backbench stars Tom Tugendhat, Johnny
Mercer and James Cleverly, all began to be talked about as possible
candidates. Over the summer, online campaigners were even to advance
the prospects of professional eccentric Jacob Rees-Mogg under the
banner of 'Moggmentum'. It was in all their interests for May to survive
another two years.

The plotters had worked for four weeks to foment a rebellion in the
parliamentary party. What they found was a party simmering but not yet
ablaze. In the aftermath of the Grenfell disaster it looked like the next
breath of wind might topple May. By mid-July MPs were making clear to
the conspirators that she would have to mess up again before they would
contemplate action. 'After that flatfooted response to the Grenfell Tower
thing, at that point she was one other problem away from literally saying,
"I just can't continue," and I think there would have been the numbers.'
At that point it 'would have been fair' for Davis 'to step up to the plate',
one conspirator said.

'Once they managed to struggle through to the recess, the process was
on ice,' said a former minister. 'I'd say fifteen to twenty people were of the
opinion that she ought to go. For the time being, she's our prisoner in
Number 10.' One of May's former staff who wanted her gone said, 'I
think it is cruel to keep her. It is like the scene in a Bruce Willis movie
where the terrorist that is already shot gets used as a human sandbag to
help him get from point A to point B. That is what the party is doing with
her at the moment.'

For now, though, Theresa May was safe. All she had to do now was deliver Brexit – but that was about to blow up in her face again.

FLORENCE AND THE MAYCHINE MALFUNCTION

Michael Gove read the paper and scribbled notes. He read it again, wanting to be sure he understood what it meant. It was 7 September 2017, two weeks before Theresa May was due to make another of her big set-piece speeches on the European Union. After a summer of drama and infighting, the Brexit talks with Brussels were stalled. The prime minister was due to head to Florence, the birthplace of the Renaissance, in the hope that she could inject some life into the process. Compromises would be needed if the prime minister was going to uncork the blockage. Until now Gove had no idea that this much compromise was planned.

The environment secretary was one of nine senior cabinet ministers invited, in great secrecy, to read the paper. Philip Hammond, David Davis, Liam Fox, Damian Green, Michael Fallon and the chief whip Gavin Williamson were all there with Gove. There were two notable absentees. Amber Rudd was in Turkey and the foreign secretary, Boris Johnson, was in the British sovereign territory of Anguilla, inspecting the damage caused by Hurricane Irma, which had ripped a trail of destruction through the Caribbean that week.

The document was written by Oliver Robbins, the prime minister's envoy to the EU. What Gove read quickened his pulse. Over the summer, cabinet discussion about the kind of deal Britain might strike with Brussels had focused on the details of a transitional deal, but the time was coming when a choice would have to be made about the 'end state' relationship with the EU. Two broad options were on the table: 'EEA minus', a solution like that of Norway, where Britain would remain in close alignment with the rules and regulations of the single market, but more loosely than the Scandinavians; and 'Canada plus', an enhanced version of that country's trade deal that would place Britain in a more remote orbit away from the EU. The proposal outlined by Robbins suggested the prime minister was heading towards a Norwegian solution. When the ministers finished reading, there was a frank discussion during which Gove expressed his doubts. As they got up to leave, officials politely but firmly asked them to hand back the document and confiscated their notes. After the meeting, Gove phoned Boris Johnson and said, 'There's something you need to know ...'

Halfway round the world, the foreign secretary was furious that such an important meeting had gone ahead while he was out of the country. Eight days later, in a breathtaking act of defiance, Johnson was to shock Westminster by filing a 4,200-word essay on Europe to the *Daily Telegraph* which sought to pre-empt May's Florence speech. The article would unleash a new firestorm of leadership plotting and fresh salvoes in the Conservative Brexit civil war. This in turn was to disfigure the Tory Party conference, culminating in one of the most spectacular meltdowns ever seen by a party leader.

The genesis of the row had come in the first week after the general election. With Theresa May now tethered prey at the mercy of her colleagues, the senior Remain-supporting ministers took their chance to press for a new approach to Brexit negotiations. In the cabinet committee, which met on the Wednesday, as May was reeling from the Grenfell Tower disaster, and a separate meeting of the smaller Brexit negotiations committee, Amber Rudd and Philip Hammond argued that the young people who had flocked to the polls to back Labour 'felt they didn't have a voice' in May's Brexit settlement. 'Younger people who voted last year to remain feel they weren't listened to and we need to show a level of commitment to get this right, to bring everyone together,' Rudd said. The chancellor stressed that the Brexit settlement should not endanger the City: 'My responsibility is the economy. I can't be seen to be going recklessly over a cliff-edge.' The same case had been made publicly by the prime minister's new chief of staff, Gavin Barwell, who had lost his Croydon seat thanks, in part, to a backlash from Remain voters. 'In my seat the area of the constituency where Labour did best was the area that had voted heavily for Remain.'[1]

In the cabinet meetings there was vocal pushback from the Brexiteers, led by Boris Johnson. 'Hold on a second,' the foreign secretary said. 'This wasn't all about Europe, this was about public services as well. We're completely shooting ourselves in the foot if we suddenly start to decide that this election is all about Brexit.' A cabinet source said, 'Boris pushed back. DD pushed back. Philip and Amber were incredibly punchy. It was the Brexit camp against the Remain camp.' Cleverly, Johnson turned to May and said, 'Before we finish this session, I just want you to make very clear to this room, Prime Minister, is your Lancaster House speech – leaving the customs union, leaving the single market, leaving the jurisdiction of ECJ – still our plan?'

May said, 'Absolutely.'

It was round one to the Brexiteers. Hammond did not give up, though, and won agreement from May that they could soften some of the language in public. Treasury officials briefed again that the issue of customs union membership could be reopened. None of this impressed Eurosceptic backbenchers. Reminding the chancellor of his National Insurance budget U-turn, Andrew Bridgen noted dryly, 'We stood on a manifesto of leaving the customs union, but as we know Phil's not that good on manifesto commitments.'

May's position, weakened by the election result, became clearer when David Davis travelled to Brussels for the opening round of Brexit negotiations with Michel Barnier on 19 June. Before the talks, Davis claimed he was set for the 'row of the summer' over the sequencing of the negotiations, with Britain demanding that details of the divorce deal be discussed at the same time as the future trading relationship. On day one, the Brexit secretary was forced to give ground, agreeing a schedule which made clear that they would only proceed to trade talks once 'sufficient progress' – to be judged by the Europeans – was made on the exit bill, the Northern Irish border and citizens' rights. 'It's not when it starts, it's how it finishes that matters,' Davis declared.

Civil servants who had worked in Brussels always regarded Davis as naïvely optimistic about the sequencing. 'If you've dealt with them before you know that once the EU's locked on its starting position it's very difficult to shift them off it,' one said. 'Not because they're a bunch of assholes but because that's just how their process works. That's why the EU's a difficult negotiator.' Even one Downing Street official expressed surprise. 'I don't know why we kept on talking about wanting to do a divorce in parallel with a transition when they're never ever going to roll over on that. Why do we make ourselves look like prats?'

In their joint press conference after the opening exchanges, Barnier declared that a 'fair deal' was possible but added, 'I am not in a frame of mind to make concessions' and suggested the 'consequences' of Britain leaving the single market and customs union 'are substantial'. In a private meeting with the European Commission, the minutes of which emerged the following month, Barnier cast doubt on Davis's dedication to the task, telling the college of twenty-eight commissioners, 'David Davis … did not regard his direct involvement in these negotiations as his priority.' Jean-Claude Juncker expressed concern that this 'risked jeopardising the success of the negotiations' and warned Barnier 'not to accept discussions at the purely technical level with negotiators who had no political mandate'.[2]

When the second round of talks took place on 20 July, Davis turned up for just one hour on the first day, before returning to London and leaving the detailed work to Oliver Robbins, who was leading the technical discussions with Barnier's deputy Sabine Weyand. Robbins was accompanied by ninety-eight British officials. In a pep talk at the UKREP offices in Brussels he told his nervous team, 'This is the biggest negotiation any of us will do in our careers and we need to get it right.' The two sides agreed a 'technical note' outlining their different positions on citizens' rights. More seriously, Barnier suggested it would be impossible for the talks to move forward unless the British made clear what they were prepared to pay. Davis had told Parliament on 15 July that Britain's financial obligations to the EU would 'survive the UK's withdrawal' but defining these 'survivable obligations' would take five more months. One EU diplomat said, 'The impression we got so far is that the UK is not ready for these talks.' If the Brits were less well prepared than Barnier's team, that was because they had more on their plates. 'The EU didn't need to do a Lancaster House speech,' a DExEU official said. 'It didn't need to do the Supreme Court case and Article 50 legislation. They're not dealing with the political problems in the cabinet. There is excellent technical work being done here, but it's not been the only thing that these people have been doing.'

The EU's demand had now risen to €100 billion, a bill that appeared to have been arrived at by adding in future commitments announced by the Commission during Britain's membership but which the UK had made no explicit pledge to fund. 'They all agree on one thing,' a Conservative adviser said. 'Make the UK pay as fucking much money as possible for as fucking long as possible.' The week before the talks, Boris Johnson told MPs the sums demanded were 'extortionate' and suggested Brussels could 'go whistle' for the money, an intervention which did little to endear him to his cabinet colleagues or for his own reputation for statesmanship.

With the talks stalled, the government announced that they would publish a series of position papers spelling out their intentions on a range of issues including customs, fisheries, agriculture, citizens' rights, nuclear materials, data protection, ongoing court cases and Northern Ireland ahead of the third round of talks at the end of August. The papers were an anti-climax since they mostly offered a range of options and did not state Britain's preferred outcome.

August's talks were the worst of the lot, with Barnier branding the UK's approach 'nostalgic and unrealistic'. Other EU officials branded the British approach 'magical thinking'. For the Europeans, Britain was still trying to have its cake and eat it, making 'specific requests which would amount to continuing to enjoy the benefits of the single market and EU membership without actually being part of it'. Davis responded that Barnier should 'not confuse a belief in the free market with nostalgia' but the position papers had failed to move the dial. Davis and his team, led by Treasury official Mark Bowman, took the Commission line by line through their budget demands, demanding a legal justification for every item. The meeting took four hours as a thirty-nine-year-old government lawyer 'with a hipster beard' ploughed through twenty-three slides and forty-seven paragraphs of text. The meeting took so long that Bowman arranged for updates on the Test match score to be smuggled into the room hidden in official documents. Barnier's team regarded it as impertinent when the hipster suggested the EU's own preparations on the financial settlement were 'inadequate'.[3] 'They didn't like it one bit,' a source close to Davis said.

The glut of negative briefings about the British negotiating position emanating from Brussels convinced Eurosceptics that a Commission-inspired dirty tricks campaign was being run by a 'black ops' unit in Brussels. A senior businessman and a prominent QC passed details of the claims from contacts in Berlin to the desk of Steve Baker at DExEU. They named an official in the German finance ministry, who was close to Martin Selmayr, as the source of reports in the *Financial Times* and the German press bad-mouthing Britain. The official was alleged to have been involved in a previous effort to destabilise the Italian government.

When the press made enquiries about the claims, the British embassy in Berlin, DExEU, 10 Downing Street and the German finance ministry went into panic mode and denied the claims.

In the final week of the parliamentary term the Brexit war cabinet agreed that so much time had been lost because of the election that Britain should seek a formal period of transition after Brexit – but crucially not how long it would last. A month examining farm subsidies had convinced even Michael Gove that a transition period was needed. A senior cabinet colleague observed, 'Michael has been forced to engage with the reality of this problem by being given a job in DEFRA, almost a department designed to turn hardline Brexiteers into massive transitionalists.' The senior cabinet minister said Gove and Johnson, the two main faces of the Leave campaign, were alive to the potential 'negative short-term effects' of getting Brexit wrong because 'they are going to get the blame – I suspect for them that's the key motivator now.'

When Theresa May went on holiday, a few days later, Philip Hammond saw his chance to put down a marker and define the nature of the transition period. Showing an uncharacteristic flair for making news, he told the *Today* programme on 28 July that 'many things will look similar' in Britain's relationship with the EU during the transition, with free movement, access to the single market and an inability to strike separate trade deals remaining in place. 'People have talked about a year, two years, maybe three years,' he said. Even Hammond acknowledged that the transition would have to end before the 2022 general election, but his move was seen by the Brexiteers as a provocation. Hammond's claim that there was 'broad acceptance' of his views in cabinet was swiftly disproved.

Two days later, Liam Fox told the *Sunday Times* that cabinet had not agreed that freedom of movement would continue for three years and that such a move would 'not keep faith' with the referendum result: 'I have not been involved in any discussions on that.' Fox, who was not a member of the elite gang of six ministers in the Brexit war cabinet, said, 'That has to be an agreement by the cabinet. It can't just be made by an individual or any group within the cabinet.' David Jones, who wanted Davis installed as leader, issued a withering put-down in the pages of the *Mail on Sunday*, accusing Hammond of 'going on manoeuvres' the moment Mrs May went on holiday. 'This is a classic case of when the cat's away, the mice will play,' he wrote. 'All this agitation by the Chancellor and his allies is hugely discourteous to Mrs May – and undermines her authority.' Another cabinet minister accused Hammond of seeking 'his revenge' after 'all the briefing that Phil was going to get fired'.

In a bid to silence those who said he wanted to thwart Brexit, and to keep his name in the news, Hammond then struck a deal with Liam Fox to write a joint article for the *Sunday Telegraph* in which Fox would place on the record his agreement with the need for a 'time limited' transition period to avoid a 'cliff-edge' while Hammond confirmed that the UK would definitely leave the single market and the customs union in 2019.

When May returned to work, the most dedicated loyalists in her circle urged her to reassert her authority. Election post-mortems pitched Nick Timothy's world view against that of Lynton Crosby. But in Team May the narrative was clear: the election had been botched because Crosby had changed the formula which had given them a twenty-point poll lead. The conclusion of most Tory MPs, that May should never be allowed to fight another election, was not shared by the prime minister. 'It's not clear she has reconciled herself to going in 2019,' a loyalist MP said. 'I don't think she's bought into that at all.'

May was still in touch with Timothy and Hill and their influence was also felt through Jojo Penn, their protégée and still deputy chief of staff. 'I think the parliamentary party would be up to Number 10 with a burning cross and pitchforks if they were wired to how much influence they are still having over the PM,' a Downing Street official said. 'Jojo is just a proxy for Fi.' Nick Timothy had two or three conversations with the prime minister in June, and the next month signed a contract to write columns for the *Daily Telegraph*. In a launch interview with the paper, he admitted, 'I have spoken to Theresa a few times since the election but I haven't seen her and I'm not advising her on policy. They are private conversations, people catching up.' Penn, alongside the chief whip Gavin Williamson, was at the head of a group of 'Save May' uber-loyalists. One MP said, 'Those around her who inflicted her on us want her to carry on because they keep their jobs.' At the suggestion of the loyalists, May began a charm offensive on her return, inviting MPs and their spouses to Chequers for informal dinners. One compared her greeting him at the door to 'meeting the custodian of a National Trust house'.

When an opportunity for May to assert her right to fight on presented itself, she grasped it with both hands. The occasion was a trade trip to

Japan. The previous weekend the *Sunday Mirror* had run a report that May would stand down before the end of August 2019 having delivered Brexit, a report that encapsulated the conventional wisdom of the vast majority of Conservative MPs. When, on the plane out, the prime minister was quizzed by Francis Elliott, the political editor of *The Times*, about whether she would fight the next election as prime minister, May's aides primed her to say 'I'm not a quitter' – a memorable quote which would not pin her down to a particular timetable. May fudged her answer and failed to use the line. Following discussions with her new director of communications, Robbie Gibb, who was in London, it was agreed that she should 'lean into' the question if asked it again.

Once in Japan, May did three broadcast interviews and delivered three slightly different lines. To the BBC, she said, 'I'm here for the long term.' When Sky News asked if she would fight the next election, she answered bluntly, 'Yes,' to the consternation of her aides, and of the broadcasters who had been told to expect something requiring more interpretation. Only during the third interview, with ITV, did May finally deliver the line she had planned, 'I'm not a quitter.'

Some MPs applauded her boldness but others reflected that May should have answered less explicitly to avoid another media circus over the leadership. 'God knows she has enough experience of not answering questions,' one MP observed. Those who had suppressed their anger at May found it welling up again. To this group, her comments were dangerously reminiscent of Margaret Thatcher's infamous 1987 promise to 'go on and on', which crystallised the dissent against her into a lethal force. Grant Shapps added three names to his list. 'It's completely delusional,' one MP said. 'It's yet another reminder that she's not that good.' Another of the Shapps signatories added, 'I think she's just signed her own death warrant. She lost our majority in an election she didn't have to call. Anyone else would have fallen on their sword. The only people propping her up are the hardline Brexiteers. She'll fuck up again and then she'll be taken out and shot.' Even a May loyalist expressed concerns: 'The priority should not be worrying about 2020, it should be about surviving conference.' They were prescient words.

On 26 August, Labour announced that they would back membership of the single market and customs union in a transitional period after March 2019, and Keir Starmer left the door open to Britain staying in both for good. Revealing the change of approach in the *Observer*, Starmer said, 'Remaining in a form of customs union with the EU is a possible end destination for Labour, but that must be subject to negotiations. It also means that Labour is flexible as to whether the benefits of the single market are best retained by negotiating a new single market relationship or by working up from a bespoke trade deal.' The wording of the customs union section was little different from Conservative plans to negotiate 'a form of' customs union as part of the new deal. But the suggestion that a bespoke trade deal might not be the preferred option put clear red water between Labour and the Tories on the end-state solution.

After going into the election with a policy of constructive ambiguity, the new stance was an important victory for Starmer, who had watched as Labour's Europe policy descended into chaos throughout June and July. On 11 June, John McDonnell had declared that staying in the single market after Brexit would mean 'not respecting that referendum'. On 23 July, Corbyn appeared to agree, telling the BBC's Andrew Marr that membership of the single market was 'inextricably linked' with being a member of the EU, ignoring the example of Norway. McDonnell was pushing the classic 'Lexiteer' argument from the left that single market membership would stop a socialist government from using state aid to help key industries. Corbyn, one frontbencher said, 'is not interested in the detail – he's just been told you can't be in the single market unless you're in the EU'. Seumas Milne, a colleague said, wanted Labour to make 'big progressive statements', not 'get bogged down in technical Brexit stuff'. A senior Labour source said, 'The leader's office thought the best way to deal with this was to not really deal with it.' Starmer argued that if Labour won power they might inherit the Brexit negotiations before they were complete, meaning it was better to encourage the government to seek a status quo transition to minimise disruption. 'I'm worried that if the government gets this wrong we might get ourselves in the position where we pick up such a mess we can't unravel it,' he warned.

The issue came to a head the day after Corbyn's Marr interview when Barry Gardiner, the shadow international trade secretary, wrote an article for the *Guardian* arguing that staying in the customs union after quitting the EU would be 'a disaster' and leave Britain as a 'vassal state' of the EU. His intervention had not been cleared by the leadership and was an attempt to face down Starmer. Formerly pro-Remain, Gardiner had concluded that immigration had driven the referendum result, and had advocated a harder line on that and the EU. 'Keir and Barry were at loggerheads,' a shadow cabinet member said. 'Barry took a very dogmatic view that we had to be absolutely out the single market, out the customs union, and pretty well away from transitions too.'

The publication of the Tory position papers on Brexit made the internal disputes more acute. 'Every time we responded I thought we were making our own position worse,' a Labour frontbencher said, 'because instead of taking a punch at government it was, headline: "Government doesn't know what it's doing on Brexit", next line, "nor does Labour"'. A Starmer ally commented, 'Ambiguity was descending into a lack of coherence.' A negative reaction to Gardiner's piece from the trade unions helped Starmer to persuade Corbyn and McDonnell to agree a policy change for the transitional period which would give Labour a distinctive position and end the infighting. Once it was agreed, the deputy leader Tom Watson announced that Labour were now the party of 'soft Brexit'.

The new policy was also a victory for Chuka Umunna, who had put his name to a motion to amend the Queen's Speech which called on the government to 'rule out withdrawal from the EU without a deal, guarantee a Parliamentary vote on any final outcome to negotiations, set out transitional arrangements ... and proposals to remain within the Customs Union and Single Market'. Forty-nine Labour MPs defied a three-line whip to back the motion, which went far further towards reversing the referendum decision than Starmer was yet comfortable doing. But Umunna had put down a marker. The Team 2019 group of Tory Remainers voted with the government but told Umunna his willingness to defy the Labour leadership would embolden them too.

Labour's move to embrace the single market during a transition period proved that Corbyn and McDonnell were prepared to put the necessities of effective opposition ahead of their views on the EU. Similar discipline was in evidence during Labour's party conference in Brighton at the end of September. Delegates, whipped by Momentum and the unions, supported a decision not to have a vote on the party's Europe policy which might have proved divisive and instead toured the convention centre and the hotel bars excitedly talking about the prospect of being in government. Ever since the election, Corbyn had been on a tour of sixty marginal seats, keeping the party in full campaign mode. He was now a political rock star of such stature that he was invited to the Glastonbury music festival. From the main pyramid stage, Corbyn told the cheering crowd that politics was about 'what we dream' as he handed a copy of the Labour manifesto to the festival's founder, Michael Eavis. Backstage, Eavis asked him when he was going to be prime minister. Corbyn replied, 'In six months.'

While the leadership tried to look like a government in waiting, they also sought to strengthen the left's stranglehold on the party. When Kezia Dugdale quit as Scottish Labour leader on 29 August, the Corbynistas finally had a majority on the NEC, opening the door to a purge of Labour headquarters. Jon Lansman put himself forward for a seat on the committee. The resignation of Patrick Heneghan from Southside 'by mutual consent' a week later, after five general elections, further weakened the moderates. In the main conference hall, delegates approved a plan reducing the number of MPs needed to get on future leadership ballots from 15 per cent of the PLP to 10 per cent.

Under pressure from prominent Corbynistas, broadcasters began to regularly feature young left-wingers – The Canary's Kerry-Anne Mendoza appearing on *Question Time* and Novara Media's Ash Sarkar on *Newsnight*. But the leadership also made overtures to the mainstream media, McDonnell giving an eve-of-conference interview to the *Sunday Times*, offering to support the government if it acted to ease the burden of tuition fees. Yet in a fringe address to the Labour Representation Committee, the shadow chancellor outlined plans for the hard left to seize key posts throughout the Labour Party. Calling it a 'make or break' year, McDonnell said, 'In addition to having Jeremy as leader [and] all of the shadow cabinet now being solidly on the left, we've got to populate every aspect of constituency parties and elected office now with socialists. We've got to populate it at every level.'[4]

To the moderates this looked like the beginnings of a purge. One official at headquarters said, 'Their next plan is trigger ballots. If you've ever said anything critical of the Dear Leader they think you should be gone. They seem to be completely blind to the fact that Jeremy Corbyn spent thirty years in Parliament opposing his own leader. They don't see that in any way as relevant.'

* * *

Labour were not the only ones calling for single market and customs union membership during the transition. In the first week of July the CBI – Britain's biggest business group – launched a pincer movement. Carolyn Fairbairn, the CBI's director general, gave a speech at the London School of Economics insisting that the status quo would have to remain in place for as long as it took to negotiate a free trade deal because companies could not cope with 'multiple cliff-edges – in tariffs, red tape and regulation'. She said, 'Instead of a cliff-edge, the UK needs a bridge to a new deal.' Some of the CBI's biggest hitters repeated the same message at a business summit hosted by David Davis at Chequers, the first time the Brexit secretary had used the facility.

Having sat out the election, the man whose referendum had sparked a year of turbulence was also beginning to flex his muscles. In calls with leading Remainers, inside and outside the cabinet, David Cameron was arguing for Britain to pursue a 'Norway plus' deal with Brussels. 'He thinks that's the way forward,' one former aide said. 'He's made that clear to lots of people.' Cameron had spent his first year out of power making lucrative speeches at £150,000 a go but was looking for a purpose in his life.

In the months after the referendum, friends said he was sanguine about the situation. 'The thing about David is, he's a self-confident, secure person, and he doesn't hold grudges, or sit awake at night,' one friend said. 'He's more interested in what animal he's going to shoot, or what claret he's going to have for lunch, or where he's going to shag Sam next! He's not a political obsessive, which is one of his great strengths.'

When the former Israeli premier Shimon Peres died in October 2016, Cameron found himself on the same plane as Boris Johnson, his nemesis in the referendum campaign. The two Old Etonians made up over a scotch at the King David Hotel. Johnson told a friend later, 'He's a guy who feels he was doing a bloody good job as prime minister and then suddenly he wasn't allowed to be prime minister any more. He's pissed off. You can't blame him.'

Yet as 2017 went on, the Cameroon set grew concerned about their leader, who was easily bored, confiding that he was becoming depressed by the implications of Brexit and the state of his life. One friend recounted how he had been to see the former prime minister and found him 'asleep in front of the tennis'. Another recalled how Cameron had phoned around trying to find someone to play tennis against and found all his old associates too busy to see him. Television presenter Kirstie Allsopp briefly lifted the lid in an interview in September 2017, saying the Camerons were both 'utterly, utterly, utterly broken over Brexit'. Another family friend confirmed, 'Sam is worried about him. He's very down about Brexit.' Cameron refrained from making his views public. An MP friend said, 'There's a former PMs' club where they know what these things are like, and are much less willing to say how awful their successors are because they know the challenges.'

The same could not be said of George Osborne, who even allies believed was cheerleading for a stop to Brexit. 'He's so obsessed with destroying Theresa and wanting to stay in the EU,' one old colleague said. 'There is a scenario he sees where it precipitates the destruction of the Conservative Party but we stay in Europe. If the business community thinks this thing is going to fall they will stop investment decisions. Inward investment will stop. Suddenly – and I think this is what George has calculated – you're into recession. Then all bets are off. Someone, be it Philip or a member of the younger generation, will say, "Let's stop this madness."'

The Eurosceptics were also growing depressed at what they saw as a coordinated effort to thwart Brexit. Suspicion was fuelled by reports from within Whitehall to leading Brexiteers that Jeremy Heywood and Oliver Robbins, egged on by Damian Green, the first secretary of state, were now driving the government's policy towards 'Norway minus' and that David Davis had been captured by the officials. Having asserted themselves during May's post-election collapse, the mandarins had not let go since. A senior mandarin close to Heywood said, 'Jeremy is very active. Being part of the EEA was hard wired into people in the civil service of his generation. Many cut their teeth going through the various institutions in the EU.'

On 9 July, David Jones fired a broadside, accusing pro-EU Conservative MPs of hatching a 'cunning plot to stymie Brexit'. In an article for the *Mail on Sunday*, he wrote that the Remainers wanted the UK to exit the EU 'on such ludicrously pro-Brussels terms, we might as well have stayed exactly where we were. We will have left but not left. Just like the Eagles' Hotel California, we can check out but we can never leave.' Dominic Cummings, who still had contacts across Whitehall – and a longstanding belief that Heywood should be removed – had several conversations with Boris Johnson and Michael Gove to express his concerns.

Cummings believed the victory they had all won the year before was being thrown away. He told them, 'The DExEU process is dysfunctional.' He advised the ministers to create a Brexit task force of fifteen to twenty officials from the Treasury, the Foreign Office and DExEU to take control of negotiations – and suggested that Victoria Woodcock, a former Cabinet Office official who was operations director for Vote Leave, take charge. 'Davis has totally bogged it,' he said. 'It's time to call the A-Team, and Vics is Hannibal and B. A. Baracus rolled into one.'

A source close to Johnson told the author in July, 'There's a sense from a lot of Brexiteer ministers and backbenchers that DExEU are trying to slow Brexit down. DD is not being as robust as some think he should. Philip is the ardent slow-it-all-down man. DD and Hammond are talk-ing.' The foreign secretary was growing fearful that together these estab-lishment forces would delay things long enough for an economic downturn to force a public rethink. 'If you have a three-year transition period, you could have an election in two years' time, when you still haven't left,' the friend said. 'All it takes is a slump in economic perfor-mance and perversely the chancellor's hand is strengthened.'

Even pro-EU officials recognised that failure to time limit a transition period might have the same effect. 'What I observe as a diplomat is that transitional agreements have a funny habit of becoming quite long last-ing,' one said. 'Once you've got an agreement it's often very hard to move off it.'

On 12 September, Hammond gave evidence to the House of Lords Economic Affairs Committee and sought to enshrine the CBI's view as the new reality. 'There is general agreement that it would not make sense to ask business to face two sets of changes and that implies that a transi-tion or interim period would need to look a lot like the status quo,' the chancellor said. In the following forty-eight hours journalists were briefed that the prime minister was prepared to continue paying in around €10 billion a year to the EU budget during a two-year transition period – guaranteeing there would be no black hole in the budget. The fix was in.

The view that the Whitehall and City establishment was taking over was fuelled by an announcement a week later that Oliver Robbins was to relinquish his post as senior mandarin at DExEU and to return to the Cabinet Office to 'strengthen cross-government coordination of the next phase of negotiations'. He was replaced by Philip Rycroft, who had been brought in as Robbins' deputy in April to cover for his long absences. David Davis initially encouraged the move. 'He wanted Robbins fired,' said a close ally. But he quickly came to realise that the centre of gravity had shifted decisively away from DExEU. 'He was furious with Olly, who used to go behind his back to Number 10,' a source said. 'DD thought he was resolving that problem. He made it one hundred times worse. Now Olly is reporting straight to Jeremy [Heywood] and Theresa. He doesn't even have to report to DD. DD has knocked himself out of the fight.' Robbins began recruiting twenty more of the best officials in Whitehall to join what looked like a civil service war cabinet for Brexit, a step towards what George Bridges, Ivan Rogers and Dominic Cummings had all recommended over the past year.

When the members of the cabinet were called in to read Oliver Robbins' policy paper on 14 September, it was obvious to his colleagues that Davis was not fully in the picture. 'It looked like DD had not seen the document before and wasn't even aware it was being prepared,' one cabinet source said. 'It was a draft think-piece of what a communiqué of an EU–UK agreement to move to the next stage of the talks might look like. It revealed what the UK's negotiating hand was and what the UK was prepared to put up with.' Despite a year of cabinet discussions about the shape of Brexit, it was the first time most of the ministers had seen anything written down from central government on the direction May was heading. 'As initially drafted, it was EEA minus, and so close to the EEA that the minus scarcely featured at all,' a source who read the document revealed.

May rejected such labels, but they helped to describe how Britain would respond to the issue which had come centre stage in cabinet ministers' minds – the degree to which Britain would use its new-found freedom to diverge from the rules and regulations of the single market and how that relationship would be managed going forward. In essence, Hammond and the business community felt it was sensible to mirror changing EU rules in order to minimise friction at the borders, staying in a kind of perpetual near-earth orbit with the EU. The Brexiteers wanted to make more use of Britain's freedom of manoeuvre to do things differently. Michael Gove was already agitating to ditch the Common Fisheries Policy during a transition period and beef up animal welfare rules. He also had designs on unshackling the UK from the Common Agricultural Policy.

The key issue was how Brussels would respond when Britain chose to diverge. Switzerland had seen some of its agreements with the EU suspended when it sought to tear up freedom of movement. The Brexiteers did not want to have to decide in advance the areas in which the UK would seek to assert its sovereignty, since that would be dictated in part by future events that could not be predicted. The reason the Robbins paper was so controversial was that it appeared to be conceding this point. 'It was creating a mechanism where we would have to ask to diverge at any point,' a cabinet minister said. 'If we decided we wanted to change the wheelnuts directive we would have to negotiate that change rather than be in a situation where we could diverge.'

The ministers were given twenty minutes to digest the contents. When David Davis spoke, he provided a 'political analysis', predicting which issues would cause problems for Leavers and which for Remainers without making clear where he stood.

Gove said, 'I'm not really sure about this.' When he called Boris Johnson in the Caribbean to tell him about the meeting, the foreign secretary 'went ballistic'. When the foreign secretary returned home they met for crisis talks. Johnson had been planning to make a big speech of his own on Brexit, earlier the same week, but he had been banned from delivering it by Downing Street because it was scheduled to clash with crunch votes on the second reading of the EU Withdrawal Bill in the Commons. The 4,200-word text, which had been worked up in conjunction with Dominic Cummings, was sitting on his laptop.

After the row erupted, a close ally of Theresa May said the paper was not official policy and would never have been circulated to ministers if Nick Timothy had still been in Downing Street. 'That paper put the wind up Boris and Michael Gove, understandably,' the source said. 'There's no way Theresa would have gone that far. Nick would have taken one look at that paper and had it burnt.'

Yet the paper had been floated by Downing Street as the kernel of May's Florence speech by her most senior Brexit adviser. Johnson also got wind that Gavin Barwell, the chief of staff, was ringing round cabinet ministers floating two ideas that 'got alarm bells ringing' – namely that May should 'promise not to use the money to hold the process hostage', and should propose a model of the post-transition 'end state' that looked a lot like the Norway-lite model. 'We would promise to stay within single market rules and mirror ECJ judgments with some kind of undefined quasi-ECJ overwatch,' a source said. 'Both Boris and Michael thought it sounded fairly disastrous.' A source who discussed the issue with DExEU officials that week said, 'Olly Robbins was telling people in DExEU that he'd got this where he wanted it and EEA minus was in the speech. They thought they had got it stitched up. The officials said, "That's not what DD thinks is happening." Robbins said, "Well, me and Jeremy have squared the prime minister, so that's what's happening."' According to May loyalists, this interpretation was alarmist.

Under David Davis's analysis, shared with his cabinet colleagues, there were three ways of approaching the issue of divergence. 'In areas where it doesn't have any effect on the single market we can diverge; in other areas we might want to say we want the same outcomes as the EU but we will get there by a different route; and in some areas we will keep the EU's way of doing things,' a cabinet minister explained. 'Phil [Hammond]'s point is that it's the last of those that should be absolutely dominant. The worry was that the Phil approach would mean we would have had to go to the EU and say, "We're planning to diverge in this area, is that okay with you?"' There was a logic to Hammond's position, as even Gove could see, because it meant the EU could act as a brake on a Corbyn government, were Labour to win power, but the Brexiteers saw it as a negation of taking back control.

An ally of the pair said, 'Fundamentally what Boris and Gove are saying is this: a transition is okay but it must end before the next election and we must be able to say that whatever the party manifestos are going into the 2022 election we can deliver them in full and we are not going to be bound by the ECJ. We can pass legislation and regulate our own economy. You start off completely compliant but from day one you start changing things. The Hammond–Treasury view is that you start off compliant and aim to remain almost totally compliant for the foreseeable future.'

As the face of Brexit, and yet one whose department was not central to delivering it, Johnson felt under growing pressure. He knew he would be the one blamed by the public if things went wrong, but throughout the summer he had watched as Hammond asserted his influence and Davis had his high-profile meetings with Barnier. The phrase that was increasingly used by MPs in the House of Commons tea room was that Johnson was 'a busted flush'. Over the summer he had even been eclipsed by his fellow Old Etonian, Jacob Rees-Mogg, who had been hailed as a leadership contender by 'Moggmentum' online activists. Boris's one attempt to insert himself into the Brexit debate – telling the EU to 'whistle for it' on the money – had been seen as a gaffe which confirmed his lack of seriousness.

Had Johnson had a better year, he might have seemed the inevitable choice to replace May after the general election. He might already be prime minister. Now there were reports that he might be fired in the next reshuffle. Two weeks earlier, on 29 August, the *Times* columnist Rachel Sylvester had penned a wounding article headlined 'Our foreign secretary is an international joke'; it claimed that even the Trump White House 'don't want to go anywhere near Boris', while European foreign ministers saw him as 'a clown who can never resist a gag'.

Johnson felt vulnerable. He had stopped calling some of the MPs who supported his leadership bid. 'Boris has moved on from a lot of people,' a friend said. His special adviser Liam Parker had decided to leave because the hours were not conducive to life with his young family and he and Johnson had clashed over certain briefings to the media. A friend said that week, 'Boris is worried about his future, he's worried about Brexit and he's worried about the government collapsing.'

The foreign secretary had told friends that he had one more leadership bid in him, but he was also concerned he would be eclipsed by the younger generation. Johnson had breakfast with Amber Rudd and confided in the home secretary, 'I really hate it when people say the Tory party should skip a generation – and go to Amber Rudd.' The joke was that Rudd was fifty-four, a year older than Johnson, though she had entered Parliament nine years after he was first elected. In ConservativeHome's monthly survey of the Tory grassroots, Johnson had slipped to fifth, far behind Jacob Rees-Mogg as their pick for the next leader.

The Sylvester column included the observations of a Whitehall source who said, 'He doesn't know what he thinks so he flies by the seat of his pants.' Flying by the seat of his pants was what had kept Johnson's career on the go and, facing what he saw as a personal political crisis, he resolved to do so again. At lunchtime on Friday, 15 September, Johnson 'hit the panic button' and told Downing Street he would be publishing an article in the *Daily Telegraph* the following day. He did not tell Gove and Cummings what he was planning. Number 10 did not see the text

– a reworked version of his speech – until late afternoon and had no opportunity to change it.

The stage was set for a Brexit battle royal.

The article was a sensation. The *Telegraph* cleared an entire spread for the four thousand words and devoted its front page to a picture of the foreign secretary emerging purposefully from 10 Downing Street under the headline, 'Boris: Yes, we will take back £350m from the EU for NHS'. The article was an upbeat paean to Britain's 'glorious' Brexit future, written with Johnson's customary gusto, dismissing those who 'think we're going to bottle it'. At its centre was an attempt to deliver on the promises he had made during the referendum campaign. 'Once we have settled our accounts, we will take back control of roughly £350m per week. It would be a fine thing, as many of us have pointed out, if a lot of that money went on the NHS.'

Johnson had driven around the country during the referendum campaign in Vote Leave's bus, emblazoned with the pledge to spend £350 million a week – Britain's gross contribution to the EU – on the NHS instead. Critics called it 'a lie' because the sum did not include the rebate won by Margaret Thatcher or the funds returned to projects in the UK. Johnson wanted to answer that charge and was arguing in cabinet that Hammond should use the budget to begin fulfilling the pledge to the health service. Neither he nor Gove could understand why the government's election promise to increase NHS spending by £8 billion a year – an extra £150 million a week – had not been advertised as a down payment on the referendum pledge. 'She could have stood up and said, "I didn't make these commitments, but I recognise that people want more money for the NHS,"' a Tory adviser said. 'It would have taken the toxicity out of everything.' Johnson and Gove wanted May to commit to an extra £100 million a week for the NHS when Britain left in 2019, at a cost of £5 billion, with another £5 billion to follow by 2022, bringing the total to an extra £350 million a week. Hammond was not interested, telling friends Vote Leave's pledges were 'their problem' not his.

Johnson's article unleashed claims that he was trying to oust May and provoked criticism from the head of the UK Statistics Authority, Sir David Norgrove, that he was guilty of 'a clear misuse of official statistics'. Amber Rudd accused the foreign secretary of 'backseat driving' the Brexit process. Ruth Davidson and Will Tanner – a former May aide –

both criticised him for choosing to file the piece on the day of a terrorist attack on the London tube, which fortunately caused no fatalities. 'Astonishing that Boris thought this self-serving posturing, disloyal at best of times, would reflect well in the hours after a terror attack,' Tanner tweeted.

Furious as Downing Street was, Gavin Barwell contacted both Johnson and Gove the following week and asked them to help rework May's Brexit speech. Johnson helped inject some more soaring rhetoric. 'He feels the language was more constructive and positive,' an ally said.

On Thursday 21 September, the day before May's Florence speech, the cabinet met to discuss the text. Ministers were given half an hour to read the draft, then each of them had their say. The speech outlined plans for a transitional period of 'around two years' during which trade would continue on the same terms, with Britain continuing to 'honour commitments' to the EU budget. May did not put a figure on it, but that meant £18 billion to £20 billion in total. Hammond appeared to have won, but the chancellor was sporting 'a face like thunder'. He suggested the transitional period might not be long enough. He was backed up by other Remainer ministers. 'Phil was saying it should be extended, as was Justine [Greening, education secretary] and [David] Gauke [work and pensions secretary],' a source said. 'They want three years or longer.' Greg Clark, the business secretary, also backed the chancellor. His department had, at one stage over the summer, advocated a five-year transition period, in order to give business some certainty and stability. One of the Brexiteer ministers said, 'It was a load of bollocks from people who have never done any business planning and spend their time talking down business. It was like they were speaking from the same script.'

The second reason for Hammond's ire concerned what was not in May's speech. The prime minister made no reference to the 'end state' that the government would be seeking after Brexit. The Norway option was explicitly ruled out because it 'could not work for the British people'.

In the cabinet meeting, a handful of ministers made coded attacks on Johnson's grandstanding. The Tory chairman, Patrick McLoughlin, said, 'We owe it to all our colleagues to be supportive.' Justine Greening also lashed out: 'The stuff last week was not helpful.' But other ministers were grateful that Johnson's intervention had forced May to give the whole cabinet a say on Brexit. 'What he did last weekend actually forced the issue to the table,' said one. Extraordinarily, it was the first time they had ever discussed it at full cabinet – a point made by Andrea Leadsom, who complained to May, 'It is strange we are having a discussion about the speech the day before the speech when we need a policy discussion.' Another cabinet minister said, 'The person who has been most heroic on this has been Boris. By busting things out into the open, he changed the terms of the debate. Even though he has profoundly irritated some people he has done a brave and good thing.'

Johnson's intervention had not won the war but it had changed the face of the current battle. One leading Brexiteer described the speech as a '4–1 victory for Heywood and Hammond' because mirroring EU regulations was still 'a practical possibility'. He added, 'The Boris–Gove position has massive support among Tory members, strong support among Tory voters and majority support in the country. However, they are against the two most powerful forces in Britain – Jeremy Heywood's Cabinet Office and the Treasury, with Number 10 stuck in the middle.'

Still May did not decide what the endgame would look like. 'We're in a situation where she might have to choose between Boris resigning or Philip resigning,' one Downing Street aide said. 'At the moment it looks like she has decided that she can't afford to have Boris resigning.' It was a judgement she would soon have grounds to regret.

May's Florence speech, delivered in the Catholic church of Santa Maria Novella – where Galileo was first accused of heresy – on 22 September was the least substantial of the prime minister's big speeches but it still represented a long road travelled in a year. However lacking in detail, the prime minister had managed to take the Brexiteers in her cabinet willingly to a realisation that Britain would be entwined with the EU until at least 2021 – without the accusation of heresy being levelled against her. May's secretive nature and ponderous decision making were proving as virtuous as Corbyn's constructive ambiguity before the general election. She had also put money on the table in a bid to unblock the Brexit talks. 'The ball is in their court,' said Boris Johnson as he began a European tour to explain the speech to Britain's EU partners.

Michel Barnier described the speech as 'constructive' and said the prime minister had shown 'a willingness to move forward', but there was no immediate breakthrough. When he sat down with David Davis three days later for the fifth round of talks the EU's chief negotiator again complained that Britain was not offering enough money to show 'sufficient progress' to begin trade talks. In fact, Barnier was privately arguing that the EU should try to meet Britain halfway, commencing talks on a transition deal before the exit deal was finalised so May could see that Florence had changed the terms of trade. However, when he made the case at a meeting of EU ambassadors on 5 October, Barnier was shot down by the Germans and French, who were not ready to reward the personal political risks May had taken. 'Barnier was told that he had a mandate and he should stick to it,' said an EU source. One EU ambassador coldly remarked, 'We are not here to save the Tory Party.' A series of trips by ministers to EU capitals to make the case for compromise backfired.[5] It looked, for a moment, as if May's gamble had failed.

Outside the cabinet, the Eurosceptics were nervous. Leave Means Leave issued a statement saying, 'We are deeply concerned that her proposals could lead to nothing changing either during or after the implementation period. She has fallen for the trap laid by senior civil servants, the Treasury and the CBI.' Jacob Rees-Mogg took to the studios to declare that free movement ought to end in 2019 not 2021 and that the ECJ ought to have no jurisdiction in the UK after Brexit. He added, 'For us to be guaranteeing money, which the speech practically does, so early on, concerns me considerably.' Another gloomy Brexiteer said, 'All it did was confirm that we can't leave the EU properly until five years after the referendum. We know precious little about the terms on which we'll leave. We're committed to an additional two years' subscriptions. They'll pocket it and demand much more.'

Having got some of what he wanted with his *Telegraph* article, Johnson overplayed his hand. Aides briefed the press that he had been responsible for steering May away from a Norway-style soft Brexit, a claim which prompted David Davis to declare, 'I don't think there has been any change in policy in the last few weeks.' Even one ally said, 'He didn't need to go and try and claim credit for changing the Florence speech.'

Apparently emboldened, Johnson went further, giving an interview to the *Sun* on the Saturday before the Conservative conference in which he laid out four personal red lines on Brexit: a transition period of 'not a second more' than two years; accepting no new ECJ court rulings during the transition; no payments for single market access after that; and no 'shadowing' of EU rules as part of a new deal. The first point sought to impose a hard deadline where May had wanted flexibility, the second directly contradicted her plan and the other two were darts aimed at the

Treasury. Having achieved an awkward cabinet truce after a summer of infighting, May had seen her foreign secretary tear it up within eight days. 'There is no point in coming out of the EU and then remaining in rotational orbit around it,' he said. 'That is the worst of both worlds.' Johnson also roamed off piste on public sector wages, declaring, 'I want people to be paid more,' a subject so far outside his Foreign Office purview that it prompted further leadership speculation. The interview had been authorised by Downing Street, but on the eve of a conference where May was desperate to reboot her premiership, this second intervention in a fortnight was an act seen as treachery by May's aides. A senior cabinet minister accused Johnson of trying to oust her: 'He should colour inside the lines, not set his own red lines. He wants to see the boat tip over and see if he can clamber in.' Another minister said, 'Either she sacks Boris or she goes. It's that simple.'

With the storm clouds gathering, May was in as much trouble as Johnson. Allies of the foreign secretary warned that Tory donors were preparing to move their money offshore because the prime minister was 'driving the party into the ground'. One said, 'I detect a change of weather among MPs and donors. People who said to me in July that she must stay until 2019 are now saying. "I don't think she'll make it" or "She shouldn't make it."' Others claimed that Johnson was deliberately trying to get sacked because – after years of earning more than £400,000 for his day job, a column and book deals – he was struggling to manage his extensive family responsibilities on a cabinet minister's salary of £141,505.

Whatever else Johnson had achieved, as the Tory conference opened in Manchester, no one was talking about him as a busted flush. The ConservativeHome leadership survey that weekend had Johnson back at the top of the pile. A cabinet colleague remarked sharply, 'Boris is no longer yesterday's Jacob Rees-Mogg.'

Johnson's antics overshadowed an £11 billion package of announcements by May as conference began that were designed to appeal to young voters by easing the pain of university tuition fees and helping them onto the housing ladder. May announced that she would freeze tuition fees at £9,250 a year and raise the threshold at which graduates started paying off their debt from £21,000 to £25,000, at a cost to taxpayers of £1.2 billion. There was also a £10 billion cash injection to extend the Help to Buy scheme for first-time buyers. In the face of Labour promises to scrap tuition fees altogether, the Tory proposals, which would save graduates just £360 a year, were both ruinously expensive and a politically meagre offering, one which caused despair among MPs that May had decided to bring a peashooter to a gunfight on Corbyn's home turf. As a senior backbencher put it, 'When you go over the top you don't stop in no man's land, you have to keep advancing and take the opposition trench.'

Even these lacklustre proposals had been the subject of a bitter stand-off between the prime minister and the education department. May's chief of staff Gavin Barwell, her policy chief James Marshall and Mike Crowhurst, her education adviser, wanted the PM to use her conference speech to announce a cut in tuition fees, with variable charges based on the cost of the course and its worth to the pupil. The effect would have been to cut the price of arts courses, which are cheaper and do less to boost graduate earning power than so-called STEM degrees – science, technology, engineering and maths. Justine Greening, the education secretary, and the universities minister Jo Johnson, refused point blank. 'Justine and Jo both literally said no,' one senior source recalled. In a fraught series of meetings in Downing Street, the week before conference, Greening told Number 10 officials that making STEM degrees more expensive 'is the opposite of how you plug the skills gap' and argued that ministers should bring back maintenance grants to help poor students with the cost of living and slash interest rates on loans instead, both of which they regarded as more progressive.

Faith in Downing Street's wisdom was dented when Barwell and Marshall argued that the government should also promote two-year-long degree courses. 'They seemed oblivious to the fact that we had literally just passed a Technical and Further Education Act to do just that,' a DfE source said. 'It seemed like they did not have a good grasp of policy.'

Both Greening and Johnson were also horrified to learn that May was planning to announce a major review of tuition fees as well lasting up to a year, something they both thought was a hostage to fortune when it was unclear what outcome the prime minister wanted, and a move that would allow the issue to fester for another twelve months. With May downstairs in Number 10 preparing to do an eve of conference interview, in which she wanted to announce the review, her aides shuttled between the PM and Greening, waiting in a meeting room upstairs, to thrash out a deal. Greening argued, 'We should not constrain ourselves for a full year in order to do something that Jo and I could quite quickly do ourselves.' A source familiar with the exchanges said, 'Justine insisted on an agreement that Theresa would not use the "review" word. She could say we would "look at tuition fees" instead.' The first Greening knew that May had reneged on the arrangement came when May announced in her speech, 'We will undertake a major review of university funding and student financing.' The education secretary had, though, blocked an immediate cut in tuition fees, something that led to her departure from cabinet within three months.

Later, the prime minister's allies – including Nick Timothy – complained that other interesting ideas had been blocked by the Treasury. 'All the significant and interesting stuff that Theresa might have been able to announce was nixed at every stage by Phil,' a cabinet minister said.

Even before May's speech, the mood at the conference in Manchester was sombre and flat. One minister said the four-day event was something to be 'endured rather than enjoyed', while a former minister's verdict was less polite: 'It's absolutely shit!' The only people (other than the couple discovered having sex in the ladies' loos) who seemed to be enjoying themselves were David Davis, who told delegates that he was allergic to orange juice as he hit every party in town, and Jacob Rees-Mogg, whose legion of fans mobbed him demanding selfies. On Sunday night, Rees-Mogg, who addressed nine fringe events, held a private dinner with family and friends to celebrate his status as a potential leadership contender. 'To Moggmentum and Downing Street,' they toasted him with champagne.

May's team, which included Chris Wilkins again, worked on the speech throughout Tuesday night to sharpen it. A key passage on consent for organ donations, which had been due to be announced to Parliament the following week, was hastily added at the last moment to beef up the content. May did not get to bed until gone midnight. With her back to the wall, she had endured a gruelling week of receptions and media interviews that left her drained and listless in some private encounters. May was missing the chiefs. 'Fiona would have torn out half the events and put her to bed,' one MP remarked. It was another mistake in a week of many.

Around 11.30 a.m. on Wednesday, May began her speech well, apologising for her role in the general election debacle, admitting the campaign had been 'too presidential'. She then struck a more personal tone, discussing why she was in politics and talking about her sadness that she had never had children. Then disaster struck. Not once, but three times.

Cabinet ministers watched in stunned silence as a comedian called Simon Brodkin, whose stage name was Lee Nelson, interrupted the prime minister as she was in mid-flow to hand her a fake P45, with the words 'Boris asked me to give you this.' A look of fear briefly flashed across May's eyes, as the recognition hit her that the interruption might derail her big moment. She calmly took the piece of paper and placed it on the floor, but now the room was in pandemonium as Brodkin approached Johnson and asked him if he was happy with his work. The comedian looked surprised he had not yet been pulled away by police protection officers. In the aftermath of the shambles, May said, 'There was nothing about his body language that gave me cause for alarm,' but the fact that Brodkin had obtained a security pass and was allowed to remain feet from the prime minister was hugely embarrassing.

Johnson and David Davis muttered to each other that the interloper was 'a tosser'. The foreign secretary shouted, 'Keep going, Theresa.' Davis – a former member of the Territorial SAS – told friends later, 'He's lucky I didn't hit him. He'd have been down for a long time.' It was left to Amber Rudd to take the lead, ushering Brodkin aside with her arm and a schoolmarmish, 'Leave now.'

Just as May got going again, the cough which had already interrupted her a few times struck with a vengeance. First it disrupted her flow and then she was reduced to great hacking spasms, doubled over as she gulped cold water which only constricted her throat and made the coughing worse. As journalists flicked through the speech and realised May had nine more pages to croak her way through, Rudd ordered Johnson to his feet for a standing ovation designed to buy the prime minister time. When Hammond passed her a cough sweet, May joked, 'It's the chancellor giving something away for free.' Behind the stage, May's team wondered whether to pull her off stage or turn out the lights. May said she never thought about quitting. 'I am a very determined person. I am not someone who gives up.' On she ploughed for another half hour, through numerous bouts of coughing that brought her to a halt.

To cap it all, the slogan on the wall behind May began to fall off, letter by letter. It had been attached, bizarrely, with magnets. When it was over,

Brandon Lewis, the immigration minister, summed up the feelings of many when he said, 'What the actual fuck was that?'

As soon as May had uttered the last syllable of her speech, husband Philip leapt to his feet to comfort his embattled wife. Drawing her close to him, he whispered to her, 'I am so proud of you,' before delivering a pep talk. 'You battled through, battled through, battled through,' he repeated robotically, facial expression fixed as he waved for the cameras. Earlier in the week friends of Philip May from the City had confided that he was worried about the toll the job was taking on his wife. 'They have a very strong marriage and Philip loves her dearly and has clearly been very worried about her,' one friend said. 'She has been unwell and depressed since the election.'

Behind the stage May made a face at one of her aides to suggest she had let the side down. But those around her rallied to express their support as the group met in an upstairs room in the conference centre. May also received a number of supportive text messages from the cabinet, telling her she had been a 'trouper'. 'She felt like she had let us down but we felt that we had let her down,' an aide revealed. Despite claims that she was emotional, aides said May did not cry. But she did flee the conference centre to return to her constituency home, leaving her usual travelling aides behind. Senior figures who tried to contact her that night say they could not get through. 'The whips couldn't get hold of her,' a minister said. 'She did a bunk and turned her phone off.' Her friends wondered if this would finish her for good. It was left to Philip May to urge her not to resign. Gavin Williamson, the chief whip, eventually reinforced that message.

Within a few hours of the debacle, the chief whip was worried by a growing insurrection on the backbenches. Williamson got reports that Grant Shapps was phoning his colleagues to see if more of them wanted to join a delegation to tell May to resign. That evening a former minister texted Williamson, 'She has got to go.' He replied, 'Thanks, that's what I need to know.' Just as it had after the Grenfell Tower disaster, May's career hung in the balance. By 10 p.m. on Wednesday evening, Shapps was confident he had thirty backers. He wanted forty-eight – the number necessary to trigger a vote of no confidence.

MPs were shellshocked by the speech. A backbencher on Shapps' list said, 'There's no way back from that. That was not a car crash, it was an entire motorway pile-up. The driver doesn't get three points, they get a lifetime ban. She'll never be allowed behind the wheel again.' Sympathy for May's plight meant some hesitated before giving Shapps the green light. 'My wife says it would look bad to pick on her when she's had a bad day,' one otherwise rebellious MP said. But others saw a prime minister broken by the strains of office: 'There needs to be a mercy killing.' May's coughing fit had distracted attention from a content-free speech where the big announcement – a freeze on energy prices – was not new, having been a feature of the party's election manifesto. MPs were also contacting party officials to say that May did not look well. 'There is a growing view that she is only staying because she feels it is her duty and that it would not be disloyal to get rid of her, it would be a relief for her,' one official said. 'People are genuinely worried about her.'

Unusually, since chief whips are usually seen and not heard, Williamson had given a platform speech before May, playing up to his reputation for the dark arts. 'I don't very much believe in the stick, but it's amazing what can be achieved with a sharpened carrot,' he quipped with sinister camp. Now he sought to live up to his reputation. When newspapers outed Shapps as the mastermind of the coup on Thursday evening, the MP believed it was Williamson who had named him. In fact, Westminster journalists had known about his role for three months and some had tired of the subterfuge. It suited Williamson to claim the credit too, since it looked like a masterstroke as MPs broke cover to denounce the former party chairman. Shapps doubled down, taking to the airwaves when the first edition of *The Times* dropped and doing more interviews on the Friday. He might have been wiser to keep his head down until he had the numbers.

A self-made man who was one of the Tories' best local campaigners, Shapps ought to have been a man to admire, but too many colleagues remembered the Walter Mitty streak that had led him to make a living selling get-rich-quick schemes under the alter ego Michael Green, a feature of his past that had persuaded David Cameron not to give him a major cabinet post after the 2015 election. MPs who had agreed to support him on the grounds that nothing would happen until there were sufficient rebels were alarmed when he began doing interviews. Others did not see Shapps as a leader to follow. Nicholas Soames took to Twitter and declared, 'Winner of nominees for the person one would least like to go to war with: unanimous decision @grantshapps #shutup.' Thirty MPs from the 2017 intake agreed on their WhatsApp group collectively not to get involved. Shapps was deliberately added to the main MPs' WhatsApp group by colleagues so he could see them venting about his behaviour. Therese Coffey, an environment minister, offered the pithy 'STFU' – shorthand for 'shut the fuck up'.

Not everyone was put off, though. One of Shapps' four former cabinet ministers received an email that read, 'After the lamentable performance of Theresa May, surely it's time for a change of leadership.' The writer urged the MP to 'join forces with Grant Shapps to remove the hapless May'.

The WhatsApp group became an arena for vigilante justice. James Cleverly, the MP for Braintree, had been tipped – not least by himself – as a possible future leader. When Shapps was exposed he urged him to 'just stop'. But Cleverly was then accused of being one of the names on Shapps' list. Cleverly responded by calling his accusers 'wankers' and appealing for an end to the 'witch hunt', which he labelled 'political masturbation'. James Duddridge, the MP for Rochford, told him this was 'far to[o] graphic', prompting Nadine Dorries to accuse Duddridge of being a plotter as well. 'Perhaps you can deny that is the case while you are here,' she wrote. When Duddridge did not reply, Dorries fired another shot: 'You read my message three minutes ago – how long does it take you to type "not true".' Dorries went on to name Bob Neill and Owen Paterson as conspirators. Each of them denied backing Shapps. MPs claimed Cleverly had joined the plot after the election and had then been 'bought off' by the whips with a post as a parliamentary private secretary. 'He told colleagues that Theresa had to go and discussed lists,' one MP said. 'He only pulled out when Downing Street got wind of it and gave him a job.'[6] Mike Penning, a former minister fired by May after working on her leadership campaign, and also known to be disgruntled, was handed a knighthood just five days later.

Shapps was an irrepressible character. As far as he was concerned, the coup was on hold. It had not been defeated. He had more names on his list than he had a week ago. He had also spent his time consulting veterans involved in the successful plot to topple Iain Duncan Smith in 2003, which took three weeks to unfold after a disastrous party conference. On Friday evening, Andrew Mitchell was the guest speaker at Shapps' association annual dinner. The following week Shapps was approached by several MPs who had publicly condemned him. Robert Halfon apologised for calling him a 'knucklehead'. Shapps replied, 'I had no idea that's what you had said.'

Gavin Williamson took the plaudits for a coup crushed. Theresa May lived to fight another day and Amber Rudd declared that the prime minister had 'the absolute support of her entire cabinet'.

The truth was very different.

One day after May's meltdown, three members of her cabinet decided her time was up. It was Thursday afternoon when one picked up the telephone, called a colleague and said, 'It can't go on like this.' To the ministers the speech farce was more than just unfortunate, it was a metaphor for a government that had been paralysed since the general election setback. They talked to a third minister – one of many in the cabinet who entertained leadership ambitions. The third minister agreed it was only a matter of time before May would have to stand down. One of the ministers – very far from a usual suspect in the plotting game – picked up the phone to the *Sunday Times* and said: 'I think it's very difficult to see how this is a long-term proposition. It's a when question now. It feels to me that this is over before Christmas.'

The minister said discussions were under way about trying to find a 'Michael Howard option' – mirroring the period of calm ushered in by the former Tory leader after the implosion of Iain Duncan Smith's leadership in 2003. There was talk of sending former leaders like Howard and Sir John Major to tell May her time was up. 'Michael Howard wears a grey suit,' one minister said. This minister favoured Boris Johnson as leader, but would also have been happy with David Davis or Amber Rudd. 'Boris is the biggest winner, but the party may not wear it,' the minister said. 'But we're in a position where any of the acceptable candidates is better than the current position. The PM wanted to do some exciting things at the conference speech, but she wasn't able to do so because she wasn't able to impose her authority on the rest of the cabinet. You think: whether it's on Brexit or domestic policy, nothing is happening, no grip is being exercised, no leadership is being shown.' A fourth minister said on Friday, 'The big change from Wednesday is that there is no prospect now of the prime minister leading the party into the next general election. I do think the prime minister has to be thinking about: how do I achieve an orderly transition?'

At least one cabinet minister was also in touch with Shapps that week. Other plotters received calls from MPs supporting Johnson's leadership cause and at least one discussed his intentions with Davis on Wednesday evening. Boris, who had whisked his wife Marina away for a holiday in Italy while the drama was unfolding, sent a message to the Tory MPs' WhatsApp group urging them to read a loyalist article by Amber Rudd. He said,

> Folks I am away but just read this!
> See amber piece this am
> She is right right right
> We have JUST HAD AN ELECTION and people are fed up with all this malarkey
> Get behind the pm. Ordinary punters I have spoken to thought her speech was good and anyone can have a cold
> Circle the wagons turn the fire on Corbyn and talk about nothing except our great policies and what we can do for the country.

Privately, senior civil servants also warned ministers not to move against May ahead of the European summit in Brussels at the end of October, which would decide whether the olive branch she had offered in her Florence speech would be accepted. The cabinet coup stalled.

May sought to stabilise her position with a light-hearted but resolute interview for the *Sunday Times*, in which she denied crying over her speech setback: 'One minute journalists are accusing me of being an ice maiden or a robot, then they claim I'm a weeping woman in dire need of a good night's sleep!' she said. 'The truth is my feelings can be hurt, like everyone else, but I am pretty resilient.' Explosively, May hinted she would like to move Boris Johnson in her next reshuffle. 'I didn't come into politics for an easy life,' she said. In a private conversation that week she had said, 'There is not a binary choice between keeping Boris and sacking Boris', implying that demotion was also an option. Johnson's friends claimed he would resign rather than walk away.

That was a problem for another day. May had survived the humiliation of conference but weakened and demoralised she still had to get an EU deal. In the days after Birmingham it became clear again that her cabinet was still bitterly split and the Florence speech had failed to persuade the other member states to meet her halfway. May's position was again under threat. However, initially it was Philip Hammond whose head was on the block.

'SUFFICIENT PROGRESS ...'

Cabinet on 10 October, six days after May's conference meltdown, laid bare the bitter divisions among her senior ministers. The dispute concerned the slow pace of government preparations for the 'no deal' scenario with Brussels and the belief among Brexiteers that Philip Hammond was deliberately dragging his feet. The issue had come up before. Before the Florence speech, both Sajid Javid and Jeremy Hunt had urged Hammond to release funds so their departments could make preparations. The chancellor refused. Now Michael Gove raised the subject, arguing that there should be regular updates to cabinet on the status of each department's plans for Brexit and a no-deal option in 2021. 'The credibility of your position is greater if you are prepared to walk away,' he said. 'I'm just a bit worried that we need to do more.'

Ministers had been annoyed to discover that under Treasury guidance, ministers could not spend any money on infrastructure or IT contracts until after the Withdrawal Bill received royal assent. That would make it difficult to prepare for the world after March 2019, let alone prepare contingency plans for all eventualities in March 2021. 'The business case for spending money had to go through four separate government agencies to be approved before they could spend a single penny,' a cabinet minister explained. Treasury rules meant that money was supposed to be spent in ways that got the greatest return for the taxpayer. Spending on day-to-day projects might garner £1.50 of benefit for every £1 spent, whereas preparing for a no-deal scenario might produce worthwhile gain, say £1.20 per £1 spent, but not as much. It gave Hammond power of veto over no-deal preparations.

Unbeknownst to most cabinet ministers – but Hammond probably was aware – Gove and Boris Johnson had both written a pointed memo to May, which the foreign secretary had delivered by hand to Gavin Barwell, the prime minister's chief of staff, with the instruction that it was 'for your and Gavin's eyes only'. The memo combined faint praise for the prime minister's 'sensible pragmatism', a demand that Brexit must lead to Britain becoming 'a fully independent self-governing country by the time of the next election' and a scarcely veiled complaint about Hammond and 'those who wish to frustrate that end'. The memo, which leaked a month later, read, 'We are profoundly worried that in some parts of Government the current preparations are not proceeding with anything like sufficient energy. We have heard it argued by some that we cannot start preparations on the basis of "No Deal" because that would undermine our obligation of "sincere co-operation" with the EU. If taken seriously, that would leave us over a barrel in 2021.' Gove and Johnson warned that the 'Whitehall machine' and its 'ossified ways of working' cannot be 'left to its own devices' and called on May to 'clarify the minds' of all ministers 'whatever their original positions during the referendum'.[1]

Gove's hand had been strengthened by May's decision to add him to her smaller Brexit 'war cabinet'. In the meeting on 10 October his call for the Treasury to spend immediately on no-deal planning was supported by Johnson and Chris Grayling. Hammond disagreed. 'No, we should delay spending until the last possible moment,' he said, winning support from Amber Rudd. 'We shouldn't spend money before we need to,' said the home secretary. 'That's what the implementation period is for.' May listened to the arguments before telling Gove, 'We should have a discussion about this, but I don't think we need weekly updates.'

Irritated by the ambush and thinking he had May's support, Hammond went back into Number 10 later in the day and got permission to write an article for *The Times* designed to reassure business that the government had the preparations in hand. However, the piece submitted contained a sentence which read, 'We are planning for every outcome and we will find any necessary funding and we will only spend it when it's responsible to do so.' Hammond's aides later claimed he was seeking to reassure taxpayers he would be parsimonious with their cash. But, coming just a few hours after a cabinet row in which the chancellor had refused to open the nation's chequebook, the wording was incendiary. When the op-ed was shown to Downing Street, May's media team took one look at it and announced that if the line remained as it was the story would be a cabinet split. The Treasury ignored them. When *The Times* splashed on 'Hammond refuses to budget for hard Brexit', the Eurosceptics went into orbit.

A cabinet minister said, 'It was pretty clear he thought he needed to slap down the Brexiteers for trying to ramp up the no-deal scenario.' The mutual suspicion was such that Hammond feared preparing for no deal would allow the Brexiteers to make that their preferred option, while Gove and Johnson feared that failure to prepare for no deal would allow the chancellor to bounce them into accepting whatever deal was on offer from Brussels.

Hammond doubled his stakes telling MPs on the Treasury select committee the same morning that he did not want to 'waste' money preparing for the UK to crash out of the EU in March 2019 when there was still a chance of a deal with Brussels. At Prime Minister's Questions, May overruled him, telling the Commons that £250 million was being handed to departments such as the Home Office and HM Revenue & Customs. 'Where money needs to be spent, it will be spent,' she said.

The chancellor's actions were the final straw for Nigel Lawson. The former chancellor called for Hammond to be sacked, saying, 'What he is doing is very close to sabotage.' He added, 'The really important thing now is that we prepare for the no-deal outcome and it is grossly irresponsible if we don't prepare.' Later, Lawson and Owen Paterson said Britain should unilaterally announce that it was pulling out of the negotiations and going to WTO rules, something for which Davis, Johnson and Gove knew the customs authorities were not prepared.

The *Daily Mail* splashed the following morning with 'SACK SABOTEUR HAMMOND', branding him a 'dismal, defeatist, relentlessly negative' Eeyore. A day later, the paper revealed that he had enjoyed a seafood lunch before the Conservative conference with arch-remainer George Osborne, proof, the paper claimed, that they were part of a 'LOBSTER PLOT' to block Brexit. What the paper would have made of the fact that Gove had dined with Nigel Lawson earlier that week is anyone's guess.

Eurosceptic nerves were already strained by an interview May had given to LBC's Iain Dale on the Wednesday, in which she refused to say how she would vote if there were another referendum on Brexit. 'I don't answer hypothetical questions,' the prime minister said, effectively refusing to endorse her own government's main policy. Pressed, she added,

'What I did last time round was I looked at everything and I came to a judgement and I would do exactly the same this time round. But we are not having another referendum.'

On a trip to the US later that week, Hammond sought to remove the heat from the debate, using a broadcast clip to stress where the cabinet agreed. 'I understand that people have very strong views but we are going to the same place,' he said. 'We all have the same agenda. The enemy, the opponents are out there on the other side of the table.' Characterising the rest of the EU as 'the enemy' caused further uproar and cemented the view of Hammond's cabinet colleagues that he was doing their cause as much harm as good. Within an hour the chancellor had posted an apology on Twitter, but that weekend even senior Remain cabinet ministers were privately suggesting he should be fired. Reflecting on his series of disastrous media outings, one said, 'Philip is an inept political operator in quite a crowded field.' A second senior cabinet minister told colleagues that May should appoint Gove as chancellor since he would be more likely to devise imaginative policies and, as a Brexiteer, should take responsibility for finding the £350 million for the NHS.

When allies of Hammond sought to get back on the front foot, briefing that his plans for a safety-first budget were being torn up and the chancellor was looking at lower tax rates for the young, May's aides were furious. 'Why the fuck would anyone talk up a budget a month out like that?' one asked. 'It's rule number one: manage expectations.' Seven months on from the National Insurance U-turn, Hammond seemed not to have learned his lesson. The following day, the *Evening Standard* suggested that the plan to axe stamp duty for first-time buyers – floated before the election and examined and rejected before party conference – was back in play.

May had made her Florence speech hoping to unite her cabinet around a common cause and persuade the European Commission that Britain had moved enough to justify the start of trade talks. Nineteen days later she knew she had failed. The prime minister had just one card left – to appeal directly to her fellow EU leaders.

May had telephone conversations with Angela Merkel and Emmanuel Macron, the leaders of Germany and France, spelling out her predicament. 'She stuck it to them,' a source said. May gave a broad indication that, on top of the €20 billion she had indicated it would pay during a transition, the UK was prepared to pay future liabilities amounting to around the same amount again. Given the prime minister's precarious position, neither leader was prepared to accept private promises. In their separate conversations Merkel and Macron both pressed for Britain to move further on the money and submit written pledges that would formalise the signals in the Florence speech. Merkel remained firm that it was not her responsibility to solve Britain's problems. The chancellor had been up that road before during David Cameron's renegotiation and it had not ended well for either of them.

It was a measure of May's weakness that she then appealed first to the man who had betrayed her trust the last time they had broken bread – Jean-Claude Juncker. On Monday, 16 October, three days before the European Council meeting that would help to decide the future of the talks, May sat down for dinner with the Commission president in his dining room on the thirteenth floor of the Berlaymont building. Michel Barnier was also present. May was accompanied by David Davis and Oliver Robbins, Juncker by Martin Selmayr, the chief of staff blamed for leaking the details of their last supper in April. On that occasion, May had used the leak to project strength at the start of the general election campaign. This time, her only trump card was her weakness.

In her understated way, the prime minister threw herself on the mercy of the EU officials, quietly but firmly making the case that she had expended what was left of her political capital to move the government's position in the ways demanded by Brussels. Britain had spelt out more of its approach in the position papers over the summer and made a detailed offer on the rights of EU citizens. Most of all, she had risked the ire of the Eurosceptics by offering up money with no strings attached which would ensure there was no black hole in the budget for the other twenty-seven member states. Now, she needed help. She had softened her position, she needed them to do the same. Davis had impressed upon May that Barnier and the others were assiduous readers of the English newspapers. They were intimately familiar with her conference disaster and the soap opera surrounding Boris Johnson. Had they not seen how her enemies hovered in case she stumbled?

Juncker pushed back, saying the UK still needed to pay up. British sources said the exchanges were 'something close to a row'. As they left the dinner, May and Davis heard Juncker turn to Selmayr and say, 'We won't have any leaks of this, will we Martin,' a remark received with 'hilarity'. After the dinner, a joint statement was issued agreeing to 'accelerate' the talks but without providing concrete details. It described the meal as having taken place in a 'constructive and friendly atmosphere'.

When May arrived at the summit on Thursday it appeared that the other leaders might be more prepared to help. Merkel announced that there were 'encouraging' signs that trade talks could begin in December. As they entered the council room, Merkel and Macron walked with her, the three leaders locked in conversation. They were talking about the Iranian nuclear deal, as it happened, rather than Brexit, but that did not matter. May had pictures of her being taken seriously, supported even, by the Council's two key power brokers. It was a far cry from the lonely pose she often struck on these occasions.

Over dinner with her fellow leaders on Thursday evening, the prime minister said she was prepared to break the impasse by going further on the money. 'The financial settlement will not be easy for me,' she said, 'but Florence was not my last word.' Merkel acknowledged that the EU27 would need to move as well to formulate a new negotiating mandate to move things forward. If they were not yet prepared to start trade talks, they were prepared to start talking among themselves about how they would approach those talks.

When May had left the room, the other leaders sent the notetakers out so they could discuss her plight frankly. 'Three or four' leaders – among them Mark Rutte, the Dutch premier, and Leo Varadkar, the Irish prime minister – advocated giving May a helping hand. The leaders warned that failure to move now would push May to breaking point, could lead to her being ousted or to Eurosceptics pushing Britain into a turbulent crash out of the EU. Dalia Grybauskaitė, the forceful Lithuanian president, warned, 'We need to be careful, we don't want to cause chaos. We can't let the government collapse.' The leaders agreed that May was the best prime minister on offer. They did not want to deal with Boris Johnson. Others said it was not the EU's role to settle internal Conservative Party disagreements. Merkel urged caution and order. She still wanted a commitment from Britain to move closer towards the EU's €60 billion demand before stage two of the talks could get going. However, the leaders agreed that they would be prepared to help May if she moved first. When they were done, Donald Tusk – the Council president – announced, 'I hope we will be able to move to second phase talks in December.'

Just when it looked as if May could enjoy the positive outcome, the same newspaper which had printed the account of her dinner with Juncker in April, the *Frankfurter Allgemeine Sonntagszeitung*, produced another lurid account of their new encounter, written by the same journalist as before, Thomas Gutschker. The article claimed May had 'begged for help', that she was 'anxious', 'despondent', 'discouraged' and 'tormented'. 'She wears deep rings under her eyes,' the report said. 'She looks like someone who does not sleep at night.' If this was hurtful for May, there was a positive aspect to her weakness. Her parlous state had convinced her fellow leaders that she should not be allowed to fall. 'Better to negotiate with a realistic May than with the dream dancer Johnson,' the report concluded.

Freed of the necessities of silence, Nick Timothy called out Martin Selmayr on Twitter: 'After constructive Council meeting, Selmayr does this. Reminder that some in Brussels want no deal or a punitive one.' Selmayr hit back, denying the allegation, which he had not done in April: 'This is false. I know it doesn't fit your cliché, @NickJTimothy. But @JunckerEU & I have no interest in weakening PM'. He claimed it was 'an attempt to frame the EU side and to undermine talks'. Selmayr's claims of innocence were possible since Juncker had debriefed the Commission's Brexit task force after the dinner, dramatically widening the pool of potential leakers. Gutschker was known to speak directly to Juncker. David Davis blamed the Commission duo: 'There were only six people in the room and Barnier wouldn't do that.'

Whoever was the source, their actions might have even helped May. In Berlin, Merkel reacted with fury. 'It is known that she has lost patience with the British Conservatives but the last thing she wants is for Theresa May to be replaced in the middle of the Brexit negotiations,' a source said. Juncker also denied the newspaper's account. 'I had an excellent working dinner with Theresa May. She was in good shape, she was not tired, she was fighting as is her duty.' No national leader wants to be pitied, but at that point it was the most effective weapon in her armoury.

Yet there were grounds for thinking the description of May's demeanour was accurate too. The following week, a report emerged of May as 'stricken and stunned' in meetings. 'On one occasion she sat in silence for almost ten minutes while the visitor she had invited to see her waited for her to lead the conversation. He left the meeting deciding she no longer wanted to be prime minister.'[2]

Those who were there say similar agonising pauses characterised May's interactions with her chancellor ahead of the budget on 22 November, now a make or break event for Hammond. He was in a tight spot. The Treasury had received preliminary estimates from the independent Office of Budget Responsibility (OBR) that the productivity figures were to be downgraded, meaning a good portion of the headroom Hammond had maintained in the public finances would evaporate and the prospect of wage growth – a key measure for hard-up voters – receded further. The OBR downgraded estimates of GDP growth to 1.6 per cent up to the next election.

Both prime minister and chancellor acknowledged that, following the failures of conference, something big was needed on housing. Officials say there were 'heated' exchanges, as Hammond fought off Sajid Javid's calls for £50bn of borrowing to build and initially pressed May to allow building on the green belt. May told the chancellor, 'Absolutely no way. That will not fly.' In the end Hammond also realised that he risked breaking Tory manifesto pledges – his mistake in March's budget – and backed down. 'They're both quite difficult characters,' a source who witnessed the exchanges said. 'They're a little bit awkward with each other. He can be quite patronising to her.' Downing Street aides instead wanted to revive Nick Timothy's pre-election plan for a stamp duty cut for first-time buyers. The policy had now evolved into the abolition of stamp duty – at that point levied on sales over £125,000 – for first-time buyers on all properties up to £300,000, with those valued at up to £500,000 exempt of tax on the first £300,000. Hammond resisted. 'Number 10 twisted his arm. He had to be shown polling,' a source said.

Relations at the top were not improved when Michael Gove twice used cabinet meetings at the start of November, and again the week before the budget, to 'audition' for the role of chancellor, trotting out a surprising knowledge of EU directives on financial markets one week and, in the words of one colleague, deploying 'lots of long, economicky words' as the big day approached.[3]

Hammond remained his own worst enemy. The weekend before the budget, the chancellor had negotiated an interview with the *Sunday Times* with aplomb, joking that he was no Eeyore, speaking passionately about helping young people onto the housing ladder and even discussing his children. But after posing for some statesmanlike pictures, Hammond inexplicably let down his guard and said, 'Now one for those difficult economic figures,' pulled a gurning expression and scratched his head like a latter-day Stan Laurel. The resulting image undid much of his good work. That Sunday, in an interview with the BBC's Andrew Marr, Hammond claimed, 'Where are all these unemployed people? There are no unemployed people', an assertion that was just 1.42 million out. He was later forced to apologise.

Nonetheless, Hammond was confident enough to open his budget speech with a joke about May's conference meltdown. Two days earlier he had asked her, 'If it's all right with you, I'd like to do a joke about the cough.' May replied, 'I'll bring some Strepsils.' Yet even Hammond did not know that the prime minister was going to turn up in the Commons with a packet of the cough sweets and brandish them at the key moment. 'That wasn't rehearsed,' an aide said. Hammond also found time to make a dig at Gove, telling MPs that the section on macroeconomic forecasts was 'the bit with the long economicky words in it'.

In the speech Hammond talked the language of prudence but quietly loosened the purse strings by £25bn over the forecast period, pumping £2.8bn into the NHS and £1.5bn to ease problems with universal credit. 'He spent £25bn saving himself,' one colleague remarked. However, Hammond's luck held. Despite some analysis that the stamp duty cut would drive up house prices, polls suggested the policy was popular. Jeremy Corbyn's response to the speech was widely panned as a rant and in a series of broadcast interviews John McDonnell was the one who looked evasive, refusing to say by how much borrowing would rise under Labour. When the following day a Downing Street official prepped May for an interview, with Hammond in the room, the aide said, 'I'm sorry about this, chancellor, but they will ask, "Has the chancellor done enough to keep his job?"'

May replied, 'Yes, of course.' Both laughed.

Even Hammond's aides still could not quite believe it had gone so smoothly. That Thursday there was a relaxed mood in Number 10. 'It has landed well,' one of May's aides said to a close ally of the chancellor. Fearing that he could yet seize defeat from the jaws of victory, the Treasury official replied, 'Don't say that; he's still got two hours of opening his mouth.' This time Hammond did not come a cropper and one opinion poll that week even put the Tories ahead of Labour. A fellow minister said, 'It's the first week since the general election debacle that we have looked like a government.'

The most significant event of budget week might not even have been the budget. On Monday 20 November the prime minister held a cabinet committee meeting on Brexit in which the arch-Brexiteers Boris Johnson and Michael Gove agreed she could make a new financial offer to Brussels in an attempt to uncork the stalled talks. In effect, they gave May a free hand to double her offer to around €40m. In return, Gove won the right to demand that Britain be allowed to leave the Common Fisheries Policy and take back control of its sovereign waters during the two-year transition period. The prime minister asked each of the ministers present to make a solemn pledge that they would not even discuss the contents of the meeting with their own special advisers – in order to prevent leaks to journalists. 'There was a vow,' one aide confirmed. 'I poured a bit of wine down him and he still didn't tell me.'

There was still cabinet angst about the way the EU was seeking to enshrine the powers of the European Court of Justice in the UK by insisting that the ECJ rule on disputes involving EU citizens living in the UK. Both Johnson and Gove raised the issue. In the following fortnight, David Davis helped broker a deal in cabinet and then with Barnier that British courts would be supreme but could apply to take into account the judgment of the ECJ. Davis was also instrumental in pushing May to secure a sunset clause meaning ECJ influence would lapse after eight years. A cabinet minister recalled later, 'The concern was that the role of the ECJ be both time limited and restricted to requests by the UK courts, rather than being a requirement.' After a torrid summer, Davis had some of his old mojo back. 'The EU wanted the ECJ to be a direct court of appeal with the right it currently has to adjudicate cases and impose fines,' said one DExEU official. 'They also wanted the Commission itself to have a "monitoring" role over citizens' rights in the UK. They've got none of that. At various points, the text involved compulsory reference for interpretation, no sunset clause, a fifteen-year sunset clause and each time DD said he wouldn't sign it off.'

If that looked like a win for Britain, the EU27 could scarcely believe how quickly May had agreed to double her financial offer on the exit bill. By 23 November the deal had been briefed to the rest of the EU. The

€40bn–€45bn offer was only two thirds of the original demand and less than half the more recent and speculative figure of €100bn. Yet one senior EU source claimed 'jaws dropped' when it became clear that Britain had even agreed to pay into a fund to recompense the Turks for deterring migration from Syria to the EU. 'We got everything we wanted,' the source added.[4]

It was just as well progress had been made on the money and citizens' rights because the issue of Northern Ireland now blew up, threatening the entire deal. The first portent of disaster came on 3 October, when the European Parliament – following talks between Barnier and Guy Verhofstadt's Brexit steering group – voted to grant Northern Ireland 'special status' in which avoiding a hard border with the Republic would mean 'the United Kingdom stays in the customs union or that Northern Ireland stays in some form in the internal market and customs union'. The British government's approach was that the ultimate arrangements in Ireland could only be determined when the parameters of the final trade deal were known. But May, Robbins and Davis had not reckoned with the determination of the Commission and the Irish government to use the border as a wedge issue.

On Wednesday 8 November, the day before the sixth round of talks, Robbins was handed a Commission talking points document with a sting in the final paragraph. It said to avoid a hard border it would be 'essential' that there be 'no emergence of regulatory divergence' between the North and South in Ireland. Robbins went 'apeshit', demanding of Sabine Weyand whether this was a new red line. He was assured it was not, but it was a serious complication.[5] Nine days later, May met Leo Varadkar at an EU summit in Gothenberg. In private and public, Varadkar issued a stark warning that his government would block progress to phase two of the talks at the December Council meeting unless the UK guarantee that there would be no hard border. 'We want that written down in practical terms in the conclusions of phase one,' he said. He was openly insulting to May: 'Sometimes it doesn't seem like they have thought all this through.'

After months of assuming that the nature of the post-Brexit border could be resolved through fudge, remote technology to track consign-ments of goods and a casual blind eye turned to smuggling – the same arrangements that for two decades had kept the peace process on track – ministers were faced with the suggestion that the only way to prevent a hard border was for Britain to stay in the customs union, something May had ruled out and the Brexiteers would not accept, or for Northern Ireland to stay in it, something that would move the practical border to the Irish Sea and was anathema to the DUP, on whose votes the Conservative government depended for its survival. Varadkar was facing an election and keen to take a stand for domestic political reasons, but his intervention was no less dramatic for that.

On Saturday, 2 December, the weekend before May hoped to finalise the deal with Juncker, Varadkar's intervention was weaponised by Brussels. Donald Tusk, the president of the European Council, made explicit that Ireland had a veto over the deal, stating that if the UK's offer on the border 'is unacceptable to Ireland it will be unacceptable to the EU'. Tusk went further, perhaps revealing the EU's real game – to use the Irish situation to coax Britain into close regulatory alignment with the EU – when he said, 'The key to the UK's future lies, in some ways, in Dublin, at least as long as Brexit negotiations continue.' In Downing Street, Gavin Barwell regarded Tusk's words as 'a major outrage', according to one confidant of the chief of staff. Barwell told one colleague, 'The Irish are behaving very badly. The EU is not the issue. The issue is Ireland.' A friend added, 'He was extraordinarily annoyed at the attempt to bounce us.'

That Saturday night, Arlene Foster, the DUP leader, used a speech at her party's Lagan Valley association warning the UK not to 'isolate' Northern Ireland. May was also under pressure at home from the hardline Brexiteers. On Sunday, 3 December, senior Eurosceptics fired a warning shot, issuing seven new 'red lines' she should not cross when she met Jean-Claude Juncker the following day to try to finalise the phase one deal with the EU. In their letter to the prime minister, more than thirty former cabinet ministers – including Owen Paterson, John Redwood, David Jones and Nigel Lawson – business leaders and economists demanded that May gave no money to Brussels and walk out of the negotiations unless their conditions were met. She was already planning to agree a deal which violated at least five of them: that she demand a free trade agreement without tariffs by the end of March 2018; an end to 'any jurisdiction' by the European Court of Justice in the UK; an agreement from Brussels that the UK will be free to negotiate, sign and implement trade deals during the two-year transition period; that no new EU regulations would apply during the transition; and that freedom of movement be scrapped.

On the Sunday, as Davis went back and forth with Number 10 and Barnier's team, new language was drafted that would see the UK promise to 'maintain full alignment' between the UK and the EU in the event that other solutions to the Northern Ireland border were not forthcoming. It was a classic EU fudge. The British government could argue that other solutions would present themselves while Barnier's team had inserted the thin end of the wedge under May's position if, as the Commission fervently believed, such a solution was a chimera.

As May and Davis flew to Brussels on the Monday morning, where they were met by Robbins, who was armed with the latest text, Juncker briefed the European Parliament Brexit team about the deal. The MEPs were surprised May had agreed to the wording on 'full alignment' and questioned the Commission president as to whether Downing Street had really signed it off. No one thought to ask if she had Arlene Foster's seal of approval. The DUP only had the text read to them that morning, shortly before May was due to sit down to lunch with Juncker in his offices on the thirteenth floor of the Berlaymont, the Commission headquarters.

It was 1.16 p.m. in Brussels, where May and Juncker were tucking into a lunch of turbot, when the first draft of the agreement, suggesting there would be 'no regulatory divergence' between Northern Ireland and the Republic, leaked to the Irish broadcaster RTE. In another comedy of errors, RTE tweeted again a few minutes later to clarify that the draft had already been abandoned and replaced with 'continued regulatory alignment' – but by then it was too late. The DUP were already spooked. To some – with Ian Paisley Jr to the fore – it looked like a bid to bind the province closer to Dublin than London. To Eurosceptics it seemed like a bid to keep Ulster inside the single market and the customs union.

In a statement, DUP leader Arlene Foster said, 'We will not accept any form of regulatory divergence which separates Northern Ireland economically or politically from the rest of the United Kingdom.' It should not have been a surprise. The previous Thursday the DUP had threatened to rethink its deal with the Conservatives if it was 'treated differently than the rest of the UK'. After the failure to land the confidence and supply agreement for weeks after May had told the Queen she had done so, this was further evidence of shambolic naivety in Number 10 about the necessity of nailing down the Democratic Unionists. One factor was the move, a month earlier, of the chief whip Gavin Williamson to become defence secretary, something that robbed May of her chief interlocutor with the DUP. MPs complained that Williamson's replacement Julian Smith and his deputy Esther McVey should have man-marked Nigel Dodds and Jeffrey Donaldson, the senior DUP figures in Westminster. 'While Theresa and DD were in Brussels, the whips office should have been sitting with the DUP, explaining what was happening, holding their hands,' one said. A normally loyal minister also blamed Damian Green, the man who was supposed to have May's back: 'It's extraordinary. Julian should have been holding their hand. Damian should have been on the phone to them.' Another MP said, 'They've negotiated the Good Friday Agreement and everything else in Northern Irish politics – of course they're going to be good negotiators. You can't piss around with the DUP. We should have known that.' Others noted that the lack of political grip would have been unthinkable under Nick Timothy and Fiona Hill and, for the first time since the election, some MPs privately voiced the view that Timothy should return. 'There was no one on the political side of May's team who had any experience of these types of negotiations or a political brain to foresee any of the dangers,' one source said.

Desperate to get the DUP back on board, May took over Juncker's office while the Commission president and his aides retreated to a neighbouring, and much smaller, study. May was patched through to Foster's mobile, watched by Davis and Robbins. The call lasted more than an hour while an increasingly agitated Juncker and his team remained cooped up next door. When it was over, the DUP had still refused to budge. One source in Juncker's entourage revealed that he lost his temper with May – claims hushed up by both sides afterwards but which reached the ears of at least one EU head of state. Juncker's team had made it clear to Downing Street that May should not come to Brussels unless she was ready to do a deal. Now the Commission president accused her of 'failing even to speak for her own government', adding, 'You can't come here to negotiate if you don't have a mandate.'

May had survived as prime minister because Eurosceptics had concluded that she was best placed to deliver the Brexit they wanted. With that in doubt, for the fourth time in six months – after the general election setback, the Grenfell Tower disaster and her meltdown at the party conference in October – May's humiliation unleashed the beginnings of a campaign to oust her.

The finger of blame was also pointed at Robbins, who Eurosceptics believed was using the Irish issue to usher in the civil service's preferred solution: permanent regulatory alignment with the EU across the whole of the UK. A former minister said that week, 'The whole process of Brexit is being run by Robbins, who has the PM's ear. Olly is very keen on this maximum alignment end-state scenario and is willing to trade anything to get over the line. There's no check on him.' Iain Duncan Smith, the former work and pensions secretary, spoke to May and Robbie Gibb, the Downing Street director of communications, warning them that Eurosceptics would not tolerate any moves that would keep Britain a de facto member of the customs union. He told them not to just 'take a line' from the civil service. In fact, the government's position was that it would not accept EU rules in relation to Northern Ireland but would achieve them by equivalent means – and only in areas such as energy and agriculture where there are already all-Ireland arrangements. Yet Downing Street had failed to explain this. Gibb, a very hands-off spin doctor, told his staff they should not seek to firefight every crisis and was happy to let the row play out in the belief that it would be quickly forgotten. That meant the coverage on twenty-four-hour media as the crisis unfolded that week was shaped by the Irish government, the DUP and Commission sources, while Number 10 appeared paralysed. A Tory special adviser recalled, 'There was no grip at all – a complete inability to make decisions.' Officials in DExEU complained that they put in papers to Number 10 for a decision and received instead just a note saying 'thanks'. One career civil servant even ventured, 'Bring back Gordon Brown, all is forgiven. That's how bad it is.'

In the cabinet there was despair that another set piece had descended into chaos. That Monday afternoon, a cabinet minister texted a prominent backbencher their assessment of the prime minister: 'She's fucking useless.' By Tuesday a small group of MPs who had defended May after the conference setback began openly discussing whether they should submit letters to the backbench 1922 Committee demanding a vote of no confidence. On the night of Tuesday, 5 December, some fifty MPs in the Tory 92 Group gathered for dinner at the Vincent Rooms, a private dining room in Westminster. Philip Davies, the MP for Shipley, got to his feet and – according to three witnesses – made clear that he thought a different leader should be found to deliver Brexit. 'Philip Davies gave a speech about how crap Theresa May is,' one MP said. A former minister present added, 'He was very blunt. He essentially said we should find a way of replacing her.' Davies denied he had gone as far as calling for May's head but did admit, 'I was asking about how we might go about achieving what we want to achieve in terms of Brexit. I posed some questions. I mentioned the leadership of the party.' The intervention was telling, in part, because Davies was in a relationship with the deputy chief whip, Esther McVey. Chris Grayling, the transport secretary who had chaired May's leadership campaign, made a plea for loyalty. But another MP present said, 'The leadership was the sole topic of discussion around the table. People were very unhappy with the Arlene Foster debacle.'

The following morning, a man was charged with planning to use an improvised explosive device to blow up the gates of Downing Street before entering Number 10 to kill May. The story prompted one mutinous MP to remark, 'MI5 has not uncovered all the plots to bump off the prime minister.' After prime minister's questions, Barwell sought one-to-one meetings with prominent backbenchers like Nadine Dorries, apparently fearful that some might break cover to denounce May. Andrew Mitchell, David Davis's closest parliamentary ally, invited members of the 2015 and 2017 intakes to his office for a drink. The rebels did not even trouble to hide. During a late vote that week, May saw Zac Goldsmith, the former London mayoral candidate, talking to Brexiteer Andrew Bridgen and Grant Shapps, who had been gathering support for a move against her in October. 'She gave them quite a glare,' said one witness. Goldsmith was not intimidated, telling colleagues, 'My four-year-old daughter could do a better job.' He openly discussed with colleagues whether to submit a letter calling for a vote of no confidence.

The sense of a government under siege was compounded when MPs called for David Davis to be held in contempt of Parliament after the Brexit secretary told a select committee that officials had not prepared formal Brexit 'impact assessments'. DExEU had been ordered to hand over the documents following complaints to the Speaker by Chuka Umunna. Davis had previously claimed that fifty-eight papers on the impact of Brexit on different sectors of the economy went into 'excruciating detail'. When his department eventually passed them on, the papers were sketchy and much of the information was redacted. In an agonising outing at the DExEU committee, Davis insisted these were not, strictly speaking, impact assessments – a very precise term in Whitehall – but 'sectoral analyses'. A lack of precision by his opponents had given Davis a way out, but the Institute for Government think tank, pompously but accurately, said he had 'shown contempt for the principle of making decisions based on thorough evidence and analysis'.

This troubled Davis more than his reputation as a public bruiser would suggest. He and the Tory whips privately told Conservative MPs on the Brexit committee not to cause him trouble as it might mean the end of his career. 'DD has been going around telling people he might have to resign,' a senior Tory confided that week. 'He was very down and muttering to people that he might have to go,' a close friend and former minister confirmed. Both Jacob Rees-Mogg and Peter Bone, stalwarts of the European Research Group, 'initially took quite a purist view, but ultimately voted to back DD,' an ally recalled.

On Tuesday, 5 December, Downing Street began talks again with Barnier, conscious that in order to secure a deal at the Council meeting that month they would have to seal it by the following weekend. Failure to get a breakthrough looked like it could imperil May's premiership. In an important move, the Northern Ireland secretary James Brokenshire was drafted in to talk to the DUP alongside the chief whip, Julian Smith, and Simon Case, now the point man on Ireland in Brussels. The Unionists sent Jeffrey Donaldson, Nigel Dodds and Emma Little-Pengelly to the talks in 9 Downing Street. Discussions continued into the small hours of Wednesday, the participants fuelled by Chinese takeaway, pizza and foul-tasting filter coffee. A DUP source made clear they were in no rush to give in: 'This is a battle of who blinks first, and we've cut off our eyelids.'[6]

Downing Street staff, hopeful of a deal that would take them to Brussels, went to work with overnight bags on Wednesday but the talks continued into Thursday. May spoke to the Irish prime minister Leo Varadkar mid-morning while officials went to and fro with the Commission, the Irish and the DUP. The Unionists secured six changes to the text, the most important of which was a new paragraph 50, in which the UK pledged that 'no new regulatory barriers' would be imposed between Northern Ireland and the rest of the UK and that it would enjoy the 'same unfettered access' to the UK internal market. That day, May received warnings from the Treasury that unless she got the DUP on board by the end of the week there would be market turmoil for ten days.

While the DUP talks continued, Gavin Barwell was keeping the senior Brexiteers informed of what was happening. He spoke to Michael Gove by phone, while Boris Johnson visited May in 10 Downing Street at 5.30 p.m. on the Thursday, a picture of which Julian Smith was to tweet much later to show that the Brexiteers had been consulted. May and Davis got little respite: 'Both the PM and DD have been absolute troopers: both in their sixties and they worked all weekend last weekend, taking calls, reading, analysing and clearing bits of text late into the night on Sunday and Thursday.'

The crunch came in two phone calls between May and Arlene Foster, the first at 9 p.m., the second after 11 p.m. While May talked on the phone to the DUP leader, the sounds of karaoke and drunken laughter from the Downing Street staff Christmas party carried down from the state rooms upstairs. Officials clutching bottled beer lurched past the prime minister's door. May argued that the document was not perfect but it would allow the talks to move to phase two. Foster was still not happy. In another scene from *The Thick of It*, thanks to a technical fault a tired-looking May had to move to her outer office for the second call. Her officials, who would usually have listened in, listened anxiously to just her side of the call while May sat cross-legged and hunched making her argument.[7] Foster did not give way. As she explained later, she 'cautioned the prime minister about proceeding with this agreement in its present form, given the issues which still need to be resolved and the views expressed to us by many of her own party colleagues'.

It was at this point that May made a highly courageous decision. She told Foster she was going to Brussels anyway to sign the deal. 'We understand there are concerns but we are taking a decision in the national interest,' she said. Perhaps the PM had little choice, but this showed a willingness to make some political moves that belied her cautious reputation. May returned to her constituency home near Maidenhead, leaving Julian Smith and Simon Case to continue negotiations. Barwell left for home at 1 a.m., tweeting that it had been a 'long day'. Other Number 10 staff slept in their offices. Around 2 a.m., two tiny tweaks allowed the DUP to climb down with grace. May's gambit had worked. By 4.30 a.m.,

May was at Brize Norton, boarding a pre-dawn flight to Brussels.

On arrival, she breakfasted with Juncker and Barnier. At 6.06 a.m. Martin Selmayr tweeted a picture of white smoke, the traditional signal that a new Pope has been selected. The deal was done. At the press conferences to announce the details, both Juncker and Donald Tusk, the European Council president, seemed as pleased as May as they announced that 'sufficient progress' had now been achieved to move to phase two of the talks. A former minister said that week, 'The extraordinary thing is that Juncker and Barnier are now propping her up, they are so fearful of her going.'

As with many of her other key decisions on Brexit, May had not consulted her cabinet before testing Foster's mettle. Yet the relief was such that even the Brexiteers expressed effusive delight at the outcome. Gibb cleverly sent Michael Gove to do the flagship interview on the *Today* programme, where his expressions of support for the prime minister – a 'personal political achievement' – were so elaborate that one colleague described them as 'almost ejaculatory enthusiasm'. Minister after minister took to Twitter in a bid to outdo each other. A more cynical MP compared the orgy of adulation to the Politburo-style support for Iain Duncan Smith just a fortnight before he was ousted: 'It was like the orchestrated standing ovations at IDS's last party conference speech.'

As a showcase of May's resilience and determination it was her best day in government since her Lancaster House speech in January. On the detail, it was clear that a fragile house of cards had been constructed which undeniably eased Britain into a position where customs union membership was more likely. If May had survived, there was little illusion that she had won, a feeling reinforced in a triumphalist press conference by Leo Varadkar. 'The whole point of the EU love-bombing Ireland was to allow it to climb down,' a senior Tory said. 'But instead of that Varadkar did a press conference in which he went out of his way to say that alignment and convergence were the same thing.' The document was a matter of interpretation, but it was clear that Dublin and Brussels saw the consequences very differently. Efforts were made to convince the Brexiteers that the language had not tied May's hands for phase two, the trade talks. 'They tried to reassure Boris with magic words,' a prominent Eurosceptic said. 'But if you concede alignment now it's difficult to turn around later when you're talking about the end state and say we won't be aligned. That is the problem.'

Julian Smith and Stephen Parkinson, one of May's Downing Street aides, began a ring round of the Tory backbench awkward squad, urging them not to 'rock the boat'. In a bid to calm their fears, Smith told MPs that the notion of equivalence between EU and UK law 'does not mean anything'. Michael Gove told friends, 'As I read it, we only stay in alignment in those areas which are necessary to North–South cooperation as part of the Belfast agreement and, in addition, if we can't solve that problem through trade deals. I've been told straight that alignment doesn't mean copying all the same rules, it can mean achieving the same goals through different means – so it doesn't mean a lack of divergence across the whole of UK competences.'

More controversially, Barwell told Gove and Johnson that the deal was not legally binding, an interpretation that found its way to the *Sunday Telegraph* and was then repeated by David Davis, who told the BBC's Andrew Marr that Sunday, the deal was 'more a statement of intent than it was a legally enforceable thing'. This was technically true, but the deal was to be written into a legally binding text by March. Davis's intervention was greeted with incredulity in Brussels, where it looked like an effort to tear things up before the ink was even dry. Guy Verhofstadt condemned Davis for 'undermining good faith'. Barnier thundered, 'We will not accept any backtracking from the UK.'

Later that week, the EU27 agreed with the Commission assessment that 'sufficient progress' had been achieved. May could contemplate starting 2018 with a spring in her step. It was a significant milestone for May but also a sobering one for phase two. An EU official said, 'It took nine months to come up with fifteen pages for the deal agreed on Friday. The EU-Canada trade deal has 1,598 pages – so make your own calculations.' The conundrum of the Irish border remained, a solution to it as fondly and forlornly sought as nineteenth-century naturalists searched for a unicorn. In one of the great quotes of the age, a senior UK negotiator summed up the state of play: 'We all know unicorns don't exist. The question now is whether everyone can agree to make do with horses with shells glued to their foreheads.'[8]

In thirteen months Theresa May had made three big speeches on Europe. The first, at the Tory Party conference of 2016, had described which parts of Europe Britain wished to leave behind – the single market, the customs union and the jurisdiction of the European Court of Justice. The second, at Lancaster House, had formalised that position and suggested that Britain would be interested in a transitional arrangement to a new world but would be prepared to walk away if a comprehensive trade deal was not forthcoming. The third, in Florence, had described what Britain was prepared to swallow as part of divorce proceedings with the European Union.

In the meantime, May's entirely understandable decision to call a general election, the shambolic campaign and her own limitations as a leader in the modern media age had almost fatally undermined her authority and emboldened the strong personalities in her cabinet to press their violently contradictory answers to the key outstanding question – what Britain's final relationship with the EU should look like. After Florence, she battled the refusal of the Commission to acknowledge the risks she had taken and the truculence of the DUP to seal a phase one deal.

At home, if May allowed herself a celebratory drink, the vultures still circled. One of the October plotters said, 'She's bought herself some time until the next crisis, but the crisis will come.' They didn't have long to wait. Within a week the prime minister had suffered a defeat in the House of Commons on her Brexit bill and, within a fortnight, the resignation of her third cabinet minister in the space of a month.

But that is another story.

Conclusion

MAY WAS WEAK IN JUNE

The Conservative Party won the 2017 election. They got more votes and far more seats than Labour. Yet for those involved it felt like a defeat. 'I had the most miserable seven weeks of my entire life,' one special adviser remarked, comparing those who lived in the war room to 'post-traumatic stress disorder survivors'. 'It was just joyless. The whole thing was like crawling through shit.' James Chapman, who resigned as David Davis's chief of staff at the Department for Exiting the European Union in April 2017, told friends the previous twelve months, wrestling with the EU referendum result and the most complicated bureaucratic task since the Second World War, had been 'the worst year of my life'.

We may never know how Theresa May really feels about the events described in these pages since it is not her style to offer her innermost thoughts to the world. Yet no peacetime leader of recent years has known adversity like it, certainly not one so untested at the pinnacle of politics. Like all political leaders, her strengths and weaknesses were exposed as coterminous. May's resolution and stoicism under fire were also stubbornness and inflexibility. Her healthy disdain for chasing the next headline was exposed as brittle nervousness when questioned by the media or the public. The inviolability of her provincial English vicarage Tory principles and the firmness with which she cleaved to decisions taken masked a surprising level of personal insecurity which allowed her views to be shaped by her two principal aides whose approach would not have found favour at a parish tea party.

It is far too early to know what the 2017 general election will mean for British politics or what Brexit would mean for the UK. May's first year made clear how she would deal with both – with methodical but secretive precision and pathological caution leavened with moments of great boldness.

It is hard to fault May's boldest gesture, calling the election in the first place. As a party leader with a twenty-point lead in the polls it would have been negligent to have allowed such an opportunity to pass her by. The ghost of Gordon Brown was not a role she wished to reprise. Even afterwards, May said, 'I don't regret calling it, I think it was the right thing to do at the time.'[1] Having gone to the country, however, May and her team seem not to have understood that calling a snap election meant she needed to try doubly hard as a national leader to justify that decision to an electorate weary of voting and more suspicious of the political class than in previous generations. George Freeman said, 'Calling the election broke the spell around Theresa as a reluctant leader. It was seen as an act of tactical partisan advantage.'

If May did genuinely believe that the election was to strengthen her hand in Brexit talks she should have done more to dramatise that during the election. She appeared to be behaving for party political advantage precisely because she had nothing new to say on either her strategy for the talks or what lay beyond. A minister said, 'What country do we want to be at the end of all of this? We needed to answer that question.' Instead, May was hamstrung by the tone she had struck on Brexit in the first nine months. If it had been necessary to take a firm line on immigration and the jurisdiction of the European Court of Justice early on to keep the Brexiteers in her party and cabinet happy, the election was the perfect opportunity to offer a broader and more upbeat vision that could have reached out to the 48 per cent who voted Remain. May and her manifesto were largely silent on the subject. There was no way May could sustain a seven-week election campaign on Brexit when she had so little to say on it.

Where ambiguity on Brexit was an impediment to May, it was a strength for Jeremy Corbyn. The policy of 'six tests' put in place by Keir Starmer allowed MPs in Leave areas to stress that the party was respecting the referendum result while Remainers could say Labour was aiming for a soft Brexit.

May and Corbyn had much in common. They were both conscientious constituency MPs regarded as unfashionable by their previous party leaderships and fighting their first election on the national stage.

Both would find themselves presiding over a profound dispute between an inner circle who regarded them as transcendent leaders and campaign professionals whose judgements were formed by polling data. While May called an election she wanted but did not know what to run on, Corbyn was caught by surprise but immediately knew what he would offer voters.

May's second problem with calling an election at such short notice was that she and her team seemed oblivious of how unprepared Conservative Campaign Headquarters was for an election. Vote Leave had won the referendum with a small and agile team under Dominic Cummings, who had spent eighteen months thinking about his strategy. David Cameron had scraped an unexpected win in 2015 after giving Lynton Crosby four years of preparation time and almost dictatorial control. The most revealing aspect of researching this book was that of dozens of senior Tories the author spoke to about the Conservative campaign, not one of them gave a straight answer to the question: 'Who was in charge?'

Nick Timothy and Fiona Hill felt like they had handed over control to Crosby and Stephen Gilbert, but responsibilities remained split. Crosby and Gilbert chaired the key meetings, but the chiefs were May's essential confidants and the embodiment of her authority in the war room. It was them not Crosby who talked to May. Crosby and Jim Messina barely saw the prime minister. When Hill and Timothy did not want something done, like tweeting during the terrorist attacks, it did not happen. Timothy took himself off to write the manifesto, but he did so without any supervision from Crosby. Hill took the meaningful decisions about communications and the cadre of special advisers in the war room looked to her every bit as much as to Crosby. For months, ministers and special advisers had complained that three people was too few to run a government. But at precisely the moment it would have been advisable to impose a dictatorship, power was fatally diluted between Crosby, Hill, Gilbert, Timothy, Messina, Mark Textor and Tom Edmonds.

Nick Timothy and Chris Wilkins deserve credit for positioning Theresa May in a way that had broadened support for the Conservatives. Afterwards they regretted their failure to continue with the projection of May as a candidate for change which Wilkins had mapped out at Chequers in February. Yet Crosby also had a point that a political strategy designed to win the 2020 election might need altering to win a snap election which had created its own uncertainty. Timothy and Wilkins would be on stronger ground in arguing their plans should have been dominant if the changes mapped out in the manifesto were not so unrelentingly grim. May, Hill and Timothy all knew what campaign Crosby would run. He had used the same playbook in every election for a decade: do your research, find a message that frames a choice for the electorate, hammer it until the media's ears bleed and voters are just beginning to pay attention. Crosby's stance on stability versus change was clear from the Chequers summit. If May and the chiefs did not want that campaign they should have hired someone else.

Crosby also was at fault. He should have sought more guarantees and demanded a direct line to the candidate. The impression many had was that he thought it would be an easy win which he could add to his list of triumphs without having to grip the apparatus. When he and Textor had doubts about the manifesto they never demanded anything but minimal changes. 'If he could hand that £4m back and have his reputation back instead he would do that,' a friend said.

The upshot was that two diametrically opposed visions of the campaign were allowed to co-exist from the start. To begin with Crosby's was dominant. Timothy's took over with the publication of the manifesto. When things went wrong the inherent incompatibility of these visions made resolution difficult. Either vision run with full commitment would have been likelier to get a better result than this botched hybrid. 'One of the great ironies is that Nick and Fi let go of the campaign,' a close ally said. 'I'd argue that the lack of Nick and Fi was the problem.' Ultimately, it was Theresa May's job to choose what sort of campaign she wanted. She did not. 'She's the Prime Minister, she signed off on the campaign,' a consultant said. Later May voiced her regrets: 'We didn't get across more the ... vision that I set out when I became Prime Minister [and] stood on the steps of Downing Street.'[2]

Chris Wilkins said, 'I have no doubt that if the election campaign had been based around the Plan for Britain strategy and the team that together built a significant lead in the polls, secured a great result in the Copeland by-election and delivered a local election result that surpassed our expectations, then we would have achieved a very strong result indeed. Sadly the campaign went in a different direction. If feels like we were twenty points ahead with fifteen minutes to go. All we needed to do was see out the game by sticking to the plan that was working so well, but instead we changed the team, ripped up the game plan and ended up squandering the lead we had so painstakingly built.'

Where the Mayites and the consultants agreed – and were both at fault – was in projecting the prime minister into a spotlight she loathed and, in an age when emotion was driving politics, for which she was almost uniquely unqualified. Crosby was driven to the conclusion by the polling data, Hill and Timothy by a determination that May should be allowed her own triumph. Both should have realised she was not equipped to deal with the scrutiny.

The seven-week campaign gave more time for these problems to emerge. In retrospect, Andrew Bridgen was onto something when he suggested an election on May 4th to coincide with the local elections. Had May announced it when she triggered Article 50 it would have been much easier to frame it as a Brexit election.

The internal tensions in the Conservative campaign burst into the open when the manifesto was published. A campaign that had sustained a healthy poll lead depicting May as 'strong and stable' was now forced to sell a document offering a vision of May's Britain with tough choices on social care, free school meals and winter fuel allowance, with few compensatory 'retail' offerings. 'It confused the electorate,' a senior aide said. 'They went, "You're not who we think you are, we don't get it any more."'

The manifesto process, with the whole document kept from ministers until the day of the launch, was problematic. The contents of the manifesto were reckless. Timothy and Gummer had been warned by Crosby and Textor that their lead was wide but shallow and that it depended on maintaining the public view that May was a different kind of Conservative. The manifesto, serious and grown up as it was, seemed almost designed instead to confirm voters' worst fears.

This was most evident in the social care policy, a brave plan for a serious problem. One of the authors said, 'I would beat myself up if I had written something which was disingenuous or wrong or designed for political effect and it had all gone wrong.' But the problem was not that the manifesto was designed for political effect, but that it was not. Timothy and Gummer forgot the first rule of manifestos – that they are there to win elections. So confident were they about victory that this seems to have been barely a factor alongside securing a stronger mandate for government. A minister said, 'Nick was so arrogant that he thought he could write whatever he wanted and we'd win and that wasn't the case.'

Voters did not understand that they already had to pay for care – let alone the distinction between residential and domiciliary care. The campaign had no time to 'roll the pitch' and the comms operation was not able to explain the progressive benefits of May's policy – hardly surprising when Hill's media team was given just twenty-four hours to prepare. This was a policy turd immune to spin-doctor polish.

A former cabinet minister said, 'It's perfectly reasonable to say to someone, "You have a house, rather than making your postman pay tax to look after you, you have to sell your house and pay for your own care." That's perfectly reasonable. But it's not very popular and if you're going to try and sell it to the public, you better prepare the ground. And if you start by launching that policy with a *Daily Mail* story that says, "At last! Victory for people who want to keep their own home", you're launching on a false prospectus, which very quickly unravels, the Tory Party then has a panic attack and it falls apart.'

Whatever the rights and wrongs of the plan, every single Tory campaign chief with access to the internal data says that the public reaction was immediate and catastrophic, with support dropping 'off a cliff' in a way that veterans had never seen before. The real problem was not the headline number, which gradually recovered, but the effect on May's brand. 'It could clearly be portrayed as demonstrating Theresa May had been hiding the traditional face of the Conservative Party,' a campaign official said. 'It was really damaging for that reason.' May was no longer seen as a different sort of Tory. The U-turn a few days later – which most who were there agree was necessary – undermined May's claims of stability. Her insistence that 'nothing has changed' appeared both disingenuous and delusional. A senior official in the London Labour Party said, 'It was a policy that smashed their core vote in the balls and a U-turn that tore their slogan to pieces.'

The Tory meltdown was so damaging because it came after Labour's manifesto launch had proved a roaring, if somewhat accidental, success. Emily Thornberry spoke for many when she said, 'The star of the show was the manifesto. People think it was Jeremy, and I love Jeremy, but the star of the show was the manifesto.' Labour's manifesto went with the grain of the campaign and a sixty-eight-year-old leader who was finding that the things he had believed and argued for four decades were suddenly resonant with a public tired of stagnant wages and arguments from politicians that everything was fine. The cruel way to sum this up is to say that a stopped clock is right twice a day, but Corbyn's team did have a philosophical approach to politics that gave them freedom to be themselves, when Labour politicians had agonised about doing so for a decade. The manifesto was the document of which they had always dreamed.

While the leader's office and Southside were locked in a bitter standoff over tactics, LOTO – backed up by Momentum – fought the campaign they wanted to, showcasing Corbyn's enthusiasm and a raft of policies that cost billions but captured the imagination of the young and middle-class professionals. A former Tory Treasury official said, 'I think it was very clever, a bunch of good retail policies. They're also raising some serious tax. It's a proper go at socialism.' Manuel Cortes, General Secretary of the Transport Salaried Staffs' Association said, 'It told the British public what we were thinking, and actually what we were thinking was what they were thinking.'

John McDonnell, while sometimes flirting with political violence in private, showed himself an astute mainstream campaigner with his tax lock and attempts to cost the manifesto, a decision which handed Labour a huge boost when the Conservatives – moronically – failed to publish their own. Corbyn's office correctly deduced that pumping out a huge number of policies would allow them to dominate the broadcast coverage. Their campaign strategy, such as it was, seemed based on faith in Corbyn's ability to turn votes, rather than data. But, despite their differences, they received useful support from the Southside operation under Patrick Heneghan, which succeeded in getting £2m worth of leaflets out of the door in a week at the start of the campaign and showed the flexibility to switch from defensive to offensive seats when the polls began to close.

A former member of the shadow cabinet said the manifesto was like a swing for the fences in cricket, conditioned by a belief even among Corbyn's allies that he could not win but would make the best case for his beliefs: 'It's like being the night watchman. You can be batting away trying to get the odd six, because you've got absolutely fuck all to lose, and if you're a memorable night watchman it can win the test, but people forget that most of the time you were dead lucky and missed five out of six balls. But if you want to win and you start that far behind, it gives you that freedom.' A source who worked on Ed Miliband's campaign said, 'We could never have done that with Ed, when he was ahead in the polls, when you're actually thinking you may be in government.'

The other star was Corbyn who had spent decades learning which lines worked with his target audience. 'Jeremy has spent a lot of time getting middle-class people motivated about the politics of the left,' a Labour official said. 'He's very good at that.' Corbyn didn't just harness anger and enthusiasm for the underdog, he also grasped the need for hope. A Conservative official said, 'Why did people in the depression fall in love with Busby Berkeley movies? You know that Corbyn's stuff is all bollocks, but when you've got "Here is some more misery and gloom" and "Here is happiness and sunny uplands and all the cash you could possibly want" – I kind of get it.'

Corbyn also showed that he was willing to learn. Snippy and irritable in the first eighteen months of his leadership when questioned by the media, Corbyn got media training and, in the words of one aide to Theresa May, 'He took the biggest chill pill in modern history and he was so zen-like.'[3]

Afterwards, Labour moderates, who had reined in Ed Miliband's left-ist tendencies, had the humility to admit they had learned from Corbyn that the public were prepared to be led further left than they believed. 'Some of the things proved much more popular than I thought they would be,' a Labour director said. 'One of the lessons of populism is that you can kind of get away with a lot more now than you could have done.' Richard Angell, director of the moderate Progress pressure group, added, 'The irony of the 2017 election was the moderates had convinced the world that Corbyn was unelectable. The election was all about how big Theresa May's majority was going to be, not whether the government changed. Voting Labour became a consequence-free activity. They clipped May's wings and gave Corbyn an inadvertent shot in the arm and, thankfully, killed off the nonsense idea of a new party.'

The view of May, Hill and Timothy that they should avoid David Cameron's playbook – coupled with the marginalisation of Philip Hammond after the budget bust-up – meant the Tory campaign did little until it was too late to scrutinise the economic implications of Labour's plans, a staple of every previous Conservative campaign since the war.

Here, Crosby's belief that Brexit alone should be front and centre, multiplied rather than mitigated the mistake of the chiefs. By the time they realised their error, on the final weekend of the campaign, the London Bridge terror attack drowned out coverage of Labour's garden tax and triple tax whammy. David Cameron lost the EU referendum, in part, because he put the traditional Tory economic arguments at the heart of the campaign. Theresa May stumbled in the 2017 general election, in part, because she did not.

Some Conservatives believe Timothy's approach to the economy, with its depiction of big business as rogue, made it harder to combat Labour. 'By conceding that capitalism was flawed, it became almost impossible to attack Corbyn's socialism,' a special adviser said. 'The entire campaign was being fought on Labour's ground.' More serious was the failure to provide retail policies to help those who had seen enough of austerity. A senior Cameroon said, 'David Cameron thought he had to offer something that people want. May's people said the 2015 manifesto had too much of that, therefore, do none of it. That's crazy logic. People went on the doorstep and talked people round on social care but when they asked, "What good things are you going to do for me," they were scratching their heads.'

The sum total of the two manifestos was a game changer in terms of momentum and morale. 'We had this terrible situation where one group of people were spooked and the other looked like they were fighting for something,' a Tory consultant said. 'It was like a rugby game where a team gets a lead and holds it so tight they effectively strangle themselves, lose momentum and allow the other team to overtake them.'

The two terror attacks not only fossilised the campaign at a bad time for the Tories, they highlighted another way in which the Mayites had distanced themselves from the Cameroons – the wilful disregard of social media campaigning, which the chiefs seemed to regard as a bizarre gimmick you add on to a campaign, rather than one of the foundations of modern voter outreach. Another Cameron aide said, 'The desire from Number 10, Theresa and her spads to do everything possible to distance themselves from anything Cameron has done, blinded them to a point where they started to do things that were massively disadvantageous to their own campaign.'

The atrocities at Manchester Arena and London Bridge sparked two social media campaigns – one on Jeremy Corbyn's past terrorist sympathies and the other on Theresa May presiding over police cuts – both of which ended up hurting the Tories. In the end May's record as home secretary seemed more relevant to voters than Corbyn's dalliances with the IRA three decades earlier. 'We might as well have been talking about the Boer War,' a Downing Street official said. George Freeman believed the 'negative personal attacks on Jeremy Corbyn' convinced voters the Conservatives didn't care about his concerns about public services. 'We were contemptuous of him and it looked like we were contemptuous of those issues.'

Corbyn channelled media hostility into public sympathy, like a boxer on the ropes. 'It was the rope-a-dope strategy,' a Labour adviser said. 'When you've been beaten up by a savage bully, you pick yourself up off the ground. You might be a withered old man, but you've got a few punches in you. You get up and the crowd roars. You still lose but you lose like *Rocky*.'

If Corbyn was Rocky Balboa, when it mattered – after the manifesto meltdown and in the televised Q&As – Theresa May displayed all the charm and emotional intelligence of his Soviet opponent in *Rocky IV*, the robotic Ivan Drago played by Dolph Lundgren. May was unable to live up to the billing of her own campaign. She was like a new actress in her first Hollywood blockbuster with her name above the title and she had neither the ability to carry the big scenes or the charisma to disguise that fact as some of her predecessors had managed. A former cabinet minister said, 'They built a personality cult around someone who doesn't really have a personality.'

Throughout the campaign, she regarded media interviews as a threat rather than an opportunity to project herself and her message to a public that was initially well-disposed to her. A civil servant who witnessed attempts to prepare May for these encounters found the experience painful: 'She'd say, "Well why do they want to know that? That's ridiculous. Why would anyone be interested in that?" She did get quite nervous.' May's reluctance to project empathy caused her difficulty when confronted with the nurse in the *Question Time* debate; again in her speech in Downing Street after the election, when she expressed no humility or concern for defeated colleagues; and finally – and nearly fatally – after the Grenfell Tower disaster, when her failure to meet the victims and plunge into something close to a breakdown convinced many of her colleagues she had to go. In the words of one minister, 'She's a decent human being, a good person, but she became a rather severe, humourless, childless woman who looks rather unpleasant up close.'

When public support began to plummet in the final fortnight of the campaign, May's confidence had taken a knock and she retreated further from challenging her advisers, while her closest aides adopted a bunker mentality and just wished the Australians gone. Here, Crosby and the other consultants expected May to erupt and demand changes. Instead, she backed Crosby and Timothy's view that the campaign was working – this despite at least some data suggesting that she might not make meaningful gains. Messina's final model ended up being more accurate even than YouGov's but it is strange indeed that the chiefs seem to have been unaware of this.

The manifesto changed the seats that were in play and the turbulence in the modelling after the manifesto meant this was not spotted until it was too late for many MPs. George Freeman said, 'There was a whole catalogue of failures in CCHQ. A lot of Conservative MPs who knew their seats were vulnerable were told they were fine, that the polling had been done and to go to marginals and then they both lost.' Those looking for one explanation of what happened should look no further than the manifesto. A Labour adviser said, 'It was a game of unforced errors on both sides, but one side made a catastrophic one, literally getting the racquet and twatting themselves in the head with it.'

Timothy immediately admitted his mistakes over the care policy. The consultants were not so frank about their own roles. Another voice who was silent after the election was Fiona Hill, arguably the senior figure with the greatest grounds for complaint. While most of her subordinates in government found her difficult to work with, all but a couple of Hill's campaign colleagues say she was hard done by during the campaign. Hill made two big political gut calls – that the care policy should be ditched and that the campaign should be recast in the final ten days. On both she was at odds with Nick Timothy. On both history will judge that she was right. On both Theresa May sided with the wrong chief. No one else has suffered more from the mistakes of others. While Hill licked her wounds, Nick Timothy began to rebuild a reputation as a public intellectual and continue to make the case for his brand of Conservatism – but given the scale of the cabinet revolt against them it is impossible to see either of the chiefs returning to government this side of a general election. 'He's ruined it for himself,' a colleague said. 'He's got to live with that.'

The campaign they helped to run was not a total failure. A source close to May said, 'We got 42.5 per cent. We got more votes than Blair ever got. There were shortcomings during the campaign and I have regrets about the campaign but it's not quite simple enough to say, "We blew it."'

But any election that a sitting government calls in order to boost its majority which concludes with it in humiliating retreat cannot be considered a success.

The question for Labour was whether the fourth worst defeat in their modern history could be considered a victory. It certainly felt like one. Corbyn had added thirty seats and 9.6 per cent to Labour's vote share. His 12.9m votes were the best performance since Tony Blair's second landslide in 2001. However, a Labour official said, 'Jeremy's programme moved people and the Tory campaign was a disaster but the reason we were up 9 per cent was that the Liberal Democrats and Ukip have basically ceased to exist. Once you remove their decline, the swing to us was only 2 per cent. That is not a big swing. Our haul of seats is the fourth worst in our history since 1935. By those definitions it's not a good result. But it's a great result because we were so far behind.' A source close to McDonnell said, 'We'd gone through a year of people telling us we were going to take the Labour Party to the dogs and now we've given it the first injection of life it has had in ten years. We've energised politics on the left.'

The issue debated in the party post-election was whether Labour were at 'peak Corbyn'. A Labour adviser on the moderate wing of the party said, 'Jeremy reached the limits a protest movement allied to a series of giveaways, minus economic credibility, can do against even the most catastrophic Tory campaign that has ever been run. Even against that, we still got a bigger deficit of seats to the Tories than Gordon got.' Corbyn trailed May by fifty-five seats, seven more than Brown's deficit to Cameron.

Kent provided a case study of the election in microcosm. John Spellar, a veteran MP who had been fighting the hard left for three decades, said, 'There are two Kents. There's the Kent of the village pubs and the rolling land and the university. It's an astounding result to win Canterbury for the first time in history. However, there's another Kent all along the Thames where we used to have eight seats. We now don't have one and the Tory majorities are all around nine thousand and require a 10 per cent swing. These were seats we held during the period of the Labour government, even in 2005.

'That pattern is replicated elsewhere. We won Warwick and Leamington but we didn't win back Nuneaton, which used to be a safe Labour seat. We didn't win North Warwickshire, Rugby, Redditch, Dudley South or Halesowen and Rowley Regis. That's a big mountain to climb. We've done well with the tertiary educated but not with the skilled workers. They are the bedrock of the party and geographically concentrated. We're building up huge majorities in places where people are footloose and come to work in London, but the places they have left behind are drifting away from us.'

Party moderates and even some allies believed Corbyn's success was as much luck as judgement. A senior trade unionist said, 'Basically, they got lucky but campaigns do bring out the best in Jeremy.' Yet even moderates who thought he was wrong as well as unelectable had to admit that Corbyn had confounded their expectations. Those who thought he was merely unelectable reassessed. A Southside official said, 'Some of the PLP who were insistent that the whole thing was awful drank the Kool Aid. You realise it was everything to do with wanting to win their seat again. Now they've won their seat again, they don't care.' Others dug in for a fight. A Labour adviser said, 'This generation's war is over. Blair won the first battle, the Trots won the second battle, and now we're talking about a new battle. We just need to make sure that we get as many decent people in there as possible who aren't certifiable fucking lunatics.'

Scenting power, Corbyn's supporters kept up their campaigning after the election. Momentum's Adam Klug said the group would seek to install its cadre of young activists in Westminster. 'We do want to bring a whole generation of people to stand as councillors and as MPs and create a parliament more representative of wider society,' he said. 'We'll keep getting large numbers of people out to canvass in marginal constituencies and we'll be ready for that general election as soon as it comes.'

Corbyn got himself into training. After forty years of oppositional politics, he spent the autumn of 2017 receiving training from Lord Kerslake, the former head of the civil service, about how to operate in government. Win or lose, he had already done enough to be seen as a key leader in Labour's history, unpicking the work of Neil Kinnock and Tony Blair to marginalise the hard left in the twenty-four years between 1983 and 2007 in just twenty-four months. 'A lot of the project has been successful,' a union official said. 'The Labour Party is now an anti-austerity party and there is a clear difference between Labour policy and the Tories in a way that people didn't feel that there was before. The party has a renewed base of young people. The 2015 intake and the 2017 intake is more left wing. If Jeremy did decide he wanted to go tomorrow, he could draw up a good score sheet of how the party has changed under him.' A close ally puts it in a way likely to most offend the Blairites: 'He is now the moderniser of the Labour Party.'

For his closest political ally, there was no prospect of Corbyn retiring. 'Never in my lifetime did I think we would see a socialist prime minister in Number 10,' John McDonnell said. 'I never thought it would happen, not in my lifetime. It's going to happen.'[4]

Whether Labour would be taking on Theresa May would be defined by her Brexit negotiations.

Theresa May's challenge of handling a bitterly divided cabinet in the midst of Brexit negotiations was perhaps best summed up by the comedian Frankie Boyle, who said, 'The Tories are at pains to make sure that Brexit is being done by the book; sadly, that book is *Lord of the Flies*.' The cabinet debates seemed at times as much about past positions and the prospect of future advancement as they did about the details of departing the EU.

Just as with the decision to call the election, Britain's Brexit strategy was decided, with minimal consultation, by a tiny group around the prime minister, of whom Nick Timothy was the most dominant. Several of the decisions made in those first weeks of May's premiership failed to stand the test of time.

There was a political logic to leaving the single market and escaping the jurisdiction of the European Court of Justice, but it is clear that the full implications of these decisions were only slowly comprehended by the cabinet. In her haste to placate the Eurosceptics, May began Brexit as a partisan of the 52 per cent and missed an opportunity at her first party conference to cement herself as a national leader with the thoughts of the 48 per cent in mind as well. May's determination to play her cards close to her chest was also understandable but led to the kind of obfuscation over her intentions that was habit forming and led to disaster during the election campaign.

There may have been some benefits to a dedicated Brexit department, but it could have remained in the Cabinet Office, with which other departments were used to interacting as the provisional wing of Downing Street. Creating DExEU as player and referee in the same game caused unnecessary upheaval and confusion. 'A lot of instability and movement which cost time and effort was spent just building up the department,' a DExEU official said. Creating DIT effectively set in stone the decision that Britain should leave the customs union four months before May claimed that it was decided. Similarly, the decision to give Oliver Robbins a dual role was also flawed, periodically enraging David Davis as work was commissioned behind his back and setting up a conflict of interest for junior officials unsure whether they were reporting to him or to Robbins. May's decision to ban her own Lords minister from seeing the relevant cabinet paperwork was absurd and contributed to George Bridges' resignation.

May and Fiona Hill saw the negotiation as a mirror of the talks they had engaged in with Brussels on justice and home affairs, when May opted out of more than one hundred directives then back into her chosen thirty-five. An official who saw her then said May was 'the most reliable' cabinet minister on difficult issues. 'Once she decided what she was going to do it she stuck there. She had a terrible time over the European Arrest Warrant. I always found her completely steadfast.' That issue was instructive because the Paleosceptic 'theologians' who resisted the opt-ins made their argument on the basis that ECJ could not be allowed jurisdiction in the UK. On that occasion May resisted them. When it came to the post-Brexit talks, she took the opposite position with equal vigour, a move some officials believed limited the UK's options. Having made up her mind, May was not for turning. 'She's totally inflexible,' a former mandarin said. 'That's both the strength and the weakness. She doesn't do flexibility or speed.' Some officials believed that May's team were naïve in the Brexit talks about the degree to which mutual economic benefit would be allowed to compete with the political integrity of the EU. An official said, 'In that JHA negotiation the incentive on the other side of the table – much as they resented the fact we were doing this at all – was to maximise the number of things they got us back into. It's not like that in this negotiation.'

May's appointments, equally hurriedly delivered, shaped the cabinet debates. In David Davis she picked a resolute but flawed Brexit secretary. A fellow minister called him 'really good under fire' but an official said, 'the swashbuckling bravado can get a bit wearing'. Civil servants were not always convinced by his command of detail and his optimism that apparently intractable problems could be negotiated away. Davis was shrewd enough to stay out of the worst of the cabinet infighting and to help guide Philip Hammond towards compromise.

The chancellor dealt with Brexit as he dealt with most things, with an eye on the bottom line and a political tin ear which rubbed his colleagues up the wrong way. Depending on your perspective, Hammond was either an obstruction to fulfilling the democratic decision of 23 June 2016, or the last bulwark between Britain and a car-crash Brexit. He was also temperamentally opposed to much of May's domestic agenda and the prime minister's team came to regret his appointment and his inability to use the powerhouse of the Treasury for imaginative political policymaking.

Boris Johnson played a lesser role in the Brexit policymaking than Davis or Hammond. Nonetheless when it looked, in the autumn of 2017, as if he could be quietly written off, Johnson wrote himself back into relevance with his *Daily Telegraph* article. As a cabinet colleague who disagreed with him on Brexit puts it, 'Boris is quite iconic because many people see him as the face of Leave and what he has to say about an outcome will become important to the way that many people who can't be bothered to do the reading themselves will interpret it.'

No personnel issue was as mishandled as the events that led to the resignation of Ivan Rogers, Britain's ambassador to the EU in January 2017. Rogers was right to warn that the other EU member states would hold together and resist British efforts at divide and rule. He was right that triggering Article 50 would put Britain on the clock, allowing Brussels to apply time pressure – a situation made worse by May losing two months on a failed election gambit. Rogers was right that it would take more than two years to negotiate a trade deal. He was right that Robbins' doing two jobs was impractical. Yet these warnings were dismissed as negativity. Infuriating character that he could be, it would have been better to find a way of accommodating his expertise and institutional memory.

Brexit might have meant Brexit but by October 2017 the public and the cabinet were still working out what Brexit would actually mean.

Some delay can be attributed to May's laboriously methodical way of working and the lack of clarity to her temperamental secrecy. What is not clear was whether this infuriating ambiguity was also a proactive strategy. If it was, it was one which had slowly but surely manoeuvred her cabinet forwards without letting one of the many violent disagreements tear the government completely apart. Remainers had been forced to accept that Britain was leaving the single market and the customs union, Brexiteers that there would be a transition period of two years and that the UK would pay an exit bill of at least €20 billion and more likely double that. In a Cabinet Room full of gunpowder with ministers like Johnson or Hammond dancing on the table juggling pinless hand grenades, having a prime minister not given to sudden movements was not the worst thing in life. To May's credit, her willingness to call the DUP's bluff before heading to Brussels in December 2017 was brave and effective.

What is undeniable is that ministers concealed the potential problems from the public. When the fifty-eight sectoral assessments of the economic impacts of Brexit were eventually published, they appeared to some MPs to have been cobbled together in haste – and even then DExEU redacted the most damaging details. That ministers and officials, daunted by what they found, chose to walk away was disturbing. So convinced were some officials that Brexit would one day result in a Chilcot-style inquiry into what went wrong that in the summer of 2017 they began sending internal emails with the express intention of showing that they had taken the risks seriously and attempted to mitigate them. It was not necessary to be a fully paid up Remainer to conclude that May might have been better to level with the public about the challenges she faced.

A DExEU official said, 'Liam Fox has said this is going to be the easiest deal in human history. That is spectacularly irresponsible. There's been no expectations management. People think we're going to leave the EU, snap our fingers and get a trade deal, pay no money, have no foreign judges seeing over anything even in areas where people don't care about it. All these millions of people who voted leave on the basis of the £350 million for the NHS are going to be extremely angry.'

A May loyalist put the counter view. 'What I'd say to any Remainer is, "Don't be insane, this is absolutely the best thing for the country." It really is. I'm really really excited about it. It's in no one's interests across

the twenty-seven to have this be a failure. We're a massive trading partner. We're probably the biggest security partner for the rest of Europe.'

In the end, most aides agreed the trade deal would only come about
when May went for 'a walk in the woods' with Angela Merkel and
Emmanuel Macron. 'She's intensely shy: that's what worries me,' a
mandarin said. Questions remained about whether May had the adapt-
ability to thrash out a deal at 3 a.m. in a world where Nick Timothy and
Fiona Hill were no longer in the next room. 'All the stories build up to a
very weak character who was primed over a very long period to be the
front woman, but totally unsuited to being it,' a former aide said. 'She still
takes instruction. It's just there are different puppet masters. She's brilliant at learning a script but she's less good when she has to improvise.'
Another former Number 10 aide said, 'She is a Sphinx without a riddle.
People think that she is thinking something really deep, but the truth is
she doesn't know what to think. I once sat in a room with her in silence
and I thought there must be a lot going on in there. But there is
nothing.'

May's allies did not deny that she was Sphinx-like but claimed that
countenance concealed a fully worked out plan for Brexit. 'I work for a
woman who works her balls off and absolutely loves her country and will
do anything and everything possible to make sure she gets the right
thing for the country,' one of her closest advisers said. 'Theresa has got
six years of experience being at the heart of Europe negotiating. She
knows what she's doing and how she'll do it. Sometimes she doesn't tell
us what's in her head. But she has this kind of confident, relaxed, knowing look in her face, which I take great comfort from.'

There could be no denying the stakes – the future of the prime minister,
her party and the country. Some saw only disaster. A minister said, 'The
Conservative Party is dying, impaled on the spike of Brexit.' Some saw
opportunity. A leading Cameroon said 'Brexit will be like the French
Revolution. It will go on consuming people until everyone is dead. At the
end of it we'll reappoint the king.' Those who saw any Brexit outcome
splitting the Tories preferred another historical parallel. 'The Armageddon
scenario is that it will be like the Corn Laws,' a senior backbencher said.
'We will save the country but destroy the Conservative Party.'

The question Conservative MPs had to ask themselves was whether
Theresa May would help or hinder them winning their seats next time.

George Osborne tells a story about meeting Lynton Crosby for the first time in 1996 when he was director of the Liberal Party of Australia and Tony Blair was heading for a landslide. Crosby asked, 'What are you going to do when you lose this election?' The reply was, 'John Major will go.' Crosby said, 'Well why are you not getting rid of John Major now?' The Labour Party's political graveyards are scattered with the bodies of those who wish they had moved against Gordon Brown in 2009. Some Tories were determined not to make the same mistake.

It is impossible to know what the political landscape will look like in 2019, let alone 2022. Those looking for lessons from 2017 might conclude that the Conservatives lost their majority because neither the Timothy–Wilkins change strategy nor the Crosby Brexit strategy was properly pursued and the manifesto undercut both of them; there was a problem with the spinning of the manifesto; there was a problem with the data that led them to fight the wrong seats; there was a problem with the Tory machine which meant that even where they knew the battleground they failed to contest it properly. Finally, there was a problem with the candidate. Of those, the only one that could not be fixed while Theresa May remained leader was the leader herself.

Looking back, if Boris Johnson had not been so gaffe prone or so obviously ambitious, if David Davis had not reined in his friends or been persuaded to join Philip Hammond's triumvirate, if George Osborne had not abandoned Parliament or if Ruth Davidson had decided she wished to join it, Theresa May might have been gone within a week of the election, certainly after the Grenfell Tower debacle cruelly exposed her shortcomings once more. Once again she was the beneficiary, as she had been a year earlier, of the absence of serious rivals from the battlefield. The fate of Osborne and Davidson – who may well yet lead her country – was proof that the first rule of politics is that you have to be in it to win it.

May accumulated considerable respect for battling on in the eye of the storm, seeking a path through the valley of Brexit with cannons to the right and left of her. 'There is still a lot of animus for Cameron for leaving as soon as he lost,' a senior cabinet minister said. 'The fact that she got on with the job gave her a lot of credit with the Tory grassroots. She is the toughest and most resilient person I've ever known.' May's example conjured echoes of the words of Teddy Roosevelt quoted at the front of this book: 'It is not the critic who counts; not the man who points out how the strong man stumbles, or where the doer of deeds could have done them better. The credit belongs to the man who is actually in the arena.' Or in this case, the woman. Whatever else Theresa May did wrong, the prime minister along with Nick Timothy, Fiona Hill, David Davis, Oliver Robbins, Philip Hammond and Boris Johnson were prepared to put themselves in the arena.

In the most turbulent times of my life, it is hard to see how anyone could have negotiated their way without error through the turbulent fall out from Brexit. We should be grateful someone was willing to try.

Appendix 1

RESULTS OF THE 2017 LOCAL ELECTIONS

LOCAL COUNCIL ELECTIONS, 4 May 2017

Party	Pop. Vote	Councils	Councillors
Con	38% (+8)	28 (+11)	1,899 (+563)
Lab	27% (−4)	9 (−7)	1,152 (−382)
Lib Dem	18% (+3)	0 (nc)	
Ukip			
Green			
SNP		0 (−1)	431 (−7)
PC		1 (nc)	202 (+33)

MAYORAL RESULTS

Cambridgeshire & Peterborough – James Palmer (Con)
Greater Manchester – Andy Burnham (Lab)
Liverpool City – Steve Rotheram (Lab)
Tees Valley – Ben Houchen (Con)
West Midlands – Andy Street (Con)
West of England – Tim Bowles (Con)

RESULTS OF THE 2017 GENERAL ELECTION

EXIT POLL – 10 p.m.

Conservative – 314 seats
Labour – 266
SNP – 34
Lib Dems – 14
Plaid Cymru – 3
Green – 1
Ukip – 0
Others – 18

FINAL NATIONAL RESULTS

Party	Seats	Vote share	Votes
Con	317 (–13)	42.3% (+5.5)	13,636,690
Labour	262 (+30)	40.0% (+9.5)	12,877,869
Lib Dem	12 (+4)	7.4% (–0.5)	2,371,861
Ukip	0 (–1)	1.8% (–10.8)	594,068
Green	1 (nc)	1.6% (–2.1)	525,665

SCOTLAND

Party	Seats	Vote share	Votes
SNP	35 (–21)	36.9% (–13.1)	977,568
Con	13 (+12)	28.6% (+13.7)	757,949
Labour	7 (+6)	27.1% (+2.8)	717,007
Lib Dem	4 (+3)	6.8% (–0.8)	179,061

NORTHERN IRELAND

Party	Seats	Vote share	Votes
DUP	10 (+2)	36.0% (+10.3)	292,316
Sinn Fein	7 (+3)	29.4% (+4.9)	238,915
SDLP	0 (–3)	11.7% (–2.2)	95,419
UUP	0 (–3)	10.3% (–5.7)	83,280
Alliance	0 (nc)	7.9% (–0.6)	64,553

WALES

Party	Seats	Vote share	Votes
Labour	28 (+3)	48.9% (+12.1)	771,354
Con	8 (–3)	33.6% (+6.3)	528,839
Plaid Cymru	4 (+1)	10.4% (–1.7)	164,466
Lib Dem	0 (–1)	4.5% (–2.0)	71,039

Appendix 3

CHRIS WILKINS' STRATEGY

EXTRACTS FROM A PAPER PRESENTED AT CHEQUERS SUMMIT, FEBRUARY 2017

1. Summary – what is the political strategy of this government?

Between now and 2020, we have a unique opportunity to move forward and gain ground, fortifying our existing support and gaining votes in new parts of the electorate. The Labour Party is currently divided – torn between its pro-EU base and the Leave-voting marginals it needs to win – and viewed as irrelevant by many voters. UKIP is fast morphing into more of a threat to Labour's traditional working class than to Conservative supporters. And Brexit allows us to own key motivating issues that we could not lay claim to in 2015. In effect, a whole group of voters has been unlocked for us by last year's referendum and the impact it has had – the large portion of the population who describe themselves as working class, who are often in skilled blue-collar or unskilled white-collar jobs, who struggle with everyday costs, and who see the parties that traditionally represented them fading into obscurity. They are not Labour's inner-city vote (who remain out of reach), but are voters across England and Wales who look for which party best channels their views and increasingly see the Conservative Party under Theresa May as the most viable option.

Brexit also provides an opportunity to address a deep discontent with and mistrust in the political class – much of which played a part in the referendum, which was a vote for a fundamental change to how the country works as well as a vote to leave the EU. For years people have felt their concerns have been ignored by politicians – and in the context of the rise of populist parties and figures across the globe, addressing people's concerns and representing their identity and values is more important than ever. Not doing so, and failing to provide or to be seen to provide the change that people want, risks another political force filling the void. This underpins the thinking behind our Plan for Britain: as we leave the EU, we must also change the kind of country we are. Our research contains initial signs of promise that people are starting to understand our intentions in this regard; it suggests people in our target groups, some for the first time, cautiously feel that the Prime Minister and the government she leads is starting to address these concerns.

We must of course be realistic. The public, particularly in the current political climate, are unlikely to enthusiastically welcome us with open arms, and it is questionable whether they will ultimately think we are any more trustworthy than the rest of the political elite. Elections are usually won on less lofty terms, on the political cut and thrust of who can better run the country. We must also be ready for the current positive situation to change – of the possibility of a Labour Party without Corbyn, or of the possibility of an adjustment in the economic situation.

But – as things stand – we are poised to increase our support from the last election, and we have the potential to make gains in areas and with groups we may not have previously considered and who may not have previously considered us. The key strategic challenge will be to be bold and to do so while – in a context of uncertainty, with a public largely still divided on Remain or Leave lines, and a resurgent Liberal Democrat presence – retaining our support among the diverse coalition of voters that helped deliver the 2015 election victory. Defending this flank will be important as we go forward.

That means planting ourselves firmly in the centre ground: presenting ourselves as moderate, open and outward looking, identifying the unifying strands that bring voters on either side of the EU debate together, and making it clear that we can represent and work for everyone in Britain. It means always being the party of competence and custodian of the economy, building on the strengths that delivered us victory in 2015. But it also means clearly demonstrating that we are the 'change candidate', that we are the government and the Party which will change Britain and continue to do so, and understanding that we must win the values and identity argument. It means focusing on new groups of voters available to us – not so much Middle England as Working Class England –

more resolutely than before, with the knowledge that that is where the electoral prize lies. In short, it means being bold – and capturing the rare and unique opportunity this government now has to win over people across the country. Such an approach forms the bedrock of the real and true modernisation of the Conservative Party.

4. Strategy – what does this mean for our political strategy?

It is clear from this research that we must:

1. Frame our priorities with our key target groups in mind. Our segmentation has produced two key target sections of the electorate – the 'Working Class Struggler' group, and the 'Conservative Leaner' group. We performed well with both groups in 2015, and the Conservative Leaner group in particular helped to deliver many of the seats we won from the Liberal Democrats. Our challenge now is that the vote in the EU referendum cuts differently across the two groups. The 'Working Class Strugglers' identify as working class, are less well-educated, are often struggling with everyday costs, and feel like politicians have ignored their concerns in recent years – they prioritise immigration as an issue, and tend to have voted Leave in the EU referendum. The latter group tends to consist of slightly younger voters, who are more politically engaged and better educated, often living in areas that are more cosmopolitan – they tended to vote Remain in the EU referendum last year. Together these two groups – alongside our traditional base of support (where we have already won significant support back from UKIP) – are the pillars of a future General Election victory.

2. Focus our energy on reaching out to working class voters who no longer feel Labour represents them. Initial analysis suggests they are where the true electoral prize lies: they are located in marginal seats across England and Wales, and are turning away from Labour. By continuing to drive at this group – and being bold in doing so – we have the potential to make significant inroads across England and Wales.

3. Work to retain support amongst groups which were a key part of the 2015 voting coalition. The younger, more affluent (though by no means well-off), Remain-voting and well-educated Conservative Leaner group formed a key part of the 2015 voting coalition. They had a particular presence in seats we gained from the Liberal Democrats, and were also behind our support in more cosmopolitan or university seats. They were the group which most warmed to the previous Prime Minister's language about a modern and compassionate Party. In June 2016, they tended to vote Remain – quite different from our other target group. Instead of gaining ground with this group since July, we have lost some support to both Labour and the Liberal Democrats. People in this group are less likely than working class voters to identify with the government, and their support continues to fall – and this is likely to intensify as the negotiations take place. As we move towards the election, we will need to work to retain the support of this group by stressing the unifying factors that bring the public together, setting out a vision for the country, as well as focusing and emphasising competence and clear dividing lines with other parties.

4. Hold on to the Traditional Conservatives won back since the referendum. The biggest shift of support since the referendum has been amongst the Traditional Conservatives group – older, more affluent people who also voted Leave. Here, the people who voted UKIP in 2015 have changed their preference, and we have been the only beneficiaries. These are the people who voted UKIP because of concerns about the EU, or immigration, or because of other issues associated with the previous Prime Minister. They now not only very much like the current Prime Minister, but believe we are now delivering for them on immigration and leaving the European Union. These voters held us back from gaining some Labour marginal seats in 2015, where the UKIP vote was high. We must ensure these voters now stay with us – and that UKIP continues to be a threat to Labour's base rather than ours.

We face then, the need to act to hold and secure support in three quite different groups: our base, which is at its most supportive; the more liberal pillar of our 2015 victory, which needs to be reassured about our trajectory; and working class voters, who are beginning to nervously identify with us. To do these things, we will need to:

a. Plant ourselves firmly in the centre ground, and focus on the issues that unify these groups. Even though people do not necessarily hold 'centrist' views, they perceive themselves to be in the centre ground and want their government to be the same. This does not mean echoing the same message as under the previous Prime Minister – indeed, many people's concept of the centre is quite different to that – but does mean projecting an image that we are a party for everyone.

b. Stress, emphasise and maintain competence at all times. One of the main drivers behind the PM's approval ratings – and one of the things that helped deliver the 2015 election victory – was the perception that we were the most competent option. So on leadership, on the economy, on the ability to manage the country, we must continually put competence at the top of our agenda and ensure we have the clearest possible distinction with our rivals on this issue.

But we must also:

c. Unapologetically and clearly present ourselves as the change candidate. People are angry with the political class. They feel they have been ignored for too long, and part of the reason they voted to leave the European Union was down to this frustration. And the public, particularly that key electoral group – the Working Class Strugglers – are now looking for someone to deliver wider, comprehensive change to how our country works. We must show we can represent people's frustrations through a mainstream political process, and must prove that we can – to quote a favoured phrase – 'change to conserve'.

d. Talk to people's values and speak to people's concerns, learning and embracing the lessons of 2016. Though they are different in many respects, one of the key similarities between Brexit and the election of Donald Trump in 2016 was how much these votes were about identity and values. Many – particularly those with a lower level of education (which, statistically, almost totally explains people's voting patterns in both elections) voted because the candidate and cause they liked put what they were thinking into short, easy and understandable terms which resonated with how they felt in their everyday lives. We must therefore think in terms of people's attitudes, concerns and values: the public wants a PM and a Government which clearly aims to represent their voice, not one which is managerial and distant.

So, while focusing on the centre ground and competence to ensure we are attractive to all groups across the electorate, we must also be bold in our outreach to the people who want and demand change – and in so doing make electoral gains. To realise this in practice we must:

i. Own the referendum result, and clearly project our interpretation of it. With Brexit being the prism that most of the public are seeing issues through, and the key issue over the next few years, it is essential that we clearly own the result of the referendum and make clear our interpretation of the consequences of it. That means being clear that the referendum vote was a vote to leave the European Union, but also one to change the country as a whole.

ii. Clearly present our Plan for Britain – both during the negotiations but after Brexit too. The Plan for Britain is the crystallisation of this interpretation of the referendum result, and is our plan for change as we leave the European Union. It recognises that the public see almost all issues through the prism of Brexit and that our success will be rated on these terms. It also demonstrates that we are committed to pursuing wider change to the country, and that we are firmly on the side of ordinary working people. We must ensure that this is not a plan which ends the moment we leave the EU, but continues beyond that and forms a key part of our campaign in 2020 as we put our plan for post-Brexit Britain to the British people.

iii. Frame our messages in terms of people's values – and prove we are putting those values into practice.

iv. Harness the strength and popularity of the Prime Minister when it is appropriate. The Prime Minister is more popular than the Party with the public, and is seen by many as a credible and convincing conduit of our message and aims. But one of the very things people like about her approach is that it is business-like, and that she is quietly getting on with the job, and not always in the public spotlight. Ideally, then, the 'visibility' of the PM should be controlled – she should front and intervene at the right and strategic moments. The very power of the PM's presence is that she is not always present – we must continue to emphasise and harness that strength.

Appendix 4

LYNTON CROSBY'S STRATEGY

2017 ELECTION STRATEGIC NOTE – APRIL 2017

ABOUT THIS RESEARCH:
C|T|F Partners conducted two pairs of focus groups among soft voters (those undecided how they will vote, or likely to change their mind) from marginal seats in both London and the North West. In addition, we have completed a nationally representative political benchmark poll of n=1000 voters.

SUMMARY
The research shows there is clearly a lot of risk involved with holding an early election – and there is a real need to nail down the 'why' for doing so now. Voters are actively seeking to avoid uncertainty and maintain the status quo, and yet by calling an election the Conservatives are the ones who are creating uncertainty. Therefore, Theresa May must be able to show that by holding an election now she is minimising future uncertainty and instability.

Furthermore, if an election was held today there is a risk that the Conservative vote share would end up broadly similar to that the party secured in 2015. And as earlier research has shown, there is the potential for a significant number of seats won from the Liberal Democrats in 2015 to return to Tim Farron's party – largely based on the performance of incumbent MPs compared to their predecessors.

Theresa May is the most favourably viewed individual tested, while Jeremy Corbyn is the least favourably viewed. Of all the other Conservative individuals tested, only Ruth Davidson has a net favourable rating.

There is a strong preference for the Conservatives to be in Government after the next election with Theresa May as Prime Minister. But there are also exceptionally high expectations that this will be the outcome of any election held now. Both quantitatively (in Liberal Democrat seats) and qualitatively (in Labour seats) this is leading voters to believe that they can vote for the best local MP, or not reject their current good local MP, while still remaining secure in the knowledge that Jeremy Corbyn will not be Prime Minister. Thus the Conservatives must urgently work to ensure that any election is seen through a national prism.

Voters do not want the uncertainty that an election will cause, in large part because they are worried about the risk of potential election outcomes – namely a hung Parliament creating chaos over the delivery of Brexit and Nicola Sturgeon calling the shots, and the spectre of Jeremy Corbyn as Prime Minister.

Instead voters desire a better future where Brexit is a success, the economy stays strong, and they maintain their standard of living. To win this election, the Conservatives must demonstrate how only a vote for them can provide the leadership and stability needed to secure this better future.

The consequence of not voting Conservative is that Brexit negotiations will stall and fail – either through a hung Parliament creating chaos and stasis, or Prime Minister Jeremy Corbyn messing up negotiations with the EU – and that will mean Britain could fall behind other countries, damage the economy, and lead to lower living standards.

WHAT THE CONSERVATIVES MUST DO:

1. Be clear why this election is needed now – to prevent future uncertainty that would hamper Britain's ability to make a success of Brexit, maintain economic competitiveness, and improve voters' standard of living.
2. Ultimately frame the election as a choice between continuity and stability, or chaos and uncertainty.
3. Demonstrate the only way to secure a better future is through strong leadership, backed up by a stable and united party, that voters can trust to make the right decisions.
4. Demonstrate the only way to secure strong leadership (and Theresa May as Prime Minister) with the stable government

needed to secure a good deal for the UK and a better future is by voting Conservative.

5. Use Theresa May as the campaign's main communication vehicle – and take every opportunity to contrast her with Jeremy Corbyn.

Appendix 5

SEUMAS MILNE'S STRATEGY

MILNE'S POWERPOINT PRESENTATION TO LABOUR'S NATIONAL EXECUTIVE COMMITTEE, 19 APRIL 2017

GENERAL ELECTION 2017 STRATEGY

Why a snap election U turn?

- Theresa May says she's challenging the opposition to stop 'blocking' Brexit
- Reality is she wants to forestall unpopularity as reckless Brexit unravels and living standards turn down

What kind of Brexit?
Making this a referendum re-run is a trap. Brexit is settled. But what kind of Brexit is not.

The choice:

Tory reckless Brexit

- Britain a low-wage tax haven
- Workers' rights 'unsustainable' (Liam Fox)

Or a people's Brexit

- Access to the single market to protect jobs and living standards
- Workers' rights and consumer and environmental standards secured

- Building a new economy – investing in infrastructure, skills, new technology, green industries

Tories – evading scrutiny

Seven years of Tory austerity, aided by LibDems, has meant:

- Economic failure
- Most families worse off
- NHS and public services cut and plundered by privatisation
- Housebuilding at its lowest since 1920s
- Attacks on disabled and other vulnerable groups
- Schools facing cuts and rising class sizes

Tories – a Britain only for the richest – Tax handouts (2016–2022)

- Corporation Tax – £63.8 billion
- Inheritance Tax – £3.6 billion
- Capital Gains Tax – £0.8 billion
- Bank Levy – £5.4 billion

Labour's core theme

Instead of a country run for the rich …
　　Labour wants a Britain where all of us can lead richer lives

Labour – 10-day policy 'blitz' just a taster

- Free primary school meals to help learning and health
- Increasing the carer's allowance
- Giving pensioners dignity and security
- An environment for small businesses to grow
- A £10 minimum wage
- Ending high street bank closures

Labour – a real alternative for Britain

Core strategy for investment, job creation and upgrading the economy

- A national investment bank
- Regional investment banks

- Modernising infrastructure
- Creating a high-skill, high-tech, green economy
- Employment rights for good jobs

The challenge we face

Polling advice:

'Party is in a weak position with undecided and considerers, and simply attacking the Tories tends only to worsen our position.'

How do we project our alternative?
Not by business as usual

Framing of arguments:

- Empathy – start where people are
- Causes and context – who and what is to blame
- Answer – our alternative

How do we cut through?
We have to surprise:

- Turn Tories' creation of a Britain for the rich against them
- We want a richer Britain. We want people to live richer lives
- But we want a richer Britain for the many, not the few

Labour's election strapline
Labour – for the many, not the few

Tory attack on us
Core attack – Corbyn would bankrupt Britain

Secondary attacks:

- Spectre of the SNP
- Divided on leadership and Brexit
- Weak and extremist

Trust on the economy
Real challenge among older voters:

- Legacy of 2008 banking crisis – may have been global but it was on Labour's watch
- Legacy of 2010 – 'there is no money'
- Confusion over debt for investment and the deficit

Tories are the real extremists

- Failed to clear the deficit to give tax handouts to richest
- Driven more and more into poverty and low pay
- Auctioned off industries and outsourced services
- Let infrastructure crumble and failed to upgrade economy
- Pushed our NHS into crisis – leaving people on trolleys in corridors

Labour – key targets include

- Low and middle income voters
- Older voters and pensioners
- Young people and students
- Ethnic minorities
- Self-employed and small business owners
- People with disabilities and carers
- WASPI women
- Public service professionals

Campaign issues

- Push for head-to-head TV debates
- Offensive and defensive seats
- Manifesto launch and policy blitz
- May 4 elections significance – change polling narrative
- Fundraising – online £150,000 in six hours

ILLUSTRATIONS

Fiona Hill and Nick Timothy sitting on a sofa (Andrew Parsons/i-Images)

Hill sticking her tongue out (Ben Cawthra/London News Pictures)

Nick Timothy outside the Conservative Party HQ (Chris J. Ratcliffe/Getty Images)

Katie Perrior leaving the Royal Society (Steve Back/Barcroft Images/Barcroft Media via Getty Images)

Prime Minister Theresa May at home (Sunday Times/News Syndication)

May holding hands with Donald Trump at the White House (Christopher Furlong/Getty Images)

May signing Article 50 (Christopher Furlong/WPA Pool/Getty Images)

Philip Hammond at the Treasury, preparing his 2017 budget speech (Carl Court – WPA Pool/Getty Image)

Jean-Claude Juncker arriving at Downing St for dinner (Mark Thomas/Alamy Stock Photo)

Oliver Robbins walking behind May (Mark ZC/Splash News)

Martin Selmayr at a function in Brussels (Thierry Tronnel/Corbis via Getty Images)

David Davis with Michael Barnier over talks at the Commission (Isopix/REX/Shutterstock)

Nicky Morgan and Anna Soubry on Downing St (Rex Features)

Ivan Rogers in Westminster (Simon Dawson/Bloomberg via Getty Images)

Gina Miller at the Supreme Court in Parliament Square (Leon Neal/Getty Images)

Jim Messina, Lynton Crosby and Mark Textor leaving No. 10 (Steve Back/Barcroft Media via Getty Images)

Headshot of Patrick Heneghan (Twitter)

Stephen Gilbert (Lord Gilbert of Panteg) in Downing St (WENN Ltd/Alamy Stock Photo)

Headshot of James Kanagasooriam (James Kanagasooriam)

Leader of the opposition Jeremy Corbyn and Karie Murphy at the Labour HQ (Daniel Leal-Olivias/AFP/Getty Images)

Corbyn and Seumas Milne at Broadcasting House in London (Dominic Lipinski/ PA Archive/PA Images)

Theresa May on the Daily Mail front cover from 19 April 2017 (© Daily Mail)

Ariana Grande at a Manchester benefit concert after the attack (Dave Hogan/One Love Benefit/REX/Shutterstock)

Concertgoer following the attack at Manchester Arena (Dave Thompson/Getty Images)

Corbyn at the Manchester Arena terror attack vigil (Martin Rickett/PA Wire/PA Images)

Corbyn holding up the Labour Manifesto (Leon Neal/Getty Images)

Labour's John McDonnell on the campaign trail (Simon Dawson/Bloomberg via Getty Images)

Diane Abbott during a TV interview (Simon Dawson/Bloomberg via Getty Images)

Theresa May visiting Gresford, North Wales during the election (Andrew Price/ REX/Shutterstock)

Crowd at the Tranmere Libertines concert (Splash News)

Corbyn at Tranmere Rovers where 'oh Jeremy Corbyn' began (Visionhaus#GP/ Corbis via Getty Images)

Corbyn speaking to Emma Barnett on R4's *Women's Hour* (© BBC Motion Gallery/Getty Images)

Boris Johnson arguing with Ian Lavery (© BBC Motion Gallery/Getty Images)

Ruth Davidson on the campaign trail, in Giffnock, south of Glasgow (Andy Buchanan/AFP/Getty Images)

Michael Gove in a cabinet meeting after the election (Leon Neal – WPA Pool/ Getty Images)

Sajid Javid during cabinet after the election (Steve Parsons/PA Wire/PA Images)

May meeting police after Grenfell Tower (Dan Kitwood/Getty Images)

Corbyn hugging a victim of Grenfell (David Mirzoeff/AFP/Getty Images)

Grenfell tower smoking (Carl Court/Getty Images)

Peter Brookes cartoon (Peter Brookes/The Times/News Syndication)

Grant Shapps at a Tory Party Forum in Manchester (Paul Ellis/AFP/Getty Images)

Andrew Mitchell in Westminster (Jack Hill/The Times)

Theresa and Philip May on *The One Show* (Photo by The Conservative Party via Getty Images)

Boris Johnson arguing with Andrew Gwynne (Stefan Rousseau/PA Wire/PA Images)

May choking with coughs during the Tory conference (Lindsey Parnaby/Anadolu Agency/Getty Images)

May being handed a P45 (Paul Ellis/AFP/Getty Images)

Tory Conference slogan collapses behind Theresa May (Carl Court/Getty Images)

May and Richard Jackson boarding her plane at Brize Norton (Number 10/flickr)

NOTES

Introduction: Four Minutes to Ten

1. Katie Perrior, May was right then and she's right now, *The Times*, 19 May 2017
2. Nick Timothy: why the election went wrong and how the Tories can beat Corbyn next time, *Daily Telegraph*, 5 August 2017
3. The prime minister ruined by her gruesome twosome, *Sunday Times*, 25 June 2017
4. Katie Perrior, May was right then and she's right now, *The Times*, 19 May 2017
5. Nick Timothy: why the election went wrong and how the Tories can beat Corbyn next time, *Daily Telegraph*, 5 August 2017
6. A Decent Woman Betrayed By Her Gruesome Twosome, Standpoint, July/August 2017

Chapter 2: 'No Running Commentary'

1. Hard Brexit could cost £66bn a year, *The Times*, 11 October 2016
2. Don't mansplain to May or her team, Whitehall warned, *The Times*, 19 November 2016
3. Nick Timothy: why the election went wrong and how the Tories can beat Corbyn next time, *Daily Telegraph*, 5 August 2017
4. Ivan Rogers, evidence to Exiting the European Union Committee, 22 February 2017
5. Ibid.

6. Ibid.
7. Leak reveals low-priority industries for Brexit talks, *The Times*, 10 February 2017
8. May's revenge: Brexit memo firm pulls out of contracts, *The Times*, 21 December 2016
9. 'Chaos' and confusion over plans for Brexit, *The Times*, 16 November 2016

Chapter 3: The Enemy Gets a Vote

1. Ivan Rogers, evidence to European Scrutiny Committee, 1 February 2017
2. Ibid.
3. Theresa May Is So Dependent On Two Key Advisers They Had To Rejoin Government After The Terror Attacks, Buzzfeed, 6 June 2017
4. Ivan Rogers, evidence to Exiting the European Union Committee, 22 February 2017
5. *Evening Standard* comment: We should unilaterally allow EU citizens to stay, 23 June 2017
6. Philip Hammond in Cabinet row over accusations he is trying to 'undermine Brexit', *Daily Telegraph*, 16 October 2016

Chapter 4: Enemies of the People?

1. Garvan Walshe, The Government is making the same five strategic mistakes on Brexit that we made in Iraq, ConservativeHome, 20 October 2016

2. Don't trust Brexit 'three blind mice', says Tory former minister, *Guardian*, 2 October 2016

3. No 10's toxic texts … over PM's trousers, *Mail on Sunday*, 11 December 2016

Chapter 5: How Do You Solve a Problem Like Boris?

1. Bumbling Boris's Brexit 'blunder' (part three), *Mail on Sunday*, 20 November 2016

Chapter 6: Ivan the Terrible

1. Ivan Rogers, evidence to Exiting the European Union Committee, 22 February 2017

2. Ivan Rogers, evidence to European Scrutiny Committee, 1 February 2017

3. Ibid.

Chapter 8: The White House

1. Britain's plan to tame Trump, *Sunday Times*, 13 November 2016

2. Tim Ross & Tom McTague, *Betting the House: The Inside Story of the 2017 Election* (Biteback, 2017), in *Mail on Sunday*, 9 September 2017

3. Brexit will be a great thing, *The Times*, 15 January 2017

4. Donald Trump begs Theresa May to fix a 'warm welcome' for his state visit – and says he won't set a date for it until he knows he's going to get 'a better reception', *Sun*, 15 July 2017

Chapter 9: Triggered

1. It's time for Labour moderates to jump ship, *The Times*, 9 May 2017

2. Brexit faces fresh hurdles, leaked Whitehall papers reveal, *The Times*, 14 March 2017

3. Revealed: How the Cabinet plotted to exploit EU's fear of Vladimir Putin during Brexit talks, *Sunday Telegraph*, 2 April 2017

Chapter 10: 'Economically Illiterate'

1. Prints of darkness, *Sun*, 19 March 2017

Chapter 11: The Snarling Duds of May?

1. Working in No 10, I was staggered by the arrogance of Nick Timothy and Fiona Hill, *The Times*, 10 June 2017

2. Nick Timothy: why the election went wrong and how the Tories can beat Corbyn next time, *Daily Telegraph*, 5 August 2017

3. Nick Timothy and Fiona Hill: How civil servants lived in fear of the terrible twins at No 10, *The Times*, 17 June 2017

4. Inside Team Theresa, *The Times Magazine*, 15 July 2017

5. Working in No 10, I was staggered by the arrogance of Nick Timothy and Fiona Hill, *The Times*, 10 June 2017

6. Blond ambition: Boris Johnson plans one last attempt at becoming Prime Minister, *iNews*, 29 September 2017

7. The prime minister ruined by her gruesome twosome, *Sunday Times*, 25 June 2017

8. Ibid.

9. Working in No 10, I was staggered by the arrogance of Nick Timothy and Fiona Hill, *The Times*, 10 June 2017

10. Fiona Hill and Nick Timothy: the story being told about Theresa May's top advisers is inaccurate and unfair, *Daily Telegraph*, 10 June 2017

Chapter 12: Bolt From the Blue

1. Nick Timothy: Where we went wrong, *Spectator*, 17 June 2017

2. Nick Timothy: why the election went wrong and how the Tories can beat Corbyn next time, *Daily Telegraph*, 5 August 2017

3. Tim Ross & Tom McTague, *Betting the House: The Inside Story of the 2017 Election* (Biteback, 2017), serialised in the *Mail on Sunday*, 10 September 2017

4. *The Inside Story of Election '17*, Radio 4, 26 July 2017

5. Ross & McTague, *Betting the House* (Biteback, 2017), *Mail on Sunday*, 10 September 2017

6. 'The walks give clarity': how Wales hike helped PM decide on next step, *Guardian*, 22 April 2017

7. How Theresa May lost, it, Politico, 11 June 2017

8. *The Inside Story of Election '17*, Radio 4, 26 July 2017

9. Ibid.

10. Nick Timothy: why the election went wrong and how the Tories can beat Corbyn next time, *Daily Telegraph*, 5 August 2017

11. *The Inside Story of Election '17*, Radio 4, 26 July 2017

12. Ibid.

13. Nick Timothy: why the election went wrong and how the Tories can beat Corbyn next time, *Daily Telegraph*, 5 August 2017

14. Ibid.

15. *Election 2017: What Just Happened?*, BBC2, 12 June 2017

Chapter 13: Leninists and Lennonists

1. Inside Corbyn's office, Jacobin, 26 April 2017

2. Ibid.

3. *The Inside Story of Election '17*, Radio 4, 26 July 2017

4. *Election 2017: What Just Happened?*, BBC2, 12 June 2017

5. Inside the Corbyn campaign team, *Influence*, 13 July 2017

6. *Election 2017: What Just Happened?*, BBC2, 12 June 2017

Chapter 14: 'Another Galaxy'

1. How Theresa May lost it, Politico, 11 June 2017

Chapter 15: Strong and Stable

1. Revealed: how Theresa May's two aides seized control of the Tory election campaign to calamitous effect, *Evening Standard*, 16 June 2017

2. Katie Perrior, Better to be the underdog going into battle, *The Times*, 1 June 2017

3. Listen to her fans and you'd think Theresa was bigger than One Direction, *The Times*, 6 May 2017

Chapter 16: From Sharks to Minnows

1. Arron Banks, *The Bad Boys of Brexit* (Biteback, 2016, paperback edition), p.344

Chapter 17: Manifesto Destiny

1. John McDonnell welcomed the financial crash and called himself a Marxist, newly found footage shows, *Daily Telegraph*, 15 September 2017

2. Labour's next great battle, *Spectator Life*, 11 June 2016

3. *Election 2017: What Just Happened?*, BBC2, 12 June 2017

4. Ibid.

5. Ibid.

Chapter 18: 'Nothing Has Changed!'

1. How Theresa May lost it, Politico, 11 June 2017

2. *Election 2017: What Just Happened?*, BBC2, 12 June 2017

3. Ibid.

4. How Theresa May lost it, Politico, 11 June 2017

5. Katie Perrior, Better to be the underdog going into battle, *The Times*, 1 June 2017

6. The Tory 'dementia tax' could backfire for Theresa May, *Spectator* blog, 18 May 2017

7. *The Inside Story of Election '17*, Radio 4, 26 July 2017

8. *Election 2017: What Just Happened?*, BBC2, 12 June 2017

9. Michelle Lowe: Social care. May ducking TV debates. Fox hunting. What sank our candidacies in the West Midlands, ConservativeHome, 13 June 2017

10. *The Inside Story of Election '17*, Radio 4, 26 July 2017

11. *Election 2017: What Just Happened?*, BBC2, 12 June 2017

12. Ibid.

13. Gareth Baines: How good Tory candidates in Wales were betrayed by a dire central campaign, ConservativeHome, 16 June 2017

Chapter 19: Manchester

1. Inside the Corbyn campaign team, *Influence*, 13 July 2017
2. *Election 2017: What Just Happened?*, BBC2, 12 June 2017
3. Inside Corbyn's office, *Jacobin*, 26 April 2017
4. *Election 2017: What Just Happened?*, BBC2, 12 June 2017
5. Ross & McTague, *Betting the House* (Biteback, 2017), *Mail on Sunday*, 17 September 2017

Chapter 20: 'This Isn't Working'

1. Nick Timothy: why the election went wrong and how the Tories can beat Corbyn next time, *Daily Telegraph*, 5 August 2017

Chapter 21: I, Maybot

1. Theresa struggles to take back control – from her own Maybot, *Guardian*, 8 November 2016
2. Michelle Lowe: Social care. May ducking TV debates. Fox hunting. What sank our candidacies in the West Midlands, ConservativeHome, 13 June 2017
3. *The Inside Story of Election '17*, Radio 4, 26 July 2017
4. Ex-No10 spin doctor: 'When May became PM she ditched everything Cameron had done', *Sunday Express*, 30 July 2017

Chapter 22: The Corbyn Surge (and Why Almost No One Spotted It)

1. https://www.youtube.com/watch?v=slBGDqCjE5M, Copa90, 31 May 2017
2. *Election 2017: What Just Happened?*, BBC2, 12 June 2017
3. *The Inside Story of Election '17*, Radio 4, 26 July 2017
4. Ibid.
5. Inside Corbyn's campaign team, *Influence*, 13 July 2017
6. Ibid.
7. *Election 2017: What Just Happened?*, BBC2, 12 June 2017

8. The US Bernie Sanders campaigners lending Jeremy Corbyn a hand, *Guardian*, 30 May 2017
9. Ibid.
10. Inside Corbyn's campaign team, *Influence*, 13 July 2017
11. Hamish McFall: Tellers' work wasted. Invaded privacy. Computers that spewed gibberish. How CCHQ bungled this election campaign, ConservativeHome, 16 June 2017
12. Inside Corbyn's campaign team, *Influence*, 13 July 2017
13. Here's how Labour ran an under-the-radar dark ads campaign during the general election, Buzzfeed, 6 July 2017
14. Dan Watkins: What I learned as a Tory candidate in South West London, ConservativeHome, 22 June 2017
15. Seeing off the Tories, *Jacobin*, 27 June 2017
16. *The Inside Story of Election '17*, Radio 4, 26 July 2017
17. Michelle Lowe: Social care. May ducking TV debates. Fox hunting. What sank our candidacies in the West Midlands, ConservativeHome, 13 June 2017
18. *The Inside Story of Election '17*, Radio 4, 26 July 2017
19. Gareth Baines: How good Tory candidates in Wales were betrayed by a dire central campaign, ConservativeHome, 16 June 2017
20. Ibid.
21. Anatomy of a doomed campaign, *Economist*, 13 June 2017
22. Michelle Lowe: Social care. May ducking TV debates. Fox hunting. What sank our candidacies in the West Midlands, ConservativeHome, 13 June 2017

Chapter 24: London Bridge

1. George Osborne's revenge, *Esquire*, 13 September 2017
2. Iain Watson, Twitter, 7 June 2017

Chapter 25: Mayday!

1. Theresa May interviewed by Emma Barnett, Radio 5 Live, 13 July 2017
2. Ibid.
3. Jeremy Corbyn's Big Night: How The Labour Leader Learned His 'Surge' Was Real, Huffington Post, 12 June 2017
4. Ibid.
5. *Election 2017: What Just Happened?*, BBC2, 12 June 2017
6. James McGrory, Twitter, 9 June 2017
7. *Election 2017: What Just Happened?*, BBC2, 12 June 2017
8. Jeremy Corbyn's Big Night: How The Labour Leader Learned His 'Surge' Was Real, Huffington Post, 12 June 2017
9. 'They should be on bended knee apologising': Chris Williamson warns Corbynsceptic Labour MPs, *New Statesman*, 23 June 2017
10. Nick Timothy: why the election went wrong and how the Tories can beat Corbyn next time, *Daily Telegraph*, 5 August 2017
11. Theresa May interviewed by Emma Barnett, Radio 5 Live, 13 July 2017

Chapter 26: Shellshock

1. *Andrew Marr Show*, 11 June 2017
2. Nick Timothy: why the election went wrong and how the Tories can beat Corbyn next time, *Daily Telegraph*, 5 August 2017
3. Robert Peston, Twitter, 3.58 p.m., 9 June 2017
4. Garvan Walshe, Twitter, 9 June 2017
5. *Election 2017: What Just Happened?*, BBC2, 12 June 2017
6. Nick Timothy: why the election went wrong and how the Tories can beat Corbyn next time, *Daily Telegraph*, 5 August 2017
7. Jeremy Corbyn's Big Night: How The Labour Leader Learned His 'Surge' Was Real, Huffington Post, 12 June 2017
8. Michael Crick, Twitter, 9 June 2017

9. Andrea Leadsom demanded high-profile role as price of demotion, *The Times*, 5 July 2017
10. Jim Waterson, Twitter, 12 June 2017

Chapter 27: The Four Horsemen

1. Here's three ways Theresa May can show the Conservative Party that she's still the boss, *Sun*, 7 October 2017
2. Implosion of the plotters, *Mail on Sunday*, 7 October 2017
3. How 'shameless' PM begged David Cameron for help in a crisis, *The Times*, 3 July 2017
4. Brexit chief David Davis is urged to stand for leader, *Mail on Sunday*, 24 June 2017
5. May must quit now, says chief Davis ally, *Mail on Sunday*, 5 July 2017
6. Davis allies accused of smearing PM's husband, *Sunday Times*, 16 July 2017

Chapter 28: Florence and the Maychine Malfunction

1. *Election 2017: What Just Happened?*, BBC2, 12 June 2017
2. Barnier backs Davis after questioning Brexit talks engagement, Reuters, 7 Sep 2017
3. The inside story of how Theresa May and Britain's Brexit team secured the deal with the EU, *Daily Telegraph*, 15 December 2017
4. McDonnell confirms plan to take over Labour HQ, Guido Fawkes, 19 October 2017
5. The inside story of how Theresa May and Britain's Brexit team secured the deal with the EU, *Daily Telegraph*, 15 December 2017
6. Implosion of the Plotters, *Mail on Sunday*, 7 October 2017

Chapter 29: 'Sufficient Progress …'

1. Boris and Gove plot to 'Hijack' No. 10, *Mail on Sunday*, 12 November 2017
2. Westminster's hall of mirrors is about to shatter, *The Times*, 24 October 2017

3 Gove uses economicky words at cabinet, *The Times*, 16 November 2017
4 The inside story of how Theresa May and Britain's Brexit team secured the deal with the EU, *Daily Telegraph*, 15 December 2017
5 Ibid.
6 May's bid to save bill, *Sun*, 6 December 2017
7 The inside story of how Theresa May and Britain's Brexit team secured the deal with the EU, *Daily Telegraph*, 15 December 2017
8 Ibid.

Conclusion: May Was Weak in June
1. Theresa May interview with Emma Barnett, BBC Radio 5 Live, 13 July 2017
2. Theresa May interview with Emma Barnett, BBC Radio 5 Live, 13 July 2017
3. *The Inside Story of Election 17*, Radio 4, 26 July 2017
4. *Election 2017: What Just Happened?*, BBC2, 12 June 2017

INDEX